Photons

Propel Your Ascension

ALSO BY LORI TOYE

A Teacher Appears

Sisters of the Flame

Fields of Light

The Ever Present Now

New World Wisdom Series

I AM America Atlas

Points of Perception

Light of Awakening

Divine Destiny

Sacred Energies

Temples of Consciousness

Awaken the Master Within

Soul Alchemy

Building the Seamless Garment

Sacred Fire

The Twilight Hours

Golden Cities and the Masters of Shamballa

Evolutionary Biome

Awakening: Entering the Ascension Timeline

Freedom Star Book

I AM America Map

Freedom Star Map

6-Map Scenario

US Golden City Map

PHOTONS
propel your
ASCENSION

The ASCENDED MASTERS
received through

LORI ADAILE TOYE

I AM AMERICA PUBLISHING & DISTRIBUTING
P.O. Box 2511, Payson, Arizona, 85547, USA.
www.iamamerica.com

© (Copyright) 2022 by Lori Adaile Toye. All rights reserved. ISBN: 978-1-880050-09-5. All rights exclusively reserved, including under the Berne Convention and the Universal Copyright Convention. No part of this book may be reproduced or translated into any language or utilized in any form or by any means, electronic or mechanical, including photocopying, recording, or by any information storage and retrieval system, without written permission from the publisher. Published in 2022 by I AM America Seventh Ray Publishing International, P.O. Box 2511, Payson, Arizona, 85547, United States of America.

I AM America Maps and Books have been marketed since 1989 by I AM America Seventh Ray Publishing and Distributing, through workshops, conferences, and numerous bookstores in the United States and internationally. If you are interested in obtaining information on available releases please write or call:

I AM America, P.O. Box 2511, Payson, Arizona, 85547, USA.

www.iamamerica.com
www.loritoye.com

Graphic Design and Typography by Lori Toye
Host and Questions by Lenard Toye

Love, in service, breathes the breath for all!

Print On Demand Version

10 9 8 7 6 5 4 3 2 1

"The Photon Belt and Plasma Field continuously arc the Gold and the Aquamarine Ray into the heart of the Eight-sided Cell of Perfection. This great cell mirrors in fractal symmetry the magnificent Golden Cities of Light."

- Saint Germain

CONTENTS

AUTHOR'S INTRODUCTION.. xix

A Living Crystal   25

LIGHT CALIBRATES THE ASCENSION PROCESS 25
PURPOSE OF THE GOLDEN CITIES 26
LIVING, PLASMIC LIGHT 26
THE LIGHT IS WITHIN, THE LIGHT IS WITHOUT 27
LIVING CRYSTAL CITIES OF LIGHT 28
DARKNESS IS LIMITED 28
AMERICA HOLDS THE LIGHT FOR THE WORLD 28
THE SOUL'S CHOICE 28
THE TIME OF SHAMBALLA INCREASES THE LIGHT 29
FREEDOM STAR 29
GROW IN THE LIGHT OF ASCENSION 30
LIGHT SHINES ON THE DARKNESS 31
BONDAGE OF THE DARK ONES 31
USE OF GROUP MIND 31
ENLIGHTENMENT AND HU-MAN ENERGETICS 32
THE CELLULAR AWAKENING 33
DETACHMENT AND CULTIVATING TRUE MEMORY 33
DIET AND DNA FREQUENCIES 34
ASCENSION THROUGH THE VIOLET FLAME 34
SHAMBALLA'S INTENTION 35
EACH GOLDEN CITY MODELS SHAMBALLA 35
EVOLUTIONARY BIOME AND THE ONE 35
PORTALS OF LIGHT 36
THE WHITE RAY 36

Gatekeepers of Light — 39

FREEDOM, CHOICE, AND FREE WILL 39
THE EIGHT-SIDED CELL OF PERFECTION
  AND THE GOLDEN CITY 39
THE LIGHTED STANCE 40
VIOLET FLAME AND THE GROUP MIND 40
THE ANCIENT SHAMBALLA SCHOOLS 41
TEMPLE GATEKEEPERS 41
THE SHAMBALLA SCHOOLS ARE LOWERED 42
ENLIGHTENMENT IN THE STAR 42
THE GOBEAN SCHOOL 42
TESTS OF THE RIGHT-HAND PATH 43
FREEDOM FROM TIME 43
THE MALTON SCHOOL 44
GENETIC KINGDOMS OF LIGHT 44
MOVEMENT OF LIGHT 45
HARMONY OF THE RIGHT-HAND PATH 45
ONESHIP 46
RULE OF LAW 46
VIOLET FLAME OF FREEDOM 46
CHOICE AND THE CO-CREATIVE POWER OF THE I AM 47
FREEDOM STAR 47
ADVANCED HEALING IN SHALAHAH 48
TECHNOLOGY AND THE GROUP MIND 48
THE HEALING PLANT KINGDOM 48
A DECREE FOR LONGEVITY 49
WHITE FIRE OF KLEHMA 50
DIVINE TIMING OF THE WHITE RAY 50
DIVINE DNA ACTIVATION 51

Elder of Light — 53

THE MALTESE CROSS 53
THE LIGHT BEING 54
ANAYA OF THE AQUAMARINE AND GOLD RAYS 54

A TIME OF CRITICAL MASS 55
DIVINE DNA 55
"OF THE LIGHT, AND FOR THE LIGHT" 56
DARKNESS 56
KNOWLEDGE OF THE ONE 56
CUP CEREMONY 57
UNITED AS ONE 58
KINGDOMS OF THE FOURTH DIMENSION 58
ANOINTING OILS 59
ACTIVATION 59
DIVINE DNA CONNECTION 59
PHOTON ACTIVATION 60
INCREASE THE LIGHT 60

Enlightenment Pilgrimage   63

"CHOICE IS HOW HUMANITY EVOLVES" 63
BABAJI'S ASSISTANCE 63
CHOICE AND EVOLUTION 64
EARTH'S DESTINY AS FREEDOM STAR 65
PHOTON BELT: THE ATOMIC MALTESE CROSS 65
THE ENLIGHTENING 65
MOVEMENT OF THE WHITE RAY 66
"MAKE A COMMITMENT FOR YOUR FREEDOM" 66
CARDINAL LEI-LINES CONDENSE THE ENERGIES 66
YOUR PURIFICATION 67
CALL UPON THE BE-INGS OF LIGHT 67
ONE-HOUR MEDITATIONS 68
THE OVERLIGHTING 68
"INSIDE OUT…OUTSIDE IN" 69
THE COOPERATION POINT 69
"A STEP-DOWN TRANSFORMER OF LIGHT" 70
NEW ENERGY BODIES 70
MANTLE OF THE BUDDHA 70
THE ANGELS OF INITIATION 71
FIRE CEREMONY 71
SACRED PACT OF THE RIGHT-HAND PATH 71

INTEGRATION AND STILLNESS 72
"PROCLAIM THIS UNTO SELF" 73
FOLLOW THE CARDINAL LEI-LINE 73
A PILGRIMAGE OF INITIATION 74
THE PREPARATION OF ENERGIES 74
CLEANSING IMPURITIES 74
"MOVE WITHIN THE LIGHT" 75
LORDS OF VENUS ARE ON EARTH 76
EARTH'S EVOLUTION 76
STEP-DOWN ENERGIES 77
TRUST AND KNOW 77

FREE, HUMANITY SHALL BE   79

THE DIVINE COMPLEMENTS OF THE GOLDEN CITIES 79
FREEDOM STAR—A SUN OF VIOLET LIGHT 80
BEINGS OF LIGHT 80
SHAMBALLA REMAINS OPEN 80
NOTHING CAN STOP THE GOLDEN AGE 81
SHAMBALLA'S OPENING ASSISTS PILGRIMAGES 81
GOLD AND AQUAMARINE RAYS 82
THE MASTERS OF SHAMBALLA
    AND THE GOLDEN AGE OF LIGHT 82
"IT IS OUR HONOR TO SERVE" 83
ASCENSION IN THE LIGHT 83
"FREE, HUMANITY SHALL BE!" 84
"A LESSENING OF KARMIC BURDEN" 84
FRACTAL ENERGY 84
HEALING AND RESTORATION 85
A THOUSAND ADJUTANT POINT HIERARCHS 85
WATER AND THE CUP CEREMONY 86
THE LORDS OF VENUS STEP-DOWN
    ESSENTIAL ENERGIES 87
"SHARE WILLINGLY" 87
APPEARANCE OF THE MASTERS 88
SERVICE 88

Umbilicus of Light — 91

- AN UMBILICUS PORTAL 91
- GOLDEN CITY VIBRAL CORE AXIS 92
- TWIN UNIVERSES 93
- GALACTIC LIGHT AND SOUND HARMONICS 94
- THE WHITE RAY 94
- HUE AND OM 95
- SUBTLE FREQUENCIES OF SOUND AND LIGHT 95
- "EXERCISE THE DIFFERENT FREQUENCIES" 95
- A PLEIADEAN GENESIS 96
- THE SEVENTEEN GOLDEN CITIES OF INNER EARTH 96
- A CREATOR SOUND FREQUENCY 97
- REORGANIZE LIGHT-FIELDS AND DNA 98
- SOUND FREQUENCIES AND DOLPHINS 98
- DIVINE HU-MAN 98
- A DIVINE INFORMATION PORTAL 99
- ANCESTRAL PLANET SANJANA 100
- AMERICA IS ACTIVATED 100
- THE PHOTON IS LIGHT, SOUND IS PLASMA 100
- ANCESTRAL FIELD 101
- THE COLOR RAYS 101
- TRUE NORTH VERSUS MAGNETIC NORTH 102
- VENUSIAN GOLDEN CITIES 102
- THE EARTH PLANE AND THE EARTH PLANET 103
- GOLDEN CITY FLUCTUATION 103
- USE OF THE AWAKENING PRAYER 104
- SAINT GERMAIN AND BELOVED SUSAN 104

Energy-for-Energy — 107

- "THE PREMISE OF ENERGY-FOR-ENERGY" 107
- THE COMMUNICATION PORTAL 108
- SOULS WITH SPECIAL ABILITIES 108
- THE MASTER YEARS 109
- "SCRAMBLE FOR THE TIMELINES" 109

CONCENTRATION OF THE WHITE RAY 110
DEVELOPMENT OF THE NEW ENERGY BODIES........................ 110
ANCHORING GOLDEN LIGHT 110
DIVINE INTERVENTION 111
THE STEP-DOWN TRANSFORMER 111
BUILD THE SHAMBALLA GRID 112
OVERCOME LIMITATION THROUGH SPIRITUAL PRACTICE.. 113
LEVELS OF VIBRATION AND SPIRITUAL EVOLUTION 113
THE EVOLUTIONARY BIOME... 114
A FULL-FORCE GOLDEN AGE 114
BREATH TECHNIQUE... 115
A THREEFOLD ACTIVITY 115
THE TRINOMIAL LAW OF THE BIOME 116
THE LIGHT PREVAILS... 117

PILGRIMAGE OF LIGHT   119

SHAMBALLA REMAINS OPEN 119
ASCENSIONS IN THE GOLDEN CITY ASHRAMS 120
SAINT GERMAIN'S BLESSING 120
SANANDA'S CUP 121
EL MORYA'S SHAMBALLA BLESSING 121
GOD OBEDIENCE 122
"PILGRIMAGES THROUGHOUT THE YEAR" 123
THE HIERARCHS OF LIGHT 123
GODDESS TI OF THE LIGHT 123
THE HARMONY POINT 124
THE CARDINAL POINT.. 124
REJUVENATE WITH MEDITATION 125
EARTH'S IMMERSION INTO THE PHOTON BELT 126
GOLDEN CITY INTERVENTION 127
"WE MEET YOU IN RECIPROCITY" 127
ALL FOR ONE!... 128

The Photon — 129

A TRANSMISSION FROM THE MAP ROOM 129
THE MALTESE CROSS 129
ACTIVITY OF THE PHOTON 130
CHAOS AND ORDER 131
LEI-LINES CARRY THE VITAL ENERGY 132
THE MONOATOMIC PHOTON 132
GOLDEN CITY PILGRIMAGE 133
THE GOLD AND AQUAMARINE RAYS 133
GOLDEN CITIES ARE CAPACITORS OF LIGHT 133
THE PLASMA FIELD 133
THE MOVEMENT OF PHOTONS 134
THE MONOATOMIC GOLDEN CITIES 134
SACRED GEOMETRY OF THE PHOTON 135
THE MULTI-DIMENSIONAL HU-MAN 135
THE ALIGNMENT PROCESS 136
USE OF THE HUE MANTRA 136
WORKING REMOTELY 137
ENTER THE GROUP MIND 138
LIGHT WITHIN THE PHOTON 138
A HEALING TECHNIQUE 138
A TIME OF CHOICE 139
STEP-DOWN TRANSFORMER: THE PILLAR OF LIGHT 140
SPIRITUAL METABOLISM 140

Appendix A: *Golden City Vortex* 143
Appendix B: *The Advanced Light Fields of Ascension* 145
Appendix C: *The 51 Golden Cities* 149
Appendix D: *The Photon* 153
Appendix E: *Arcing of Ray Forces to Golden Cities* 155
Appendix F: *The Eight Pathways to Ascension* 156
Appendix G: *Sensing the Flux of Golden City Adjutant Points* 159
Appendix H: *Shamballa and Sanat Kumara* 161
Appendix I: *Temples of Shamballa* 173

Appendix J: *The Four Doorways of a Golden City* 175
Appendix K: *The Cycle of the Yugas* 179
Appendix L: *The Group Mind and
 Visualization to Achieve Group Mind* 185
Appendix M: *Decrees for the Healing of the Nations* 191
Appendix N: *Part One: Evolutionary Points and Pyramids* 197
Appendix N: *Part Two: Golden City Adjutant Points, Lei-lines,
 and Golden City Ashrams* 205
Appendix O: *The Evolutionary Field* 217
Appendix P: *The White Ray and Modulated Ray Forces* 265
Appendix Q: *The Right-hand Path* 287
Appendix R: *Diagram of the Eight-sided Cell of Perfection
 with the Unfed Flame and the Monad* 289
Appendix S: *Human to HU-man Light fields* 291
Appendix T: *The Violet Flame* 297
Appendix U: *El Morya* 299
Appendix V: *Akhenaton* 301
Appendix W: *The Will Chakras* 303
Appendix X: *Agreement Formation* 305
Appendix Y: *Lord Sananda* 311
Appendix Z: *Saint Germain the Holy Brother* 313
Appendix AA: *Timelines and Consciousness* 317
Appendix BB: *The Cup Ceremony* 321
Appendix CC: *Devas and Elementals* 324
Appendix DD: *The Heart of the Dove* 327
Appendix EE: *Fire Ceremony* 329
Appendix FF: *The Enlightenment Pilgrimage* 331
Appendix GG: *Spiritual Hierarchy* 336
Appendix HH: *The DAHL and DERN Universes* 345
Appendix II: *The Soul Ray of Purpose
(An excerpt from New World Wisdom Three with Master KH)* 347
Appendix JJ: *The New Shamballa Grid Pilgrimage* 349
Appendix KK: *Movement of the Photon as the Golden City* 351

GLOSSARY	353
INDEX	389
DISCOGRAPHY	413
AWAKENING PRAYER	414
ILLUSTRATIONS/PHOTOS ENDNOTES	415
INVOCATION FOR THE VIOLET FLAME AT SUNRISE AND SUNSET	416
BIBLIOGRAPHY	417
ILLUSTRATIONS RESOURCES	419
ABOUT LORI AND LENARD TOYE	421
ABOUT I AM AMERICA	423
I AM AMERICA BOOKS	424

Author's Introduction

Recent research by a team of physicists at the University of Warsaw provides compelling evidence that the Photon—the subatomic presence of light—takes the shape of the Maltese Cross. Through reconstructing a series of 2,000 repetitious flashes of two intersecting photons, the geometry of the sacred cross appeared. The Photon, historically defined by scientists as both a particle and wave, has been represented in religious and spiritual iconography for hundreds of years. It has been known as the Ethiopian Coptic Cross, the Eight-pointed Cross of Saint John, and is hidden within the eight-sided Bagua or Pa-k'ua, the iconic foundation of Taoist cosmology.

Perhaps the Photon's most recognizable symbology is the emblem of Malta, a series of geometric concave arrowheads, and the abiding signature of Saint Germain.

A Photon is a particle of light whose primary purpose is to create and deliver light into denser structures of matter. It is conscious, alive, and aware. Photons are widespread through all dimensions of light, and have the ability to adapt to every frequency. They are not limited in size, or dimensional expansion. The Photon exists microscopically within the evolving HU-man as the Eight-sided Cell of Perfection, and it appears again, as the wondrous and extensive Golden City.

The Master of the Violet Flame first introduced the insignia of light in his earliest I AM America Teachings, and defined its heavenly perimeters as a Golden City, an ethereal area of spiritual sanction and safety. Saint Germain further explained the Golden Cities as large Vortices, and prophesied they'd play an important role in humanity's ongoing Ascension Process through "interaction with spiritual energy."

Golden Cities play a fundamental role in Ascended Masters Teachings as their energies can immediately revitalize and restore our spiritual heritage, while infusing evolutionary light and sound frequencies into our auras through their vital portals and surging lei-lines. Golden Cities act as a capacitor of Galactic Light. Their sacred geometry reflects in the Eight-sided Cell of Perfection the source of divinity within each evolving HU-man. This cell doubly mirrors the image of the subatomic Photon, and the Maltese Cross reappears throughout the sprawling infrastructure of the Golden City, constructed with a precise series of dimension-spanning pyramids. Saint Germain quotes Hermetic Law when commenting on its remarkable metaphysical symmetry, "As within, so without."

The Golden City quickens our inner light through creating simultaneous Third-, Fourth-, and Fifth-Density experiences. Adjutant Points appear where major Golden City lei-lines intersect and coalesce, and refine the Galactic Light spectrum. Fifty-one Golden Cities, total, cover the globe. Each Golden City progresses our collective planetary Ascension. As we evolve through this unique biome of Photonic energies our interaction with the Nature Kingdoms becomes heightened through telepathy, manifestation, precipitation, bi-location, and teleportation. Naturally, this contemporary interface takes practiced time and experience to develop, but even beginning aspirants on the spiritual path can experience invaluable multi-dimensional communication with the Evolutionary Biome.

Alongside the development of the wondrous Golden Cities, our solar system has recently entered a large oceanic ionic field of plasma. The Master Teachers refer to this anomaly as the *Plasma Field*. Plasma is in a constant state of colliding, a movement that creates a strong magnetism. A simple example of ever-colliding plasma is the magnificent Aurora Borealis (North), and Aurora Australis (South), a brilliant show of lights familiar at the poles of our Earth. The continuous friction of colliding ions is significant, and the constant hurtle and crash creates an ionic bond with energetic bursts. This synergistically expands levels of human consciousness into multi-dimensional experiences with the Seven Rays of Light and Sound. This monoatomic presence affects the human absorption of high-frequency Ray Forces with an expanded division of cells, and unique cell replication, resulting in the increase of lifespans for thousands of years. Naturally occurring monoatomic elements conduct a vital life force that assists rapid repair of the body through increased cellular communication. Monoatomic elements are known to produce the M-state, a super-conductive electromagnetic condition that produces the ability to traverse multiple dimensions, receive spiritual enlightenment, increase intelligence and memory function, and repair genetics.[1] Throughout history monoatomic substances have been well-known by alchemists as the *Philosopher's Stone*, the *Elixir of Life*, the *Ark of the Covenant*, and *White Powder Gold*.[2]

A Plasma Field is concentrated, not disbursed. It is known to carry inaudible sound pitches, (B-flat, D, and G at varying octaves), that step-down from the Great Central Sun — the center of our galaxy. Like all creation, plasma and its sound and light frequencies travel with a spinning motion.

---

1. Monoatomic Gold. https://monoatomicgold.org/.
2. What Is the Connection between David Hudson and Monatomic Gold? Monatomic Orme, December 9, 2021. https://monatomic-orme.com/what-is-the-connection-between-david-hudson-and-monatomic-gold/.

Currently our solar system and our galaxy are moving through the highly-charged Plasma Field, which the Earth has just begun to cross. Our recent convergence into this life-expanding process heralds the birth of a full-force Golden Age for many millions of Earth-years. This includes an ever-increasing spectrum of light and sound frequencies that expands the seven traditional Rays with new, unique Ray Forces. Current examples of this evolutionary progression are the newfound presence of both the Gold Ray and the Aquamarine Ray, and the appendices of this book feature a special section dedicated to the identification and qualities of the new modulated Ray Forces.

Photons organize and concentrate into group effort, and regularly move in condensed currents of energy similar to immense river waterways that course throughout the galaxy. The *Photon Belt* is a main thoroughfare of such conscious convergence that flows within the evolutionary Plasma Field. Photons attract one another, and they build and collect, divide and replicate, throughout the dimensions.

The Photon Belt is interrelated to the oceanic Plasma Field, and presently Earth is traveling through a Gold Ray-infused current of Photonic energy. Because of this, we are experiencing the Seven Rays in a much fuller spectrum and encountering a remarkably new, monoatomic galactic atmosphere. This is the foundation of the Evolutionary Biome.

Throughout the pages of *Photons Propel Your Ascension*, Saint Germain explains this Golden Age science that propels conventional science and religion and unites physics and spirituality. Earth's movement into the light-surging Photon Belt envelops and develops her biologic and ecological systems into a synergistic symmetry of conscious spiritual evolution. For many, this provokes a profound inner awakening which later affects change within our social systems. Through this process we will see the transformation of our world economies and money systems, innovative and revolutionary discoveries within our medical and healthcare practices, and the positive abolition of politics and advancement of human rights. Change is not easy, however, and there will likely be challenges during this transition. Saint Germain reinforces that the Golden Age has begun and avidly states, "Nothing can stop this time of bounty, abundance, light, and Ascension for humanity!" For many, including Saint Germain, this historical tipping point is known as the *Great Awakening*.

To ensure a more comfortable passage into the Golden Age, for the last several years the Ascended Masters, Beloved Archangels and Elohim, and the great Cosmic Beings who oversee and protect humanity and Earth's spiritual development have purposely kept the Fifth-Dimensional Golden City of Shamballa open. Typically, when the sublime Golden City is opened on an annual basis, Earth is flooded for a short-period of time with a boon of spiritual energy from the heavenly city. This energy provides essential spiritual nourishment for humanity at many levels during the Shamballa season. Throughout the seasonal period, Ascended Master students may enter the sublime city during meditation and dreamtime. It is claimed that this is an important period for extensive training and one-on-one teaching with the Masters of the Shamballa lineage. Spiritual practice, ceremonies, and pilgrimages performed during this time period are considered more effective and spiritually potent. After a full-month's time, the golden gates are closed until the next Shamballa season. In the meantime, entrance is granted to only those who have spiritually developed the extrasensory "eyes to see, ears to hear."

Obviously, and especially now, Earth and humanity may need the additional boost. Recently we have experienced the 2020 Pandemic, untenable unemployment, the war in Ukraine, unpredictable power grid failures alongside historic cold and heat, and a continued, intense polarization with public debate over vaccines, abortion, racism, and continued insidious political turmoil. Contrarily, the Golden Age begins. Has our world reached the pinnacle of polarity, with a seeming perpetuity of clashing ideas, viewpoints, and beliefs? Through ongoing conflict our passage into light initiates a new HU-man infrastructure with the activation of our Divine DNA, and the expansion of new energetics and light-fields. Yes, we are truly experiencing the Cellular Awakening.

The teachings presented in *Photons Propel Your Ascension* are designed to increase your spiritual insight to gain familiarity with the Golden Age. After all, before now we've experienced tremendous spiritual darkness and ignorance through the reduced light-spectrum of Kali Yuga. As the Gold Ray triggers our Divine DNA, our awareness expands into new principles of spiritual growth and development. In these pages the Ascended Masters will direct your attention to the conscious use of free will, the inherent power embedded within each personal choice, and the enduring tenets of the Right-hand Path. Saint Germain, along with Lord Sananda, El Morya, Kuthumi, and the Pleiadean Master Anaya share and guide this simple, yet unique and precise instruction.

This teaching would be incomplete if not accompanied by the distinctive, experiential spiritual practices that were once secretly held in the venerated Shamballa Lineage. You will intensify your knowledge and use of the Violet Flame for your Ascension Process with specific decrees for HU-man Development and strengthen your service as a Step-down Transformer of Light. The mysteries of the White Fire Spiral of Ascension are revealed and further developed through engaging specific Spiritual Pilgrimages and Cup Ceremonies. You will learn the karma-freeing knowledge of "Energy-for-energy," while Co-creating a useful Information Portal to Fourth- and Fifth-Dimensional knowledge.

Each page of *Photons Engage Your Ascension* is filled with the new science and spiritual nuance of the Evolutionary Biome. Saint Germain introduces the foundation of trinomial mathematics, the basic physics that build the Golden Age. He offers the captivating fractal science of the Photon, which empowers the Golden Cities as electromagnetic capacitors of light. A new multidimensional construct of our Earth is presented through the descriptions of Inner Earth, and his insights explore how multiple, sensitive timelines calibrate with thoughtful, purposeful HU-man Consciousness. Undoubtedly, the Time of Change is now!

Most importantly, the almost forgotten spiritual heritage of freedom, our Ascension in the Light, is now reinstated. It is perhaps our most important HU-man right, and is gratefully received after the bondage of numerous lifetimes. Raise your right hand, and courageously accept the Mighty Gift as you proclaim unto self:

> "I AM a Divine HU-man—a BE-ing of Light!
> I call forth the Victory of the Violet Flame,
> To stream throughout my worldly karmas.
> The Ascension heals, restores, glorifies,
> And expands my Light!
> My Light Ascends to both
> Fourth and Fifth Dimensions.
> I AM the perfected balance of
> Divine Mother and Divine Father!
> I AM Awakened and Realized through
> The Christ Consciousness!
> I proclaim my Ascension
> And eternal Victory!
> So be it!
> Amen."

Photons

A Living Crystal

other names, and it increases your evolution exponentially.[8] (The Photon Belt) is assisted by the Gold Ray and its influx—that originates from the Great Central Sun—and arcs itself into the core of your Earth, into the inner Sun, and radiates through the Golden Cities.[9] Then the Golden Cities are qualified by Beloved Babajeran and the various Hierarchs, but primarily by the Hierarch of each Golden City who qualifies its first primary Ray Force. We have discussed this in detail. Each of the Golden Cities, as they move, is absorbing this Plasma Field.[10] A way to understand this is that their rotational fluxes expedite these energy frequencies to the HUman. For the Golden City is indeed a Golden City of living, plasmic light. From this viewpoint, the Golden City is a living and breathing crystal and it holds within the re-fraction of the energy and the coalescing and condensing of the energy.

THE LIGHT IS WITHIN, THE LIGHT IS WITHOUT

This promotes both an inner and outer Awakening. As I have said before the light is *within* and the light is *without*. This creates an acceleration of the light bodies and allows you to enter into a form of timelessness. For you see, Dear ones, we have always taught that it is indeed the neutral zone where the Ascension is achieved.[11] This is the energy and the frequency of balance. This also comes through the energies and the frequencies of the Golden Cities.

---

multi-dimensional experiences of the current of the Seven Rays of Light and Sound. This monoatomic presence affects the human absorption of high-frequency Ray Forces with an expanded division of cells, and unique cell replication, resulting in the increase of lifespans for thousands of years.

A plasma field is concentrated, not disbursed. It is known to carry inaudible sound pitches, (B-flat, D, and G at varying octaves), that step-down from the Great Central Sun—the center of our galaxy. Like all creation, plasma and its sound and light frequencies travel with a spinning motion.

Currently our solar system and our galaxy are moving through a highly-charged plasma field, of which the Earth has just begun to cross. Our recent convergence into this life expanding process heralds the birth of a full-force Golden Age for many millions of Earth-years. This includes an ever-increasing spectrum of light and sound frequencies that expands the seven traditional Rays with new, unique Ray Forces. Current examples of this evolutionary progression are the newfound presence of both the Gold Ray and the Aquamarine Ray. More life-expanding Rays will be identified and experienced in the future.

A Photon is a particle of light whose primary purpose is to create and deliver light into denser structures of matter. It is conscious, alive, and aware. Photons are widespread through all dimensions of light, and have the ability to adapt to every frequency. They are not limited in size, or dimensional expansion.

Seldom independent, Photons more commonly work together. Through organizing and concentrating their efforts, they move in condensed currents of energy similar to large river waterways, or the thermohaline circulatory system of the ocean. The Photon Belt is a main thoroughfare of such conscious convergence within the evolutionary plasma field. Photons attract unto one another, and they build and collect, divide and replicate, throughout the dimensions.

The Photon Belt is interrelated to the oceanic plasma field, and presently Earth is traveling through a Gold Ray infused current of Photonic energy. Because of this, we are experiencing the Seven Rays in much-fuller spectrum, and encountering a remarkably new, monoatomic galactic atmosphere. This is the foundation of the Evolutionary Biome.

8. See Appendix D: *The Photon.*
9. See Appendix E: *Arcing of Ray Forces.*
10. Golden Cities move like a Human Chakra.
11. See Appendix F: *The Eight Pathways of Ascension.*

LIVING CRYSTAL CITIES OF LIGHT

As you enter each of the Adjutant Points you may feel them only within a two-and-a-half-mile to five-mile flux; but, for those who have a more sensitive Kundalini system, and have developed their light bodies, they may feel an Adjutant Point up to sixty, sometimes eighty miles.[12] The sensitive human Kundalini system develops itself into its majesty of light, then each of the Adjutant Points is sensed within the entire Golden City and it becomes a resonating frequency of light—the living crystal of light. This is why so many times we have referred to the Golden Cities as the Golden Crystal Cities, for this is another way to understand how they function in this time of the Golden Age.

DARKNESS IS LIMITED

The dark frequencies are curious, and also understand this science. We know that you have protected the locations of the Adjutant Points, but it is important for you to understand that even they (the dark ones) may initiate a process through touching these Adjutant Points. Then, they become activated for the light and by the light. Dear ones, darkness has limitation, whereas light is always expanding and working toward freedom and the ultimate Ascension in the light!

AMERICA HOLDS THE LIGHT FOR THE WORLD

At this time America is at a threshold of great light, for it is by no mistake that the first five Golden Cities of the United States were activated (first).[13] Indeed, it is America's destiny to hold the light for the rest of the world.[14] The five Golden Cities: Gobean, Malton, Wahanee, Shalahah, and Klehma currently hold the light for the rest of the world.

THE SOUL'S CHOICE

It is important to remember that humanity always has free will, has their choice, do they not?

---

12. See Appendix G: *Sensing the Flux of Golden City Adjutant Points.*
13. The five Golden Cities of the United States are: Gobean, (Arizona, New Mexico), Malton, (Illinois, Indiana), Wahanee, (Georgia, South Carolina); Shalahah, (Idaho, Montana), and Klehma, (Colorado, Nebraska, Kansas).
14. According to the I AM America Prophecies, Saint Germain says that the people of America have a unique destiny in the New Times. America contains within it a unique anagram:
A M E R I C A = I A M R A C E.
The I AM Race of people is a unique group of souls who lived in America as Atlanteans. But their destiny has evolved since those ancient times. Instead of sinking on a continent destroyed by the misuse of technology and spiritual knowledge, their active intelligence continues to develop in modern times. Their service is focused on the Brotherly love of all nations. In the I AM America Earth Changes Prophecies Saint Germain states, "America will be the first to go through the changes, and then give aid to the rest of the World."

Response: *Yes.*

This is most important to know and to understand. For one cannot be forced to absorb the light. One must come to the light through the choice within their soul; however, once that choice is made it is very difficult to turn back. Now, let us move forward in our teaching regarding the Golden City Vortices.

THE TIME OF SHAMBALLA INCREASES THE LIGHT

During this Time of Shamballa we dispense even more information that can help you by ten, twelve, even up to fifteen, sometimes as much as twenty percent more radiance of light.[15] However, until one turns their will completely over to the Divine Will, it is very difficult to absorb these truths. We shall continue in our dispensation of (this) knowledge, especially during this Time of Shamballa as these energy frequencies grace the Earth right now.[16] America shall hold the light for the rest of the world, and the light shall expand over into the Greening Lands, and then over into the Lands of Exchange.

FREEDOM STAR

The Earth is to become that great Freedom Star of Light, a light that is held within the galaxy itself. She (will become) like a luminous Violet Sun that will hold the light for a new galaxy.[17] (This is) a new time period that is coming and will glorify the freedom of choice and the freedom of the Light BE-ing.

---

15. Over four weeks (twenty-eight days), esoteric followers, including Ascended Masters, honor the Celebration of the Four Elements during the Shamballa festivities. It begins December 17 — accompanied by lighting of the Eternal Flame Candle, or the Fireless Light — on the altar of the main temple. This etheric celebration is divided into the following four parts:
  1. Week One: December 18 to December 24. Element: Earth. The celebration and thanksgiving offered to Mother Earth. Ceremonies and rituals for Earth Healing are held at Shamballa during this time. Bowls of salt, which represent earth united with spirit, are placed on all the altars in the Temples of Shamballa.
  2. Week Two: December 25 to December 31. Element: Air. Celebrations of gratitude and thanksgiving to the World Teachers and the messengers of the Great White Brotherhood who have selflessly served humanity are held this week. Krishna, Jesus Christ, Buddha, and other well-known avatars and saviors are also lauded. Doves of Peace are symbolically released this week.
  3. Week Three: January 1 to January 7: Element: Water. A thanksgiving for our Soul Families is held during this week. This phase of Shamballa Celebration is about revering love and friendship, and performing Cup Ceremonies. A Cup Ceremony is a water ceremony that celebrates the union of Mother Earth and Soul Families. A cup of water is passed and infused with the prayers of the devoted. The prayer-charged water is then poured on the Earth.
  4. Week Four: January 8 to January 14: Element: Fire. This week is a celebration of Spiritual Fire. This time is set aside for personal purification, intentions, reflection, and meditation for the upcoming year. This is an important period for the Brotherhoods and Sisterhoods of Light to review plans for the following 365 days. Candles for each of the Seven Rays, representing the seven Hermetic Laws, are lit this week.
  5. The Sealing of Divinity: January 15 and 16: Celebrations of Unity — Unana — and the ONE.
  6. The Closing of Shamballa: January 17: the light of the Eternal Flame returns to Venus.
16. See Appendix H: *Shamballa and Sanat Kumara.*
17. The Ascended Masters prophesy that Earth will eventually break away from its current solar system, and evolve into a Violet Star. Later, it is claimed this star develops into a Sun, with its own

GROW IN THE LIGHT OF ASCENSION

In past Shamballa (seasons), we gave you much discourse upon the functioning of Shamballa, the weeks of the celebrations, and the many Temples of Light.[18] During this Shamballa, we will not focus upon these activities, for while they will be in the background for the many chelas and devotees of the Great White Brotherhood to celebrate and to experience, we will place our focus upon giving you more information so that you can grow in the light of Ascension. We will focus our discourse upon the Golden Cities, upon the Doorways,[19] and how they function within the Ray Forces. There will also be numerous messages that will come forward from the many Adjutant Point Hierarchs, for they, too, give their service at this time.[20] Now, Dear ones, before I proceed, do you have any questions?

Response: *Just one.*

Proceed.

Response: *Please help the students, the seekers, to have an experience of Shamballa during this Shamballa season.*

I will send my Mantle of Consciousness[21] to touch each of them at their highest frequency and level of light. This will activate them in their time of meditation and also in their time of sleep so they may enter the Golden Gates of Shamballa and partake of the many festivities, the many feasts, and the celebrations.

Ascension is the focus, is it not? This is the purpose of the HU-man — to achieve its evolution and liberation within the light. Of course this is always carried forward through the free will, and Ascended Master Teaching and the great Hierarchy of Light stress how important *free will* and *choice* is. Dear ones, it is through the energy and vibration of the Mighty I AM Presence that the light can continue to express its growth and evolution in perfection. This, too, is a lineage that has been brought forward not only from the Halls of Venus but also from Halls of the Pleiades and that great light of the DAHL.[22] For it (the teaching) has grown in its own evolution and now its light cannot be held back!

---

scheme of planets. Earth, in this new state, will be known as *Freedom Star*. As a breakaway civilization, the new solar system will host a total of seven moons, and will be the home for many Ascended, free Light Beings.

18. See Appendix I: *Temples of Shamballa*.
19. See Appendix J: *Golden City Doorways*.
20. An Adjutant Point Hierarch is the Master Teacher, Angel, Archangel, or Elohim associated with a certain ethereal Ashram located within a Golden City Vortex. Adjutant Point Hierarchs serve the Ray Force of their particular Golden City, which is overseen by the Golden City Hierarch.
21. A Mantle of Consciousness assists one to a new level of conscious awareness that produces tremendous change and spiritual development.
22. The parallel, twin universe to our universe. The Dahl Universe is spiritually and technologically advanced, and it is alleged that members from the Dahl Universe visit our Universe, known as the DERN, at timely junctures for spiritual evolution and intervention.

LIGHT SHINES ON THE DARKNESS

The darkness that is now being experienced upon the Earth Plane and Planet is like that *Last Waltz of the Tyrants*.[23] This is their last grasp upon humanity, for they know they are losing control of their darkness. They know that they, too, have this great Light of God shining upon them and this is illuminating even their own DNA.

BONDAGE OF THE DARK ONES

There was a time upon the Earth Plane and Planet when the dark forces abounded, not only in Third Dimension, but Fourth and Fifth Dimension.[24] Dear ones, this was that dark time of Kali Yuga[25] and they were given, shall we say, *their choice*. However, now in this time of great light—the Golden Age—the choice of humanity reigns supreme.[26] The dark forces were bound by Archangel Michael many decades ago, we have also discussed this. They were bound through the Fourth Dimension, and onward into the Fifth Dimension. Now there are those who would say that these demons and deities are still coming through (from Fourth and Fifth Dimension) and many of them come through Subjective Energy Bodies.[27] This, too, held in the Group Minds of those of evil.

USE OF GROUP MIND

We have instructed you in the great Group Mind of holding light, for each Group Mind as it is formed holds the light like a brilliant beacon on the Earth Plane and Planet.[28] When it aligns itself and coalesces with the light of the Adjutant Points and the Star of a Golden City it is increased not only a thousand-fold but ten thousand-fold, so it is important to know and understand Group Mind. Listen to tape. Hold your Group Mind practice as this has great power. It is most important to form a Group Mind with chelas at physical Adjutant Points and at the physical Golden

---

23. A seminal work based on the channeled works of Ramtha that details the history of the world's controllers. Received in the late 1980s, this prophetic information accurately portrays the drastic economic and political change we are now experiencing.

24. In *A Teacher Appears*, Saint Germain explains, "For it was Archangel Michael who came to bind and bound the foreign entities. They have been taken from your Earth Planet and Plane at this time, so the entities that you encounter are those which have been created through the thought form of mankind."

In *Fields of Light*, he shares further insight on this subject, "You are all of the opinion that Princes of Darkness have free access to your world. Well they do not! They have been removed, so the Children of Light may grow in their light and ascend. The darkness you see around is created by the human beings after 1952. The begetters of darkness are gone. The only evil, or backward living, is all created by humankind, out of the Karmic memory you all have. Give up the memory of darkness and choose the memory of light!"

25. The Age of Iron, or Age of Quarrel, when Earth receives twenty-five percent or less galactic light from the Great Central Sun.

26. See Appendix K: *The Cycle of the Yugas*.

27. This type of energy is similar to a thought-form, which causes behavioral changes when triggered. They are created through intense emotions, addictive behaviors, and the use of addictive substances, and often contain elements of lower consciousness.

28. See Appendix L: *The Group Mind and Visualization to Achieve Group Mind*.

City Star(s)—this is the greatest coalescing of light.[29] This is why the Adjutant Point Hierarchs are (present) at the Adjutant Points. This is why the great Hierarchs of the Golden Cities reside in the Golden Cities, for they hold within them the nexus (connection) of the Group Mind that streams from the energies of that grand Golden City and Shamballa.

During the Time (opening) of Shamballa, light streams from the seven Temples of the Mighty Rays into the hearts of all fifty-one Golden Cities on Earth.[30] This reinvigorates and recharges the Golden Cities and each of their Doorways into a majestic expression of and for the light.

Last year you were instructed and sent upon several Pilgrimages, this builds and fortifies your light fields. We sent you for the *Healing of the Nations* and while I know you could not complete all of these Adjutant Points, you were present at several of them and this was most important.[31] Through this process you have grown, have you not? Your will has become a bit stronger, has it not?

Response: *Most certainly, yes.*

ENLIGHTENMENT AND HU-MAN ENERGETICS

This year, if you so choose, you can continue onward with your Pilgrimages into the Southern Door.[32] However, this year there will be an emphasis that will be placed upon the Western Door. For the entire year of 2021 is a continued year of healing, but also a year of illumination and enlightenment. This comes through the energetics of the Western Door of all Golden Cities, and we will give discourse upon how to achieve this enlightenment, to increase the effectiveness of your decrees, and increase the effectiveness of your Group Mind, and enter into the great solace of meditation. This all is achieved (enhanced) through the energetics of the Western Doors of Golden Cities. This is not to say that the other Golden City Doorways are not important, for all of them, at any time, can help you to grow and to learn within the light frequencies. While you may spend some of your time within the Southern Door, and move through your Ascension Process, this year we will work with you to expand your light and help you to identify *with* the light. This is true *En-lighten-ment*.[33]

---

29. The apex, or center of each Golden City. All spiritual practice, especially prayer and meditation, is extremely effective while one is located in any Star area of a Golden City Vortex.
The Stars of Golden City Vortices function with a unique similarity to a technique developed by the late Dr. David Hawkins whose research mapped states of human consciousness known as critical-point analysis. In his book *Power Versus Force*, Hawkins explains his process: "Critical point analysis is a technique derived from the fact that in any highly complex system there is a specific critical point at which the smallest input will result in the greatest change. The great gears of a windmill can be halted by lightly touching the right escape mechanism; it is possible to paralyze a giant locomotive if you know exactly where to put your finger."

30. To learn more about Shamballa and the Temples of Shamballa, see *Evolutionary Biome*.

31. See Appendix M: *Decrees for the Healing of the Nations.*

32. This is the *Ascension Pilgrimage*; for more information see *I AM America Atlas, 2020 revised edition.*

33. This is an advanced process of Cellular Awakening, and the physical cells of the human body literally fill with spiritual light.

THE CELLULAR AWAKENING

Enlightenment is the light that pours through that mighty shushumna of energy, and into your Kundalini. Then (the light) expands through each of your cells. This is that magnificent Cellular Awakening that we have spoken about in past discourse.[34] The Cellular Awakening rouses your mental body, it stimulates all the faculties of the physical body, it develops your Astral Body and your Causal Body. Now I know that all of you have achieved to some degree the knowledge and the experience of the use of these light bodies, however, this year it will be exponential (multiplied). Why is this so? Again, this is due to the great Plasma Field and the Golden Cities as living crystals of light.

Dear ones, understand that there will be many time anomalies this year. Time weaves the illusion, like each thread within a rope. However, it is important to understand time as a *field of experience*. This, too, I have taught, exampled by each of the Evolutionary Pyramids that express in the Golden Cities of Light.[35]

DETACHMENT AND CULTIVATING TRUE MEMORY

These (Golden City) fields of experience can predicate the types of experiences that you may have.[36] This, too, is traced through time; however, I hope that you will have more experiences within these experiential fields of time. This will assist you to recognize, know, and understand not only the anomalies of Time Compaction along with the anomalies of timelessness. Timelessness reverses the aging process of the physical body, as you accede to surf through time. This is known as True Memory, and you begin to distinguish and recognize experiences, without personal judgment.[37] You are able to view experiences *just as they are* with detachment. Of course, through the use of the Mighty Violet Flame you can achieve great levels of detachment; however, within the fields of experience in the Golden City, this, too, can be magnified. Now, I sense your questions…proceed.

---

34. A spiritual initiation activated by the Master Teachers Saint Germain and Kuthumi. Through this process the physical body is accelerated at the cellular level, preparing consciousness to recognize and receive instruction from the Fourth Dimension. Supplemental teachings on the Cellular Awakening claim this process assists the spiritual student to assimilate the higher frequencies and energies now available on Earth. Realizing the Cellular Awakening can ameliorate catastrophic Earth Change and initiate consciousness into the ONE through the realization of devotion, compassion, Brotherhood and the Universal Heart.
35. See Appendix N: *Part One: Evolutionary Points and Pyramids*.
36. See Appendix O: *The Evolutionary Field*.
37. Memory, as defined by Ascended Master teachings is not seen as a function of the brain, or the soul's recall of past events. Instead, True Memory is achieved through cultivating our perceptions and adjusting our individual perspective of a situation to the multiple juxtapositions of opinion and experience. This depth of understanding gives clarity and illumination to every experience. Our skill and Mastery through True Memory moves our consciousness beyond common experiences to individualized experiences whose perceptive power hones honesty and accountability. The innate truth obtained from many experiences through the interplay of multiple roles creates True Memory, and opens the detached and unconditional Law of Love to the chela.

DIET AND DNA FREQUENCIES

Question: Yes. At a DNA and RNA level, light fields of consciousness penetrate our human physiology and the other levels of DNA that we carry in our physical bodies. Are Ray Systems expanded at an auric level and at a physical genetic level?

This is true, Dear one, and certain Star seeds have more of a propensity to absorb light, while other Star seeds have a much more difficult time. This is why we set up the different requirements for the diet.[38] We realize that it may not match perfectly. Sometimes the DNA frequencies that you hold in your physical body have great difficulty. It (the diet) does help them to break through. Do you understand?

Response: *Yes, I do.*

ASCENSION THROUGH THE VIOLET FLAME

It is important to always ensure that your light frequencies take on a daily practice of meditation, but also the work with the Violet Flame. For lower energies, (as) the dross of the karmic residue is burned away, this allows for a change of the DNA itself. Now, I know you have questioned this in the past, but it is true. This is how the Ascension can be achieved through focus upon that Mighty Violet Flame.

> Violet Flame, I AM.
> Come forth in the majesty of the Seven Rays.
> Come forth and raise my body,
> My physical body, my Astral Body, my Causal Body and all of my light bodies,
> Into the freedom of the Ascension!
> So be it.

Response: *So be it.*

As you call upon and focus upon that Mighty Violet Flame, this, too, is another pathway through which you can achieve your eternal freedom in the light.

---

38. Saint Germain's advice on diet in, *A Teacher Appears:* "I would like to verse you, too, on your diet. Take in only that which is pure and clean, for the stress of the many vibrations are hard upon the physical vehicle. At the end of your day, spend time in solitude and meditation to cleanse your system from this. Put only the freshest and most valuable foods to your system. Before you eat, charge them with a directed activity of the I AM, for are you not taking in that which is of the ONE Source? Recognize this in all that you do. And are you not taking in of the ONE Source as you travel and people are placed in your path? See that, as they give to you, you also give to them."
Similar advice given by Saint Germain in *Fields of Light:* "Saint Germain also introduced a technique to purify food and drink: that of visualizing Green and Gold energy streaming from your ring finger, on your left or right hand, whichever you prefer. Apparently, this is a type of individualized energy that streams directly from your I AM Presence, and carries a unique vibration and blessing that alchemizes a distinctive and matchless elixir into your food and beverages."

SHAMBALLA'S INTENTION

Dear one, since I have introduced the course of which we shall travel, I am here to guide, assist, and help you. Know, Dear hearts, that Shamballa is open for all, for those seekers of light, for those who ask, "Is there more...is there a way that I can achieve more knowledge, more information, more experience through the Mighty I AM?" This was always the intention of Shamballa, to be open for the spiritual seeker of light, but also, to preserve its great ancestry of teaching.

EACH GOLDEN CITY MODELS SHAMBALLA

As we have stated in past discourses, the Mighty Golden City of Shamballa is modeled after the grand Venusian Cities and the Pleiadean Cities of Light; but, it is also true that the great Golden Cities are modeled after Shamballa. Each contains their Mighty Temples of the Ray Forces, their Mighty Temples of the Angelic Host, and Mighty Halls of Wisdom that are overseen by the Elohim. It is important to understand that at the center of each Golden City is a Mighty Temple of Unity that mirrors that Mighty Temple of Unity as it exists in Shamballa, and those who enter into the Star frequencies feel this uniting of energies, feel the camaraderie and the Brotherhoods of Breath, Sound, and Light...feel each of the Ray Forces come together, coalescing, and working together as ONE.

EVOLUTIONARY BIOME AND THE ONE

When I say the ONE, this is indeed what you term the Evolutionary Biome. Dear ones, this is the mighty understanding of unity that *all works together* as ONE and is as ONE. In the future we all know that the Evolutionary Biome will assist and help many to become free of the tedious tasks of the physical plane, but it will also allow humanity to enter into that Time of Transportation.[39, 40] This, you know, Dear ones. This, you know, Dear heart. Questions?

Response: *Yes, the Age of Transportation, the Time of Ascension...*

---

39. The Evolutionary Biome is the seamless connection, interaction, and cooperation with Creation at multi-dimensional levels through the HU-man senses. The premise of Evolutionary Biome is cultivated through the fractal experience of the Evolution Points in the Eight-sided Cell of Perfection; it is further aided through the Oneness, Oneship, and ONE of the Golden City Adjutant Points, Temples, Retreats, and Stars. The Evolutionary Biome is the evolutionary process that leads Earth and humanity to the Ascended Master state of consciousness known as Unana.

40. A prophesied epoch on Earth humanity will experience once we leave the current Information Age (late eighties through the twenty-first century). The Transportation Age will see humanity's consciousness evolve into Mastery beyond the human maxims of time and space. During this period, which is prophesied to run concurrently with several periods of the Golden Age — the Age of Cooperation and the Age of Peace — humanity will begin interstellar travel, alongside leaps in evolutionary growth resulting in telepathic communication, spiritual technologies, and bi-location.

Not only is it a Time of Ascension, it is a time when lifespans of the physical body will be extended not only to eight, nine-hundred years, but up to twelve-hundred years, and more. This will change much of how human life is lived and perceived. This human extension of life will create an extensive change throughout Earth's cultures. This will allow for an exploration that will occur upon the Earth Plane and Planet, but will extend throughout your solar system and move on into other great galaxies of light. This, too, is another important aspect and attribute of the living crystals of light—the Mighty Golden Cities—for they connect you timelessly and assuredly with the Evolutionary Biome, the ONE, the Mighty Unana, and they connect you to other galaxies of experience.

PORTALS OF LIGHT

This (connection) is often first achieved in the Star. This is why we have identified the Stars as the most critical points within the Golden Cities.[41] Now, the Adjutant Points can carry almost as much energy and frequency of light, however, they also serve to protect that Mighty Star. They are like a web of Golden Light that coalesces, yet also contracts and expands in a breath of expansion. One can enter through these mighty, grand portals of light, and their consciousness may stream into other galaxies of experience. This will be more fully understood as more light streams forward to the Earth Plane and Planet. Dear one, questions?

Question: *So, would it be helpful for students and chelas traveling to the Southern Door to follow the normal sequences that have been outlined, or to follow the sequences that have been outlined in the Western Door?*

THE WHITE RAY

Each is a choice...each is given with a timing and an intention. For last year the brilliant White Ray was streaming into the Southern Door, this year the brilliant White Ray streams into the Western Door.[42] This we follow, for it allows us to increase more effulgent light within the light fields. This energy streams from Venus and is stepped-down from the Pleiades, and that mighty DAHL. This is also part of the great lineage

---

41. The Stars of Golden City Vortices function with a unique similarity to a technique developed by the late Dr. David Hawkins whose research mapped states of human consciousness known as critical-point analysis. In his book *Power Versus Force,* Hawkins explains his process: "Critical point analysis is a technique derived from the fact that in any highly complex system there is a specific critical point at which the smallest input will result in the greatest change. The great gears of a windmill can be halted by lightly touching the right escape mechanism; it is possible to paralyze a giant locomotive if you know exactly where to put your finger."

All spiritual practice, especially prayer and meditation, is extremely effective while one is located in any Star area of a Golden City Vortex for World Peace. The Ascended Masters' instruction focuses on Lord Sananda's Heart Meditation and recommends that a group of seven individuals focused on this meditation can effect personal change for global peace. In essence, this technique is a force field of light, especially when applied within the Star of a Golden City Vortex, where the least amount of energy exerts the greatest effect.

42. See Appendix P: *Periodic Movement of the Rays in Golden Cities and Modulated Ray Forces.*

of Shamballa. We understand and know the nuance of the White Light, how it holds within it the full spectrum of the Seven Rays of Light and Sound...this potentiates the new Rays of light. Yes, this is brought forward through the Plasma Field and the Gold Ray, but it also streams forth with a provenance and a certain ancestry. We follow the energies of the White Ray, for this is indeed our pledge to the Right-hand Path.[43] Proceed.

Response: *I see. So the White Ray appears in each of the Doorways in a succession?*

Indeed, Dear one, and today is the day of that great churning of the clock. This is the time frame that we work with on the Earth Plane and Planet. As the White Ray moves from the Southern Door, it begins to arc energies into the West, and it will proceed as it moves through all the Doorways. Sometimes this happens on an annual (yearly) basis; however, sometimes it can take longer and sometimes it can be shorter. This depends on the positioning of the Golden Cities, and the Gold Ray[44] as it streams forth from the Great Central Sun and into your solar system. Do you understand?

Response: *Yes. Are we the only solar system affected by the Gold Ray and the Plasma Field?*

This is correct; however, only the Golden Cities are affected by the White Ray. The White Ray, the middle way, is the provenance and the true understanding of Shamballa. This is the balance of karma and dharma. It is the understanding of the Right-hand path and that humanity is to become free.

Response: *Yes, freedom is very different than liberty. Freedom is permanent. Our process of attaining our freedom and helping others is to guide, inspire, and assist others in this Earth Plane. As these Doorways open up for every Golden City, and I am assuming it's not just the ones that we would refer to as being activated, it could be every Golden City throughout this Plane and Planet?*

---

43. See Appendix Q: *Right-hand Path*.
44. The Ray of Brotherhood, Cooperation, and Peace. The Gold Ray produces the qualities of perception, honesty, confidence, courage, and responsibility. It is also associated with leadership, independence, authority, ministration, and justice. The Gold Ray vibrates the energies of Divine Father on Earth. Its attributes are: warm; perceptive; honest; confident; positive; independent; courageous; enduring; vital; leadership; responsible; ministration; authority; justice. The Gold Ray is also associated with the Great Central Sun, the Solar Logos, of which our Solar Sun is a Step-down Transformer of its energies. According to the Master Teachers, the Gold Ray is the epitome of change for the New Times. The Gold Ray is the ultimate authority of Cosmic Law, and carries both our personal and worldwide Karma and Dharma (purpose). Its presence is designed to instigate responsible spiritual growth and planetary evolution as a shimmering light for humanity's aspirations and the development of the HU-man. The Gold Ray, however, is also associated with Karmic justice, and will instigate change: constructive and destructive. The extent of catastrophe or transformation is contingent on humanity's personal and collective spiritual growth and evolutionary process as we progress into the New Times. The dispensation of the Gold Ray to Earth calibrates the movement of the Color Rays, including the White Ray of Venus, throughout the Golden City directions.

This is true, Dear one, however, the Great Activation of 2020 helped the White Ray to stream into the Southern Doors and move this year (2021) into the West. This is of vast importance.[45]

Now I shall like to also indicate that I will be carrying forth discourse next Thursday on a weekly basis as we continue our journey into not only the expansion of knowledge, but also more into this provenance of the White Ray of Ascension and Freedom.

Response: *Thank you.*

And now, unless if there are other questions I shall take my leave and return at the appointed time.

Response: *I have only one question.*

Proceed.

Question: *Is there a specific decree to be said in the Western Door Adjutant Points?*

There will be specific decrees that will be given for each Adjutant Point.

Response: *Then I thank you for your grace, blessings, and compassion. Shamballa to you and all who gather.*

May light stream forth into the hearts of humanity! For humanity is to be free and ascended as ONE in the light. So be it!

Response: *So be it.* Hitaka!

Hitaka.

---

45. An acceleration of the activation of certain Golden Cities that hastens our entrance into the New Times. Golden Cities participating in the Great Activation are: Braun, Afrom, Ganakra, Mesotamp, Shehez, and Adjatal.

CHAPTER TWO

Gatekeepers of Light

Shamballa Imbues Energies to the Golden Cities

Greetings, Beloveds, I AM still here. I AM Saint Germain and request permission to come forward.

Response: *Please, Saint Germain, come forward and thank you for your patience.*

FREEDOM, CHOICE, AND FREE WILL

I never left your side, Dear ones. I was always guiding you, setting a vibration within your residence so that you could continue with this discourse. As I was just saying, we at the Hierarchy and especially during the time of Shamballa, oversee the great liberty and freedom of humanity. As you well know, one must have their freedom in order *to choose*.

One does not come to the understanding of the Ascension without free will. Free will plays a most important role, for choosing is the great fulcrum of the will itself. This allows the individual to activate that Mighty Unfed Flame of Love, Wisdom, and Power, but it also helps to bring forward a great activation of the Divine DNA, the Eight-sided Cell of Perfection.

THE EIGHT-SIDED CELL OF PERFECTION AND THE GOLDEN CITY

The Eight-sided Cell of Perfection is the nexus[1] of liberty, freedom, and liberation. Within and after the Ascension many move on in their service, not only (service) to humanity, but (service) to many others, planetary life-streams, and Planes of Consciousness that are focused within the Galactic Web. Also, you know, Dear ones, during Shamballa we all have the ability to give a *little bit* more. The (Spiritual) Hierarchy gives a little bit more to humanity so that you may gain and grow in your own spiritual evolution. This is a form of an energetic, a *shakti* of energy[2] that comes forward at this time (that is) activated within the light fields, and also within the divine DNA—the Eight-sided Cell of Perfection.

The great Photon Belt and Plasma Field also help to arc more continuously the Gold and the Aquamarine Ray into the heart of the Eight-sided Cell of Perfection.[3]

---

1. Connection, link, tie, or center of.
2. Shatki is a form of energy that is Co-creative, sustaining, and can initiate spiritual growth and development.
3. See Appendix R: *Diagram of the Eight-sided Cell of Perfection with the Unfed Flame and Monad.*

This great cell mirrors in fractal symmetry the magnificent Golden Cities of Light. We at Shamballa serve and assist the great Golden Cities and the Vortex structure mirrors—as within, so without—that mighty Eight-sided Cell of Perfection. (Through this) we can serve at a much higher level every individual's spiritual evolution and ultimate freedom in Ascension.

THE LIGHTED STANCE

We have given you much information regarding the Adjutant Points of Light and I mentioned in my first discourse that this Shamballa Season is a year of enlightenment. Dear ones, enlightenment is not only a philosophical and spiritual tenant, it is also the great light that enters into the Mighty Eight-sided Cell of Perfection. There, it is able to refract and arc into each of the individualized light fields. As this occurs, the enlightenment is the precursor to the Lighted Stance—I have spoken of this before. Right now, I stand in the Lighted Stance, as I have lowered my energies from Fifth Dimension into the Fourth Dimension.[4] I embrace you within my light and within the stance of God Power so that you can rise in vibration to the Fourth Dimension and receive my energy and this lesson!

VIOLET FLAME AND THE GROUP MIND

The Lighted Stance is sustained through the use of that Mighty Violet Flame. Dear Ones, the Violet Flame promotes states of detachment, compassion, and forgiveness within the Mental Body. It also creates an alchemy that clears the way within the divine DNA so that greater light can move within the light bodies…arcing and melding the light bodies. This melding is of vast importance, for you perceive them as separate layers, yet we know them only as ONE light.[5] This is the Lighted Stance of Enlightenment. It is ONE body of light, yes, and sometimes we refer to this ONE body of light as the Christ Consciousness. However, it is the Oneship that is contained and held within our Group Mind.

Use of the Violet Flame allows you entrance into our Group Mind that we have held from time immemorial. The Violet Flame [6] has an exacting history with a provenance from the DAHL to the Pleiades, onward to Venus, and then into the Earth Plane and Planet. It is true that the Violet Flame was held by Archangel Zadkiel during the epoch of Atlantis.[7] It has also been applied many times at a spiritual level to clear the etheric fields of the Earth so that humanity could have a more pristine environment in which to spiritually evolve. The Violet Flame allows you entrance into

---

4. The Lighted Stance is also known as the *Diamond Mind*. It is a powerful energy field that can pierce illusion. This energy is also part of the development of the Tenth Energy Body, or Tenth Light field of HU-man Development.
5. See Appendix S: *Human to HU-man Light Fields*.
6. See Appendix T: *The Violet Flame*.
7. The Brotherhood of Zadkiel was established there, and today remains as an ethereal temple over Cuba.

the Group Mind held at Shamballa and many other sanctuaries of light and the Violet Flame engenders within all of you your great Divine Destiny.

THE ANCIENT SHAMBALLA SCHOOLS

Dear ones, Dear hearts, as you move forward in your Ascension you will each be given an opportunity to serve. Many of you may choose to come forward into the great Ashrams of Light at the Adjutant Points.[8] Some of you may choose to serve in the magnificent Ashrams that are present in the Star and some of you may choose to arrive at these great halls of Shamballa to serve in one of the many temples.[9] In our last Shamballa season I introduced many of the different (Shamballa) temples, so that you may begin to understand the expansive knowledge that is contained at Shamballa. You may also receive extensive spiritual knowledge when you meditate during the Time of Shamballa, or when you sleep and enter its mighty gates. Each Shamballa School has been present during every epoch of Earth's history. They have held the most perfect philosophies, religions, and dispensed the Cosmic Laws that have been (subsequently) enacted upon the Earth Plane and Planet. You can access any of this information at any time during (the opening of) Shamballa, and be given exact instruction to touch these etheric, Akashic Records. (This access is) through what is known as the Gatekeeper of each of the schools.

TEMPLE GATEKEEPERS

Each Gatekeeper holds and protects the Ancient Scrolls of Life[10] that are contained within each temple. The Gatekeeper accepts within their ashrams the students who come to learn various esoteric subjects from time immemorial upon the Earth Plane and Planet. These are sometimes known as the great libraries, similar to the great libraries that exist on the planet Venus. These, too, are held at the etheric level of Shamballa. During greater epochs of light upon the Earth many of these schools existed upon the Earth; however, because of the lower vibration of humanity and

---

8. See Appendix N: *Part Two: Golden City Adjutant Points, Lei-lines, and Golden City Ashrams.*
9. See Appendix I: *Temples of Shamballa.*
10. This is in reference to the Akashic Records, which are spiritual records that document and affirm every lifetime and experience that a soul encounters throughout their evolutionary process and spiritual development. Reference to the Akashic Records is mentioned in the Holy Bible Book of Jubilees, as the *Book of Life*, where the Creator allegedly enters each soul's many names and their subsequent deeds, both good and bad. Good deeds are recorded in the *Book of Life*, and impure deeds are documented in the *Book of Death*. This is the principle of karma, and from its Sanskrit root, *kri*, means *actions, both good and bad*. The Ancient Mysteries assign the holder of these karmic records to the Ancient of the Ancients, who is sometimes known in Ascended Master Teaching as the Ancient of Days, the formidable Venusian leader of the Great White Brotherhood, Sanat Kumara. Manly Hall writes, "He is knowable and unknowable. In the Zohar, his robes are said to be white, but they are shown as red to signify that the garments of Divinity partake of the nature of cosmic activity. His face is declared to be the likeness of a face vast, luminous, and terrible. He sits upon a throne of flaming light and the flashes of the fire are subject to his Will. The White Light streaming from his head illumines four hundred thousand worlds. The glory of this Light shall be given unto the just." He is considered the "Concealed of the Concealed Ones," the "Eternal of the Eternal Ones," and the "Mystery of the Mysteries."

especially at this time—until humanity is able to rise into higher vibration—this information is guarded and kept securely in the Mighty Halls of Shamballa.[11]

THE SHAMBALLA SCHOOLS ARE LOWERED

Many who are drawn to I AM America may have rekindled a memory of a time period upon the Earth when they served in these remarkable schools of light and wisdom. These (schools), Dear ones, not only prepared the mind, but moved the chela (quickly) into the realm of the initiate, and from the initiate into the Arhat, and assisted their education and experience with ease into the Adept, and onward to Master.[12] These schools held the venerated knowledge that could free the soul into higher levels and realms of light. Each of these schools now exists in a different form at Shamballa, and (currently) we lower their energies and their frequencies into the center of the Golden Cities during Shamballa. This is how you are able to access their information.

ENLIGHTENMENT IN THE STAR

During periods of Shamballa it is important to retreat within the Star frequencies so you can access the pure knowledge as (their) energetics are lowered to the Earth Plane and Planet. I have spoken of these schools before, and today I would like to give more detail regarding their function during this opening of Shamballa, and how you may receive greater insight, knowledge, and wisdom. Dear ones, this is also the *true enlightenment*.[13] This is the spirituality that exists *within you* as an open heart—ready to receive this information. This, too, is the lineage of Shamballa, and the energetic that streams forward from our heart to your heart. You are ONE with us, and we are ONE with you. So be it. Before I proceed do you have questions?

Response: *Not at this time, please proceed.*

THE GOBEAN SCHOOL

The majestic school of Gobean is overseen by beloved El Morya.[14] Here, he teaches and steps-down frequencies from the Gatekeeper of the Temple of the Blue Ray and its school of knowledge. It is a school that streams, yes, from ancient Egypt. This school is active at this time, for two of its noble teachers of Unity Consciousness—Akhenaton

---

11. It is claimed that Shamballa is home to numerous Temples, Schools, and Retreats of the Ascended Masters and Beings of Light. For more information see Appendix H: *Shamballa and Sanat Kumara.*
12. See the Seven Levels of human evolution and their initiatory processes in Appendix H: *Shamballa and Sanat Kumara.*
13. Enlightenment is the act of gaining spiritual wisdom and insight. According to the Spiritual Teachers, this process literally increases the light of the Human Aura. From a Buddhist perspective, it is a final state of spiritual growth and evolution, and is defined by the lack of desire and human suffering.
14. See Appendix U: *El Morya.*

and Nefertiti—serve within the Southern Door of Gobean.[15] The illustrious school of Egypt focused upon the Blue Ray, and held within it the purity of the Ascension knowledge. This is the knowledge of the freedom of the soul, and includes teachings of soul travel through meditative techniques. Students could travel beyond the Earth, enter the Galactic Web,[16] and move among the various Golden Cities of Light of the Earth, and Golden Cities of other solar systems. This is achieved through the tempering of the Will Chakras.[17] Yes, the frontal chakras are very important in this knowledge, but the will carries within it the ability to hold energetics intact of the physical incarnation. This allows that Mighty Golden Thread Axis to extend itself as a silver thread of light between it and the traveling Astral Body. This was produced through a series of anointings, and a series of initiations.

TESTS OF THE RIGHT-HAND PATH

Yes, indeed, some initiations were brought about though the tempering of the soul in a religious manner, but any test is given through the Right-hand Path. A test is never physical, but a spiritual test. That is why we have given you so many different Pilgrimages, for each Pilgrimage presents a test for you, does it not? Do you have the resources to travel within the physical plane? Do you have the strength to carry on spiritually, from one point to the next? Can you move forward with great joy in your heart, and love for the spiritual path? This is true initiation. Each test prepares one for even greater knowledge that is held in the grand schools of Gobean. In the future, knowledge of the science of the soul, will be taught here. This is the knowledge of soul travel, and that sound frequencies are interrelated to the concept of time. We have somewhat discussed this and the possibility of time travel, is this not true, Dear one?

Response: *It is so.*

(Time travel) has always been taught in the schools of the Blue Ray. For *time,* Dear one, *is perception* is it not?

Response: *Yes it is.*

FREEDOM FROM TIME

Time controls the many vast experiences—this was always taught in the great schools of the Blue Ray. When one frees themselves from the physical plane and enters into the freedom of the Fourth and the Fifth dimension, they free themselves *from time,* and this allows one to travel not only into the future, but also, into the past. This

---

15. See Appendix V: *Akhenaton.*
16. The Galactic Web is a large, encircling galactic grid, created by the consciousness of all things in the galaxy—human, animal, plant, and mineral. Magnetic Vortices, namely the Golden Cities, appear at certain intersections of the Galactic Web.
17. See Appendix W: *The Will Chakras.*

is known as the recapitulation or a re-collection process.[18] One begins to understand how the past has played a vital role in creating the present, and the present plays a vital role in creating the future. However, from this viewpoint, all are ONE and held within the unity and the sanctity of the teaching.

THE MALTON SCHOOL

Let me move on to that Mighty Golden Gate held in Malton. This carries the frequencies and the energies of the knowledge of the Elemental Kingdom and one may enter into a greater union with Beloved Babajeran. I have given a basic outline of the Elemental Kingdoms, but what is not known is that the human body contains within many of these great kingdoms: the Kingdoms of the Fairies, of the Gnomes, of the Sylphs, Undines, Brownies, and Elves. All are contained within the human body.[19] Sometimes you see Elementals expressing themselves in different human form, and this remarkable school of the Ruby and the Gold influence comes forward to assist mankind to understand its Divine DNA and relationship to the Fourth Dimension.[20]

GENETIC KINGDOMS OF LIGHT

As one begins to travel through the many Kingdoms of Creation that exist upon the Earth Plane and Planet, the Eight-sided Cell of Perfection further activates and one begins to understand their vast connection as ONE. This, Dear ones, Dear hearts, is important. This is another form of *true enlightenment* and each of you contains genetics of the Elemental Kingdoms. I am not speaking of only earth, water, air, and fire...I

---

18. This is the process of recalling the past, including past lives. From this overview, the soul gains knowledge of their unique, individualized spiritual development and evolution.

19. Interestingly, all plants and animals share only one kind of DNA. However, this vital DNA contains different codes and sound frequencies that signal genes and vital amino acids and enzymes that define and build life. Esoteric scientists link both Pleiadeans and Earth's elven genomes with an ancient Lyran alien race. It is claimed that both species have a profound ability to heal, live primarily on a vegetarian diet, and are peaceful. Their spirituality relies on allegiance to fairness and equality, and they self-govern through the philosophic Right-hand Path of the White Council. Elves often intervene to assist humanity during times of evolutionary crisis.

Elven biology mirrors human biology, with only a 0.2 percent difference. Their hearing range is considerably higher than the human. Humans hear sounds from 400 to 20,000 hertz, while their elemental counterparts can discern sound from 1,000 to 30,000 hertz. Elves can separate colors at subtle levels and adjust their eyesight to ably see in the dark. Remarkably, Elves live long lives, sometimes past 600 years, and often live their entire life disease free, without physical degeneration and the ravages of old age.

20. Spiritually and philosophically the principle of Divine DNA draws from the words of the John 1:14, "The Word became flesh and dwelt among us." This is the practical underpinning that governs the presence of the Christ Consciousness. However, in the I AM America Teachings, our Divine DNA is activated within our hearts, literally and metaphorically, through the Eight-sided Cell of Perfection. Divine DNA carries the flawless realization of the HU-man while it simultaneously removes the death urge, the decay of disease and death, and transmutes human patterns of negativity. Divine DNA acts in accordance to each individual's free will and responds harmoniously with each personal choice, and unique spiritual development. Its activities unite the individual with the I AM Presence and cultivate the HU-man super senses.

am speaking of the great Kingdoms of Light that you experienced as you traveled into the Southern Door of Malton.[21]

MOVEMENT OF LIGHT

There were other epochs on the Earth Plane and Planet, especially as Earth lowered frequencies from Dvapara Yuga into Kali Yuga and the Elemental Kingdom came forward to help preserve the great truths of humanity. In the past, humanity was always interfacing with the Elemental Kingdom and there was a deep understanding of the Earth as a system. Notable schools of geography, geology, and (Earth's) culture are held within Malton. This is another characteristic of the Divine Aspect of the Arhat.[22] The Arhat cultivates and gains control over the Elemental Kingdom through *balance*. This is always achieved through the Right-hand Path, functioning through the will to know and understand these magnificent Kingdoms. (These Kingdoms) willingly give, and humanity willingly receives and directs. This activity assists the production of the great seasons of life that exist upon the Earth Plane and Planet. The Elemental Kingdom functions at the most rudimentary levels and esoterically creates the great precession of these seasons (equinoxes). Yes, the light that moves from winter to spring, from spring to summer, from summer to fall, is moved through the Elemental Kingdom…even the rotation of the Earth is held through the Elemental Kingdoms who perfected their consciousness as the great Elohim of light and sound. This knowledge steps down its frequencies into the Star of Malton during Shamballa. Before I move on, do you have questions?

Response: *Just one.*

Proceed.

HARMONY OF THE RIGHT-HAND PATH

Question: *In the interaction with the Elemental Kingdom, is this achieved primarily by agreement and a plan?*

---

21. During this Spiritual Pilgrimage the author directly encountered the Elemental Kingdom of the Gnomes, Master Kuthumi states in *Golden Cities and the Masters of Shamballa,* "There was also another being who jokingly left his belt for you, this was the being Thronana, for Thronana is of the Earth Kingdom (gnome) and represents a village of Earth Beings who exist primarily in the Fourth Dimension. He did this jokingly, and he is happy that you saw it, examined it, and left it."
22. Two types of spiritual archetypes inhabit the metaphysical terrain of the Arhat, the Shaman and the Sorcerer. They differ considerably, however. The Shaman spiritually travels both Third and Fourth Dimension, with the ability to shape shift into animal and plant form while journeying into the spirit world. The Sorcerer commands the elements of Fourth Dimension, and can adeptly swirl them, changing the weather and the surrounding natural world of the Third Dimension. Both the Shaman and the Sorcerer can psychically read and communicate with the nature kingdoms, thus accurately prophesying and predicting upcoming worldly events. The realm of the Arhat is often accompanied by seasoned Feng Shui practitioners and experienced Astrologers who interface the interactive spirituality and metaphysics of both Third and Fourth Dimensions.

Always, through agreement. Dear one, when one moves through the great teachings of the Blue Ray, they learn the differences of the Right-hand and Left-hand Path. The Elemental Kingdoms move forward with great accordance and harmony. This is an attribute of the Right-hand Path. Do you understand?

Response: *Yes.*

ONESHIP

In my beloved Wahanee, (in) the great Star, the Gatekeeper of that Mighty Temple of the Violet Ray steps-down frequencies to help guide humanity in relationship. What are these relationships? They are (present in) the governments. They are the remarkable organizations that guide civic activity and onward to the knowledge of brotherhood, sisterhood, and light. In the purest form (relationship) is a Oneship, however, it is the one thing that so disrupts humanity! Who shall guide? Who shall lead? What rules shall be followed?

RULE OF LAW

This has always been known culturally as that Mighty Rule of Law, and Wahanee holds as a focus to address this great need alongside the evolving human freedom and liberty for all. In its purity, the Rule of Law functions like a *shakti of energy*—this is freedom engendered in the heart.[23] It is true, Dear ones, I was present at the founding of this nation and I have presented myself to every president of this United States, who has the *eyes to see* and the *ears to hear*.[24] Now, we well know that not too many of late can qualify for this, can they?

He's chuckling a bit.

Response: *That is an understatement, yes.*

VIOLET FLAME OF FREEDOM

I engender through this great school of light the energy of liberty and freedom to my chelas, not only of I AM America, but to the many chelas who practice The Mighty Violet Flame in action!

---

23. Rule of Law: The condition where the laws of a nation or country are obeyed and upheld by their institutions and courts.
24. This indicates that the person must also have the spiritual consciousness and level of evolution to recognize and receive the blessing from Saint Germain.

> Violet Flame come forth,
> In the liberty and freedom
> Of the I AM That I AM.
> Hold in your purest form
> Liberty and freedom for humanity!
> May all governments of the world pursue the Ascension!
> In that Mighty Christ, I AM.

CHOICE AND THE CO-CREATIVE POWER OF THE I AM

Dear Ones, we know that the dark forces have penetrated and attacked this Mighty Freedom of Ascension that is engendered for humanity. During this Time of Shamballa, we lower (our) frequencies to the Earth Plane and Planet, and the purity of my heart leaps into the heart of those who hold the pristine ideal of the Violet Flame. This creates a promise and a sacred pact for the Ascension. It also holds and engenders within (an intention) to create and Co-create governments of freedom… governments that hold the Co-creative power of the I AM, entrusted and engendered within each and every one. This is the new Mighty Bill of Rights! For each has the right to choose, each has the right to affirm their Ascension, each is at liberty to experience within their own liberty, for only *in experience* can one become free. Because of this, the Violet Flame is most critical at this time, and during this Time of Shamballa, we will hold vigil for the United States and for the entire planet. For you well know, this is the time when *Freedom Star* is activated.[25]

FREEDOM STAR

When I speak of Freedom Star I am speaking of that immense inner Sun that exists within the inner Earth and holds within a coalescing and condensed energy from the DAHL.[26] For the Earth has been cradled and held by great ancestors of light from Venus, the Pleiades, and the Lords of the DAHL. Before I move on, do you have questions?

Response: *Yes.*

Proceed.

Question: *Your vigil for the freedom of humanity and the entire planet…as the United States so goes the rest of the planet?*

---

25. Freedom Star is the Ascended state of the Earth.
26. This is in reference to the central core of Inner Earth. Not the mantle of the Earth that is honey-combed and filled with underground tunnels and bases.

It is so. However, know that the Light of God never, ever faileth! We hold our continuous vigil within Wahanee as the light develops and shines within the heart of all, do you understand?

Response: *Yes, I do.*

ADVANCED HEALING IN SHALAHAH

Now, let me proceed to the Golden City of Shalahah. As we lower frequencies into the Star of Shalahah more knowledge will be given of healing processes. I discussed in my last discourse that the human body lives much longer than 120 years…it can live ten times this amount, and with the proper vibration and energies, can live thousands and thousands of years! However, because of the light frequencies that the Earth has experienced, lifespans have been radically shortened and are presently only a fraction of what is possible. There is enormous knowledge held in both sound and light frequencies. The knowledge of healing presents for humanity and begins to affect the Earth as magnificent beams of light generate from Shamballa and enter into the Golden City of Shalahah. All will be given the opportunity for this shakti of energy to increase their lifespan. This is another form of true enlightenment.[27]

TECHNOLOGY AND THE GROUP MIND

Humanity's healing is also realized through the appropriate care and feeding of the human physiology. Many new technologies based on light and sound frequencies come forward. Their science is based upon an understanding of the Collective Consciousness that holds frequencies that can be accessed. This is why I have given so much information regarding the Group Mind.

THE HEALING PLANT KINGDOM

Shalahah holds a unique relationship with Malton and the Deva Kingdoms because Shalahah holds within a specialized knowledge of the Plant Kingdom. Dear ones, for every disease that humanity encounters there is also a balanced placement of a plant upon the Earth Plane that can cure that problem. This process occurs through higher levels of consciousness, for consciousness is really the builder, is it not? We have always stated, "Mind is the builder." Contacting the consciousness of the healing plant engenders and promotes a healing process. This, too, is possible as our physical body holds elements of the Plant Kingdom. This is the essence of that Mighty Green Ray. Lord Sananda holds this healing frequency in his heart, and those in his presence or

---

27. True Enlightenment is not a philosophic or spiritual teaching. It is a metaphysical process that ensues after the development of the Ninth Energy Body and it fills the Mental Body with light. This is the cultivation of the Diamond Mind, and it assists the attainment of the Lighted Stance. True Enlightenment is recognized as the third approach in the Eight Pathways of Ascension.

vibration encounter healing. This was also true when Lord Sananda was incarnated as Jesus Christ upon the Earth Plane and Planet.[28]

Gobean holds within it the mineral consciousness. Malton holds within it the Deva and the elemental consciousness. Wahanee holds within it the HU-man consciousness, and Shalahah holds the plant consciousness. All of these (Golden Cities) work together in a proper form and manner to educate and enlighten. This is why we state, "the human is a great Co-creation, for all of these kingdoms are contained within…as within, so without." I stated last year during the Shamballa season that more miracle healing cures will come forth for humanity, and this year those who travel to the Star of Shalahah will receive in their highest mind various formulas and the technological understanding for many cures that may move humanity's health and hygiene forward thousands of years. Questions?

Response: *Yes.*

Proceed.

A DECREE FOR LONGEVITY

Question: *Is there a specific decree, which is a sound frequency, to aid and assist in this longevity?*

> Om Hunana.
> Om Sunana.
> Om Banandra.

This decree invokes the Mighty Gold and Aquamarine Rays to come forward within the light fields.[29] If there are not other questions, I would like to proceed.

Response: *Please continue.*

---

28. See Appendix Y: *Lord Sananda.*
29. This is another form of the Golden Ray Mantra, however it is arranged differently. Mantras are alchemical sounds that are chanted for protection or for enhancement of specific Ray Forces. The Golden Ray Mantra promotes the presence of the Golden Ray in our aura, or enhances the affect of the Ray throughout our light fields. The structure of the mantra is: "Om Banandra, (2x), Om Hunana, (1x), and Om Sunana, (1x)." Its language is Owaspee, the divine language of the Angels, often used by the Master Teachers for specific spiritual phrases and Golden City Names.
The etymology of the Golden Ray Mantra breaks down like this:
Om: Invokes the presence of our solar Sun that step-downs the sublime energy of the Great Central Sun, the Galactic Center.
Banandra: Means "delight," or "of the light."
Hunana: A melodic version of the "HU," a bija-seed mantra that invokes the presence of all of the Rays, and primarily the transformative Violet Ray.
Sunana: Invokes the presence of Sanat Kumara, the ancestral Ascended Master who now resides in the higher dimensions of Venus. Sanat Kumara was the venerated leader and master planner of Shamballa that serves as the formative template of all Golden Cities.

WHITE FIRE OF KLEHMA

The Mighty White Ray of Ascension and the Flame of White Fire is lowered by Serapis Bey and the Gatekeepers of the White Ray Temple into the Star of Klehma. This holds the histories of humanity and the powerful knowledge of how we are all connected as ONE. When I say we are connected as ONE, I speak of the histories of the White Ray of Venus, in the Pleiades, and in the DAHL. This, too, you can obtain through meditation and dream time spent in the Star of Klehma. This history is significant.[30]

DIVINE TIMING OF THE WHITE RAY

When one comprehends the extraordinary history that is held within their Divine DNA, one becomes more attuned to the frequencies of freedom and their Ascension. Expansion of knowledge into these Akashic Records transmits the Divine Order, timing, and the clockwork of the solar system. The White Ray enters the Western Doors of all Golden City Vortices this year; and the White Ray dispenses at the Star frequencies of Klehma. The White Ray streams forward for the freedom of all humanity, and (carries) a Divine DNA combining many Kingdoms of Light.[31] I sense I have expanded your knowledge. Do you have questions?

Response: *Yes.*

Proceed.

Question: *So as I understand the White Ray presents itself in the Southern Door, then the Western, then the Northern, and then finally to the Eastern Door of every Golden City as we proceed in this expansion and evolution?*

Yes, this is the White Ray, the White Fire, the spiral of Ascension, do you understand?[32]

Question: *And its purpose is to set up the spiral of Ascension?*

---

30. The purifying White Flame, also known as the White Fire, is used to cleanse the aura especially during the use of Group Mind. The White Flame is also critical for the Ascension Process and is applied throughout the attainment of many of the HU-man energy fields. The White Flame was perfected in the Temples of Venus and anchored in the Shamballa Temple of the White Ray. Its alchemic mantra is, "All is as ONE, ONE is as Service." The emanating light of the White Flame is symbolized by a flaming circle of light which signifies unity, Oneness, the Oneship, and the ONE.
31. See Appendix P: *Venus through the Golden City Doors, 2021–2065.*
32. The Ascension Spiral is a visible, spiral of the White Flame. It is often noted appearing in the energy field prior to one obtaining the freedom of Ascension. It resembles a spiral staircase, and is depicted in the Holy Bible as Jacob's Ladder.

DIVINE DNA ACTIVATION

This is true, indeed. This is why we send you to numerous Adjutant Points in Pilgrimage, so you can familiarize yourself with the energy of each Point, to enter into the Evolutionary Biome of each experience, and carry that frequency of sound and light within your heart. As you breathe the (Point's) air and take in vital chi, this begins to further activate the Divine DNA within. This is of vast importance. Proceed.

Question: *So as we travel to these Adjutant Points, is the White Ray being re-established in our own physiologies, in our own energies, to create the Seamless Garment?*

Indeed, Dear one, and in my next discourse, I shall be accompanied by a remarkable Pleiadean teacher who has appeared before. Her name is Anaya, and she will share information on integration within the Evolutionary Biome of the Adjutant Points. Now, unless if there are other questions, the channel tires and I shall take my leave from your frequency.

Response: *Thank you and Shamballa.*

Hold within your heart the great freedom and knowledge of Ascension. I AM your Brother of the Light, and in service to humanity. So be it.

Response: *So be it. Hitaka.*

Magic Angel

CHAPTER THREE

Elder of Light

Saint Germain and Lady Anaya

Greetings, my beloveds. Shamballa and blessings to all of you. As usual, Dear ones, I request permission to come forward.

Response: *Please, Saint Germain, come forward, and Shamballa to you.*

Today is a blessed day. Yes, it is the first day of the New Year, and this is the first day of our beloved Cup Ceremonies at Shamballa. Dear ones, Cup Ceremonies bring us all together as ONE, within our Group Mind and pour a blessing upon the Collective Consciousness.[1]

THE MALTESE CROSS

Today, as I promised, I have brought with me another Ascended Being of Light. She has served the Hierarchy for many years, not only as a Master Teacher, but as a distinguished Elder of Light who helps oversee many of the festivities at Shamballa, but also on an ongoing basis throughout the year. She appears during certain periods of light. Dear ones, we travel upon the light and while it is true that we also function through sound, our primary focus is *of the light*.[2] Dear heart, the Maltese Cross is a representation of the light and the Maltese Cross represents within you the atomic structure of all of your light fields.[3] This light is a Photon, and is life-giving and all life-serving. For those who have the eyes to see, and the ears to hear, it is life-demanding! When you call upon any decree that I have given, or another member of this Hierarch, you are calling upon the Light Supreme and the law that leads and guides it.

At the basis of this (great law) is my beloved Maltese Cross,[4] or what you have come to understand as the Photon.[5] This is one of the building blocks of the universe. In fact, on Earth, it is one of the most basic building blocks. There are, however, others that do exist, but this one is the most venerated in our teaching. Dear ones, you contain within you the genetic code that identifies a *light being*. What is a light being?

---

1. The higher interactive structure of consciousness as *two or more*.
2. Sound creates the path for the light. The Eight-sided Cell of Perfection is created through two Maltese Crosses or Photons.
3. This is the Eight-sided Cell of Perfection.
4. The Maltese Cross, a symbol often used by Saint Germain, represents the Eight-sided Cell of Perfection, and the human virtues of honesty, faith, contrition, humility, justice, mercy, sincerity, and the endurance of persecution.
5. See Appendix D: *The Photon*.

THE LIGHT BEING

A light being is composed of the light and responds to the light. There are two forms of light beings that exist upon the Earth, those who evolve upon the surface of the Earth, and those who evolve within the inner Earth.[6] A great inner Sun exists within the Earth, and it guides and leads the evolution of many civilizations and beings of light of the inner Earth. "As within, so without," and this saying is true of the Earth. Without further delay, I shall introduce beloved Lady Anaya.

ANAYA OF THE AQUAMARINE AND GOLD RAYS

Let me describe Lady Anaya. She is quite tall, with flowing blond hair almost down to her waist. She is wearing a gown of aquamarine light, and upon it are seventeen golden stars. On the bodice of her gown and similar to Saint Germain, is a golden Maltese Cross. She steps forward.

Good morning, Shamballa, and blessings to all of you, Dear ones. I am Anaya, and I request permission to come forward into your energy fields.[7]

Response: *Dear Anaya, please come forward. You are most welcome and Shamballa to you.*

I have come before upon that beam of the Golden Ray, and today I stream forward again upon the Golden Ray of Light, and upon the Aquamarine Ray of Light.[8] Dear ones, as Saint Germain would say, "There is still much to be accomplished upon the Earth Plane and Planet, to raise humanity into higher vibration." This higher vibration of light is difficult to achieve unless the human can understand and accept the light. The acceptance of the light comes first, of course, at a physical level, but it also must penetrate into the Astral-field and onward into the Solar-field—the Causal Body. This has a great effect upon the Mental Body.[9]

When I first came forward many years ago, the I AM America teachings were just beginning to be known and understood. Now, they are reaching a new threshold where they will be understood by many. This is of no mistake.

---

6. There are many Ascended Beings that reside within the inner Earth, and they oversee seventeen fully activated Golden Cities.
7. Anaya is an Ascended Master from the Pleiades. She serves the Aquamarine and Gold Rays and holds a continuous focus for humanity's unity and entering into the consciousness of Unana. Anaya also assists individual comprehension of the ONE and this relationship to both science and technology.
8. The Aquamarine and Gold Ray represents the opening of the Divine Heaven and the realization of Divine Man. This Ray Force is associated with perception, unity, sensitivity, intuition, cooperation, integration, spirituality, idealism, and self-realization. Its gemstones are turquoise and aquamarine. Its scents are hydrangea, bayberry, and sage. The Aquamarine and Gold Rays are served by the Archangel Chrystiel and the Archeiai Clarity. The Elohim are the Elohim of Unity who serves alongside its feminine counterpart Rainbow (also known in some teachings as Iris).
9. In Jyotish, Vedic Astrology, the Astral Body is read through the Chandra Lagna, the Moon Chart. The Causal Body is determined through the placement of the Sun, and the Mental Body is defined through the placement of Mercury. In this form of astrology, Moon represents the mind (emotion), and Mercury represents the intellect.

A TIME OF CRITICAL MASS

Let me give you a bit of my own history and the role that I play with I AM America. I am an Ascended Being from the consciousness of the Pleiades. I stream my consciousness from the Pleiadean Golden Cities and I am most happy to serve. For you see, my beloveds, I have worked for a long time with I AM America and within the mighty halls of Shamballa to stream knowledge, information, and enlightenment to those of the Earth Plane and Planet. We (the Pleiadeans) are the progenitors or ancestors of the human race, and come forward in conscious expression at times of critical mass.[10] The beloved Earth is like one of our outposts, but not only is it an outpost; it carries within the streaming light of the Pleiades.[11]

DIVINE DNA

We come forward in various time frames upon the Earth Plane and Planet to assist different civilizations of light. Now what does this mean? It means that when the mass of humanity has awakened, then it is ready to receive the gift of the Ascension. This happens through a maturation of the light fields and through the acceptance of light not only from without, but primarily from within. This, of course, comes through your Divine DNA.

---

10. The Pleiades, also known by astronomers as M45, comprise over a thousand star clusters, but is primarily known by a small group of its luminous planets: the mythological daughters of Atlas and Pleione, Alcyone, Merope, Electra, Celaeno, Taygeta, Maia, and Asterope. The brightest seven are also known as the Seven Sisters of the Pleiades and have been observed since ancient times. The star cluster is located 445 light years from our Earth, and is located in the Taurus constellation. The Pleiades are near the umbilicus connection that links the twin universes the DAHL-DERN. According to the Master Teachers, Earth is an ancient Pleiadean outpost and our previous civilizations claim periods of interaction with Pleiadean beings of light, who have interjected science and technology into our culture during critical phases of evolution. Native Americans, and the ancient Egyptian, Mayan, and Hindu culture allege interaction with the highly evolved Pleiadeans and purposely aligned numerous architectural structures, pyramids, and temples to commemorate their brilliant location in the heavens. Researchers claim that the Egyptians worshipped the Pleiades as the Divine Mother, and considered the star system sacred and heavenly. The Mayans associated the Pleiades with Quetzalcoatl, the feathered serpent of Divine Wisdom. Esoteric scholars consider the Pleiades as the cradle of human consciousness and the source of spiritual hierarchy.

Pleiadeans are alleged to be humonid, tall, and Nordic in appearance. Their diet is strictly vegetarian as their spiritual vibration is attuned to both Fourth and Fifth Dimensions. Pleiadean science and technology is remarkably advanced with both interdimensional and time travel. Political structures are nonexistent, and are apolitical; Pleiadeans allegedly are pledged to a Galactic Oath of Noninterference based on the evolutionary premise of choice. It is claimed that the foundation of their spirituality is an in-depth knowledge and practice of love and the Oneness that is love's natural byproduct. Their culture is primarily nonviolent; however they will fiercely defend the ideals of personal choice and the unfair treatment and victimization of the weak. Some Pleiadean contactees claim that the Pleiadeans evolved from the Lyran race, and naturally possess a strong healing ability. Pleiadeans live for thousands of years and their planets host many mature and active Golden Cities of Light, the model for the now nascent Golden Cities of Earth that will develop and advance throughout the Golden Age. Many Pleiadeans protect and assist humanity's current spiritual growth into the light of the New Times.

11. Vital HU-man evolving energies stream from the Pleiades to Venus, and from there step-down into our Earth. Golden Cities also carry and disburse energies from Pleiadean and Venusian starcraft, through their central lei-lines and Adjutant Points. As described in this lesson, energies also stream from the Galactic Center and the unbilicus connection between the DAHL-DERN.

Saint Germain[12] has introduced aspects of this Divine DNA containing five elements of the different Kingdoms of Light.[13] It is time for you to accept, and move into your HU-man experience. As taught before, everything within and without is ONE. The Earth is ONE with you, and you are ONE of it. Babajeran accepts and receives light not only from the Galactic Center, but she accepts and receives prescient light that streams from Venus. This light is stepped-down from the Pleiades and originates from the umbilicus (connection) that exists to the DAHL. It is now time for Earth's evolution in the light, and to move forward to a greater understanding and expansion of the light.

"OF THE LIGHT, AND FOR THE LIGHT"

I mentioned before that we have come forward during many different tipping points upon the Earth. We are the progenitors of the great race of beings that exist in your inner Earth, and yes, it is true, there are other Star seeds that coexist alongside our Divine DNA. Yet, we hold the original DNA as it was deemed from the Co-creation. This great Co-creation was the birth of the DAHL and the DERN, side-by-side, twin universes that would serve those *of the light* and *for the light*. There have been many invasions from other universes that try to arrest the light, or in most instances, were working to learn of the light. This has caused great polarity and conflict.

DARKNESS

One of the greatest conflicts that have occurred in this universe occurred upon Earth. For Earth is known as a great fulcrum, from the Moon to Venus, and from the Venusian Golden Cities to the Pleiadean Golden Cities...light streams and activates the Divine DNA. Dear ones, those (dark ones) who have interfered with the progression of humanity must be put aside. This darkness has no role or place upon the Earth Plane and Planet. You may have sensed or noticed that many of the Pleiadean brothers and sisters of light are now here, not only within the atmosphere of the Earth, but some are present in spacecrafts. Many are present through our Group Mind, and we project our energies from the Golden Cities of the Pleiades. We are here, assisting and protecting the Earth at this time.

KNOWLEDGE OF THE ONE

Last year it was deemed that beloved Saint Germain could remove the Golden Belt of Light.[14] Yes, it is true that many in the Collective Consciousness have shifted into a

---

12. See Appendix Z: *Saint Germain*.
13. The Kingdoms of Light include the Mineral, Plant, Animal, Elemental-Deva, Human and HU-man Kingdoms. The five elements are: Earth, Air, Fire, Water, and Ether (spirit).
14. See *Evolutionary Biome*, page 259. The Golden Belt or Golden Band of Light was placed around the Earth in the 1950s through the efforts of the Ascended Master Saint Germain. It held back catastrophic Earth Changes until humanity had a better chance to evolve. This Belt of Light dissipated

new timeline and evolution of understanding…leaving behind the old ways of death and destruction—resurrecting into the Ascension of the ONE.[15] Dear ones, there are also many Pleiadean ancestors who reside in the light fields of the Earth. Many of these progenitors of light come forward within the Golden Cities and serve within the Adjutant Points. You have many names that you call them within your historical accounts. They come forward to honor the Photon of light, the Maltese Cross that Saint Germain reveres. We will give you more science to lead you into this great and celebrated knowledge of the ONE.

> For it is the ONE that you seek,
> It is the ONE that you are of,
> And it is the ONE of how you shall attain
> Your liberation and Ascension in the light.
> We are ONE in fellowship,
> ONE in Sisterhood,
> ONE in Brotherhood of Breath, Sound, and Light!

This vast ONE permeates all things, and as you have come to know and understand, the next evolutionary process is for you to begin your conscious knowledge of the Fourth Dimension. This, of course, is the connection to the Evolutionary Biome—a biome of light and sound frequencies, matrices of light that stream from the Great Central Sun, the mighty Galactic Center of Light, and from the umbilicus of light that exists between the DAHL and the DERN. This energy is stepped-down from the Pleiades, moves onward into Venus, and streams into the heart of the Earth itself. Yes, and at the center of (Earth) the golden ball of light, that mighty frequency of Sun, sound, and light, is yet another Photon—a great, Mighty Eight-sided Cell of Perfection.

CUP CEREMONY

This year will be a year of increasing the light *within*, so the light can be expressed *without*. As you move forward in your evolutionary process, know that I am present with the Gold and Aquamarine Rays. Call upon me into your meditation, into your spiritual practice, and into your Cup Ceremonies. The Cup Ceremony is a distinguished tradition that originates from the Pleiades.[16] Water holds both light and sound frequencies, and contains within it at the most atomic level a structure that is akin to the Photon—the Maltese Cross. Water assists the translation of your prayers and your divine thoughts into the Collective Consciousness. Water is also the basis of life, and contains within it the ability to unite the Collective Consciousness. That

---

during the Shamballa Season of 2019-2020, and its Golden Threads were woven into each of the Fifty-one Golden Cities. This act declared Earth's and humanity's passage into the Golden Age.

15. See Appendix AA: *Timelines and Consciousness.*
16. See Appendix BB: *The Cup Ceremony.*

is why the Water Ceremony is one of the most venerated ceremonies at Shamballa during this week of water.

UNITED AS ONE

The great civilizations came under the duress of the precession of the yugas of time, and this lowered their frequencies. Lower energies allowed doubt and suspicion to creep among humanity.[17] Humanity is meant to be united as ONE, and to function as ONE…for how can you separate the light? You are ONE *within* and you are ONE *without*. The ONE is the foundation of your Ascension Process.

Attune yourself to the Evolutionary Biome, and as you enter into each Adjutant Point of Light attune yourself to your mighty Photon within, that is the Eight-sided Cell of Perfection.[18] In its movement of perfection, you mirror (perfection) within your energy fields and onward (onto) the light. The Golden Cities have been brought Co-created to mirror this mighty teaching in a greater scope (or) field of understanding.[19] Still, you are ONE with it and ONE without it, for you are of *it* and *it* is of you.

KINGDOMS OF THE FOURTH DIMENSION

The kingdoms of the Fourth Dimension, the great beings of the Nature and Deva Kingdoms, live in a greater purity and understanding of the ONE.[20] This is the great gift they have to share, for you are ONE with them, and they are ONE with you. Many Kingdoms hold great tasks upon the Earth Plane and Planet. Some of them fasten and stitch together the Kingdoms of Plants, the Kingdoms of the magnificent trees and forests of your planet, while some of them secure the Kingdoms of Water. Yet, others protect the Kingdoms of Air. The Gnomes shelter the remarkable Earth Kingdoms, though differing they all work together as ONE. The impressive Salamanders of Fire work as ONE within each of these kingdoms. It is important for you to attune yourself as you enter into the Adjutant Points to become aware of the multidimensional kingdoms that exist at each point of light. Dear one, I sense your questions.

Question: *Traditionally, we perform a Cup Ceremony when we travel to each Adjutant Point and we are of the opinion that this helps to activate the Adjutant Point. My concern is that sometimes we are not exactly clear what Ray Force is present. We know that the White Ray is now moving to the Western Doors of the Golden Cities throughout this plane and our planet, and we also know that these Adjutant Points are dealing primarily with enlightenment and the knowledge on the Western Doors and so the question that I have is, are we aiding the Elemental Kingdom in its interface with humanity?*

---

17. See Appendix K: *The Cycle of the Yugas.*
18. See Appendix R: *The Eight-sided Cell of Perfection.*
19. See Appendix J and N: See how the Eight-sided Cell of Perfection overlays the Golden City, creating both an energetic microcosm and macrocosm.
20. See Appendix CC: *Devas and Elementals.*

It is so and I would add one thing, before you perform your Cup Ceremony to sprinkle a circle of salt around your circle before you begin, this will allow the purity of the Elemental Kingdom to come forward. Dear ones, this is a form of the Sacred Fire.

ANOINTING OILS

You can also perform a sacred anointing before the Cup Ceremony. I suggest using oils of sandalwood and myrrh. You also can use frankincense as well. These are the divine anointing oils that came originally from the Pleiades and are also used within the DAHL.[21] These are the higher essences of the plant kingdom that come forward and immediately lift the energy fields into higher vibration. It is no mistake that they, too, were used in the holy anointing of Jesus Christ as he took incarnation upon the Earth Plane. They are used also in the sacred cups of the priests and priestesses of Melchizedek.[22]

ACTIVATION

Now when I state this, do not get too caught up in form. These are ways that you can begin a purification process and interface with the Elemental Kingdom of Light. Call them forward as you enter into each Adjutant Point of Light, for you are ONE with them, and they are ONE with you. They, too, will serve your Divine Plan and assist and help you in your activation of each point. They will also assist you in your Ascension Process, for each of you contain their Divine DNA. This can lift you into harmony as ONE with the Earth and harmonize you into the next Adjutant Point of Light. Do you have further questions?

DIVINE DNA CONNECTION

Question: Yes, *you just brought up something about the Divine DNA, so it is the fulcrum of the Divine DNA that is in everything that is the connection of the ONE?*

---

21. Electrical frequency, when measured in the number of oscillations per second is a Megahertz (MHz). This is vibrational motion, and one hertz equals one oscillation per second. It is claimed that negative thoughts lower our vibration by 10 to 15 MHz. Prayer and positive thought heighten our vibration by 15 MHz. Essential oils can immediately uplift our vibration. The MHz rating of several essential oils are:
Sandalwood, 96 MHz.
Myrrh, 105 MHz.
Rose, 320 MHz.
Sacred Mountain (a Young Living Blend), 176 MHz.
(Source: gf-oils.com/frequency).
22. The righteous, royal priests of the Old Testament. The Melchizedek priests were claimed to be the "most high," and offered both bread and wine to God the Creator. King David and Jesus Christ are claimed to be of this distinct lineage. In the Ascended Master tradition, both water and oil are offered in the Cup Ceremony.

It is the connection of the ONE, for the beloved Elemental Kingdoms and Devas of Light contain the Divine DNA that came forth in the shape of the Photon. This, of course, has not been received by many others throughout the universe and I think you know what I speak. Proceed.

Response and question: *Yes, it was in the last transmission that I became aware that the Divine DNA was something above the human DNA. I had always thought of it as the super human DNA, but in essence, it is Divine so everything matriculates from Divine DNA into this three-dimensional form, true?*

This is true. The Divine DNA connects you as ONE. ONE to the Elemental Kingdom, and to all of their kingdoms and Devas of Light, ONE to Babajeran, ONE within a Group Mind, ONE to another HU-man, ONE to the Spiritual Hierarchy, ONE to the Lords of Venus, ONE to the Lords and Priestesses of the Pleiades, ONE to the great umbilicus of light that connects the mighty DERN and DAHL, ONE to the frequencies of the Galactic Center. This, you see, is your Divine Inheritance. We have reiterated this, have we not?

Response: *Yes.*

It is what is activated in order to reclaim your heritage as a light being. Proceed.

Response and question: *So the experiences that we have in this denser form gives us this sense of separation but the separation is not a fact?*

PHOTON ACTIVATION

There is no separation; however, the human consciousness it is so Co-creative that it has even used the dark force as a way to move forward in evolution. However, it is easier to remove this shadow substance from your light fields. This is achieved in understanding the Photon of light as it exists upon the Earth Plane and Planet through the Golden Cities. This great plan of light activates not only the Photon of light as the Eight-sided Cell of Perfection; it activates numerous (other) Photons of light. We have described this before…this is the duplication of perfection within the light fields that affects the body. The body is designed to *receive* and *be* of the light, to be responsive to the light, and to Co-create with the light. You are ONE with it, and it is ONE with you, do you understand?

INCREASE THE LIGHT

Response and question: *Yes. For the dissolution of darkness, we have utilized the Violet Flame to dissolve attachment to darkness. Is there a specific decree that you could share with us that would help us along this path?*

Not a decree, but I shall be happy to give you different spiritual principles and practices that can increase the effulgent light within your light fields. First, when you are present at an Adjutant Point, and after you have performed the Cup Ceremony, sit within your circle of salt and visualize first the Gold Ray streaming then the Aquamarine Ray of light within your circle. Both Ray Forces are purifying and they also increase the light within your own light fields (aura) do you understand?

Response: *Yes I do. It is true that the visualization process is part of the Co-creative activity that we, as humans, possess.*

Dear ones, and now I shall take my leave from your physical plane. I will return to give further teaching in the future.

Response: *Thank you and Shamballa.*

Blessings to all…Shamballa.

Anaya backs away, and Saint Germain comes forward.

Beloveds, I know that it is difficult for a new frequency to come and there are still adjustments that need to be made to your home. This can be aggravating…do you understand?

Response: *Yes*

So now, Dear ones, I shall return to the festivities of light at Shamballa.

Response: *Thank you.*

He is backing away from the podium.

I AM your brother in the light and in service to humanity.

Now let me explain…Saint Germain and Anaya move into a great golden ball of light and leave the Earth Plane.

Response: *Thank you.*

Meditating Buddha

CHAPTER FOUR

Enlightenment Pilgrimage

Through the Western Door with Saint Germain

Greetings, my Beloveds, I AM Saint Germain, and I stream forth on that Mighty Violet Ray of Mercy, Transmutation, Forgiveness and Compassion. As usual, Dear hearts, I request permission to come forward into your energy fields.

Response: *Please, Saint Germain, come forward. You are most welcome and Shamballa.*

"CHOICE IS HOW HUMANITY EVOLVES"

Shamballa. Greetings and Good Morning to both of you. Today, indeed, is a blessed day for we are rejoicing and celebrating in the mighty halls of Shamballa, and as the Earth and the nation of America is in great turmoil at this moment, we send our radiance to beloved America. For America is to be free…free, so that its citizens can make choices! Dear ones, it is free will and choice that the Great White Brotherhood and Sisterhood of the Right-hand Path engender. Choice is how humanity evolves. If choice is removed upon the Earth Plane and Planet, the evolution of humanity will stall, and it would be difficult for personal development to move forward. Choice is the fulcrum of evolution, and choice must always be protected.

BABAJI'S ASSISTANCE

I remember long ago you asked for this (the I AM America messages) to never become political, but you see, Dear ones, the turmoil of the dark ones upon the Earth Plane and Planet is rising to an even greater pitch. And I assure you, Dear ones, that in the mighty temples, halls, and schools of Shamballa, we send our radiance into the heart of America—to that Mighty Galactic Heart (Earth's), the Heart of the Dove.[1] There, Babaji extends this radiance to assist each Golden City.[2] This (energy) engenders true liberty, true justice, true freedom for the evolution of humanity.

---

1. See Appendix DD: *The Heart of the Dove*.
2. Babaji is a timeless and immortal Being of Light who is said to possess a birthless, deathless body. He frequently takes on a physical body for different spiritual missions on Earth, and is commonly known as the "nameless one." He is often revered as a form of Shiva, and in Ascended Master Teachings works closely with the Four Pillars: El Morya, Kuthumi, Saint Germain, and Lord Sananda. Some esoteric researchers claim that the Four Pillars are the Four Horsemen of the Apocalypse, mentioned in the Book of Revelations.
Babaji is primarily known for his teachings of *Kriya Yoga*, a breath and meditation yoga that rapidly accelerates spiritual growth and evolution. It is claimed that the technique was taught by Krishna

CHOICE AND EVOLUTION

(Personal) Evolution is how one moves forward in their spirituality and in their understanding of the sciences, philosophies, and religions of the world...evolution is how humanity ascends. The dark ones know this, for the first right that they trample upon is your freedom of choice. America is to be free, and as I have said so many times before, "America is to hold the light for the rest of the world. As America is free, so is the rest of the world." When I speak this, I am referring to the *surface* of the planet and the Mighty Light Beings who occupy it—the Earth Plane and Planet.[3]

---

to Arjuna, from Christ to his disciples, and later from Babaji to his chela Lahiri Mahasaya. Lahiri Mahasaya taught Sri Yuteswar, the astrologer and guru to Paramahansa Yogananda. Yogananda popularized the technique and introduced the yogic method through the establishment of the *Self Realization Foundation*. Clearly, the teachings of the Violet Flame and its various applications produce a similar result to Kriya Yoga.

Some biographers of Babaji claim that he is the Archangel Metatron, the savior of mankind. Babaji oversees the *Heart of the Dove,* that calibrates vital energies to every Golden City on Earth. It is claimed that Babaji resides with his sister Mataji, who wears a white, cotton sari with a green border and red sash. Their spiritual Ashram is located in the Garwhal region of the Indian Himalayans and is built near a series of caves surrounded by sheer rock cliffs, along with two waterfalls. The spiritual retreat and Ashram emits a continuous light force and contains a spiritual force-field that protects the location within the radius of one mile.

The Ascended Masters often refer to Mother Earth as *Babajeran*—the feminine of the Avatar Babaji. In reality, the etymology of Babajeran translates to mean, "the grandmother rejoices."

The appearance and alleged incarnations of Babaji into physical form is somewhat controversial. As incarnated into a physical form near the north Indian village of Haidakhan, Babaji lived and taught in a nearby Ashram. *In Babaji, Gateway to the Light,* by G. Reichel Verlag, Babaji was a proponent of the cultivation of the Christ Consciousness. Verlag writes, "Babaji gave a short speech stating that Christ was present. He said, people must let go of their envy and hatred that makes them feel separate, and instead regard themselves as connected and belonging to a single unity, which was the true state of reality. He added that anyone who opened oneself to Christ's energy would receive a Christ vision."

Haidakhan Babaji left our world on February 14, 1984. Several days before his departure, he imparted this teaching:

> "Love and serve all humanity.
> Help everyone.
> Be happy. Be courteous.
> Be a dynamo of irrepressible joy.
> Recognize God and goodness in every face.
> There is no saint without a past and no sinner without a future.
> Praise everyone. If you cannot praise someone...let him/her go out of your life.
> Be original. Be inventive.
> Be courageous. Take courage again and again.
> Do not imitate. Be strong. Be upright.
> Do not lean on the crutches of others.
> Think with your own head. Be yourself.
> All perfection and every Divine Virtue are hidden with you—reveal them to the world.
> Wisdom, too, is already with you—let it shine forth.
> Let the Lord's Grace make you free.
> Let your life be that of a rose—in silence, it speaks the language of fragrance."

3. Saint Germain prophesies, "America is a great focus of light for the Earth. They are the torchbearers, the people who hold great light for the rest of the world. Yes, there will be changes elsewhere, but America will be the first to experience the changes and the first to overcome them and again hold the light. Look to your Higher Self at all times for the answers. Within the Higher Self is the Mastery of all things."

EARTH'S DESTINY AS FREEDOM STAR

The Being of Light that carries the Divine DNA of the HU-man, moves forward in transcendence and is assisted by the Gold and Aquamarine Rays. However, (evolutionary) energies flow from the Galactic Center and from the Pleiades that step-down onto Venus, and again step-down to the center of the Earth. I have spoken before about the great civilizations of Light Beings who live in the center of the Earth. Currently, they too, hold light for the rest of the world and (for) the Mighty Planet Babajeran, as she is to become Freedom Star.

This is the Divine Destiny of Earth. For Earth is to be known as a wondrous and Mighty Planet of Freedom, a place where all Light Beings and others with different genetic structures can come to and reach their Ascension through Spiritual Liberation. Indeed, liberty, justice, and freedom are the divine tenets of free will and choice!

PHOTON BELT: THE ATOMIC MALTESE CROSS

My beloved Golden City of Wahanee and also Gobean hold within them the energies of freedom. Gobean holds the Blue Ray, and Wahanee holds the Mighty Violet Ray. This balance of freedom is also held through Beloved Mother Mary on the Pink Ray, and Beloved Kuan Yin through her aspect of the Pink Ray. The Golden Cities of Light assist this process (of freedom), for the Earth is moving through the Plasma Field and the Photon Belt.[4] The Photon Belt is filled with smaller, atomic Maltese Crosses, and each contain within themselves the ability to catapult the Divine DNA.[5] I have explained before that the Maltese Cross is a representation of the Divine HU-man. I cannot help but overemphasize this fact, for this structure causes the enlightening of the cells.

THE ENLIGHTENING

Dear ones, 2021 is to be a Year of Enlightening—a year of the Lighted Stance, and a year of moving into higher mental knowledge and the physical processes of enlightenment.[6] This is carried forward through Pilgrimage to the Western Doors. As I stated in my last discourse, the White Ray carries the energetic directly from the DAHL Universe into the DERN. The energy flows through the umbilicus connection of the two twin universes from the Pleiades, onward into Venus, and to some degree arcs through your Moon, and then into the core of the center of the planet (Earth). There, the energy is qualified again through the great Golden Cities of Light and the

---

4. The Photon Belt is contained with the Plasma Field, and is a flowing current of monoatomic, flowing light energy. This is also influenced by the galactic presence of the Gold Ray.
5. This is due to the constant colliding presence of the Photon Belt, which produces monoatomic anomalies.
6. Saint Germain later announced that this annual influence continues through the year 2025. The Pleiadean-Venusian spiritual practice of Spiritual Pilgrimage follows the flow of the White Ray through the four doors of the Golden City. For more information see Appendix P, *Venus through the Golden City Doors, 2021-2065*.

Ascended Beings, Archangels, and Elohim. These Light Beings refine the energy yet again, as it moves into and throughout each of the Golden Cities.

MOVEMENT OF THE WHITE RAY

This mighty force of light was felt last year in all the Southern Doors of the Golden Cities, and by the close of this Shamballa it will have moved its radiance from the Southern Door into the Western Door. Now, this does not change on an annual basis. Sometimes it changes every twelve years, and sometimes it changes every twenty-four years.[7] However, as mankind and humanity move into their Ascension Process, the Spiritual Hierarchy accelerates its force to move into the Western Doors of all Golden Cities this year. This (White Ray energetic) will stay for a number of years (in the West) to allow an enlightening process to occur. Last year the White Ray was purposely sent into the Southern Door to help humanity heal from the insidious forces of evil that have inundated Earth for so long.

"MAKE A COMMITMENT FOR YOUR FREEDOM"

It is important to take on your Lighted Stance and make a commitment for your freedom in Ascension, for this is the highest path you can travel at this time. Yes, it is true that the dark forces move upon the Earth Plane and Planet…and yes, it is true they will try to remove many of your freedoms. However, the great choice you can make is for your freedom. This is your choice for personal justice, and instills liberty and spiritual freedom. I have given you the science behind each of the Adjutant Points, and now will share some of the science behind the Western Door Pilgrimage of Enlightenment. But before I move forward, do you have questions?

Response: *Please continue.*

CARDINAL LEI-LINES CONDENSE THE ENERGIES

This Pilgrimage is very interesting, for it first follows all of the Cardinal lei-lines.[8] These are the mighty lei-lines of light that move throughout the Golden City Vortices. I know you are familiar with them, for I have taught this previously in the Northern Door Pilgrimage.

Cardinal lei-lines contain the greatest condensation of energy.[9] This is similar to Outer Child and the Inner Child Points, also known as Outer Cardinal or Inner Cardinal Points. They coalesce and carry an immense force of energy.

This is due to the convergence of lei-lines, but it also has to do with the natural movement of the Photon. The Photon you see is (naturally) oriented to move in the

---

7. For more information see Appendix P, *Venus through the Golden City Doors, 2021-2065.*
8. See Appendix N, Part Two: *Golden City Adjutant Points, Lei-lines, and Golden City Ashrams.*
9. In Ascended Master Teaching on the Golden Cities, lei-lines are current of energy that form lines between two Adjutant Points. Lei-lines vibrate with both an electric or magnetic energy flow. Golden City Lei-lines can have a width of one to five miles, with a measurable, rhythmic pulse.

cardinal directions, which are the directions of pure North, pure South, pure East, and pure West.[10]

YOUR PURIFICATION

As you enter the Cardinal lei-line, seek purification at a physical level through fasting and the removal of animal products. I also suggest that you use the Mighty Violet Flame.

> Mighty Violet Flame come forward and purify my light bodies,
> Readying me for the spiritual liberation of enlightenment!
> Mighty Seamless Garment come forward in full force and power,
> Surround my light fields with the ONE light the ONE true Christ, of I AM.

Call upon this decree and prayer, memorize it, and take it (energetically) unto the great and mighty silence.[11]

CALL UPON THE BE-INGS OF LIGHT

This Pilgrimage of Light begins in the Golden City Star, where you shall enter for a forty-eight hour (period of) meditation. This coalesces your energies (aura), and prepares them (your light fields) for the mighty work at hand. Focus upon the decree I have just given you and the Awakening Prayer, gather into both Cup and Fire Ceremonies. This assists the coalescing of your energies as you call upon the light *within* and the light *without*. As you embark upon your Mighty Enlightenment of the I AM, you are assisted by the mighty BE-ings of Light who reside in the Inner Earth. Call upon them, for they, too, shall accompany you and assist you in your Enlightenment Process.[12] They help and assist you to become a true BE-ing of Light,

---

10. In calculating the locations of Adjutant Points, especially for anchoring ceremonies, it is suggested to use true North.

11. The Master Teachings encourage a contemplative period of quiet and stillness to intensely apply spiritual energies in certain circumstances and situations. This period of tranquil power is often referred to as the *Great Silence*. This period of stillness allows for integration and to restore our personal spiritual equilibrium.

12. The Inner Earth is commonly known as *Agartha*, where it is claimed lies a continent of land, with oceans, seas, and an inner Sun. It is populated with both humans and evolved HU-mans who once existed on the surface of the Earth and it is theorized that they escaped to the Inner Earth to avoid various catastrophes and periodic Earth Changes experienced on Earth's surface. There are also Venusians and Pleiadeans who have helped to guide and shape the culture of Inner Earth where humans quickly evolve and enter the Ascension Process. There are many Ascended Beings and Masters in the Inner Earth, along with spiritually developed HU-mans who live in physical bodies for thousands of years.

Since the center has no gravitational flux, it also serves as a multi-dimensional portal to other planets and galaxies. It is claimed that the major entrances to the Inner Earth exist at both the North and South Pole, however, there are also several entrances scattered about the Earth. Researchers claim that the Inner Earth has four unique rivers that flow to the four directions. Saint Germain speaks about the seventeen Golden Cities that inhabit Inner Earth and drive spiritual evolution onward to the surface of the planet.

It is claimed that the inhabitants of Inner Earth enjoy a utopian culture, and most are highly evolved and use advanced technology based upon the Evolutionary Biome. Meditation, astral projection, and the science of the Angelic Kingdom are taught in their schools, along with typical subjects. There is

a BE-ing engendered with free will and personal choice, a BE-ing who affirms the Right-hand Path of Righteousness. This, Dear ones, is your entrance into our Mighty Hierarchy...*as within, so without.*

ONE-HOUR MEDITATIONS

I ask for you to meditate within these forty-eight hours. This may include a minimum of four to sometimes as much as six hours per day. You can space this out into one-hour meditations throughout the day. I know this shall be long and arduous, but I shall be there assisting and helping you. We are realizing the mighty tenets of the Freedom Star! Hold within your heart the great Flame of Freedom! Visualize throughout your light bodies the Mighty Violet Flame.

> Mighty Violet Flame,
> Come forth and free me now!
> To serve Beloved Babajeran
> As Freedom Star!

Affirm this over and over again (to permeate) into your consciousness. This is your mighty first step.

THE OVERLIGHTING

Within these forty-eight hours of meditation and prayer, when you feel complete, turn your will over to the mighty Right-hand Path. You will feel my soft overlighting, and you may feel the gentle presence and overlighting of Archangel Zadkiel.[13] Beloved Portia will reveal herself, for we stand as stewards of your process.[14]

---

little crime and no poverty. They farm and cultivate lush gardens, filled with orchards, fruits, and vegetables of many varieties. Many of their cities are filled with buildings and temples featuring Golden Domes. Buildings are constructed of *livingstone*—a unique form of stone that originates from Venus and is similar to Saint Germain's monoatomic glacium.

The inhabitants of Inner Earth are aware that the humans of the Outer Earth are waiting to experience the Evolutionary Biome of the Fourth Dimension. There are several Light Beings of the Inner Earth who have revealed themselves telepathically and are willing to help humanity and their ongoing Ascension Process. They are:

Rodon: An ambassador of the higher dimensions who teaches others how to live within a Fourth Dimensional framework.

Mikos: Head librarian of the Library of Portho-logos, a municipality located in a Golden City of the Inner Earth. This remarkable library covers over 456 miles of terrain.

Master Adama also known as Adamus: High priest from the City of Telos. He has been incarnated in the same body for six hundred years and teaches Ascension techniques.

13. The process of Overlighting by an Ascended Master is sometimes referred to as "shadowing" or "overshadowing." This is a natural progression for the Master Teacher when they have chosen to educate and oversee the development of a certain student or chela. The Master Teacher is in constant rapport with their disciple and can assist the course of events destined to evolve their pupil's HU-man development. This process can include guidance and direction at important junctures, including the transference of energy. This can include Divine Intervention from difficult karmas, through their transmutation, amelioration, or lessening their negative results.

14. The Goddess of Justice and Opportunity. She represents Divine Justice on Earth. Her action is balance, expressed as the scales. Harmony holds balance. Some say her electronic pattern, a

"INSIDE OUT...OUTSIDE IN"

Move to the next Adjutant Point. This Pilgrimage begins from the inside out, and ends (with Pilgrimage from) the outside in.[15]

THE COOPERATION POINT

The next point that you shall travel to is the Cooperation Point. You shall feel cooperation surging within all your cells.

> Mighty I AM!
> Come forth and produce Cooperation,
> For my Enlightenment Process!

Cooperation[16] is an integration of the Mighty Will in Action, but it is also an integration process with the (Divine) Feminine...(this leads to) an integration with both Divine Mother and Divine Father. These three energetics come forward (into your aura). Face to the West and claim your freedom!

> I AM ONE within the light!
> And I AM free within the light!
> I AM a manifestation of the Right-hand Path,
> And Beloved Freedom Star.
> So be it.

You may stay at this Adjutant Point for twenty-four to forty-eight hours. Call upon the Mighty Violet Ray in (its) action and activity. Call upon the force of the Mighty Gold Ray.

If you wish to travel with a group of chelas, you may do so. The Cooperation Point is one of the best points to form your Group Mind. However, if you are traveling as an individual or in partnership you, too, may call upon the Group Mind by calling forth mine and Beloved Portia's assistance. We shall be there, always helping, guiding, and assisting.

---

mandala, is the Maltese Cross. Portia serves as hierarch of Eabra, a Golden City for feminine balance of the Earth, located in the Yukon and a part of the Land of Co-creation

15. See Appendix FF: *The Enlightenment Pilgrimage*.
16. The seventh of the Twelve Jurisdictions advises joint actions, work, and assistance to faithfully adhere with fairness, honesty, and the acknowledgment of the Divine Presence. This process helps us to make choices that are both intuitive and balanced. This creates equilibrium with the energies of Divine Mother (nurturing) and Divine Father (protection). Divine Mother is the soul and inner beauty of all Creation. Divine Father is the spark and the divine authority of Creation.

"A STEP-DOWN TRANSFORMER OF LIGHT"

The Cooperation Point begins to fill the cells with Photons of gold light. This is the beginning of your Enlightenment Process. You will feel a difference—a lightening, you will feel your light bodies expanding and moving to 100 feet, sometimes up to 200 feet in their expanse. This is the ultimate Pilgrimage for the Step-down Transformer and (at this point) you shall become as a Step-down Transformer of Light.[17]

The next step of the Pilgrimage moves you onward to the outer parameters to the Central Gateway Point…you know this to be the Outer Child Point. This point coalesces with mighty energies. This is the Photon's cardinal force of enlightenment.

NEW ENERGY BODIES

After you settle within this point, perform your Cup Ceremony. Call your Mighty I AM Presence with gratitude and appreciation for all that has been given to you throughout your many successive embodiments. This (ceremony and gesture) will be an acceptance of your Eighth and Ninth Energy Body, and you will clearly feel the seating-in of the Tenth energetic (Tenth Energy Body) at this point.[18]

Now I know I have given you other Pilgrimages[19] that settle this energetic in as well, but as I have stated before, sometimes we must practice, practice, practice for something to become permanent, do we not, Dear ones, Dear hearts?

Response: *Yes.*

MANTLE OF THE BUDDHA

Again, this will require your intense focus. Call upon the Violet Ray of Mercy, Compassion, and Forgiveness. (At this point) You will take on the Mantle of the Buddha,[20] moving within the gateway of enlightenment. Many of you will sense the Fourth Dimensional Kingdoms of Light, and they may come and dance at your feet. It is best to be in nature as you move into these points, for you want your connection to Beloved Babajeran to overflow with innocence and purity.

---

17. The processes instigated through the Cellular Awakening rapidly advance human light bodies. Synchronized with an Ascended Master's will, the awakened cells of light and love evolve the skills of a Step-Down Transformer to efficiently transmit and distribute currents of Ascended Master energy — referred to as an Ascended Master Current (A.M. Current). This metaphysical form of intentional inductive coupling creates an ethereal power grid that can be used for all types of healing. Energies are typically used to anchor Adjutant Points for Divine Intervention, or securing the transmission of healing energies in a crisis or at a specific location.

18. See Appendix B: *The Advanced Light Fields of Ascension*, and Appendix S: *Human to HU-man Light Fields*.

19. Saint Germain is referring to the Ascension Pilgrimage. For more information see *Evolutionary Biome*.

20. Buddha means *the awakened one*; free from faults; filled with mental clarity and awakened from the sleep of ignorance.

Stay for another forty-eight hours. Meditate in nature if possible, and call upon the clarity of the Buddha. This process is essential, for it raises energies from Christ Consciousness into the Buddha, and onward to the Bodhisattva of Compassion.[21]

This, Dear hearts, is also your enlightenment...it is the seating-in of the Seamless Garment through the Photon of Light.[22] Visualize energies moving from your Root Chakra, up through your united Kundalini, the Golden Thread Axis,[23] and into your Crown Chakra. You will feel a pulsation of light as you meditate during the Pilgrimage and at this specific migration (location).

THE ANGELS OF INITIATION

Dear ones, at this location, call upon the Angels of Compassion, call upon the Angels of Transcendence, call upon the Angels of that Mighty Violet Ray![24] They have existed from time immemorial in the sacred halls of Shamballa, and now leap from the flame of its altar into your heart! *This is your initiation.* You will feel heat and a burning within the Heart Chakra. This is the sign that you have received this initiation, and now it is time to complete your migration of the Western Door of Enlightenment.

FIRE CEREMONY

When you move back to the Cooperation Point, you will perform a very specific fire ceremony.[25] This fire ceremony, Dear ones, is the same fire ceremony that the biblical prophets once performed. It works with internal fire, but is a representation of the eternal fire, which is the eternal Violet Flame.

SACRED PACT OF THE RIGHT-HAND PATH

This fire ceremony is performed again at the Cooperation Point. Call upon my presence (Saint Germain) and Portia, and the Elohim Arcturus to come forward. Anoint yourself with frankincense, myrrh, and lavender. These three oils, when com-

---

21. It is claimed that the Bodhisattva embodies the four divine qualities of kindness, joy, empathy, and equanimity. The Bodhissattva is a step in Mastery, and are able to bear the pain of others. Some consider this to be a manifestation of Amitabha Buddha, an incarnation of both mercy and wisdom. The Bodhisattva intentionally postpones their liberation to assist others in their Spiritual Awakening.
22. The Ascended Masters wear garments without seams. This clothing is not tailored by hand, but perfected through the thought and manifestation process. The later stages of the Ascension Process include the transfiguration of light bodies and Fifth Dimensional contact through the super-senses as the magnificent Seamless Garment manifests its light. It is claimed that the Golden Cities assist the Ascension Process at every stage of development.
23. See Appendix W: *The Will Chakras.*
24. Legions of Violet Flame Angels are claimed to carry the energies of the transmuting Violet Flame whenever they are called upon. The Angels of the Violet Flame protect the flame in its purity and dispense its transforming vibration. Violet Flame Angels can be called upon for a healing crisis.
25. See Appendix EE: *Fire Ceremony.*

bined together, create a special form of alchemy which is the Alchemy of Freedom.[26] Anoint your Third Eye, and accept the Sacred Fire. Raise your right hand:

> I accept the Sacred Fire within my heart.
> I AM ONE with the Spiritual Hierarchy.
> I AM ONE with Freedom Star.
> So be it!

Response: *So be it.*

This is the sacred pact, brought through the heart of love—the heart of compassion and the enlightenment of Ascension. This, too, builds the Seamless Garment of light and sound frequencies. Chant the bija-seed mantra, HUE,[27] no less than forty-nine times. This seals the process. Do you understand?

Response: *Yes.*

INTEGRATION AND STILLNESS

Now, move into the Western Door Retreat. Call upon the energies of stillness, and settle yourself before you prepare yourself to enter into the Star frequencies. This is yet another twenty-four to forty-eight hours. Perform your Cup Ceremony. This is a time of stillness and integration, a time to settle the energies within the Golden Thread Axis, and to realize the immense energetic movement you have made, both externally and internally.[28]

---

26. Sandalwood is 96 MHz, Myrrh is 105 MHz, and Lavender is 118 MHz.

27. In Tibetan dialects, the word hue or hu means *breath*; however, the HU is a sacred sound and when chanted or meditated upon is said to represent the entire spectrum of the Seven Rays. Because of this, the HU powerfully invokes the presence of the Violet Flame, which is the activity of the Violet Ray and its inherent ability to transform and transmit energies to the next octave. HU is also considered an ancient name for God, and it is sung for spiritual enlightenment.

28. There are various Ascended Master techniques for integrating subtle energies of new light bodies and Golden City energies. The first is the salt bath. Use one cup of salt natural or Himalayan Salt is preferred, but any type will work, in bath water with essential oils. You can also use a salt scrub in the shower. The salt helps to capture and hold negative energies that rinse away in the water. Walks in nature are also helpful, and preferably in a slight wind if possible. The wind elements help to cleanse the auric field. Sitting near a fire is also good, as it cleanses negative karmas. Use of certain incense and essential oils is also helpful, as they help to raise the vibration of a room. Play music that is calm and soothing, such as classical music or mantras. Construct a small home altar and place pictures of the Master Teachers and Archangels. Activate the altar with incense, a candle, and fresh flowers. This is a perfect location for meditation and decree.

Spiritual practice is perhaps one of the best techniques for integration. This includes the use of the Three Standards, Violet Flame Decrees, the Awakening Prayer, and the Violet Flame at Sunrise and Sunset. Apply meditation and the Violet Flame Breath Technique at both sunrise and sunset.

Diet can also significantly help the integration process. Fasting is always best, but if that is too difficult, try one meal per day. Focus on foods that contain no to low animal products.

"PROCLAIM THIS UNTO SELF"

After you feel complete within this Pilgrimage (step), move back into the Star frequencies and call upon the Mighty White Ray and Violet Ray. Accept the White Ray within your being, for you have just carried and seated Cooperation within your light fields. You will enter as a member of the Spiritual Hierarchy of the Great White Brotherhood and Sisterhoods of Light.[29] Now, proclaim this unto yourself and realize your Oneship.

Again, call upon the Hierarch of that Golden City to assist you in your entrance into the Great White Brotherhood, and to receive your sacred anointing of light. You will take your beginning steps into your Seamless Garment.

This, too, is accomplished by your Cup Ceremony, but also by your prayer and your meditation. Now do you have questions?

Response: *Yes.*

Proceed.

FOLLOW THE CARDINAL LEI-LINE

Question: *So as I understand this (Pilgrimage) we start in the Star, then we travel to the Western Door and onward to the Southwest Door?*

No. This (Pilgrimage) travels along the Cardinal Lei-line and its points to the West. From the Star (go to the Star Retreat), then move to the Cooperation Point, onward from the Cooperation Point, move to the Cardinal Point of the outer Western Door.

Response: *Okay.*

Then move back to the Cooperation Point, to the Western Retreat, and then onward to the Star. Are we clear?

Response: *Very clear. This is similar to the Northern Door Migration that El Morya gave us.*

It mirrors it, however, I am sponsoring this migration for my many chelas in this year of 2021 so you may all begin to understand, know, and utilize the Mighty Seamless Garment of Light.[30] For until you have taken on the Seamless Garment, you have yet to understand what freedom is. Proceed.

Question: *Shall we share this as soon as possible with the other students?*

---

29. See Appendix GG; *Spiritual Hierarchy.*
30. Saint Germain, Beloved Portia, and Archangel Zadkiel are sponsoring chelas who engage this important Pilgrimage through the year 2025. In 2026 the White Ray moves to the Northern Door of all Golden Cities.

A PILGRIMAGE OF INITIATION

All that I give in my teaching is for all the students of I AM America. I share this willingly and from the Great Violet Flame within my heart. This, you see, is a Pilgrimage of Enlightenment that fills you with the Violet Flame of Freedom; it also is a Pilgrimage designed to initiate you into the Great White Brotherhood of Light.

Some may be physically contacted by members of the Hierarchy in this Pilgrimage. This can happen at many levels, through inner guidance, or an appearance—I will not limit the form as it can have many.[31] Do you understand?

Response: *Yes I do.*

Proceed.

Question: *Then my question…should we do this sooner than later?*

THE PREPARATION OF ENERGIES

Move with haste, Dear ones, but I suggest that you begin after the close of Shamballa. Right now the energies are settling into the Western Door and currently the Hierarchy that is gathered at Shamballa is making certain that the energies are properly prepared for you. Do you understand?

Response: *Yes.*

Proceed.

Question: *Back to the knowledge of our choices being tampered with…is there anything you wish for us to do?*

CLEANSING IMPURITIES

It is important to drink the purest water that you can find to flush your system of the impurities, use a pure salt—this I know you have identified.[32] Remove all chemicals if you can from your diet. Eat fresh and organic foods. I always mention to remove animal products, and I have a reason for this. It has a tendency to hold the fear substance. Of course you can use prayer and the use of the Green and the Gold Rays through your ring finger as you bless it (your food), do you remember?[33]

---

31. The Ascended Master is never limited by form.
32. Real Salt is a non-refined, natural salt. It is not processed or stripped of natural trace minerals.
33. Saint Germain shares this guidance in *Evolutionary Biome,* "Indeed, there is, Dear ones, Dear hearts. I taught this many years ago in the teachings and it is important to charge your food with your own energy before consumption. This can remove the fear substance, but it also enlivens the food and allows it to contain a higher energetic that is derived from your own spiritual practice."

Response: *Absolutely yes.*

That, too, can purify any type of food that you take into your being. Dear ones, Beloved Sananda has taught many times, "it is not so much what you put into your mouth, but it is indeed the intention and the words that you speak." Work for purity of heart, a clear intention, and a clear mind. This is the purpose of the diet, for it clarifies the body at a physical level.[34] Do you understand?

Response: *Yes I do.*

Do you have further questions?

Response: *Yes.*

Proceed.

"MOVE WITHIN THE LIGHT"

Question: *We have always striven to never interconnect with any political interactivity; however, the freedom of our nation is extremely important for the overall plan of the Spiritual Hierarchy. Is there anything you need us to do at a spiritual level?*

Saint Germain's advice on diet in, *A Teacher Appears:* "I would like to verse you, too, on your diet. Take in only that which is pure and clean, for the stress of the many vibrations are hard upon the physical vehicle. At the end of your day, spend time in solitude and meditation to cleanse your system from this. Put only the freshest and most valuable foods to your system. Before you eat, charge them with a directed activity of the I AM, for are you not taking in that which is of the ONE Source? Recognize this in all that you do. And are you not taking in of the ONE Source as you travel and people are placed in your path? See that, as they give to you, you also give to them." Similar advice given by Saint Germain in *Fields of Light:* "Saint Germain also introduced a technique to purify food and drink; that of visualizing Green and Gold energy streaming from your ring finger, on your left or right hand, whichever you prefer. Apparently, this is a type of individualized energy that streams directly from your I AM Presence, and carries a unique vibration and blessing that alchemizes a distinctive and matchless elixir into your food and beverages."

34. Saint Germain shares this insight regarding cleansing the physical body: "The best way to prepare the body is to fast. I suggest no longer than a full three-day fast. However, at that time, be sure that you are getting a proper amount of hydration along with the essential salts. As you break your fast, you can use lemon juice, some vinegars, and of course very small amounts of fruit juice mixed with water. This helps the body to cleanse. That is, to remove impurities. Of course, you can also focus on a spiritual fast that is heightening your spiritual practice. This can be done through four hours a day, focused upon the Violet Flame, and a combination of Violet Flame, along with salt baths. For you see, this too will increase your connection to the spirit world, along with cleansing the physical body. Now, as I have always suggested, stay off animal products. This is for several reasons. Animal products, you see, Dear ones, are very polluted today. Of course, if you can find those that are very pure, have been fed the highest amounts of nutrition, that is, high amounts of chlorophyll, these too can assist you, but be sure to remove, through the techniques I have taught you in blessing, the fear substance."

Pursue your Ascension in the light, Dear one! As you become freer and freer from the constraints of duality and the evil dark force, then you will move within the light and attract more light. This is the Law of the Photon.[35] Do you understand?

Response: *That's very interesting...I accept that, yes.*

Light attracts more light unto itself, and darkness, too, attracts more darkness unto itself. Call upon my assistance, Dear ones. I shall be there.

LORDS OF VENUS ARE ON EARTH

It is important to understand that many from the Pleiades are now within the Earth Plane, giving their assistance. They will come forward soon, and reveal themselves; also, currently many great Lords of Venus[36] are present upon the Earth in physical form. They are taking physical form to hold the light for America. America *is* the great light of freedom! From this great light the Earth shall become as ONE with Freedom Star. Do you understand?

Response: *Yes I do.*

Do you have further questions?

EARTH'S EVOLUTION

Response: *So technically, Freedom Star is the Higher Self of our planet?*

It is the highest frequency that Earth will hold as Bhurloka.[37] For remember, she is not the highest or the lowest in terms of the consciousness of the solar system. She is to become a great light that is free! She shall free herself from the bounds of duality, and travel through the remarkable Photon Belt of light. She will open as a new classroom for many new Star seeds of consciousness. Do you understand?

---

35. Law of the Photon: Light attracts more light.
36. A group of Ascended Masters who came to serve humanity. They once resided on the planet Venus. Sanat Kumara and Serapis Bey were with an ancient group of Master Teachers from Venus. Some Ascended Master teaching also associated the Seven Holy Kumaras as originating from Venus.
37. According to the sacred Sanskrit text of Hindu philosophy, the Bhagavad-Gita, fourteen planetary systems exist in the intangible universe. The highest is Satyaloka where residents grasp advanced spiritual knowledge. Sanat Kumara and Sananda—who in Vedic culture is referred to as Sanandana Kumara—are two of the four sons of Brahma and inhabit the second-tier planetary system of Tapaloka. Earth, known as Bhurloka, falls seventh in line. It is determined to exist in the middle range of evolution, not the highest or the lowest.
   Each planetary system creates a unique experience for its dwellers—the sentience of the space-time continuum and the manifestation of the physical being differentiate higher from lower beings. Residents of enlightened strata perceive time durations in millennia, have no sense of fear, and do not confront disease or the aging of the body. In the lower planetary systems, residents experience shorter life spans, marked fear, widespread disease, and increased apprehension.

Response: *Yes I do.*

STEP-DOWN ENERGIES

This is a process that is being engendered through the center of the Earth itself, and radiating to the surface. As Light BE-ings you become as Step-down Transformers of light, and this is also the purpose of the Enlightenment Pilgrimage. As you move from Adjutant Point to Adjutant Point, you step-down frequencies of the purest form of God Light and God Protection *into* and *onto* the Earth Plane and Planet. Do you understand?

Response: *Yes.*

> America is to be free,
> And Freedom Star shall be!

Response: *Hitaka.*

Do you have further questions?

Response: *I have only one.*

Proceed.

Question: *Since we are now going to share this with the other students, shall we share everything that has come through as soon as possible?*

As I have always said, Dear ones, my work is given to you so you may liberate as quickly as possible to reunite with your Mighty I AM Presence, and to realize the fullness of Ascension.

Response: *I understand I have no further questions.*

TRUST AND KNOW

Throughout your Pilgrimage, I shall give guidance and many lessons along the way.

> Trust and know,
> That I AM there.
> Trust and know,
> That the fullness of your Ascension is at hand.
> Trust and know,
> That you are free!

I AM your Brother in the Mighty Violet Flame, and the knowledge of the I AM That I AM, Saint Germain.

Response: *Om Manaya Pitaya Hitaka. Shamballa.*

Hitaka!

CHAPTER FIVE

Free, Humanity Shall Be

Shamballa's Energies Assist the Golden Age on Earth

Greetings, Beloveds, in that Mighty Christ I AM Saint Germain and I stream forth on that Mighty Violet Ray of Mercy, Transmutation, and Forgiveness. As usual, Dear ones, Dear hearts, I request permission to come forward.

Response: *Dear Saint Germain please come forward and Shamballa, greetings, and love to all.*

THE DIVINE COMPLEMENTS OF THE GOLDEN CITIES

Shamballa and greetings to you, as well. You may have noted there are many of us here today to give our message of peace and blessing to humanity.

Now let me describe. Saint Germain steps forward, and on his arm is Beloved Lady Portia. El Morya is also present and he is complemented by the energies of Desiree. Master Kuthumi is also present and he is complemented by the energies of Lady Nada. Lord Sananda is present and he is complemented by the energies of Lady Miriam. Beloved Serapis Bey is present and he is complemented by the energies of Lady Luxsor. Saint Germain will step forward to speak.

Dear ones, as you see we are all present today with our Divine Complement[1] of Energy to serve as an adjunct[2] (Hierarch) in each of our Golden Cities. As you know, Dear ones, this is a blessed time of Shamballa and energy is pouring forth upon the Earth Plane and Planet. (During this time) we come forward in our Collective Consciousness as a Group Mind to also pour our blessing upon the Earth, to I AM America, to the students of I AM America, and primarily to the beloved Golden Cites

---

1. Each Ascended Master, Divine Being, and Archangel is alleged to be paired with a divine complement of energy. Each divine pair manifests and streams energies into the corporeal worlds through the Hermetic Law of Gender. Hence, one is masculine in quality, while the other is feminine. Similar to a Twin Flame, Divine Complements differ in that they are ascended and purposely divide their efforts to assist Earth and unascended humanity. In the higher realms they are ideally ONE energy, and serve upon one individualized Ray Force.
It is also apparent that occasionally different Ascended Masters and their Divine Complements change for different missions and divine work together. Again, Ascended Masters are never limited by form.
2. Adjunct: Joined, or added.

of Gobean, Malton, Wahanee, Shalahah, and Klehma. These five Golden Cities hold the fulcrum of light within America and as you well know, America indeed holds the light for the rest of the world.

FREEDOM STAR—A SUN OF VIOLET LIGHT

As America matures, she, too, shall hold the light for beloved Freedom Star.[3] This we have prophesied and the Freedom Star is to be a great light within the solar system! She shall enter into an evolutionary process where the Earth will become a Sun of the Violet Light.

BEINGS OF LIGHT

You know that the Sun is a planet where, yes indeed, great Beings of Light occupy the great Sun of Light.[4] We have also spoken about the Ancestral Planet[5] and the many Beings of Light who also inhabit her, not only at a consciousness level, but also at a physical level.

Currently the surface of the Earth is in great turmoil. We realize this, and the great Beings of Light within the Inner Earth are holding a mighty lighted vigil for the Beings of Light at the surface. This, too, has been complemented by the energies of Shamballa.

SHAMBALLA REMAINS OPEN

When I came forward and gave my request that we would be giving weekly teachings, I also mentioned that this would begin during the opening of Shamballa and through the energy of these beloved Dear ones. We all stand together in stewardship of these teachings. And in our Mastery of the Earth Plane and Planet, Shamballa shall remain open this year throughout the entire year.[6] This is being done to help assist humanity at this time and to guide and direct her during this sensitive tipping point.[7] This will help many of the chelas to readily mature and to realize their own Great

---

3. The Earth's prophesied new name as the Earth and humanity evolve throughout the Golden Age. *Freedom Star* is both a state of consciousness that is associated with Ascension and spiritual liberation, and is a new light body that planet Earth will develop in the New Times. In advanced Ascended Master teaching, Freedom Star is considered Earth's ascended state.

4. In Ascended Master teaching, the Sun is inhabited. Its heat is claimed to be a defensive forcefield generated by the great beings of light who live upon its surface and within it.

5. A hidden planet, whose view is obscured by the dark, twin Sun. Its inhabitants are highly evolved Spiritual Beings who assist humanity during times of evolutionary darkness. Saint Germain shares teachings on the Ancestral Planet in *Awaken the Master Within*, "It is true that there is another planet that exists behind your solar Sun. It has contained within it, the ancestry of the genetic strains that exist upon the Earth Plane and Planet. Some of this information has been recorded within your history. Some of it is correct and some of it is not."

6. This is an inordinate event that has continued beyond 2021 and the Ascended Masters claim may continue for many more years. This helps to rapidly advance the spiritual evolution of humanity, through increased energies in the Golden Cities.

7. A tipping point is a critical point where an unstoppable change or series of events could occur.

Awakening. You see, Dear ones, the five Golden Cities hold this energy for the Planet throughout this entire year. Yes, it is an anomaly, and it will close again within one year's time — after the closure of Shamballa from 2021 to 2022.

It was decreed long ago that *if* the Golden Age were to erupt upon this Earth Plane and Planet, especially during this extraordinary time that many of you have known as Kali Yuga, that Shamballa would usher in this New Time.[8] Last year I gave you information regarding the Golden Belt[9] and how each of its tiny threads and numerous firmaments of light were woven into each of the Golden Cities. This, too, was a confirmation that this time — the Golden Age — would commence and contribute to HU-man evolution.

NOTHING CAN STOP THE GOLDEN AGE

For you see, the dark ones in their evil and insidious plan have worked through, shall we say, a science of consciousness to try to corrupt the timeline of the Golden Age.[10] Now you well know, Dear hearts, and as it has been decreed by this Hierarchy of Light, the Golden Age is well upon its way. Nothing can stop this time of bounty, abundance, light, and Ascension for humanity!

SHAMBALLA'S OPENING ASSISTS PILGRIMAGES

Shamballa's Fifth Dimensional energies of light permeate through the Fourth Dimension, and onward into the Third Dimension. Shamballa will shed its radiance for an entire year upon the Earth Plane and Planet. This, too, will allow many of your Pilgrimages to continue in a magnificent Lighted Stance. Yes, it is true that we have given you a Pilgrimage of the Lighted Stance (the Enlightenment Pilgrimage), but

---

8. This is a reference to the Fourth and Fifth Dimensional Timeline Two.

9. This etheric Golden Belt, or Golden Band of high-frequency energy was in place since the early 1950s through the efforts of the Ascended Master Saint Germain. It held back catastrophic Earth Changes until humanity has a better chance to evolve. The belt also played a significant role in mankind's spiritual growth. The Golden Belt was dissipated during the Shamballa Season of 2019-2020, and its Golden Threads were woven into each of the fifty-one Golden Cities. This act declares Earth's passage into the Golden Age.

10. If you consciously observe the I AM America Map, two unique timelines are presented. One is Earth Changes — almost apocalyptic — and the other is the birth of the New Times, the Golden Age. We've discussed this before in previous messages, but recent events guide us to remind you again of this prophetic message.

The recent volcanic eruptions (La Palma), earthquakes from Australia to South Carolina, and a summer filled with constant wildfire reiterate the Earth Changes theme of the I AM America Map. Is Timeline One gaining momentum? Right now, humanity's consciousness is in a battle for the timelines. This pattern may appear many times throughout the next twenty years.

Timeline Two is the Timeline of the Golden Age. It is also the remarkable timeline of entering Fourth Dimension as humanity's Global Consciousness enters the Great Awakening. This is the time of Peace and Cooperation that the Masters prophesied — of balance, truthfulness, harmony, and cooperation.

We suggest that as you view your I AM America Map, recite the Awakening Prayer. Keep your consciousness, intentions, and loving actions tuned into the vibration of love. "If you live with love, you will create love," and affirm the presence of Timeline Two.

even those who wish to continue in their progression of any Pilgrimage, will do so with great success.[11]

GOLD AND AQUAMARINE RAYS

Today, we stand as sponsors of this New and Mighty Time of the Golden Age, and each of us holds in our mind's eye the Gold and Aquamarine Rays' force of great purity and strength. Also, it is important to understand that the best way to segue your energies into this time of golden light is through the Mighty Violet Ray and the use of Mighty Violet Flame of Mercy, Compassion and Forgiveness.

> "Mighty Violet Flame,
> Come forth and blaze throughout humanity!
> Pave the pathway for this New and Mighty Time,
> The Golden Age of Abundance."

Dear hearts, the Violet Flame prepares the light fields to receive the energies of the Gold and the Aquamarine Ray. I have given you many teachings upon this, and I am always available for your questions if you need review.

The Gold Ray raises the Earth into a new vibration of light. This is also accompanied by the Aquamarine Ray. The Aquamarine Ray provides necessary healing at new levels of energy for humanity. During this time of great light of the Golden Time, new healing modalities will come forward through the Aquamarine Ray. That is why I have prophesied that many can live for thousands of years in this Time of Light.

THE MASTERS OF SHAMBALLA AND THE GOLDEN AGE OF LIGHT

Shamballa is supported by the Mighty Masters of the Pleiades, and the Lords of Venus alongside the Great Lords and Goddesses of the DAHL. It was long decreed that if this time should come forward (on Earth) then light supreme would rule again upon the Earth. The children of the Mighty God and the Christ Consciousness of Light would be able to advance and realize their fullness of liberty and freedom in Ascension.

Normally, these would be our final weeks of closure at Shamballa; however, because of this special condition—which was set into play through the Great Activation of the Golden Cities of Europe and the Middle East. This is now possible!

While the ten of us stand in conscious effort to usher in the Golden Age of Light, it is also important to understand that the Fifty-one Hierarchs of Golden Cities of Light also play a tremendous role.[12] Our intent and timing comes forward in service and glory to the light! This too, was issued through the edict and service of Sanat

---

11. To learn more about Golden City Spiritual Pilgrimage and their unique Migration Patterns see the *I AM America Atlas for 2021 and Beyond.*
12. To learn more about the fifty-one Hierarchs of the Golden Cities see *Golden Cities and the Masters of Shamballa.*

Kumara and Beloved Lord Apollo.[13] All come forward for this time period upon the Earth Plane and Planet. The Great Beings of Light in Inner Earth also are assisting.

"IT IS OUR HONOR TO SERVE"

I have mentioned before, Dear Ones, that there are many Golden Cities of Light that exist within the center of the Earth. Not as many as the surface (of Earth), but seventeen glorious Golden Cities of Light that hold the Christ Consciousness gestated through the kernel of the Quetzalcoatl consciousness. This is the energy of compassion, love, and mercy that is held within the Eight-sided Cell of Perfection in the heart.[14] This is the culmination of your Divine DNA and as it activates becomes the activity of the Unfed Flame of Love, Wisdom, and Power. In adjunct to this is that Mighty Flame of Desire,[15] for the desire for freedom has brought us here, and kept us here! Dear ones, we come in service to humanity through the Brotherhoods and Sisterhoods of Breath Sound and Light. It is our honor and our privilege to serve humanity at this most glorious Time of Awakening.

ASCENSION IN THE LIGHT

It is important to understand that throughout this year there will be many more Ascensions. In fact, it is important to understand that in your previous year there were over 10,000 Ascensions that were achieved. This is through the (additional energy of the) Golden Cities of Light. Also, I announce that one of your great servants of light—Beloved Elaine—has achieved her victorious Ascension in the light.[16] This she has achieved through her service within the Golden City of Wahanee, and now she shall serve at an Adjutant Point of Light within the Golden City of Afrom.[17] She has individualized (her consciousness) upon the White Ray of Service. Of course some of this came through her mighty service to I AM America alone! We also recognized

---

13. A God of healing, truth, music, and Prophecy. This Ascended Master is a venerated scholar of the Ascended Master tradition and is considered a guru, or Master Teacher, of many contemporary Ascended Masters.
14. The Quetzalcoatl Energies, as explained and taught by Lord Meru, are akin to the Christ energies when applied in the esoteric Western Christian tradition. This ancient spiritual teacher, however, predates Christianity and likely has its roots in alchemic Atlantean (Toltec) teaching. Quetzalcoatl, in contemporary terms, is the Incan Christ.
15. The Ascended Masters claim that the physical presence of the Flame of Desire lies within the heart nestled inside the Eight-sided Cell of Perfection. As students and chelas perfect the Co-creation process, some teachings suggest the Flame of Desire evolves alongside the Three-Fold or Unfed Flame of Love, Wisdom, and Power into the Fourfold Flame. In this physical, progressed state it develops as the fourth White Flame of Creation. The cultivation of the Jurisdiction Faith (as Hope) engenders and protects its development. The Flame of Desire is said to be another important innate link to the source of creation and is protected through chanting the "OM."
16. Elaine Cardall, (1945-2016), was an editor for many of the I AM America Books. An advocate of the I AM America Teachings, Elaine lived in the Star of Malton. She led study and decree classes in her Golden City area based upon the Ascended Master Teachings. An alumni of Brown University, Elaine's unique insight and loving devotion to the I AM America Teachings will be forever remembered and cherished.
17. A Golden City Vortex of the White Ray located in Hungary and Romania.

that you have another Beloved Sister of Light who is waiting on the wings for her Ascension.[18] For now, she shall continue her service of light within the Golden City of Shalahah.

"FREE, HUMANITY SHALL BE!"

Dear ones, this time of Shamballa and its magnificent and celebrated opening upon the Earth Plane and Planet will allow many new energetics to flourish within the HU-man, physiologically. This will allow the Eighth, Ninth, and Tenth Energetic to become firmly secure within your capability. You will have unyielding access of these energies of light. This prepares you for Eleventh Energetic, and we all know what lies beyond this…yes, your glory and freedom in the light! For free, humanity shall be! Now, I sense your questions.

Response: *Momentarily I am speechless, and filled with love and devotion. Please continue on.*

"A LESSENING OF KARMIC BURDEN"

Our love and devotion streams forward to each and every one of you, chelas of I AM America, and other chelas of the Great White Brotherhood and Sisterhood of Light. This shall be a grand and glorious year, a year of the turning of the Wheel of Karma.[19] This means that those who have followed the lesson(s) and the teachings of the light will find a lessening of their karmic burden. But those who proceed on a path of darkness will suffer even greater ramification of karmic burdens, until they accept into their heart the Mighty Love and Light of God that never fails!

FRACTAL ENERGY

Throughout this year each and every one of you shall receive direct downloads of information that will direct you to various Adjutant Points of Light. Many of you will pursue your own Spiritual Pilgrimages to the Adjutant Points of Light and while I have given you many of these Pilgrimages, you may also be guided to just one Adjutant Point of Light where you will experience its fractal energy. Each Adjutant Point of Light contains within it a microcosm of seventeen Points of Light, and its own energetic Star and Doorways. This, too, is for your wondrous discovery.[20] Many new Adjutant Point Hierarchs are being appointed and serving in these mighty

---

18. Susan Liberty Hall, (1945-2020), friend and contributor to the I AM America Maps, books, and teachings.
19. The Wheel of Karma, fed by insidious, lower desires, is the cycle of actions, outcomes, and the resulting new action. It is the basis of reincarnation and as we enter our Ascension Process and the Fourth Dimension the polarity and duality of the Wheel lessens. As we gain enlightenment, our mind intervenes through choice and will, and the use of spiritual practice, primarily the Violet Flame, transmutes lower desires into the Flame of Divinity, *of the source.*
20. See *Seventeen Points*, Appendix N.

Golden Cities of Light. The firmament of Heaven is open for humanity to receive the gift. As always, Dear ones, this is through the fulcrum of choice and free will.

HEALING AND RESTORATION

It is important that I give you more information on healing and integration. We recognize and know that healing will be a tremendous issue this year, for humanity has been assaulted at many levels. This has happened through your news media, through various chemtrails, and the corruption of your food stuffs.

To restore your will, carry out Pilgrimage to the Western Door...for this is also a Pilgrimage of Light that is considered a Pilgrimage of the Divine Will and restores your vital connection to your Mighty I AM Presence. This can open the pineal gland so that you may receive vital knowledge directly. Sometimes this knowledge is given in higher realms as you sleep at night, sometimes it is given through a dream experience, sometimes it softly brushes into your consciousness as you are in meditation, and sometimes it comes through an intuitive urge. The intuition is cultivated and healed through your Pilgrimage in Eastern Doors.[21] All of these Pilgrimages unite and serve as ONE. Dear ones, it is the great gift that streams forward and heralds the New Time of Light—the Mighty Golden Age. Do you have questions?

A THOUSAND ADJUTANT POINT HIERARCHS

Question: *Yes, you mentioned the fractal seventeen for each of the Adjutant Points...does that mean that there are additional Step-down Hierarchs for these Fractal Points?*

Indeed. Do you remember after the events of 9-11, and the Hierarchy dispensed thousands of Adjutant Point Hierarchs to enter into the Golden Cities?[22] This was

---

21. See *Evolutionary Biome, Golden City Eastern Door Pilgrimage* and *Awakening the Divine Feminine*.
22. From *Awaken the Master Within*: "You see, Dear ones, it was decided in this most recent Shamballa that we would begin the process of sending our, shall we call them, Sergeants and Lieutenants at Arms, those who are our most stalwart followers. They are to move forward into the Earth Plane and Planet at this time to ready the Golden City Vortices and to also bring the great assistance that the Earth needs at this most perilous time...Those beings that have freed themselves from the need to reincarnate on the physical plane, take upon a higher service. They are still under the auspice of their Master Teacher, an Ascended Master, who has freed himself also from astral and causal influence. The Master Teacher, under this auspice, still gives their sponsorship to the freed chela. This freed chela then is able to operate at a greater level of service for the Earth Plane and Planet. These are the Master Teachers that are now entering into the Adjutant Points of the Southern Doors of all Golden City Vortices. They are Masters indeed and come under the service of the hierarchy...It is now important to understand that there will come forward these Master Teachers in their great service within the Southern Doors. It was no mistake, Dear one, Dear heart, that I sent you to activate Adjutant Points in the Southern Door of Gobean. I sent you for the purpose primarily so that you could perform the service of a Step-down Transformer in these specific Adjutant Points. This brought forth a necessary influx of energy; for you see, as above, so below. All energy, when it is sustained upon the Earth Plane and Planet, is under these types of applicable laws. Now, so that you can gain further understanding into this process, many of these servants are coming forward, each of them of course through different Master Teachers. As the Gobean Vortex is sponsored by Master El Morya, there are many Master Teachers working for the influence of Master El Morya and coming forward now to assist this great influence of energy. It is true too that some of these Master

what we were speaking about, for we knew the great assault on the Light that had occurred upon the Earth Plane and Planet…knew about the evil and dark plans that were ensuing, and knew that humanity's hope, life, and freedom in Ascension would lie within the empowerment of the beloved Golden Cities of Light. It is true that as an Ascension Process you may leave from the physical plane. However, many may choose to enter into the path of Ascension through the disciplines of the Golden Cities of Light. Do you understand?[23]

Response: *Yes.*

Proceed.

WATER AND THE CUP CEREMONY

Question: *As we move through the Adjutant Points we know how to perform the Cup ceremony. Is there a specific decree for each of the Adjutant Points for the activations of the energy bodies?*

It is important to always apply the Violet Flame, for it will clear the pathways for the emboldening and the enlightening of the Light. But the Cup Ceremony is perhaps best to use at this time, for as given in my discourses at our last Shamballa, the power lies within the water itself, do you understand?

Response: *Yes, because of the composition of the water?*

This is true, Dear ones. It magnifies the energetics of that location and allows you to interface immediately with the Evolutionary Biome of Light, do you understand?[24]

Response: *Yes I do, and water, through creation, does take many forms…yet, it still is water.*

Teachers will keep their residence in the higher level, that is, in the Fourth and the Fifth Dimension. Those Master Teachers who retain an influence of the Fourth Dimension have a more Elemental or Deva type energy. They shall serve the cause of influencing weather patterns, also the Earth energy itself, and allowing an imbuing of the energies of that mighty Blue Ray to come forward for the true healing of the nations."

23. There are many forms of Ascension. For more information see Appendix F: *The Eight Pathways to Ascension.*

24. Metaphysicians are just starting to understand the science that lies within water. Japanese scientist Dr. Masaru Emoto theorized that thoughts and feelings can imbue the physical molecules of water. The result charges the water with benefic energies, or negative influences. Through the use of high-speed photography he was able to catch crystalline patterns of positive themes, such as gratitude, peace, and happiness. Discordant energies displayed figures with disarray, with no meaningful arrangement. Emoto also discovered that sound and music played a remarkable role, with prayer, mantra, and classical music creating beautifully arranged patterns within the water. Insensitive and harsh sounds created indistinct and distorted crystal arrangements.

It is the foundation of life itself, it carries within it the vital chi and the light and the sound frequencies. Do you understand?

Response: *Yes I do.*

Now, there is more that I would like to share unless if you have other questions.

Response: *Please continue.*

THE LORDS OF VENUS STEP-DOWN ESSENTIAL ENERGIES

As I stated in my last discourse, many of the Lords of Venus are now present, in physical form. This is for many and various reasons. First, they step-down energetics that are vital and essential onto the Earth planet. The Golden Age will not only be realized within the Golden Cities that accelerate your Ascension Process, but the Golden Age will be felt by many throughout the world as the Earth is realized as Freedom Star. They (the Lords of Venus) are present in many of the world's capital cities, and (some) reside in your nation's capital...they are also present in all the capital cities of the United States of America. Again, they are stepping-down energies and frequencies that are essential.[25] Some of these energies and frequencies Co-create freedom at many new levels of understanding and comprehension, yet (the energies) also carry a wave of healing that is present throughout this year. Many will feel new frequencies of Awakening to levels they have not ever experienced. This is a new experience for many, many people.

"SHARE WILLINGLY"

Dear ones, holders of the light, holders of the sacred Cup of I AM America, you are present to give assistance to those who ask the question, "Why?" and who ask the question, "How?" Be stalwart in the light, firm in your understanding of the Right-hand Path, yet hold them in the love and the compassion of Christ, for there are *no mistakes,* Dear ones. All who come across your path also thirst for the knowledge of light. Share willingly with them; yet always remember your sacred vows to the Brotherhood of Light. Do you understand?

Response: *Yes, completely. I stand with you.*

And we stand with you! The Lords of Venus will assist at many levels as new groups and parties appear. This will happen at many levels. New organizations of Light will appear with many new spiritual groups. They will come forward to serve at this time, for you see, Dear ones, many of the churches have become adulterated. Many thirst for

---

25. Some of these beings of Light manifest physical bodies, others do not and work multi-dimensionally, moving in and out of phase.

the knowledge of spirit, of their true identity, of their Divine Destiny and integration with the I AM That I AM.[26] This, too, is important, for free, humanity shall be!

APPEARANCE OF THE MASTERS

From time to time throughout the Golden City Vortices of Light, each of the Hierarchs will take upon physical form. This was prophesied years ago, and it was said that for twenty years the Ascended Masters will manifest in physical form to bring about healing for humanity. This does not mean that they will interact with humanity and the gross public, but there will be sightings. One may notice a great wall of light before them, and one of the Ascended Masters will step forward, offer the Cup, and ask, "Will you drink?"[27] This, too, shall occur throughout this year as the frequencies of Shamballa bathe Earth and the lowering of the Shamballa energies will create time anomalies. Instead of Time Compaction, you will experience *a stretching of time*, as if time *no longer exists*. This assists the Enlightening Process and a youthening of the physical body. Now I shall say no more, for I believe I have given you enough in this discourse. I open the floor for your questions.

Question: *Yes, as humanity is moving on and we utilize the Violet Flame to aid, assist, and transmute the friction and aggression, and come forward with an evolutionary process that is not in conflict…as we go through this, in our personal movements to the Adjutant Points, is it advisable that we hold this focus not only for personal but for the entire planet, true?*

SERVICE

It is true, Dear one. From each of our hearts leaps the Mighty Flame of Freedom into the heart of humanity, for free, humanity shall be! This year keep your focus upon the Awakening Prayer, so that the *right* people at the *right time* cross your path. Give them love and assistance at the most significant time within their own evolutionary

---

26. A term from Hebrew that translates to, "I Will Be What I Will Be." "I AM" is also derived from the Sanskrit Om (pronounced: A-U-M), whose three letters signify the three aspects of God as beginning, duration, and dissolution—Brahma, Vishnu, and Shiva. The AUM syllable is known as the omkara and translates to "I AM Existence," the name for God. "Soham," is yet another mystical Sanskrit name for God, which means "It is I," or "He is I." In Vedic philosophy, it is claimed that when a child cries, "Who am I?" the universe replies, "Soham—you are the same as I AM." The I AM teachings also use the name "Soham" in place of "I AM."

27. This is a reference to the "most refreshing drink." The *Refreshing Drink* is an allegory of the Universal Supply of Life. It originates from the work of Guy Ballard, who, under the pen name Godfré Ray King, authored the classic theosophical book of Ascended Master teaching, *Unveiled Mysteries*.
 Ballard's work evolves from a simple meditation during a hike on Mount Shasta. On a warm day, Ballard—asking God to define his path—finds his way to a stream and fills his cup with its water. A drink of the liquid sends an electrical current through his body. Suddenly, a young man materializes and telepathically relays this message: "My Brother, if you will hand me your Cup, I will give you a much more refreshing drink."
 The young man later on reveals himself as Saint Germain; Ballard's water flows directly from the Universal Supply, "(as) pure and vivifying as Life itself; in fact it is Life—Omnipresent Life—for it exists everywhere about us."

process. If there are those who have the eyes to see and the ears to hear, and wish to accompany you on a Pilgrimage, welcome them with open hearts and with an open mind. For this will assist them. Maybe open a chakra that has been diseased or unclean (impure) for a long time, maybe it will help to uncloud an energy field that is holding past wounds of many lifetimes. Perhaps this will instill within them the vigor within to become a new chela and to study the courses of light, to learn about their Divine Destiny and their Divine Light within. Come forward as servants of mine . . .help and assist, and serve humanity. Questions?

Response: *I am very willing to serve humanity and all that the Hierarchy is asking with love and devotion. There are students that we interact with, who would probably prefer if we took them to the Adjutant Points.*

    As the energies present themselves, it will become obvious to you when to embark upon your spiritual journey of light.

Response: *I understand. We will always be on a need to know basis as we move forward.*

    And now, Dear one, unless if there are other questions, I shall close down this discourse.

Response: *Just one.*

    Proceed.

Question: *Shall we continue on with another session next week?*

    Indeed. For a frequency has been set up within your home and energies may stream forward at the appointed time. You may have sensed that we have had to employ several adjustments. Do you understand?

Response: *Yes, those were easily perceived.*

    And now we shall retreat back to the Halls of Shamballa, where numerous preparations are being planned and placed into effect for our Beloved Earth—Freedom Star.

Response: *I am very grateful that you're continuing on with the opening of Shamballa and thank you.*

    I AM your brother and servant in the light.

I'd like to describe…they all step forward into the Star of an even greater Golden City of Light and their collective energy forms a great golden ball. As it moves to the Temples of Shamballa, it dissipates from this dimension.

Golden Light

CHAPTER SIX

Umbilicus of Light

Sound and Light, Photons and Plasma

Greetings, Beloveds, and in that Mighty Christ I AM Saint Germain. I stream forth on that Mighty Violet Ray of Mercy, Compassion, and Forgiveness. As usual, Dear hearts, I ask permission to come forward.

Response: *Dear Saint Germain, please come forward. You and all are most welcome.*

Today I come forward with two others; to my right is Beloved Anaya. She streams forth on that Mighty Gold and Aquamarine Rays of Service to humanity and to my left you may recognize a sister of mine…your Beloved Susan, who assists in this discourse. Do we all have permission to come forward?

Response: *You are all most welcome with great joy and love.*

Now let me explain. Beloved Anaya is stepping forward and they are all surrounded by a golden ball of light.

Greetings, my beloveds, I AM Anaya and I stream forth on the Mighty Gold and Aquamarine Rays of Service to humanity.[1] Do I have permission to enter your energy fields?

Response: *Beloved Anaya, you will always have permission—please come forward.*

AN UMBILICUS PORTAL

We all come forward today in service to humanity. Dear ones, humanity is now at a great precipice. Yes, humanity is ready to evolve to a new level of BE-ing…this you have known for some time as moving from the human to HU-man. This is part of your Ascension Process. Dear ones, energy streams from the Beloved Pleiades and onward into your solar system, and there are energies that stream from the Umbilicus

---

1. The Gold and Aquamarine Rays represents the presence of Divine Man through the intervention of the Divine Heavens. It is a perceptive and unifying Ray, that is also cooperative, creative, and self-realized. This Ray Force is also inordinately sensitive, and initiates the development of the HU-man senses. Because of this it is an integrative and intuitive energy. Lady Anaya is joined by Master Kona, Djwal Khul, Lady Master Leto, Helios, and Vesta. All of these Ascended Masters and Light BE-ings serve this important, evolutionary Ray Force.

connection between the DERN and the DAHL universe.[2] At the Pleiades we often interface with this energy. Sometimes our consciousness travels seamlessly through the Umbilicus, and enters into the DAHL. We are able to step-down higher frequencies and energies of consciousness into the Umbilicus Portal[3] and onward to the Pleiades. The Pleiades serve as a Step-down Transformer of this energetic, not only to your solar system, but to the entire DERN solar system infrastructure. This energy arcs from the Pleiades and onward to the Ancestral Planet of your dual Sun system, (onward) to Venus[4] and from Venus the energies resonate to the core of the Earth. The Golden Cities draw this frequency up through their own Vibral Core Axis.

GOLDEN CITY VIBRAL CORE AXIS

Each of the Golden Cities has their own Vibral Core Axis.[5] As you understand the Evolutionary Biome, they are alive and filled with the energy of the ONE. This sound frequency is similar to an energetic of the ONE; however, it has its own distinct quality.[6] It captures the genetics of the Divine Light being and helps to discard any light

---

2. See Appendix HH: *The DAHL and DERN Universes.*

3. The Master Teachers describe the Umbilicus Connection that exists between the DAHL and DERN universe as a hypersensitive point and portal that advanced civilizations may use for many purposes, including travel. The Unbilichus Connection or Portal naturally radiates and pulses with evolutionary energies, similar to our Great Central Sun, also known as the Galactic Center.

4. In Ascended Master Teaching, the planet Venus in reality is a large, biologic spacecraft. "Earth at that time was bombarded through multiple asteroids, and life upon the Earth Plane and Planet became inordinately unstable. In this greater intervention, it was then brought forward that another planet shall be brought in into your solar system. This planet would be modeled upon perfection. It would hold within it the great symphonies of harmony, light, and hold within the great Akashic records—not only of Ascension, but records of the true HU-man origin. For yes, even at this moment, the libraries of Venus hold the true timeline and histories of humanity. The Venusian libraries contain the true timeline and the histories of your solar system. There are those who will teach otherwise, but know this, Dear ones, to be the truth! Now I shall proceed even further. The planet Venus was brought in—a constructed planet of perfection held within the fulcrum of light. It held within the unlimited wisdom and knowledge, not only of Ascension, but the science that sustains an entire solar system within balance." For more information see: *Evolutionary Biome*, Chapter Nine, *Enkhail/Enoch.*

5. The Ascended Masters often refer to the Vertical Power Current as the Golden Thread Axis or the Vibral Core Axis. A portion of this major energy current links the soul to the higher mind and is known as the Hindu Antahkarana. According to the I AM America teachings, the Vertical Power Current connects to our solar Sun and its resident deities Helios and Vesta. Its energies travel to the I AM Presence and stream from the Presence through the Crown Chakra, and flow through the physical spine of the individual (Kundalini), and the current grounds into the center of Earth's core—itself considered a latent, fiery Sun. In Hinduism, the portion of the Antahkarana that enters the physical planes and the Earth's core is known as the Sutratma, or Silver Cord. In Golden Cities the Vibral Core exists in the center (Star) of the Golden City, and its energies radiate through the clockwise or counterclockwise spinning movement of the Golden City.

6. According to Saint Germain, individual mantras infuse Golden City Ray Forces into Light Bodies (auras), a practice that evolves the conscious life experience toward Ascension Consciousness. He suggests that the efficiency of a Ray is best understood when used in a Golden City Vortex, where the energy of a mantra works concurrently with the centrifugal force of the Golden City Star. Uttering mantras is most effective in the Star of a Golden City, but don't let that prevent you from the practice. If you can't make it to the Star, saying mantras in any part of a Golden City is beneficial. The following mantras should be used simultaneously with the initiatory Ray work in each Golden City.

GOBEAN, *Om Shanti:* Produces peace and harmony

MALTON, *Om Eandra:* Produces harmony and balance for the Nature Kingdoms. It is also associated with instant thought manifestation.

substances that no longer serve the being of light and catapult the being of light to the next level of evolution. This is like a clarification of your DNA.

TWIN UNIVERSES

This is a function and result of the Gold Ray as it arcs from your Great Central Sun, through the Fire Triplicity,[7] and onward to your Earth.[8] I know you understand this

---

WAHANEE, *Om Hue*: Aligns the chakras with the Vertical Power Current, or Golden Thread Axis, and evokes the Sacred Fire—the Violet Flame. Since this mantra is a Vibration of Violet Flame Angels, it invokes their Healing presence, which helps purify and heal the body.

SHALAHAH, *Om Sheahah*: Evokes the consciousness of the ONESHIP—Unana. This mantra means, "I AM as ONE."

KLEHMA, *Om Eandra*: Used as a decree for Instant-thought-manifestation of Ascension, glory, and conclusion.

7. Energies from the Great Central Sun, or Galactic Center triangulate to our Solar System through these three planets: the Sun, Mars, and Jupiter. These three planets are known as the *Fire Triplicity* and represent three forms of spiritual fire: the Sun is the spiritual leader; Mars is the spiritual pioneer; and Jupiter is the spiritual teacher.

8. The Ascended Masters Kuthumi and Saint Germain both prophesy that perhaps the Gold Ray is the most important energy force currently present on Earth. While its presence catalyzes the spiritual growth of the HU-man, it is also associated with Karmic Justice and will instigate change at all levels: Earth Changes, economic and social change. The Master Teachers prophesy that its appearance fosters the dawn of a New Consciousness for humanity, which ends the turbulence of Kali Yuga and ushers in a 10,000-year time of spiritual potential and opportunity for all—the Golden Age of Kali Yuga.

The Golden Cities are affected by the Gold Ray, and the Ray's energies ramp up the energies of the Golden City Vortices. The Gold Ray also increases the energies of Golden City Vortices through subtle activation of the individual Ray that each Golden City serves. Certain planetary configurations, especially lunar eclipse, affect the planetary energies and Golden City energies. According to Saint Germain, lunar eclipses assist the process of shedding and cleansing individual karmas. These celestial placements work alongside the Gold Ray to initiate individuals into the New Consciousness. Saint Germain gives this decree to initiate the stream of the New Consciousness within, and into the heart of the consciousness of humanity.

Mighty Golden Ray, stream forth now,
Mighty Golden Ray, bring forth new understanding.
Bring forth a new Spiritual Awakening.
Bring forth complete and total Divinity
In the name of I AM That I AM.
So be it.

This decree allows the Brotherhood to give further aid and contact to individuals who desire the Masters' help and assistance for spiritual development. The Gold Ray initiates and transforms through the spiritual principles of balance and harmony. Working through the Hermetic Principle of vibration, Saint Germain claims that the Gold Ray creates, "Absolute Harmony." The Gold Ray balances and harmonizes the great spiritual darkness that today covers the Earth by introducing enough light to balance personal perceptions of duality. The Middle Way, which is the spiritual notion that best describes the work of the Gold Ray, accepts the presence of both light and dark forces. This acceptance helps to heal our own individual dark side, which we may personally suppress—which can lead to the expression of uncontainable emotion. Saint Germain explains that "one cannot control" emotion until one experiences the full spectrum of emotion's anatomy. Each level of emotional experience and development expresses the presence and fluidity of varying Ray Forces through the unique experiences of each individual:

- Physical emotion is experienced or revealed through facial expression and body language.
- Feeling is the lower emotional body and expressed through instinct.
- Astral emotion is the higher emotional body, and manifests through dreams, goals, and desires.
- Mental/Emotional body contains the self-conscious emotions (guilt, shame, embarrassment, pride), and the higher emotions such as kindness, love, empathy, trust, respect, courage, and hope.

The degree of emotion will determine the type and intensity of action because of the philosophic idea that nothing in life is random. The Gold Ray of Consciousness helps the chela to shape and

process; however this process is a little different. While it promotes an energetic of light, it is always initiated through a sound frequency. This takes place through many from the Pleiades who enter into the Umbilicus Portal and send the harmonic into the DERN universe, but also through a pulsation of the portal itself. The Umbilicus of Light is similar to what ties one child to the next (twins). For you see the DAHL and the DERN share one Umbilicus of Creation for they are as ONE, yet they have been separated through their own dual experiences and polarities.

GALACTIC LIGHT AND SOUND HARMONICS

This Umbilicus pulsates with a life-giving sound. It is the breath of the Creator and comes forward to give sponsorship to both of these universes of light; however, one has evolved onward in their Ascension Process and the other has had difficulties. Although these difficulties have not been systemic throughout the entire DERN, there have been problems that have occurred on certain planets due to energetics of interference. I will not speak about the interference in this (discourse), but I will share information on the systems of light. Hopefully, you will begin to understand how the Earth evolves not only through Galactic Light spectrum but through the sound harmonics from the source of creation.[9]

THE WHITE RAY

Saint Germain has given much information about the Doorways of Light of the Golden Cities. Each Doorway calibrates light spectrums, but also calibrates sound frequencies. Sound frequencies bond with the frequencies of light from the Galactic Center. The White Ray responds best to these sound frequencies because the White Ray holds all of the frequencies of the light from the lowest to the highest.[10] This is the energetic that is stepped-down from your Ancestral Planet to Venus, and into the core of the planet (Earth).

---

form the will and align our emotions and inevitably our actions to the Divine Will. The Gold Ray enters into the Seventh Chakra and its current flows alongside the Golden Thread Axis (Medullar Shushumna). "All things work together for the ONE!" This principle of Unity Consciousness is the key to understand the activity of the Gold Ray. All experiences, good and bad, work together for the Divine Will. Call upon the Gold Ray for acceptance of the unacceptable—tolerance for the intolerable. The Gold Ray helps one to structure the New Consciousness into a personal psychological framework through the spiritual precept of Brotherhood and Sisterhood. Saint Germain explains, "You shall face that New Day cloaked in the glory of the Sun!"

9. From *A Teacher Appears*, Saint Germain shares introductory teachings on sound: "Sound is a principle of the God element of all elements. There is sound which keeps molecules together... Intermingled within the Law of Sound are also again the perceptual waves. Mastery of the perceptual waves is the Mastery of sound and the Mastery of time together. There are the clear notes."

10. The Ray of the Divine Feminine is primarily associated with the planet Venus. It is affiliated with beauty, balance, purity, and cooperation. In the I AM America teachings the White Ray is served by the Archangel Gabriel and Archeia Hope; the Elohim Astrea and Claire; and the Ascended Masters Serapis Bey, Lady Master Luxor, Paul the Devoted, Reya, the Lady Masters Venus and Se Ray, and the Group of Twelve.

HUE AND OM

This sound frequency has been heard since time immemorial...it is the Beloved HUE that you have chanted.[11] It is contained within the OM. These two sound frequencies hold within them the ability to bond sound and light together and begin to empower the divinity within, known as the Eight-sided Cell of Perfection. It is connected in Oneness, it is connected as a Oneship, and it is the empowered ONE... for you are of it, and it is of you. You cannot separate yourself from this Oneness, for you were always born of it, contained within it, and are the seed kernel of it. You hold within your light being the Divine Oneship of the Creator—the Creator who created the twin universes, the Umbilicus Portal, the Pleiades, and all of the other planets in your beloved system.

SUBTLE FREQUENCIES OF SOUND AND LIGHT

As these frequencies step-down into the Golden Cities of Light they help to adjust through activation, and also instigate a purification process. During your many lifetimes and different sojourns upon the Earth Plane and Planet through the re-embodiment process, you have taken on many different frequencies of light and sound through differing Star seeds. Each frequency helps to spin away impurities and lower energetics that no longer serve your Ascension Process. This is also described as moving from the Ninth to the Tenth energetic. There is another, yet very subtle process that occurs with sound, vibrating the Eight-sided Cell through the Vibral Core Axis—the Golden Thread Axis—and onward to affect each chakra, and into the light-fields (aura).

"EXERCISE THE DIFFERENT FREQUENCIES"

The reason we have given so many different forms of migration is that as you encounter each geophysical location in a Pilgrimage, you are able to adjust the frequencies of your light fields. This process strengthens them. In the same way that you must crawl before you walk, toddle a bit as you learn to walk, and then walk before you run...you must learn to exercise the different frequencies of sound and light throughout your spiritual infrastructure. This gives you the opportunity to *realize* and *know* that you are a BE-ing of Light, and it engages your Ascension Process. You begin to interface with the living crystal of light, the Golden City—the Evolutionary Biome.

---

11. In Tibetan dialects, the word *hue* or *hu* means breath; however, the HU is a sacred sound and when chanted or meditated upon is said to represent the entire spectrum of the Seven Rays. Because of this, the HU powerfully invokes the presence of the Violet Flame, which is the activity of the Violet Ray and its inherent ability to transform and transmit energies to the next octave. HU is also considered an ancient name for God, and it is sung for spiritual enlightenment.

A PLEIADEAN GENESIS

This Evolutionary Biome is interconnected with your frequencies and the frequencies of *all* of creation. As the Earth enters the Ascension Process, she too, is spinning away the dross, getting rid of the systems that no longer serve her, freeing old genetics and DNA patterns, and the frequencies and sounds that no longer serve the creation of Beloved Freedom Star.

> Free, humanity shall BE,
> And Earth shall BE
> As Freedom Star.

In other sojourns of light, many of you existed upon the Pleiades. Dear ones, you are of this Divine Star seed of Co-creation. Many of you embodied upon the Earth to (help) raise its vibration. Many of you came to explore and to learn about a new arena of light and sound. And now, Dear ones, through your call to your Mighty I AM That I AM the Divine Creator Source within, you are called home.

> Home you shall come,
> Through Sound and Light.
> Home you shall BE as ONE,
> With me.

Our teachings upon the Pleiades are the teachings of light and sound, and how they marry in grand Co-creation. These teachings were utilized upon the planet Venus, and the light and sound frequencies are glorified through the building of her numerous Golden Cities of Light. This (teaching) was mirrored again into the core of the Earth (Inner Earth), where seventeen Golden Cities of Light were formed. This creates a frequency that engenders spiritual growth and evolution for *all* of humanity and for *those* of the light—who respond to the light and are BE-ings of the light.[12]

THE SEVENTEEN GOLDEN CITIES OF INNER EARTH

The seventeen Golden Cities within the core of the Earth hold (spiritual) consciousness in its purest form. This is a form of Quetzalcoatl and Krishna; it is a form of the Brotherhood of Christ Consciousness and the compassion of the Buddha. The seventeen Golden Cities hold with clarity and purpose the Great Golden Cities of Light (on Earth's surface), and they are activated one-by-one upon your beloved Earth—Babajeran, with the assistance of the Spiritual Hierarchy—those great Ascended Masters of Light of the Earth. Mother Earth's beginning came through the

---

12. The number seventeen is considered a sacred number in Ascended Master Teaching. It is a number that signifies spiritual growth, reception, and humanity's evolution. For instance, there are three sets of Seventeen Golden Cities, that comprise a total of 51. The number fifty-one is considered a Mayan number of completion.

Sisters of the Pleiades, and this is why she, in her own harmonic, was a perfect home for those who came to raise consciousness, where many could find, know, and experience *the eyes to see and the ears to hear.*[13] Yes indeed, the greatest sound frequencies move through the White Ray.[14] Do you have questions?

Response: *Yes, I do.*

Proceed.

A CREATOR SOUND FREQUENCY

Question: *The sound frequency from the DAHL through the DERN, is that a frequency that you can hum for us?*

You may hum yourself and I shall imbue you with the sound frequencies. You can relay this on your recording. Proceed.

Now let me describe…Anaya is infusing an energetic of light and sound directly into Len's heart chakra.

Have you received this energy?

Response: *Yes, I have.*

Now you may hum it and *know it*. It is a creator sound.[15] This sound is engendered within each and every one of you as evolving light beings. As I stated before, many of you know and understand it as the HUE. Many of you have heard it before in the OM. It is the sound of rushing water; it is the perfect sound of light itself. It is a sound frequency associated with the White Ray; but, also heard in the higher reaches and octaves of the Violet Ray. This sound organizes creation in its highest order, to its highest frequency, and God-like divinity. Do you understand?

Response: *Yes I do.*

Do you have a question?

---
13. This phrase refers to the development of the HU-man senses.
14. Most of the annual requests for Spiritual Pilgrimage are founded on the premise of following the White Ray through the doors of the Golden City. The sound frequencies are intensified at Adjuant Points and influence the development, growth, and evolution of human to HU-man energetics.
15. Divine Languages are often known as form languages. My Vedic teacher once explained the etymology of Sanskrit as "a Mother tongue," similar to the syntax and semantics of computer languages. According to Vedic legend our entire Earth was programmed, or created, through the spoken words of Sanskrit. Speaking a form language is powerful and commanding, and each spoken syllable has the ability to exactly create in form and substance its subject. Perhaps the creation story of Genesis says it best, "Then God said, 'Let there be light,' and there was light." (Genesis 1:3 New American Standard Bible)

Question: *Can I hum the sound?*

Proceed.

Response: *Om HUE, Om HUE.*

Len sings the sound frequency shared by Anaya.

REORGANIZE LIGHT-FIELDS AND DNA

So Be It. This frequency shall fill your house with a harmonic energetic that will produce not only peace, but reorganize your DNA and your light-fields. I have stated before that these are certain sound frequencies that one encounters as they travel in Spiritual Pilgrimage.[16] It does take some time for integration after one has received the initiation of sound and light at a Golden City Adjutant Point. I shall turn the floor over to Saint Germain for (his) instruction on integration, but before I do that…do you have further questions?

Question: *Yes, are the OM and the HUE sufficient enough for this pitch?*

SOUND FREQUENCIES AND DOLPHINS

You may lower it, and if you can, you may take it to even higher oscillations of vibration. The dolphins upon your Earth have known and held certain sound frequencies throughout the waters of the Earth…they, too, step-down the energetics from the Seventeen Golden Cities of the center of the Earth. They are able to pick up the vibrations throughout the honey-combed Earth, and the Inner Earth's resonance frequency is delineated through the salt in the water. They carry this vibration, though sometimes not audible to the human ear, and it does produce its sound frequency which then calibrates the energetics of the Earth. There are also many plants and minerals who accomplish the same thing upon Earth.

DIVINE HU-MAN

In this time of expanding light, humanity is evolving and growing through many mechanisms that assist and allow the various combinations of Star seed genetics to recalibrate to the light. This allows the Divine HU-man to emerge, for the Divine HU-man lives in a constant state of bliss and Ascension. Questions?

Response and Question: *Yes. I can hear this pitch very clearly throughout my energy, yours, Susan's, Saint Germain's, Lori's, the house, and everything that's here! My sense is*

---

16. Each Adjutant Point contains an array of sound frequencies.

that it is now radiating past our home. My question is, can we use this pitch for alignment and purification and for any who would need the help?

A DIVINE INFORMATION PORTAL

Indeed, yes. So Be It. I would like to explain even further, because this sound pitch is Co-creative in nature, it creates an Umbilicus Connection from your home, onward to the Ancestral Planet, from the Ancestral Planet to the Pleiades, and onward to the DAHL. This creates your Divine Information Portal as you have described. Of course Beings of Light came forward many years ago to orchestrate and construct this portal (at your home). It, too, functions with an umbilicus of light that grounds to the core of the Earth, and finds sustenance in its own energetic through the Ancestral Planet. This is why we have been able to send our messages with such frequency and with such great detail.[17]

When you are functioning within the Information Portal, not only can you receive information at this level in clairaudience, but all of your HU-man senses are activated, so they can begin their reception process. This can also give much (better) reception during meditation, and assist automatic writing. It is important to learn how to receive these messages, so they can come forward with great clarity.

Each of the Adjutant Points is also a form (type) of an Information Portal, and they carry forward the clairaudient and clairvoyant energetics of the Adjutant Point's Hierarch. Understand that the energetics carry forward through the Ray of its light and its sound frequency that streams from and through the umbilicus of the DAHL-DERN. Do you understand?

Response: *Yes.*

All of these work in conjunction, and while we break them apart so you can begin to discern each of these, they all work together as ONE, and are ONE. They all need one another, and function together with an interdependence of Divine Glory. Do you have any further questions?

---

[17]. In the book, *A Teacher Appears,* on page 19, a description of the Communication Portal is shared: "Saint Germain, White Water, and Mahani are opening up the Portal of Communication through thanks and appreciation." A divinely created Communication Portal assists the medium to receive accurate information.

Later, in the mid-90s, the Spiritual Teachers of I AM America created a more developed Communication Portal. The I AM Presence directed Lori to purchase a specific lot in the Town of Payson for our home. We found the lot in one day, and after two years time, moved into our new home. This unique portal is customized for our energy systems and includes a specific resonation.

As the Communication Portal opens, it is frequently accompanied by the harmonies of celestial music or the delicate scent of roses, lavender, or orange blossom. Lori is a skilled multi-dimensional communicator, and the presence of this spiritual gateway increases accuracy to over ninety-five percent. During each session, high-frequency energy streams through the portal that can be detected for many days after its release.

Since our Communication Portal has been in use for over twenty-five years, it is inordinately strong. It carries high frequencies of both sound and light, and the BE-ings of Light oversee, calibrate, and guard its presence.

ANCESTRAL PLANET SANJANA

Response and Question: *Yes. We have never asked for the name of the Ancestral Planet. Are we permitted to have that name?*

Sanjana. This has been its name from time immemorial. Sanjana is also a distinguished greeting which basically means, "I greet you in the Divine Holiness, and I leave you in the Divine Holiness." Sanjana.[18]

Response: *Sanjana.*

Let me describe…she backs away from the teaching and Saint Germain comes forward.

Greetings, my Beloveds, I AM Saint Germain and I request permission to come forward.

Response: *Dear Saint Germain, please come forward, you are most welcome.*

AMERICA IS ACTIVATED

There is still much work to be accomplished upon the Earth Plane and Planet, and this year because of the tussle between the forces of light and dark upon the Earth Plane, much will be happening! Know that the Light of God never, never fails and that America is indeed the I AM race. Because of the opening of Shamballa, every person living within America this year shall be further activated within the light, and activated to understand the false narratives that have existed. This is through your media and within your political systems. I will not devolve the conversation too far, but it is important for you to know and understand that there is a purpose and an intention in keeping the Mighty Gates of Shamballa open throughout this year. This will give great assistance to any Pilgrimage that you undertake; it will give great assistance to your own individualized Ascension Process.

THE PHOTON IS LIGHT, SOUND IS PLASMA

Know that as Earth travels in its sojourn throughout the Photon Belt of radiant, conscious light, it is also traveling throughout (an energetic) Plasma Field. The Plasma Field activates each Photon, for the plasma holds the Divine Sound. Do you understand?

Response: *Yes, like a resonator.*

That is correct. Both of them work in tandem, in the same way that light and sound frequencies bond themselves in water. They work at an atomic level, bond together,

18. Sanjana in Hindi means, "in harmony."

and then raise and evolve consciousness. Yes, this is at an electrical level, but also at a level of magnetism. Now, Dear ones, do you have any questions upon the White Ray, and how it rotates throughout the Doorways of the Golden City Vortices?

Response: *Yes, I do.*

Proceed.

ANCESTRAL FIELD

Question: *So the very first question is about the name Sanjana, can we utilize this in our Violet Flame decrees and when calling upon the other Rays?*

You can meditate upon it as a force-field of light, for it contains within itself the energetic of the Ancestral Field. This immediately connects you to the Pleiades and their many solar systems of light. It connects you to the Umbilicus of Light that exists between the DAHL and DERN. Do you understand?

THE COLOR RAYS

Response and Question: *Yes, so back to the White Ray, we have always referred to the White Ray through the Archangel Gabriel, but each of the Rays actually have specific names, do they not?*

Yes, indeed they do. However, at this point it is important that there is no further confusion, and to express their presence as *color*. Sometimes color is immediately sensed only through the visual senses, but, color, as you well know, is also sensed at an audible level, and it is also sensed through its electromagnetic frequencies.[19]

---

19. When you observe full-spectrum light, your brain does not sense the segmentation of light frequencies and accepts sunlight as the normal, everyday radiance of the Sun. Here is a contemporary understanding of the visible light spectrum, broken down by color and wavelength:
Color and Wavelength
Red: 625-740
Orange: 590-625
Yellow: 565-590
Green: 520-565
Cyan: 500-520
Blue: 435-500
Violet: 380-435
The primary light that we interact with is white light and contains many or all of these ranges of wavelength. Light shining through a prism causes the wavelengths to slightly bend, with different angles due to optical refraction. This splits the white light into a visible color spectrum. And the shorter the wavelength, the faster the frequency; Saint Germain explains the Violet Flame and Ray is the transmuting light frequency for all of the Rays.

TRUE NORTH VERSUS MAGNETIC NORTH

This is important because I have observed some of your conversations regarding the Doorways and the vital lei-lines of Golden Cities. The vital lei-lines are given in the beginning phases to align themselves to *True North*. (Using this) allowed us to convey this concept at a primary level to those who have the eyes to see, the ears to hear.

It is well recorded that the magnetic field is constantly moving, and in flux.[20] The magnetic field is calibrated by the collective consciousness and by the movement of sound frequencies from the Ancestral Planet. Again, these sound frequencies also move from the Pleiades, and onward to the great DAHL and DERN umbilicus. Do you understand?

Response: *Yes.*

The magnetism moves in constant flux, however it is always rooted to the Earth itself—to Beloved Babajeran. This is why there is Divine Combination between the Ascended Masters of Light and Sound and Beloved Babajeran. This is a great truth that I speak, of which you will learn more.

You can use also the system of Magnetic North, but it may throw some of your calculations off to some degree.[21] Apply this with prudence and with psychic faculty. Do you understand?

Response: *Yes.*

So if you are having difficulty locating a Point within the True North directional, then use the Magnetic North directional and between the two systems comes a rectification of the process. Do you understand?

Response: *Yes.*

For the Points are always in flux…the Golden City is a living and breathing being of conscious light and sound. Do you understand?

Response: *Yes I do.*

VENUSIAN GOLDEN CITIES

This knowledge is a provenance that was practiced upon the planet Venus. It grew to a high level of the understanding and science of light and sound, and they merge, or marry as ONE. When the Venusians and Venus became a great outpost of the

---

20. In the 1990s the Earth's magnetic North Pole was drifting about nine miles per year. Since then Earth has experienced a rapid magnetic pole drift of about forty miles per year.

21. This mapping method uses agonic lines which are imaginary lines that connect magnetic North and South. It is suggested to use True North measurements until you are experienced with mapping Adjutant Points.

Divine Pleiades, it was declared that they, too, shall shed light upon the Earth Plane and Planet. They were the first (humans) to inhabit the core of the Earth (Inner Earth) and there, created and built their living and breathing crystal Golden Cities. Do you understand?

Response: *Yes.*

This was created through a harmonic resonance that is now being realized in this great time upon the surface of the Earth, for Divine Hu-mans you shall be! Questions?

THE EARTH PLANE AND THE EARTH PLANET

Response and Question: Yes, back to True North…my sense is that True North is a stabilizing point that creation may have originated from and I use the word 'may' because I am uncertain, but that Magnetic North deals with the basic activities of flux that exist here in this Plane and Planet.

True North is the *Earth* itself; Magnetic North is the *Earth Plane*. Do you understand?

Response: *Ah yes…so basically the Golden Cities that exist on their specific lei-lines are stable. But the influence of Magnetic North is a fluctuation of what's going on throughout the Earth Plane?*

Indeed, Dear hearts, therefore it *all* has an effect upon the Co-creation. Do you understand?

GOLDEN CITY FLUCTUATION

Response and Question: *Yes, so when we actually find an exact Point and we are estimating that is the exact Adjutant Point, there is still a fluctuation from that Point, because of the activity on the Earth Plane?*

True, Dear ones, in the same way that the Golden Cities themselves have a flux… sometimes the flux of a Golden City can be felt from forty to one hundred miles — this is the parameter of the Golden City of which I speak. Adjutant Points can have a flux from five miles to twenty miles, and for a highly, sensitive developed person sometimes for even forty miles![22] This creates a matrix of light that is carried throughout the entire Golden City. Do you understand?

Response: *Yes.*

---

22. See Appendix G: *Flux of Golden City Adjutant Points.*

One never really leaves the radiance of the foci of light. Do you understand?

Response: *Yes, I do.*

However, as Anaya stated, "First we must crawl, and from crawling we must toddle." I know you have found this to be true.

Response: *Extremely true.*

Do you have further questions?

USE OF THE AWAKENING PRAYER

Response and Question: *I think the questions of the magnetic versus True North have now been more completely understood and I appreciate that. Regarding the White Ray, is there a specific invocation for the White Ray that we can utilize in these Pilgrimages?*

Always call upon the Awakening Prayer, for it calls forth the Great Light of Divinity that encapsulates all Rays and sounds of creation. Do you understand?

Response: *I do.*

So be it.

Response: *So be it.*

SAINT GERMAIN AND BELOVED SUSAN

Now let me describe…Saint Germain and Susan come forward, and Susan reveals a magnificent Golden Cup. She pours a blessing of (sacred) water upon the Earth. She and Saint Germain hold the sacred chalice together…he will speak for Susan.

Your beloved Sister of Light requested to come forward at this time, for she knows that you are to receive her great inheritance of light, which she toiled in the Earth Plane to receive. This Cup that we pour is a blessing for the divine apports that will be present in your life.[23] She has entrusted them with you, and as she too grows in her light and upon her liberation within the light will reveal more of the innate secrets that they hold. For now, she comes forward in order to give recognition of their frequencies and how they step-down the beloved energies of the Ascended Masters into the Earth Plane. Many of these (apports) came forward through me and other great beings of light that hold a focus of light within the Earth Plane and Planet. You are now entrusted with these, and in your care use them for the best and the highest

---

23. An inheritance of a collection of Divine Apports, received through the mediumship of the late Rev. Keith Rinehardt.

good of all humanity. Be prepared to receive further instructions upon their use. Do you understand?

Response: *I understand and I accept this mission, as I know Lori does also.*

So be it! Now, we shall take our leave from the Earth Plane and Planet and hold you in the eternal grace of Shamballa.

I AM a Being of Violet Fire,
I AM the purity of Humanity's Desires!

So Be It.

Response: *So be it. Hitaka.*

They are all joined as ONE Golden Globe of Light and dissipate.

Sharing Energy

CHAPTER SEVEN
Energy-for-Energy

Saint Germain Explains Trinomial Energies

Greetings, Beloveds, in that Mighty Christ I AM Saint Germain, and I request permission to come forward into your energy fields.

Response: *Beloved Saint Germain, please come forward, and Shamballa to you and everyone.*

Before I proceed, Dear ones, I must perform an energetic adjustment of the room.[1]

Saint Germain blazes violet light in, through, and around the living room…a gold ball of light streams forth from his heart to cover the entire cabin.

Good Morning, and Shamballa to all of you. When I give this greeting, of course I give it to you two, but also to the many students who study the I AM America material and its message. As you know, Dear ones, there has been much work that has been completed upon the Earth Plane and Planet and still much work to be completed.

"THE PREMISE OF ENERGY-FOR-ENERGY"

The work of the Golden Cities still streams forth, and as you know at (during) Shamballa we are able to give the Earth just a little bit more energy. That is, the karmic burden of humanity is lifted at this time and (for) the beloved students of the Ascended Masters—those who are focused upon their Ascension Process can gain a momentum. We have heard your many prayers, decrees, and fiats that you have been offering, and we are grateful and thankful. For you know, Dear ones, everything is based upon the premise of energy-for-energy.[2]

Let me explain this so you have a clear understanding. As we lower our energy into the Earth Plane and Planet, (as) we exist primarily at a Fifth and sometimes

---

1. This message was received in Greer, Arizona, in the Star energies of Gobean. Saint Germain often adjusts the energies of a room, especially with his first appearance. This clears negative energies and assists the Communication Portal.
2. To understand this spiritual principle, one must remember Isaac Newton's Third Law of Motion: for every action there is an equal and opposite reaction. However, while energies may be equal, their forms often vary. The Ascended Masters often use this phrase to remind chelas to properly compensate others to avoid karmic retribution; and repayment may take many different forms.

even Sixth or Seventh Dimensional capacity, we move into the Fourth Dimension of Consciousness and then into a lower plane that you might describe as an Astral Field.[3] (As) we move into that thin barrier sheath, you must then raise your energy up, through your prayers, through your decree, through your meditation, through your write and burn(s), through your breath technique, and other spiritual applications and exercises that I have shared with you. As you keep your spiritual practice moving throughout the year, this too, creates the reciprocal energy-for-energy.

THE COMMUNICATION PORTAL

Each Master Teacher recognizes their beloved student or chela and they know and understand the most appropriate time to break through that barrier sheath and begin to stream energy for communication. This you see is what we know as a true Communication Portal. It exists between the Master Teacher and the chela. Once this is achieved it can always be reinstated or reiterated—whatever is needed. For instance, we have created such a Communication Portal at your home. If you are no longer at your home, we withdraw the energies and move with you wherever you may be. The connection is with you as the student, as a chela, as the initiate, and even as the Arhat. You carry this through the Eight-sided Cell of Perfection, that Divine Monad and Unfed Flame that exists within the heart.[4] I encourage all students and chelas, disciples of mine to create their own Communication Portal. Again, this is only achieved through the premise of energy-for-energy.

SOULS WITH SPECIAL ABILITIES

Of course there are those born unto the Earth Plane who have a special ability. They have removed the karmic burden and from the impetus of former lives carry within them the energetic resonance in order to immediately create the Communication Portal. Many of these disciples of the Ascended Masters have had many lifetimes within Mystery Schools and through their discipline in those lifetimes have the ability to immediately access communication with the Master Teacher. The Master Teacher readies them, helps them, and assists them at various junctures within their life. There are key time periods within a lifetime when the Master Teacher *knows* that the soul is readied. This is based upon the maturation of Ray Forces within the light fields. While you can follow the classic maturation tables as they are often presented, the aura or the light fields are born with their readiness intact.

---

3. As we raise our spiritual energies to meet the Ascended Master, the Ascended Master lowers their energies. Consciousness meets on a peaceful plane of reciprocity. This metaphysical practice is based on the Law of Energy-for-energy.
4. See Appendix R: *Diagram of the Eight-sided Cell of Perfection with the Unfed Flame and Monad.*

THE MASTER YEARS

I have discussed (this) before, and during the junctures of certain Master Years there is a certain readiness that comes upon this particular type of person.[5] At the age of eleven, the pineal gland is allowed to be open. Before then they may have (already) had many experiences with the Fourth Dimension. At the age of twenty-two the initiate is always touched by the Master Teacher and a form of readiness is applied.[6] They may attend a Mystery School or they are contacted in the inner planes and are led, guided, and directed to the information that they must study. This rekindles the great flame or fire of dharma within the heart. At the age of thirty-three, the Master appears again and the great work is brought forward. This is allowed many years of maturation and the subsequent master years of forty-four, fifty-five, sixty-six, seventy-seven, eighty-eight…and if possible, onward to the age of ninety-nine ensue. At each of these years a great boon of energy is released to the soul, and the soul can utilize this boon of energy and move into a new dimension of light and service.[7] This, too, assists the Ascension Process. As your life progresses, take note of these years. However, I remind you that every day that is spent in service to the Great White Brotherhood and the Ascended Masters through the lineage of Shamballa is a great blessing.[8]

The tenets of the Great White Brotherhood are also based upon this educational process that prepares the chela—the disciple, the initiate, the Arhat—for service to humanity. This service is based upon the principle of energy-for-energy, yet there are moments when the need is so great, that service must be given at every level in order to raise the vibration of the Earth. As you know, Dear ones, this was the great service and gauntlet that was in front of you.

"SCRAMBLE FOR THE TIMELINES"

The energies of the Earth were at a critical phase! We know you are aware of this scramble for the energetic timelines. I have described through the teachings of the Six-map Scenario[9] how Collective Consciousness calibrates the timelines of experience and the Earth and its evolution was possibly faced with great apocalyptic experience.[10] That is why we shared the I AM America and the Freedom Star Maps. Alongside this

---

5. See Appendix II: *The Soul Ray of Purpose*, excerpt from *New World Wisdom, Three*.
6. This may be through a visitation from a Master Teacher energetically or through the dreamstate. Often, this is a form of shatki, an energetic transference that initiates an Awakening Process.
7. Ascending to or attaining a new level of conscious awareness that produces tremendous change and spiritual development.
8. The Ascended Masters consider the principle of service to others as one of the highest spiritual principles we can apply. Their teaching reiterates, "Love, in service, breathes the breath for all!"
9. A series of six maps of the United States. The Ascended Masters prophesied this schematic to illustrate choice, consciousness, and their relationship to Earth Changes.
10. See Appendix AA: *Timelines and Consciousness*.

we also shared the opening for the Golden Age through giving the locations of the great Golden Cities of Light.

CONCENTRATION OF THE WHITE RAY

Throughout this past year we have streamed more energy into the Golden Cities, and further prepared them for humanity. This created an activation of all the Western Doors of Golden Cities with energies calibrating from Venus, through your Moon, and onward to the core of your Earth.[11] This vital energy streams upward, into the Golden Cities of Light. This produces an elevated condensation of the White Ray. Both of these planets can emit this light substance, however at times the Moon emits qualities of the Pink Ray. During the year of 2022 more energies of the Pink Ray will be imbued into your Western Door; however, the great mission of Venus will continue for several more years into both the Southern and the Western Doors. I gave you (specific) Migration Pilgrimages, and when you are ready and prepared within your light fields, I encourage you to take at least one of these Pilgrimages.

DEVELOPMENT OF THE NEW ENERGY BODIES

As you enter into each Adjutant Point there is a jostling of the sound frequencies. This calibrates and creates an energetic within your light fields, and from this new energy, bodies for the Ascension Process are birthed. I have described the energetics of Eighth, Ninth, Tenth, Eleventh and Twelfth Energy Bodies and it is important to continue these specific Pilgrimages sequentially through the points as I have given them.[12] For they build one to the next. Yes, the seed kernel for these energy fields are held within your Eight-sided Cell of Perfection, but the duplication and replication processes stabilize as they develop into their materialization. As we build each of these fields of light you will begin to experience higher senses, not only clairaudient senses, but you will experience clairvoyant senses. This will increase your sensitivity. You will notice that time no longer exists and that you exist in the Ever Present Now.

ANCHORING GOLDEN LIGHT

For the last several years upon the Earth Plane and Planet there has been much fear, of course this is that *Last Waltz* of the tyrannical energies—those who wish to suppress and control the spiritual evolution of humanity and hold it into cycles of rebirth and reincarnation.[13] I know that you are all well aware of this, Dear ones. It

---

11. Both Venus and the Moon arc the White Ray to our Earth. Venus represents the Divine Feminine. The Moon symbolizes Divine Mother. Both of these aspects are present in the White Ray.
12. See Appendix A: *The Advanced Light Fields of Ascension*.
13. *The Last Waltz of the Tyrants* by Ramtha explores the tyrannical, out-of-balance male energies and their relationship to control, suppression, and the Time of Change.

was for this reason that we made the decision, after many meetings at Shamballa, to keep the energies of the City of Shamballa open for one more year. We heard the petitions of those who are working at the Ashrams of Light within the Golden Cities, and through a consensus of their energies and the understanding that *more light* must flood into the Earth Plane at this time, Shamballa will remain open for yet *one more year*. Again, this will be on a need by need basis.[14] That is, it staying open will be based upon energy-for-energy. Most importantly, we ask our chelas to travel to Adjutant Points and complete these missions. This is the energy that is needed upon the Earth Plane and Planet to anchor this Golden Light into the Earth Plane. There is no other reason for us to have asked, and because of the premise of energy-for-energy, *you too*, gain through this process. It is always reciprocal, as within, so without, as without, so within.[15]

DIVINE INTERVENTION

The Golden Cities of Light are a Divine Intervention for humanity at this time, and we work to move the fledgling Golden Age forward one step at a time into the Mighty Light of God that never, never faileth! Now, I know I have given much information in just a few paragraphs, and I sense your questions. Proceed.

Response and question: *It is my personal desire to complete the Southern Door Migration and I go without a sense of fear or apprehension, but (with) a sense of duty and purpose. I think it is time that we go as soon as possible, do you agree?*

THE STEP-DOWN TRANSFORMER

So be it, my beloved student and friend. As you enter each of the Adjutant Points you will hear a sound vibration, and this will increase in its clairaudience as you get closer and closer to the (center of the) Point. Then it will matriculate a sublime light into your energy fields. At this moment stand upon the Earth and become a Step-down Transformer, anchoring and tethering the Light into the Third Dimensional Earth Plane from the Fourth Dimension. The Divine Intervention streams forward and the events of the Earth Plane can begin to evolve into the Evolutionary Biome. This is your great purpose. You are as farmers of this New Time of Light and Golden

---

14. The energies of the ethereal Golden City of Shamballa will continue to flood Earth throughout the year 2022.
15. This universal maxim teaches that our outer world and experiences are a reflection of our inner world. This is also known as the Law of Correspondence. On a transpersonal level, the Law of Correspondence tells us our inner world defines our outer world and vice versa: this universal tenet forms the foundation of our everyday thoughts, attitudes, and beliefs. For instance, if your insides are chaotic and miserable; if you lack confidence and self-esteem; if you're full of anger, resentment, and negativity, you'll experience a tumultuous outer reality. The grasping of this fundamental precept is the key to comprehending the Laws of Cause and Effect (karma) and the Law of Attraction. The Law of Correspondence is also described as mental equivalent. "But we know now that any outward act is but the sequel to a thought, and that the type of thought which we allow to become habitual will sooner or later find expression on the plane of action."

Consciousness. Each Adjutant Point that you tend to, place the seed within the ground, and there the seed is nourished, watered, it is cultivated, it is fertilized, and it grows. Do you see and understand?

Response: *Yes.*

As you move from Point to Point, the Web of Consciousness weaves and they (each point) are interconnected as ONE within the Biome of Light. This biome pulses as a gold energetic orb. This is why we taught you about the Group Mind,[16] so you could begin to understand the contraction and the expansion of the Orb of Light.

BUILD THE SHAMBALLA GRID

When you have completed (your Pilgrimage), see your work as service to the Hierarchy. Then the Master Teacher comes forward, and gives their service unto you…helping and assisting you to grow in the Light, to understand your path of spiritual enlightenment, and (helping you to achieve your) ultimate liberation in the Ascension. We have taught each of these processes very clearly so you can begin to understand them. This, of course, is known as building that Mighty Grid of Shamballa![17] Each Adjutant Points is connected through the Golden City of Gobi to the great Golden City (the Golden City of Shamballa), which you have known from time immemorial and as you have been taught within these teachings.[18] As we weave this magnificent grid upon the Earth, know that it plays a role in changing many things. Yes, you (change) at a personal level; however, it is important to know that (this work) will change your world. It will change your culture. It will change your science. It will change your politics. It will change your economies and your money systems. It will change businesses, and most of all it impacts the Collective Consciousness. It grows and expands through the Collective Consciousness and assists many to accept the new tenets of the Golden Age. We gave you these tenets in our earliest teachings—the Twelve Jurisdictions.[19]

---

16. See Appendix L: *Group Mind and Visualization to Achieve Group Mind.*
17. See Appendix JJ: *The New Shamballa Grid Pilgrimage.*
18. Named for the Great Desert of China, Gobi in Mongolian means "the waterless place." Ascended Masters claim the Golden City of Gobi is a step-down transformer for the energies of Earth's first Golden City—Shamballa. Gobi's esoteric definition comes from the Chinese translation of "go—across," and bi in Indonesian (Abun, A Nden, and Yimbun dialects) means "star." The Golden City of Gobi means "Across the Star," or "Across the Freedom Star." "Freedom Star" is a reference to Earth in her enlightened state.) Gobi aligns energies to the first Golden City of the New Times: Gobean. The Ascended Masters claim that Gobean disburses the vital energies of Shamballa, via Gobi, throughout the worldwide Golden City Grid. Gobi is located in Tibet, China. Gobean is located in Arizona and New Mexico, United States.
19. Twelve laws (virtues) for the "New Times," which guide consciousness to Co-create the Golden Age. They are: Harmony, Abundance, Clarity, Love, Service, Illumination, Cooperation, Charity, Desire, Faith, Stillness, and Creation/Creativity.

OVERCOME LIMITATION THROUGH SPIRITUAL PRACTICE

We realize too that you have many limitations placed upon you at times as you are living in a physical body in Third Dimension. Limitation is always overcome through the spiritual practice and principles that I have given you. Find one that suits you the best and then apply these principles especially within your Pilgrimage.[20] As I have described before, if you cannot physically attend to an Adjutant Point, you can also visit them through your meditation. I encourage this, but remember this (technique) is for a more advanced student. Do you understand?

Response: *Yes.*

Are there questions?

Response and question: *Yes, one question I do have (concerns) True North vs. Magnetic North. Magnetic North will fluctuate and change, but True North will always be stable unless there is a huge change in the Solar System…as I understand it the Golden Cities are oriented to True North?*

LEVELS OF VIBRATION AND SPIRITUAL EVOLUTION

Originally this was the best way to convey this information, but as your knowledge advances of the Golden Cities, it is true; Magnetic North may be one way to work

---

20. The Three Standards: *The Use of the Violet Flame, Tube of White Light, and the Protection of Archangel Michael.*
Call forth the Violet Consuming Fire: "In that Mighty Christ I AM, I call forth Saint Germain's Violet Transmuting Flame of mercy, transmutation, and forgiveness. Alchemize my lower energy bodies into the perfection of the Christ! Almighty I AM! (3x)" Then proceed with any Violet Flame decree. (Use seven times.) Suggestions are: "Violet Flame I AM, God I AM Violet Flame," or "I AM a Being of Violet Fire, I AM the Purity God desires!"
Call upon the Tube of Light: "Beloved Mighty I AM Presence, surround me now with the Tube of White Light, ever-sustained, ever-maintained, throughout this day and onward into night! Almighty I AM! (3x)"
Invoke Archangel Michael's Blue Flame: "Beloved Archangel Michael, surround me now with the Blue Flame of Protection! Protect my Violet Flame in its action and activity, protect my Mighty Tube of Light, giving me multiple layers of protection! Almighty I AM! (3x)"
Complete this spiritual practice with thanks and gratitude: "I love you, I love you, I love you! I bless you, I bless you, I bless you! And I thank you, I thank you, I thank you! Almighty I AM! (3x)
Close with Almighty I AM That I AM (9x) and OM HUE (9x). (This properly seals the decree and affirmation.)
It is suggested that for those who have not completely eliminated animal products from their diets to use the above sequence. For chelas and students who have eliminated animal products and adhere to a vegan diet, the sequence is as follows: first, use of the Tube of White Light; second, call upon Saint Germain's transmuting Violet Flame; third, invoke Archangel Michael's Blue Flame. Since this is a practice associated with purification and spiritual hygiene, the difference for carnivores and vegetarians is the cleansing through the Sacred Fire. Using the Sacred Fire removes the fear substance ingested through animal products from the physical body and light bodies, transmutes karmas, and prepares the auric field for the Tube of White Light. When the Three Standards is used by vegans, it is claimed the result of the Sacred Fire is intensified, as the Violet Flame can focus its entire energy upon the transmutation of karmas.

with the Adjutant Points to understand them. Now, remember, Dear ones, each student who comes unto this knowledge is at a different level or vibration of understanding, so there can be different locations where they access.[21] For in the same way that I create a Communication Portal with you, they too create their portal and they enter into the Evolutionary Biome of the Adjutant Point. Do you understand?

Response: *Yes.*

So this is also of importance, all is based upon your own evolution and from your individual evolution you enter into the collective evolution. All is interconnected as ONE. This is the Biome of Light. Questions?

Response: *My sense is at a ceremonial and intention level to do the True North first, and then to also address the Magnetic North for each point.*

Each disciple will have a different approach. It is important to move from one to the next, for this weaves the energetic grid. As you attend to (visit) each one of the points and as you return to them they grow in energy and in substance. Similar to each time you utilize the Communication Portal, the Portal grows in energy. As you enter into your home, can you feel the presence of the Masters?

Response: *Always.*

THE EVOLUTIONARY BIOME

I have described this, for there is always a residue of ethereal substance from (the process) when I pull energies from the Fourth Dimension and as you raise energies up from the Third Dimension.[22] This again is based upon that Mighty Law, *as within so without*, and there is the ONE. This is the complete understanding of the Evolutionary Biome.

A FULL-FORCE GOLDEN AGE

In the same way that the great core of the Earth is a Sun, and connected to your Solar Sun, and onward to the Sun of your galaxy through the great Rod of Power… the Galactic Sun connects to the umbilicus connection of the DAHL and the DERN. This triune force of energies creates a type of substance that is now being calibrated, shall we say, at an exponential level through the entrance of the Gold Ray and the movement of your solar system through the Photon Belt. This great field of plasma

---

21. Essentially there is no wrong or right way. Trust that you will be guided from within as you discover each sublime Adjutant Point.
22. A psychic imprint is often left from the presence of the Master Teacher. It is similar to a footprint left in mud or snow.

is activating light within the human itself, it is also activating light within the inner Sun (Earth's), light within your own Sun (Solar Sun), light within the Galactic Center (Great Central Sun) itself. You see, Dear ones, this is a time of Ascension and light. In fact, it is important to understand that as humanity moves forward, it may seem a bit slow in the beginning stages. As humanity begins to understand this, it is possible that even a full-force Krita Yuga[23] (a Golden Age), a time of great light upon the Earth, will be realized. Of course everything hinges upon the Mighty Will. For again, as I began this lesson, this result is based upon energy-for-energy. Questions?

Question: *Yes. May we keep the gold ball around Lori and I, and our home, and all the work that we do, and all that we work to protect?*

BREATH TECHNIQUE

Indeed. Now, let me give a breath for this so it (this request) is sustained. As you breathe draw the energy up from the perineum, through each of the chakras, and upon your exhale place your your left hand over your heart, right hand projecting and give the force of life—the great breath of life, to the golden ball. Do you understand?

Response: *Yes.*

A THREEFOLD ACTIVITY

Let us practice this three times. Draw the breath up…now project the energies through the palm. Repeat this yet one more time, and now repeat again. It is always a triune of energies. For the same way that the gold ball of the Inner Sun exists, so does your Solar Sun, and so does your Galactic Sun. All are held together through the energies of the umbilicus. Do you understand?

Response: *Yes.*

This calibrates and creates a Web of Consciousness throughout, and allows for *all three* to work together as ONE. This constitutes, in some respects, a pulsation similar to a heartbeat that flows through all of them simultaneously. This controls their inner connection like capillaries of light through a nervous system. This is yet another understanding of the (Evolutionary) Biome. All creation within the Biome of Light comes through a three-fold activity, and in your Pilgrimages, you will note I have always given you at least *three points at once*. This is by no mistake; there must always be at least a minimum of three movements (migrations).[24] Of course I always give you

---

23. A full-force Golden Age is also known as Krita Yuga. Krita Yuga contains seventy-five to one hundred percent Galactic Light Spectrum.
24. The term *migration* refers to the movement(s) within a Spiritual Pilgrimage.

more than three so you may move your energies of light, sometimes through random choices; but, it would appear as if you were always attending to at least three at one time. Do you understand?

Response: *Yes, and there is no separation.*

None, whatsoever! In the same way that we give (release) our energies, as we move from Fifth Dimension into the Fourth Dimension, you move from Third Dimension, up to the Fourth to receive the Fifth, from both sides there are *three* movements. Do you understand?

Response: *Yes*

THE TRINOMIAL LAW OF THE BIOME

This is the true law of the biome; it is based upon this principle and knowledge of the trinity. The trinity has been venerated within your religious traditions, but it is based upon a true knowledge of the movement of sound and light frequencies and how they interconnect. The trinomial knowledge is the mathematical system that underlies this, and I know you understand this.[25]

Response: *Yes, trinomial math. The sustainment of the residue that you spoke of is trinomial and it is also audible, because the frequencies of those sound waves never dissipate.*

This is correct and this is how they sustain themselves. As you ask "Can I keep this golden dome of light sustained?" This is how it is achieved. This achieves first the sound vibration, and from this streams the light. Questions?

Response: *Yes, and it contains the sound frequencies that we have been given by Lady Anaya.*

This is correct. Now within your own home…this is one reason why I always instruct you, at the inner level, to always place three foci of light within your home. This, too, is another way to reinforce this teaching into your everyday activity. Do you understand?

Response: *Yes.*

Questions?

---

25. The term *trinomial mathematics* indicates that there are three parts or components in a mathematical formula. Binary is the term for two components, and polynomial means that there are more than three parts. The Ascended Masters reference trinomial, or three components, as the necessary expansion that can accelerate humanity into the Ascension Process.

Question: *Can we take this focus of the gold ball and project it to other circumstances and situations that need to be restrained or to protect us?*

You can. However, we would have to instruct you at a simplistic level, and as you Master the more simplistic movement, then you can move into the trinomial movement. Questions?

Response: *As you wish, yes, so there are certain circumstances such as students suffering who I feel need protection.*

Yes indeed, I shall give this information to you at a personal level. Do you understand?

Response: *Yes, I will accept it and I am grateful for your help, thank you.*

THE LIGHT PREVAILS

Dear ones, I am happy to give more discourse, however it is important that you call upon me and during this blessed time of Shamballa we stream energies unto the Earth Plane and Planet. It is important to overcome fear at all levels, and to recognize and know that the Golden Light will prevail, and streams forth into the hearts of all. Humanity is evolving and growing. Be joyous for this!

> I AM the Light of God that never faileth.
> The Golden Age is now!

Response: *So be it.*

Do you have further questions?

Response: *This is sufficient for now, unless there is more important discourse to give us.*

I shall withdraw my energies and I will come forward again at your request.

Response: *Thank you.*

I AM Saint Germain, Lord of the Golden Cities, your brother and servant in the Light. So be it!

Response: *Shamballa, and my love always.*

"I offer my Cup."

CHAPTER EIGHT

Pilgrimage of Light

Saint Germain, Lord Sananda, and El Morya Offer a Cup Blessing

Greetings, beloved chelas. I AM Saint Germain and I stream forth on that Mighty Violet Ray of Mercy, Compassion, and Forgiveness. As usual, Dear one, I request your permission to come forward.

Response: *Dear Saint Germain, you are most welcome. Come forward on this glorious day!*

Good afternoon, Dear hearts, and Shamballa to each and every one of you. I have brought several of my beloved brothers and comrades in the light. With me to my right is beloved Lord Sananda, and to my left is beloved El Morya. They will be assisting me this day with this information.

SHAMBALLA REMAINS OPEN

As you know, we have kept the energies of the Golden City of Shamballa open for this New Year. This was a decision that was made at the higher levels of the Planetary Council that oversees Shamballa.[1] For you see, Dear ones, this was not an easy decision, but it was a decision that was reached for the good of humanity. Humanity is experiencing a great threshold, or precipice, if you will, in their collective evolution. Yes, there are many that are evolving and growing at this time through that Mighty Gold Ray. The Gold Ray helps one then to acquire the Eighth, Ninth, and even Tenth energetics (light fields). This is a great impetus for the Ascension Process and allows one to more readily access and achieve their liberation in the light!

---

1. The Planetary Council (of Justice) oversees the Earth's spiritual welfare and development. It has intervened during critical phases of humanity's development, and approved the dispensation of the Violet Flame on Earth to transmute karma. It serves alongside the Karmic Board. Apollo, Sanat Kumara, Kuan Yin, Portia, El Morya, Kuthumi, and the Eight Archangels sit on this important ruling body, alongside other venerated Cosmic Beings of Light. Currently the Planetary Council sponsors and oversees critical spiritual and scientific teaching on concurrent timelines, and their relationship to spiritual growth, evolution, and the influence of Collective Consciousness upon Earth Changes. The I AM America Teachings are sponsored through the Planetary Council. Saint Germain speaks of his mission with I AM America and the Planetary Council: "Specifically, my committed message of the Earth cleansing concerns raising from the Fifth Dimension to Seventh Dimension. We have spoken of the Violet Flame and the work of the Planetary Council at this time. You see, Dear ones, timing is crucial, and we give to you our everlasting love and project to you the energy to inspire and direct you to keep you in this work."

ASCENSIONS IN THE GOLDEN CITY ASHRAMS

There are many who will reach their Ascension this year. And as we usually report, it is important for you to understand that many more are achieving their liberation.[2] Many are achieving their Ascension through traditional courses; but, there are even more that are achieving their Ascension through the great Ashram of light. And this year we are happy to announce that 3,088 have achieved their liberation (in the Golden City Ashrams of Light).[3] They are now ready to move on...free from the need to reincarnate into the Earth Plane. It is important to understand that in this liberation process, many are still residing in the inner Ashrams of Light, where they will continue to work on healing and educational processes. As you well know, your beloved sister in the light is still serving in the Golden City of Shalahah. And within several years time upon the Earth Plane, she will be ready then to serve I AM America, for this was her great request. When she entered into the Golden City of Shalahah, we (both) offered our Cups to you. We realized the great sacrifice that you continue to make for the work of I AM America upon the Earth Plane and Planet.

SAINT GERMAIN'S BLESSING

We offer our Cups[4] to you and we understand that you, too, have been on your great Pilgrimage of Light. We heard your prayers and your requests, and now we offer and pour our energy-for-energy upon you.

Now let me describe. Saint Germain, Lord Sananda, and El Morya come forward with Beloved Susan. Saint Germain speaks.

I come forward, Dear chela.

He is offering you the Cup...

I request (that) you drink of the effervescent light.

He pours light from his Cup upon us, and into our home.

---

2. Spiritual Liberation is a temporary reprieve from the cycle of reincarnation, and the soul seeks and obtains their Ascension in higher dimensions. According to the Ascended Masters, this is often achieved through service and spiritual development in Fourth and Fifth Dimensional Spiritual Retreats and Ashrams of Light.

3. It is important to note that a significant amount of Ascensions have shifted into the multi-dimensional Ashrams of the Golden Cities. These Fourth and Fifth Dimensional abodes of spiritual development and evolution feature many Temples, Halls of Learning, and Spiritual Retreats designed to rapidly assist the HU-man Development of Ascension. Before the maturity of the Golden Cities, Ascensions were obtained through conventional means, and relied primarily on traditional religious and spiritual practice.

4. When an Ascended Master offers their Cup, this is considered an act of respect and love. The Cup literally exchanges energy from the Master Teacher directly to the chela.

This effervescent light comes forward from my heart to yours.
It is in indeed the Light of Immortality.
It is the Light of Conscious Immortality.
It is the Light of Service,
As All for ONE,
And ONE for All!

He's backing away. Lord Sananda comes forward, and he, too, offers his Cup.

SANANDA'S CUP

Dear ones, Dear hearts, I AM Sananda and request permission to come forward.

Response: *Dear one, please come forward. You are most welcome.*

I offer my Cup to you today. Dear steward, chela, I offer this Cup to you and to all the students of I AM America. Love is the ONE principle which we serve.

For in the beginning there is love,
And always in the end, there is love.

Now, I offer my Cup to you…

He comes forward and offers you the Cup to drink.

Drink of the effervescent substance of service, brought forth from the Heart of Love.

He raises his Cup to his heart.

Dear ones, I offer this cup, not only to you individually for the messenger-ship that you have brought forward, but I offer this Cup to I AM America and to the students of I AM America. This (action) gives a great boon of energy for their service within the light.

He pours his Cup and light floods the entire room and spreads throughout our home. He backs away, and El Morya comes forward.

EL MORYA'S SHAMBALLA BLESSING

Beloved Dear hearts, I AM El Morya and request permission to come forward.

Response: *Please, El Morya, come forward. You are most welcome.*

I offer my Cup for your strength and courage. Dear ones, it is through the will that any great action is ever achieved. And I have said many times,

> Choose, choose, and choose again!
> Choose the Love.
> Choose the Service.
> Choose your Ascension.

My Cup is filled with the Light of God that never, never faileth! And I offer it to you.

He's offering you the Cup.

Response: *Thank you.*

As you drink of this substance, you will feel an activation within your kundalini energies.

He offers Len a drink from the Cup, and then holds it up to the heavens.

> I charge this Cup with the energies of Gobi,
> Stepping-down energies from the Golden City of Shamballa,
> And they anchor within your house and within your heart.
> So be it!

Response: *So be it!*

Now, let me describe. All of the energies commingle and form a great Vortex of Light. Saint Germain comes forward and speaks.

GOD OBEDIENCE

Dear ones, bask within this energy. For it is yours, this is the energy-for-energy. Now, I would like to describe the Energy-for-energy Pilgrimage. Dear Ones, we know that you embarked upon a Pilgrimage, not only to your Star, but onward to the Southern Door of Gobean. You followed my instruction, exactly…and I commend your God obedience unto the light! It is important for all who wish to take Pilgrimages to always understand that, yes; you can attend to just one point. Indeed, this will give you a great energetic boost. But for those who offer themselves of service at this new level—to serve as a Step-down Transformer of Light for of the planet…I ask that you always follow through with three (points), as we have taught.[5] It can be *any* three that you *choose*. It can be of three within any doorway, three of various

---

5. Pilgrimage to any three Adjutant Points when visited sequentially in the same trip comprise an auspicious Energy-for-energy Pilgrimage.

doorways, three Adjutant Points. Three Adjutant Points…always follow (this pattern) as I have taught in previous discourse.

"PILGRIMAGES THROUGHOUT THE YEAR"

The trinomial energies carry the energies of the Christ Consciousness; this allows one to enter into neutrality. From this position, *even more* energies can stream forward for your development in the Ascension. These Pilgrimages assist beloved Mother Earth, Babajeran, and allow her to anchor more light within the Earth Planet. This is of great importance. We ask for those that have the *eyes to see and the ears to hear*, to carry through with many Pilgrimages throughout the entire year of 2022. Beloved El Morya comes forward for discourse.

Saint Germain backs away, and El Morya comes forward.

THE HIERARCHS OF LIGHT

Beloved Dear hearts, I AM El Morya. I stood by you at the Star, and I stand by you throughout all of your Pilgrimages throughout the Golden City of Gobean. I oversee many of the Adjutant Point Hierarchs who are present at each and every activation.[6] For as you place your Cup in action, I, too, place my Cup in action and pour light upon the Earth Plane and Planet. Each Adjutant Points and Hierarch comes forward in service to the Golden Cities of the great Golden Age.

Each time you enter an Adjutant Point, *more energy* is flooded into the Earth and into the Golden City of Light. I attend to each of the points through my focused attention, and many other hierarchs will present themselves, as they come forward. Know, Dear ones, that they have studied under my tutelage. It is important for you to understand that each one comes forward with a focused intent, and serves a different Ray. Each Ray gives their service of light. It is true that they can morph and change on an annual basis, however, some of their Ray Forces will stay intact throughout their entire service of the Golden City.

GODDESS TI OF THE LIGHT

The first point that you attend to (visit) in the Southern Door is the Abundance Point. This is served by the lovely Goddess of Light, Nefertiti. This is the name you recognize her by, however, in the higher realms of light, we know her as the Goddess Ti (pronounced *tee*) of the Light who serves the White Ray.[7] Because of her presence in Abundance, she (also) serves the modulated Ray Force known as the Coral or the Orange Ray.

---

6. El Morya is the Hierarch of the Golden City of Gobean, located in Arizona and New Mexico, United States. The Golden City of Gobean serves the Blue Ray.
7. Also known as the Goddess Ninti, which means *to give life*. Goddess Ninti is the spiritual deity which is the basis of Eve in the Holy Bible.

This (Ray Force) always gives you a great boon of energy...sometimes for material manifestations upon the Earth Plane and Planet, similar to a Northern Door Pilgrimage. It creates an energy so the focus of your desire can be (easily) achieved. This, you see, Dear ones, is her *right service* in the light. There is some history I would like to share with you about this beloved being, and when she is ready, she will present herself. For her teachings concern the Principle of Abundance. She once served in the great temples of the Lemurian Epoch, ages ago, and was present when the Earth (existed) as just one disk of land...floating in the Eternal Light of God.[8] She serves this Abundance Point through her knowledge of the Unity of the Light. She carried the great flame from Atlantis into the temples of early Egypt, where the veneration of beauty and balance was celebrated. She has served as a Catholic Saint, and brought purity to the scriptures through their translation. She recently reached her Ascension in the Ashrams of Light at Shamballa. There, she was awarded her Ascension through the Temple of Unity. Her service is given at the Abundance Ashram of Gobean. Now, I move forward the next Adjutant Point—the Harmony Point.

THE HARMONY POINT

This point also serves the White Ray and the Aquamarine Ray. Its Hierarch, (Akhenaton) comes forward in truth, for those that are seeking truth and transparency within their relationships may move to this Point of Harmony.[9] There, it imbues a *shakti*,[10] if you will, and moves the soul into a transmutation process; he serves with his beloved Divine Complement Goddess Ti. The Aquamarine Ray moves alongside the Coral-Orange Ray, and creates harmony in the Earth Plane and Planet.[11]

THE CARDINAL POINT

Dear ones, the (Golden City) Gateways always influence Third-Dimensional experience. As we move to the center, this (Cardinal) point holds a great coalescing of energies, based upon the uniting of Harmony and Abundance! There, you will find the Beloved Archangel who works in service with his Divine Complement, serving and helping the White Ray and Gold Ray to infuse its evolutionary process for the Ascension of humanity.

Cresta[12] will also come forward in future sessions to share teachings upon the unity within. Dear ones, I also realize that you performed yet another Pilgrimage

---

8. Saint Germain teaches in *New World Wisdom, One*, "Remember, Dear ones, there was the time when the land was only a continuous disk. It floated on a continuous body of water. And inside your planet, the waters. It was primarily a planet of waters with a fiery core."
9. See Appendix V: *Akhenaton*.
10. An energetic transference.
11. These are the new Modulated Ray Forces that assist humanity's entrance into the HU-man Development of the Golden Age.
12. Archangel Cresta serves on the White and Gold Rays, a new modulated Ray Force. He is accompanied by the Archeia Christa, who serves at the Gobean Gateway to Love Ashram (Eastern Door). Cresta and Christa are twin Archangels, brother and sister, who often assist Chrystiel and Clarity, the Archangels of the Gold and Aquamarine Rays. This Cardinal Point contains both the Gold and

to the Service Point, and service unites the soul in their great Divine Purpose. As you serve as Step-down Transformers, it is important to call forth your service.

> I align my will to the Divine Will!
> I serve as a Step-down Transformer of Light,
> May the energies of Shamballa to Gobi surge within me and affirm themselves,
> For love, in service, breathes the breath for all!
> So be it!

He's now backing away. Saint Germain comes forward.

REJUVENATE WITH MEDITATION

Dear ones, I too will come forward throughout several more sessions this year for you. I realize that your schedules have been busy. However, we too would like to share more information with you regarding the expansion of consciousness within the Earth Plane. As you well know, each time that you visit an Adjutant Point in Pilgrimage, you expand your light fields. Sometimes there is tremendous fatigue that can overtake the body. I suggest to combat this fatigue to use a salt-water bath, as I have suggested in the past. I also ask that you meditate and surround your body with a Golden Ball of Light. For the Golden Ball of Light meditation will rejuvenate and restore. Now, I know there are several questions and I open the floor for your questions.

Question: *In the next Pilgrimages, shall we complete in the Southern door of Gobean... and the Convergence Points?*

Yes. This will carry forward your great Pilgrimage into the light for the Southern Door. However, we also ask that you attend to (visit) three at a time. Follow the Migration Pathway for this particular (pattern of) Pilgrimage and you will receive yet another great energy-for-energy exchange. Do you understand?

Response: *Yes, I do.*

Proceed.

Response: *My sense is that we should complete our understanding of these locations of points, and to do the Pilgrimage as soon as possible!*

Work upon your own schedule, for it is important that you attend to the work of I AM America as well. For this year, there will be several new books that will be published that are of great import to the Great White Brotherhood. They will carry

Aquamarine Rays and the White and Gold Ray. As we move into the new twenty-year period, Period Nine, the White and Gold Ray will dominate.

forward more information on the Plasma Field, the Photon Belt, and the structure of the Photon. Do you understand?

Response: *Yes.*

Proceed.

Question: *Well, considering that you've brought it up, what do you wish to share with us regarding the Photon Belt and the Plasma Field at this time?*

EARTH'S IMMERSION INTO THE PHOTON BELT

As you well know, Dear one, we have been infusing this information upon the Earth Plane for nearly twenty years. The Earth in its position within its solar system is now immersed within the Photon Belt. This allows a different convergence of timelines to occur. As you well know, Dear ones, last year a great war for the timelines occurred through those dark and evil forces with the forces of light. That is why it was decided that we shall keep the energies of Shamballa flowing into the Earth Plane and Planet at this time. For Mother Earth holds back many of the Earth Changes, knowing that the Apocalyptic Timeline could be induced (through) the activities of HAARP[13] and chemtrails. However, the plan of light is great, is it not? And the light of God, as El Morya says, "Never, never faileth!" Higher-level timeline strands for the Earth Plane and Planet contain instantaneous cures for the current pandemic.[14] Dear ones, the pandemic was planned by the dark forces to tip the (Earth's) balance into the Apocalyptic Timeline.[15] There are also many other miracle cures of light that can come forward!

For those who seek and need healing, within the Plasma Field are the many Photons that rearrange themselves at a monoatomic level. This, you see, Dear ones, accelerates

---

13. High-frequency Active Auroral Research Program.

14. The Ascended Masters explain that time is different from one person to another. A small child perceives five minutes as an hour; an older personal perceives an hour as five minutes. Metabolic rate influences differences in perception. According to the Master Teachers time exists to literally keep track of events and organize life experiences. It seems that time governs both our lives and our social values. Is time travel possible? The Ascended Masters explain that time travel is part of the Co-creative expansion, and the Ascension Process. They further explain simultaneous timelines, and from their viewpoint there are many timelines with many Co-creative perceptions guided by the ONE. A good example to understand simultaneous timelines is to observe a twelve-inch section of a 1.5-inch diameter rope—I recommend that you purchase a foot of rope at your hardware store. In this diameter of rope there are three tightly wound bundles of hemp, and around the outer portion of rope there are many other strands that hold the bundles together. Each strand in a bundle is a Collective Consciousness group, held together by culture and belief systems. Interestingly, the three bundles represent the Trinomial Creation. Notice how closely each bundle with individual strands are interwoven. It is intricate, and our many time (strand) experiences overlay one another. We can easily move our consciousness from one (time) strand to another, and therefore have many varied experiences, calibrated by perception.

15. According to the Master Teachers the Earth and its sensitive environments respond psychically, physically, emotionally, and spiritually to the mass Collective Consciousness. This consciousness, subsequently, calibrates the many threads of time that evolve into two distinct timelines: one timeline is Apocalyptic, the other is the Golden Age.

the Ascension Process, especially when one is present at the Adjutant Points. This is a higher coalescing or condensation, if you will, of the Photon itself. It functions very much like orgone or chi, as you have noted in the human aura. As you were present at the Abundance Point, did you not notice the unusual cloud formations?

Response: *Yes.*

GOLDEN CITY INTERVENTION

These were the Venusian and Pleiadean star crafts, which allow the energetic of the Photons to infuse into the Adjutant Point and into the vital lei-line(s).[16] As you and others achieve more Pilgrimages, you'll notice more of this phenomenon, Dear ones. This is all within a careful plan as the Golden Cities increase their light upon the Earth Plane and Planet. As the new twenty-year cycle comes forward many of the Masters of Light will lower (their energies) from Fifth and into the lower reaches of Fourth Density (Dimension).[17] This will allow for much teaching and healing to occur among the masses. It will also set humanity firmly upon the Ascension Timeline! Questions?

Question: *Is there anything specific that I can do to help Mother Earth or the timeline? Is there anything specific that you would like for me to do?*

"WE MEET YOU IN RECIPROCITY"

Regarding each Energy-for-energy Pilgrimage…(each) builds one upon the next to the next. So as you achieve three of these, there is a great impetus. As you achieve nine, another impetus…as you achieve twelve, yet another impetus! Each of these build energy—one to the next, in the same manner as we lower our energies from the Fifth Dimension to the Third, as you attend to your Pilgrimage, you are heightening your energies through each layer of the field of Third Dimension, onward into Fourth, and then into Fifth Dimension. It is an achievement, indeed, to carry this work into the Earth Plane and Planet. For as you give your energy, we can meet you *in reciprocity* and because of the energies of Shamballa, we can give again yet *a little more.* Do you understand?

Response: *Yes, I do.*

Questions?

Question: *Can we go to the Western Door this year?*

---

16. Several crafts were observed during our Pilgrimage to the Gobean Abundance Point, located near Rodeo, New Mexico.
17. This twenty-year cycle begins in the year 2024, and is known in Chinese Feng Shui as Period Nine.

Indeed. However, as you complete the Western Door, I also ask for you attend to the Eastern Door (first), to keep the energy balanced.[18]

Response: *I see. It will be done!*

If you have questions, I am always available for discourse.

Response: *Thank you.*

Now, unless if there are other questions I shall leave and return upon your signal.

Response: *I thank you for your aid and assistance…and for the three of you giving so graciously of your energies. I am here. I love you. I am in service. So be it.*

ALL FOR ONE!

Now, they're gathering altogether.

> We are ONE within the light,
> ONE within Shamballa,
> ONE for All,
> And All for ONE.
> So be it!

Response: *So be it.*

---

18. This is a reference to the Eastern Door Pilgrimage. For more information see: *Golden City Eastern Door Pilgrimage and Awakening the Divine Feminine,* Appendix FF, *Evolutionary Biome.*

CHAPTER NINE

The Photon

Saint Germain Explains the Spiritual Science of the Photon

Greetings in that Mighty Christ! I AM Saint Germain and I stream forth on that Mighty Violet Ray of Mercy, Transmutation, and Forgiveness. As usual, Dear hearts, I request permission to come forward into your energy fields.

Response: *Dear Saint Germain, please come forward. You are most welcome*

A TRANSMISSION FROM THE MAP ROOM

Greetings, Good morning, and Shamballa to each and every one of you today. Dear ones, I would like to describe where I am sending this transmission from…yes, it is true, I have lowered my energies from the Fourth Dimension into the upper reaches of Third Dimension. I am transmitting to you visually and I am in that Mighty Map Room—the (same) room where we carried forward many discourses.[1] This (room) carries an energy that streams from the Temple of Unity at Shamballa. And from there, it streams into a lower Fourth Dimensional construct, so that you may be impressed with its visual representations. You have known this to be the Green Room, sometimes filled with (constructed of) marble.

THE MALTESE CROSS

Today I will share a series of illustrations and give instruction upon the Maltese Cross,[2] or what you also know as the Photon. The Maltese Cross, or Photon, is perhaps the most efficient way for light to transmit throughout the entire universal structure. In fact, the Maltese Cross is a parcel or packet of light. It carries within the seed-kernel of light itself—sound vibration. This (parcel) holds a sound vibration from the purity of the Mental Body and the Co-creative activity. I have taught the

---

1. Since the earliest days of receiving the I AM America Teachings, Saint Germain describes his presence in a large room with a table where many of the I AM America Maps were unrolled and revealed in the higher dimensions of light. Here is a description in *New World Wisdom, One,* as we are entering this magnificent room at Shamballa: "Once again, I am ascending the steps into the marble room that is back-lighted. I see Saint Germain to my right, Archangel Michael to my left. Sanat Kumara is again seated at the desk. Sananda is behind him, standing to his right."
2. The Maltese Cross, a symbol often used by Saint Germain, represents the Eight-sided Cell of Perfection, and the human virtues of honesty, faith, contrition, humility, justice, mercy, sincerity, and the endurance of persecution.

Maltese Cross within the Golden City construct. This knowledge begins with the four important doorways.[3]

Now he's drawing the Maltese Cross with four triangles...one to the North, one to the South, the East, and the West. In the center he draws a circle.[4]

The circle, Dear ones, is a representation of the Sun that holds and contains light. The light is stimulated through sound vibration. Perhaps the simplest way to understand this is the Bible verse, "In the beginning, there was the word, and the word was made manifest."[5, 6] Dear ones, this is how the Maltese Cross is empowered. Some would say this creates through the mental construct of the mind. Or, does the mind think the sound and then whisper the sound into the ethers? Or, is the sound perpetual? Does the perpetuity of the sound hold the universe together at a Third, Fourth, and Fifth Dimensional level?[7]

ACTIVITY OF THE PHOTON

Perhaps all of these contain the truth. Today I will present the working model, so you can begin to understand the Photon. The activity of the Photon, especially in a

---

3. The *Four Directions within a Golden City Structure*, from *New World Wisdom, Volume Two*: "The northern portion of the Vortex is referred to as the Black Door. This represents discipline and hard labor. It also represents the material world and how everything 'appears.' Hence, this portion is based on the Law of Opposites, or the Law of Attraction and The Law of Repulsion. These two laws synergize as the Law of Rebirth. Here, all service is given to life through the cosmos.
The southern portion of the Vortex is referred to as the Red Door. Symbolically, the Vortices represent our passage to immortality and four areas show the course that our soul chooses. Saint Germain often says, 'Once you choose...it is done. You have entered your great work.' The Red Door represents the Healing of the Nations through enlightened love, non-judgment, and faith. A momentum of healing is established through the Law of Rhythm. Service is rendered through choice, courage, and ultimately, the surrender of animal desire to the Law of Land. Here, all service is given to life through humanity.
The eastern portion of the Vortex is known as the Blue Door. This portion of the Vortex asks for purification and sacrifice but with the great reward of Alchemy. The Ascended Master Law of Non-judgment and Surrender is known as the The Elixir of Life—the fusion of the ONE, expressed in The Law of Group. Here, service is expressed through self.
The western portion is the last section, known as the Yellow Door, also the Philosopher's Stone. It is the path of adeptship, perfection, and often the last path taken before entry into the apex, or what symbolizes, 'the star that you follow.' Here, the great Law of Love and service for others is expressed in Brotherhood and Sisterhood."
4. See Appendix KK: *Movement of the Photon as the Golden City.*
5. Saint Germain is paraphrasing John 1:1, "In the beginning was the word, and the word was with God, and the word was God." The word *manifest* appears in John 1:14, "And the word was made flesh, and dwelt among us, full of grace and truth."
6. A fiat is a Creation Word spoken by a Cosmic Being, or with the human voice. A decree is a rhythmic version of the fiat, designed to permeate and change consciousness and can activate physical matter. The Write and Burn technique is the densification of the sound and words to transmute and Co-create. Written word captures the sound in a slower form. It is suggested to read the I AM America Spiritual Teachings aloud, from the book.
7. In *A Teacher Appears,* Saint Germain shares teachings on sound. He explains that sound holds physical molecules together. Sound frequencies constantly vibrate from the Source. This is the eternal outbreath of Creation.

Golden City begins at the Northern Door. (The activity) travels to the East, onward to the Southern Door, then to the West and migrates to the center. However, the center (Star) contains all of the (energies of) the doorways, coalescing their energies. This location is the greatest condensation (concentration) of the source (energy).[8] The Maltese Cross contains many Adjutant Points and vital lei-lines. The Adjutant Points represent where the vital lei-lines intersect, and these intersections cause sub-Vortices that exist within the Golden City. Let us return to what I have drawn upon the board.

Let me explain. He is pointing to the diagram that displays the Northern Door and the Southern Door Photons.

CHAOS AND ORDER

Yes, indeed, (Photons) sometimes travel in a chaotic pattern, but this chaos contains a predicated movement that is important to understand.[9] It begins by orienting itself to the magnetic North. For the purposes of understanding the Golden City Vortices upon the Earth, I use true North. True North aligns to Beloved Babajeran and the Earth Planet (Mother Earth) will make a difference in the interaction of the Golden City energy. Next, travel from the North to the South. This creates a type of a Vertical Power Current that exists within the Golden City.[10] This also influences the magnetic pulse, for North and South rule, the (Golden City's) magnetism. Then energies move from East to West. This is the electricity of the Vortex. So you see, Dear ones, it is indeed an electromagnetic flux, or I should say more of a magnetic-electric flux! This (energy) creates an interaction between all of the Doorways…moving almost like a dove in flight—similar to the movement of the great Heart of the Dove.[11,12] However, this movement engenders an activity toward the center (Golden City Star).

---

8. Each direction of the Maltese Cross, or Golden City structure is a sound frequency of the Ray arcing through the direction. The sound(s) change as the Ray Forces migrate through the doors of the Golden City.
9. Photons align and harmonize to the Collective Consciousness that bridges to True North.
10. Also known as the Golden Thread Axis, in the human body is physically composed of the Medullar Shushumna, a life-giving nadi physically comprising one-third of the human Kundalini system. Two vital currents intertwine around the Golden Thread Axis: the lunar Ida Current, and the solar Pingala Current. According to the Master Teachers, the flow of the Golden Thread Axis begins with the I AM Presence, enters the Crown Chakra, and descends through the spinal system. It descends beyond the Base Chakra and travels to the core of the Earth. Esoteric scholars often refer to the axis as the Rod of Power, and it is symbolized by two spheres connected by an elongated rod. Ascended Master students and chelas frequently draw upon the energy of the Earth, through the Golden Thread Axis, for healing and renewal by using meditation, visualization, and breath techniques.
11. The Heart of the Dove is located in Kansas and Missouri, United States. Its movement is not like a Vortex, and mirrors the movement of a bird in flight. Its energies flutter, rush, and glide as its doorways move energies between Third, Fourth, and Fifth Dimension. The energy anomaly expands and contracts.
12. The Dove overlaid the Golden City distributes the head and tail on the North/South axis. This represents magnetism. East/West are the wings in a rotational movement. This creates the electrical charge. When the Dove flies vertically, the movement is from the Golden City Apex, and enters Fourth and Fifth Dimension. This represents the spin of the Vortex.

This causes the spinning motion of the Vortex. In this case, even at a microcosmic level, the Photon movement is a spinning action. As I have described before, it moves in a clockwise motion to take energy in; counterclockwise to remove energies.[13]

LEI-LINES CARRY THE VITAL ENERGY

This movement is mirrored within all of the Adjutant Points, and calibrates those mighty lei-lines. The lei-lines, you see, Dear ones, also carry many vital energies throughout the Photon, and the Golden City Vortex. They work together as ONE continuous system. It is as if the Adjutant Points are the meridians as represented in the physical body.[14] Lei-lines resemble the circulatory system, and the movement or the spin of the Vortex carries the vital breath or the chi throughout the Vortex.

THE MONOATOMIC PHOTON

You will find this similarity in smaller sub-vortices or Adjutant Points. Light is parceled or packaged in such a fashion, with Third, Fourth, and Fifth — even Sixth, Seventh, and sometimes Eighth Dimensional attributes. This is the monoatomic aspect that exists within the Photon of Light.[15] The Photon of Light moves human consciousness from Third Dimensional constraint into Fourth…and sometimes Fifth! This instigates the Ascension Process. This is the purpose of the Golden Cities, for they instigate within the human, a movement of the Kundalini System and assist the building of the higher bodies of light. This affects the overall Collective Consciousness of the Earth.

---

13. This is the classic movement of a Golden City Vortex.
14. The human body contains major and minor energy meridians. Some are yin—feminine; others are considered yang, masculine. The Evolutionary Biome of the Golden City mirrors a similar biologic infrastructure.
15. A monoatomic element is a single atom that does not bind to another and is usually derived from rare earth elements, i.e., gold, platinum, rhodium, iridium, titanium, silver, and copper. Since monoatomic atoms have a ceramic property, they are also superconductive. Recent research has proven that monoatomic substances exist throughout the Earth and in nature. Superconductivity creates a non-polarized energy field—best known as a Meissner Field. In fact, our own human aura is a type of Meissner Field. The appropriate use of monoatomic substances can expand and further develop your Meissner Field. According to researcher David Hudson, "You light up the room when you walk in...the gifts that go with this are: perfect telepathy, you can know good and evil when it is in a room with you, you can also project your thoughts into someone else's mind. You can levitate; you can walk on water because it's flowing so much light within you that you don't attract gravity. And when you understand that when you exclude all external magnetic fields, when you exclude gravity, you are no longer of this space-time. You have become a Fifth Dimensional being." In *Soul Alchemy*, Saint Germain states, "Now, this Eight-sided Cell of Perfection is mirrored too within a Golden City Vortex. For so you see, it too can super conduct, in its own monoatomic state, to bring forward a greater transcendence upon the Earth and its relationship to the Galactic Center and Galactic Web."

GOLDEN CITY PILGRIMAGE

Dear ones, your Pilgrimages work within the different (Golden City) Doors of light…some work in the Northern Door, some in the Southern (Door), some in the Eastern (Door), and some in the Western Door. There are Pilgrimages that many take only to the (Golden City) Stars. You have recently learned about the Energy-for-energy Pilgrimages, and how they create a Divine Intervention within your life.[16]

THE GOLD AND AQUAMARINE RAYS

Now, more anomalies are occurring upon the Earth Plane and Planet. The first is the Gold Ray that streams forth from the Great Central Sun (the Galactic Center). It is a higher energy, sometimes known as the Eighth Ray and in other teachings it is known as the Tenth Ray. It joins in purpose and vision with the Aquamarine Ray. The Aquamarine Ray and the Gold Ray are activated in your solar system through the two planets of Neptune and Saturn.[17] When I mention Saturn, I am speaking of a higher aspect of this planet.[18] There are different energies that qualify from the central source of each planet. We have explained this before in detail. These two planets play a large role in calibrating the Aquamarine Ray and the Gold Ray to the Earth. However, there are other influences that also play even a larger role. Of course it is the triune aspect of energy moving from your Solar Sun, to your Inner Sun. These two sources arc energies to and fro, yet the source of all of this is the Great Central Sun. So indeed, we have a triune effect—a trinomial intervention. This affects Earth, primarily at its inner core and radiating to the surface.

GOLDEN CITIES ARE CAPACITORS OF LIGHT

This is the purpose of the Golden Cities, for they act as capacitors of light that draw the energy up from the Inner Sun. They disperse these energies throughout the Earth Plane and Planet.[19] This has an effect upon humanity, dispersing the Gold Ray throughout humanity to affect culture, politics, societies, and above all a huge influence upon the (spiritual development of) the individual. This is the greatest work of the Gold and Aquamarine Rays.

THE PLASMA FIELD

There are other aspects that involve the Earth, and its position in its solar system, and location within the DERN (Universe). Now, Earth is passing through a huge

---

16. For more information on various Spiritual Pilgrimages recommended by the Ascended Masters, see *I AM America Atlas*, "Golden City Spiritual Pilgrimages."
17. The Gold Ray works through Saturn to help humanity to quickly transmute and transcend difficult karmas. The Aquamarine Ray is metaphysically linked to Neptune and is spiritual, sensitive, and intuitive.
18. Fourth and Fifth Dimensional aspects.
19. See Appendix E: *Arcing of Ray Forces to the Golden Cities*.

Plasma Field. The Plasma Field is a type of energetic charge and contains within it billions of small particle-like Photons.[20]

THE MOVEMENT OF PHOTONS

Photons charge themselves and sometimes move in a circular (clockwise) motion, sometimes in a counter (clockwise) circular motion. They do not orient to North or South; however, they carry a huge influence on the planet that comes under their sway.[21] Remember, I mentioned that the Photons have a monoatomic flow and sometimes they are functioning at a Sixth Dimensional level.[22] Sometimes they are functioning at a Fourth Dimensional level and even into Third, even Second, and First Dimension…they have the ability to move through matter with a sense of timelessness.[23] Therefore, the Photon is a symbol of life eternal and conscious immortality. (The Photon) is the kernel of life and creates light through sound into the manifestation process.[24]

THE MONOATOMIC GOLDEN CITIES

The Golden Cities also engender a monoatomic experience. When you hear the high-pitch ring, when you see that flash of light, when you sense something about you; and yet, you do not see it or perceive it through typical human senses. Indeed, you are having a monoatomic experience. Your consciousness is traversing through the dimensions and functioning at a new level of perception and comprehension. This is one of the major purposes of the Golden Cities, for they allow human consciousness to interact with Third, Fourth, and Fifth Dimensional constructs, and their purpose is to engender this at a much higher level…so humanity can be prepared for their Ascension Process. Lord Sananda has said, "The awakening is at hand. The time has come for man to receive the gift." Receive this mighty gift, for it comes with love from the source of creation, love from the Creator, and inspires the activation of the great divinity within—the Eight-sided Cell of Perfection.

---

20. Remember, the Photon Belt exists within the Plasma Field. The Photon Belt is inordinately monoatomic, and creates multi-dimensional experiences that promote the Ascension Process.
21. Many solar systems have been experiencing the movement of the Plasma Field with currents of monoatomic Photons for both hundreds and thousands of years. This process advances their civilizations spiritually and scientifically. Our solar system is one of the last in our Universe to experience this evolution of life and human consciousness.
22. According to Saint Germain, Third Dimension is .317 revolutions per milisecond. Fourth Dimension add .063 revolutions per milisecond; six times to reach Fourth Dimension. Fifth and Sixth Dimension are unknown at this time.
23. This produces the anomalies of both Time Compaction and Time Contraction.
24. In form language the sound pitch is key, alongside the spoken word.

SACRED GEOMETRY OF THE PHOTON

The Eight-sided Cell of Perfection mirrors the Photon, for what is man? He is composed of sound and light frequencies, and the first kernel is held within the heart.[25] This is the Divine Construct of the Maltese Cross or the Photon, and it is perhaps the most sacred of all geometry. It holds within the square, the triangle, the rectangle, and above all the circle, which expands life in glory and vision.[26]

THE MULTI-DIMENSIONAL HU-MAN

As you enter into different Adjutant Points and lei-lines, you'll begin to have varying experiences of Fourth and Fifth Dimension. This is purely natural and not meant to be paranormal. Indeed, you are a multidimensional HU-man Being! You have only been in the slumber of lesser light,[27] and now it is time for you to fully awaken into the grand HU-man!

> I AM the HU-man of life!
> I AM the HU-man of Ascension!
> I AM the HU-man of Divinity!
> So be it!

Response: *So be it.*

Many of the spiritual practices, decrees, meditations, and prayers that we have given you are meant to open your Third-Dimensional faculties to these Higher Dimensions. They prepare your light fields to receive this mighty gift of your multidimensional light. When you enter into Spiritual Pilgrimage, you are attuning your light fields to higher frequencies and energies by observing your Third-Dimensional world. You begin to open and sense Fourth- and Fifth-Dimensional nuance. As the Earth moves through even more intense Plasma and Photon Belt activity, there will be even more *ahas* and awakenings. Many of these occur in Earth's scientific world, in health and healing, and in politics and society. There will be many changes as this Great Awakening floods the Earth.[28] Indeed, as I have said before, it is an awakening (incited) through the Gold Ray. It is an awakening quickened through the Golden Cities. It occurs through (both) the Plasma Field and the Photon Belt. Indeed, this is the awakening of your divinity within! I sense your questions. Proceed.

---

25. The Eight-sided Cell of Perfection is constructed of two Maltese Crosses. One is oriented to the cardinal directions, the second to the intercardinal directions. The Golden City mirrors this sacred construction.
26. The Energy Grid in the human aura exemplifies this.
27. Due to the influence of Kali Yuga.
28. The Great Awakening is the time period humanity is currently experiencing marked by political and societal turmoil alongside humanity's collective Spiritual Awakening. As one moves through extreme polarity, the soul awakens to its divine and innate Co-creatorship that initiates the Ascension Process. The Great Awakening transpires concurrently with the turbulent Time of Change.

Question: *Each of the Adjutant Points has a specific hierarchy and Ray Force that functions within each Golden City. Are we absorbing within the Pilgrimage Process this Ray? And are we interacting with this specific (Adjutant Point) Ray along with the dominant Ray of the Golden City?*

THE ALIGNMENT PROCESS

Perhaps the best way to understand is that during your Pilgrimage you engage an Alignment Process[29] to the Ray. This creates balance. Your light fields receive the Ray Force and balance the Ray Force. For the human sojourn to the Earth Plane, and especially during the times of Kali Yuga, is imbalanced. As you travel to Adjutant Points, Ray Forces and their deficiencies can be triggered. If a Ray Force overflows within the Aura, (the Pilgrimage) tones (the imbalance) down and balance is restored.

USE OF THE HUE MANTRA

Perhaps the best mantra to use when you enter into an Adjutant Point is the OM HUE. Chant this mantra fifty-one times, and this balances your energy with the Adjutant Point. You may also feel the Adjutant Point (Fourth Dimensionally), and she may reveal her many Nature Kingdoms through this process. Do you remember when I gave you the spiritual experience of *rocking* your land? You chanted the HUE, and the Nature Kingdoms responded.[30]

Response: *Yes, they did.*

This is one way to assure that your energy is balanced within the Adjutant Point, and can be added to your ceremonial activity. The Cup Ceremony is yet another way for you to enter into the Adjutant Point. This assists your entrance into the Evolutionary Biome. However, (chanting) the HUE can also accomplish this through its sound

---

29. To bring into balance.
30. The Golden City Stone Technique is a remedial measure to raise the vibration of land to calibrate with the four doorways of a Golden City. Collect small stones, around one to two inches in size. Try to find stones that contain silicon (obsidian, granite, diovite, and sandstone) felds par, quartz, and quartz crystal. These types of minerals hold Golden City energies best. Collect stones from all four Golden City Doorways and Adjutant Point locations. Mix the stones together in a large container or wheelbarrow so the energies meld. (We used our pickup bed for this.) Fill a small bucket that can be easily carried, a fanny pack (this works best), or a small backpack with the stones, and drop a stone every twenty feet on your property. Before you let go of the stone, hold the stone close to your mouth and imbue the mantra "OM HUE" directly into it. Or, you can use this decree suggested by Saint Germain:
> "Mighty Violet Flame, blaze forth from the heart of the Central Sun,
> Transmuting all discord, all disharmony, upon this land forever,
> In the name of I AM That I AM."

This method purifies land from subjective energy bodies, negative influences, and dark energies. It also raises the vital energy of the land through the transcendent energies of the Golden City Doorways.

activity. Listen carefully, and during your great silence at an Adjutant Point,[31] you will hear the higher humming as it emits from the Ashram of Light. Do you understand?

Response: *Yes.*

Questions?

Question: *Traditionally, we accept that there are seven layers of the Aura, but my understanding is that are many more layers and the Ray Forces at the Adjutant Point activates these higher energy bodies?*

It is true, Dear one. Currently your seven fields of light are somewhat under the control of the human. Of course, some of them are (controlled) through unconscious and autonomic experience. However, they have been brought into their own accord through the epoch of the Aryan. Now we are entering the epoch of the HU-man.[32] This is a new time that humanity is traversing and entering. Indeed, this is being instigated through many factors, and there is not just one (reason). This is a *New Time* and we welcome it, do we not?

Response: *Absolutely, yes.*

WORKING REMOTELY

Now it is important to understand that in the practice of Spiritual Pilgrimage, one can also work remotely with an Adjutant Point. This can be achieved in many ways. I realize with the current economic system, that sometimes there are restraints placed upon a chela or student…they may experience (economic) limitation. Therefore, it is important to engage your own study, and discover the location of an Adjutant Point. First, use True North, and then apply magnetic North. This, too, assists the visualization process. Take a photograph of the (Adjutant Point's) Map and place this upon your altar for your meditation. Psychically enter into the Adjutant Point. You may locate a picture of the Adjutant Point, and you can enter (the location) through your Fourth and Fifth Dimensional awareness. Another way is to hold a flower, leaf, small rock, or pebble that comes from the Adjutant Point. This impresses the energetics of the (Adjutant) Point. As you locate each Point, I suggest spending twenty-four hours at the location. Enter into meditation for a minimum of twenty minutes upon the entering (the physical) location, homing in within yourself, discovering more about it, defining it at a multi-dimensional level, (including) the Ray Force and its Hierarch. These are suggestions that you may find useful. Questions?

---

31. A time of silence is always encouraged when visiting Adjutant Points. This allows for integration of subtle, yet essential Golden City Energies.
32. A period of time when the human realizes and uses their transcendent HU-man abilities.

Response and question: *Yes. Back to the initial teaching on the Photon, can we apply the sacred shapes for healing, Co-creation and spiritual upliftment?*

ENTER THE GROUP MIND

When you enter into an Adjutant Point, either through meditation (remotely) or in Pilgrimage, join into Group Mind. If you are by yourself, attune to the Hierarch of that Adjutant Point and ask for the Gold Light to flood within your being. This begins with the Eight-sided Cell of Perfection. You will feel it as a large Gold ovoid... a warmth within. This expands and covers your entire field (Aura). This is the Gold Ball of light of which I have instructed you before. The Gold Ball carries within the vital chi of the Adjutant Point. Of course, this technique works best when you are (physically) present at the location. However, it can also be formed remotely. Do you understand?[33]

Response: *Yes.*

LIGHT WITHIN THE PHOTON

The Gold Ball represents the circle of light that is within the Photon, and it represents the circle of light that is the movement of the Photon. It represents the Inner Sun within your Earth. It represents your solar Sun, and it also represents the Great Central Sun. This ovoid of light moves between you and your Mighty I AM Presence! Call upon your Mighty I AM Presence to help form this ovoid of light. From the physical plane to your Mighty I AM Presence and to the Ashram of Light, call forth the Mighty I AM Golden Ball of Light:

> Golden Ball of Light I AM,
> Come forth into my physical plane.
> Carry the energy of the Photon throughout me,
> For healing, health, and vitality!
> So be it.

Do you have questions?

A HEALING TECHNIQUE

Response: *If we are praying for someone else's health or recovery, as we are with two of your students, can we visualize the Gold Ball of light around them?*

Indeed, this can be done from an Adjutant Point, working remotely visualize the Adjutant Point, move the energetic through your Mighty I AM Presence. First, a

---

33. For more information on Group Mind and formation of the Golden Ball of Light, see *Golden Cities and the Masters of Shamballa.*

small nucleus of golden light appears, and it gains its momentum. See the light roll through the lei-lines of light and settling into the heart of those that you visualize healing for. The light expands through your breath and (through) your Mighty I AM Presence. Draw your breath up as I've instructed you, (move the energy) through the perineum — this opens the doorway to the Great Central Sun of your Inner Earth. The energy moves to the light within your heart and your Mighty I AM Presence. The breath expands this ball of light within, for those you seek the healing for. Their own ball of light begins to expand around them. This can also be performed with a picture of the person you are working to help, or visualize their image. Whatever way to mentally form the construct. Do you understand?

Response: *Yes.*

It is important also to understand that at the core of this great Golden Ball of Light, again, is that mighty Photon — the Maltese Cross — the most perfect geometric shape for the human.

Response: *That's actually very clear. We have a dear loved one, who has been very ill. Is there anything specific that we can do to help her? In addition to the instruction you have just given?*

Hold her in prayer and call upon my Mighty Violet Flame Angels and they will minister to her. Call upon Archangel Zadkiel, for he too, can send the Violet Flame in, through, and around this beloved one of light to transmute any residue of Karmic action. Do you understand?

A TIME OF CHOICE

Response: *Yes, I will do this. We have a similar situation with another student who lives at the Star of Gobean. It seems she has lost her faith and determination.*

This time upon on the Earth Plane and Planet is a *Time of Choice*, is it not?

Response: *Yes.*

There are many who will be leaving. As I have said before, many are ready to work in the higher planes of light and their time in mortality (is) closing quickly. However, there are others who choose to be here, to anchor the light within their heart as a Pillar of Light, as a Step-down Transformer. This Dear one may be ready to work in the higher realms of light. I cannot say, for this a *choice of the individual*. However, whenever healing is the choice, healing shall occur. For a Divine Intervention call forth beloved Archangel Zadkiel and the beloved Healing Flame Angels of the Violet Ray. Sometimes it is best to anchor a healing vision through the write and burn technique. In certain cases, this is the best way to convey these energies directly into the physical plane. Also, keep a candle burning (for her), for the light represents the *light within*. She may realize that she carries the light, and not all is lost! Do you understand?

Response: *Yes, I do.*

STEP-DOWN TRANSFORMER: THE PILLAR OF LIGHT

The work of the Step-down Transformer is perhaps one of most effective that the chela, the initiate, and even the Arhat can take upon at this time. Each day make the choice to serve as a Pillar of Conscious Light within the Earth Plane. Serve as a Pillar of Light, to infuse more light—the radiant Gold Light—within the Earth Plane. This can be performed at any location, at any time. It can be performed when you're sitting, but is best when you're standing. Stand and hold your hands (out) to receive the light, breathe up through the Root Chakra. Feel the light as it moves and draws from the Sun, throughout all of the Chakra Centers. As you establish your Pillar of Light, turn your will over to the divine and declare:

> I AM a Step-down Transformer of Light!
> I AM an anchor of the Golden Age of Light.
> I AM in service to the Great White Brotherhood of Light!

Immediately, a Divine Intervention occurs and more light streams, not only from your Mighty I AM Presence, but from the Inner Sun, the solar Sun, and the Great Central Sun. Do you have questions?

Response and question: *Yes. In effect, since 'All is ONE,' we are Step-down Transformers of the Great Central Sun?*

Indeed. Remember, you carry within the Eight-sided Cell of Perfection. What is this? But the Photon of Light! The Photon is within, the Photon is without, and it is commanded through sound…the I AM That I AM.

SPIRITUAL METABOLISM

Question: *So in years past, when you described the 0.1, two, or four revolutions per millisecond…you were speaking about the movement of the Photon, the activation of matter, and how it is held together?*

Indeed, Dear one. This is a form of (spiritual) metabolic health. This metabolism is energy and it is important to always understand your personal spiritual metabolism. Your focus upon the great and Mighty Divine Light within calibrates your spiritual metabolism.[34] Do you understand?

---

34. In earlier I AM America Teachings, the Masters often referred to this principle as "interdimensional mathematics."

Response: *Yes.*

This is the energy force that will move you from Third to Fourth, from Fourth to Fifth (Dimension) and onward. It is the nexus of your Ascension Process and it will inevitably free you. Do you understand?

Response: *Yes, we must spiritually practice and stay present in our focus to literally interact with matter at the higher levels.*

That is correct, Dear one. Now let us return to our lesson, so I can clarify points on North, South, and East and West.

Response: *Please do.*

There is a movement that occurs with the Photon, through the electromagnetism and the metabolic rate. This comes through the spinning movement, and the Doorways seem to fold in upon themselves. This creates a Sun unto itself, its own Golden Ball of Light that generates, again, a duplicating and a replicating process. I am describing at a microcosmic level, how the Photon Belt is created. Do you understand?

Response: *Yes. So this occurs at the time of Ascension, when the chakras move at that faster rate of speed?*

This is how the energy transmutes and moves from one dimension to the next. The Golden Ball is the result of the monoatomic movement. Do you understand?

Response: *Yes.*

I think for this day, I have given enough. Do you have questions?

Response: *I think the Golden Ball can be used for protection…*

It can be used for a number of things. In fact, the Golden Ball will become the center of the new medicine, health, and vitality for the Age of the HU-man.

Response: *Thank you for that key. I am very grateful. Shamballa and my love to all of the Spiritual Hierarchy.*

I AM yours in Golden Light, your brother and servant, Saint Germain.

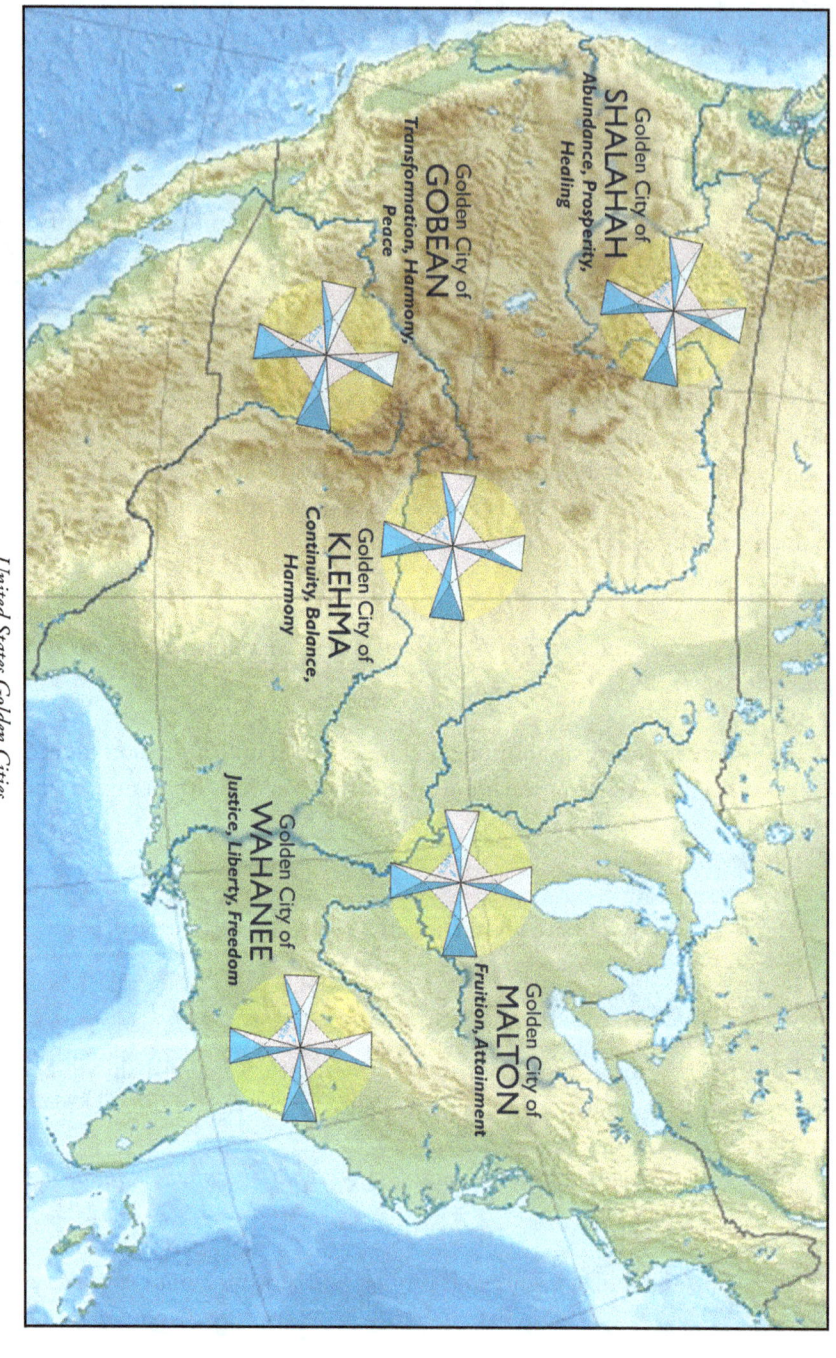

United States Golden Cities

The five Golden Cities of the United States are: Malton, located in Illinois and Indiana. Wahanee, located in Georgia, South Carolina, and North Carolina. Klehma, located in Colorado and Kansas. Shalahah, located in Idaho and Montana. Gobean, located in Arizona and New Mexico.

APPENDIX A
Golden City Vortex

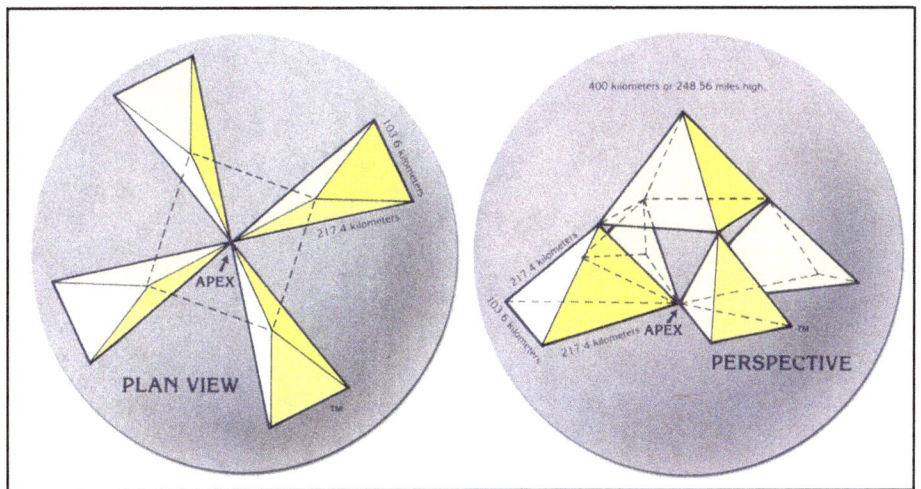

Golden City Dimensions
The above illustration gives the dimensions of the Golden Cities in both kilometers and miles. The height of a Golden City is 248.56 miles. A Golden City Gateway is 64.37 miles. The Golden City Cardinal lei-line is 135.09 miles. However, it is important to note that Golden Cities can vary in size due to their cyclic and varying activity.

A Golden City Vortex — based on the Ascended Masters' I AM America material — are prophesied areas of safety and spiritual energies during the Times of Changes. Covering an expanse of land and air space, these sacred energy sites span more than 400 kilometers (270 miles) in diameter, with a vertical height of 400 kilometers (250 miles). Golden City Vortices, more importantly, reach beyond terrestrial significance and into the ethereal realm. This system of safe harbors acts as a group or universal mind within our galaxy, connecting information seamlessly and instantly with other beings. The Master Teachers coin this phenomenon the Galactic Web.

Fifty-one Golden City Vortices are stationed throughout the world, and each carries a different meaning, a combination of Ray Forces, and a Divine Purpose. Some are older than others; some Vortices are new; and some shift locations. The activation of Golden City Vortices occur in patterns — that's the crux of the numbering system. The Master Teachers call the Earth Beloved Babajeran.

Although the Masters, as a group, oversee all Golden Cities, each stewards his or her own Vortex. A Golden City Vortex works on the principles of electromagnetism and geology. Vortices tend to appear near fault lines, possibly serving as conduits of inner-earth movement to terra firma. The Gobean Vortex near the fissure-filled Mogollon Rim of Arizona; the Malton Vortex of the Midwest, adjacent to the New Madrid fault line; and the Shalahah Vortex of Idaho, an ancient cleft near the Snake River and Hells Canyon, lend credibility to this theory.

Geology has a profound effect on the potency of a Vortex. Not surprising, the five Golden City Vortices rest on areas of highly magnetic geologic

Golden City Meditation
Development of the HU-man senses is claimed to accelerate in Golden Cities. The energy of Golden Cities also improves prayer, meditation, and spiritual practice.

formations. The iron-rich content of basalt pillars and ancient-lava deposit serve as natural conductors of electromagnetic energy; igneous rocks, according to geologic data, create more magnetic pull than sedimentary rocks. That's why Gobean exudes so much energy. Landmarks — such as Mount Baldy in Arizona, the apex of the Southwestern Vortex, and the Golden City Vortex of Shalahah — are filled with basalt and iron-rich rocks.

Water also drives the disbursement of Vortex energies. The Gobean Vortex sits atop the largest aquifer in the Southwest. Shalahah, too, surrounded by three, huge freshwater lakes near Coeur d'Alene and Pend'Oreille, Idaho, and Flathead Lake in Montana, draws power from water.

Visitors to Golden Cities experience spiritual and psychic development — they feel a heightened sense of balance, harmony, and peace. Natural places of meditation, connection with spirit guides, and contact with past-life experiences, Vortices can instantly align the human energy field (aura). During your first stay in a Vortex, you may sleep more while your body adjusts to powerful energies. As you acclimate, you'll undergo a rejuvenation of the body and the spirit. After the shock subsides, many Vortex-seeking pilgrims will engage in prayer and group ceremonies with friends and spiritual mentors, awakening deep connections among fellow humans.

APPENDIX B
The Advanced Light Fields of Ascension

As human spiritual evolution advances, we begin to develop new energy bodies of light, sound, and experience. The Spiritual Teachers mention that the HU-man, the developed God Man, can acquire fifteen new distinct energy bodies beyond the initial, primary Seven Light Bodies. It is claimed that the Fifteenth Energy Body propels the soul out of duality, free from both Third and Fourth Dimension.

An Ascended Master contains and influences twenty-two light bodies. Apparently, Light Bodies Eight through Ten have the ability to contend with varying light spectrums beyond Third Dimension and can manage space-time, including time contraction, time dilation, and time compaction. But more importantly, the development of the HU-man Energy system implements the ever-important Ascension Process. The following information shares descriptions of the HU-man Energy Bodies Eight through Twelve.

Eighth Light Body

Known as the *Buddha Body* or the *Field of Awakening*, this energy body is initially three to four feet from the human body. It begins by developing two visible grid-like spheres of light that form in the front and in the back of the Human Aura. The front sphere is located three to four feet in front of and between the Heart and Solar Plexus Chakras. The back sphere is located in front of and between the Will-to-Love and Solar Will Chakras. These spheres activate an ovoid of light that surrounds the entire human body; an energy field associated with harmonizing and perfecting the Ascension Process. This is the first step toward Mastery. Once developed and sustained, this energy body grants physical longevity and is associated with immortality. It is known as the first level of Co-creation and is developed through control of the diet and disciplined breath techniques. Once this light body reaches full development, the spheres dissipate and dissolve into a refined energy field, resembling a metallic armor. The mature Eighth Light Body then contracts and condenses, to reside within several inches of the physical body where it emits a silver-blue sheen.

Ninth Light Body

This body of light is known as *The Divine Blueprint*, as it represents the innate perfection of the divine HU-man. It is an energy field that is developed through uniting dual forces and requires an in-depth purification of thought. In fact, this energy field causes the soul to face and Master those negative, dark, forces that the Spiritual Teachers refer to as a type of *mental purgatory*. This energy body processes extreme fears and transmutes them. The transmutation completely restructures beliefs and purifies energies held in the lower mental bodies accumulated throughout all lifetimes. This produces an alchemizing, divine, HU-man Mental Body that develops approximately thirty-six feet from the human body.

This energy field first appears as nine independent triangular-gridded spheres. Apparently, the nine glowing spheres grow in circumference and inevitably morph into one glowing energy body. As the Ninth Light Body develops, it is extremely responsive to telepathy and group thought and progresses to act and influence collective thought and consciousness.

In its early to mid-stages of development, this energy body emits a high frequency violet light that evolves into the alchemic Violet Flame. The Spiritual Teachers claim that the decree, "I AM the Presence of Collective Thought," is its energetic mantra. The refined energies of the mature Divine Blueprint inevitably contract and concentrate in a similar manner to the Eighth Light Body. As it draws its auric field closer to the physical body, within two to four inches, it radiates gold and then a bluish-silver light that reflects the strength of its protective shield.

Tenth Light Body

This is the final level of three protective HU-man light bodies, which is formed through the purification of desires, and is known as the *Diamond Mind*. Because this energy body gathers thought as light, it is a substantive and sizeable light body. The Spiritual Teachers often refer to the three protective HU-man energy bodies as the *Triple Gems* and together they are strong enough to pierce human illusion. Combined with the four higher primal energy bodies — the Fourth Light Body to the Seventh Light Body — the total sum of these energy bodies produces the alchemic number seven. In this septagonal order, the Diamond Mind helps to produce the *Lighted Stance* and the inevitable attainment of the *Seamless Garment*.

Eleventh Light Body

While you are building the energies of the Eleventh Energy Body you may experience changes in physiology, affecting the breath and metaphysically altering sound and light frequencies. Since this is an Energy Body of Transfiguration, you will notice differences in your perception of reality, with the ability to simultaneously experience Third, Fourth, and Fifth Dimension. This is the beginning of sensing the Evolutionary Biome — the experiential ONE of Fourth, Fifth, and Sixth Dimensions.

The Eleventh Energetic is alleged to be quite large and can extend for over one-hundred feet, but typically begins to form a light field of twenty to forty feet around the body. (This depends on the energetic mass of the Ninth and Tenth Energy Bodies.) Its spiritual focus cultivates the essential "stillness of the mind" that inevitably leads to the inner presence of the Mighty Silent Watcher.

As the Eleventh Energetic develops the Master begins to experience bi-location, precipitation (physical manifestation), time and multi-dimensional travel. Its color is filled with the individualized light of the Ray that the Master chooses to serve. This Color Ray is apparent and is readily discernable throughout the energy body. Undoubtedly, the Eleventh Energy Body in its early stages of cultivation produces the Adept who spiritually matures into the Master. The Adept-Master is in constant rapport with the higher planes of consciousness, the Great White Brotherhood, Shamballa, and the ethereal retreats and Golden Cities. Naturally, the Eleventh Energy Body precedes the Twelfth Energetic — the Energy Body of Freedom, Spiritual Liberation, and Ascension.

Twelfth Light Body

The Twelfth Energetic is the energy body of freedom, and it is cultivated in the Great Silence. This process of development is purposely held in mystery, as it a diverse experience for every spiritual Master on the path of liberation. The law of energy-for-energy in still in effect until the great soul gains their eternal Freedom and Victory in the Ascension. Once the Twelfth Energetic

Changes within the Human Aura

As the Ascension Process enues, the light fields of the human aura change and transform. Colors morph into brilliant, radiant tones with each newly developed layer. This induces a remarkable transformation of both the physical body and traditional human psychology, Fourth Dimensional attributes include the ability to bi-locate with multi-dimensional phasing and travel, the experience of spontaneous healing for self and others, and regeneration at many levels. Psychic ability expands beyond conventional norms and telepathy becomes the ordinary means of communication.

is obtained, the shadow presence of duality dissolves, and the Master steps into the vibration and energy of an Ascended Master, forever freed from the need to reincarnate into a physical body upon the Earth. The Ascended Master has achieved the Mantle of Consciousness of the Mighty Alpha and Omega, holding the light and sound frequencies of both the beginning and the end of time, in service to both humanity and God — the Divine Creator.

Sanat Kumara
Sponsor of the Golden Age
Venusian Lord

Lord Apollo
Sponsor of the Golden Age
Galactic Sun

Saint Germain
Lord of the Golden Cities
Sponsor, I AM America Map
Hierarch of Wahanee

Mother Mary
Sponsor, I AM America Map
Manu of the New Children
Hierarch of Marnero, Swaddling Cloth

Kuan Yin
Sponsor, Greening Map
Hierarch of Jehoa

Lady Nada
Sponsor, Map of Exchanges
Hierarch of Denasha

El Morya
Sponsor, Map of Exchanges
Hierarch of Gobean

Kuthumi
Sponsor, Map of Exchanges
Hierarch of Malton
and Gandawan

Founders of the Golden Age on Earth

Pictured above are the Ascended Masters that have played critical roles through the I AM America message of the Golden Age. Sanat Kumara and Lord Apollo are considered sponsors of the Golden Age, including oversight of the building of the ethereal Golden Cities. Saint Germain is the current Lord of the Golden Cities, an office first held by Lord Sananda. He and Mother Mary are the sponsors of the I AM America Map. Saint Germain oversees Canada and the United States; Mother Mary ministers to Mexico, Central, and South America. Kuan Yin is the sponsor of the Greening Map. Lady Nada and El Morya are the sponsors of the Map of Exchanges and protect and assist both Europe and the Middle East. Kuthumi is also a sponsor of this Map, with his guiding focus upon Africa.

APPENDIX C
The 51 Golden Cities

GOLDEN CITY	VORTEX Activation Year	STAR Activation Year	MASTER TEACHER	Ray Force	COUNTRY
GOBEAN	1981	1998	El Morya	Blue	United States
MALTON	1994	2011	Kuthumi	Ruby-Gold	United States
WAHANEE	1996	2013	Saint Germain	Violet	United States
SHALAHAH	1998	2015	Sananda	Green	United States
KLEHMA	2000	2017	Serapis Bey	White	United States
PASHACINO	2002	2019	Soltec	Green	Canada
EABRA	2004	2021	Portia	Violet	Unites States, Canada
JEAFRAY	2006	2023	Archangel Zadkiel, Holy Amethyst	Violet	Canada
UVERNO	2008	2025	Paul the Venetian	Pink	Canada
YUTHOR	2010	2027	Hilarion	Green	Greenland
STIENTA	2012	2029	Archangel Michael	Blue	Iceland
DENASHA	2014	2031	Nada	Yellow	Scotland
AMERIGO	2016	2033	Godfre	Gold	Spain
GRUECHA	2018	2035	Hercules	Blue	Norway, Sweden
BRAUN	2020	2037	Mighty Victory	Yellow	Germany, Poland, Czech Republic
AFROM	2020	2037	Claire, Se Ray	White	Hungary, Romania
GANAKRA	2020	2037	Vista	Green	Turkey
MESOTAMP	2020	2037	Mohammed	Yellow	Turkey, Iran, Iraq
SHEHEZ	2020	2037	Tranquility	Ruby-Gold	Iran, Afghanistan
ADJATAL	2020	2037	Lord Himalaya	Blue, Gold	Afghanistan, Pakistan, India

PHOTONS

GOLDEN CITY	VORTEX Activation Year	STAR Activation Year	MASTER TEACHER	Ray Force	COUNTRY
PURENSK	2022	2039	Faith, Hope, Charity	Blue, Yellow, Pink	Russia, China
PRANA	2024	2041	Archangel Chamuel	Pink	India
GANDAWAN	2026	2043	Kuthumi	Ruby-Gold	Algeria
KRESHE	2028	2045	Lord of Nature, Amaryllis	Ruby-Gold	Botswana, Namibia
PEARLANU	2030	2047	Lotus	Violet	Madagascar
UNTE	2032	2049	Donna Grace	Ruby-God	Tanzania, Kenya
LARAITO	2034	2051	Lanto, Laura	Yellow	Ethiopia
MARNERO	2036	2053	Mary	Green	Mexico
ASONEA	2038	2055	Peter the Everlasting	Yellow	Cuba
ANDEO	2040	2057	Archeia Constance, Goddess Meru	Pink and Gold	Peru, Brazil
BRAHAM	2042	2059	Goddess Yemanya	Pink	Brazil
TEHEKOA	2044	2061	Pachamama	Pink	Argentina
CROTESE	2046	2063	Paul the Devoted	Pink	Costa Rica, Panama
JEHOA	2048	2065	Kuan Yin	Violet	New Atlantis
ZASKAR	2050	2067	Reya	White Ray	Tibet
GOBI	2052	2069	Lord Meru, Archangel Uriel	Ruby-Gold	China (Gobi Desert)
ARCTURA	2054	2071	Arcturus, Diana	Violet	China
NOMAKING	2056	2073	Cassiopea, Minerva	Yellow	China
PRESCHING	2058	2075	Archangel Jophiel	Yellow	China, North Korea

GOLDEN CITY	VORTEX Activation Year	STAR Activation Year	MASTER TEACHER	Ray Force	COUNTRY
KANTAN	2060	2077	Great Divine Mother, Archangel Raphael	Green	China, Russia
HUE	2062	2079	Lord Guatama	Violet	Russia
SIRCALWE	2064	2081	Group of Twelve	White	Russia
ARKANA	2066	2083	Archangel Gabriel	White	Russia
MOUSSE	2068	2085	Kona	Aquamarine-Gold	New Lemuria
DONJAKEY	2070	2087	Pacifica	Aquamarine-Gold	New Lemuria
GREIN	2072	2089	Viseria	Green	New Zealand
CLAYJE	2074	2091	Orion	Pink	Australia
ANGELICA	2076	2093	Angelica	Pink	Australia
SHEAHAH	2078	2095	Astrea	White	Australia
FRON	2080	2097	Desiree	Blue	Australia
CRESTA	2082	2099	Archangel Chrystiel	Aquamarine-Gold	Antarctica

The I AM America Dove
According to the Ascended Masters, the Dove of Peace is a symbol for the New Times and the Golden Age. It is said to represent, "One Age merging into another."

PHOTONS

Symbolism of the Photon
The symbolism of the Photon, compared to the Golden City Structure (center). (Top left) Maltese Cross, 1699. (Next) Bagua, China, 1370. (Bottom, right) Ethiopian Coptic Cross, 20th Century. (Bottom, left) Eight-pointed Cross, Sweden, 1526.

APPENDIX D
The Photon

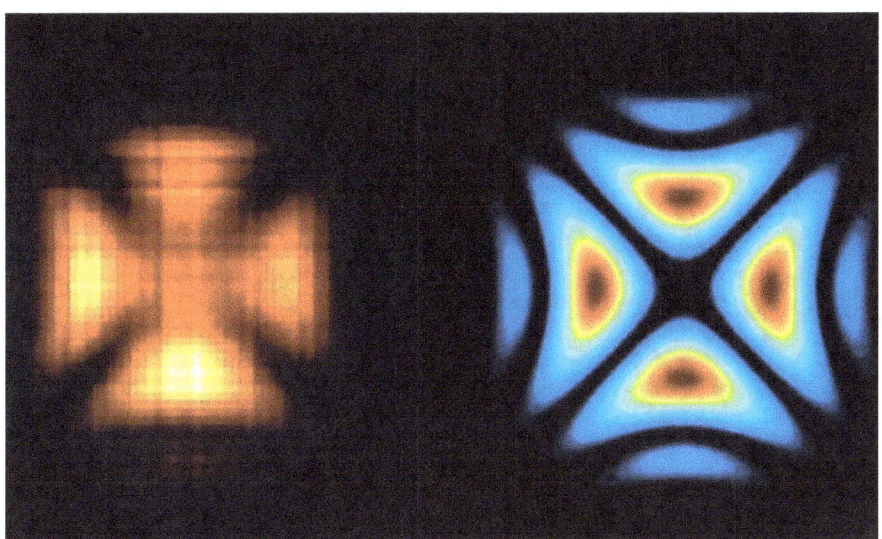

Photon Hologram
Photograph of two Photons intersecting and their interaction creates a Maltese Cross.

The Science of the Maltese Cross

Recent scientific research has created the first ever hologram of a single light particle—the Photon. Einstein resolved the argument about whether light was wave or particle when he created the quantum theory of light that conceived that light exists in microscopic packets or particles that he called Photons. He also knew that the flow of Photons is a wave—so light contains its own form of polarity, and it is both particle and wave. These two properties allow light, as a Photon, to create both refraction and diffusion.

So when scientists wanted to view exactly what a Photon would look like, they knew that they would be looking at something that might be tricky to detect: the shape of the wave fronts of a single Photon.[1] Physicist Erwin Schrodinger, an Austrian scientist, disliked the dual terminology of wave and particle. He set out to theorize in waves only, which led to the basis of wave mechanics, wave equation, and quantum wave function. This corroborates the recent research of physicists at the University of Warsaw. After reconstructing a series of 2,000 repetitious flashes of two Photons intersecting and their subsequent interaction, they were able to create a hologram image and the shape of the Photon's wave function: a Maltese Cross. (*See photo above.*)[2]

The four directions of the Golden City represent the refraction and diffusion of light into the four doorways. They are: Northern Door, black; Eastern Door, cyan; Southern Door, magenta; and the Western Door, yellow.

---

1. Jessa, Tegga. "What Are Photons—Universe Today," December 24, 2015. Accessed November 14, 2016. http://www.universetoday.com/74027/what-are-Photons/.
2. O'Connell, Cathal. "What Shape Are Photons? Quantum Holography Sheds Light." *Cosmos Magazine.* July 20, 2016. Accessed November 14, 2016. https://cosmosmagazine.com/physics/what-shape-is-a-Photon.

Since a Golden City is prophesied to be 400 kilometers or 248 miles high, its elevations contain both terrestrial and spiritual significance that relate to atmosphere as well as planes of consciousness. It breaks down like this:

0 to 28 miles in elevation: Physical Plane (stratosphere).

28 to 191 miles in elevation: Astral Plane (ionosphere, mesosphere, thermosphere).

191 to 400 miles in elevation: Causal Plane (ionosphere, exosphere).[3]

---

3. Zell, Holly. "Earth's Atmospheric Layers." NASA. July 30, 2015. Accessed November 14, 2016. http://www.nasa.gov/mission_pages/sunearth/science/atmosphere-layers2.html.

Milky Way Spiral with Aurora Borealis
An example of the ever-colliding Plasma Field is the Aurora Borealis.

APPENDIX E
Arcing of Ray Forces to Golden Cities

Arcing of Ray Forces to Golden City Vortices

The Seven Rays of Light and Sound originate from the Great Central Sun — or Galactic Center — as it is known in Hindu and Mayan cultures. Ray Forces are an unseen type of energy that are said to function like a non-visible, quasar–type of light. Since Ray Forces control many human evolutionary aspects, they distribute their energies by arcing through the planets of the Fire Triplicity of our Solar System to Earth: Mars (Aries, the spiritual pioneer); Sun (Leo, the spiritual leader); and Jupiter (Sagittarius, the spiritual teacher). Vedic Rishis and Master Teachers concur that the amount of galactic light streaming to Earth as the Seven Rays controls lifespans, memory function, ability to absorb and respect spiritual knowledge, and access to the Akashic Records. Golden City Rays arch primarily through our solar sun and enter the earth's core. The movement of Golden City Vortices draws the Ray Force through, to the center of the Vortex — the Star. Energies of the Ray are disbursed from the Star throughout the entire Vortex.

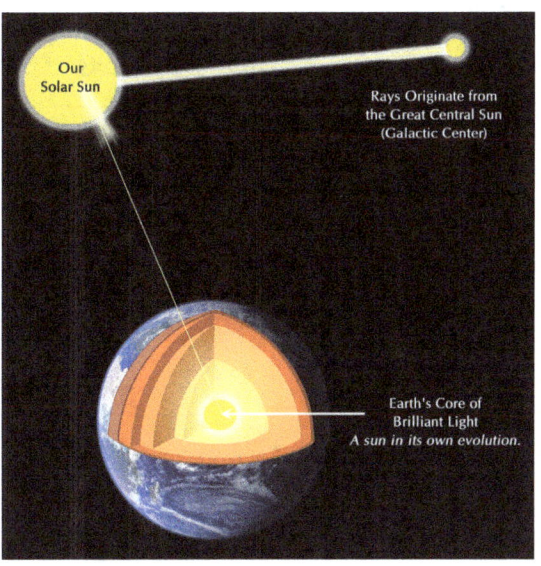

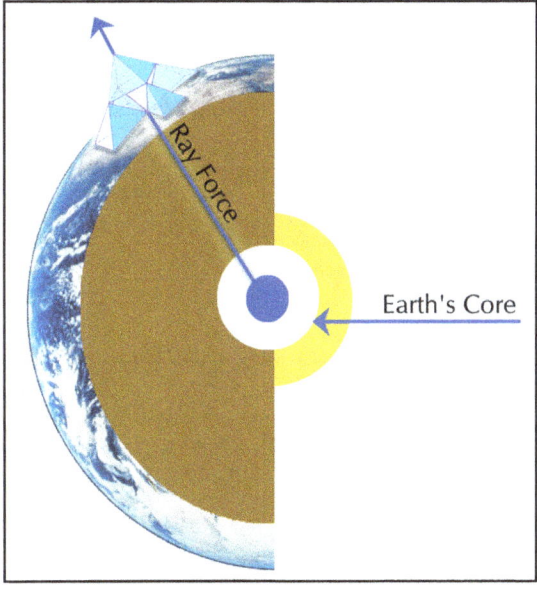

Ray Forces and Golden Cities
(Above) Rays originate from the Galactic Center.
(Next) Ray enters Golden City.

APPENDIX F
The Eight Pathways to Ascension

Form of Ascension: Rapture
Ray Force: Blue Ray.
Provenance: Egyptian Mystery Schools; Christianity.
Techniques: Devotion through belief systems.

Form of Ascension: Spiritual Liberation, "As above, so below."
Ray Force: Pink Ray.
Provenance: Indigenous.
Techniques: Oneness, Oneship, and the ONE through unifying the individual light fields with Mother Earth.

Form of Ascension: Enlightenment.
Ray Force: Yellow Ray.
Provenance: Buddhist; Contemporary.
Techniques: Purification of the Mental Body through spiritual practice.

Form of Ascension: Neutral Point.
Ray Force: White Ray.
Provenance: Contemporary.
Techniques: Balancing the light fields through the principle of love. This influences the Mental Body and the reincarnation process is no longer required.

Form of Ascension: Liberation from the body; dropping the body.
Ray Force: Green Ray.
Provenance: Vedic.
Techniques: Yogic techniques create harmony through healing, and the consciousness moves from the physical body to the Astral Plane, and onward.

Form of Ascension: Ceremonial worship and the Group Mind.
Ray Force: Ruby Ray.
Provenance: Late Lemurian culture; Atlantis.
Techniques: The power of the Group Mind lifts the participant's consciousness into the Astral Plane (Heaven).

Propel Your Ascension

Elijah the Prophet
Nicholas Roerich, 1931.

Form of Ascension: Sacred Fire.
Ray Force: Violet Ray.
Provenance: Saint Germain.
Techniques: The Alchemy of the Violet Flame activates throughout the human kundalini system and dissolves karma. The karmic need for a physical body dissipates. Consciousness moves to the Astral Plane, then onward to the Causal Plane.

Form of Ascension: Golden City.
Ray Force: Gold Ray in tandem with the Yellow Ray during the Golden Age of Kali Yuga.
Provenance: Shamballa, Sanat Kumara, and Sananda.
Techniques: Refinement of the Mental Body through spiritual practice from all of the Seven Rays of Light and Sound, use of Group Mind, and Spiritual Pilgrimage. Ascension is obtained after physical or astral entrance into a Golden City Ashram, Temple, or Retreat.

Hagia Sophia, Istanbul
Many of the ethereal temples and retreats of Shamballa and the Golden Cities mirror famous temples on Earth.

APPENDIX G
Sensing the Flux of Golden City Adjutant Points

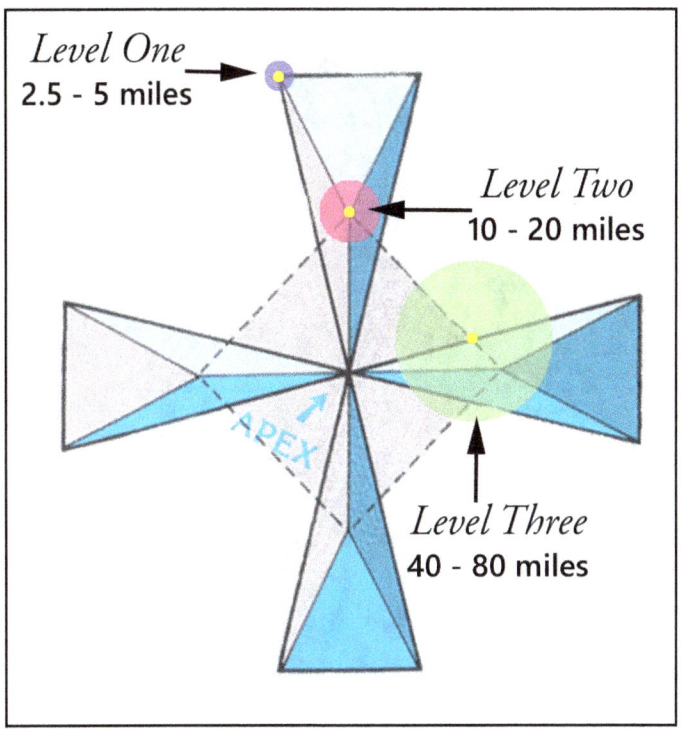

Development of HU-man Consciousness
The development of HU-man Consciousness includes many steps, and as your consciousness evolves from chela to initiate, and onward to the Arhat and Adept, you will notice subtleties and differences with each level of observation, intuition and feeling, and innate psychic ability. According to Saint Germain, the capability to sense the presence of Golden City Adjutant Points progresses through several stages. They are:

Level One, Calculated
The location of Adjutant Points is based upon the use of instruction, maps, and measurements. You may sense the flux of the point within two and a half to five miles.

Level Two, Intuitive — Psychic
You will experience heightened sensitivity as you enter the flux of the point. Sound frequencies and inner guidance, along with instruction from your dreams will be strong. You may identify and read the surrounding landform of the Adjutant Point, and employ the use of pendulums, dowsing, and certain crystals for accuracy. Sensing of the Adjutant Point is from ten to twenty miles.

Level Three, Developed Energy System
You may employ the methods of both Level One and Level Two; however, you will also receive direct contact with the Hierarch of the Adjutant Point. Since you are in constant rapport with the spiritual ashram's Teacher, you may

Crystal Energy
You can develop your Golden City Adjutant Point sensing ability through the use of crystals, pendulums, and dowsing to define and tap into lei-lines.

see and identify surrounding lei-lines and minor energy portals, while receiving both clairaudient and clairvoyant information. You will sense the flux of the Adjutant Point from forty to eighty miles.

Level Four, HU-man

You are adept at Levels One, Two, and Three, and you are in rapport with the Evolutionary Biome of the entire Golden City Vortex, and know its many types of Adjutant Points and Ashrams of Light. You may bi-locate or engage remote viewing to visit a spiritual ashram. Or you may travel to various Adjutant Points in your contemplation or meditation. At this level of development, you receive direct perception and knowledge of each unique Adjutant Point, their beloved Hierarch, and the Ashram's teachings and Ray Force. While this process can be engaged remotely, it is strengthened in Star locations, where you cultivate the ability to enter the Galactic Web and other Golden Cities of Light.

APPENDIX H
Shamballa and Sanat Kumara

Shamballa and Sanat Kumara

Shamballa, which means to *make sacred*, is the Earth's first Golden City. The notion of Shamballa represents peace, happiness, and tranquility. It's a place of spiritual cleanliness and divine dominion; it's the ethereal home and sanctuary of Sanat Kumara.

To understand Shamballa's metaphysical antiquity is to grasp its complex timeline. According to modern occult literature, this mystic metropolis existed more than 60,000 years ago. Other sources suggest that Sanat Kumara's legion of volunteers descended to Earth millions of years ago to build and inhabit the first incarnation of Shamballa. Over its long and calamitous history, the White City experienced a series of cataclysmic Earth Changes that destroyed it three times during sensitive alignments with the Galactic Light of the Great Central Sun. This cosmic susceptibility occurs when the progression of yugas (periods of Vedic timekeeping) move from one age of light to another. Sanat Kumara's followers rebuilt Shamballa twice; the third time the White City ascended beyond the physical realm where it now exists in etheric perpetuity. This is the thirty-sixth Golden City Vortex of Gobi, known today as the City of Balance. It is located in China over the Qilian Shan Mountains next to the Gobi Desert.

The Venusian Volunteers

This City of White served a specific purpose: to save the Earth and humanity from certain annihilation. Stories like this in the Bible abound. Man's faith falters; his connection with God dims; and moral, physical, and spiritual depravity prevail — as was the state of the Earth before the Time of Shamballa. In a theosophical sense, universal principles demand a certain level of spiritual enlightenment for an entity to exist. The Earth and its inhabitants, however, consistently fell short; so a cosmic council of divine luminaries, including Sanat Kumara, voted to destroy the unfit planet.

But the compassionate Venusian Lord wouldn't allow Earth to fall into oblivion. Instead, he offered his light to balance the planet's metaphysical darkness and disharmony. As word spread of the Master's plans, devotees — 144,000 of them — volunteered to accompany their Guru on his karmic Mission. One-hundred of Sanat Kumara's stalwarts arrived on Earth 900 years beforehand to proliferate light; propagate the Flame of Consciousness; and prepare for the coming of Shamballa.

But, Sanat Kumara's volunteers paid a heavy spiritual price: karma. No longer would their Venusian souls enjoy the fruits of constant consciousness. Instead, as terrestrial bodies bound to the wheel of embodiment, they would follow the Laws of Earth — death, birth, and the passing of forgotten lifetimes — as their incarnating light energy lifted the consciousness of Earth.

Esoteric teachings say fellow Venusian Serapis Bey served as Sanat Kumara's first volunteer. With an affinity for architecture, this Master Teacher — along with the Seraphic Hosts he served with on the planets of Mercury, Aquaria, and Uranus — offered to oversee the creation of Shamballa.[1] Serapis Bey, the exalted being of light, performed one of the greatest sacrifices in Ascended Master legend by descending — as the light of heavens dimmed — into a physical body. On Earth, with his legions of seraphim, Serapis Bey oversaw the building of the White City for nine centuries. His sacrifice awarded him the honor of the Divine Architect of Shamballa.

---

1. Tellis Papastavro, *The Gnosis and the Law* (Tucson, AZ: Group Avatar), page 28.

This legend is analogous to the Hindu deity Tvashtri, later known as Vishvakarma, the celestial architect credited with the designing of the Universe and its contents.[2] Vishvakarma represents the power of regeneration and longevity. Serapis Bey later incarnated as Phidias, the great designer of the Parthenon, the classical sculptor of the Statue of Zeus, and the architect of the Temple of the Goddess Athena.

The Design of Shamballa
The builders of Shamballa modeled it after the opulent Venusian Cities of the Kumaras. On a white island in the sapphire-colored Gobi Sea (present-day Gobi Desert), workers erected the Elysian metropolis of light and consciousness. An ornate bridge of marble and Gold connected the White Island to the mainland. They adorned the city with hundreds of white, dome-and-spire-capped temples — that's where Shamballa earned its moniker, the City of White. Against this whitewashed backdrop, the luminous Temples of the Seven Rays and their corresponding hues — blue, pink, yellow, pearl-white, green, ruby, and violet — stood prominently along a landscaped avenue. At its terminus rose the Temple of the Lord of the World, Sanat Kumara's annular, Golden-domed sanctuary. Here, the Ascended Master; three other Venusian Kumaras (lords); and thirty high priests, also known as Lords of the Flame, held conscious light for Earth to sustain her place in the solar system. During his time in Shamballa, Sanat Kumara provided more than a spiritual safe harbor for the Earth's denizens. He also formed the Great White Brotherhood — the fellowship of the Ascended Masters.

Thus, Shamballa defined itself as the earthly seat of selflessness. Divine beings, including the unascended, flocked there to volunteer their efforts and services. To elevate their consciousness, and prepare them for upcoming lifetimes and undertakings, Sanat Kumara magnetized their energies with his Divine Love. Others seeking the Master's Heart Flame trained as messengers at Shamballa's numerous temples. Many of these servants became initiates of the Great White Brotherhood.

The Ethereal City
During Shamballa's physical existence on Earth, ascended and unascended members of the Great White Brotherhood returned annually for sanctuary, retreat, rejuvenation, and instruction for the upcoming year. After the third destruction of the city, and Shamballa's subsequent Ascension to the Fifth Dimension, ascended beings continued this tradition. But, without their aid, earthbound souls could no longer enter the City of White. To gain access, ascended members escorted the unascended to the etheric temples of the City of White by accelerating their Light Bodies during meditation and dreamtime.

For now, Shamballa will continue to exist in the ether, but Sanat Kumara prophesies its return:

"[It] shall remain there until it is lowered again, permanently, into the physical appearance world as the Golden Age proceeds and mankind, individually and collectively prove themselves worthy to sustain it for all eternity. It will be My Gift to the evolution that I have loved, and will remain a part of the Star of Freedom, long after I have returned to my home ... "[3]

---

2. Hart Defouw and Robert Svoboda, *Light on Life: An Introduction to the Astrology of India* (London: Penguin Books Limited), page 232.

3. Tellis Papastavro, *The Gnosis and the Law* (Tucson, AZ: Group Avatar), page 103.

Propel Your Ascension

Message from Shambhala
Nicholas Roerich, 1933.

Mythical Names for Shamballa from other cultures:
Hindu: Aryavarsha
Buddhist: Shambhala, a hidden community of perfect and semi-perfect beings.
Chinese: Hsi Tien, Western paradise of Hsi Wang Mu, the Royal Mother of the West.
Greek: Hyperborea
Russian: Belovodye and Janaidar
Jewish and Christian: Garden of Eden
Celtic: Avalon
Esoteric: Shangri-La; Agartha; Land of the Living; Forbidden Land; Land of White Waters; Land of Radiant Spirits; Land of Living Fire; Land of Living Gods; Land of Wonders.[4]

Sanat Kumara

Sanat Kumara, the venerated leader of the Ascended Masters, is best known as the founder of Shamballa, the first Golden City on Earth. He is also known in the teachings of the Great White Brotherhood as the Lord of the World and is regarded as a savior and eminent spiritual teacher. Sanat Kumara is revered in many of the world religions as the familiar Ancient of Days in Judeo-Christianity, Kartikkeya in Hinduism, the Persian deity Ahura Mazda in Zoroastrianism and as Moses' challenging teacher and the Sufi initiator of Divine Mysteries Al Khdir. C. W. Leadbeater and Alice Bailey referred to Sanat Kumara as the Youth of Sixteen Summers — a paradox to his Ancient of Days identity — and the One Initiator, as the Master of spiritual ceremonies of initiation. According to esoteric historians, Sanat Kumara was one of the few Ascended Masters who revealed his fourfold identity as the Cosmic Christ: first

---
4. Mary Sutherland, *In Search of Shambhala*, http//www.living in the lightms.com (2003).

Sanat Kumara
The Venusian Leader of Shamballa.

as Kartikkeya, the Hindu commander of God's Army; second, as Kumar (Kumara), the holy youth; third, as Skanda, son of Shiva; and fourth, as Guha — a Sanskrit term for the secret place in the heart, as he lives in the cave of all hearts.[5]

Sanat Kumara's Vedic and Buddhist Connection

The leader of the Spiritual Masters of the World appears historically in Vedic religious texts as a rishi who was one of the four sons of Brahma, the Creator. The four sons are born as liberated souls, and in early life take vows of celibacy. Since they are young, unmarried males, this becomes their eternal appearance, and the four sons are naturally attracted to devotional service to humanity. The four sons, or Kumaras, are known as: Sanaka Kumara; Sanandana Kumara (Sananda); Sanatana Kumara; and Sanat Kumara.

In Sanskrit the name Sanat Kumara means eternal youth. Vedic scholars claim that the four sons are actually one incarnation manifesting on different planes of spiritual and physical reality.[6]

Santana Kumara	Supra Cosmic Plane
Sanaka Kumara	Solar Plane
Sanandana Kumara	Earth Plane
Sanat Kumara	Earth Planet

Sanat Kumara's affiliation with the Earth is often referred to by esoteric researchers as the station or office of Planetary Logos — a soul whose evolutionary journey leads them to oversee entire planets. Dr. Joshua Stone describes this cosmic position: "The job of the Planetary Logos is to set up a framework on the physical level for all evolving life forms which allows them all to evolve and grow. The Planetary Logos could be symbolically likened to a mountain and the paths on the mountain which the life forms travel to evolve. The Planetary Logos is also at the top of the mountain so he can guide all life forms toward the top."[7] Perhaps this understanding alone gives explanation for Sanat Kumara's abiding presence in Shamballa, known in ancient India as the true spiritual center of Earth, akin to Earth's Sahasrara — Crown Chakra.

The Vedic epic of ancient India, the Mahabharata, states that Sanat Kumara is reborn as the son of Lord Krishna, Pradyumna. Pradyumna was an incarnation of the God of Love — Kama — and met a Karmic death at Dwaraka, one of the seven sacred cities of ancient India. With this final Earthly Karma completed, Pradyumna resumes his cosmic identity as Sanat Kumara and secures his rightful seat as the Planetary Lord of Shamballa.

---

5. Wikipedia, *Sanat Kumara*, http://en.wikipedia.org/wiki/Sanat_Kumara, (2011).
6. Wikipedia, Sanat Kumara.
7. Joshua Stone, *The Complete Ascension Manual: How to Achieve Ascension in This Lifetime*, (Light Technology Publishing, 1994, Sedona, AZ), pages 178–9.

Buddhist lore defines Shambhala (Shamballa) as the place of happiness, tranquility, and peace; and where the records of the Kalachakra Tantra — advanced spiritual practices, spiritual philosophies, and meditation techniques — are claimed to be safeguarded. The teachings of Vajrayana Buddhism declare the King of Shambhala as King of the World, and this royal lineage descends from the Kalki Kings who maintain the integrity of the Kalachakra teachings. Early Tibetans claim Shambhala's location to be North of Lake Manasarovar, the highest fresh-water lake in the world, and nearby Mount Kailash, which derives its name from the phrase the precious one and is considered a sacred mountain of religious significance to the Bon, Buddhism, Hinduism, and Jainism. This area is considered the hydrographic center of the Himalaya, and its melted snows are the source for the Brahmaputra River, the Indus River, and Karnali River — an important tributary of the Ganges River. It is thought that all of the Earth's dragon currents — energy lei-lines — intersect at Mount Kailash.[8]

Evolution and Training of a Planetary Logos

Sanat Kumara's evolution is said to have occurred primarily on an Earth-like planet located in the Milky Way Galaxy. It is claimed that after sixty-nine lifetimes, he achieved the Ascension. After a brief study of the Music of the Spheres, he elected the path of Planetary Logos. This training was arduous and spiritually challenging and the Master divided his consciousness into 900,000 fragments with each portion strewn to a different planet of the galaxy. From there he wove each individual piece back into the ONE through unconditional love and equanimity. After this great test of Mastery, Sanat Kumara was required to take on a physical body to continue his training on the Planet Venus, where he encountered the cosmic being Adonis who became his Guru. It is claimed that Sanat Kumara was educated in the beautiful Fourth Dimensional temples of Venus for 2,000 years. During his epoch tenure on Venus, Sanat Kumara was assigned to work with the Venusian Planetary Logos. As the Master grew in experience and knowledge of planetary infrastructure and patterns, he evolved his spiritual Mastery to embrace Unity Consciousness, integration, balance, and the power of choice. These important spiritual precepts ultimately groomed the young Lord for his chief assignment: Earth.[9]

Some esoteric texts claim Shamballa existed more than 60,000 years ago, while others claim Sanat Kumara was sent to Earth to build the restorative Golden City more than 18,000,000 years ago. This complex timeline may be explained by the cosmic susceptibility to the progression of the Yugas (periods of Vedic timekeeping) and their correlation with cataclysmic Earth Changes. The provenance of Shamballa states that the wondrous City of Light was destroyed and rebuilt three times. The first Golden City on Earth, however, was in all of its various stages of planning, construction, destruction, modification, and transformation, under the stewardship of Sanat Kumara. His assignment was simple but relatively complex: raise the consciousness of humanity. Should he fail in his mission, Earth would likely be destroyed. The compassionate Venusian Lord offered his light to balance the planet's metaphysical darkness and disharmony.

Prior to Sanat Kumara's descent to Earth, he was given a well-deserved vacation of fifty years. Upon his return, he was given a party where it was announced that Sanat Kumara would be accompanied by the Venusian

---

8. Wikipedia, *Sanat Kumara*.
9. J. Stone, *The Complete Ascension Manual*, page 179.

The Four Kumaras
The four youthful, immortal Brothers are depicted in this Indian print.

volunteers Lord Gautama and Lord Maitreya. Along with the angelic Serapis Bey, these two Lords would play invaluable roles in humanity's spiritual history and development.[10]

As Sanat Kumara entered Earth, his three Brothers — the immortal Kumaras — held their focused energies to assist the heavenly incarnation. Today this is known as the Astrological Spiritual Trinity transmitted to the Earth through Jupiter, the Sun, and Mars. And to this day, energies of the Galactic Center triangulate to the Earth through these planets. While Sanat Kumara's incarnation took effect immediately, another 1,000 years was needed to properly seat the celestial powers and link the supreme consciousness to Earth. During this 1,000-year period, occult historians claim the Earth's atmosphere was filled with electrical storms. Sanat Kumara and his stalwart volunteers patiently calibrated the Earth's energy fields and established their spiritual headquarters located near the Himalayan Mountains, near the present-day Gobi Desert.[11]

Sanat Kumara: Shamballa and the Great White Brotherhood

H. P. Blavatsky first coined the phrase "Lords of the Flame," to describe Sanat Kumara's association with humanity's Divine Evolution. Yet it was the theosophists Leadbeater and Annie Besant who claimed Sanat Kumara deployed thirty Lords of the Flame to accompany him on his spiritual mission to Earth. Classic Ascended Master teachings concur with this legendary story, however Sanat Kumara's group numbered 144,000 Venusian volunteers — pledged to enlighten Earth at a time of collective spiritual darkness.

One-hundred of Sanat Kumara's volunteers arrived on Earth 900 years beforehand to proliferate light, propagate the Flame of Consciousness, and prepare for the coming of the Golden City of Shamballa. Esoteric teachings say fellow Venusian Serapis Bey served as Sanat Kumara's first volunteer. With an affinity for architecture, this Master Teacher — along with the Seraphic Hosts he served with on the planets of Mercury, Aquaria, and Uranus — offered to oversee the creation of Shamballa. Serapis Bey, the exalted being of light, performed one of the greatest sacrifices in Ascended Master legend by descending into a physical body. On Earth, with his legions of seraphim,

---

10. J. Stone, *The Complete Ascension Manual*, page 181.
11. Ibid., page 182.

Serapis Bey oversaw the building of Shamballa — the City of White — for nine centuries. His sacrifice awarded him the honor of the Divine Architect of Shamballa.

The builders of Shamballa modeled it after the opulent Venusian City of the Kumaras. On a white island in the sapphire-colored Gobi Sea (present-day Gobi Desert), workers erected the Elysian metropolis of light and consciousness. An ornate bridge of marble and gold connected the White Island to the mainland. They adorned the city with hundreds of white, dome-and-spire-capped temples — that's where Shamballa earned its moniker, the City of White. Against this whitewashed backdrop, the luminous Temples of the Seven Rays and their corresponding hues — blue, pink, yellow, pearl-white, green, ruby, and violet — stood prominently along a landscaped avenue. At its terminus rose the Temple of the Lord of the World, Sanat Kumara's annular, golden-domed sanctuary. Here, the Ascended Master; three other Venusian Kumaras (lords); and thirty high priests, also known as Lords of the Flame, held conscious light for Earth to sustain her place in the solar system. During his time in Shamballa, Sanat Kumara provided more than a spiritual safe harbor for Earth's denizens. He also formed the Great White Brotherhood — the fellowship of the Ascended Masters.

Sanat Kumara's Return to Venus

Before Sanat Kumara's appointment as Lord of the World, Sri Magra held the office in Earth's spiritual-political hierarchy. After millions of years of service to Earth, Sanat Kumara was granted his freedom on January 1, 1956 and the noble Lord returned to his beloved Venus and his Divine Consort, Lady Master Venus. His three beloved Venusian volunteers — Lord Gautama, Lord Maitreya, and Serapis Bey — had successfully developed and advanced their sacred mission.

Serapis Bey became renowned as the World Architect and was also revered as the Hindu deity Vishvakarma.

Lord Maitreya became the leader of the Great White Brotherhood as a representation of the Cosmic Christ. He is the magnificent Guru of Jesus, Kuthumi, El Morya, Saint Germain, and many other Masters, saints, and spiritual teachers. Through the process of overshadowing (overlighting), this avatar "enfolded Jesus in His Cosmic Consciousness through Jesus' form." [12] The overshadowing process is described by Joshua Stone, PhD, in The Complete Ascension Manual:

"Overshadowing was a process of melding his consciousness from the spiritual world into the physical body and consciousness of Jesus. In a sense, they shared the same physical body during the last three years of Jesus' life. Most people do not realize this. Many of the miracles and sayings attributed to Jesus were really those of Lord Maitreya who holds the position in the Spiritual Government as the Christ. Jesus so perfectly embodied the Christ Consciousness that it enabled the Lord Maitreya, who is the Planetary Christ, to meld his consciousness with that of Jesus."[13]

Using the same technique initiated by Lord Maitreya as the World Teacher, Sanat Kumara overshadowed and accelerated the Earth's spiritual development through Venusian Lord Gautama's earthly embodiment as Prince Siddhartha Gautama, an Indian prince (563–483 BC). Through Sanat Kumara's careful guidance, their consciousness melded as ONE, and Lord Gautama became the

---

12. J. Stone, *The Complete Ascension Manual,* page 138.
13. Ibid.

Enlightened One and qualified as Earth's first Buddha. According to A.D.K. Luk in the Law of Life, the activity and service of a Buddha is, "to step-down the high spiritual vibrations and radiate them to nourish, expand, and sustain the light in all beings during their development on the planet. He is to radiate God's love to a planet and its evolutions; to draw and hold the spiritual nourishment around a planet for all evolving lifestreams on that planet both while in and out of embodiment, sustaining them spiritually and developing their inner God natures especially the emotional bodies. He guards and sustains the flame of the least developed soul, so that it will not go out. A Buddha's work is through radiation, by radiating."[14]

Buddha's radiation of the indwelling spiritual consciousness of humanity paved the pathway for the development of humanity's conscious mind and the Christ activity, or Christ Consciousness in self-realization. Lord Buddha also assumed Sanat Kumara's vacant position at Shamballa as present-day Lord of the World, an honor bestowed from the now seasoned Planetary Logos: Sanat Kumara — mentor, Guru, and friend.

The Spiritual Contributions of Sanat Kumara

The spiritual role played by Sanat Kumara in Earth's history and humanity's spiritual enrichment is truly invaluable and, without question, almost impossible to measure. There are, however, several significant and remarkable accomplishments worth noting.

Sanat Kumara spearheaded the mission to graft the sublime Unfed Flame — a Flame of Divinity and spiritual consciousness — to the carnal human heart. The Unfed Flame urges humanity to evolve beyond its present state of spiritual consciousness through Co-creative thought, feeling, and action and the Divine Tenets of Love, Wisdom, and Power. This empowers humans to achieve a higher sense of consciousness, thereby assuring humanity a type of spiritual immortality. With an etheric silver cord, Sanat Kumara connected the Unfed Flame to every life stream incarnation on Earth. This ensured the development and growth of spiritual consciousness among individuals.

During the 1,000-year period while Earth energies were purified to receive the spiritual presence and teachings of Sanat Kumara, the esteemed Lord performed yearly Sacred Fire ceremonies to clear Earth's etheric atmosphere of darkness. These ceremonies assisted the spiritually awakened to maintain contact with their I AM Presence. It is claimed that many attended these rites, and each attendee would take home a piece of the sacred wood used for the fire — likely sandalwood — to keep throughout the year. These ceremonies forged an indelible bond between Sanat Kumara and those he once served. A. D. K. Luk writes, "Sanat Kumara came ages ago to give assistance to the Earth when it would have been dissolved otherwise. He offered of his own Free Will to supply the light required to sustain her and keep her place in the system until enough of mankind could be raised to a point where they could carry the responsibility of emitting sufficient light ... Now when people first come in contact with his name they usually feel a sense of happiness come over them. This is because of his connection with their lifestreams through radiation during the past."[15]

The sacred City of Shamballa is said to be both "a location and a state of consciousness."[16] Sanat Kumara's service to advancing spiritual students is never

---

14. A. D. K. Luk, *Law of Life*, (A.D.K. Luk Publications, 1989, Pueblo, CO), Book II, page 310.
15. Ibid., page 306.
16. J. Stone, *The Complete Ascension Manual*, page 185.

Propel Your Ascension

The Ancient of Days
by William Blake (1757 — 1827)
Sanat Kumara, portrayed by the visionary artist William Blake as *The Ancient of Days*, holds his spiritual compass as if to engineer the spiritual city Shamballa. This portrait is housed in the British Museum, London, and is claimed to be Blake's final painting, commissioned by Frederick Tatham.

static and always unfolding; and along with various counsel meetings among the Spiritual Hierarchy, Sanat Kumara's purpose at Shamballa is to continue the initiatory process of students and chelas and to provide a haven for those who have successfully passed the fifth initiation. The seven levels of human evolution and their initiatory processes are:
1. The spiritually un-awakened, yet Conscious Human.
2. The Aspirant — a newly awakened, ambitious student.
3. The Chela — the disciple who has entered a formal student relationship with a guru or teacher.
4. The Initiate — personal experience by degree, test, and trial that is encountered morally and mentally.
5. The Arhat — one who has overcome antagonistic craving, including the entire range of passions and desires — mental, emotional, and physical.
6. The Adept — one who has attained Mastery in the art and science of living; a Mahatma.
7. The Master — "human beings further progressed on the evolutionary pathway than the general run of humanity from which are drawn the saviors of humanity and the founders of the world-religions."

"These great human beings (also known by the Sanskrit term *Mahatma* 'great self') are the representatives in our day of a Brotherhood of immemorial antiquity running back into the very dawn of historic time, and for ages beyond it. It is a self perpetuating Brotherhood formed of individuals who, however much they may differ among themselves in evolution, have all attained mahatma-ship, and whose lofty purposes comprise among other things the constant aiding in the regeneration of humanity, its spiritual and intellectual as well as psychic guidance, and in general the working of the best spiritual, intellectual, psychic, and moral good to mankind. From time to time members from their ranks, or their disciples, enter the outside world publicly in order to inspire mankind with their teachings."[17]

In metaphysical terms, Sanat Kumara may be seen as a mastermind of Earth's spiritual evolutionary process. A mastermind contains organized effort — a true measure of everlasting power. Sanat Kumara had the ability to hold the focus of the Elemental and Fourth Dimensional energies to create Shamballa on Earth and then actively engage the help of literally thousands of Lords, Masters, sages, saints, angels, Elohim, and adepts throughout our galaxy. Esoteric scholars claim that the entire spectrum of the Seven Rays are indeed embodied in Sanat Kumara and distributed through the synthesizing radiance of the Lord of the World.

Sanat Kumara Today

Presently the ethereal City of Shamballa is open to all who have acquired the eyes to see, and the ears to hear from December 17th to January 17th on an annual basis. During this time, Sanat Kumara returns to Shamballa and gives guidance to the Brotherhoods and Sisterhoods of Light for their yearly plan for humanity's spiritual growth and progress. Sanat Kumara's visit is accompanied by the Celebration of the Four Elements: a twenty-eight day festivity centered on devotional sacraments dedicated to the elements of earth, air, water, and fire in conjunction with thanksgiving, gratitude, love, friendship, intention, and unity. (For more information see: Points of Perception, and The Celebration of the Four Elements.)

---

17. *Encyclopedic Theosophical Glossary,* http://www.theosociety.org/pasadena/etglos/etg-hp.htm, (2011).

Sanat Kumara is the guru of four of the Twelve Jurisdictions, spiritual precepts on Co-creation designed to guide human consciousness into the New Times. As he gave this important wisdom, his ethereal presence was often accompanied by the Golden Radiance of the Solar Logos: Apollo. Here is a synthesis of Sanat Kumara's four teachings.

Stillness
The principle of stillness is a spiritual teaching that Sanat Kumara shares in the Twelve Jurisdictions.

The Masculine Principle of Cooperation

The spiritual teachings of Cooperation, the seventh of the Twelve Jurisdictions, are taught by both Lady Master Venus and Sanat Kumara. Cooperation is the spiritual knowledge that teaches every individual to honor their divinity. Both Lady Master Venus and Sanat Kumara share their philosophies on this topic. Lady Master Venus gives the feminine point of view. Sanat Kumara elaborates from a male perspective. In his teachings Sanat Kumara states, "Your enlightenment has always been and will always be. That is unchangeable. Bring your conscious awareness, your focus, to the sustaining, and cooperate with yourself in this great magnificence that you are. Cooperate with all others in the great magnificence that they are."

The Principle of Charity

The eighth of the Twelve Jurisdictions is the spiritual guidance to live with love and equity. Sanat Kumara advises, "Charity is a distribution, and it is the equalizer when there is un-justice and inequity."

The Principle of Desire

The ninth of the Twelve Jurisdictions is based on a new perception of desire based on the true etymology of the word. *De* is a French word that means *of,* and the English word *sire* means *forefather, ancestry, or source.* From this context, Sanat Kumara teaches the Heart's Desire is the source of creation. He states, "Desire springs not only from the heart, it comes from the soul, the spark of creativity."

The Principle of Stillness

Stillness is the eleventh of the Twelve Jurisdiction and Sanat Kumara explains this important spiritual knowledge as the Law of Alignment. The practice of this immutable law was likely perfected during the creation of Shamballa, and the Lord of the World states, "Stillness is the space where energy is gathered and aligned to come forth in a manifestation."

Building of the Temple of Jerusalem
Jean Fouquet, 1470.

Propel Your Ascension

APPENDIX I
Temples of Shamballa

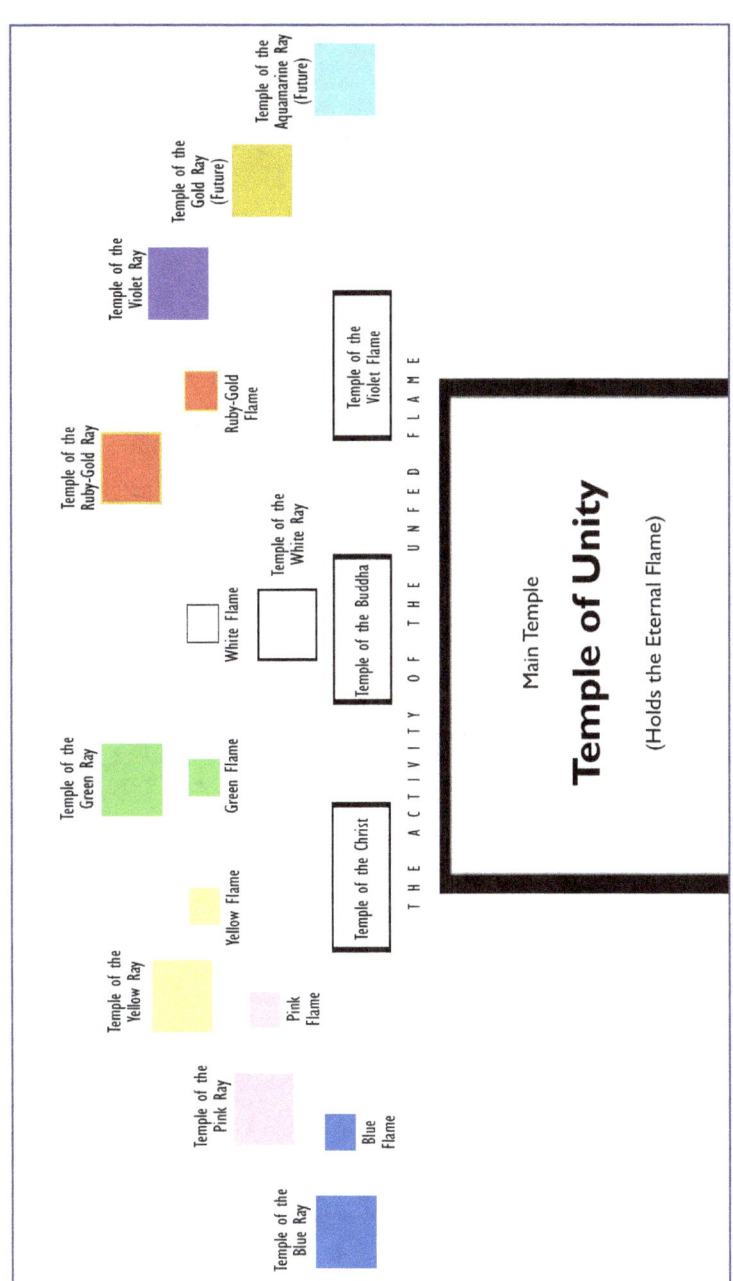

The Temples of Shamballa

Diagram of a group of the many temples at Shamballa. Included are the Nine Temples of the Rays, with the Temple of the Gold Ray and Temple of the Aquamarine Ray contemplated in the future. The Temples of the Rays surround the Main Temple (Temple of Unity) and the minor Temples. The Seven Temples of the Flames hold the conscious activity of each Ray's Flame within the Earth Plane and Planet. The Temple of the Christ, the Temple of the Buddha, and the Temple of the Violet Flame hold the Activity of the Unfed Flame for humanity.

PHOTONS

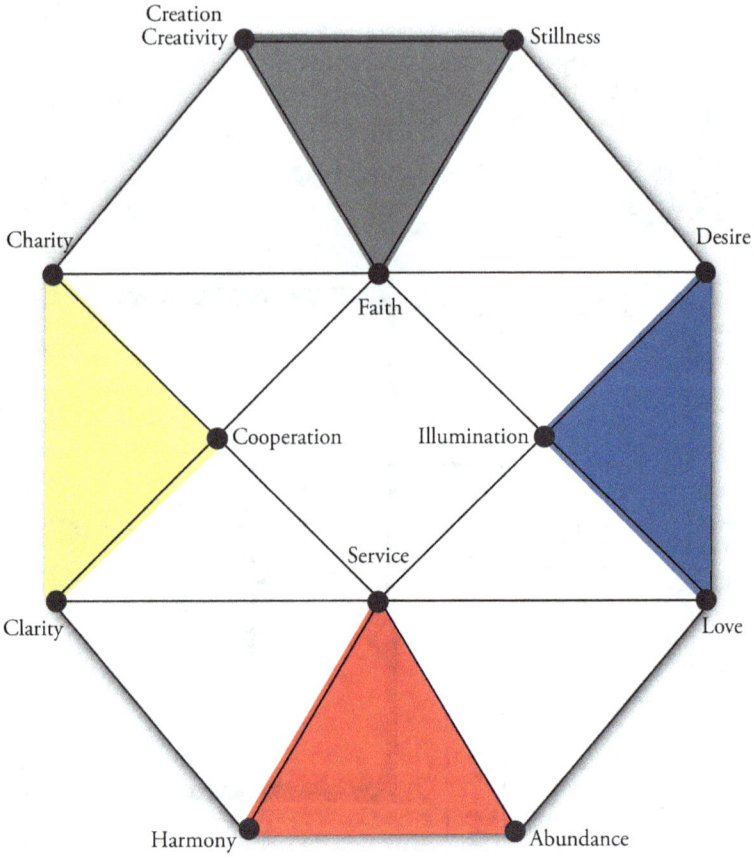

*The Eight-sided Cell of Perfection
with the Four Vortex Doorways and the Twelve Jurisdictions*
The Eight-sided Cell of Perfection as a Golden City Vortex identifies
the Adjutant Points as the Twelve Jurisdictions.

APPENDIX J
The Four Doorways of a Golden City

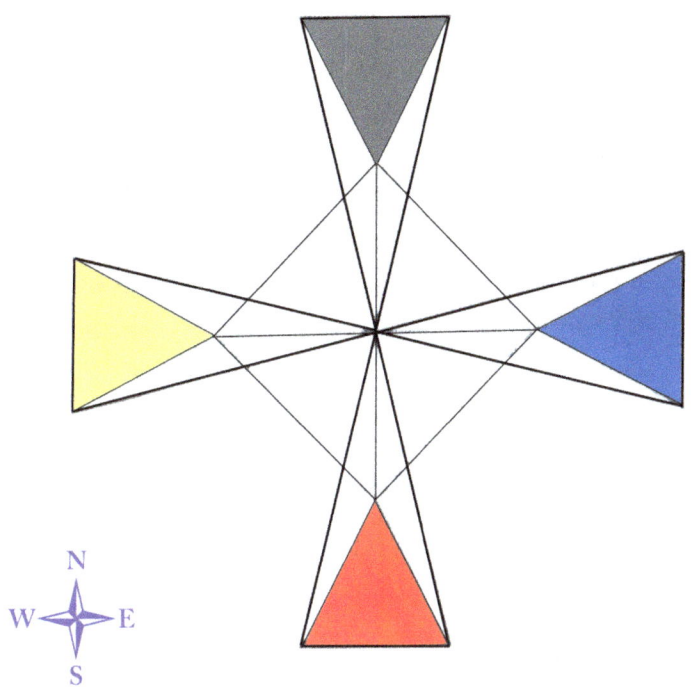

The Four Doorways of a Golden City
The Four Doors, (Black, Blue, Red, and Yellow), are also known as Gateways.

Doors (gateways) of the Golden Cities
The four doors of the Golden Cities signify the four directions, and each represents certain attributes and characteristics. They also represent four spiritual pathways or spiritual initiations.

The Black Door
Direction: North
Esoteric Planet: Earth, Saturn, Mercury
Qualities:
1. Discipline and Labor
2. Physical Abundance
3. Worldly Benefits
4. Transmutation and Forgiveness
Attributes: The Northern Doors represent discipline and hard work. Spiritually, they denote self-control achieved through transmutation and forgiveness. Some say the Northern Doors manifest abundant consciousness and gratified wishes. The prophecies of the New Times foretell bountiful and prolific crops; this doorway is best for commercial and business endeavors.

The Blue Door
Direction: East
Esoteric Planet: Moon
Qualities:
1. Purification and Sacrifice
2. Alchemy
3. Often referred to as, "the Elixir of Life"
4. Friends, Family, Helpful Acquaintances

Attributes: According to the Master Teachers, time spent in contemplation at this doorway can resolve relationship and family problems. Prophecies of the New Times say the Eastern Doors of Golden City Vortices are perfect locations for communities, group activities, residential homes, and schools for children.

The Red Door
Direction: South
Esoteric Planet: Mars, Jupiter
Qualities:
1. "The Healing of the Nations"
2. Enlightened Love
3. Nonjudgment
4. Faith and Courage

Attributes: The energies of the Southern Door induce physical, emotional, and spiritual regenerations; and miracle healings are commonplace. That's why this doorway is a great place for hospitals, clinics, retreats, and spas.

The Yellow Door
Direction: West
Esoteric Planet: Sun
Qualities:
1. Wisdom
2. "The Philosopher's Stone"
3. Adeptship and Conclusion

Attributes: The Western Door terminates the four pathways and acts as a portal to the "Star of Knowledge." Here, Golden City inhabitants will find universities and schools of higher, spiritual learning. The Master Teachers say the energies of this doorway create the hub of civic activity: Golden City government, including its administrative structure and capitol will reside here.

The Star
Direction: Center
Esoteric Planet: Venus
Qualities:
1. Self-Knowledge
2. Empowerment
3. Ascension

Attributes: The "Star" also known as the "Star of Self-Knowledge" punctuates the center of every Golden City. This area, the most powerful of the Vortex, produces self-knowledge and self-empowerment. The energies of the four doorways coalesce here—that's why it's identified as the absence of color, white. Its power reaches beyond the boundaries of the Golden City. Forty miles in diameter, a Star's healing qualities can extend as far as sixty miles. Here,

Golden City Star
The energies of Golden City Stars promote detachment, self-knowledge, and freedom. This initiates spiritual liberation and the Ascension Process.

spiritual growth in the New Times happens: the Star's energies encourage self-renunciation, meditation, and spiritual liberation. During the Time of Change, the purity and beneficence of a Star's power will attract the Ascended Masters, who will then manifest in physical form. And the city's inhabitants will flock here to absorb spiritual teaching, miracle healings, and Ascensions.

Krishna-Lel
Nicholas Roerich, 1935.

APPENDIX K
The Cycle of the Yugas

The Cycle of the Yugas

Vedic Rishis claim the evolutionary status of humanity is contingent upon the quality of Ray Forces streaming to Earth as a non-visible quasar light from the Galactic Center—the Great Central Sun. While the Rays are invisible to the naked eye, their presence contains subtle electromagnetic energy and psychics may detect their luminous astral light. Ancient astrologers visually observed and experienced the Seven Rays of Light and Sound. Their astronomy, advanced beyond today's science, maintained that our solar Sun was in reality a double star. Our Sun rotates with a companion—a dwarf star which contains no luminosity of its own. This theory suggests that as our Solar System orbits the Great Central Sun, Earth experiences long periods of time when the dwarf star impedes the flow of the Rays from the Galactic Center; likewise, there are times when this important stream of light is unhampered. Since the light energy from the Central Sun nourishes spiritual and intellectual knowledge on the Earth, the Vedic Rishis expertly tracked Earth's movement in and out of the flow and reception of this cosmic light. This cycle is known as the Cycle of the Yugas, or the World Ages whose constant change instigates the advances and deterioration of cultures and civilizations. There are four Yugas: the Golden Age (Satya or Krita-Yuga); the Silver Age, (Treta-Yuga); the Bronze Age, (Dvapara Yuga); the Iron Age, (Kali Yuga). The dharmic Bull of Truth—a Vedic symbol of morality—represents this cyclic calendar. According to Vedic tradition the bull loses a leg as a symbol of Earth's loss of twenty-five percent of cosmic light with each cycle of time. During a Golden Age, the Earth receives one-hundred percent cosmic light from the Great Central Sun. In a Silver Age, Earth receives seventy-five percent light and in a Bronze Age, fifty percent light. We are now

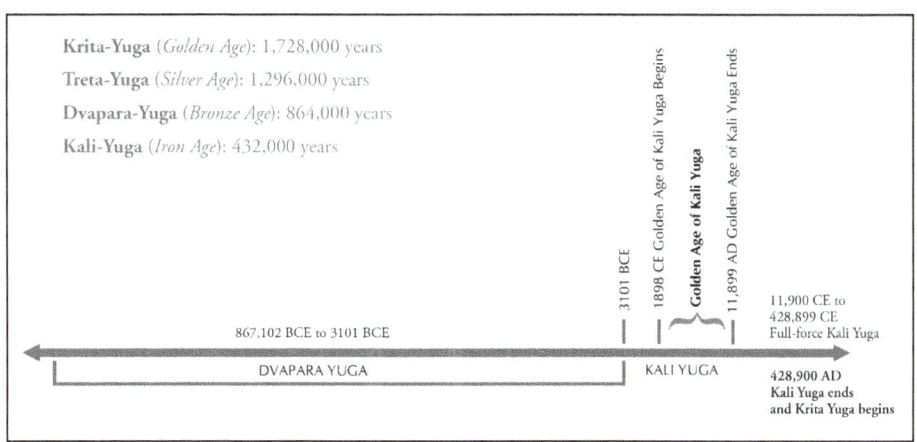

Classical Calculation of the Yugas

The classical calculation of the Yugas is depicted above, with Kali Yuga beginning in the year 3,101 BCE with the death of Krishna. According to Vedic Prophecies the Golden Age of Kali Yuga begins in the year 1898 CE and ends in the year 11,900 CE. The above illustration includes the prophesied 10,000-year period of the Golden Age of Kali Yuga.

living in Kali Yuga: the age of materialism when Earth receives only twenty-five percent light.

The science of Vedic Astrology—Jyotish—was given to humanity in a time of greater light on Earth. Vedic and esoteric scholars speculate that the calculation for the timing of the Yugas may be faulty, and we are living in the infant stages of Dvapara Yuga. This opinion is based on the calculations of Sri Yuteswar, guru of Paramahansa Yogananda. Some Vedic adherents of the Puranas—ancient, religious texts—allege we are currently experiencing a minor upswing of Galactic Light, the Golden Age of Kali Yuga. It is important to understand the Golden Age of Kali Yuga is not a full force one-hundred percent Krita-Yuga; however, the Master Teachers claim it is possible Earth may receive up to seventy-five percent Galactic Light, equal to a Silver Age Treta-Yuga at the height of this ten-thousand year period.

The Four Gifts for Kali Yuga

According to ancient texts, the world entered Kali Yuga, or the Age of Quarrel, thousands of years ago when Maharaja Yūdhisthira noticed the Vedic antagonist darkening his kingdom. The king ceded his throne to his grandson Raja Parikshit, and the court, including its wise men, retreated to the Himalayas.

Wise and benevolent souls knew the dire consequences of the lessening of Galactic Light on Earth, so the Seers, the Vedic rishis, and the Master Teachers gave humanity the following three gifts: the written word, Vastu Shastra, Jyotish, and the science of the Golden Cities.

The sages prophesied that humans would suffer from diminished recall and an inability to sustain oral tradition, thus losing historical knowledge to oblivion—that's why they bestowed the alphabet on humanity. Vastu Shastra, the ancient science of geomancy, was the world's second gift. Maharaja Yūdhisthira's exile in the mountains created a dearth of Vastu knowledge among the Hindu people.[1] So, the ancient practice, in effect, reincarnated in another culture. Legend says Vastu Shastra leaped across the Himalayas where it conceived a child—the practice of Feng Shui. Most of all, the wise men knew humanity would need spiritual liberation from the cycle of death: the gift of Jyotish, the personal and intricate science of moksha (liberation). The ancient gurus imparted this knowledge of the soul's journey on Earth and its relationship with the Astral and Causal Bodies.

Evolutionary Biome and the Golden Cities

Finally, the Golden Cities possess the ability to enhance the Evolutionary Biome—the Consciousness of Unana—through their network of intricate Adjutant Points. This accelerates humanity's spiritual evolution and Ascension Process. Remember, the Golden Age of Kali Yuga is not a one-hundred percent Galactic Light spectrum Satya Yuga. Yet, the waves of increased light from the Galactic Sun and our solar system's entrance into a highly charged plasma field that potentiates Galactic Light rapidly evolves life on Earth. The Ascended Masters claim that the Golden Cities can further increase evolution during this relatively short evolutionary period of ten-thousand years to the heights of a full-fledged Treta Yuga. This is a Silver Age with seventy-five percent Galactic Light spectrum!

According to the prophecies of the Ascended Masters, we noticeably entered the Golden Age of Kali Yuga in the year 2,000 CE. This is when the Earth and

---
1. Sri Yukteswar, *The Holy Science*, (Los Angeles: Self-Realization Fellowship), page 15.

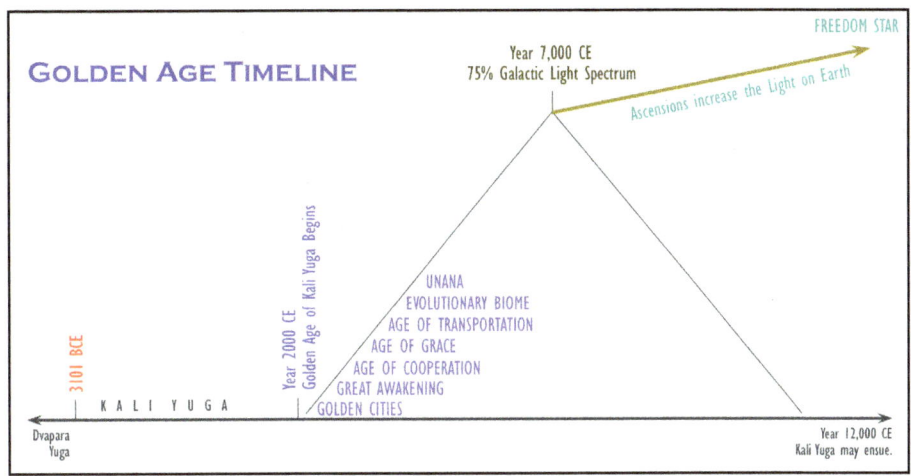

Golden Age Timeline

This chart represents the beginning of Kali Yuga, our entrance into the Golden Age of Kali Yuga, and the anticipated rise of energies. The principles of the Ascended Masters, i.e. the Golden Cities, the Age of Cooperation, and Unana are not presented as a timeline. They are listed to remind the reader of the important philosophical and scientific principles that help to create the New Times. It is prophesied in the year 7,000 CE, energies will either continue to rise, or begin a decline.

humanity began to demonstrate effects from the energies from the Galactic Center, alongside our solar system's entrance into the light enriching plasma field that researchers often refer to as the Photon Belt. We will experience a growth of energies for 5,000 years until the year 7,000 CE. After the zenith of energies in 7,000 CE, the next 5,000 years cycle into a progressive decline of energies until the year 12,000 CE. Then our solar system exits the energy-calibrating plasma field and the Galactic Light spectrum decreases, resulting in Earth's return to a full force Kali Yuga. The Ascended Masters concur that the ongoing evolution and Ascension of humanity may alter this scenario altogether, and evolution on Earth may continue to increase from the year 7,000 CE forward. This is due to the Evolutionary Biome of Ascension on Earth as self-sustaining light propels Earth onward into the Freedom Star. [For more information see: New World Wisdom, Book Two.]

The Vedic viewpoint concerning the Golden Age of Kali Yuga, however, is quite different with varying cycles of ascending and descending Galactic Light.

Yugas and the Yuteswar Theory

Galactic Light is said to regulate the intelligence of humanity during the Cycle of the Yugas, and some Vedic teachers claim the mathematical calculations made during the darkness of Kali Yuga are inaccurate. This is the theory of Sri Yukteswar, disciple of the Avatar Babaji and Paramahansa Yogananda's Master Teacher. He writes in The Holy Science:

> "The mistake crept into the almanac for the first time about 700 BCE, during the reign of Parikshit, just after completion of the last Descending Dvapara Yuga...together with all the wise men of his court, (he) retired to the Himalayan Mountains, the paradise of the

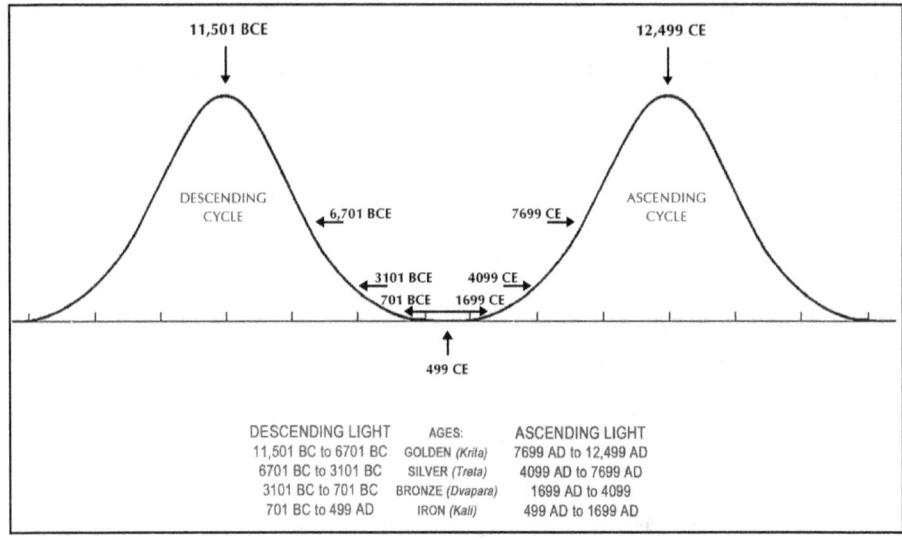

Contemporary Method of Calculating Yugas
This table represents the contemporary method of calculating Yugas, advocated by Sri Yuteswar, taught to him by the Avatar Babaji.

world. Thus there were none in the court of Raja Parikshit who could understand the principle of correctly calculating the ages of the several Yugas."[2]

The Yukteswar Yuga Cycle theorized the use of a shorter cycle with 24,000 years completing a cycle of four yugas. The longer, traditional Yuga Cycle contains a total of 4,320,000 years with 432,000 years allotted to the fourth cycle—Kali Yuga. Here's a comparison, using the Yukteswar approach, Kali Yuga ends in the year 1700 CE and by the year 2010 CE, Earth has experienced 310 years of Dvapara Yuga in an ascending cycle of light. It is also important to note that the Yukteswar Yuga Cycle, also known as the Electric Cycle, is based on the movement of light through both declining and ascending cycles. This descending cycle ceases at the lowest point and then begins an upward motion in the ascending cycle to the highest point of light. From a practical point of view, this makes sense as the longer method of calculation prophesies a Golden Age to immediately arise after the completion of the darkest hours of Kali Yuga. From this perspective, the Yukteswar method reflects a more natural progression of light—i.e., the flow of the seasons from spring to summer; fall to winter; dusk to dawn; twilight to night-time.

According to both Vedic systems, the cycle of Kali Yuga began in the year 3102 BC; however, the longer method presently places humanity's development approximately 5,000 years descending into the mire of 432,000 years of spiritual darkness. The shorter cycle positions humanity at the onset of evolution in the cycle of Dvapara Yuga.

---

2. Sri Yukteswar, *The Holy Science*, (Los Angeles: Self-Realization Fellowship), page 16.

The Golden Age of Kali Yuga

Optimistically, the shorter cycle is a much more pleasant viewpoint, marking an obvious upward trend for humanity's growth and evolution. It is, however, entirely possible that we are currently experiencing both cycles simultaneously. This is the position of contemporary Ascended Master teachings that prophesy humanity's entrance into a cyclic Golden Age filled with opportunity for spiritual growth, enlightenment, and liberation—the Ascension Process. While some global devastation and tragedies may be endured, this destruction is almost necessary in order for humanity to recognize, re-assess, self-actualize, and then re-construct a sustainable paradigm and global infrastructure that aligns and harmonizes with the New Times. Present-day Vedic scholars concur that the timing of the traditional Yugas may be interrupted with a small, minor upward cycle of Galactic Light prophesied in the Brahmavaivarta Purana to occur 5,000 years after the beginning of Kali Yuga, known as the Golden Age of Kali Yuga.[3] Dr. David Frawley, Vedic authority and teacher of the ancient wisdom, addresses the issue:

Sri Yuteswar
Revered guru of Paramahansa Yogananda and the author of *The Holy Science*, a comprehensive outline of the four yugas and their relationship to human evolution.

> "I see humanity to be in a greater dark age phase, because even in the Golden and Silver Ages of the lesser cycle as evidenced in the Vedas, the great majority of human beings appear to remain on a materialistic or vital plane level, concerned mainly with the ordinary goals of family, wealth, and personal happiness. Only the higher portion of humanity, the cultural elite of a few percent, appears to experience the full benefits of the ages of light. This is the same as today, when the majority of human beings live on the same emotional level as before, and only a few really understand the secrets of science and technology, though all benefit from them."[4]

The Hindu avatar Krishna prophesies a Golden Age of 10,000 years to begin in the descending cycle of light 5,000 years after the beginning of the Age of Kali Yuga. In essence, Vedic scholars describe the Golden Age of Kali Yuga as an age within an age. It is important to remember that this period of time is not a full force, or one-hundred percent, Galactic Light Krita-Yuga Golden Age. Instead, this is a minor short cycle of ascending light within the larger

---

3. Stephen Knapp, *Vedic Prophecies*, http://www.stephen-knapp.com, (2003).
4. David Frawley, *The Astrology of the Seers, A Guide to Vedic (Hindu) Astrology* (Passage Press, 1990, Salt Lake City, UT), page 59.

descending influences of Kali Yuga. It is claimed that the 432,000-year cycle of Kali Yuga begins in 3102 BCE; this places the commencement of the Golden Age of Kali Yuga around the beginning of the twentieth century. Krishna's prophecy and the timing of the short-cycled Golden Age give confluence to the I AM America prophecies. According to this calculation, we may have experienced over one-hundred years of this short ascending cycle of light, a little over one percent of the total 10,000-year cycle. It also explains the overall downward and material influence of Kali Yuga on our governments, political leadership, technologies, cultures, and societies. The I AM America interpretation of the Golden Age explains the sudden influx of positive energies that drive the Great Awakening. [Editor's Note: Vedic scholar Stephen Knapp places the beginning of the Golden Age of Kali Yuga around 1500 CE, with the birth of Lord Caitanya (Sri Caitanya Mahaprabhu) who placed a great emphasis on congregational devotional singing and chanting the names of God to elevate consciousness as a means for spiritual liberation. According to Knapp's timing, we have already experienced approximately 500 years of the Golden Age of Kali Yuga.[5]]

The crest of enlightened energy during the Golden Age of Kali Yuga is realized in the year 6899 CE. Subsequently, light energies incrementally decline when the 10,000-year cycle ends in 11,899 CE. At that time, Vedic authorities claim, the full effects of Kali Yuga will ensue. Many prophecies in Vedic texts describe the decline of life on Earth throughout the remaining 417,000 years of the Age of Kali Yuga.

---

5. Stephen Knapp, *Vedic Prophecies,* http://www.stephen-knapp.com, (2003).

Taj Mahal at Sunset. Agra, India.

APPENDIX L

*The Group Mind and
Visualization to Achieve Group Mind*

The Group Mind

The Group Mind is a conscious, intentional energy, created through the visualizations, meditations, and thoughtful intent of a small or large assembly of persons of like mind. Group Mind is often used for a specific focus and directs energies for the collective healing or the evolution of humanity, or to carry forward a spiritual, cultural, or social ideal to germination, development, and manifestation in the mass consciousness. Traditions, cultural mores, and societal ethics drive the heart of the Group Mind. Movement against a powerful and strong Group Mind can face numerous obstacles and disruptions, and the instruction for its creation is invaluable. More importantly, the application of its influence and command can significantly alter polarized and negative social events such as violence, injustice, discrimination, and calm the Collective Consciousness during extreme swings of emotions.

Group Mind is a type of thought-form—a phenomenon produced through strong concentration, deliberate meditation, and purposeful and directed intensity. Fiat, decree, and repeated prayer can create a personal form of Group Mind. Continuity of attention, repeated use of spiritual techniques, and an enduring, conscientious focus reaffirms the life and health of the Group Mind. In its formative stages, the positive thought-form requires care and continuous stewardship. As its energies strengthen and consolidate it is no longer dependent upon its Co-creators, and begins to function independently, with unique, individualized characteristics.

We can feel the energies of the Group Mind when we are present in certain buildings, churches, or historical sites. In Golden City Adjutant Points we can sense the high frequency Fourth and Fifth Dimensional influence of the Golden City Hierarch, the Elohim and Angels of the Ray Force, and the Adjutant Point Hierarch—a Group Mind. Our attraction, affinity, and alignment to this Group Mind often determines the types of events, negative or positive, that we will experience during Spiritual Pilgrimage. Dion Fortune, Theosophical scholar and founder of the Society of the Inner Light writes, "Each newcomer to the group enters into this potent atmosphere, and either accepts it, and is absorbed into the group, or rejects it."[1] Saint Germain often recommends that a minimum period of twenty-four hours is allowed to lapse between visits to Adjutant Points. This interlude promotes personal reflection and for one to properly receive the energies of the Spiritual Migration—an integration process with the Golden City's Group Mind.

Dion Fortune was perhaps one of the greatest advocates for the use of the Group Mind to engender the momentum and manifestation of spiritual growth and evolution among humanity to address specific human problems. She observed that as a Group Mind grows in power and influence, its prominent characteristics, negative or positive, supply additional attention and vital energy, "Anything that differentiates a number of individuals from the mass and sets them apart forms a Group Mind automatically. The more a group is segregated, the greater the difference between it and the rest of mankind, the stronger is the Group Mind thus engendered."[2] Fortune adds, "Persecution

---
1. Dion Fortune, *Applied Magic*, (Weiser Books, 2000, Boston, MA), page 15.
2. Ibid., page 16.

gives vitality to a Group Mind. Very truly is the blood of martyrs the seed of the Church, for it is the cement of the Group Mind."

The power of intent and the focus of intention is the essential seed-thought that empowers the Group Mind. Through its powerful force, participants can be lifted out of confining circumstances, transcend human limitation, and personally expand conscious awareness. In essence, as one encounters a powerful Group Mind, they are elevated out of themselves. This explains the intense feelings one often shares and engages in at sporting and social events, or religious ceremonies—these promote participation in a Group Mind. Later, these same deep emotions can become activated through auto-suggestion, the power of ritual, and associated symbols. Ideally, Group Mind is intended to empower the positive Co-creative nature of Collective Consciousness; however, it is often used for darker means. Mind control and mass hypnotic manipulation through the media are just a few ways that Group Mind is used to disempower HU-man growth and evolution.

During World War II, Dion Fortune began a program founded upon the fundamentals of Group Mind to impede the movement of the Third Reich. Her collection of memoirs, teachings, and archives from this effort are documented in her book *The Magical Battle of Britain*. Her program led to further discovery and knowledge regarding Unity Consciousness and the science of the ONE, whose underpinnings are the Group Soul. She explains:

> "The Group Soul is to a nation what the subconscious mind is to an individual; it contains the cumulative experience of the past. It acts as a counterpoise against all shifts of the wind of changing circumstance so that, instead of being blown hither and thither, the trend of the crowd mind will be steadfast and predictable. But the Group Soul of a nation is much more than a center of stability; it is a source of inexhaustible dynamic energy, and we, as individuals draw on it...The Group Mind, on the other hand, is comparatively superficial, shifting and veering with the surface currents and the winds of circumstance. It can be compared to the surface of consciousness of an individual. But though it is superficial in itself, it rests on the solid foundation of the Group Soul. It is for us who understand the nature of the invisible realities and have trained ourselves in their use, to bring all our force to bear to hold life firmly together as a unified whole, welded to a spiritual basis like a house built upon a rock that cannot be moved."[3]

She adds, "We are all members of one another."

Visualization to Achieve Group Mind

Moderator may lead the following (four) preparations for protection and connection, in order to focus energies together as ONE.

Individual's Participation

1) Begin with the group in a sitting or lying position with a straight spine. Close your eyes, and for a few moments allow your breath to slowly and deeply move in and out. Feel the cool breath coming in through the nose, and down—filling the lungs and creating a state of alert relaxation.

---

3. Dion Fortune, *The Magical Battle of Britain*, (Golden Gates Press, 1993, Bradford on Avon, Wiltshire, Great Britain), pages 4-5.

Illustration for Vyšehrad
Artur Scheiner, Czech Republic, 1863-1938.

Archangel Michael

2) Call forth the Mighty Violet Flame in action by repeating the following decrees together: "I AM the Violet Flame in action in me now. I AM the Violet Flame, to Life and Ascension I bow." (Or) "Violet Flame I AM, God I AM Violet Flame."

3) Decree for Protection: "I AM the God Protection of All Life. I AM the God Protection imbued within the Blue Ray Force. I AM God Protection that is engendered through the Mighty God I AM. We call upon Archangel Michael's Blue Flame of Protection:

Mighty Blue Flame,
I call you forth in full force activity!
Empower me with the
Blue Flaming Sword of Protection.
Surround my Physical Body,
Surround my Fourth Dimensional Body,
Surround my Fifth Dimensional Body,

All my light fields and my Chakra System.
Mighty Blue Flame in Action,
I call you forth, Now!

4) Prayer to Align the Divine Will: "I call forth my Mighty I AM Presence—that Mighty Stewardship of the God within—to align my will to the Divine Will and Holy of Holies. May I serve the plan of the Great White Brotherhood, the Right-hand Path, the Alpha and the Omega—the beginning and the end."

Visualization Exercise to Create the Golden Orb

1) Call forth the Mighty Violet Flame in action, commanding it with the "HUE" in vibration and force. Inhale deeply this Mighty Violet Flame, and exhale with a "HUE" seven times.

2) Visualize a Golden Spiral, like a whirlwind enveloping everyone in the group. We begin at the First Root Chakra, inhaling the spiral around it, and exhaling "HUE." With each new inhalation, swirl the spiral up to each successive chakra, ending again with an "OM HUE" up through all seven chakras. The whirlwind is controlled by your breath.

Visualize the whirlwind emerging from the Crown Chakra—as a spinning Golden Orb of Light, moving up into the Eighth Energy Body.

3) See this Mighty Golden Orb as the source of the tornadic activity. Close your eyes and visualize the orb encompassing the group, and spinning in a circular motion.

See the Orb begin with a lower rate of spin and gradually increasing with each new breath. From the base of the Golden Orb comes a swirling tornado, moving energy between everyone in the group. It is connecting all of the group's higher chakras—the Throat, the Pineal, and the Crown Chakra. You control the rate of spin of the Orb with your Third Eye (Pineal) Chakra. Visualize this.

Golden Orb for Healing

Once achieving this focus, continue to see the tornado connecting our higher chakras as ONE. Repeat this decree: "Mighty Green and Gold Ray, (for healing), stream in and around my light fields leading me into the unison of the Group Mind."

You may choose a location that you all know and gather there in your visualization. See the Mighty Golden Orb spinning over this location. Feel the connection between all and the Golden Orb.

If performing a healing for someone, visualize the Green Ray and Gold Ray and ask Archangel Raphael and Lord Sananda to fully heal this person. You may add other Masters, Elohim, attributes, etc.

4) Gradually disconnect by slowing the rate of spin of the tornado, as it dissipates back into the Orb. Open your eyes and reach out and touch the Golden Orb.

5) Finally, in your Mind's Eye, separate away from one another and call upon that Mighty White Flame of Purity to seal the Golden Orb from discharging back into the Earth.

6) Observe that you are no longer linked at your chakras or energy fields and see the Golden Orb as much smaller; yet, it still exists. Hold the eternal Golden Orb in the White Flame of Protection and Purity. It will continue its function and activity until you all unite again and call upon its force.

Hitaka!

[Editor's Note: *Visualization to Achieve Group Mind,* contributed by Lee Emerson and Tesha Bananda.]

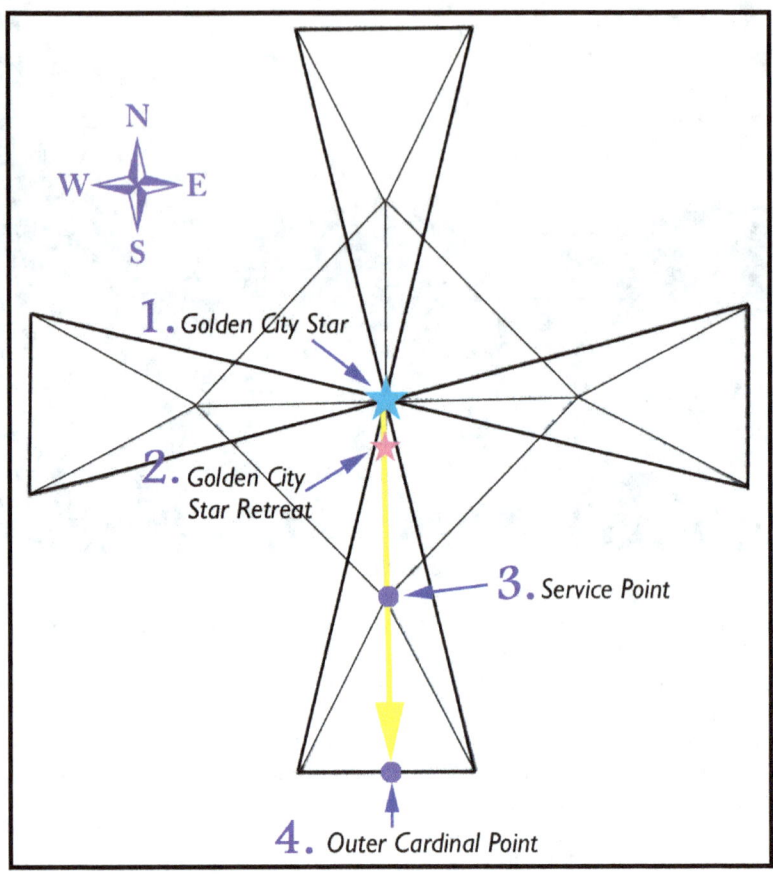

The Four Migrations of the Southern Door Healing Pilgrimage
Southern Door Healing Pilgrimage is for mental, emotional, spiritual, and physical healing of any type. Begin the Pilgrimage in the Star, migrate to the Golden City Retreat Adjutant Point, onward to the Southern Heavenly (Cardinal) Service Point, and conclude at the Outer Cardinal Point of the Southern Door.

APPENDIX M
Decrees for the Healing of the Nations

The *Healing of the Nations* is the Ascended Masters' response to the pandemic and the social and political turbulence of 2019-2021. The following decrees, however, may be applied at any time to assist Earth's entrance into the Golden Age. They can also be spoken aloud or utilized in prayer or meditation while on Pilgrimage to any Golden City Adjutant Point. This series of decrees is especially effective when used in tandem with any Pilgrimage to Southern Doors of Golden Cities, as Southern Doors and their Adjutant Points aid and assist healing process of all kinds. It is also suggested to apply these decrees as you progress through the *Southern Door Healing Pilgrimage* (see illustrated Migration Pattern, left), or while engaging the *Healing of the Nations Pilgrimage*. For more information on the *Healing of the Nations Pilgrimage* and its unique Migration Pathway through Gateway, Cardinal, Convergence, and Temple Points of Golden Cities see *I AM America Atlas, 2020 revised edition*.

Healing of the Nations: Blessing for America and I AM America

In the Name of the Mighty I AM Presence, we decree that the Americas, starting as I AM America and its Seventeen Golden Cities, shall manifest as Nations of Ascended Masters through the Christ Consciousness, to lead the rest of the Earth as the Freedom Star into the Eternal Glory and Victory of the Ascension.

America, we love you!
America, we love you!
America, we love you!
And our Love and call to the Mighty I AM Presence
Is great enough and unending,
To bring forth your perfection now,
And keep it forever sustained.

We charge you, our Beloved America, with the Ascended Masters' Eternal Victory of the Light of God that never fails, and the Mighty Mastery of the I AM Presence, expanding its perfection everywhere within your borders.

So long as the stars remain and the heavens send down dew, so long shall our Beloved America carry the Grail of Light high, and feed the rest of the Earth—Beloved Babajeran, with the Ascended Masters' Outpouring of Freedom and Perfection of the Mighty I AM Presence.

May the Golden Cities radiate and emanate their infinite Golden Light of Blessing above, upon, and within our Earth, so long as our Beloved I AM America carries the Grail of Light into the Golden Age and feeds the Beloved Freedom Star with the Ascended Masters' Outpouring of Freedom and Perfection of the Mighty I AM Presence.

America!
I AM America!
Beloved Freedom Star!
We enfold you in our Mantle of Light and Love,
Within, it is All Power.
We hold you sealed within our hearts,
And within our Divinity,

The Eight-sided Cell of Perfection.
May your Mighty Victory manifest every hour,
To the Glory of the I AM and the Ascended Ones forever!

Violet Flame for the Healing of Nations

Further, we command the Violet Flame in the name of I AM That I AM to transmute and Heal the Nations of the discord, disharmony, agitation, and insurgency throughout the World. May the Violet Flame move throughout the Earth, starting with I AM America, spreading onward throughout the Greening Lands, and progressing to the Lands of Exchange. May the Violet Flame engulf and surround Mother Earth, Beloved Babajeran, and flood our entire planet, transforming Earth into the perfect beauty, balance, and harmony of Freedom Star and its Fifty-one Golden Cities of Light.

> Violet Flame of Mercy, Compassion, and Forgiveness,
> Blaze and transmute anger, apprehension, fear, and anxiety,
> Throughout our World's Nations.
> Archangel Zadkiel and Holy Amethyst, Elohim Arcturus and Diana,
> Beloved Kuan Yin, Lady Portia, and Saint Germain,
> Guide and direct the Violet Flame throughout humanity,
> And liberate humanity and the Earth,
> From shadow governments and leaders of darkness.
> Violet Flame, I AM,
> God I AM, Violet Flame!

> Violet Flame of Mercy, Compassion, and Forgiveness,
> Blaze and transmute fear, abuse, and suffering,
> Throughout our Earth and the Inner Earth.
> Archangel Zadkiel and Holy Amethyst, Elohim Arcturus and Diana,
> Beloved Kuan Yin, Lady Portia, and Saint Germain,
> Guide and direct the Violet Flame for all of Earth's children.
> Free, liberate, and protect our children, and the New Children to come,
> From oppression, bondage, cruelty, and evil.
> Violet Flame, I AM,
> God I AM, Violet Flame!

> Violet Flame of Mercy, Compassion, and Forgiveness,
> Blaze into, through, and around our Earth and her Nature Kingdoms.
> Render insidious and inhumane technologies impotent, powerless, and ineffective.
> Archangel Zadkiel and Holy Amethyst, Elohim Arcturus and Diana,
> Beloved Kuan Yin, Lady Portia, and Saint Germain,
> Guide and direct the Violet Flame into our skies,
> Onto our lands and waters,
> And throughout God's Created Kingdoms of Earth.
> Heal Minerals, Plants, Animals, Elementals, Devas,
> Humans, and HU-mans.
> Purify, cleanse, and restore!
> Violet Flame, I AM,
> God I AM, Violet Flame!

Blessing for our United States Flag

Mighty I AM Presence, Great Host of Ascended Masters, Mighty Legions of Light, Great Angelic Host, Mighty Cosmic Beings who guard our Beloved United States of America!

Charge forth into the feeling of everyone within our borders the Ascended Masters' Consciousness of love and loyalty to the United States of America—our country—the I AM Country, God's Country, the Land of the Light of God that never fails!

Drench them with the Ascended Masters' substance, light, and respect for our flag! Compel everything unlike that within the United States to annihilate itself, this moment and forever!

Through the Hearts and Minds of everyone within our borders, activate light and love at every level necessary to do this now and keep it forever self-sustained.

We thank thee, it is done!

Blessing the Americas, I AM America, and Freedom Star

Mighty, Blessed, Beloved I AM Presence, Great Host of Ascended Masters, Mighty Legions of Light and Great Angelic Host, Great Cosmic Beings, to the Mighty Hierarchs of all Seventeen I AM America Golden Cities, and the Great Presence who guards our Beloved America! Come forth in the full power of the Unfed Flame, the Three times Three, and the Cosmic Light of the Seven Rays of Light and Sound!

Take possession of the Americas, their governments, and their people. Control their resources, direct their activities, give them Invincible Protection, Limitless Supply, Infinite Cosmic Light, Almighty Ascended Master Consciousness, Infallible Directing Intelligence in all they do, and the fullness of Your Power of Divine Love acting everywhere in the physical life of all the Americas.

Produce your Perfection!
Hold your Dominion!
Flood them with your Light and Substance,
And let the Americas stand as Nations of Ascended Masters,
Releasing their Light to the rest of the Earth until all mankind is Free.

To you, our Beloved United States of America, and the Americas, we say:

America, we love you!
America, we love you!
America, we love you!
With a Love that is Infinite, Eternal and Almighty!
Our Love shall guard you with Invincible Power
Forever, forever, and forever,
Against everything that is less than the Ascended Masters' Perfection!

I AM America, we love you!
I AM America, we love you!
I AM America, we love you!
With a Love that is Infinite, Eternal and Almighty!
Our Love shall guard you with Invincible Power
Forever, forever, and forever,

Against everything that is less than the Ascended Masters' Perfection!

Freedom Star, we love you!
Freedom Star, we love you!
Freedom Star, we love you!
With a Love that is Infinite, Eternal and Almighty!
Our Love shall guard you with Invincible Power
Forever, forever, and forever,
Against everything that is less than the Ascended Masters' Perfection!

The Light of God that never fails shall rule forever within the Americas, and so long as the stars remain and the heavens send down dew, so long shall the Americas remain the "Land of Light and Love."

The Light of God that never fails shall rule forever within I AM America, so long as the Golden Cities send their infinite Golden Light of Blessing upon and within our Earth, so long as our Beloved I AM America carries the Grail of Light into the Golden Age and feeds our Beloved Freedom Star with the Ascended Masters' Outpouring of Freedom and Perfection of the Mighty I AM Presence.

I have spoken in the Name of the Mighty Infinite I AM Presence. I have commanded by the Power of the Unfed Flame, the Three times Three, and the Cosmic Light, and so shall it be established to the people of the Americas forever, to the people of I AM America forever, to the people of our Earth as Beloved Freedom Star.

May the Healing of the Nations come forward, may this healing be forever blessed by the Light of God that Never Fails, and held and fed eternally by the Great Host of Ascended Masters, Mighty Legions of Light, Great Angelic Host, Mighty Cosmic Beings, and the beloved Hierarchs of the Fifty-one Golden Cities of Freedom Star!

We thank Thee, it is done!

Healing of the Nations

Through the Mighty I AM Presence, the power of the Unfed Flame and the Divine Trinity of Love, Wisdom, and Power, through the infinite Cosmic Light of the Seven Rays of Light and Sound, the Great Galactic Suns, and the Golden Ray of love and light through the Hierarchs of the Fifty-one Golden Cities:

I call forth the Healing of the United States!
I call forth the Healing of the United States!
I call forth the Healing of the United States!

I call forth the Healing of the Americas!
I call forth the Healing of the Americas!
I call forth the Healing of the Americas!

I call forth the Healing of the Greening Lands!
I call forth the Healing of the Greening Lands!
I call forth the Healing of the Greening Lands!

I call forth the Healing of the Lands of Exchange!
I call forth the Healing of the Lands of Exchange!
I call forth the Healing of the Lands of Exchange!

I call forth the Healing of the Nations!
I call forth the Healing of the Nations!
I call forth the Healing of the Nations!

I call forth the Healing of our Beloved Freedom Star!
I call forth the Healing of our Beloved Freedom Star!
I call forth the Healing of our Beloved Freedom Star!

We thank thee, it is done!
So Be It!
Om Manaya Pitaya Hitaka!

Moving Into the HU-man
Mighty Galactic Center,
Come forth in your supreme light,
Guide and direct this force of light,
Through which I AM!
Guide and direct this light
For liberty and freedom.
Guide and direct the United States,
As a leader of our free world.
Mighty Galactic Light,
Come forward and free humanity,
Into the HU-man.
So be it,
It is now done.

Freedom I AM, Freedom I AM, Freedom I AM!
Liberty I AM, Liberty I AM, Liberty I AM!
Human to HU-man, Human to HU-man, Human to HU-man!
I AM That I AM, I AM That I AM, I AM That I AM!

[Editor's Note: Portions of this information is derived from *George Washington's Visions and Prophecies*, decrees from the *I AM Activity*, and prayers, decrees, fiats, and calls from the *I AM America Teachings*.]

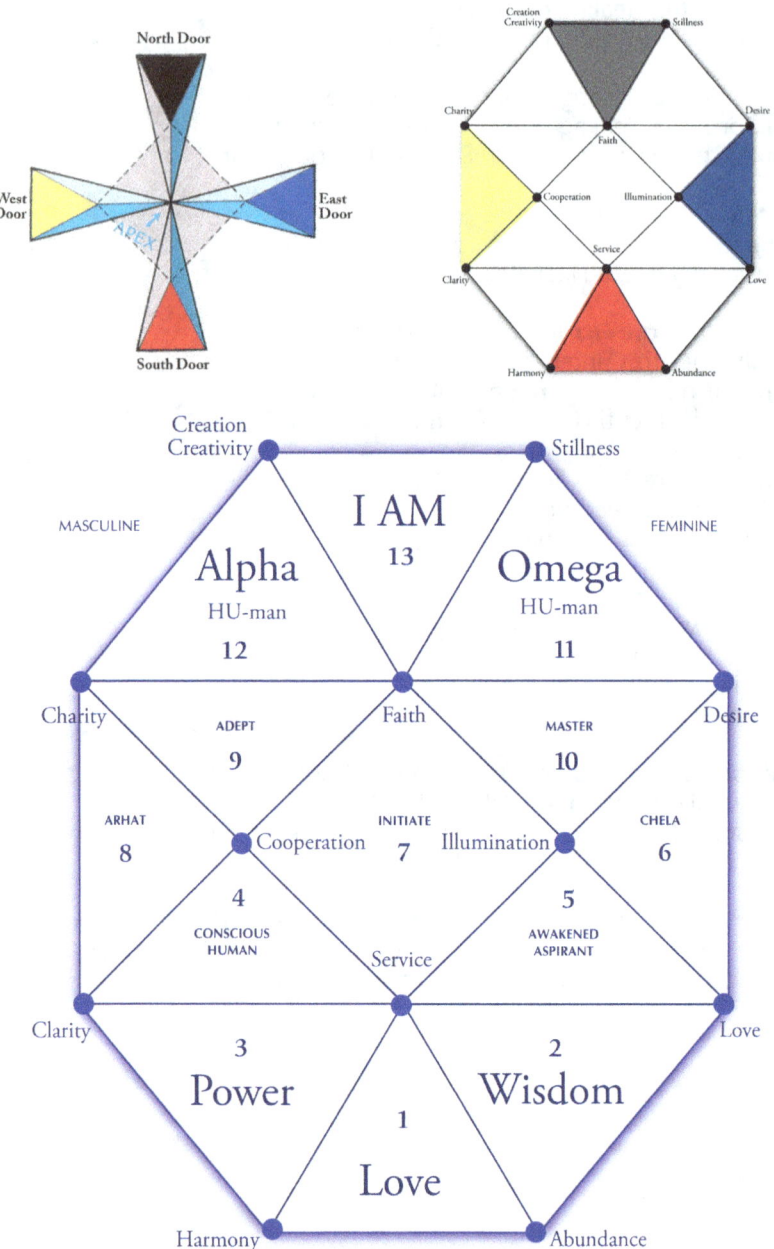

Evolutionary Points and Pyramids.
The Thirteen Initiatory Pyramids (stages) of the growth of the HU-man and their states of consciousness depicted in the geometry of the Eight-sided Cell of Perfection. Also shown are the Twelve Evolution Points (Twelve Jurisdictions). The Eight-sided Cell of Perfection as a Golden City Vortex identifies the Adjutant Points as the Twelve Jurisdictions. For more information on the Thirteen Initiatory Pyramids, see "Divine Destiny," or "Awakening, Entering the Ascension Timeline."

APPENDIX N
Part One: Evolutionary Points and Pyramids

The Eight-sided Cell of Perfection

The Eight-sided Cell of Perfection provides a direct link to the core of the Great Awakening during the Earth Changes and Time of Change. According to the Ascended Masters, within each person lies one perfect cell known as the Eight-sided Cell of Perfection. It is associated with all aspects of perfection; it contains and maintains a visceral connection to the Godhead, e.g. the God within, the God realization, and the God manifestation in all creations and perceptions. This cell is located in the Chamber of the Heart, surrounded by a mandala of energy: the Unfed Flame of Love, Wisdom, and Power. The vibral-core axis (Golden Thread Axis) provides a material connection to the Eight-sided Cell of Perfection in physical form. Located near the Solar Plexus Chakra, it serves as the central energy current that runs through the human body. Here, the aura ties to the seven chakras (energy centers); the core of the planet; and the spiritual over-soul. The over-soul is also known as the energy system that incorporates the Christ-self and the I AM Presence. As earthly energies increase in vibration and frequency, the Eight-sided Cell of Perfection awakens, stimulating Cellular Awakening and spiritual growth.

Evolutionary Points

Twelve Points of Evolution are contained within the Eight-Sided Cell and represent twelve perfected spiritual virtues. Three Evolution Points assemble as a field of consciousness where congruent spiritual laws and Co-creative processes may be applied throughout the New Times. The Evolutionary Points are analogous to the ten Sephirots of the Kabbalah Tree of Life—ten illuminating spiritual processes: Keter (Crown); Chokhmah (Wisdom); Binah (Understanding); Chesed (Kindness); Gevurah (Severity); Tiferet (Beauty); Netzach (Eternity); Hod (Splendor); Yesod (Foundation); and Malkuth (Kingship). Their emotional-psychological qualities bear resemblance to the consecutive Catholic Stations of the Cross (Via Dolorosa—the Way of Sorrows, or Way of the Cross); and Carlos Castaneda's shamanic Assemblage Points. However, it is important to remember the Ascended Masters consider the Evolution Points as attributes of godly perfection that lead to the development of the HU-man, the Evolutionary Biome, and the Ascension Process.

Adjutant Points

The sublime Eight-sided Cell of Perfection is also contained within the Golden Cities. Evolutionary Points, however, are known as Adjutant Points. Adjutant Points form where the lei-lines of the geometric Maltese Cross formation of a Golden City traverse or intersect. Adjutant Points support the infrastructure of a Golden City, both geometrically and spiritually, and assist and disburse the unique energies held by Babajeran, the Ascended Masters, and the Golden City's Ray Force.

Like Evolutionary Points, Adjutant Points produce layers of conscious radiation that is intuitively sensed and psychically known as one moves forward in their unique Ascension Process. Evolutionary Points define the microcosmic development of the HU-man, while Adjutant Points embody and formulate

the macrocosmic growth and development of the Golden Cities. They literally mirror one another through the Hermetic Law, "As within, so without."

The Twelve Jurisdictions

The twelve foundational Evolutionary and Adjutant Points contain the Twelve Jurisdictions. These spiritual tenets are practiced and personally applied in our everyday lives. Likewise, their qualities are magnified in Golden City Adjutant Points. As each consciousness expanding ideal penetrates your consciousness, revealing deeper layers of Spiritual Awakening and Ascension, their commanding presence overlights each Golden City. This powerful energetic transforms the Earth's Collective Consciousness, and shepherds in the Evolutionary Biome and the Golden Age.

Point One: Harmony

The Law of Agreement is the Genesis of the HU-man. Through this vital Evolution Point, individual consciousness evolves through synergy, synthesis, and the recognition of Christ Consciousness.

Point Two: Abundance

The Law of Choice is a vital Evolution Point and develops the individual Will. Spiritual recognition of Universal Bounty and Manifestation leads to discernment and the acknowledgement of cause and effect through the Law of Attraction.

Point Three: Clarity

Clarity is the Law of Non-judgment; the birth of Conscience, and recognition of the Divine Will. The Evolution Point of Clarity evokes the light of the Spiritual Awakening and opens the individual mind to the Co-creative possibilities of purpose and intention.

Point Four: Love

Service is the Law of Allowing, Maintaining, and Sustainability; the manifestation of Light as intellect and knowledge. Cultivation of this point is crucial in order to attract appropriate spiritual teachers, an ancient tradition known as the Guru-Chela relationship.

Point Five: Service

The Law of Love; the manifestation of the Cellular Awakening as Devotion, Brotherhood, and Compassion; the Universal Heart. In the Eight-sided Cell of Perfection this significant point creates the Eye of Horus, a spiritual representation of the individualization process completed through touch, taste, hearing, thought, sight, and smell. Evolution through this vital point births the HU-man, activates the spiritual Kundalini, and the consciousness of immortality through the development of the Clair Senses: Clairaudience, Clairvoyance, Clairsentience, Claircognizance, Clairgustance, Clairalience, Clairtangency, Clairempathy, and the Channel. Spiritual development through the Evolution Point of Service cultivates the apex of indivualization and is critical as the conscience develops and expands. For the Initiate, Service advances the vital contact with the guru—the spiritual teacher.

Evolutionary Point

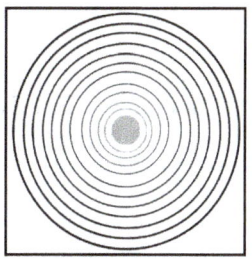

This illustration depicts the circular development of the Evolution Point. It is claimed that after twelve distinct radiations of each virtue is complete, the Evolution Point assembles, or integrates, and the individual's consciousness ascends to the next successive Evolution Point. The Evolution Point appears through conscious focus upon the spiritual virtue; each ring progresses through expanded spiritual perception and spiritual understanding. The Golden City Vortex is similar. As the Adjutant Point matures, its energies are felt for many miles. The beginning stage is a five-mile radius, but later stages can be sensed from a 25, even a 40 mile-radius. This is also contingent on each individual and their development and affinity of Fourth and Fifth Dimensional energies and the strength of the Evolutionary Biome.

Point Six: Illumination
This is the ability to live without fear or judgment; the Light of Awakening as True Memory; Wisdom, Alchemy, and Co-creation. This essential Evolution Point advances the Initiate to the birth of the guru within: contact with the inner light. This prepares the Initiate to enter into the initiatory consciousness of the Arhat.

Point Seven: Cooperation
Cooperation is the ability to live with Beauty, Honor, and recognition of innate Divinity; the birth of the HU-man and entrance into the consciousness of the ONE—Unana. As this point is cultivated, conscience develops into devout principles and ethics which are critical for the Arhat. First, extremes may be experienced; and, as this Evolution Point progresses, the Middle Way is realized as balance, poise, and stability.

Point Eight: Charity
This principle focuses on the ability to live with love and equity; this Evolutionary Point creates a humane detachment that results in spiritual transfiguration. The Eighth Evolution Point is associated with the Arhat—the Buddha who has destroyed greed, hatred, and delusion; and the Adept who has the ability to control the Elemental Kingdom. The Ancient Chinese Sovereign Fu Xi, or Fu Hsi, is an archetype of this Evolution Point and, according to legend, is the inventor of calligraphy and taught the important arts of basic survival to humanity, including cooking, fishing, and hunting. Fu Xi is the acclaimed creator of the I Ching, the oriental spiritual system that governs the arrangement of Heaven and Earth, and is the foundation of Chinese Classical Feng Shui. Some esoteric scholars claim the myths of Fu Xi mirror the western Christian Biblical patriarch Enoch, who is similarly credited as the inventor of writing and a Master of astronomy and mathematics. Enoch means initiated and is also associated with the angel Metatron—the Divine Communicator of God's word. According to Judeo-Christian scholars, Enoch

was taken directly to Heaven and received the title of Safra rabba—the great scribe.[1] This suggests that spiritual cultivation of the eighth Evolution Point of Charity may directly lead to the achievement of the Ascension, circumventing the ninth and tenth Evolution Points. The Divine Tolerance, Divine Compassion, and Divine Benevolence inherent in Charity can quickly accelerate one from Arhat to Adept, and the attainment of the Buddha. This delicate balance of choice and the Divine Will interplays through theme and variation in the higher domain of the Fourth Dimension as its perimeters touch into the causal vibration of the Fifth Dimension.

Point Nine: Desire

The Heart's Desire is the source of creation and enlightenment. This point reassembles the individualization process, and consciousness identifies with individuus: one who cannot be divided. The ninth Evolution Point is affiliated with the esoteric Christian Magus or Mage from which the word Magi evolved. In Chinese culture, Magi is synonymous with the term Shaman or Sorcerer (Wu); albeit this level of attainment and Mastery over the Fourth Dimension has many degrees of realization, including Shapeshifting, White Magic, and the performance of miracles. A Shaman invokes their experience and knowledge through numerous of out-of-body experiences for transformation; a Sorcerer remains consciously aware and invokes spirits to take command of the elements. Both may employ the principle of devotion (bhakti) to invoke certain spiritual deities. While the Arhat and Adept often serve human culture and social order, the Shaman and Sorcerer often assist at a personal level, healing both physical and psychic trauma. As a mediator between the Fourth and Fifth Dimensions, the Ninth Evolution Point of Desire opens the individual heart into the collective heart of humanity and retrieves the Divine Blueprint of the soul. This significant recovery of Divinity is analogous to the myth of the virgin birth, and represents the innate perfection of the Divine HU-man. Thus, the ninth Evolution Point is also affiliated with spiritual archetypes of Healing, Recovery, Spiritual Re-birth, and Transformation: Mithra, Quetzalcoatl, Zoroaster, Dekanawida, John the Baptist, and Jesus Christ.

Point Ten: Faith

This is the important point of Ascension, and its evolutionary location creates complete trust in the Divine Creative Birthright. This position is also referred to as the Lighted Stance and the attainment of the Seamless Garment. This important point in the Eight-sided Cell of Perfection creates the Eye of Providence, or the All-seeing Eye of God. The Rays of Light and Sound stream into the Fourth and Third Dimension from this Evolution Point and epitomize the light and wonder of God. Faith represents Divine Protection, Divine Intervention, and Divine Guidance in the affairs of humanity by the Spiritual Hierarchy. In Buddhism this critical point is known as the Triple Gem, or the Three Refuges. The Triple Gem is reflected in the Third Dimension as the Unfed Flame held in the physical heart. In the Fifth Dimension, the Triple Gem embodies three important processes for humanity's spiritual unfoldment: 1) recognition of the innate Divinity that exists within all; 2) practice of the spiritual teachings that lead to liberation—Dharma; and 3) active membership among the community of those who have attained enlightenment and liberation: the Great White Brotherhood. Buddhists attribute the spiritual

---

1. *Wikipedia*, Enoch (ancestor of Noah), http://en.wikipedia.org/wiki/Enoch_(ancestor_of_Noah), (2011).

PYRAMID	DIMENSION OF EXPERIENCE	PURPOSE
1. Love	Third	Individualization
2. Wisdom	Third	Individualization
3. Power	Third	Individualization
4. Conscious Human	Third and Fourth	Conscience
5. Awakened Aspirant	Third and Fourth	Spiritual Awakening
6. Chela	Third, Fourth, and Fifth	Spiritual Discipline
7. Initiate	Third, Fourth, and Fifth	Spiritual Experience
8. Arhat	Third, Fourth, and Fifth	Spiritual Control, Buddha Consciousness
9. Adept	Fourth and Fifth	Spiritual Mastery
10. Master	Fourth and Fifth	Spiritual Liberation
11. Omega	Fourth and Fifth	Christ Consciousness
12. Alpha	Fourth and Fifth	Ascension
13. I AM	Fourth and Fifth	Ascended Master: I AM That I AM

The Multi-dimensional Thirteen Evolutionary Pyramids.
The Thirteen Evolutionary Pyramids that drive spiritual evolution. Each Pyramid adjusts Galactic Light to specific dimensions and creates certain qualities and attributes of spiritual experience.

consciousness of the Triple Gem to the creation of the "diamond mind which can cut through illusion."[2]

Point Eleven: Stillness
The Law of Alignment is the eleventh Evolution Point. It is considered the most advanced of the feminine points contained in the Eight-sided Cell of Perfection and is distinctively Yin. Theosophists concur that this point is affiliated with the Assumption, or the process of the physical body and the soul entering Ascension. Religious texts of the Koran similarly document Muhammad's physical Ascension in The Night Journey. Orthodox Christian Catholics, however, view this process as the Dormition—falling asleep, or the sleep of human death before entering heaven. Ascended Master teachings maintain that the Point of Stillness or the Great Silence of Consciousness spiritually configures the soul for its evolutionary journey into Ascension and the Fifth Dimension. The esoteric symbol of the resurrection of the spirit through the stillness of Ascension is the Fleur-de-lis which is a symbol of royalty and literally means lily flower.[3] Like the Triple Gem of the Buddhists, some Ascended Master teachings compare the Fleur-de-lis to the Unfed Flame; however, it is more accurately portrayed as the sacred iconography of the Christian Annunciation, Mother Mary, and Archangel Gabriel. The Eleventh Evolution Point of Stillness comprises the final point in the Omega Pyramid of Consciousness and signifies the end of an initiatory series of lifetimes and the graduation of the soul's entrance into the immortal consciousness of the I AM.

---
2. *Wikipedia*, Three Jewels, http://en.wikipedia.org/wiki/Three_Jewels, (2011).
3. *Wikipedia*, Fleur-de-lis, http://en.wikipedia.org/wiki/Fleur-de-lis, (2011).

Point Twelve: Creation-Creativity

The Law of Divine Order is the Twelfth and final Evolution Point. This final point is considered masculine and therefore deemed Yang. Creation and Creativity are associated with the Christian ideology of the Annunciation—the declaration of the birth of Christ by the Archangel Gabriel to the Virgin Mary. In a universal context this Evolution Point is associated with the announcement of the Ascension of a Son of God. Since this is the final point in the entire series of Evolution Points, it may also be a beginning point for the soul's experience in the new realms as an Ascended Master; the point is also regarded as the commencement for a new soul's entrance into the Ascension Process. Creation and Creativity include the spiritual round of births and deaths; beginnings and endings. This Evolution Point is the cycle of life expressed as both the Creator and the Creation. It is the final point that completes. This is contradictory since Alpha—a Greek word—means first. Alpha, however, derives its meaning from the first letter of the Ancient Phoenician alphabet Aleph. Aleph's historical mysticism is associated with truth, the Oneness of God, and assists the Hebrew formation of the name of God as I AM That I AM. The sacred cycle of life through the Evolution Point of Creation-Creativity is best understood in the repeating text of the Bible's New Testament in the books of Matthew, Mark, and Luke that reiterates the message, "So the last shall be first, and the first last."

Evolutionary Pyramids and Galactic Light

Contained within the Eight-sided Cell of Perfection is a pyramidal grid which reflects individual states of spiritual evolution and conscious focus at a personal, microcosmic level. At the macrocosmic level, this grid of Evolutionary Pyramids is contained within the Golden City and is designed to accelerate the Collective Consciousness of Earth into the Evolutionary Biome of the Golden Age.

Each Evolutionary Pyramid is composed of three vital points that create a field of conscious experience. At a fractal level, this field of experience is similar to a regulating lens that affects light and sound frequencies. The Evolutionary Pyramids' presence in Golden City Vortices is created by three vital Adjutant Points, and connected by dynamic lei-lines of energy and is known as an *Evolutionary Field*. This energetic infrastructure creates a large, multidimensional lens that can focus, magnify, refract and calibrate Galactic Light spectrum.

Ascension and the Evolutionary Biome

Contemporary Native American Metis spiritual teacher Thunder Strikes refers to the Eight-Sided Cell as the Octagonal Mirror, and this template of energy resides near the heart and has "eight faces or camera filters called cognitive modes which determine how you will receive light."[4] The Eight-sided Cell of Perfection contains thirteen initiatory Evolutionary Pyramids through which the individual spiritually progresses, develops, and inevitably attains spiritual liberation and Ascension. Each individual's spiritual growth and evolution determines which pyramidal lens tempers life's personal experiences and distinguishes the initiatory spiritual path for that specific lifetime. However, it is interesting to note that many Avatars and Christ-Consciousness archetypes

---

4. Thunder Strikes, *Song of the Deer: The Great Sun Dance Journey of the Soul* (Jaguar Books, 1999, Malibu, CA), Book II, pages 265–66.

Pyramid	Evolution Points	Virtues
Love	1,2,5	Harmony, Abundance, Service
Wisdom	2,4,5	Abundance, Love, Service
Power	1,3,5	Harmony, Clarity, Service
Conscious Human	3,5,7	Clarity, Service, Cooperation
Aspirant	4,5,6	Love, Service, Illumination
Chela	4,6,9	Love, Illumination, Desire
Initiate	5,6,7,10	Service, Illumination, Cooperation, Faith
Arhat	3,7,8	Clarity, Cooperation, Charity
Adept	7,8,10	Cooperation, Charity, Faith
Master	6,7,9	Illumination, Desire, Faith
Alpha	8,10,12	Charity, Faith, Creation and Creativity
Omega	9,10,11	Desire, Faith, Creation and Creativity
I AM	10,11,12	Faith, Stillness, Creation and Creativity

The Thirteen Evolutionary Pyramids and the Twelve Jurisdictions. The Evolutionary Pyramids listed with their Evolution Points, and the Jurisdictions that they represent.

often enter life as advanced Initiates, and move seamlessly through the next successive six Evolutionary Pyramids to demonstrate the attainment of the Ascension within one lifetime.

Traveling to Golden City Adjutant Points and experiencing each Evolutionary Field's energetic lei-lines can enhance states and levels of spiritual development that lead one further into their Ascension Process. Spiritual Pilgrimage to these power points activates a living field of conscious energy and empowers the Evolutionary Biome.

PHOTONS

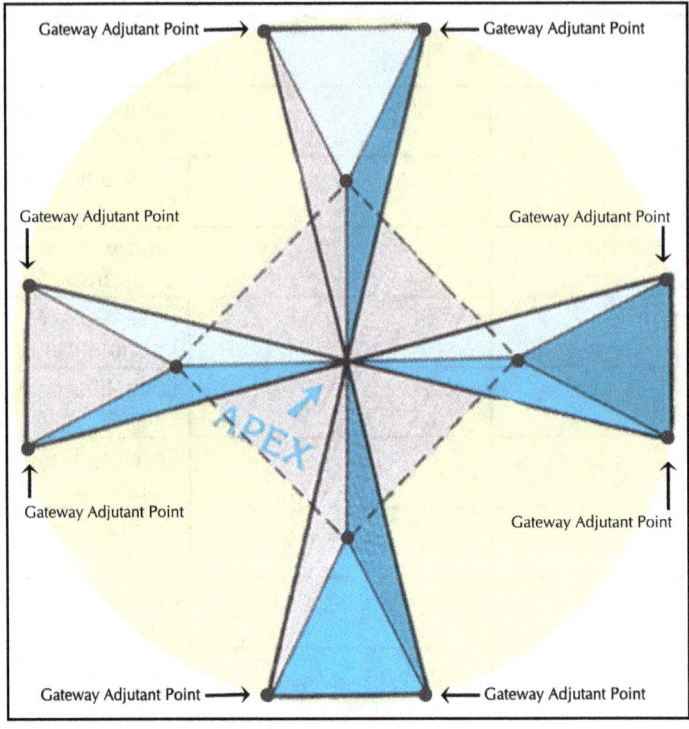

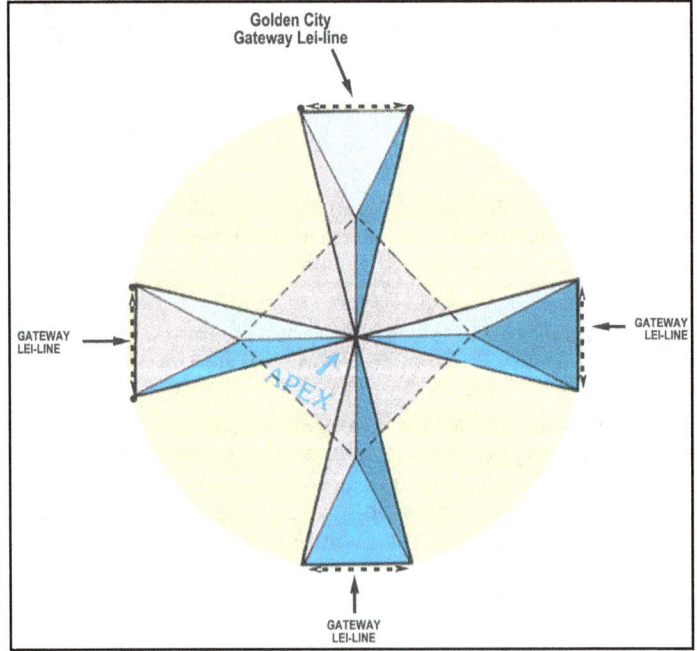

Golden City Gateway Adjutant Points and Golden City Gateway Lei-line

APPENDIX N

Part Two: Golden City Adjutant Points, Lei-lines, and Golden City Ashrams

Gateway Adjutant Points

Two Golden City Points are locations on either side of each directional gateway of a Golden City Vortex and situated to the outer perimeter of the Vortex. They protect the span of each gateway—103.6 kilometers, just over 64 miles. Since there is one pair of points per doorway, one masculine Father Point (electrical) and the other is the feminine Mother Point (magnetic), there are a total of eight Gateway Adjutant Points in each Golden City Vortex, two for each of the four directions. Each power point carries a concentration of the Golden City's Ray Force, and its unique attributes and qualities. Adjutant Points are alleged to step-down and distill the energies of the ethereal Fifth and Fourth Dimension into our physical Third Dimension with strength and intensity. Adjutant Points are spiritual locations for multiple, yet smaller, etheric retreats that exist exclusively within a Golden City Vortex that are overseen and inhabited by certain Spiritual Teachers, Angels, and Elohim.

Golden City Gateway Lei-line

A lei-line is a line of spiritual energy that exists among geographical places, ancient monuments, megaliths, and strategic points. Since a Golden City Gateway Lei-line manifests between a pair of Gateway Adjutant Points—the energy of the lei-line is electromagnetic. The length of this Golden City arterial lei-line is 64 miles.

Cardinal Adjutant Point

This power point is energetically defined by the merging of both masculine and feminine Gateway Adjutant Points. The Peak Adjutant Point is also referred to as an Golden City Outer Child Point, as it contains and expresses a pure and concentrated energy of the two gendered points of the Golden City Doorway. Outer and Inner Child Points produce the energies of Christ Consciousness. This Adjutant Point is located exactly in the center of the Vortex doorway's lei-line, approximately 32.19 miles from either side. [Editor's Note: Cardinal Points, both outer and inner, are defined by the Master Teachers through several names: Peak Points, Child Points, and Cardinal Points. Peak Points are inordinately strong in energetic force, while Child Points carry the purity and love characterized by Christ Consciousness. Your level of HU-man Development will determine the energetics you experience. Both names help to define energies, however, it is best to memorize this Adjutant Point as either an Outer Cardinal Point or Inner Cardinal Point.]

Cardinal Lei-line

This arterial lei-line of a Golden City is formed through energies surging from two points. Point one is the Golden City Doorway's Cardinal Adjutant Point and extends to the Golden City Star, the second point. There are four Cardinal Lei-lines per Golden City, often referred to as Peak Lei-lines. A Cardinal Lei-line is 217.4 kilometers, or approximately 135 miles. This lei-line is especially dynamic, and at its approximate halfway point—about 67.5 miles—Golden City Fifth Dimensional energies can be easily detected and utilized.

PHOTONS

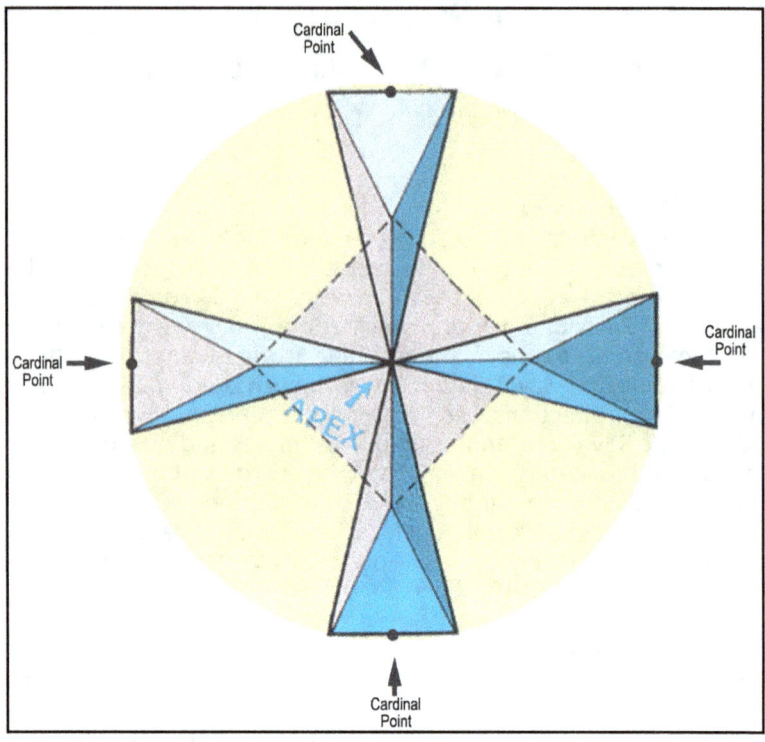

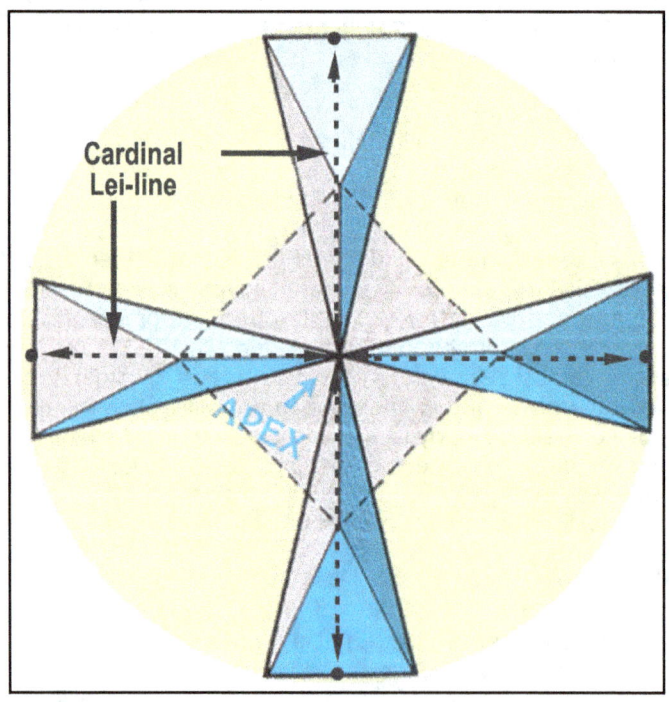

Golden City Cardinal Adjutant Points and Golden City Cardinal Lei-line

Tiger's Nest Monastery, Paro, Bhutan

Golden City Ashram
There is a great difference between an Ascended Master Retreat and a Golden City. An Ascended Master Retreat comes under the guiding sponsorship of the Maha Chohan, the Lord of the Seven Rays. The Maha Chohan oversees both Etheric Temples and Spiritual Retreats of specific Ascended Masters. These are the ethereal homes of the Masters, and where the Master radiates energies to Earth for the benefit of humanity. Spiritual Retreats and Temples often contain the Ascended Masters' focused school of light that radiates their individualized Ray Force. It is said that Ascended Master Retreats contain the records of past civilizations and previous Golden Ages. Many chelas study in these magnificent schools of light in between lifetimes to properly prepare for specific incarnations with special missions for the Great White Brotherhood.

Golden Cities fall under the auspice of the venerated Shamballa Lineage and were overseen in their beginning stage by the Lord of the Transition, Lord Sananda and presently by Lord of the Golden Cities, Saint Germain. Golden Cities are one of the four categories ascribed to Shamballa through the Planetary Hierarchy.

A Golden City Sanctuary is not dissimilar to the singular, ethereal retreats and temples of the Ascended Masters. Golden Cities, however, contain numerous Sanctuaries of Light. A Golden City is an interconnected multi-dimensional network of numerous ethereal ashrams, temples, and retreats, replete with minor and major lei-lines, power points, small and large sub-vortices, powerful landforms and mountain ranges, rivers and lakes, canyons and valleys, streams and meadows, fields and forests that unite energies with our Mother Earth—Babajeran—and the Spiritual Hierarchy. Remember, Shamballa is the notion of living in spiritually perfected community. Each Golden City is fashioned as a replica of the Fifth Dimensional City of White and steps-down the unique Shamballa energies. And each Golden City

PHOTONS

John's Vision of the Golden Cities
The New Jerusalem, described in the Holy Bible's Book of Revelations.

Ashram, Temple, and Retreat is stewarded by a certain Master Teacher, Elohim, Angel, or Archangel of Light.

Currently, many new Ascended Masters and Beings of Light are making themselves known and available for spiritual teaching and healing in Golden Cities. Because of this, Golden Cities are desired locations for spiritual Pilgrimage. Golden City Spiritual Journeys accelerate an individual's Ascension Process and amplify one's spiritual techniques and practices.

Golden Cities function multi-dimensionally and radiate and imbue evolutionary energies that assist and lead mankind into the Golden Age. They promote everyday human spiritual development into the Divine HU-man and onward to Ascension. In essence, Golden Cities are a Divine Intervention for this time—the Golden Age of Kali Yuga, to assist humanity's Global Ascension.

Four Categories

The Spiritual Ashrams of Golden Cities fall into four categories: Gateway, Cardinal, Heavenly, and Convergence. Each doorway contains seven primary Adjutant Points, and each point has their own distinct energy, guiding Hierarch, and Color Ray of Focus.

Located at the Evolutionary Points of the intercardinal directions, lay the four Heavenly Temples of Perfection. These Temples are interdimensional, and entrance is for those who have developed, "the eyes to see, the ears to hear."

There are five Golden City Star Retreats per Golden City. Four of the Golden City Retreats are located at the cardinal, directional radius of the Golden City Star—twenty miles. The final and most powerful point of a Golden City is its Star. The following list breaks down the thirty-three Golden City Sanctuaries of Light:

Golden City Gateway Ashrams: Eight per Golden City
Golden City Cardinal Ashrams: Four per Golden City
Golden City Heavenly Ashrams: Four per Golden City
Golden City Convergence Ashrams: Eight per Golden City
Golden City Temples of Perfection: Four per Golden City
Golden City Star Retreats: Five per Golden City

Gateway Ashrams

Golden City Gateway Ashrams are focused at each Adjutant Point/ Evolutionary Point. (For more information on Evolutionary Points see: Section Sixteen, Part One.) The eight Gateway Ashrams are:

1. Gateway to Harmony Ashram
2. Gateway to Abundance Ashram
3. Gateway to Love Ashram
4. Gateway to Desire Ashram
5. Gateway to Clarity Ashram
6. Gateway to Charity Ashram
7. Gateway to Stillness Ashram
8. Gateway to Creation/Creativity Ashram

Cardinal Ashram

Golden City Cardinal Ashrams are focused at the Outer Marriage-Child Points, also known as Peak or Cardinal Points. (For more information see: Golden City Series, Book Four, Sacred Energies.) These four Ashrams unite the energies of two Evolutionary Points per Golden City Doorway and are located on the cardinal directions of each Golden City.

1. The Cardinal Ashram of Harmony and Abundance
2. The Cardinal Ashram of Love and Desire
3. The Cardinal Ashram of Clarity and Charity
4. The Cardinal Ashram of Stillness and Creation/Creativity

Remember, Gateway Ashrams and Cardinal Ashrams can often be identified through physical anomalies and distinct energetic characteristics. Adjutant Points can flux, with a five to ten mile circumference; however, they often physically affix to dynamic landforms and bodies of water. [Editor's Note: As you begin to identify Adjutant Point locations, use a five to ten mile flux. As you develop your HU-man sensing ability, you may detect the Adjutant Point's presence up to forty miles radius.]

Heavenly Ashram

Golden City Heavenly Ashrams are Fourth Dimensional. These Adjutant Points and their inherent Ashrams of Light assist the Deva and Elemental Kingdoms. Their presence and life force are remarkably robust. Since these points shift our human consciousness into Fourth Dimension, we often experience Time Compaction or Dimensional Rifting while visiting these points. These are extraordinary locations for meditation, astral travel, and lucid dreaming. Golden City Heavenly Ashrams have concentrated energies that can align human energy fields to receive contact through the super-senses. Golden City Heavenly Ashrams are located at the Inner Marriage-Child Points. They are:

1. Heavenly Service Ashram
2. Heavenly Illumination Ashram
3. Heavenly Cooperation Ashram
4. Heavenly Faith Ashram

Convergence Ashram

Golden City Convergence Ashrams are similar in energy to the Cardinal Ashrams as they unite Evolutionary Point energies. There are two per doorway:

1. Convergence Ashram of Service and Cooperation
2. Convergence Ashram of Service and Illumination
3. Convergence Ashram of Illumination and Service
4. Convergence Ashram of Illumination and Faith
5. Convergence Ashram of Cooperation and Service
6. Convergence Ashram of Cooperation and Faith
7. Convergence Ashram of Faith and Cooperation
8. Convergence Ashram of Faith and Illumination

What is the subtle difference between an Ashram of Service and Cooperation and an Ashram of Cooperation and Service? The difference is the location—the directional location of the Golden City Doorway. The first Ashram is located in a Southern Door; the latter is located in a Western Door. A Southern Door is known as the Red Door of Healing; a Western Door is known as the Yellow Door of Knowledge.

Heavenly Temple Ashram

Located between each Golden City Convergence Ashram is yet another set of intercardinal power points. These are the physical locations of ethereal temples that prepare the soul to enter into the five Star Retreats. These locations are known as the four Golden City Temples of Perfection, and their energies are primarily Fourth and Fifth Dimension.

1. Temple of Service and Cooperation
2. Temple of Cooperation and Faith
3. Temple of Faith and Illumination
4. Temple of Illumination and Service

The Star Retreats

The Four Golden City Star Retreats comprise the final set of magnificent Golden City Sanctuaries. They work directly with the primary Ray Force of the Golden City. These Golden City Retreats function mainly at the Fifth Dimensional level and are extremely evolved in their energy and vibration. Unless you are attuned to their frequency, they may be difficult to detect physically—best to identify in dream, psychic, or trance states. The outer four Retreats are located at approximately twenty miles, in the four cardinal directions from the center of the Golden City Star. They are:

1. Southern Star Retreat
2. Eastern Star Retreat
3. Western Star Retreat
4. Northern Star Retreat

The Golden City Star

The final, fifth Golden City Sanctuary is the Golden City Star that functions at every level of spiritual energy, with Third, Fourth, and Fifth Dimensional frequencies. The Star coalesces and refines the energies of all of the doorways and is perhaps one of the best locations to seek spiritual refuge, retreat for

Song of Shambhala
Nicholas Roerich, 1943.

reinvigorating vacations and weekends, and to perform ceremony and recite decree in groups.

In total, there are thirty-three Sanctuaries of Light dispersed throughout every Golden City. The first twelve Ashrams oversee the outer mysteries (the Gateway and Cardinal Ashrams), and the second twelve administer initiations into the inner mysteries (the Heavenly and Convergence Ashrams). The four Temples of Perfection ready the soul on its path of Innate Divinity and Perfection, preparing it for the liberating energies of the Star. The five Golden City Star Retreats assist the divine HU-man in their Ascension Process, with the fifth and final retreat—the Star—the most powerful. Illustrations follow.

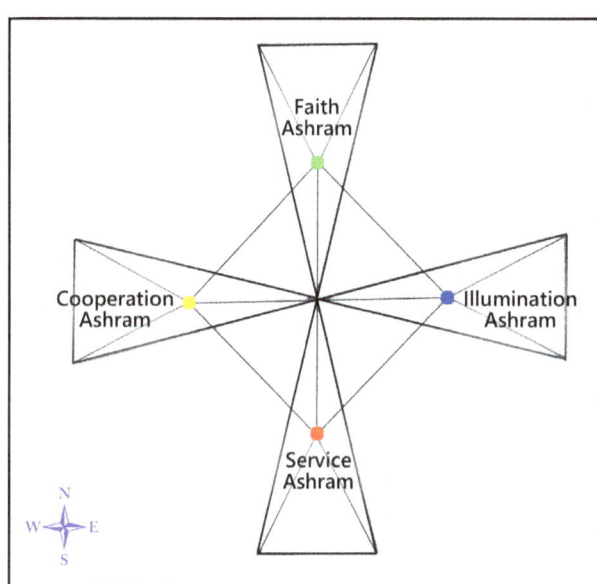

Heavenly Ashram Point (Inner Cardinal)

Heavenly Ashram Points (left) are also known as Inner Cardinal or Inner Child Points. They are especially dynamic, as they imbue the energies of powerful Evolutionary Points through the Twelve Jurisdictions—Faith, Illumination, Service, and Cooperation. They are located approximately 67.5 miles due North, South, East, or West from the Outer Cardinal Point. Locating a

PHOTONS

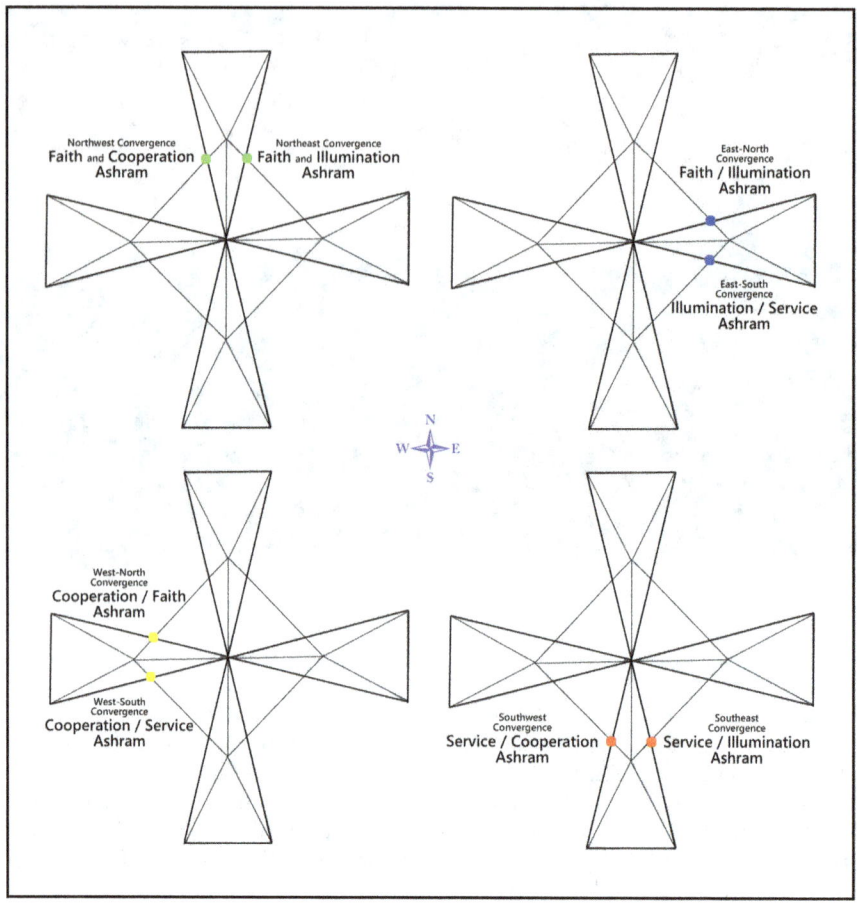

Heavenly Ashram requires developed HU-man skills as these locations contain a combination of Third, Fourth, and Fifth Dimensional Golden City energies. Heavenly Ashrams bridge Fourth and Fifth Dimensional frequencies. Hence, their name "Heavenly." Once discovered, you will notice that their energy is peaceful and sublime, and these are excellent locations for all types of spiritual practice, especially meditation and prayer

Saint Germain teaches, "This is where a direct interface exists between Third Dimension and Fourth Dimension. This causes one to begin to sense those great Fourth Dimensional Kingdoms of Creation: the Elemental Kingdom, the Deva Kingdom, and also to some degree the Great Beings—the Elohim of Creation. This also serves a great impetus for the human aura itself. It allows you to begin to understand your more intuitive side...your feeling nature in its state of evolution. This is where many of the psychic abilities begin to express themselves such as telepathy, known as the clair-senses. And these points are ideally used to help develop a rapport with not only the Deva and the Elemental Kingdoms, but also when you are working to achieve connection with your own Master Teacher."

Convergence Ashram Point

Convergence Ashram Points (above) are located at a ninety degree angle (intercardinal) from each Heavenly Ashram Point. According to the Ascended Masters the Convergence Point Hierarchs are the Mighty Elohim. "They have a type of direct influence upon the physical aspect of life in that Golden City. That is, they control to some degree the weather, the winds, the geologic formations, and the mighty elements as they move through the Golden City Vortices." There are two Convergence Ashrams per Heavenly Point, so there are a total of eight Convergence Ashrams Points per Golden City Vortex. The eight Convergence Points unite the energies of the vital Evolutionary Points of Faith, Illumination, Service, and Cooperation. Like the Heavenly Points the Convergence Points blend Third, Fourth, and Fifth Dimensional energies, although their focus is primarily upon Fourth and Fifth Dimensional experience. Because of this, developed HU-man skills are needed to accurately locate these Golden City power points.

Golden City Temple Points

The four Temple Points (right) of each Golden City are located on the intercardinal directions—Northeast, Southeast, Southwest, and Northwest. The Golden City Hierarchs of each Temple Point is an angel of the Ray Force affiliated with that Golden City. Saint Germain explains, "Temple Points, you see, are where the Angelic Kingdoms reside in each Golden City. For you see, in my Golden City of Wahanee, at these four points are

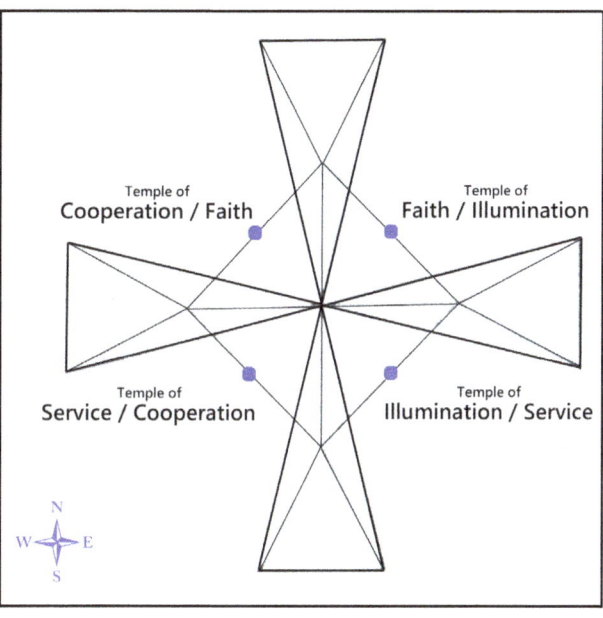

the residences at the ethereal level of the Great Violet Flame Angels. For this reason alone, these points can be sought for healing, and in the future as energies begin to accelerate into this Great Golden Age, many will travel to these points where they can experience spontaneous healing. Each of the Angelic Kingdoms qualifies themselves along the Ray Forces, each with their own understanding, intent, and purpose."

Temple Points are inordinately ethereal, and their energies are Fifth Dimensional, although their presence has an inordinate influence on the Elemental and Deva Kingdoms and Third Dimension surrrounding and overlighted by their presence. Convergence Points aid and protect the Golden City Temple. The Temples, in turn, protect the Golden City Retreats

Prayer, devotions, contemplation, meditation, and spiritual ceremonies are encouraged in these unique, sacred locations.

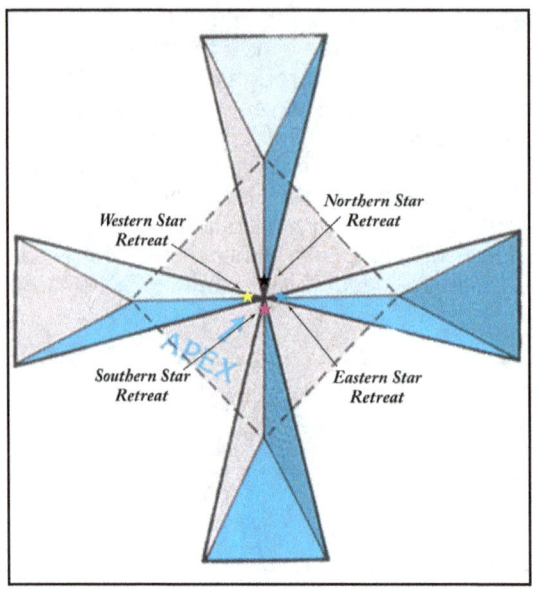

The Star Retreats

Next to the Golden City Star, the Star Retreats (below) contain and calibrate the highest levels of Galactic Light of the primary Ray Force assigned to each Golden City Vortex. There are four retreats total, with one for each of the Golden City Doors: the Black Door, the Blue Door, the Red Door, and the Yellow Door. These pristine Ashrams are located twenty miles on the Cardinal Lei-line from the Star of each Golden City. Since their energies are Fifth Dimensional, they can be sensed for five to ten miles radius and add tremendous force to the energetic infrastructure of the Star.

The Star Retreats shield and defend the Golden City Hierarch and are stewarded by Beings of Light who focus upon devotion, loyalty, and unwavering commitment to their Golden City Hierarch. They are also fierce warriors for the light. Because of this many are Archangels; however, some Ashram Hierarchs were devotees of various Golden City Hierarchs throughout Earthly incarnations. Saint Germain explains, "The Star Retreats protect the Mighty Hierarch of the Golden City."

The Star Retreats are essential in Spiritual Pilgrimage as their energies assist one to integrate the energies of the Golden City's Ray Force that assists and supports their individualization process within the Ascension.

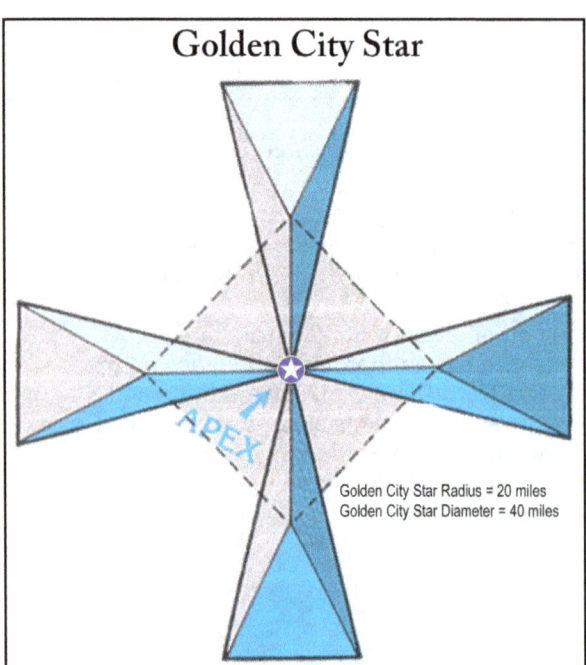

The Golden City Star

The Golden City Star is the most powerful location in a Golden City Vortex.

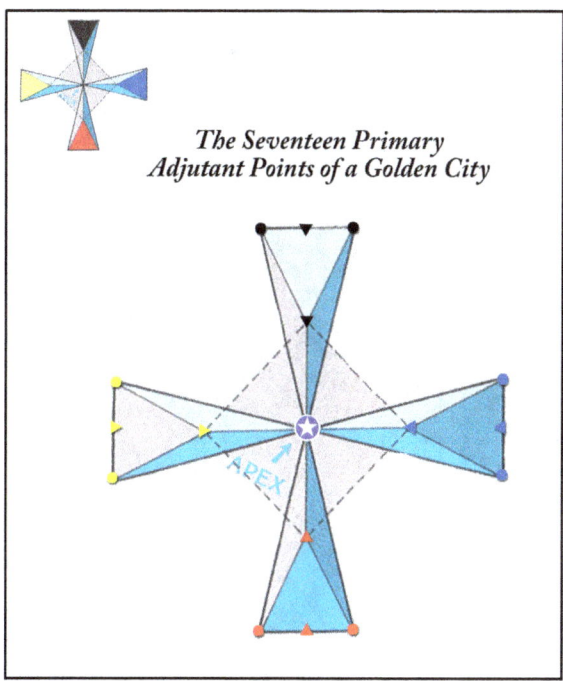

The Seventeen Primary Adjutant Points of a Golden City

Seventeen Points
The seventeen primary Adjutant Points of a Golden City include the Star.

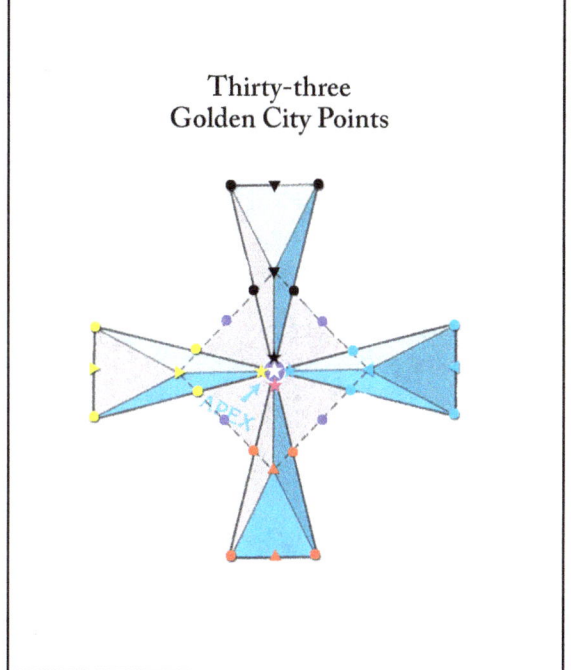

Thirty-three Golden City Points

Thirty-three Points
The thirty-three points of a Golden City include Ashrams, Temples, Star Retreats, and the Star.

A Golden Triangle
Most Evolutionary Fields are composed of triangles; however, some are square or rectangular, and a few are circles and contain a spiraling motion.

APPENDIX O
The Evolutionary Field

Evolutionary Fields are distributive regions within the infrastructure of a Golden City. They differ from the Evolutionary Pyramid, as they lie within the expanse of the Golden Cities. (Fractal pyramids lie within the Eight-sided Cell of Perfection.) They are defined through the presence of three Adjutant Points—where lei-lines intersect, and contain Third-, Fourth-, and Fifth-Dimensional energies. These areas are filled with life-changing and spiritually transcendent energies that infuse the light fields. This expansion greatly assists spiritual development and the Ascension Process, and can rapidly progress HU-man evolution.

Sacred Geometry and Geometric Language
Evolutionary Fields contain aspects of Sacred Geometry that easily interface with the evolving Light Being. Most fields are triangular in shape, but they also encompass circles, rectangles, and squares. In Feng Shui, shape symbolizes the presence of certain vital elements.

Rectangle: Wood Element
Square: Earth Element
Circle: Metal Element
Triangle: Fire Element
Spiral or wave: Water Element

According to the Ascended Masters, Geometric Language has many attributes, including philosophy, spirituality, and metaphysics. Its historical root, however, is hidden in Pythagorean mathematics and some esoteric historians claim that geometrical symbols adorned the walls of ancient Egyptian temples. The philosopher Plutarch assigned the power of the triangle "expressive of the nature of Pluto, Bacchus, and Mars...properties of the square of Rhea, Venus, Ceres, Vesta, and Juno."[1] However, throughout the years, the Masters of the I AM America Teachings have shared their insight of the profound symbology of shapes.

Rectangle
The rectangle is known to obstruct negative energy, and will produce positive, flowing energy. This energy is constructive and can shape and build, while encouraging and supporting the Co-creative Process.

Square
This shape is considered an energetic storehouse, as it holds and carries energy. The square represents alignment processes and the spiritual principle of balance.

Circle
The circle expands energy and is used for multi-dimensional growth and development.

---

1. Manly Hall, *The Secret Teachings of All Ages: Pythagorean Mathematics*, page 69, Diamond Jubilee Edition (Los Angeles: Philosophical Research Society, Inc.), 1988.

Triangle
The triangle—which is one half (diagonal) of a square—is claimed to duplicate energies. It is known to sustain new energies as they develop and mature. According to the Pythagoreans, triangles signify the beginning of the creative process and are considered a significant progenitor of life.

Spiral
Spiral: The spiral represents the movement of energies, or signifies a passage through certain progressive phases. It characterizes the movement of energy from one dimension to the next.

Master Teachers and Sacred Geometry
Similar to Ray Forces, sacred geometrical shapes can denote the presence of certain Master Teachers, who infuse the microscopic shapes to convey a specific movement or flow of energy to heal and transform. These subatomic geometric forms permeate the light fields of a student or chela with a precise and timely shakti. Lord Sananda utilizes the hopeful regeneration of the rectangle; while Soltec establishes spiritual equilibrium through the square. The triangle is favored by Serapis Bey, which reproduces the fires of inspiration, enthusiasm, or the cleansing, purifying process of Ascension. Saint Germain and Kuthumi prefer the expansive circle, as it can quickly develop, intensify, and increase spiritual knowledge and the alchemy of HU-man development.

Forms of Triangles, Side and Angle
Since Evolutionary Fields comprise the geometric face of the large, crystal-like dimensions of the Golden City, the triangle is its most common surface. This includes all three types of triangle defined by their sides: scalene, isosceles, and equilateral. Triangles, defined by angle are acute, obtuse, and right triangles. The center Evolutionary Field of the Golden City—the Initiate—contains four isosceles triangles, creating yet another additional smaller set of triangles, both isosceles and scalene. Golden City Doorways or Gateways are large isosceles triangles. Within each Doorway is yet another subset of five triangles, both isosceles and scalene.

The Isosceles Triangle
An isosceles triangle has two of its three sides in equal length. This is the metaphysical Golden Triangle which is known to carry remarkable power, alongside innate mystery. The ancients believed that the isosceles triangle was the symbol of both heaven and Earth. These are Golden City Evolutionary Fields where one may encounter intense spiritual initiations that unite our spiritual and physical worlds. This launches our spiritual development into the divine Ascension Process.

The Scalene Triangle
Each side of the scalene triangle is a different measurement, and no side is equal. The ancients ascribed the scalene triangle with secrecy, and claimed that it held the key to every genetic pattern on Earth.[2] Scalene triangles are known to produce time anomalies along with increased psychic insight and telepathic ability. Dimensional rifting is common in this type of Evolutionary Field, building strength, mobility, and agility through multi-dimensional experience.

---

2. M. Hall, *The Secret Teachings of All Ages: Pythagorean Mathematics*, page 68.

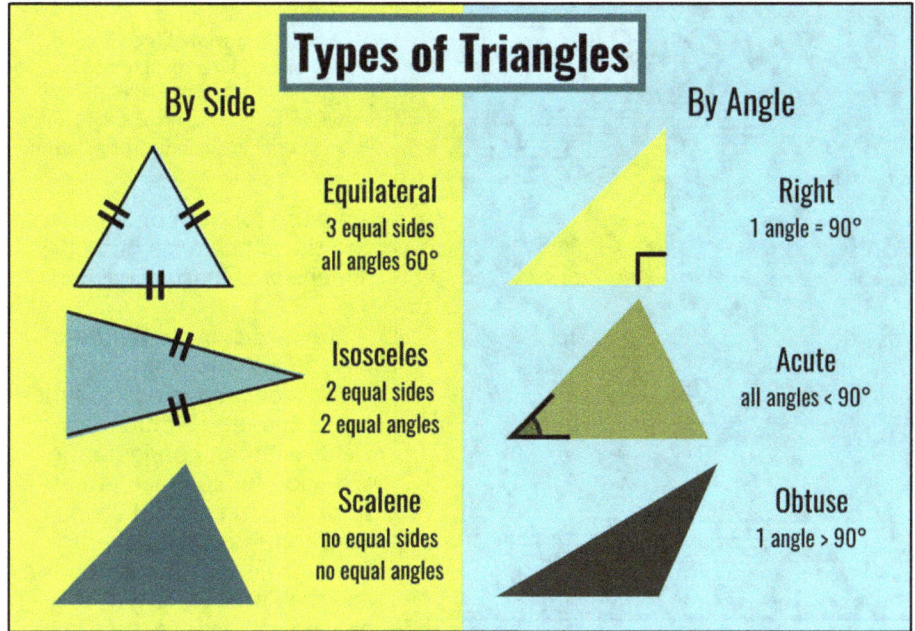

The Six Types of Triangles
Triangles are classified by the length of their sides and the degree of their angles.
(Illustration from sciencenotes.org.)

The Equilateral Triangle
Equilateral triangles contain the same measurement on all sides. Pythagoreans considered this triangle to represent the threefold creation as mind, body, and spirit. In Christian symbology, the triangle represents the father, son, and Holy Spirit. The yantra, a mystical Hindu diagram, often contains equilateral triangles. The Sri Yantra symbol contains nine interlocking equilateral triangles, and symbolizes the divine meeting of both masculine and feminine energies. Equilateral triangles create balance, harmony, peace, and Brotherhood throughout their Evolutionary Fields. They are excellent for curative and healing processes at all levels.

The Acute Triangle
An acute triangle is created when all the interior angles are less than ninety degrees. These Evolutionary Fields are inordinately sensitive and can give rapid results. Pilgrimages within these fields help one to quickly overcome obstacles and delays. They are best used, however, to assist perception and discernment. As one develops the energies of this Evolutionary Field, they can assist entrance into other worlds and the multiple dimensions present throughout the Galactic Web.

The Obtuse Triangle
Obtuse triangles contain at least one angle that is greater than ninety degrees. This Evolutionary Field is intense, with expansive spiritual experiences. These Evolutionary Fields are best to forge connection and communication with the Fourth and Fifth Dimension. HU-man senses may quickly develop in these fields, with increased access to Akashic Records through direct instruction and teaching from its three Adjutant Point Hierarchs. These fields

Yantra
The Sri Yantra symbol is composed of nine interlocking triangles. This powerful emblem is placed in the center of the yantra, pictured left, and illustrates the divine union of polarities.

are good for both bi-location and the appearance of multi-dimensional Master Teachers.

The Right Angle Triangle

A triangle that contains a ninety degree angle is a Right Angle Triangle. Evolutionary Fields with this configuration are good for spiritual retreat, spiritual practice, and various ceremonies. They can induce remarkable shifts in perception, and may produce physical healing and regeneration, along with spiritual renewal.

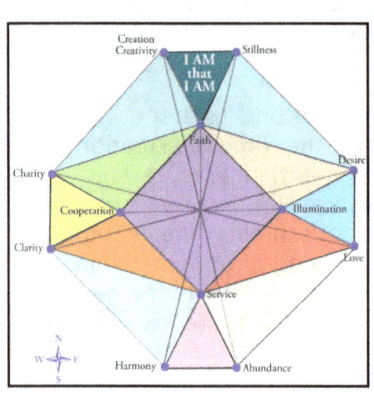

Fourteen Human to HU-man Evolutionary Fields

There are fourteen Human to HU-man Evolutionary Fields of Energy within a Golden City. They are:

1. Love: Acute Equilateral Triangle.
2. Wisdom: Acute Isosceles Triangle.
3. Power: Acute Isosceles Triangle.
4. Conscience and Consciousness: Obtuse Scalene Triangle.
5. Spiritual Awakening: Obtuse Scalene Triangle.
6. Spiritual Discipline: Acute Equilateral Triangle.
7. Vision and Compassion: Square.
    a. Four, Right Angle Equilateral Triangles.
    b. Four, Acute Equilateral Triangles.
    c. Eight, Acute Scalene Triangles.
8. Science of Spiritual Wisdom: Acute Equilateral Triangle.
9. Strengthen the Soul: Obtuse Scalene Triangle.
10. Mastery: Obtuse Scalene Triangle.
11. Omega: Acute Isosceles Triangle.
12. Alpha: Acute Isosceles Triangle.
13. I AM That I AM: Acute Equilateral Triangle.
14. Golden City Star: Round, with varying diameters of intensity. This is the center of the Golden City Vortex. The center of each Golden City Star transmits the spiraling light and sound energy of their respective Ray Force.

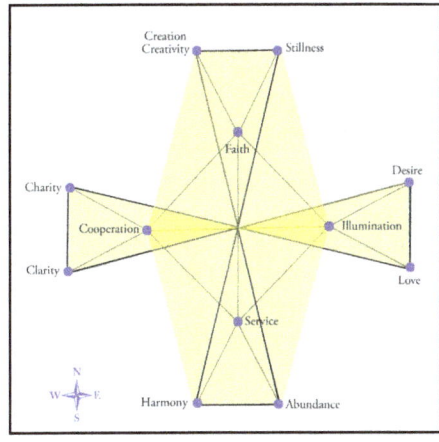

Eight Principles of the Right-hand Path

The Golden City infrastructure features eight distinctive Evolutionary Fields that support the positive, ambient energies of the Great White Brotherhood. Each of these eight principles reinforces the effectiveness of the Right-hand Path, and instills the values, ideals, and standards of the Ascended Masters. They mirror the profound, yet perceptive teachings of Buddha's Noble Eightfold Path, and convey the Ascended Masters' precious Shamballa Tradition. These Evolutionary Fields are configured as Acute Isosceles Triangles—Golden Triangles.

1. Lineage of Gurus, (right effort), Creation-Creativity, Stillness, Faith, the Star: Acute Isosceles Triangle.
2. Mysticism, (right view), Stillness, Illumination: Acute Isosceles Triangle.
3. HU-man Psychology, (right conduct), Desire, Love, Illumination, the Star: Acute Isosceles Triangle.
4. Prayer, (right samadhi), Abundance, Illumination: Acute Isosceles Triangle.
5. Prophecy, (right mindfulness), Harmony, Abundance, Service, the Star: Acute Isosceles Triangle.
6. Beauty of Nature, (right livelihood), Harmony, Cooperation: Acute Isosceles Triangle.
7. Ceremony, (right resolve), Charity, Clarity, Cooperation, the Star: Acute Isosceles Triangle.
8. Decree, (right speech), Cooperation, Creation-Creativity: Acute Isosceles Triangle.

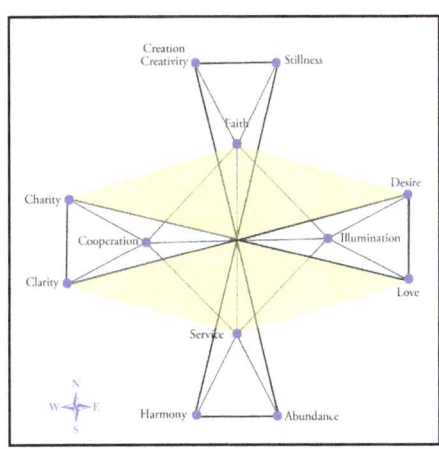

The Four Pillars

Hidden within the intercardinal directions of the Golden Cities are the Four Pillars. Each of these Evolutionary Fields is sponsored by a specific Ascended Master throughout all the fifty-one Golden Cities on Earth. Each region, along with their Ascended Master sponsor, works in tandem with the Adjutant Point Hierarchs and the Master Teacher of the Golden City. Their shapes are configured as auspicious Golden Triangles. [Editor's note: To learn more about the intercardinal directions of the Four Pillars, see *A Teacher Appears*, pages 125-128.]

- Pillar One, El Morya, Southwest: Acute Isosceles Triangle.
- Pillar Two, Kuthumi, Northeast: Acute Isosceles Triangle.
- Pillar Three, Saint Germain, Southeast: Acute Isosceles Triangle.
- Pillar Four, Lord Sananda, Northwest: Acute Isosceles Triangle.
- The Star, Serapis Bey, the center of the Golden City Vortex: Circle and spiral.

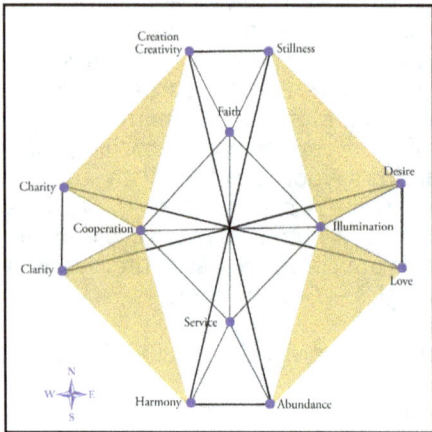

Fourfold Flame Evolutionary Fields

Activity of the Fourfold Flame

To the outer edge of the intercardinal directions, lie four additional Evolutionary Fields that complement the energies of each of the Four Pillars. These areas are known as the activity of the Fourfold Flame, and are overseen by a complement of energy to each of the Four Pillars.[3] They are:
- Fourfold Flame of Desire, Lady Desiree, Southwest: Acute Isosceles Triangle.
- Fourfold Flame of Wisdom, Lady Nada, Northeast: Acute Isosceles Triangle.
- Fourfold Flame of Power, Lady Portia, Southeast: Acute Isosceles Triangle.
- Fourfold Flame of Love, Lady Miriam, Northwest: Acute Isosceles Triangle.
- The Star, Lady Luxor, the center of the Golden City Vortex: Circle and spiral.

Nine Heavenly Gates

Pivoting off of the Four Heavenly Ashrams, (Faith, Illumination, Service, and Cooperation), and the Golden City Stars are the Eight Heavenly Gates. Each Evolutionary Field is assigned to its respective Color Ray and Archangel and aligns to the Esoteric Color Wheel of the Nine Perfections. These Eight Evolutionary Fields are:
1. Star of the Golden City: (Center), all of the Color Rays, Circle and Spiral. This is the Unfed Flame, located within the heart of the Eight-sided Cell of Perfection.
2. Archangel Raphael: Northern Door (West), Green Ray, Obtuse Isosceles Triangle. Protects personal finances, abundance, and the *Aboundness of Choice*; protects and guides the world economies.

---

3. Lady Desiree is a "complement of energies" to El Morya's energies of the Blue Ray. She is the Golden City Hierarch of Fron, the Golden City of Western Australia. In some Ascended Master Teaching, Lady Clair—the Queen of Light—is stated as Kuthumi's Twin Flame. However, in the I AM America Teachings, Kuthumi and Lady Nada are often paired together, although never stated as Divine Complements or as a Twin Flame relationship. In past I AM America Teachings, Lady Miriam pairs her energies with Lord Sananda in the Golden City of Shalahah. It is likely these relationships are formed through the esoteric qualities and purpose of specific Golden Cities, their complementary energies, and the current needs of Earth and humanity. Do not forget that the Ascended Masters are ever-evolving and changing to suit the needs of humanity. Ascended Masters commonly form a *Oneship* with another Ascended Master or Ascended Being of Light to accomplish the "task at hand." A complement of energy does not necessarily suggest the relationship of Divine Complement or Twin Flame.

3. Archangel Zadkiel: Northern Door (East), Violet Ray, Obtuse Isosceles Triangle. Protects and guides personal spiritual growth through timely interaction with Spiritual Teachers; oversees Earth's spiritual development.
4. Archangel Michael: Eastern Door (North), Blue Ray, Obtuse Isosceles Triangle. Archangel Michael protects each new generation of children and the New Children; protects the Kingdoms of Nature.
5. Archangel Chamuel: Eastern Door (South), Pink Ray, Obtuse Isosceles Triangle. Archangel Chamuel protects loving relationships and marriage; protects the Law of Love on Earth.
6. Archangel Uriel: Southern Door (East), Red-Gold Ray (Ruby-Gold Ray), Obtuse Isosceles Triangle. Archangel Uriel protects and guides each individual to find and realize their Divine Purpose; he also protects the human right of self-expression.
7. Archangel Gabriel: Southern Door (West), White Ray (Diamond Ray), Obtuse Isosceles Triangle. Archangel Gabriel protects every human family on Earth; he also protects and guides Earth's Divine Order and Harmony.
8. Archangel Jophiel: Western Door (South), Yellow Ray, Obtuse Isosceles Triangle. Archangel Jophiel protects and guides the dispensation of spiritual knowledge to humanity, along with humanity's Divine Right to discover and choose their form of spiritual growth. This is the Star of Knowledge—Divine Wisdom—gained through vital experience.
9. Archangel Chrystiel: Western Door (North), Aquamarine and Gold Rays, Obtuse Isosceles Triangle. Archangel Cyrstiel protects jobs, careers, and the ability to earn a worldly living through noble means. Chrystiel protects the spiritual knowledge and freedom gained through our experiences that assist our spiritual victory over illusion.

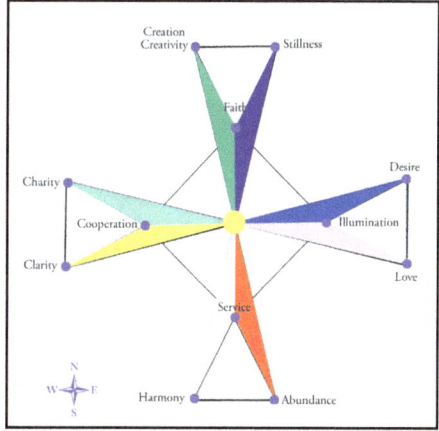

Eight Heavenly Gates Evolutionary Fields

The Elohim Evolutionary Fields

Again, pivoting off of the Four Heavenly Ashrams, (Faith, Illumination, Service, and Cooperation), are four Evolutionary Fields—the Elohim of the Golden Age. Each field is unique, and contains two Heavenly Ashrams, respectively. Encompassing two Convergence Ashrams apiece, the Elohim Field completes with one single Gateway Point of the Northern or Southern Golden City Door. Each Elohim Evolutionary Field also includes one Temple Ashram. These fields interface Third- and Fourth-Dimensional energies and express sound and light frequencies through modulated Ray Forces. Since Golden City Convergence Ashrams, "hold within themselves a direct contact to the Mighty Elohim," Elohim Evolutionary Fields assist many physical aspects

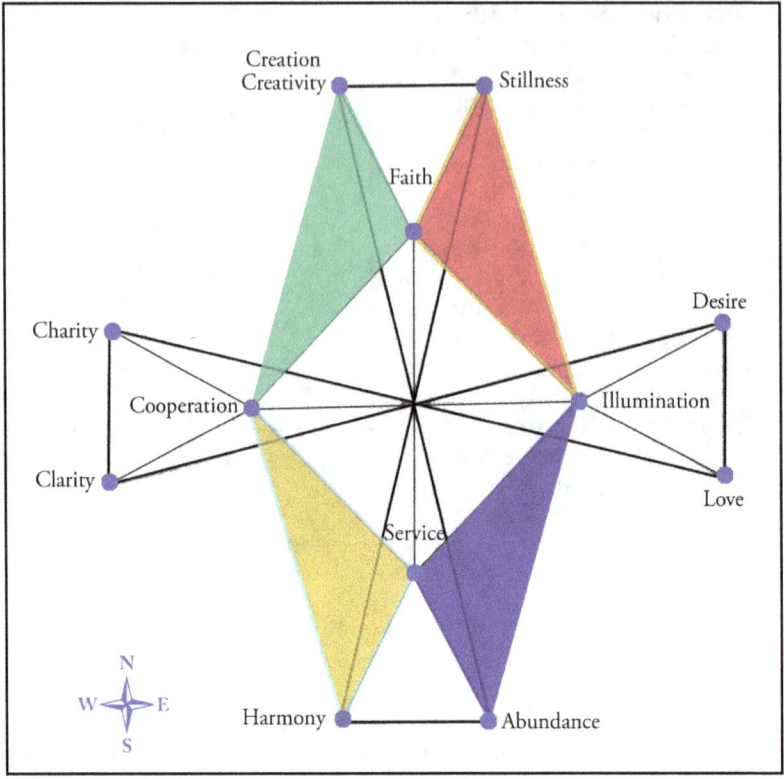

The Four Elohim Evolutionary Fields for the Golden Age

within a Golden City.[4] This includes the ability to calibrate and regulate weather conditions, the four seasons, the light spectrums of day and night, and geologic formations including lakes, river, valleys, hills, and mountains.

Elohim of Truth: Vista (Cyclopea) and Virginia, Green Ray, Northwest Region of a Golden City, Scalene Obtuse Triangle. Adjutant Points: Creation—Creativity, Faith, and Cooperation.

Elohim of Peace: Peace and Tranquility, Ruby-Gold Ray, Northeast Region of a Golden City, Scalene Obtuse Triangle. Adjutant Points: Stillness, Faith, and Illumination.

Elohim of Freedom: Arctura and Diana, Violet Ray, Southeast Region of a Golden City, Scalene Obtuse Triangle. Adjutant Points: Abundance, Service, Illumination.

Elohim of Unity: Rainbow and Iris, Aquamarine and Gold Rays, Southwest Region of a Golden City, Scalene Obtuse Triangle. Adjutant Points: Harmony, Service, and Cooperation.

---

4. Toye, Lori, *Evolutionary Biome*, (I AM America Publishing, 2020), "Gateways of Pilgrimage," page 57.

The Spiral
Circular Evolutionary Fields move energies through a spiral motion. Golden City Stars are an example of this type of field. Golden City Vortices are large Evolutionary Fields. They move in a clockwise spiral to take in energies; they move in a counterclockwise spiral to remove impurities.

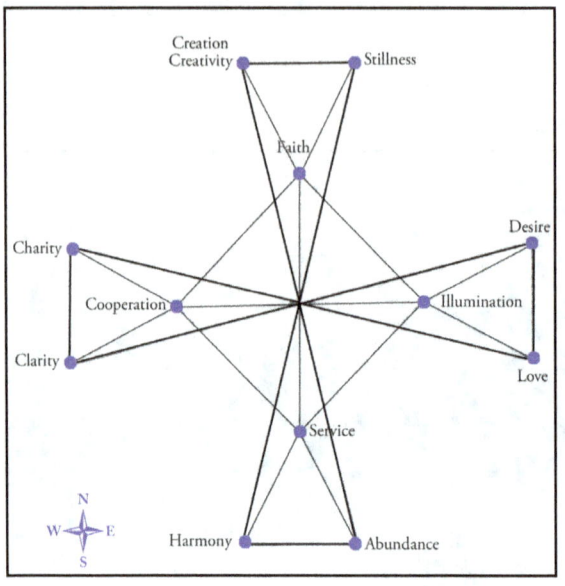

Evolution Points and the Evolutionary Fields overlaid the Golden City

The following illustrations depict the twelve major Adjutant Points and the fourteen Human to HU-man Evolutionary Fields that lie within the Golden City Vortex.

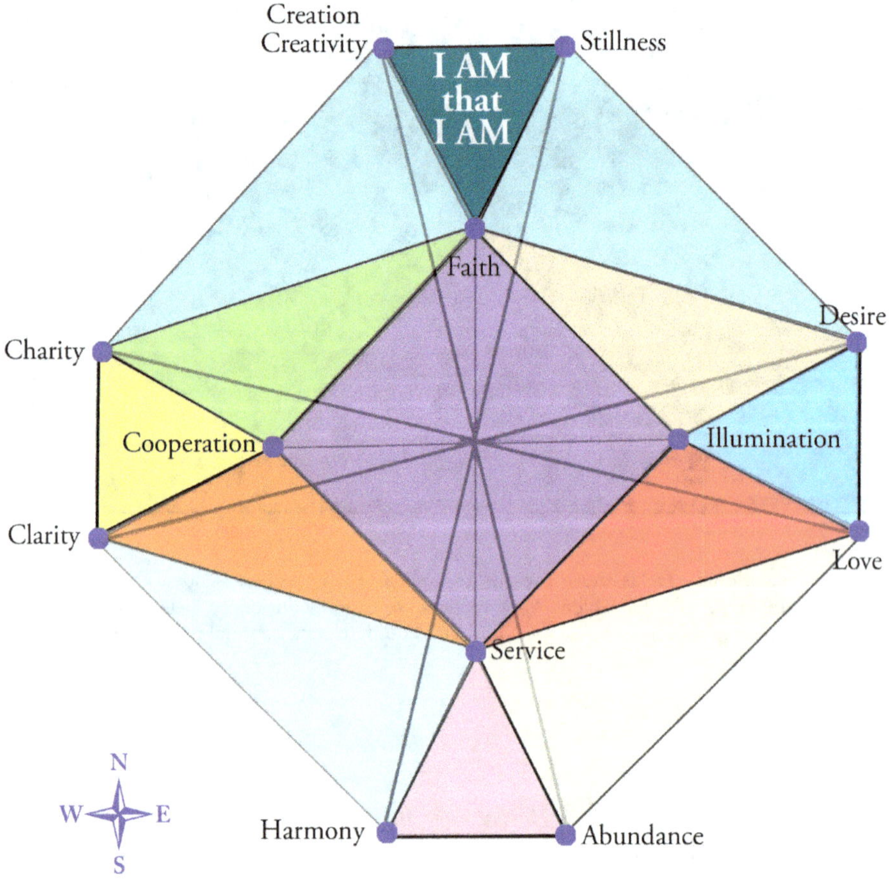

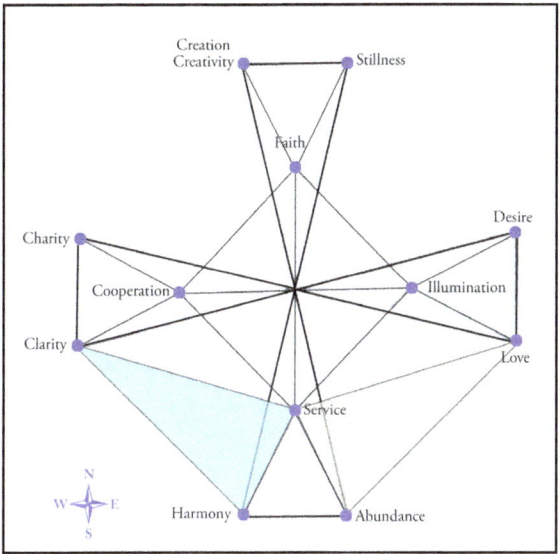

The Threefold Creation: Love, Wisdom, and Power
Unfed Flame within the Evolutionary Fields.

The Unfed Flame as it exists in the three Evolutionary Fields within a Golden City Vortex. Pink represents Love, Yellow represents Wisdom, and Blue represents Power.

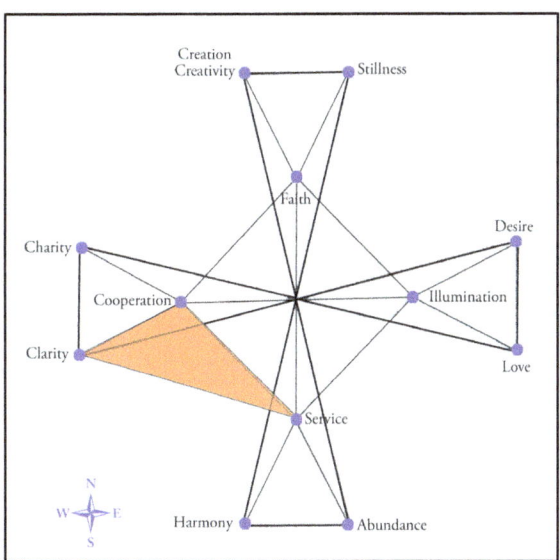

Conscience and Consciousness
The Evolutionary Field of the Conscious Human.

Located in the Golden City Vortex. This field of spiritual experience drives the development of the conscience. This location helps to create states of higher consciousness alongside changes and shifts in vibrational frequency of consciousness.

PHOTONS

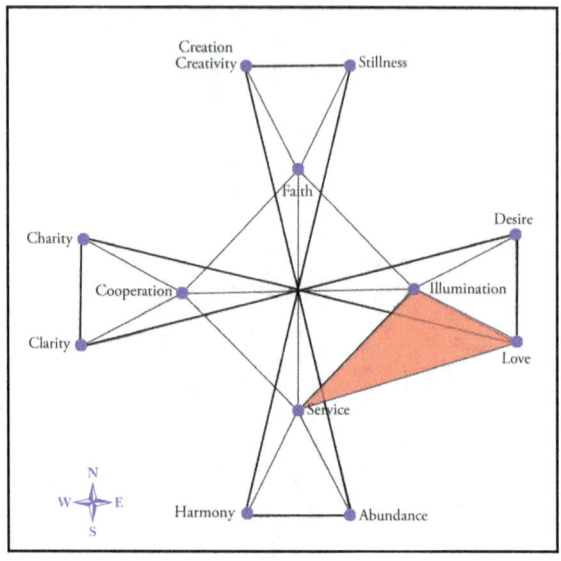

Spiritual Awakening
The Evolutionary Field of the Aspirant.
This field of high-frequency Galactic Energy creates and drives intense experiences of Spiritual Awakening.

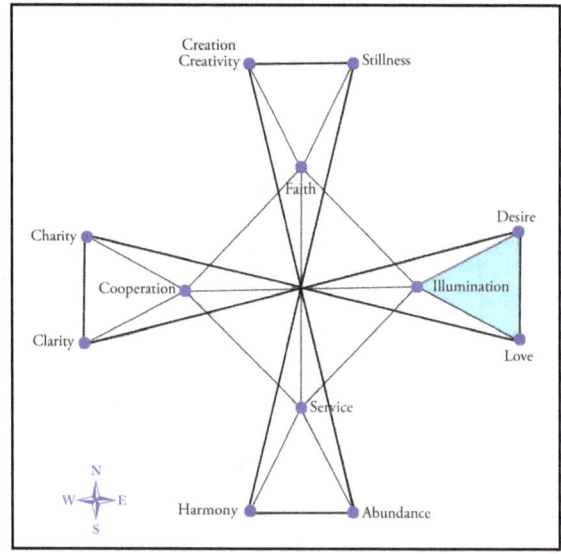

Spiritual Discipline
The Evolutionary Field of the Chela.
Located in the Eastern Door of the Golden City Vortex. This field of spiritual experience creates devotion and love for both the spiritual guru and their spiritual disciplines.

Propel Your Ascension

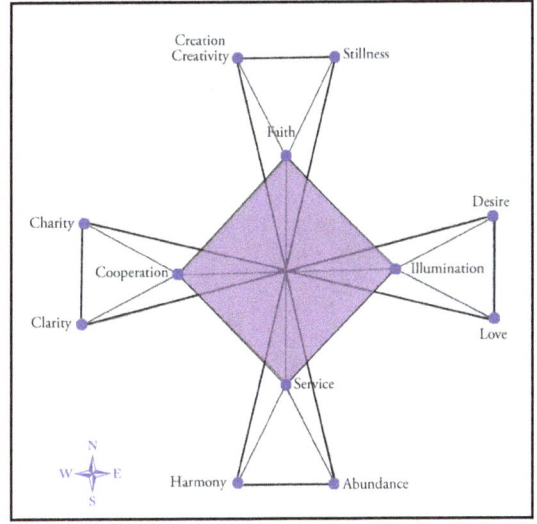

Vision and Compassion
The Evolutionary Field of the Initiate.
This Evolutionary Field drives visionary experiences. This field of energy is shaped as a square, but is actually two pyramids that represent both the Prophet and the Bodhisattva. This energy field helps to develop clairvoyance and clairaudience, "the eyes to see, ears to hear." This Evolutionary Field also cultivates deep compassion, mercy, and forgiveness for self and others through applying the spiritual tenets of Service, Illumination, Cooperation, and Faith.

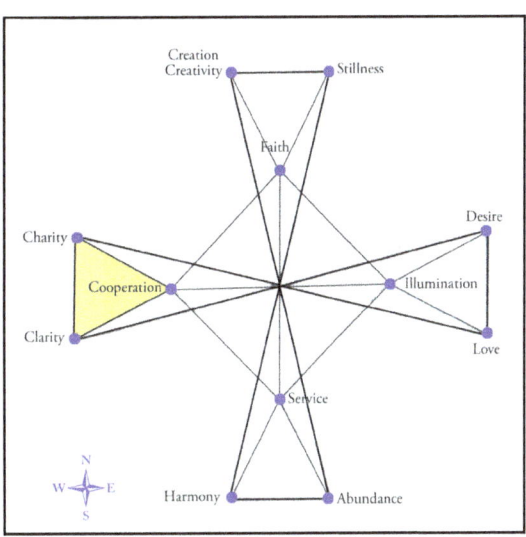

The Science of Spiritual Wisdom
The Evolutionary Field of the Arhat.
This Evolutionary Field assists individuals to cultivate and integrate the spiritual wisdom and intuition of the Evolutionary Biome. This is a field of experience that evolves spiritual intuition and insight into enlightenment. This creates profound spiritual knowledge. The Arhat is the trusted advisor, astrologer, feng shui practitioner, seasoned healer, or herbalist. In conventional thinking, the Arhat is one who has "overcome desire." This field of vibrational energy assists one to serve others through the principles of Clarity, Charity, and Cooperation.

Strengthen the Soul
The Evolutionary Field of the Adept.
This Evolutionary Field is located between the Golden City Western and Northern Doors. This field of remarkable energy produces the great soul — the Mahatma. Time spent in this Evolutionary Field can help you to strengthen your resolve to overcome duality and reinforce the use of the Right-hand Path. The cultivation of conscious, deep meditation in this energetic field can lead to Astral Travel and train the soul for bi-location.

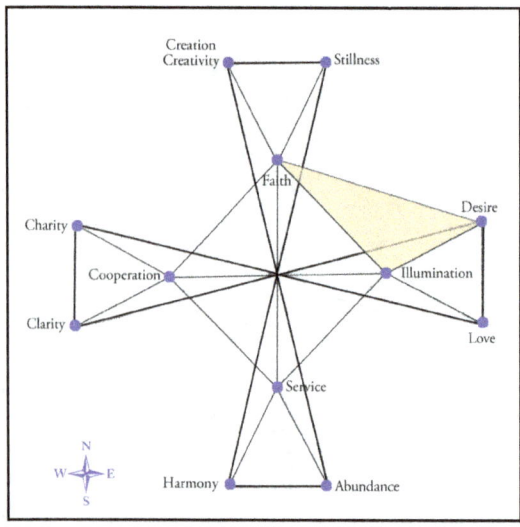

Mastery
The Evolutionary Field of the Master.
Mastery has many forms, and this field of energy helps you to realize your dharma, or great purpose. Since this Evolutionary Field focuses upon your divinity, this energetic gives ideal support to progress your Ascension Process. These energies also help to recalibrate intention and objectives to achieve HU-man Development. Mastery possesses the consummate skill of command and self-realization over individual thoughts, feelings, and actions.

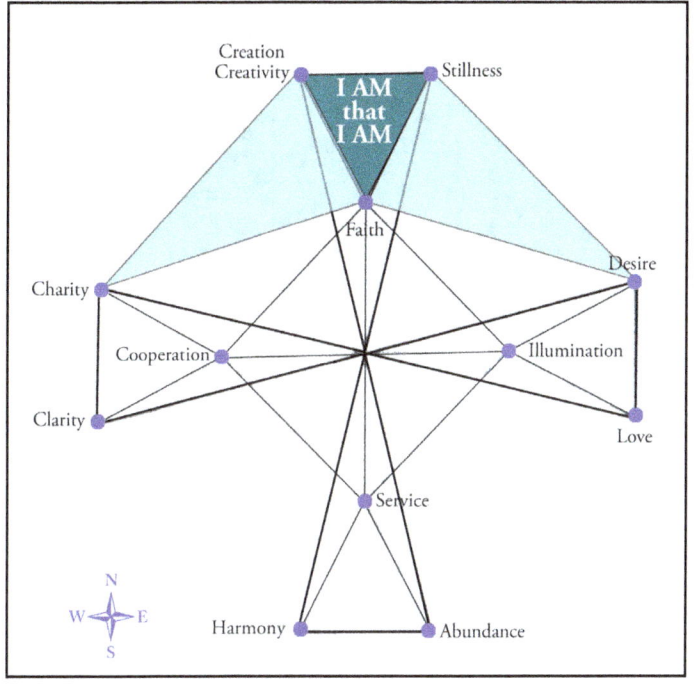

The Threefold Co-creator
The Evolutionary Fields of the HU-man and the I AM.

The three final Evolutionary Fields of the North cultivate the Evolutionary Points of Charity, Desire, Faith, Silence, and Creation-Creativity. This is the domain of the HU-man, and time spent throughout these energetic fields will assist the realization of the God-man. This is the final location to focus upon the completion of the Ascension. The Ascension is the process of Mastering thoughts, feelings, and actions that balance positive and negative karmas. This allows entrance into higher states of consciousness and frees a person from the need to reincarnate on the lower Earth Planes. The threefold aspect of the Creator mirrors and evolves the Unfed Flame of the Southern Door. These principles are known as beginning (Stillness — Omega), duration (Creation/Creativity — Alpha), and transformation (I AM That I AM).

PHOTONS

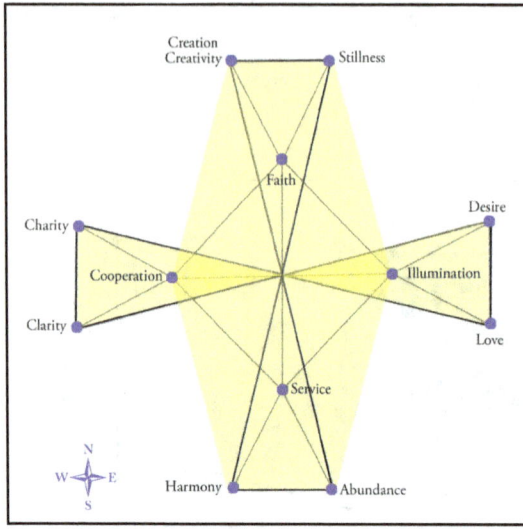

Eight Principles of the Right-hand Path

An Overview of the Evolutionary Fields:

Eight Evolutionary Fields define the principles of the Right-hand Path. All of the Right-hand Path Evolutionary Fields share one point—the Star of the Golden City. They also include two to three Adjutant Points. Their triangles create an acute isosceles shape—the Golden Triangle. Their unique metaphysical energies unite Heaven and Earth. This quickly introduces and reinforces their spiritual energies into the Collective Consciousness.

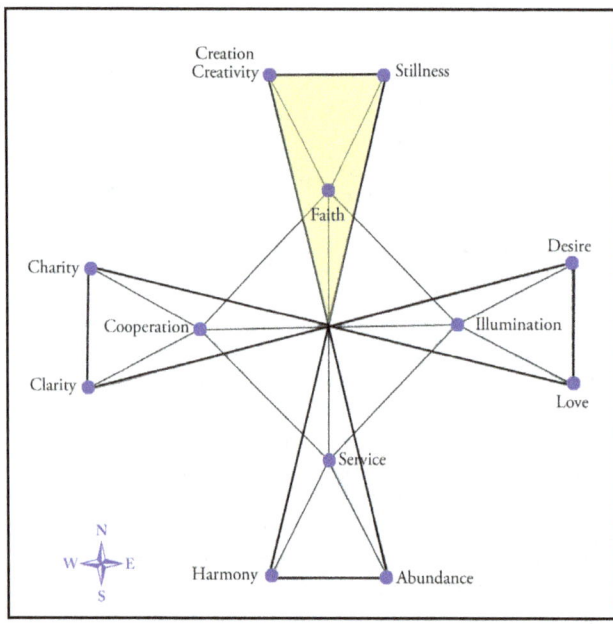

Lineage of Gurus,
Right Effort

The first Evolutionary Field of the Right-hand Path is the principle of the Lineage of Gurus. This field of energy holds an innate connection to the Ascended Masters of the Shamballa Tradition for humanity's and Earth's continued evolution into the Golden Age.

Since this field is also known as the Black Door, energies quickly acclimate into the physical plane. This field may increase your endurance and determination in all endeavors, with unshakable resolve. Pilgrimages through this unique field of energy can infuse and create a quickening, with new levels of Spiritual Awakening and devotion to the Ascension Process. There may be communication and overlighting with the ancient Elohim and the Ancestral Teachers of the Spiritual Hierarchy. Pilgrimage will increase the efficacy, simplicity, and purity of spiritual techniques, spiritual practices, ceremonies, and prayer. Northern Door Pilgrimages to connect with the lineage of Gurus are most effective during the annual Shamballa season.

Mysticsm,
Right View

The second Evolutionary Field of the Mystic increases and accentuates our ability to understand and navigate the mysteries of Ascension. This field assists our personal initiative, and the capability to follow through to develop a deep, yet transcendent Ascension Process. This field is assisted by two Adjutant Points, Illumination and Stillness. It is located in the Northeast region of the Golden City.

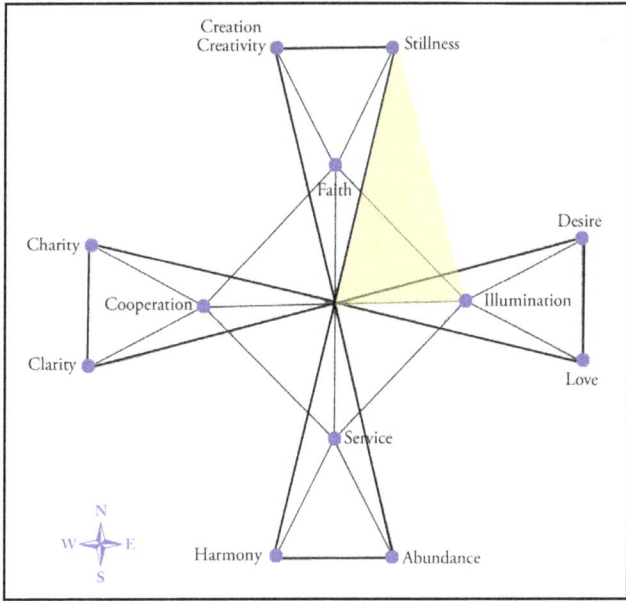

Our enlightened understanding of Ascension is spiritually supported by four seminal Ascended Master teachings, known as the *Four Pillars*—represented in this field.

The First Pillar is the fundamental spiritual intelligence that all of humanity is blessed with *innate divinity*, through the Eight-sided Cell of Perfection. Our divinity connects humanity as ONE.[1] This Evolutionary Field encourages and supports meaningful meditation and contemplation through Stillness —the remarkable Law of Alignment.

The perceptive teaching of the Second Pillar addresses the purification of the mind from karmic actions. This is achieved through the *abandonment of judging others*, and the *cultivation of self-observation*. The Evolutionary Field of the Mystic increases stillness and peace contained within the Violet Flame, and its ability to end karmic cycles.

The *freedom to choose* is the foundation of the Third Pillar. Choice is the cornerstone of freedom, and we are encouraged to not infringe on others' personal preferences. The spiritual principles of the Second and Third Pillar are further assisted by the Illumination Point. Illumination encourages us to live without fear or judgment.

The Fourth Pillar is perhaps the simplest, yet most difficult tenet to apply. This is the Law of Love, and we are asked to *love one another* without conditions. Expectation limits our love and the key to experience and share love is realized through *acceptance*.

The Evolutionary Field of Mysticsm increases the light of our Ascension through the teachings of the Four Pillars. Pilgrimages to this field increases insight and spiritual knowledge of their wisdom and grace, and these four valuable insights.

---

1. See the *Awakening Prayer*.

PHOTONS

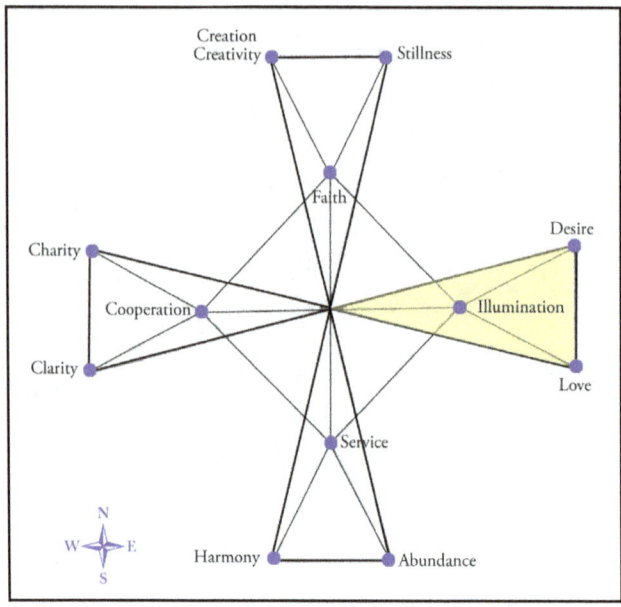

HU-man Psychology,
Right Conduct

The third Evolutionary Field is HU-man Psychology, and addresses our everyday conduct and actions while engaging the Ascension Process. This field of energy is guided by three Adjutant Points: Desire, Love, and Illumination. It also includes the energies of the Star.

HU-man Psychology embraces the energies of the Eastern Blue Door, a Golden City Doorway that addresses and transforms our closest relationships with our partners, spouse, children, or family members and friends. As we grow and develop in our Ascension Process, these types of relationships expand to include soul mates and our spiritual family.

Right conduct promotes the use of Christ Consciousness to overcome animal states, or lower, devolved conditions of consciousness. Devolved states of consciousness include the intentional use of drugs to hallucinate or escape, sex magic, blood sacrifice, and the use of magical pacts through the left-hand path. Christ Consciousness empowers cooperation, unity, and the sanctity of life through the activity of the Right-hand Path and applies these principles.

1. Light and love are realized through the *United Brotherhood and Sisterhood* of humanity.
2. Christ Consciousness is developed through adopting a *moral philosophy* and an enlightened value system. In Ascended Master Teaching, these philosophies and values are sculpted through the Twelve Jurisdictions.
3. Unlimited *love creates compassion*.
4. The energies of Christ are vast and unlimited, and not limited to Earth alone. The *Cosmic Christ* offers *redemption* as the soul grows, learns, and transforms through vital experience.
5. The energies of the Christ Consciousness weave the *Seamless Garment*, the bodies of light required to obtain the Ascension. This garment of light assures victory over death through Spiritual Immortality. This leads the soul onward in its evolutionary journey to Conscious Immortality and the ultimate freedom of Ascension.
6. The *Mighty Christ* is the realized Christ *within*.

Pilgrimages through the Field of HU-man Psychology help to refine and create value systems that realize Christ Consciousness. This Evolutionary Field is a powerful Golden Triangle where one may encounter intense spiritual initiation to overcome personal divisiveness and separation. This spiritual preparation can unite marriages and partnerships, and evolve families and groups into powerful, positive Group Minds and their group efforts.

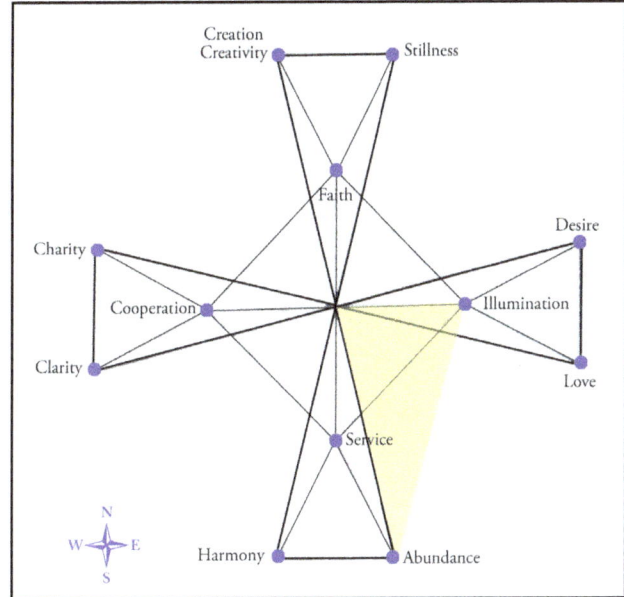

Prayer,
Right Samadhi

Prayer is an Evolutionary Field that enhances the spiritual practice of prayer, contemplation, meditation, and evolved states of trance. In Hindu and Buddhist traditions this is known as the path of *samadhi*, or deep concentration. The Adjutant Point of Abundance, which can give one the ability to open to the universal flow, and the Illumination Point, that removes the fear of others' judgments, assists this remarkable field of energy. The Golden Triangle completes with its final point resting in the energies of the transcendent Golden City Star.

Time spent in this field will enhance your concentration abilities and your capacity to control your Mental Body through peaceful, productive meditation. If it is difficult to still your mind, use the energies of this Evolutionary Field to enhance contemplation and prayer. As you develop deeper states of awareness you may receive messages and communication from the resident Adjutant Point Hierarchs. This process, however, requires that you first "empty your cup" from preconceived self-perceptions and beliefs. This Evolutionary Field will increase your ability to enter into the *plane of reciprocity*.[1] As you concentrate within your state of meditative trance, you will hear a sudden "pop." This signifies that your consciousness has phased out of Third Dimension and into Fourth Dimension. At this point you may enter into your beloved Inner Garden.[2]

Pilgrimages to the Evolutionary Field of Prayer and to its Adjutant Points increase your ability and agility with meditative states, leading to inner guidance and assistance from Spiritual Teachers and Ascended Masters. Prayer and ceremony performed is extremely effective in this field, and is alleged to be assisted by the "Light of a Thousand Suns."

---

1. As we raise our spiritual energies to meet the Ascended Master, the Ascended Master lowers their energies. Consciousness meets on a peaceful plane of reciprocity. This metaphysical practice is based on the Law of Energy-for-energy.

2. The Inner Garden is an intentional mind construct that is visualized for peace and comfort during states of meditation. As this state of consciousness strengthens, Spiritual Teachers will often join you for instruction in the sanction of this serene setting.

Prophecy,
Right Mindfulness

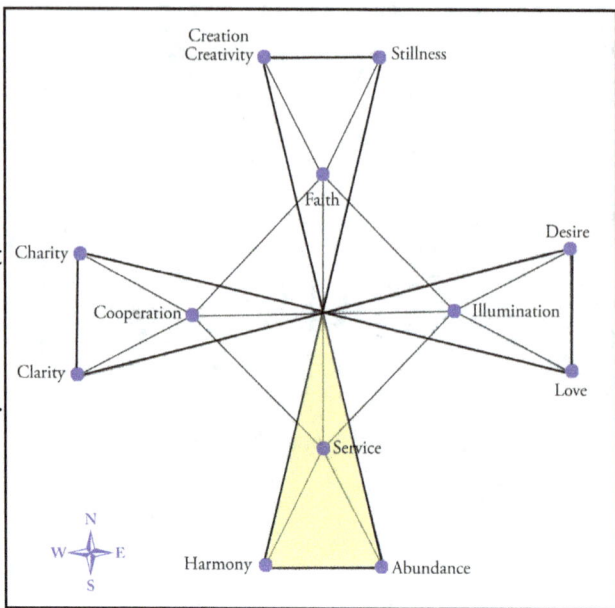

The Evolutionary Field of Prophecy is located in the Southern Door of the Golden City Vortex. This is perhaps one of the most important fields of the Right-hand Path, as it holds vital energies that connect an individual's state of spiritual consciousness to the Collective Consciousness. This Evolutionary Field helps one to define, understand, and sculpt the three significant elements of mindfulness: thought, feeling, and action.[1] Through the Southern Door's relationship to the Collective Consciousness, this field is often associated with the *Healing of the Nations*, and Pilgrimages to Southern Doors can calibrate, ameliorate, and expedite healing and restorative processes for humanity.[2]

Prophecy is associated with the conscious awareness of and the monitoring of our thoughts and feelings, and how our thoughts and feelings affect our everyday actions. This practice produces a state of watchful carefulness with our divine Co-creative energy. Pilgrimages to the Evolutionary Field of Prophecy may give us insightful glimpses into our futures, and how we may alter, change, or lessen undesired foreseen events. Prophecy is a spiritual teaching given with warning, and it is designed to change, lessen, and mitigate the prophesied insight. Its teachings are both metaphoric and literal, and outcomes are always contingent on individual choices and our state of consciousness.

As always, throughout all the Evolutionary Fields spiritual practice is extremely effective, however, in this field it is claimed that breath techniques contain an inherent efficacy. This is due to the breath's conscious ability to quickly connect body and mind.

Pilgrimage to Prophecy's Adjutant Points of Harmony, Abundance, Faith, and the benefic Star can help to mitigate negative Earth Changes events, and quell collective fear and apprehension throughout Earth's global Collective Consciousness.

---

1. In Ascended Master teachings and tradition, thought, feeling, and action are the cornerstones of the creation process. Thought represents the Mental (Causal) Body and the Yellow Ray. Feeling represents the emotional (Astral) body and the Pink Ray. Action represents the physical body and the Blue Ray.

2. Healing of the Nations Spiritual Pilgrimage: A series of Migrations through the Southern Door, and the Temples, Retreats, and Star of a Golden City. Through the Evolutionary Biome, this activates both personal healing and global healing for the nations of the world. For more information on the *Healing of the Nations Pilgrimage*, see the *I AM America Atlas* and *Evolutionary Biome*.

Propel Your Ascension

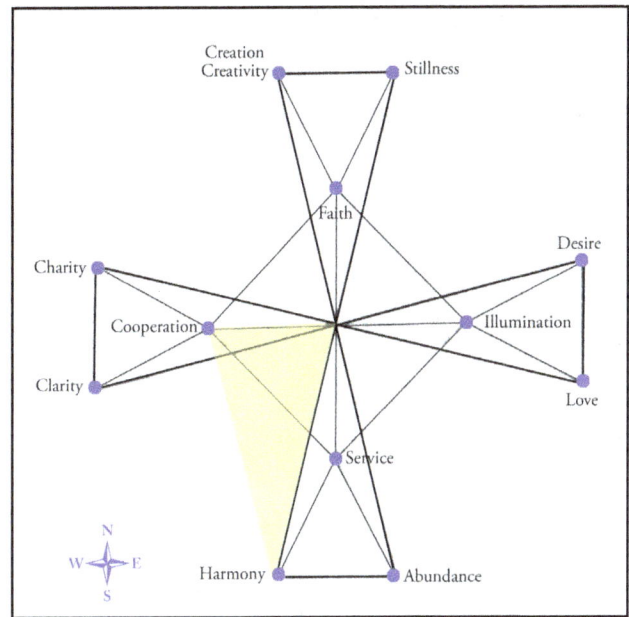

Beauty of Nature, Right Livelihood

In Ascended Master Teaching, beauty means to "Be in balance." *BE* or *BEing*, is a state of elevated, HUman awareness. The esoteric author Dion Fortune describes this field of consciousness as a mystical "love of pantheism." She writes of the ancients' love and devotion to Earth, who sought the manifestation of God in nature through "ritual and invocation with natural forces." The contemporary *School of Beauty* is in constant rapport with Nature, "through their love of her beauty, and never employ ritual."[1] Since this Evolutionary Field's Adjutant Points feature Harmony and Cooperation, our love of nature and our devotion to a deep, spiritual ecology is fortified in this Golden City location. Pilgrimages to these points, including the Golden City Star, strengthen our connection to the Evolutionary Biome and its ability to reconnect our consciousness to a Oneship, the Oneness, or the ONE.

The spiritual teachings of the Buddha reinforce the principle of Right Livelihood, and asks that our worldly professions do not harm our everyday life or others. This includes not trading in weapons, harmful drugs or medicines, poisons, and the unnecessary killing or harmful treatment of animals.[2] In Ascended Master Teaching this includes Mother Nature and her many hidden Kingdoms of Creation that exist at the Fourth Dimension. We are asked to refrain from livelihoods that destroy the natural environment, or use harmful or needless chemicals and pesticides to raise crops. This also includes excessive mining, needless drilling, and the exploitive harvest of Earth's natural resources and wildlife. The Beauty of Nature Evolutionary Field increases our ability to attune our frequencies to the hidden Kingdoms of Fourth Dimension, and receive their spiritual insight and knowledge to work in harmony and cooperation with the Earth. The *Iroquois Seventh Generation Principle* states that decisions and actions with Earth's precious environment and valuable resources should create a sustainable result seven generations into the future.[3]

---

1. Dion Fortune, *The Training and Work of an Initiate*, (Weiser Books, 2000, Boston, MA), page 65.
2. Walpola Sri Rahula, *The Noble Eightfold Path*, The Buddhist Review, http://www.tricycle.com, (2021).
3. "What is the Seventh Generation Principle?", Indigenous Corporate Training, Inc., http://www.ictinc.ca, (2021).

Pilgrimages to the Evolutionary Field of Beauty of Nature increase our love, devotion, balance, and connection to Babajeran and her many natural kingdoms. Experiences with the Deva, Elemental, Gnome, Sylph, Salamander, and the Undine and Fairy Kingdoms become amplified, along with HU-man interconnectedness to the Evolutionary Biome.

Ceremony,

Right Resolve, Intention

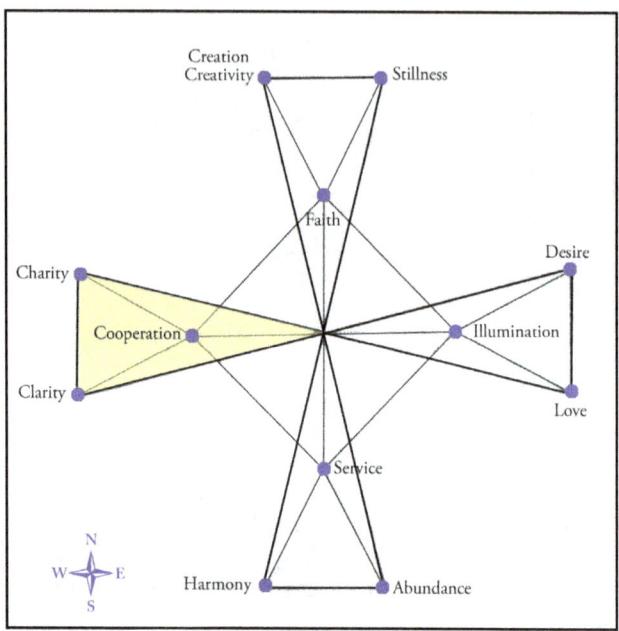

The Evolutionary Field of Ceremony infuses energetics that support our spiritual intentions, oaths, and declarations of spiritual growth, evolution, our Ascension Process, and victory in Ascension. Naturally this includes a foundation in spiritual practice, with a primary emphasis placed upon the use of the Violet Flame. The Violet Flame's energies of Mercy, Compassion, and Forgiveness help us to understand and gain the necessary detachment to spiritually integrate self and willingly serve humanity and the Great White Brotherhood.

Through the integration of the Twelve Jurisdictions, Divine Service is expressed in the Adjutant Points of Clarity, Charity, Cooperation, and the benefic Star energies. Pilgrimages throughout the Western Doors of Golden Cities help to clarify intentions and prepare us for the *Great Plan*.[1]

---

1. The overall plan of the Spiritual Hierarchy's goal for humanity's spiritual growth and evolution is sometimes referred to by Theosophists and Ascended Masters alike as the *Great Plan*. The Hierarchy's strategy focuses on the development of the strength of the Inner Government of Earth to construct a higher and more enduring civilization based upon these ideals and metaphysical precepts:
   - Humanity's recognition of the important parallels between scientific and spiritual laws.
   - Love is the great teacher; love is the great educator; love is the great evolver.
   - There is ONE Life, the limitless, incomprehensible from which all matter manifests.
   - The human will is developed and evolved through conscious knowledge of individual thoughts, feelings, and actions.
   - World conflict, combat, and division can be overcome through friendship, respect, support, service, cooperation, and equality.
   - Eastern philosophy and religion's two greatest principles are the Doctrine of Karma (Cause and Effect; Universal Causation) and the Doctrine of Reincarnation. As a result, Eastern values are focused on family and community. The Christian West places great emphasis on the value of the individual (resilience; independence) and the Ideal of Service. As a result Western values are centered on the use of strength to help the weak overcome oppression.

In the Buddhist tradition this Evolutionary Field is known as *Right Resolve* or *Right Intention*. This principle relies on spiritual renunciation, and developing compassion and good will towards others. In Ascended Master Teaching these qualities are cultivated through a two-fold application of the Violet Flame. The first practice relies on the alchemy of the Violet Flame applied during dawn—the rising of the Sun. This yang aspect of the Sacred Fire encourages true altruism and service, as the Flame transforms confusion, scarcity, self-centeredness, selfishness, and spiritual darkness. The yin characteristics of the Violet Flame are supported with meditation and decree during the setting of the Sun. This practice engenders detachment and renunciation from worldly karmas, as the Sacred Fire nurtures the growth of Love, Mercy, Compassion, and Forgiveness for self and others.

Other than Golden City Star locations, the Ceremony Evolution Field is perhaps the best location within a Golden City Vortex to perform water and fire ceremony. State new intentions and reaffirm goals during your Spiritual Pilgrimage to this Evolutionary Field. The Western Door is the Spiritual Hierarchy's choice location for the *Oath Ceremony* that initiates our entrance into the Great White Brotherhood. The energies of this field are purifying, transformational, and alchemical.

- The Great Plan concentrates on the merging of both important philosophies and cultural values to realize the Ideal of Nations as one Family, and the Ideal of Universal Peace.
- The Law of Brotherhood is the basis of civilization; the Law of Sacrifice sustains civilization. The Temple of Humanity is built with Brotherhood, Love, Amity, and Freedom.

These eight precepts were outlined by Annie Besant, an early founder of the Theosophical Movement, in four lectures she delivered in London in June and July of 1921, "Britain's Place in the Great Plan."

Fire Ceremony

Decree,
Right Speech

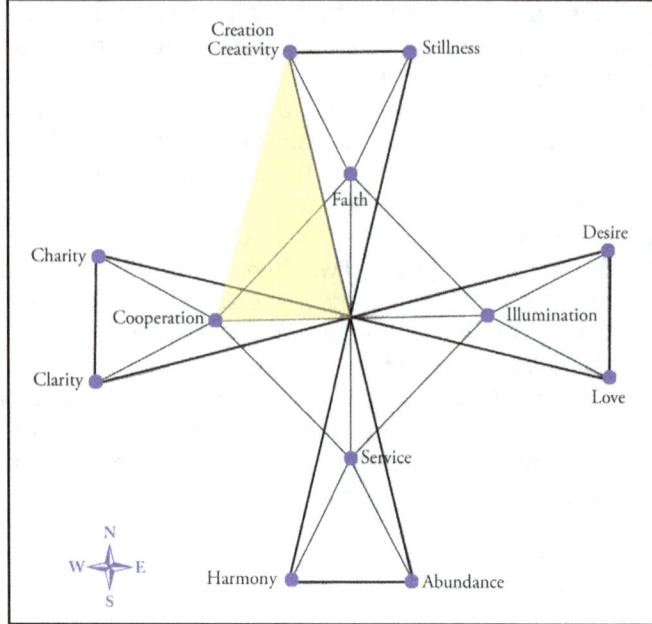

The Holy Bible states, "In the beginning was the word, and the word was with God, and the word was God."[1] Sound is the first principle of creation, and the Divine Light follows. The Evolutionary Field of Decree celebrates and reinforces this Divine Law, and infuses the spiritual pilgrim with added energy to realize the Co-creative power of the word.

In Buddhism, the principle of *Right Speech* advises one to abstain from lying, gossip, and the use of abusive words as they may cause disunity, anger, and hatred among others. Ascended Master Teaching agrees with this premise, however a Spiritual Master also understands the power of the spoken word and its undeniable ability to create. Sound does not discriminate, and thoughtless, frivolous outbursts can create negative thought-forms and unconscious Subjective Energy Bodies.[2] However, the foundation of HU-man Co-creative ability is the positive use of decree and fiat. Chelas and Initiates of the Ascended Masters hone and discipline their spiritual practice through the intentional use of *decree*—a form of rhythmic mantra, and the *fiat*—a commanding, yet simple and masterful statement.

The Evolutionary Field of Decree relies on the Adjutant Points of Cooperation, Creation-Creativity, and the Golden City Star to assist and support the powerful use of sound and the spoken word. This also involves the ability to understand the varying vibrations of tone, pitch, and octave with their important subtleties, including the meaningful use of time and place. This esoteric knowledge is honed through the Jurisdiction of Stillness. Pilgrimages through this remarkable Evolutionary Field align your meditations and inner guidance with seasoned Golden City Hierarchs who may directly share their soul-commanding knowledge.

---

1. John 1:1.
2. This type of energy is similar to a thought-form, which causes behavioral changes when triggered. They are created through intense emotions, addictive behaviors, and the use of addictive substances, and often contain elements of lower consciousness.

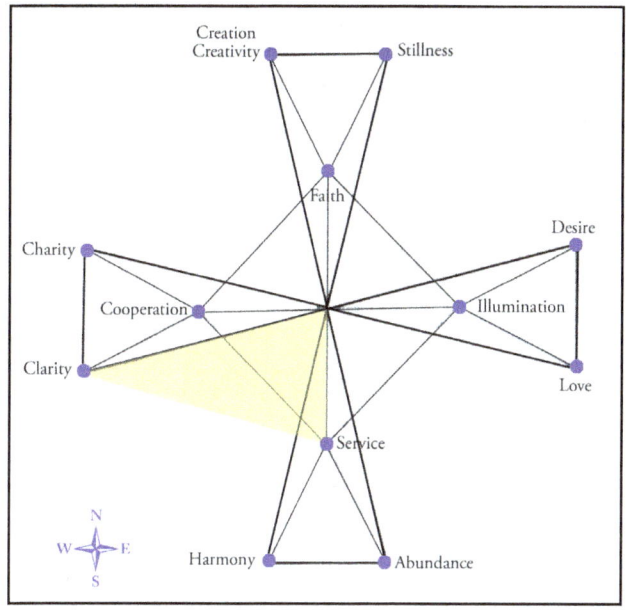

Pillar One,
El Morya

El Morya, the First Pillar, oversees the Southwest region of every Golden City Vortex. As the director of Pillar One, El Morya focuses the principle of innate divinity into this Evolutionary Field. Pillar One represents the Divine Monad within the Eight-sided Cell of Perfection, where we humbly begin our spiritual journey. This Evolutionary Field quickly develops our spiritual intelligence, as we evolve through contact and rapport with our Mighty I AM Presence. Pillar One assures our steady contact and guidance with the Mighty I AM, as we evolve from "self into selfhood." This remarkable Evolutonary Field contains the Adjutant Points of Service, Clarity, and the Golden City Star.

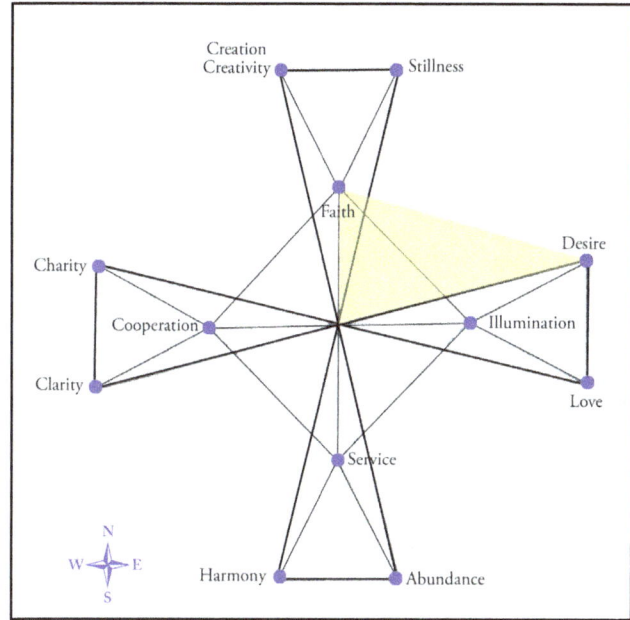

Pillar Two,
Kuthumi

Kuthumi, the Second Pillar, oversees the Northeast region of every Golden City Vortex. Pillar Two assists the purification of our Mental Body from excessive karmic action. This Evolutionary Fields helps us to overcome the judging of others and their actions through the cultivation of self-observation. The underlying spiritual law is founded upon Christ's famous *Sermon on the Mount* where he taught, "Judge not, lest you be judged."[1] When we discipline our thoughts, we begin to overcome the karmic

---
1. Matthew 5:3—7:27.

cycle and the Wheel of Karma. This Evolutionary Field assists our ability to observe and to become *the Witness*.[2] This includes integrating the Jurisdictions of Faith and Desire, since Pillar Two's Evolutionary Field is composed of these two Adjutant Points and the Golden City Star.

Pillar Three,
Saint Germain

Saint Germain is the Third Pillar, and oversees this Evolutionary Field, located in the Southeast region of every Golden City. This important field of energy assures that the spiritual principle of *Freedom of Choice* is instilled among humanity and upheld throughout our world governments. This is the third spiritual precept from the "Book of Truths," and speaks plainly regarding others' possessions, and that we must overcome the desire to possess and control others.

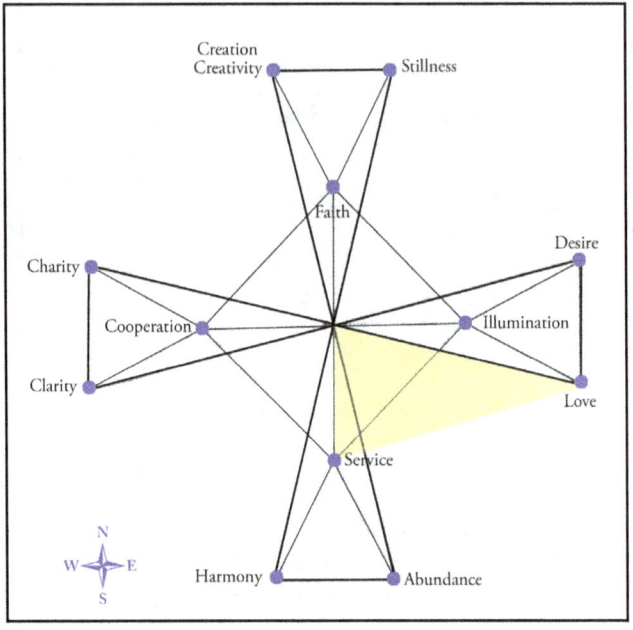

The Third Pillar is composed of the Adjutant Points of Love and Service, and the Golden City Star. Freedom of Choice is celebrated through the spiritual knowledge of allowing, and overcoming fear and judgment. This Evolutionary Field is based upon the Jurisdiction Love, as allowing, maintaining, and sustainability. We develop and perfect our love through the Jurisdiction Service, which is the activity of the Law of Love.[3][4]

---

2. The conscious state of the Witness creates neutrality within self, and develops awareness of personal thoughts and feelings. As you cultivate and develop *Witness Consciousness* you enhance the awareness of your flow of energy, a decreased state of polarity, and begin to identify and experience Oneness.

3. Perhaps every religion on Earth is founded upon the Law of Love, as the notion to "treat others as you would like to be treated." The Law of Love, however, from the Ascended Master tradition is simply understood as consciously living without fear, or inflicting fear on others. The Fourth of the Twelve Jurisdictions instructs Love is the Law of Allowing, Maintaining, and Sustainability. All of these precepts distinguish love from an emotion or feeling, and observe Love as action, will, or choice. The Ascended Masters affirm, "If you live love, you will create love." This premise is fundamental to understand the esoteric underpinnings of the Law of Love. The Master Teachers declare that through practicing the Law of Love one experiences acceptance and understanding; tolerance, alongside detachment. Metaphysically, the Law of Love allows different and varied perceptions of ONE experience, situation, or circumstance to exist simultaneously. From this viewpoint the Law of Love is the practice of tolerance.

4. To learn more about the Four Pillars and the "Truth of Ages," see *A Teacher Appears*, page 126.

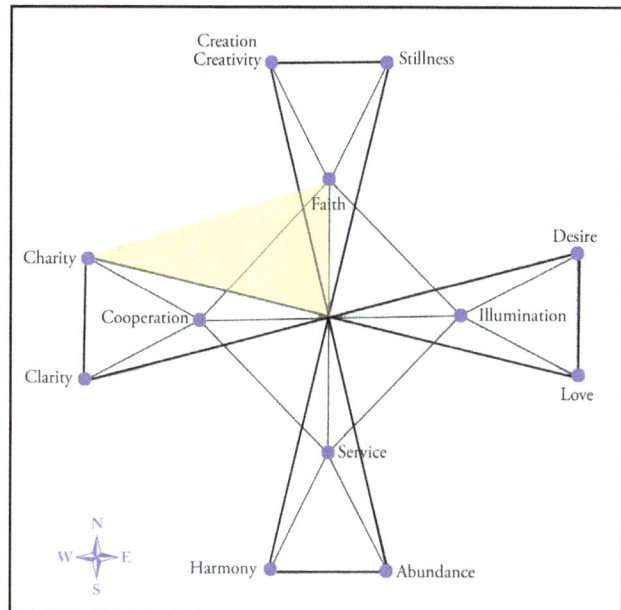

Pillar Four,
Lord Sananda

Lord Sananda oversees the Evolutionary Field of the Fourth Pillar, located in the Northwest region of every Golden City. This field of Golden City energy is based upon the simple, yet powerful action, *Love One Another.* This spiritual tenet is founded upon the release of the personal expectations we have of others. This opens our soul to the potential of unconditional love, a primary standard of the Christ Consciousness. We learn and perfect our love through *acceptance,* honed by the Adjutant Points of Charity, Faith, and the Golden City Star.

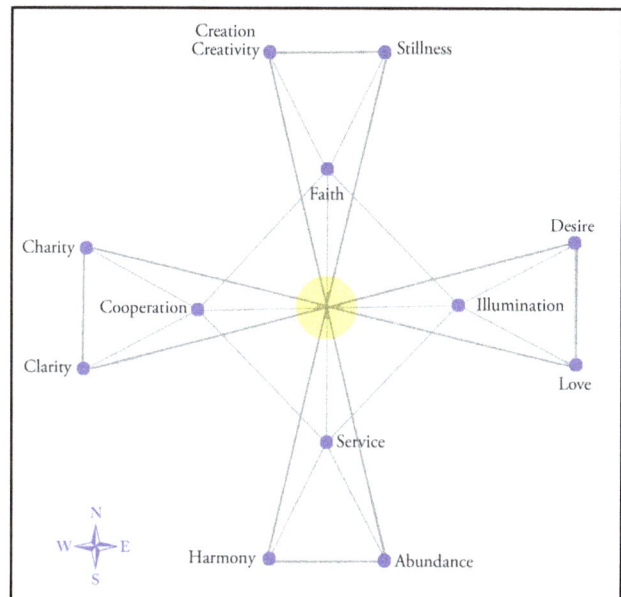

The Star,
Serapis Bey

The Evolutionary Field of the Golden City Star is overseen by the Ascended Master Serapis Bey.[1] Serapis Bey was the Archangel who purposely lowered his energies to Earth to build the first Golden City on Earth—Shamballa. He oversees every Initiate, as they progress through their Ascension Process and assists the Ascension of humanity with the energies of the White Ray. He is assisted by his energetic complement, Lady Luxor, who guards, guides, and protects the Fifth Dimensional Ascension Temple located in the Star of every Golden City.

---

1. An Ascended Master from Venus who works on the White Ray. He is the great disciplinarian — essential for Ascension; and works closely with all unascended humanity who remain focused for its attainment.

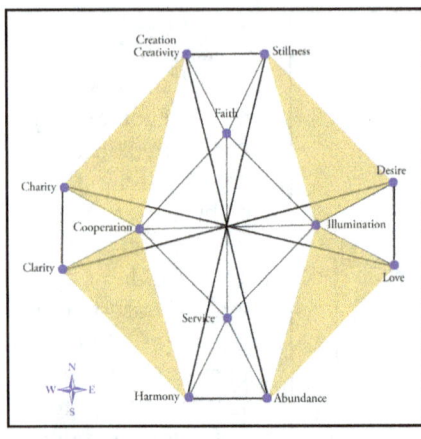

Overview of the Fourfold Flame Evolutionary Fields

The four Evolutionary Fields of the Fourfold Flame work in adjunct with the Four Pillars. Each aspect of the Fourfold Flame: Love, Wisdom, Power, and Desire, works with a complement of energy to the Four Pillars and their respective regions. A flame of a Ray Force is defined as the *activity of the Ray*, and the qualities of the Fourfold Flame act in similar fashion. Each Ascended Master of the Four Pillars holds a focused aspect of the Ascension Process, while their complementary Flame carries the energy into Earthly realization and actualization. In reality, the regionalized fields work together—a genuine Oneship. The inner Field protects, guides, and supports the human to HU-man Ascension Process. As one moves through the Evolutionary Fields of the Fourfold Flame, the teaching refines into consciousness, where it is ably applied.

Southwest Region of the Golden City: Lady Desiree works in tandem with the Ascended Master El Morya.

Northeast Region of the Golden City: Lady Nada joins forces with Ascended Master Kuthumi.

Southeast Region: Portia, the Twin Flame of Saint Germain, applies her effort in this area.

Northwest Region: Lady Miriam is the complement of energy to Lord Sananda.

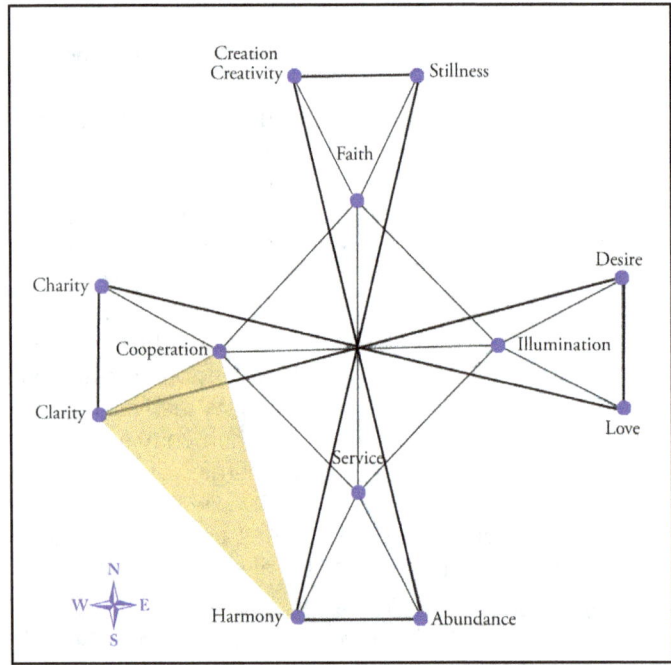

Lady Desiree, Southwest Region

Lady Desiree oversees the Evolutionary Field of the Flame of Desire, (left), that reinstates and restores our divine heritage. This includes radical changes throughout our light fields. This region specifically targets DNA, producing both subtle and intense shifts, particularly throughout the Crown Chakra. Our regal self emerges;

Propel Your Ascension

prepared to ascend the majestic throne of spiritual liberation and freedom. This Evolutionary Field is composed of three Adjutant Points: Harmony, Clarity, and Cooperation.

Lady Nada, Northeast Region

Lady Nada hones the Mental Body and our thought processes throughout the Evolutionary Field of the Fourfold Flame of Wisdom. Nada's perceptive yet tender insight helps one to overcome spiritual darkness and polarity

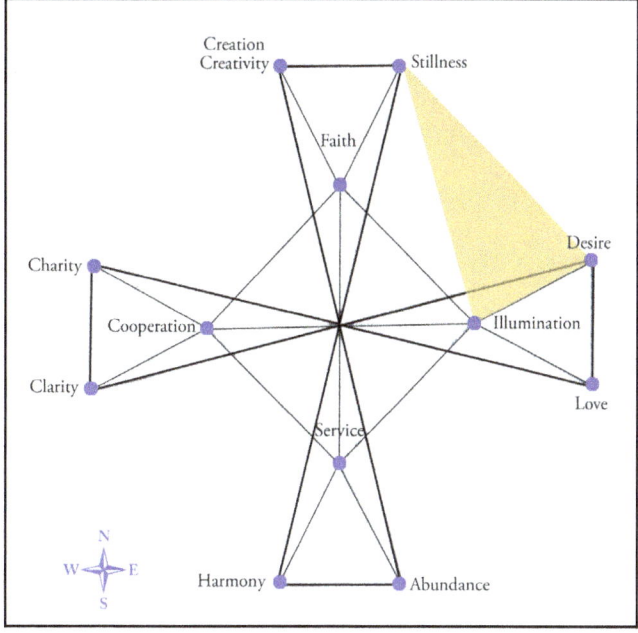

throughout this Golden City region, to fully integrate the qualities of Divine Wisdom. This Evolutionary Field, (above), is composed of the three Adjutant Points of Illumination, Desire, and Stillness.

Portia, Southeast Region

Portia, Goddess of Justice and Opportunity, and the Twin Flame of Saint Germain, refines and balances our energies throughout this field of the Fourfold Flame of Power. She assures that we align our feminine energies through the Adjutant Points of Abundance, Love, and Illumination. This field clears, stabilizes, and evolves the Heart Chakra and Third Eye Chakra, and it is claimed that its energetics can swiftly evolve the HU-man sensing ability.

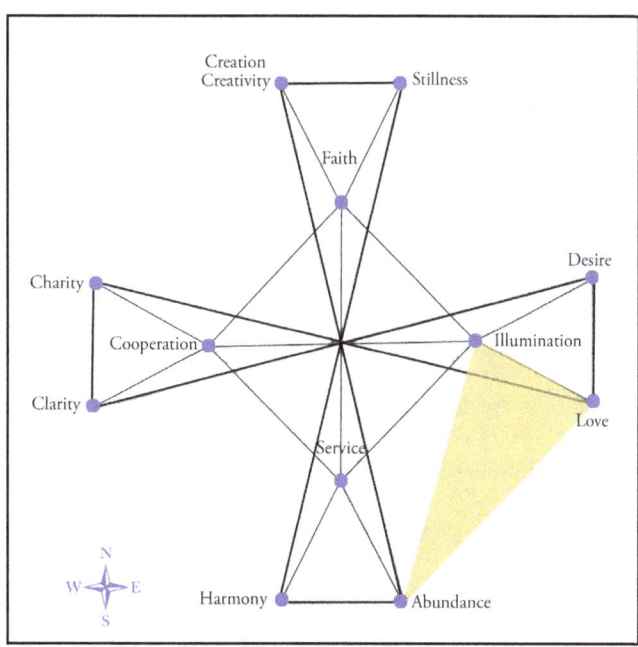

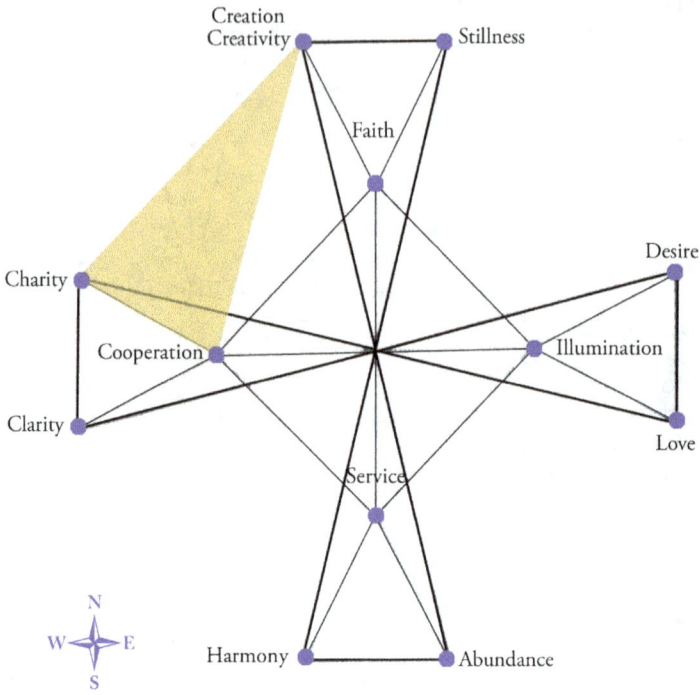

Lady Miriam, Northwest Region

Miriam, a Lady Ascended Master traditionally associated with the Blue Ray, complements the energies of Lord Sananda in this region of the Golden City. This Evolutionary Field of the Fourfold Flame of Love calibrates and refines our energy fields to readily enter the Oneness of Peace, preparing our masterful entrance into the ONE. The activity of the Flame of Love prompts our consciousness to pierce the Group Mind and calibrate Earth's Collective Consciousness for global peace and balance. This Evolutionary Field is composed of the Adjutant Points of Cooperation, Clarity, and Creation-Creativity. It is claimed that Lady Miriam's spiritual heritage is the revered lineage of Pleiadean Archangels.[1] She applies the Shalahah mantra *OM Sheahah*, as "I AM as ONE Heart." The activity of the Fourfold Flame of Love evolves our HU-man energetics for bi-location, remote viewing, shape-shifting, and time travel.

Lady Luxor, Golden City Star

Lady Luxor oversees each initiate and candidate for the Ascension alongside Beloved Serapis Bey in every Golden City Star location. It is claimed that Serapis Bey oversees the heart of the Star frequencies, within a radius of zero to twenty miles. Lady Luxor oversees the activity of the Star, from twenty to forty miles radius. Both Serapis Bey and Lady Luxor work with the White Ray of Beauty, Balance, and Purification.

---

1. *Lady Miriam, Beloved Teacher,* www.crystalwind.ca, (2015).

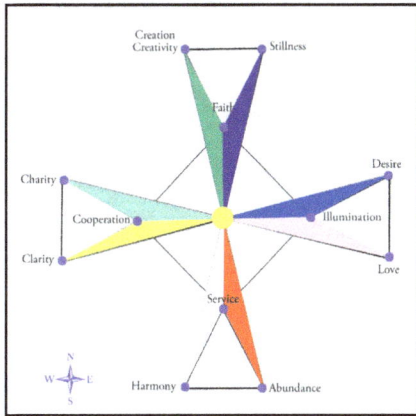

Nine Heavenly Gates

With the exception of the Golden City Star, which is the spherical center of the Golden City, eight of the Nine Heavenly Gates are obtuse isosceles triangles. Their shape creates intense and powerful energies with experiences that unite Heaven and Earth, alongside spiritual development and initiation into both Fourth and Fifth Dimension. The Golden City Star represents the activity of the Unfed Flame of Love, Wisdom, and Power and holds the energies of all Eight Beloved Archangels through the Divine Intervention of compassion, insight, and alignment to the Divine Plan.

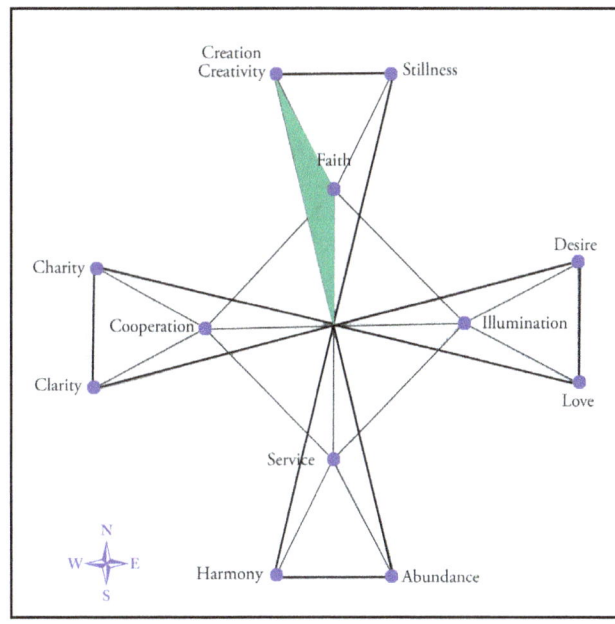

Archangel Raphael, Angel of Healing and Music

Archangel Raphael holds healing energies for individuals and humanity through an adept understanding of the Plant Kingdom and of their numerous curative powers. Since the Green Ray is also associated with truth, science, wholeness, and mathematics, energies from this Evolutionary Field assist mankind's movement into new technology through advanced medical cures and treatments. These new energies assist humanity at many levels, healing incurable diseases, illnesses, and disorders through scientific discovery.

The Green Ray is also linked to the abundant life, the principle of *Aboundness,* money, and financial freedom. This Evolutionary Field helps the new economies of the world to take shape without the need for fiat currencies.

Archangel Raphael works closely with Mother Mary and Lord Sananda. They are alleged to carry numerous thought-forms associated with our Divine Perfection, healing, herbs, alternative health, and medical intervention. Raphael is also known as the Angel of Music, and uses sound vibration for both healing and precipitation.

Archangel Zadkiel, Angel of Alchemy and Divine Justice

Archangel Zadkiel's Evolutionary Field is located on the east side of the Golden City Northern Door. Zadkiel serves the Violet Ray of alchemy, transmutation, forgiveness, compassion, and Divine Justice. His cosmic consciousness presides over this area of each Golden City, and it is alleged that the benefic energies of the Violet Ray release on Saturday, the final day of the week. The Violet Ray assists humanity to release negative karma and initiate our freedom through the Ascension Process.

The Violet Flame holds the secrets of alchemy that are founded on the spiritual principles of mercy, forgiveness, and the power of transmutation. Zadkiel is the angel of miracles, and accepts our prayers and decrees for Divine Intercession. It is claimed he is surrounded by legions of Violet Flame Angels, who work tirelessly as spiritual warriors for humanity's freedom in the light. Because of this, this Evolutionary Field is good for prayer to alleviate humanity's karmic burden and the effects of collective, mass karma on Earth.

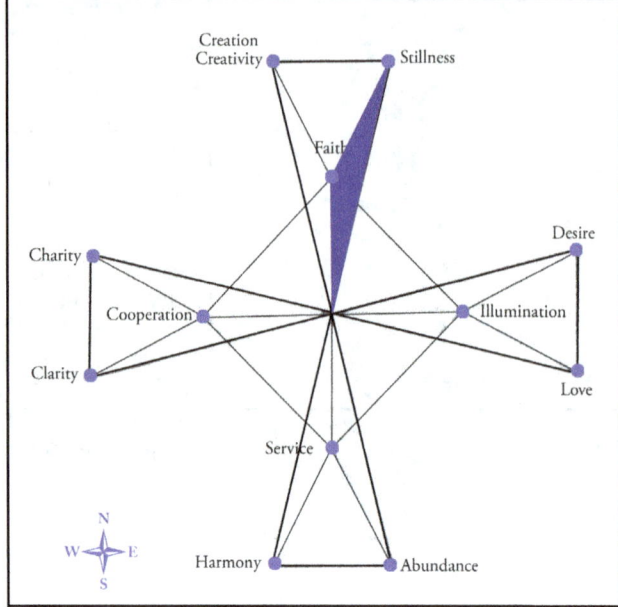

Archangel Michael, Angel of God Obedience and Strength

Archangel Michael's Evolutionary Field is located on the north side of the Eastern Door of the Golden City. Michael and his legions of Blue Flame Angels descend from Fourth Dimension and into the Astral Plane to rescue humanity from their self-created shadows and personal darkness. Those who have entered their Ascension Process may call upon them for God Protection in any circumstance and for deliverance from negativity and karmic entanglement.

The Blue Flame of Archangel Michael protects the perfection of the Christ Consciousness that is developing within the chela, and holds the blueprint of our HU-man evolution. Michael is associated with perfection, protection, and the security and safety found in our Divine Plan and Divine Will. His stalwart protection, through the principle of God Obedience, empowers our faith and victory in the Ascension.

This Evolutionary Field gives us the God Strength to fight the spiritual battle that cuts our consciousness free from negativity and karmic entrapment. Naturally, this field infuses the Blue Ray into our consciousness, and prepares our soul's majestic entrance into both Fourth and Fifth Dimensional awareness. Since the Blue Ray is a purifying force, it trains the soul to release pain and suffering and accept the glory of our innate divinity and purposeful Cosmic Service.

Archangel Chamuel, Angel of Divine Love

Archangel Chamuel's Evolutionary Field is located on the south side of the Eastern Door of the Golden City. Chamuel's energies celebrate the principle of Divine Love through the attributes of devotion, adoration, mercy, compassion, and kindness. These characteristics are

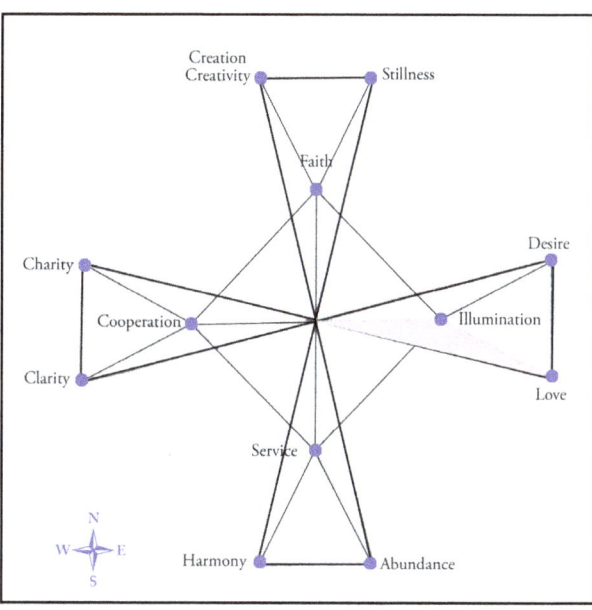

realized through the attainment of Christ Consciousness and the perfection of God's Eternal Love.

This Evolutionary Field reinforces the perfected Divine Love that is within, and forges an indelible connection with the Eight-sided Cell of Perfection, resulting in the gifts of the Holy Spirit. Communication with the Mighty I AM Presence and members of the Great White Brotherhood is realized and perfected in Pilgrimages and through time spent in this Evolutionary Field. The Flame of Love is reinforced through trust, conviction, and reliance upon the God Source—the Mighty I AM Presence. Archangel Chamuel helps one to overcome problems involving family matters, marriage, partnership, and challenging interpersonal relationships.

PHOTONS

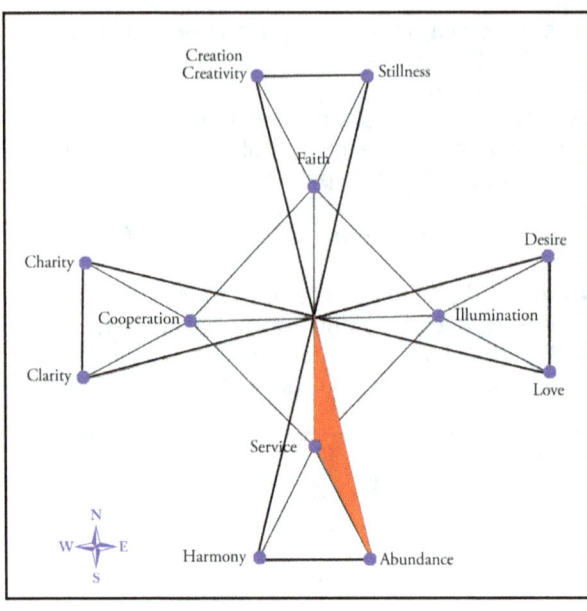

Archangel Uriel, Angel of Divine Light and Peace

Archangel Uriel's Evolutionary Field is located on the east side of the Southern Door. Uriel, the Archangel of the Ruby-Gold Ray administers the Flame of Peace to humanity which engenders the Eight-sided Cell of Perfection within every aspiring HU-man Being. Through his stewardship of God's Divine Light, Uriel also helps humanity to overcome the shadows of the lower Astral Plane and the death consciousness. In ancient teachings, it is claimed that Uriel is the Archangel of the underworld.

This Evolutionary Field, similar to the field overseen by Archangel Michael, helps us to release our shadows. Uriel guides our spiritual journey through the premise of achieving personal balance, and the harmony and tranquility found with the Peace of God. The binding of demons and evil spirits, both self-created, worldly, and other-wordly, is achieved in this Evolutionary Field. This allows the chela to release fear at many levels, and prepares the soul for resurrection, through renewal, rebirth, and rejuvenation. This transformation engenders the presence of the Resurrection Flame that penetrates darkness and separation, and initiates the Ascension Process. Uriel's Evolutionary Field promotes change, atonement, and the removal of negative karma through the recognition and self-realization of innate divinity.

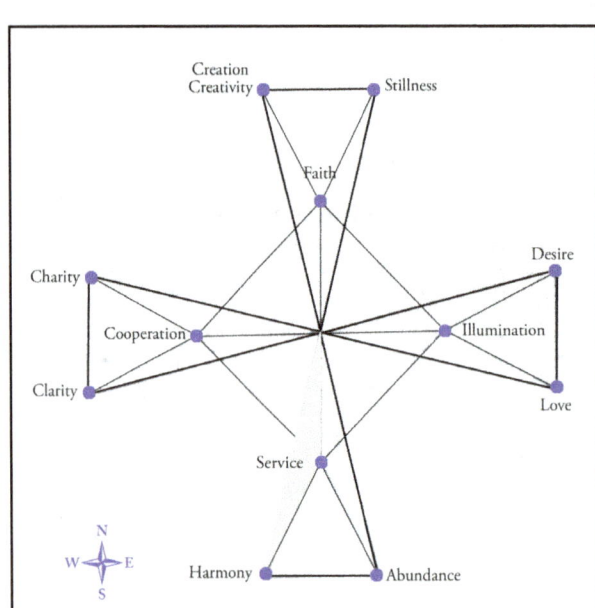

Archangel Gabriel, Angel of Purity and Divine Order

Archangel Gabriel's Evolutionary Field is located on the west side of the Southern Door. Gabriel's field of energy is devoted to the principle of purity, resurrection, and the Ascension. This Evolutionary Field connects us to our Soul Family and the essential Akashic Records that reveal our soul's lineage and incarnation through God's Divine Order. It is claimed that Archangel Gabriel protects the incoming New Children, and places a blessing on each new incoming soul to achieve Christ Consciousness and enter into the Ascension Process. This Evolutionary Field's attributes are expectancy, joy, enthusiasm, and the realization of True Memory.

Through God's Divine Order, this field of energy holds the organization and categorization of the multiple Ashrams of Light throughout each Golden City, their Ray Forces, and each Divine Purpose. This field is multidimensional in experience, with an emphasis on Fifth-Dimensional experience.

Archangel Jophiel, Angel of Divine Wisdom and Illumination

Archangel Jophiel's Evolutionary Field is located on the south side of the Western Door of every Golden City. This is an Evolutionary Field that infuses one with enlightenment, illumination, and the Divine Wisdom and Divine Right of Choice. Through the process of Divine Illumination, time spent in this field of energy illumines consciousness to overcome the gross ignorance found in conventional thinking

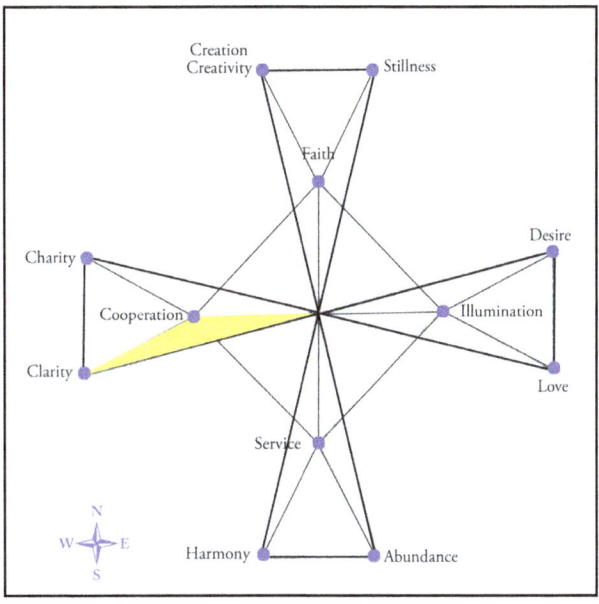

and the darkness of Kali Yuga. The "Light of God that Never Fails" lights the darkness found in politics, science and medicine, food, health, and the environment. This pristine and pure light frees the soul from addictions, unhealthy lifestyle patterns, and transforms our educational and health systems.

Jophiel empowers the soul through meditation upon the sublime Mind of God, and encourages a daily spiritual practice that inspires the soul with experiential, personal knowledge.

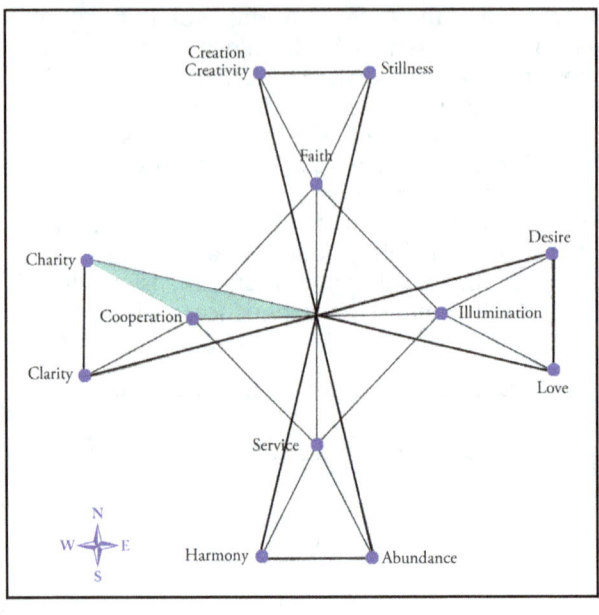

Archangel Chrystiel, Angel of the Divine HU-man

Archangel Chrystiel's Evolutionary Field is located on the north side of the Western Door of the Golden City. Chrystiel is the Archangel of the Golden Age, and the energies of this Evolutionary Field carry the attributes of conscious immortality, Co-creation ability, unity, perception, integration, and self-realization.

Through Archangel Chrystiel's transformative energies, this Evolutionary Field can quickly evolve human perception into HU-man experience through the super senses. Time spent in this Evolutionary Field evolves the senses with the higher senses of clairaudience (clear hearing), clairvoyance (clear foresight), claircognizance (clear knowing), clairintellect (clear knowing), clairempathy (clear emotion), clairsentience (clear physical feeling), clairgustance (clear tasting), clairsalience (clear smelling), and clairtagency (clear touching).[1] The Ascended Masters often refer to the super senses as, "Developing the eyes to see, ears to hear."

All dimensions interact in this Evolutionary Field, with an emphasis on Fourth-Dimensional experience that quickly evolves the human into the HU-man.

(Editor's Note: This section on the Archangel Evolutionary Fields was compiled with information from "The Masters and their Retreats," compiled and edited by Annice Booth.)

The Nine Movements of Consciousness

The Evolutionary Fields of the Archangels are represented in the nine sacred movements of energy within the Golden City. Saint Germain explains that energy moves throughout the Golden City from one region to another, creating a perfect yin-yang, figure eight. These are known as the Nine Movements of Consciousness. This sacred movement begins in the center, then moves to the South, then to the Southeast, and crosses over the Vortex to the Southwest, the energies cross again to the East, and then move to the Northeast, onward to the North, and then to the Northwest, and conclude in the West. This Migration Pattern creates the infinity sign that is eternal, unlimited, and never-ending. In essence, this energetic pattern represents the everlasting perfection of Ascension. This movement is both internal and external, and progresses through the HU-man Eight-sided Cell of Perfection,

---

1. Benilli, Colleen. "The Clair Senses." Reiki Lifestyle. Accessed February 6, 2022. https://reikilifestyle.com/wp-content/uploads/2019/09/The-Clair-Senses.pdf.

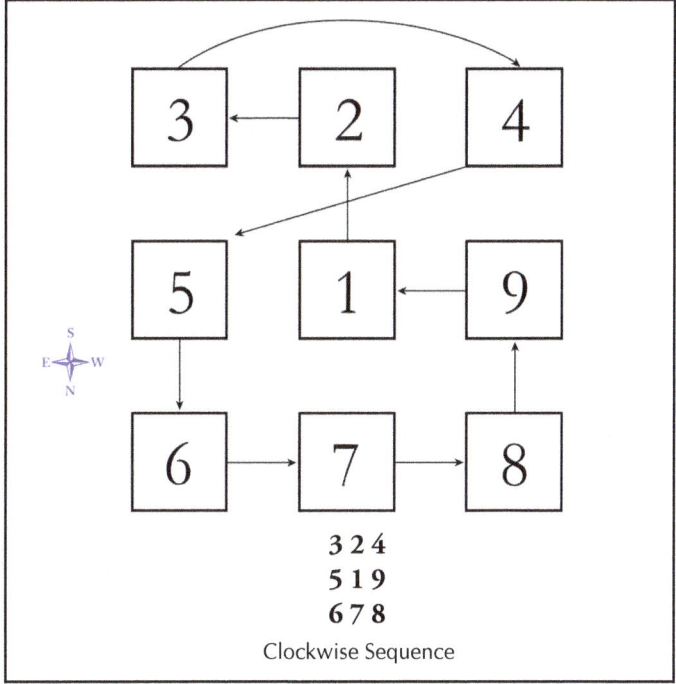

The Nine Movements of Consciousness
Through the Eight-sided Cell of Perfection the nine movements resemble the infinity sign, or the Yin-Yang formation through the figure eight.

and mirrored throughout the regions of the Golden City Vortex. It is defined through our spiritual growth and evolution, and celebrated as a Migratory Path in Spiritual Pilgrimage. An overview of the Archangels Nine Sacred Movements is:

First Movement: The Holy Temple

Our first movement is within the Eight-sided Cell of Perfection and is the recognition of the Unfed Flame. This acknowledgement in itself is considered a consecrated act, so therefore all movements that originate and continue from this point carry the Godhead of Perfection. This Evolutionary Field is represented in the Golden City Star, which is considered the Holy Temple of Self, or the evolution of BE-ing. A sublime Group Mind of all of the Archangels of Creation is present in every Golden City Star.

Second Movement: The Divine Path

Gabriel and Uriel, Outer Child Point, Southern Door: This movement into duality is one of our first steps as we begin our journey with our Divine Path. This palace is similar to the Jyotish Astrological Tenth House, and it represents skill, achievement, honor, and prestige. This palace also represents our Earthly Father and our relationship to Heavenly Father. This Evolutionary Field symbolizes the amount of status and recognition we receive in our chosen profession, and is considered the second movement of the soul as it enters duality.

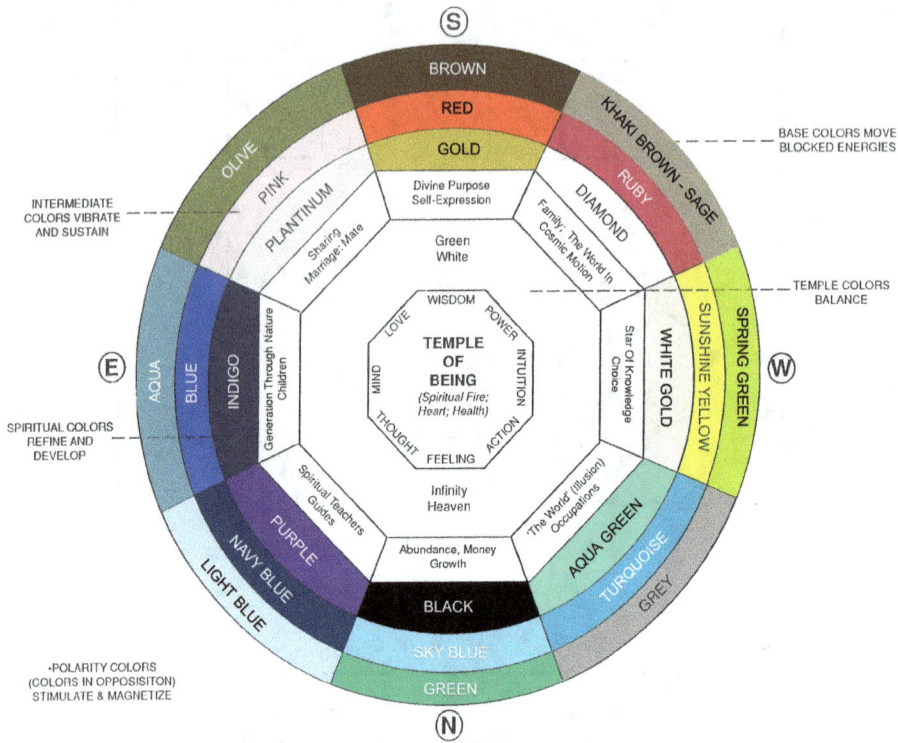

Esoteric Color Wheel of the Nine Palaces within the Eight-sided Cell of Perfection
Various colors express throughout the Nine Palaces of the Eight-sided Cell of Perfection. The colors depicted are not based upon the Color Ray system; however, Ray Forces will express through the esoteric colors.

Third Movement: Marriage and Partnership

Uriel, Southern Door (East) Evolutionary Field: This movement is associated with marriage and partnership. This palace is akin to the Seventh House in Jyotish, which indicates our husband or wife, spiritual partner, Twin Flame, and Divine Complement. This movement represents "the other," and Pilgrimages to this Evolutionary Field can improve interpersonal and intimate relationships, and develop and enhance our ability to affect others.

Fourth Movement: Family

Gabriel, Southern Door (West) Evolutionary Field: The fourth movement represents family, our genetic heritage, and includes our connection to our Spiritual or Soul Family. Similar to the Fourth House in Jyotish, this palace represents our connections to biological family, but also indicates our values. This palace is connected to our values and emotions and Pilgrimages to this point can induce healing in these arenas of life. This Evolutionary Field is deeply connected to our subconscious, and assists the formation of Group Mind.

Fifth Movement: Children and Co-creation

Michael and Chamuel, Outer Child Point, Eastern Door: The fifth movement represents our children, and at a HU-man level signifies our divine Co-creative ability. This is an extraordinary spiritual movement and unites both masculine (yang) and feminine (yin) energies throughout the energy system to empower Christ Consciousness. This spiritual process is known as the Inner Marriage.

Sixth Movement: Spiritual Teachers

Michael, Eastern Door (North) Evolutionary Field: The sixth movement represents our spiritual teachers, gurus, and spirit guides. Pilgrimage to this Evolutionary Field can instantly connect you with Fifth Dimensional teachers, Ascended Masters, and revered saints. Pilgrimage through this Evolutionary Field can release the soul's dharma and seamlessly connect your energy fields with a Master Teacher. This energetic field can also empower the overlighting process, whereby a student gains the ongoing protection, love, support, and guidance of an Ascended Master.

Seventh Movement: Abundance and Bounty

Raphael and Zadkiel, Outer Child Point, Northern Door: The seventh movement reflects the perfection of our Earth Mother—Babajeran—to us through the principle of abundance, wealth, and prosperity. Pilgrimages to this Evolutionary Field can improve personal finance, and also create new possibilities for worldly endeavors and business. Its spiritual energies empower Archangel Raphael's premise of "Aboundance." This is the spiritual acknowledgment that the Universal Substance is always present and provides a bounty of opportunity alongside multiple choices.

Eighth Movement: Worldly Career and Service

Raphael, Northern Door (West) Evolutionary Field: The eighth movement reflects our work, employment, and form of labor in the Third Dimension. This aspect of life is also linked to worldly illusion. Pilgrimages and prayers in this Evolutionary Field can improve our career, or worldly profession. When utilized at an evolved level, Pilgrimage to this area may reveal our Divine Service that can remove and burn away negative karmas.

Ninth Movement: Star of Knowledge

Chrystiel and Jophiel, Outer Child Point, Western Door: The ninth and final movement is also known as the Star of Knowledge. This is a Pilgrimage focused upon the attainment of self-actualization, and obtaining the knowledge of self through the vehicle of choice.

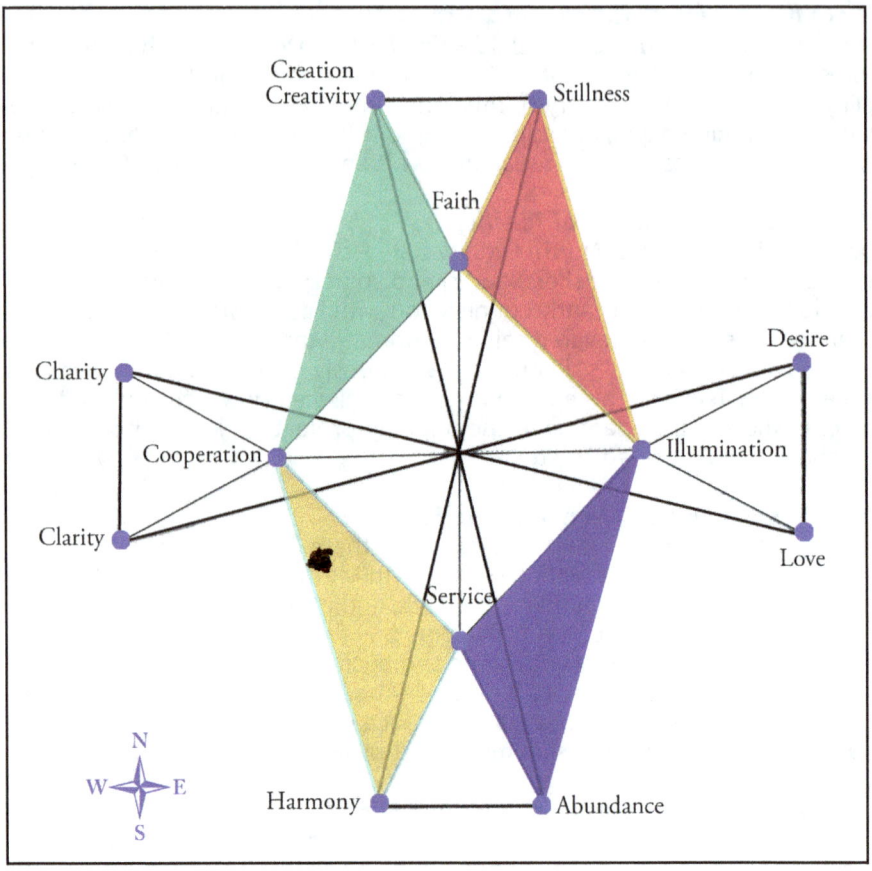

The Evolutionary Fields of the Elohim

In the Ascended Master tradition, the Elohim are considered Ascended Masters who have evolved their consciousness through the Elemental Kingdom. There is, however, another theory that the Elohim, or *Els*, are the ancient teachers of the contemporary Ascended Masters. It is claimed that many of the Ancient Elohim attained their Ascensions in ancient civilizations such as Atlantis or Lemuria. From this viewpoint the Elohim are considered the elder teachers in the lineage of the Spiritual Hierarchy, who have evolved their consciousness and teaching to higher and refined levels of simplicity, focus, and Mastery.

Four Evolutionary Fields in the Golden City are dedicated to these ancestral teachers and focus on four important principles that help to shape and define the Golden Age. The four spiritual tenets are: truth, peace, freedom, and unity. Their sacred geometry is the scalene obtuse triangle. This energy pattern holds hidden knowledge and energies that can produce intense and unique spiritual experiences and growth. These Evolutionary Fields may create time and telepathic anomalies, or dimensional rifting. These fields of energy are primarily focused upon Fourth and Fifth Dimensional experiences.

Propel Your Ascension

The Elohim of Truth: God Vision

The inner Northwest region of every Golden City is the location of the Evolutionary Field overseen by the Elohim of Truth, Vista, and Virginia. This expansive field is formed through the three Adjutant Points of Creation-Creativity, Faith, and Cooperation.

Also known as Cyclopea and Virginia, Cyclopea is known as the Elohim of Vision, hence his name *Vista*. Both Vista and Virginia embody the Mastery of the Third Eye, and this Evolutionary Field can

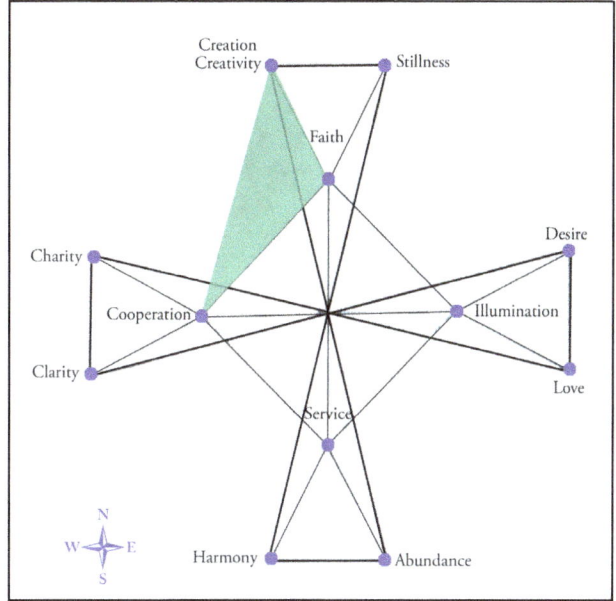

produce God Vision and insight into the Fourth Dimension that is also known as the "All-seeing Eye of God." The two Mighty Elohim serve on the Green Ray, which carries the qualities of health, healing, scientific knowledge and discovery, sound and music.

This Evolutionary Field is infused with the sublime *Music of the Spheres*,[1] and it is claimed that the celestial harmonies and songs are continuously infusing this Golden City region at both the Fourth and Fifth Dimension. These sound frequencies carry both multi-dimensional healing and balancing energies to those who spend time in this area or travel to its Adjutant Points for Spiritual Pilgrimage. It is claimed that the light of this majestic pair of Spiritual Teachers resembles the refracted light of a crystal prism, with flashing lights of emerald green, piercing blue lightning, and the laser purity of white light. Their spiritual teachings focus on the attainment of Christ Consciousness through the loving connection to the Mighty I AM Presence.

The Elohim Vista and Virginia flood you with a radiation of transmuting white light that opens your Third Eye vision to the expansive freedom of the I AM. Pilgrimages to this Golden City region infuse the Step-down Transformer with the spiritual vision to fully realize our divine blueprint, the healing of the nations and our world economies, while counteracting harmful sound waves, the effects of chemtrails on our environments and personal health, and inhumane science. This Evolutionary Field activates the Golden City biome to collectively and rapidly realize the natural, true God Science, and galvanizes the innate Science of the Soul with our achievement and victory of the Ascension.

---

1. *Music of the Spheres* is an ancient Pythagorean concept that the movement of the planets produces a specific sound vibration or pitch that is proportional, and can be relayed in shapes, angles, mathematics, and unique tones. Other esoteric researchers claim that the Music of the Spheres is also a type of Fourth-Dimensional music, composed of angelic choirs, stringed instruments, and celestial trumpets. Some report this inter-dimensional music upon awakening in the morning, especially when located in Golden City Adjutant Points and Star locations. The Music of the Spheres is inordinately healing, and can adjust our energy fields and vibrational frequencies.

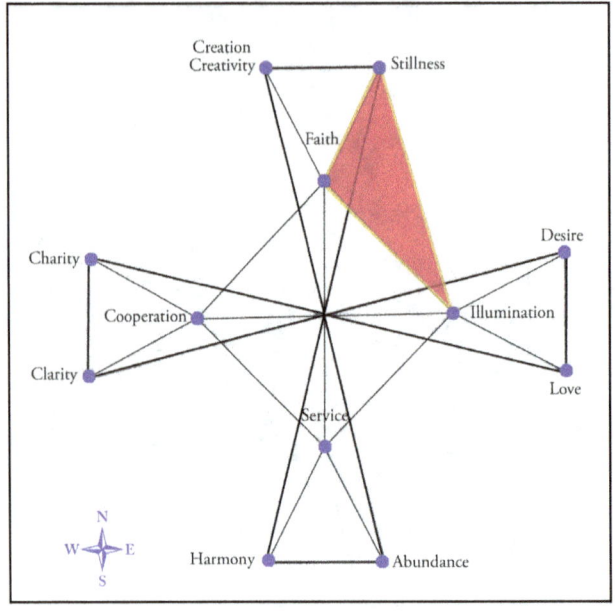

The Elohim of Peace: Cosmic Christ Consciousness

The inner Northeast section of every Golden City is served by the Elohim of Peace. The two spiritual teachers, known as Peace and Tranquility, serve this Evolutionary Field that is defined by the three Adjutant Points of Stillness, Faith, and Illumination.

The masculine Elohim Peace, and the feminine Elohim Tranquility—who is also known as *Aloha* in other Ascended Master Teaching, serves the Ruby and Gold Ray. It is claimed that Lord Sananda, in his incarnation as Jesus Christ, realized the Christ Consciousness through their teachings and that their energies illumine and radiate the Cosmic Christ throughout all Golden Cities.

Spiritual Pilgrimages and time spent in this Evolutionary Field promote the Peace of God by transmuting fear and stilling emotion. It is claimed that the energies of Peace and Tranquility perfectly balance the solar plexus from emotional disturbance or any other worldly influence. This region of the Golden City also calibrates Earth's Collective Consciousness for freedom from war and violence with the fiat, "Peace, be still and know that I AM God!"

This Evolutionary Field assists the transmutation of anger through forgiveness of self and others, magnifies the use of the Violet Flame, and enhances the personal cultivation of humility. We overcome irritation and resentment through renouncing harshness, insensitivity, and critical thoughts of others. Peace and Tranquility advise chelas to develop gentleness and kindness of spirit, and to guard our subconscious of thoughts of darkness, revenge, and greed. During Spiritual Pilgrimage to this Evolutionary Field, the Elohim Peace and Tranquility suggest meditation in the Inner Garden of Peace and visualization upon the Unfed Flame within the Eight-sided Cell of Perfection. It is also suggested to use prayer and decree and call upon Peace and Tranquility's ten-thousand angels of peace when physically present within this Evolutionary Field. It is claimed that this legion of angels can instantly deflect world wars and violence throughout the Earth, and intervene to Co-create a new world of Golden Age peace for humanity.

The Elohim of Freedom: The Freedom Flame

The Evolutionary Field of the Elohim of Freedom, Arctura and Diana, is created through the Adjutant Points of Abundance, Service, and Illumination. This exceptional field of energy is located in the inner Southeast Region of every Golden City. In other Ascended Master Teachings, the masculine Arctura is also known as *Arcturus*, and the feminine Diana is known as *Victoria*.

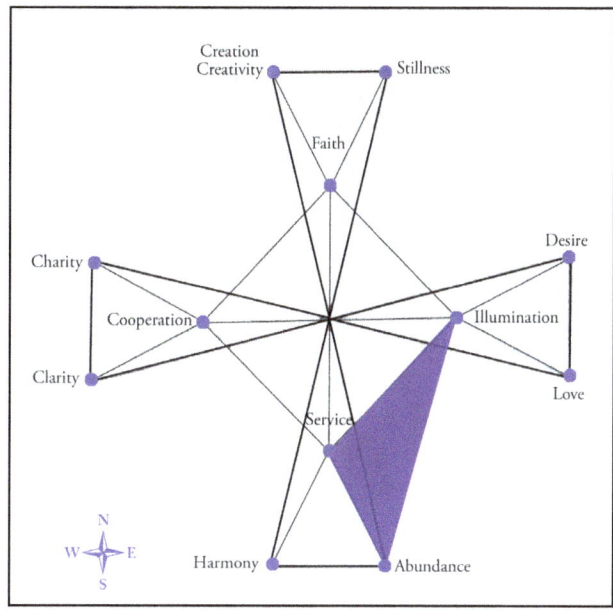

This Elohim duo focuses their energies into each Golden City for the principles of freedom, mercy, alchemy, and the victory of Ascension through the transmuting Violet Ray. The dynamic activity of the Violet Ray anchors the vibrant and forceful *Freedom Flame* into the biome of the Golden Cities.

Spiritual Pilgrimage and time spent in this remarkable Evolutionary Field can generate and intensify the Divine Intervention of the Violet Flame into any problem, dilemma, or obstacle. The secrets of the Violet Flame were once carefully guarded in the Halls of Shamballa, and its transmuting and karma ameliorating knowledge was first introduced to humanity through a special dispensation in the 1930s.[2] Today, its practice is an essential precursor to the use of the expansive Gold Ray that initiates human consciousness into HU-man experience. This Evolutionary Field sustains and maintains the Freedom Flame into the Golden City biome for humanity's spiritual development, spiritual freedom, and Ascension.

Arctura and Diana carry the ancient teachings of the Violet Flame through both spoken word and sound vibration. This extraordinary Golden City region is engendered with the spiritual velocity to transform Beloved Babajeran—Mother Earth—into the majestic *Freedom Star*.

---

2. The Violet Flame was first introduced to the public through the *I AM Activity*, which was founded by Guy and Edna Ballard in the early 1930s. Guy Ballard claims that while he was hiking on Mount Shasta he was contacted by the Ascended Master Saint Germain, who later instructed him on the application of the Violet Flame and affirmations. The Violet Flame progresses the spiritual development of the chela through ameliorating and eliminating difficult karmas. This spiritual practice can initiate the Ascension Process.

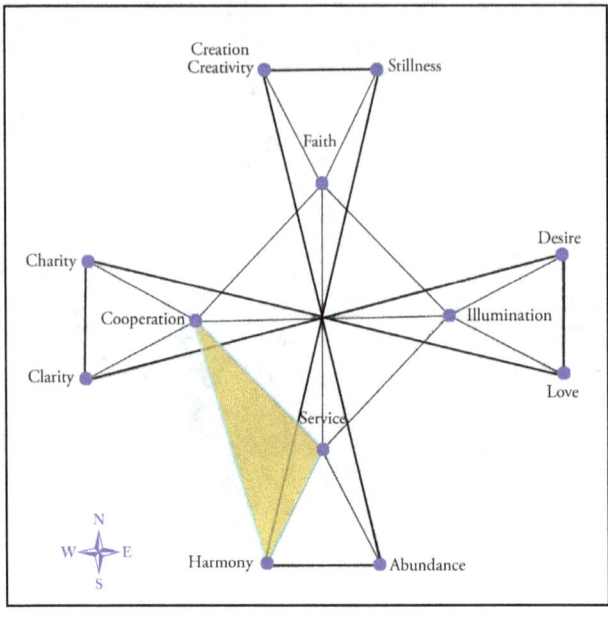

The Elohim of Unity: Heaven and Earth Unite

The Adjutant Points of Harmony, Service, and Cooperation define the boundaries of the Evolutionary Field of Unity, stewarded by the Elohim Rainbow and Iris. This area is located in the inner Southwest sector of every Golden City. Beloved Rainbow is considered the masculine force, even though his energies seem asexual and perfectly balanced with both masculine and feminine traits. Iris, too, presents balanced energies, but is considered the feminine aspect of this team of spiritual teachers.

Rainbow and Iris serve the Aquamarine and Gold Ray of the Golden Age, and its attributes are unifying and perceptive, intuitive, sensitive, and spiritual. This Ray Force unites the Divine Heaven with the Earthly Divine Man. This is an Evolutionary Field that promotes rapid advancement through spiritual development and realization of the HU-man. Pilgrimages and time spent in this Golden City region can help one to advance, "the eyes to see, and the ears to hear." As the super-senses develop, Earth experiences changes in culture, society, politics, and religion.

This extraordinary Evolutionary Field unifies humanity through shared human to HU-man experience. It plays a critical role in the realization of the Golden Age and the transformation of life in the New Times. These energies assist the development of new medical systems and cures, changes in world economies and currency systems, and assist our culture to move into an entirely new eco-system driven by the needs of evolving human consciousness.

Along with Mother Mary, Rainbow and Iris help to sponsor and educate the New Children, an incoming generation of souls who support the transformation of Earth into the Golden Age. (Editor's Note: This section on the Elohim Evolutionary Fields was compiled with information from "The Masters and their Retreats," compiled and edited by Annice Booth.)

Evolutionary Field	Adjutant Points	Attributes	Type
Human to HU-man: Love	Harmony, Abundance, Service	Threefold Creation, Human Consciousness	Acute Equilateral Triangle
Human to HU-man: Wisdom	Abundance, Love, Service	Threefold Creation, Human Consciousness	Acute Isosceles Triangle—Golden Triangle
Human to HU-man: Power	Harmony, Service, Clarity	Threefold Creation, Human Consciousness	Acute Isosceles Triangle—Golden Triangle
Human to HU-man: Conscience & Consciousness	Service, Clarity, Cooperation	Development of conscience, higher consciousness.	Obtuse Scalene Triangle
Human to HU-man: Spiritual Awakening	Service, Love, Illumination	The Aspirant	Obtuse Scalene Triangle
Human to HU-man: Spiritual Discipline	Love, Illumination, Desire	The Chela	Acute Equilateral Triangle
Human to HU-man: Vision & Compassion	Service, Illumination, Cooperation, Faith	The Initiate	Square, with Eight Inner Triangles
Human to HU-man: Science of Spiritual Wisdom	Clarity, Cooperation, Charity	The Arhat	Acute Equilateral Triangle
Human to HU-man: Strengthen the Soul	Cooperation, Charity, Faith	The Adept	Obtuse Scalene Triangle
Human to HU-man: Mastery	Illumination, Desire, Faith	The Master	Obtuse Scalene Triangle
Human to HU-man: Omega	Desire, Faith, Stillness	HU-man Consciousness	Acute Isosceles Triangle—Golden Triangle
Human to HU-man: Alpha	Charity, Faith, Creation-Creativity	HU-man Consciousness	Acute Isosceles Triangle—Golden Triangle
Human to HU-man: I AM That I AM	Faith, Stillness, Creation-Creativity	Ascended Master	Acute Equilateral Triangle

Evolutionary Field	Adjutant Points	Attributes	Type
Human to HU-man: Golden City Star	All Twelve Jurisdictions	Purification of the Initiate to Freedom in Ascension	Circle and the Spiral
Eight Principles of the Right-Hand Path: Lineage of Gurus	Faith, Stillness, Creation-Creativity	Right Effort, Connection to Shamballa, the Black Door	Acute Isosceles Triangle—Golden Triangle
Eight Principles of the Right-Hand Path: Mysticism	Stillness, Illumination, Golden City Star	Right View, Teachings of the Four Pillars	Acute Isosceles Triangle—Golden Triangle
Eight Principles of the Right-Hand Path: HU-man Psychology	Love, Desire, Illumination, Golden City Star	Right Conduct, the Christ Consciousness, the Blue Door	Acute Isosceles Triangle—Golden Triangle
Eight Principles of the Right-Hand Path: Prayer	Abundance, Illumination, Golden City Star	Right Samadhi, the Plane of Reciprocity, the Inner Garden	Acute Isosceles Triangle—Golden Triangle
Eight Principles of the Right-Hand Path: Prophecy	Harmony, Abundance, Service, Golden City Star	Right Mindfulness, Healing of the Nations, the Southern Door	Acute Isosceles Triangle—Golden Triangle
Eight Principles of the Right-Hand Path: Beauty of Nature	Harmony, Cooperation, Golden City Star	Right Livelihood, Seventh Generation Principle, Evolutionary Biome	Acute Isosceles Triangle—Golden Triangle
Eight Principles of the Right-Hand Path: Ceremony	Clarity, Cooperation, Charity, Golden City Star	Right Resolve and Intention, entrance into the Great White Brotherhood, the Great Plan	Acute Isosceles Triangle—Golden Triangle
Eight Principles of the Right-Hand Path: Decree	Cooperation, Creation-Creativity, Golden City Star	Right Speech, Divine Sound	Acute Isosceles Triangle—Golden Triangle
The Four Pillars: Pillar One	Service, Clarity, Golden City Star; West Door, South	El Morya, Southwest Region of the Golden City, Innate Divinity	Acute Isosceles Triangle—Golden Triangle
The Four Pillars: Pillar Two	Faith, Desire, Golden City Star; East Door, North	Kuthumi, Northeast Region of the Golden City, Witness Consciousness	Acute Isosceles Triangle—Golden Triangle

Evolutionary Field	Adjutant Points	Attributes	Type
The Four Pillars: Pillar Three	Service, Love, Golden City Star; East Door, South	Saint Germain, Southeast Region of the Golden City, Freedom of Choice	Acute Isosceles Triangle—Golden Triangle
The Four Pillars: Pillar Four	Charity, Faith, Golden City Star; West Door, North	Lord Sananda, Northwest Region of the Golden City, "Love One Another"	Acute Isosceles Triangle—Golden Triangle
The Four Pillars: Golden City Star	All Twelve Jurisdictions	Serapis Bey, the Golden City Star, Ascension	Circle and Spiral
Fourfold Flame of Desire	Harmony, Clarity, Cooperation	Lady Desiree, Outer Southwest Region of the Golden City	Acute Isosceles Triangle—Golden Triangle
Fourfold Flame of Wisdom	Illumination, Desire, Stillness	Lady Nada, Outer Northeast Region of the Golden City	Acute Isosceles Triangle—Golden Triangle
Fourfold Flame of Power	Abundance, Love, Illumination	Portia—Goddess of Justice, Outer Southeast Region of the Golden City	Acute Isosceles Triangle—Golden Triangle
Fourfold Flame of Love	Cooperation, Charity, Creation—Creativity	Lady Miriam, Outer Northwest Region of the Golden City	Acute Isosceles Triangle—Golden Triangle
Fourfold Flame The Star	All Twelve Jurisdictions	Lady Luxor, the Golden City Star	Circle and Spiral
Nine Heavenly Gates: the Star	Golden City Star; Center of the Golden City	Represents the Unfed Flame within the Heart	Circle and Spiral
Nine Heavenly Gates: Archangel Raphael	Golden City Star, Faith, Creation-Creativity; Northern Door, West	Personal finances, Abundance and Aboundance of Choice, World Economies	Obtuse Isosceles Triangle
Nine Heavenly Gates: Archangel Zadkiel	Golden City Star, Faith, Stillness; Northern Door, East	Personal Spiritual Growth, Spiritual Teachers and Guides, Earth's Spiritual Development	Obtuse Isosceles Triangle
Nine Heavenly Gates: Archangel Michael	Golden City Star, Illumination, Desire; Eastern Door, North	The New Generations and the New Children, Nature Kingdoms	Obtuse Isosceles Triangle
Nine Heavenly Gates: Archangel Chamuel	Golden City Star, Illumination, Love; Eastern Door, South	Loving Relationships, Marriage, the Law of Love on Earth	Obtuse Isosceles Triangle

Evolutionary Field	Adjutant Points	Attributes	Type
Nine Heavenly Gates: Archangel Uriel	Golden City Star, Service, Abundance; Southern Door, East	Divine Purpose, Human Right of Self-expression	Obtuse Isosceles Triangle
Nine Heavenly Gates: Archangel Gabriel	Golden City Star, Service, Harmony; Southern Door, West	Family, Soul Family, Earth's Order and Harmony	Obtuse Isosceles Triangle
Nine Heavenly Gates: Archangel Jophiel	Golden City Star, Cooperation, Clarity; Western Door, South	Spiritual Knowledge, Divine Right of Choice, Divine Wisdom	Obtuse Isosceles Triangle
Nine Heavenly Gates: Archangel Chrystiel	Golden City Star, Cooperation, Charity; Western Door, North	Noble, Worldly Endeavors; Victory over Illusion.	Obtuse Isosceles Triangle
Elohim Evolutionary Field: Elohim of Truth, Vista and Virginia	Creation-Creativity, Faith, Cooperation; Inner Northwest Region of a Golden City	Inner Northwest Region of a Golden City	Scalene Obtuse Triangle
Elohim Evolutionary Field: Elohim of Peace, Peace and Tranquility	Stillness, Faith, Illumination; Inner Northeast Region of a Golden City	Inner Northeast Region of a Golden City	Scalene Obtuse Triangle
Elohim Evolutionary Field: Elohim of Freedom, Arctura and Diana	Abundance, Service, Illumination; Inner Southeast Region of a Golden City	Inner Southeast Region of a Golden City	Scalene Obtuse Triangle
Elohim Evolutionary Field: Elohim of Unity, Rainbow and Iris	Harmony, Service, Cooperation; Inner Southwest Region of a Golden City	Inner Southwest Region of a Golden City	Scalene Obtuse Triangle

APPENDIX P
The White Ray and Modulated Ray Forces

According to Saint Germain the Color Rays shift their energy throughout the Golden City and create a discernable periodic influence on the Four Doorways. It is important to understand this effect that adds yet another motivation for specific Spiritual Pilgrimages during particular time periods to induce certain results. The movement of the Rays throughout the Doorways is guided by the planets in our Solar System, and their juxtaposition to our Sun, the Earth's inner Sun, the Galactic Center, and the DAHL-DERN umbilicus connection. According to Saint Germain this movement is predicated by the influence of the Gold Ray. All of these factors play a role in the absorption of the vital life-evolving energy of the Rays, especially the Gold Ray. Golden Cities act as capacitors to this fundamental life force and store and disburse light and sound energetics throughout the Evolutionary Biome.

The Presiding Ray Force
There are three methods to discern the Ray Forces within a Golden City. The first method is recognition of the Golden City's Presiding Ray Force. This is determined through the Ray Force that the Golden City's Hierarch expresses and serves. The Presiding Ray Force of a Golden City is best sensed during Pilgrimages or time spent in the Golden City Star. Some Ascended Master students can clairvoyantly see the color of the Ray Force arcing energy from the Star location. This is a permanent assignment of the Ray's influence, and carries a fifty to sixty percent weight throughout the Golden City.

The Periodic Adjutant Point Ray Force
The second influence is the Ray Force of the Adjutant Point and it changes with the twenty-year period. Disbursed throughout the Golden Cities are a total of thirty-three Adjutant Points that the Masters have currently identified. This number comprises a collection of Ashrams, Temples, Star Retreats, and includes the Star. With the exception of the Star and the Star Retreats, Ray Forces and Hierarchs change in these Adjutant Points every twenty years through the movement of the Cycle of the Elements.[1] This energy of the Ray Forces is predicated through Mother Earth, Beloved Babajeran, and the electromagnetic flux of the Golden Cities' lei-lines. We entered the Eighth Cycle of Earth in 2004, and in 2024 will enter the Ninth Cycle of Fire. In 2024 many Adjutant Point Hierarchs may change. This effect carries a twenty-five to thirty percent influence.

The Annual Influence of Ray Forces Upon the Doorways
The final influence of Ray Forces is the annual movement of the Rays throughout the Four Golden City Doorways as described above. It is important to note, however, that the movement can change on a yearly basis, or stay in position for a period of five years. Again, this influence is predicated through the movement of the Gold Ray throughout the Golden Cities. Saint Germain has shared information on the movement of the White Ray through the year

---

1. The Cycle of the Elements is founded on the Chinese Calendar. The New Year is determined by the second New Moon after the Winter Solstice. This calendar has been in place in Chinese culture since 104 BCE. The year is then divided into twenty-four parts, "fortnights," based on the longitude of the Sun, on the ecliptic.

2065. He has also mapped out the movement of the additional Ray Forces to the year 2040. This effect carries a weight of ten to twenty-five percent of influence in the Golden City location.

Use All Three Methods
When calculating the overall strength of a Ray Force all three factors should be considered: presiding, periodic, and annual. There are certain periods when one Ray Force will dominate, and can be used to calibrate specific physical, mental, emotional, and spiritual results through efforts in meditation, prayer, decree, and Spiritual Pilgrimage.

Modulated Ray Forces
The movement of the Rays through the Golden City Doorways creates new combinations of Modulated Ray Forces throughout the Golden City's intercardinal directions. Each new Ray Modulated Ray Force follows, along with a description of their qualities and characteristics.

The Gold Ray
The influence of the Gold Ray and movement of the Ray Forces throughout the Golden City Doorways create new Ray Forces that will present evolved qualities, features, and characteristics. Many of these Ray Forces combine two or more Ray Forces, and are known as Modulated Ray Forces. The addition of the Gold Ray adds a metallic tone to the Ray and produces Neon Pink, Neon Violet, Neon Green, and Neon Blue. The Ascended Masters have identified the Eighth Ray as the Aquamarine and Gold Ray. This Ray Force is a Modulated Ray Force comprised of three underlying Ray Forces to produce its specific, dynamic presence.

Pastel Green Ray
Co-creative Mastery through the spoken word. This Ray Force bestows great skill and knowledge of decree, fiat, and prayer. The Pastel Green Ray imparts an expertise in etiquette and cultural protocol, so it is associated with the elevation of HU-man culture particularly in the realms of literature and music. Unlimited imagination is the gift of this Ray Force alongside an unending fun-loving and joyful spirit. It is associated with imagination, creativity, the opened pineal gland, originality, resourcefulness, vision and farsightedness, poise, manners, self-assurance, composure, etiquette, and decorum.

Orange Ray
This Ray Force is a worldly and grounded energetic and is said to give one a timely blessing or boon that quickly improves one's life. It can enhance money matters and status. At its higher expression the Orange Ray expresses the Coral or Peach Ray, associated with Divine Purpose, joy, and infectious optimism and enthusiasm. This is a Ray Force that readily gives comfort and support to those with needs; therefore, its light guides ministers, advisors, counselors, and spiritual leaders. It is associated with reassurance, wellbeing, consolation, hope, cheerfulness, positivity, and wonder.

Spring Green Ray
This is a refreshing Ray Force of hope, renewal, and eternal life. Because of its association with restoration and growth, this Ray Force is allied with Mother Nature and the Devic and Elemental Kingdoms of Earth. At a human

level this Ray produces insightful counselors through wisdom and insight with an appetite for perceptive self-knowledge. This is an expansive and positive energetic which improves True Memory and discernibly penetrates the Akashic Records. It is intelligent, mature, subtle, and possesses a calm temperament. This Ray Force blesses one with appreciation for classical scripture, art, music, and musical instruments. It is associated with development and evolution, progress, wisdom, peace and serenity, discernment, perception, and self-realization.

Pastel Blue Ray

This is a Ray Force focused upon creating stability through enduring relationships. Energetically, it is associated with longer lifespans and the achievement of physical immortality. Its light cultivates a technical and detached viewpoint best suited for problem solving while applying a productive work ethic. Through its scientific and precise perspectives it is associated with the new agriculture and sciences of the New Times that produce new foods, pharmaceuticals, textiles, and innovative building materials. It is practical and artistic, emotionally detached, yet values historic customs and traditions. This Ray will readily embrace innovative, humanitarian technology leavened with discipline and personal effort. The Pastel Blue Ray helps individuals to embrace the New Times without forgetting our invaluable past.

The Star of Gobean
Along the trail to Mount Baldy, the center of the Star of the Golden City of Gobean. Gobean is located in New Mexico and Arizona. Its Hierarch is El Morya, and the primary Ray Force is blue.

Seventeen Initiations of the *I AM America Map*: Realization of and integration with the I AM Presence and establishment of the I AM Race.

	Golden City	Location	Presiding Ray	Master Teacher
1.	GOBEAN	United States	Blue Ray	El Morya
2.	MALTON	United States	Ruby-Gold Ray	Kuthumi
3.	WAHANEE	United States	Violet Ray	Saint Germain
4.	SHALAHAH	United States	Green Ray	Sananda
5.	KLEHMA	United States	White Ray	Serapis Bey
6.	PASHACINO	Canada	Green Ray	Soltec
7.	EABRA	Canada, US	Violet Ray	Portia
8.	JEAFRAY	Canada	Violet Ray	Archangel Zadkiel
9.	UVERNO	Canada	Pink Ray	Paul the Venetian
10.	YUTHOR	Greenland	Green Ray	Hilarion
11.	MARNERO	Mexico	Green Ray	Mary
12.	ASONEA	Cuba	Yellow Ray	Peter the Everlasting
13.	ANDEO	Peru, Brazil	Pink-Gold Rays	The First Sister, Goddess Meru, Beloved Constane
14.	BRAHAM	Brazil	Pink Ray	The Second Sister
15.	TEHEKOA	Argentina	Pink-Violet Rays	The Third Sister
16.	CROTESE	Costa Rica,	Pink Ray	Paul the Devoted
17.	JEHOA	New Atlantis Panama [The Eastern side of this Vortex is present-day Saint Lucia Island in the Caribbean.]	Violet Ray	Kuan Yin

Seventeen Initiations of I AM America

The Seventeen Initiations of I AM America is a spiritual process that helps students awaken and realize the power of the I AM Presence. As personal Mastery and command of the I AM Presence is achieved, individuals will join together to re-establish North America, Central America, and South America as ONE expression of the I AM Race. An anagram derived from the word America, the I AM race is the prophesied new breed of man destined to serve as the nucleus of the New Times. The Violet Ray, the Pink Ray, and the Green Ray are the principal Rays of I AM America Golden Cities. The Archangel Zadkiel and various Master Teachers and Elohim serve as stewards of these Vortex cities.

Seventeen Initiations of the Greening Map

Mother Earth plays a central role in the Greening Map of Asia and Australia. The migratory path of these Golden Cities is intended to restore the Earth Mother physically, emotionally, and mentally by balancing prevailing oppressive male

Seventeen Initiations of the *Greening Map*: Personal and transpersonal healing of the feminine to balance Mother Earth and awaken her ecological alchemy.

	Golden City	Location	Presiding Ray	Master Teacher
1.	ADJATAL	Pakistan, Afghanistan, India	Blue and Gold Rays	Lord Himalya
2.	PURENSK	Russia, China	Blue, Yellow, and Pink Rays	Faith, Hope, Charity
3.	PRANA	India	Pink Ray	Archangel Chamuel
4.	ZASKAR	China	White Ray	Reya
5.	GOBI	China	Ruby-Gold Ray	Lord Meru, Archangel Uriel
6.	ARCTURA	China	Violet Ray	Arcturus and Diana
7.	NOMAKING	China	Yellow Ray	Cassiopea and Minerva
8.	PRESCHING	China	Yellow Ray	Archangel Jophiel
9.	KANTAN	China, Russia	Green Ray	Great Divine Mother and Archangel Raphael
10.	HUE	Russia	Violet Ray	Lord Guatama
11.	SIRCALWE	Russia	White Ray	Group of Twelve
12.	ARKANA	Russia	White Ray	Archangel Gabriel
13.	GREIN	New Zealand	Green Ray	Viseria
14.	CLAYJE	Australia	Pink Ray	Orion
15.	ANGELICA	Tasmania	Pink Ray	Angelica
16.	SHHEAHAH	Australia	White Ray	Astrea
17.	FRON	Australia	Blue Ray	Desiree

energies with the influence of the feminine. White and Pink Rays dominate this sequence, which means spiritual initiation focuses on the balance and integration of personal and collective feminine energies. The journey of healing through the seventeen Golden Cities of the Greening Map awakens Fourth- and Fifth-Dimensional attributes of Mother Earth to the magical and sensual expression of Ecological Alchemy. This spiritual practice opens initiates to the ONE and forges an indelible connection to the Earth Mother. This Ascension method is crucial in calibrating Earth's consciousness to the incarnating New Children. Meanwhile, many new and different species of flora and fauna are prophesied to inhabit Earth throughout the New Times. The Golden Cities of the Greening Map may instigate the healing of the tyrannical male energies — in governments, religions, cultures, and economies — that have dominated Earth's timely passage in Kali Yuga. As individuals integrate and apply the energies of these feminine Golden Cities, the global culture will heal the pain of harsh, exploitive power and open the Divine Heart of Humanity. Five Archangels serve in the seventeen Golden Cities of the Greening Map and assist the awakening of Earth's light

Seventeen Initiations of the *Map of Exchanges*: Self-realization of the HU-man through the exchange of heavenly energies on Earth that usher in the Golden Age.

	Golden City	Location	Presiding Ray	Master Teacher
1.	STIENTA	Iceland	Blue Ray	Nada
2.	DENASHA	Scotland	Yellow Ray	Nada
3.	AMERIGO	Spain	Gold Ray	Godfre
4.	GRUECHA	Norway, Sweden	Blue Ray	Hercules
5.	BRAUN	Germany, Poland, Czechoslovakia	Yellow Ray	Victory
6.	AFROM	Hungary, Romania	White Ray	SeRay and Claire
7.	GANAKRA	Turkey	Green Ray	Vista
8.	MESOTAMP	Turkey, Iran, Iraq	Yellow Ray	Mohammed
9.	SHEHEZ	Iran, Afghanistan	Ruby-Gold Ray	Tranquility
10.	GANDAWAN	Algeria	Ruby-Gold Ray	Kuthumi
11.	KRESHE	Botswana, Namibia	Ruby-Gold Ray	Lord of Nature and Amaryllis
12.	PEARLANU	Madagascar	Violet Ray	Lotus
13.	UNTE	Tanzania, Kenya	Ruby-Gold	Donna Grace
14.	LARAITO	Ethiopia	Yellow Ray	Lanto and Laura
15.	MOUSEE	New Lemuria [Present-day Pacific Ocean, Northwest of Hawaii]	Aquamarine-Gold Ray	Kona
16.	DONJAKEY	New Lemuria [Present-day Pacific Ocean, Northwestern Hawaiian Islands, Midway Islands]	Aquamarine-Gold Ray	Pacifica
17.	CRESTA	Antarctica [Antarctic Peninsula]	Aquamarine-Gold Ray	Archangel Chrystiel

grids and lei lines. Archangel Chamuel, Archangel Jophiel, Archangel Raphael, Archangel Gabriel, and Archangel Uriel comprise this cadre of spiritual stewards.

Seventeen Initiations of the Map of Exchanges

The initiatory progression of the Map of Exchanges, which includes Europe, Africa, and the Middle East, is perhaps the most difficult spiritual sequence of all. It requires the guiding wisdom and focus of the Yellow Ray — the Divine Guru. The interplay of the Gold Ray in cosmic partnership with the Ruby-Gold and Aquamarine-Gold Rays helps the student realize the Yellow Ray's hidden power, or

Earth Grid
Many types of grids cover Mother Earth and include dynamic lei-lines, power points, inter-dimensional portals, and spiritual retreats.

Shatki and the Divine HU-man. The progression of Golden Cities in this particular map (Freedom Star) is prophesied to anchor heaven on Earth and usher in God-actualized humanity. It is the birth of Unana. Throughout the seventeen Golden Cities of the Map of Exchanges, a student's Fourth- and Fifth-Dimensional Light Bodies are trained to step down heavenly energies that transmute and exchange with energies of the Third Dimension. It is an extensive Ascension Process: doubt is exchanged for knowledge; fear is exchanged for courage; hate is exchanged for trust; and darkness is exchanged for light. Energies from the Galactic Center permeate the seventeen Golden Cities contained in the Map of Exchanges, lifting humanity and the planet toward the prophesied New Times and Golden Age. As Earth progresses toward the final exchange of enlightened energy, the heavenly filaments of the Galactic Web will illuminate the entire globe. This web of enlightened awareness is prophesied to link and expand individual consciousness beyond this planet and onward, toward a Galactic Consciousness that embraces the lokas — or the levels of spiritual development on all planets. Archangel Michael and Archangel Chrystiel oversee the spiritual Ascension of humanity and Earth.

When encountering inaccessible Golden Cities, such as the submerged New Atlantis and New Lemuria, travel as close as possible to the Golden City's location to absorb spiritual energies. Students can also use the Star Meditation technique, which is as follows: Enter the Star of one Golden City Vortex and access the energies of any Golden City via the Fourth- and Fifth-Dimensional Golden City Network. This technique, however, is not for the novice. It requires patience and practice. [For more information see *Points of Perception: Golden City Activations and Subtle Energies, Golden City Activation.*]

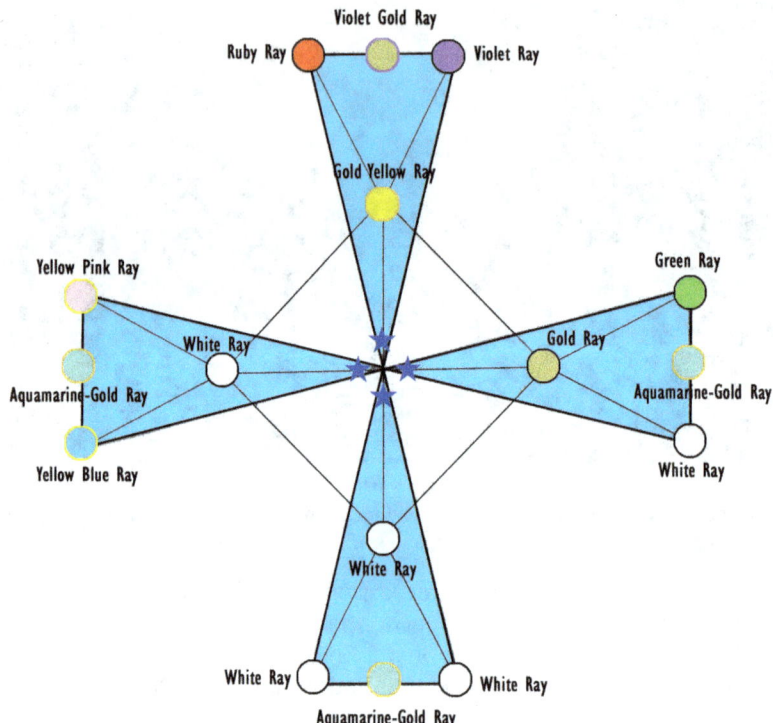

Gobean Golden City Adjutant Points with the Presiding Permanent Ray Force

The above illustration shows the Period Ray Forces of Gobean's Adjutant Points, alongside the presiding Permanent Blue Ray of Gobean. Evaluating the Ray Forces in this manner shows the efficacy of Ray Forces. For example, in the above illustration the Gobean Western Door Southwest Gateway Adjutant Point, Clarity, carries strong energies of the Blue Ray, with the Periodic and Presiding Ray Force adding up to an influence of 80 to 90%. Note that the Star Retreats carry the Ray Force of the Presiding Ray, in this case the Blue Ray.

The Twenty-year Cycles of the Elements

According to the Chinese calendar, time is not linear but moves in cycles. Perhaps the most important cycle revered in China is the sexagenary cycle, which comprises sixty years. This cycle is used in the Chinese esoteric arts, including astrology and feng-shui. One sexagenary cycle—sixty years—is known as an Era. Three Eras, a total of one-hundred eighty years, comprises the Nine Cycles. The Nine Cycles are divided into nine twenty-year portions. Energy ascends and decreases according to the energetic patterns that are connected to each sixty-year Era and to each twenty-year cycle. Below is

Era	Cycle	Starting Year	Element
Upper Era	first cycle	1864	Water
	second cycle	1884	Earth
	third cycle	1904	Wood
Middle Era	fourth cycle	1924	Wood
	fifth cycle	1944	Earth
	sixth cycle	1964	Metal
Lower Era	seventh cycle	1984	Metal
	eighth cycle	2004	Earth
	ninth cycle	2024	Fire
Upper Era	first cycle	2044	Water
	second cycle	2064	Earth
	third cycle	2084	Wood
Middle Era	fourth cycle	2104	Wood
	fifth cycle	2124	Earth
	sixth cycle	2164	Metal
Lower Era	seventh cycle	2184	Metal
	eighth cycle	2204	Earth
	ninth cycle	2224	Fire

a chart of the Nine Cycles (chiu-hun), the Three Eras (san-yüan), and each twenty-year cycle. According to Eva Wong, "Small changes occur between cycles, and large changes occur between each era."[1]

The Ascended Masters also utilize and often refer to the twenty-year cycle periods and their relationship to the elements. They teach that the Hierarchs of the Golden City Ashrams change Ray Forces every twenty years, according to the Cycle of the Elements. This creates adjustment in the Golden Cities to serve the needs of newer, evolving Ascended Beings, and to calibrate energies as Earth moves into the increasing Galactic Light of the Golden Age. While the Ashrams calibrate energies for each Golden City as the frequencies on Earth evolve and change, the primary Ray Force of each Golden City and its Star stays the same. This is also true for the Convergence Points, the Four Temples of Perfection, and the Star Retreats.

---

1. Wong, Eva. *Feng-Shui: the Ancient Wisdom of Harmonious Living for Modern Times.* Shambhala, 1996.

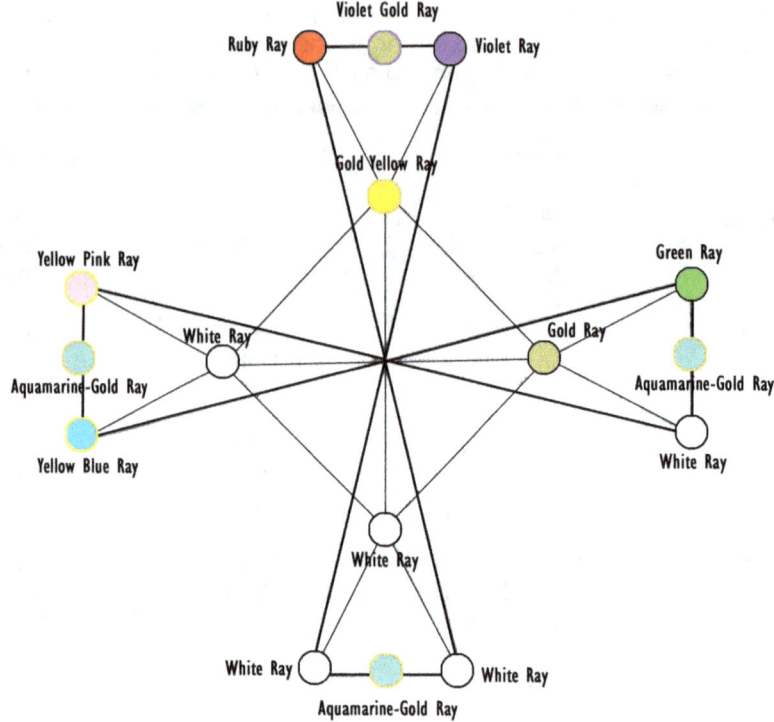

Gobean Golden City Adjutant Points with the Periodic Ray Forces
The above illustration depicts the Periodic influence of the Rays as assigned to the Gobean Gateway Adjutant Points and the Gobean Cardinal Adjutant Points. Periodic Ray Forces can change every twenty years, based upon the Cycle of the Elements. The Ray Force assigned to the various Gobean Adjutant Points may change again in the year 2024, when Periodic Nine ensues. Periodic Ray Forces carry an influence of 30 to 35% and when combined with the Annual or Permanent Ray Force, their influence may increase.

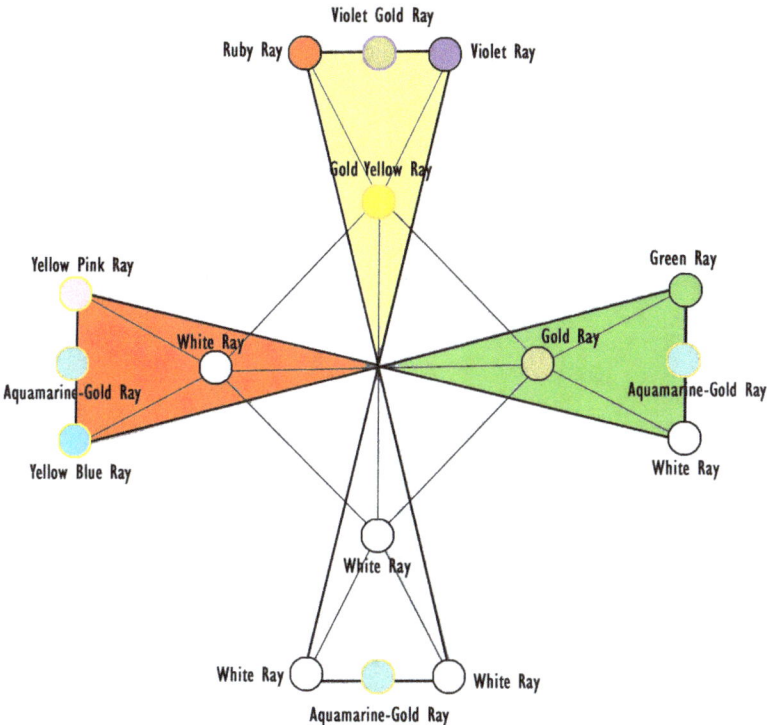

Example of Annual Influence of Rays upon the Doorways

The above illustration depicts the annual influence of the Rays upon the four Golden City Doors for the year 2020. They are: Southern Door, Venus, White Ray; West Door, Sun, Ruby Ray; Northern Door, Jupiter, Yellow Ray; East Door, Mercury, Green Ray. This illustration also depicts the Gateway Adjutant Points and the Cardinal Adjutant Points with their assigned Periodic Ray Forces for the Golden City of Gobean. Interestingly in this year, Pilgrimages to the Faith Point, increases the energetics of the Yellow Ray. Pilgrimages to the Eastern Door Desire Point, increase the power of the Green Ray. Pilgrimages to the Southern Door in this year vitally increase energies of the White Ray in the Harmony, Abundance, and Faith Points. A Periodic Ray Force can change every twenty years, according to the Cycle of the Elements. Annual and Periodic Ray Forces differ from the Presiding or abiding Ray Force of a Golden City. For example, Gobean's Presiding Ray Force is the Blue Ray, and Wahanee's Presiding Ray Force is the Violet Ray. The Presiding Ray Force of a Golden City carries an influence of 50-60%; the energy of the Periodic Ray Force is 25-35%; and the influence of the Annual Ray Force is 10-25%. Annual and Periodic Ray Forces come under the direction of the Maha Chohan and are often announced at the annual Shamballa Celebration held in the glorious City of White.

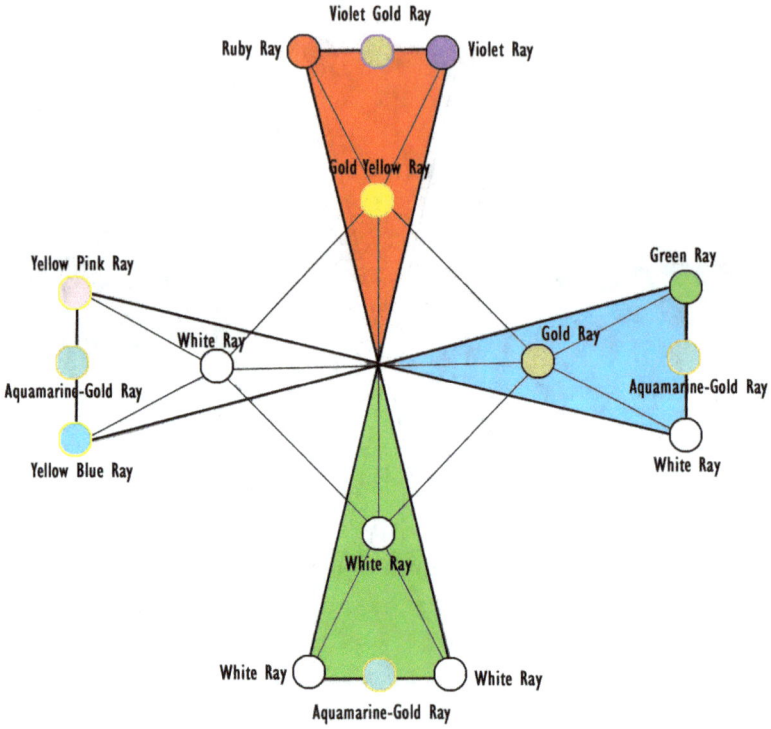

Gobean Golden City Adjutant Points with the Annual Ray Forces for 2021 - 2025
The above illustration depicts the Periodic influence of the Rays as assigned to the Gobean Gateway Adjutant Points and the Gobean Cardinal Adjutant Points, along with the Annual Ray Forces for the years 2021 through 2025. They are Southern Door, Mercury, Green Ray; Western Door, White Ray, Venus; Northern Door, Mars, Ruby Ray; East Door, Saturn, Blue Ray. Remember that Period Nine begins in the year 2024, so many of the Adjutant Point Ray Forces may change in that year and continue for a period of twenty years. If you plan Pilgrimage in the years 2021 through 2024, the dynamic energies of the White Ray, Cooperation Point, are significant. In the Gobean Northern Door, the Red Ray of Devotion is strong at the Creation-Creativity Point.

Propel Your Ascension

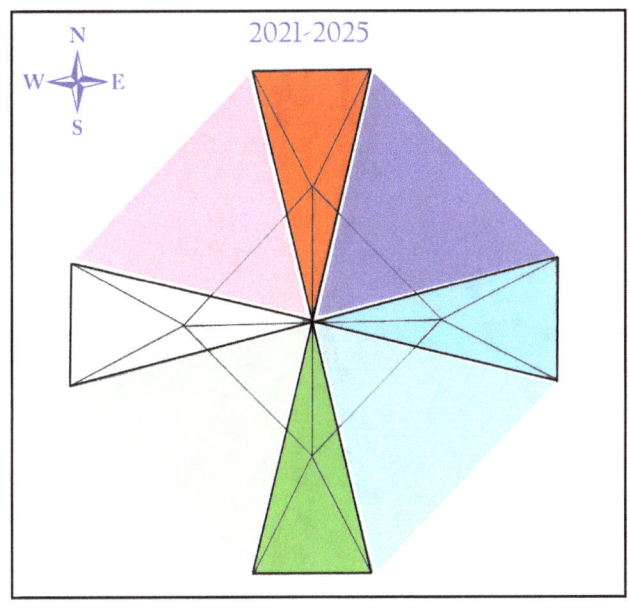

Ray Forces through the Doorways for the years 2021-2025

The Ray Forces create a rainbow of experiences for a period of five years from 2021 through 2025. Moving North and clockwise through the Golden City: The Red Ray is in the North, the modulated Ray Force of Violet presents in the Northeast, the Blue Ray is in its natural position in the East, the Aquamarine Ray presents in the Southeast, and the Green Ray is in the South, the modulated Pastel Green Ray presents in the Southwest, the White Ray is in the West, the Pink Ray is positioned in the Northwest.

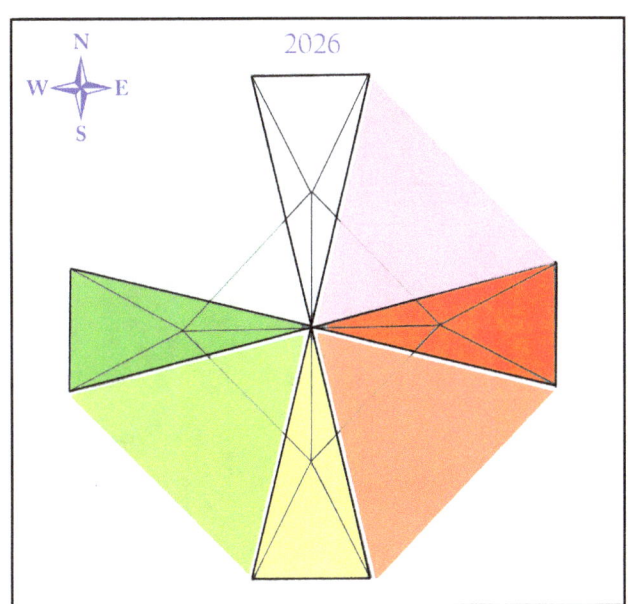

Ray Forces through the Doorways for the year 2026

The year of 2026 can create a strong year focused upon abundance, health, and technology, alongside timely benefit in worldly affairs with the modulated Orange Ray appearing in the Southeast. Moving clockwise the Yellow Ray is posited in the South, Spring Green Ray in the Southwest, the Green Ray presents in the West, the Pastel Green Ray is in the Northwest, the White Ray is located in the North, the Pink Ray is located in the Northeast, and the Red Ray is located in the East.

Ray Forces through the Doorways for the years 2027-2029

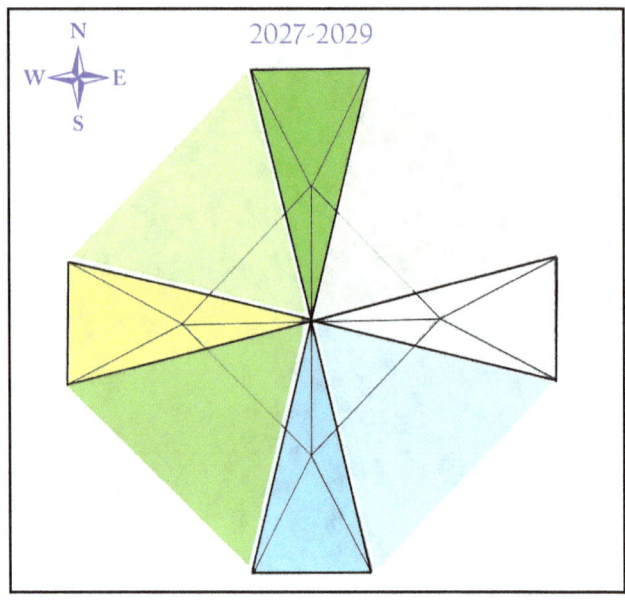

This three-year period is greatly influenced by the Green Ray, with one-half of the worldwide Golden Cities experiencing changes in economies, technology, health, and healing. Golden Cities whose Presiding Ray Force is the Green Ray will experience this phenomenon significantly. The Green Ray is in its natural position in the North, the Pastel Green Ray is located in the Northeast, the White Ray is located in the East, the Pastel Blue Ray is located in the Southeast, the Blue Ray is located in the South, the Green Ray modulates in the Southwest, the Yellow Ray is in its natural location in the West, and the Spring Green Ray is located in the Northwest.

Ray Forces through the Doorways for the year 2030

2030 will prove to be a unique year of both diversity and balance, as the Eight Rays of Light and Sound, including the Gold Ray, will present throughout the eight directions of the Golden City. The Blue Ray is located in the North, the Green Ray modulates in the Northeast, the Yellow Ray is present in the East, the Gold Ray presents in the Southeast, the White Ray is located in the South, the Pink Ray modulates in the Southwest, the Red Ray is located in the West, and the Violet Ray modulates in the Northwest.

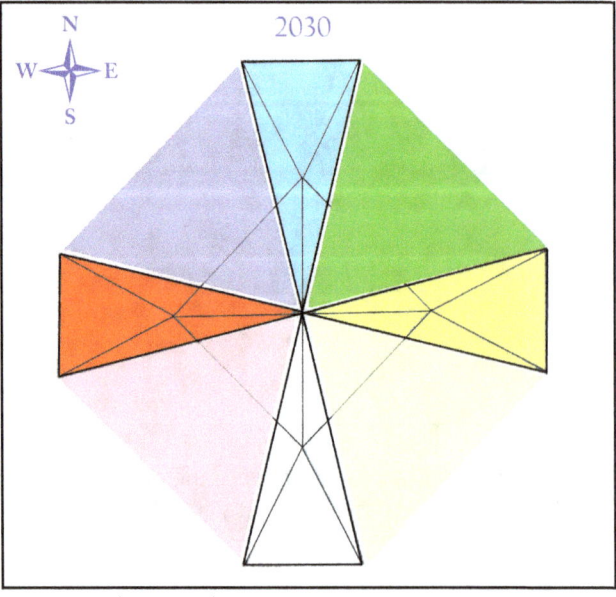

Ray Forces through the Doorways for the years 2031-2034

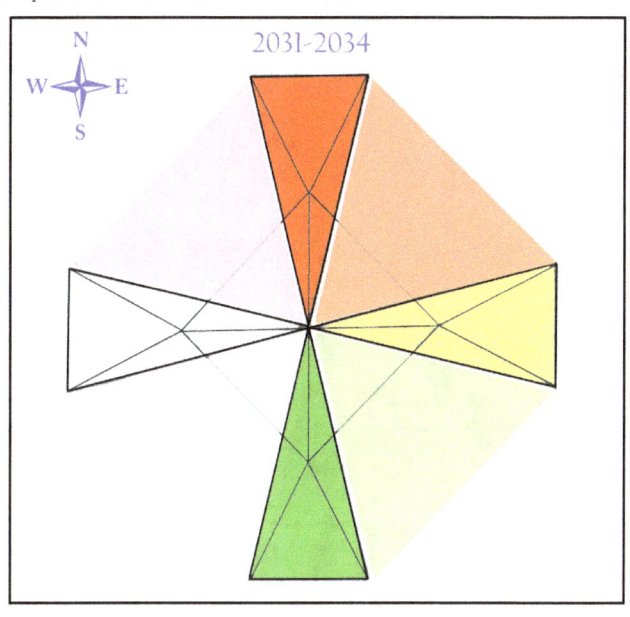

This four-year period may be an auspicious cycle for the world's overall abundance, health, and technological advancement as the Green Ray dominates the Southeast, South, and Southwest sector of every Golden City. The boon of the Orange Ray can also increase Earth's wealth at this time, and Spiritual Pilgrimage to this region can help to increase an individual's prosperity. The Red Ray is located in the North, the Orange Ray presents in the Northeast, the Yellow Ray is placed in the East, the Spring Green Ray is found in the Southeast, the Green Ray is posited in the South, the Pastel Green Ray is placed in the Southwest, the White Ray is located in the West, and the Pink Ray is found in the Northwest.

Ray Forces through the Doorways for the year 2035

The White Ray of Ascension stays in the Western Door for yet another year in 2035; however, the Color Rays change their positions for all of the other directions. The Gold Ray of Transformation and Transcendence makes its second appearance in all the Golden Cities of the World, arriving in the Southwest sector. The Green Ray is in its natural location in the Northern Door, the Aquamarine Ray is located in the Northeast Door, the Blue Ray is in its natural position in the East Door, the Green Ray is located in the Southeast Door, and the Pastel Green Ray appears in the Northwest sector.

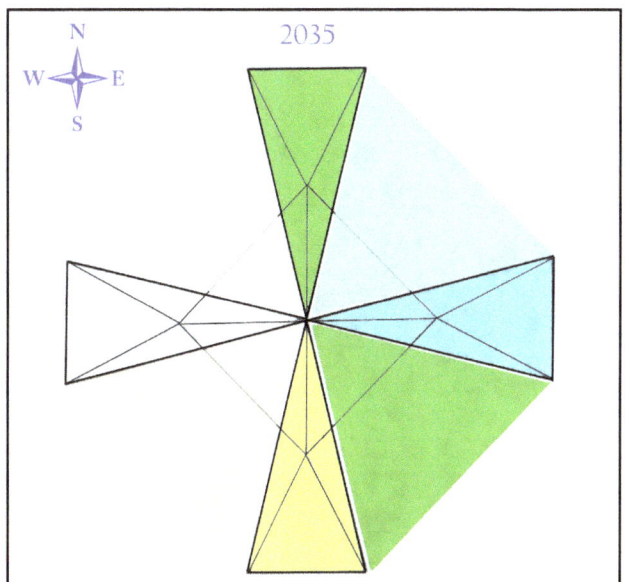

Ray Forces through the Doorways for the years 2036-2038

These three years mirror the Color Rays of 2030 with all Eight Rays appearing throughout the Doorways and intercardinal directions of the Golden Cities. However, instead of the Gold Ray, the Aquamarine Ray occupies the Southeast sector. The Aquamarine Ray helps to develop the psychic senses into the God-realized HU-man. The White Ray is located in the North, the Pastel Green Ray

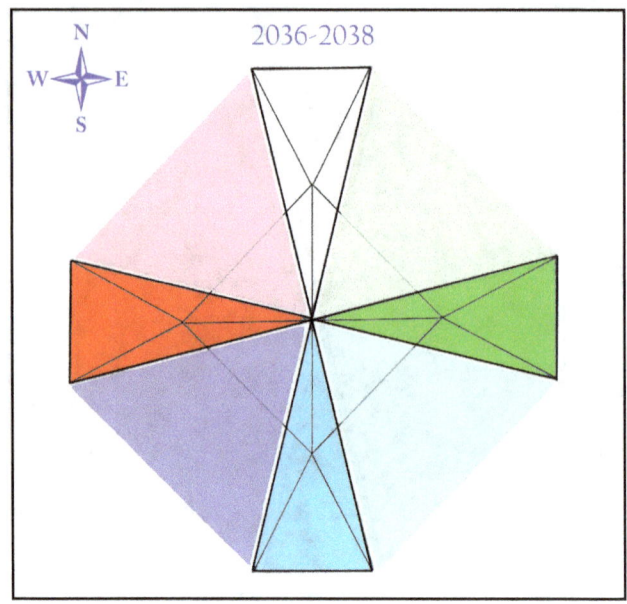

is posited in the Northeast, the Green Ray is placed in the East, and the Blue Ray is located in the Southern Door. The Violet Ray presents in the Southwest sector, the Red Ray is found in the West, and the Pink Ray graces the Northwest.

Ray Forces through the Doorways for the years 2039-2040

This two-year period will mark another period for the Eight Rays of Light and Sound with their expression throughout all Eight Palaces of the world Golden Cities. Their locations differ from the previous period, and the Gold Ray of leadership and self-realization appears in the Northeast sector. The Yellow Ray is located in the North, and the White Ray is located in the East. The Pink Ray is placed in the Southeast, the Red Ray is in its natural location in the South, and the Violet Ray is located throughout the Southwest. The Blue Ray presents in the West and the Green Ray is found in the Northwest sector.

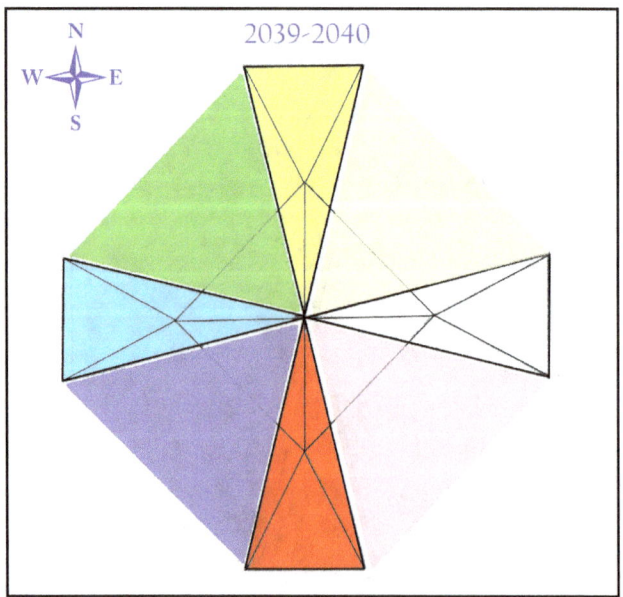

Time Period	No. Years	White Ray	Red Ray (Mars)	Ruby-Gold Ray (Sun)	Yellow Ray	Blue Ray	Green Ray
2021-2025	5	West	North			East	South
2026	1	North	East		South		West
2027-2029	3	East			West	South	North
2030	1	South	West	West	East	North	
2031-2034	4	West	North	North	East		South
2035	1	West			South	East	North
2036-2038	3	North	West	West		South	East
2039-2012	3	East		East	North	West	
No. Years and %	21 years	21 — 100%	14 — 66%	11 — 52%	13 — 62%	16 — 76%	17 — 81%

Annual Movement of the Rays through the Golden City Doorways from 2021-2041

The above table depicts the movement of the Rays through the Golden City Doorways for a total of twenty-one years. According to Saint Germain the White Ray will appear in all Golden City Doorways during this time period. Hence, he encourages timely Spiritual Pilgrimage to these Doorways as they embue the recipient Doorway with the Golden Age energies of beauty (balance), unconditional love, devotion, cooperation, and compassion. During this time period the Red Ray of Mars and the Ruby-Gold Ray appear 66% and 52%, respectively. This somewhat decreases aggression and humanity's need for authority during this time period, and violence may decrease as cultures move away from oppressive government and authoritative oversight. The Yellow Ray of Wisdom appears 62%, and gently assists humanity's overall spiritual development. The Blue Ray and the Green Ray dominate with 76% and 81%. This indicates a trend toward the transparency, hard work, honesty, and detachment of the Blue Ray, alongside the benefits of increased abundance, health, and the technological advances of the scientific Green Ray.

PHOTONS

Time Period	No. Years	Pink Ray	Violet Ray	Aqua-marine Ray	Orange Ray	Green Ray	Gold Ray	Spring Green Ray	Pastel Blue Ray	Pastel Green Ray
2021-2025	5	North-west	North-east	South-east						South-west
2026	1	North-east								North-west
2027-2029	3					North-west		South-west	South-east	North-west
2030	1	South-west	North-west			North-east	South-east	North-west		South-west
2031-2034	4	North-west	North-west		North-east	South-east	South-west	South-east		North-west
2035	1			North-east	North-east	North-west				North-west
2036-2038	3	North-west	South-west	South-east		South-east	South-west			North-east
2039-2041	3	South-east	South-west			North-west	North-east			
No. Years and %	21 years	17-81%	12-57%	8-38%	5-24%	7-33%	5-24%	8-38%	3-14%	17-81%

Annual Movement of the Modulated Rays through the Golden City Doorways from 2021-2041

The above table depicts the movement of the Modulated Rays through the Golden City intercardinal directions for a total of twenty-one years. The most remarkable trend is the appearance of the Green Ray, which appears 81% in the Doorways and 33% in the intercardinal direction. This totals to a 114% dominance in the Golden Cities for a period of twenty-one years. During the next two decades we will see tremendous changes in technology, health, science, and our economic systems. The Pink Ray and Pastel Green Ray are also both very strong presenting at 81%. This increases the feminine energies alongside HU-man development.

282

The Fourteen Ray Forces of the Golden Cities

Ray Force	Qualities	Percentage of Appearance 2021-2041
Green Ray	Communicative, thoughtful, scientific, healing, rational, awakened, the Divine Messenger or Divine Intelligence	114%
White Ray	Refined, elegant, creative, uplifting, beautiful, pure, the Divine Feminine	100%
Pastel Green Ray	Co-creative, Mastery of Sound, elevated HU-man culture, vision, originality, etiquette, the realized HU-man	81%
Pink Ray	Compassion, nurturing, hopeful, heartfelt, considerate, humane, intuitive, Divine Mother or Divine Heart	81%
Blue Ray	Steady, calm, persevering, transformational, diligent, humble, self-negating, disciplined, Divine Will or Divine Power	76%
Red Ray	Energetic, passionate, determined, dutiful, insightful, inventive, Divine Warrior or Divine Masculine	66%
Yellow Ray	Studious, learned, expansive, optimistic, joyful, generous, Divine Wisdom or Divine Guru	62%
Violet Ray	Forgiving, transmuting, alchemizing, intervening, diplomacy, magical, merciful, Divine Grace	57%
Ruby/Gold Ray	Warm, honest, confident, positive, independent, courageous, authority, justice, leadership, Divine Father	52%

Strength of the Ray Forces and their Qualities 2021-2041

The above table shows the percentage of influence of the Seven Rays and their Modulated Ray Force counterparts as they make their appearance throughout the worldwide Golden Cities. We will see an overall growth of technology and science focused on changes within our medical and economic systems. This technological change advances the quality of life through Divine Intelligence alongside the presence of the Divine Feminine. The Pastel Green Ray introduces the science of sound for spiritual growth and for technical purposes with the growth of energy medicine. The Pink Ray will also dominate, with worldwide compassion and hope as the presence of Divine Mother. Since this is the long-awaited time of the return of the Master Teachers, humanity begins a transformative process, embracing the HU-man ideals of transcendence, forgiveness, Spiritual Awakening, Innate Divinity, Ascension, and the immortality of both body and soul.

PHOTONS

New Ray Forces
The New Ray Forces of the Orange and Gold Ray
assist humanity's entrance into the New Times.

Ray Force	Qualities	Percentage of Appearance 2021-2041
Aquamarine Ray	Sensitive, creative, idealistic, spiritual, self-realized, integrative, Divine Man	38%
Spring Green Ray	Hope, renewel, eternal life, perceptive, insightful, mature, subtle, calm, evolutionary, peaceful, self-realization, Divine Earth	38%
Gold Ray	Unifying, evolutionary, transformative, Ascending, self-actualization, expansive, openness, initiatory, glory, Oneness, Divine Heaven and Innate Divinity	24%
Orange Ray	Blessings, spiritual and financial boon, joy, infectious optimism, enthusiasm, supportive, comforting, wonder, wellbeing, hope, Divine Purpose	24%
Pastel Blue Ray	Long-lived, immortality, enduring, problem solving, stewardship, precision, scientific, traditional, respectful, practical and artistic, detached, the New Times and the New Children	14%

Venus through the Golden City Doors 2021-2065

Year	Golden City Door
2021-2025	Venus in West Door
2026	Venus in North Door
2027-2029	Venus in East Door
2030	Venus in South Door
2031-2034	Venus in West Door
2035	Venus in West Door
2036-2038	Venus in North Door
2039-2041	Venus in East Door
2042-2044	Venus in South Door
2045-2046	Venus in West Door
2047-2049	Venus in North Door
2050	Venus in East Door
2051	Venus in South Door
2052	Venus in West Door
2053-2054	Venus in North Door
2055-2061	Venus in East Door
2062-2064	Venus in South Door
2065	Venus in West Door

Venus, the Divine Feminine

The Planet Venus represents the Divine Feminine as beauty, balance, purity, refinement, grace, charm, cooperation, and sensitivity. Since Venus represents the White Ray it is also associated with the Ascension Process. The Ascended Masters claim that Spiritual Pilgrimages made to the Adjutant Points within the Doorway during Venus's periodic appearance greatly assists this spiritual development.

Christ in Desert
Nicholas Roerich, 1933.

APPENDIX Q
The Right-hand Path

Ameru and the Right-hand Path
The historical provenance of America (Ameruca) — the Land of the Plumed Serpent — is the lost history of Mu, Lemuria, and Atlantis. The Plumed Serpent metaphorically represents the developed Chakra System of the Divine God-man, the Ascended Masters' HU-man. The plume of light atop the head is the developed Crown Chakra, and the serpent's coils represent the mature Kundalini system, or human energy system comprised of seven chakras. It is claimed that many Lemurians and Atlanteans had the advanced capacity to function in both the Fourth and Fifth Dimension as Spiritual Masters, Sorcerers, and Shamans where an Alchemical and spiritual battle ensued: the Left-Hand Path versus the Right-hand Path. Spiritual development at this level of consciousness endows power over the Elemental Kingdom, and the unascended Spiritual Master is often pitted between both malevolent Black Magic and constructive White Magic. (These are the prominent abilities experienced by individuals who have achieved the Tenth Pyramid of Consciousness in HU-man development. For more information, see: Golden City Series, Book Three, Divine Destiny.)

The Right-hand Path
The Spiritual Masters who fled Atlantis and re-established their spiritual temples and sanctuaries in the New Lands held their chelas to the sacred vows of the Right-hand Path which today is practiced in Buddhism and Christianity as Compassion, Tolerance, Unity, the Brotherhood of Man, Mercy, and Forgiveness. This holy vow is reiterated in the Ascended Masters' Awakening Prayer: "Great Light of Divine Wisdom, stream forth to my being; and through your right use let me serve mankind and the planet . . ."

Theologians of Ascended Master teachings claim Lord Meru's temple was founded in the New World to embrace the Western ideals of the Right-hand Path, and teach Ascension attained by way of Sainthood through the rigor of humane service in the Ninth Pyramid of HU-man Consciousness. Today, many evolved Arhats choose to circumvent the spiritually arduous lure of the Tenth Pyramid and the horrifying conflict once experienced in the final days of Atlantis. Only the Adept is capable of venturing into the dualistic nomenclature of the Spiritual Master. Initiates of the Tenth Pyramid must properly prepare and strengthen their resolve with intimate knowledge and experience regarding the pitfalls of necromancy and reinforce the spiritual practice of the Right-hand Path attained through the proper use of Alchemy, Transmutation, and God-Protection. The Master Jesus Christ fasts for forty days and nights in the desert and faces the temptations of Satan in the demanding spiritual tests inherent in the Tenth Pyramid of Consciousness. The soul-trying conflict is illustrated in this Christian story:

Jesus Christ is asked by Satan to turn stones into bread — an abomination of the Elemental Kingdom; he responds, "One does not live by bread alone..."

Satan challenges Jesus Christ to jump off a temple's rooftop; after all, since he was a Son of God, surely an Angel will catch him. Unable to misuse the Divine Power entrusted to him, Jesus Christ responds, "You shall not put the Lord, your God, to the test." Will L. Garver, metaphysical author of the Victorian

Age, clarifies this spiritual precept in the classic occult novel Brother of the Third Degree, "Remember that the Great Brotherhood requires no tests except those which are mental and moral in nature."[1]

During this period, all of the Kingdoms of Creation are revealed to Jesus Christ: the Mineral Kingdom; the Vegetable Kingdom; the Elemental Kingdom; the Animal Kingdom; the Creative Hierarchy (the Human Kingdom); and the majestic Kingdoms of the Elohim and Archangels. Again, Jesus Christ is asked by Satan to assert his complete dominion, power, and authority over their realms; yet, Jesus Christ responds: "The Lord, your God, shall you worship and him alone shall you serve," affirming the spiritual principles of Unity, Cooperation, and the Sanctity of Life through the Right-hand Path.

According to the esoteric teacher Dion Fortune, there are distinct differences between the practices of the Right-hand and Left-hand Path, referred to in her works as either White Magic or Black Magic. The evolutionary enlightenment of the Arhat relies on the rich complexities of Mysticsm, and its religions of service and adoration, the power and beauty of Pantheism, and the hidden arts of astrology, divination, trance, human psychology, ceremony, decree, and the lineage of Gurus. The hidden arts are cultivated through dedication, purification, discipline, instruction, and service, which reach their culmination through the spiritual initiations of clarity, cooperation, charity, and faith—Mastery.

The devolutionary path of Black Magic relies on the confusion created through the use of drugs, sex magic, blood sacrifice, and pacts.[2]

---

[1]. Will L. Garver, *Brother of the Third Degree* (Garber Communications, 1989, Blauvelt, NY), page 183.
[2]. Dion Fortune, *The Training and Work of an Initiate*, (Weiser Books, 2000, San Francisco, CA). page 126.

APPENDIX R
Diagram of the Eight-sided Cell of Perfection with the Unfed Flame and the Monad

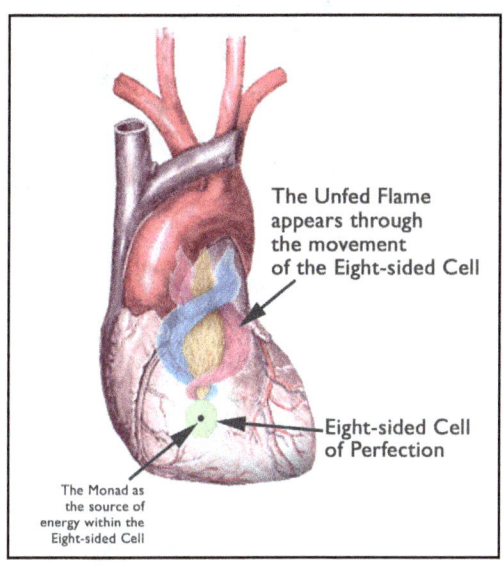

The Unfed Flame

The Unfed Flame of Love (Pink), Wisdom (Yellow), and Power (Blue) overlaid the human heart. The Monad is the source of life and energy. Its God Radiation creates the Eight-sided Cell of Perfection — a perfect cell that initiates our Ascension Process into the Evolutionary Biome. Movement within the Eight-sided Cell through the Evolution Points creates and expands the growth of the Unfed Flame. As human spiritual evolution unfolds, the Unfed Flame grows in size and intertwines around the human heart. The three flames become recognizable in the human aura and radiate soft hues of Blue, Yellow, and Pink throughout the Heart Chakra. This illustration is not to scale, and expands the Perfect Cell for visualization purposes. The Eight-sided Cell of Perfection is atomic in size, and undergoes a duplication process.

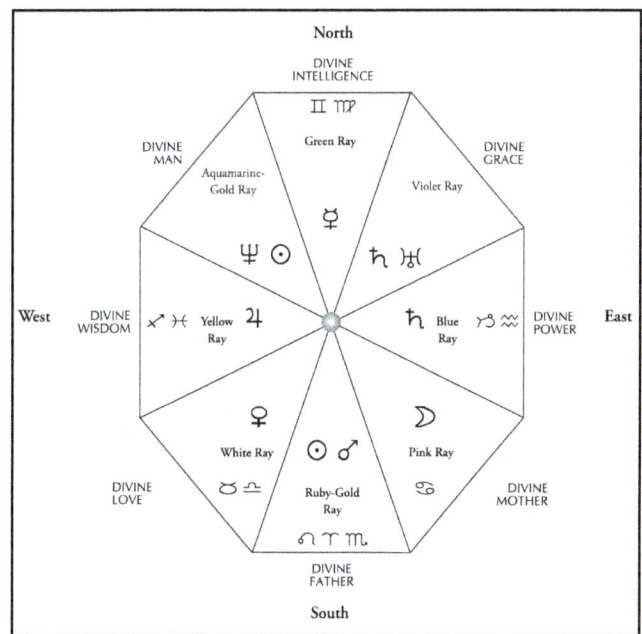

Location and Movement of the Rays through the Eight-sided Cell of Perfection
Energy Map Depicting the Rays within the Sacred Cell.

Pure Energy

APPENDIX S
Human to HU-man Light fields

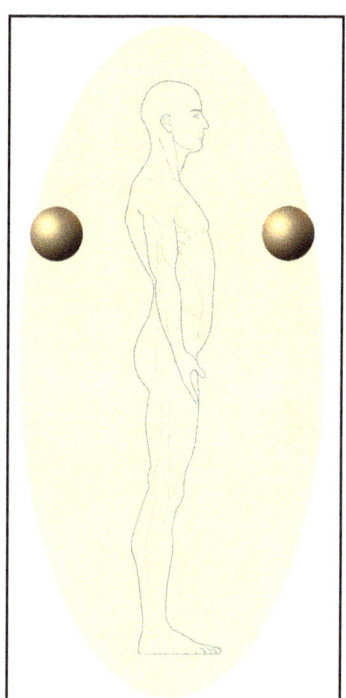

Eighth Energy Field, First Phase
The Eighth Energy Body develops in several phases. It begins with two large gold spheres forming at the front and back of the body. The front sphere is located between the Heart and Solar Plexus Chakra. The back sphere is located between the Will Chakras, Will-to-Love and Solar Will. As these spheres forms, the chela may notice a slight weight in the auric field. Exercises in Group Mind help this formation process. Eventually the spheres dissipate and release their energies into the Eighth Light Body. Repetitive Spiritual Pilgrimage helps to form this light field. (For more information see Appendix B: *The Advanced Light Fields of Ascension*.)

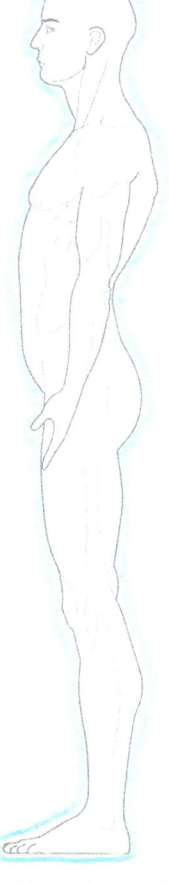

Eighth Energy Field, Second Phase
As the Eighth Energy Body further develops, the light energy refines and resembles a metallic, gold armor. The light contracts and condenses, and covers the entire body with two to six inches of silver-blue light, with a visible gold sheen. This energy field assists the sensitive development of many HU-man senses, including telepathy. This readily allows one to easily and enter into Oneness, the Oneship, and the One. Primarily cultivated through the use of Group Mind, Chelas, Initiates, and Arhats who have successfully attained this level of development can instantly assist the Group Mind formation. This light field functions through the sound and light frequencies of Christ Consciousness.

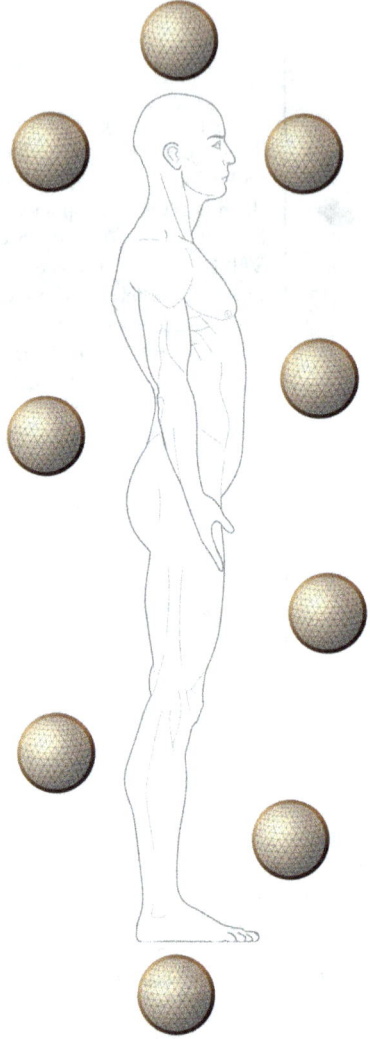

Ninth Energy Field, First Phase

The evolution of the Ninth Energy Body begins with the appearance of nine spherical globes that develop a triangular grid. They are located in an ovoid arrangement around the entire physical body. At this level, the Emotional Body responds by processing and transmuting the dual forces of the anxieties, fears, and trepidations held in the auric field. This is an intense process, and it is suggested to enter this process with the assistance of a Golden City Adjutant Point. As this process continues, the nine spheres expand and grow in size. The orbs spin, and help to raise the vibration of the physical body while the Ninth Energy Body develops into its second phase.

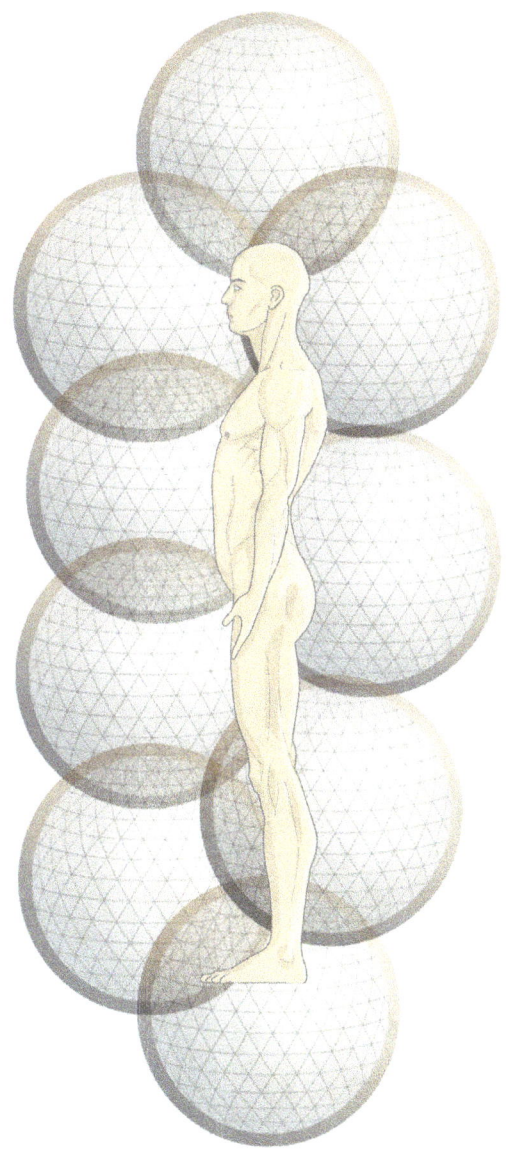

Ninth Energy Field, Second Phase
The Nine Golden Orbs continue to spin and expand, reaching a circumference of three to four feet. As they expand and diffuse energies, they begin to overlap to create one field of energy. Their spin and triangular grid inevitably disappears, as the second phase of the Ninth Energy Field completes.

PHOTONS

Ninth Energy Field, Third Phase
The energy field unites as one field of Golden Light. As this field forms, an alchemic Violet Light begins to radiate and emit throughout this layer. The energies of the tranmuting Violet Flame begin to dissolve the final fears of duality and the death urge. The energies refine in a similar manner to the Eight Energy Body, radiating a gold and then a bluish-silver light. The mature Ninth Energy Body has the ability to instantly influence the collective consciousness within dozens of miles.

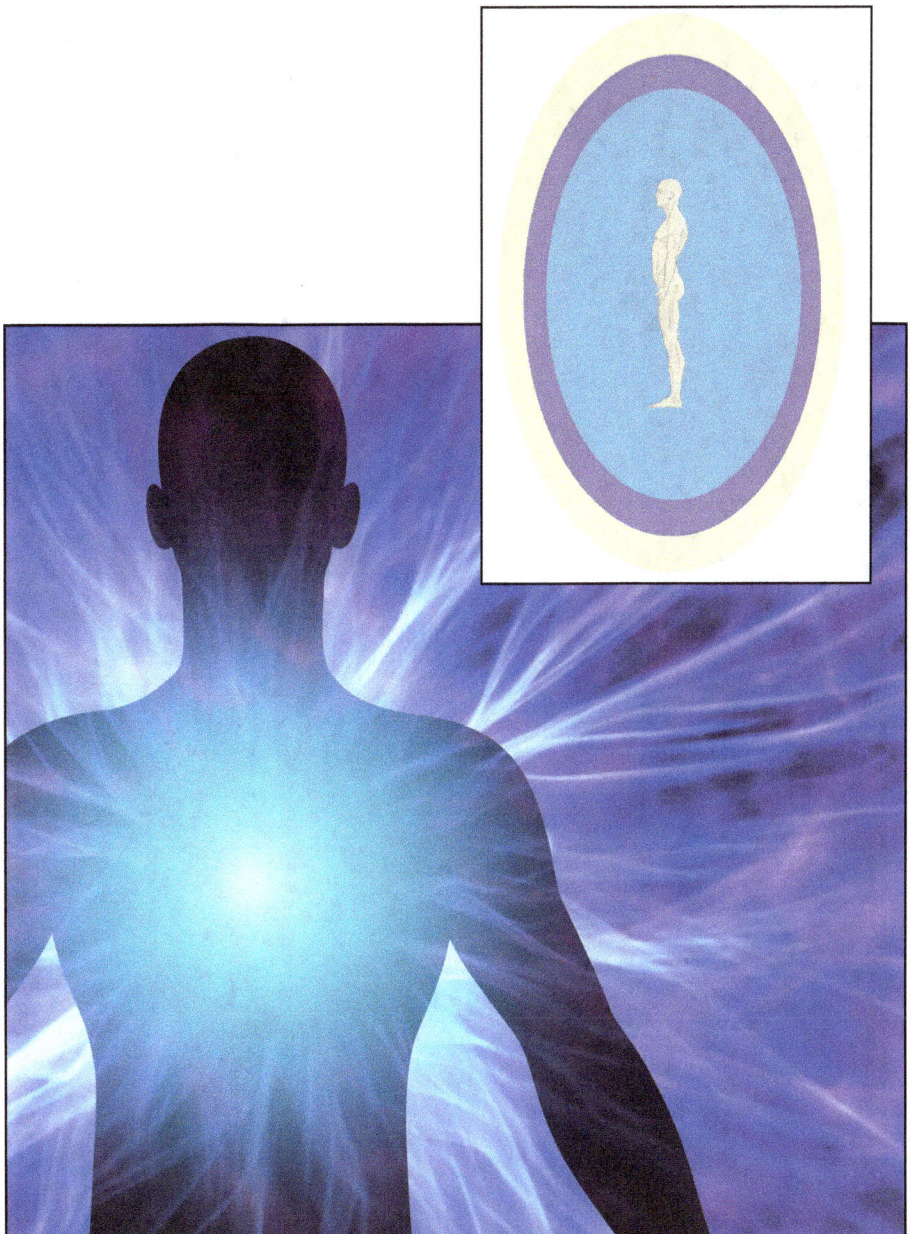

Tenth Energy Field, the Triple Gem

The Tenth Energy Field forms and then unites with the lower Eighth and Ninth Energy Field. Together they comprise the Triple Gems, three evolved fields of HU-man Light that are substantially strong and sizeable. They carry a metallic sheen of silver blue, the alchemic Violet Light, and the powerful Gold Ray. It is claimed that this light field has the ability to "cut through illusion." This energy field unites with lower light frequencies to help one to attain the *Seamless Garment*. The HU-man light produced through this field is known as the *Lighted Stance*. These states of spiritual evolution and consciousness are also known as the attainment of the *Diamond Mind*. (To learn more about the Eleventh and Twelfth Energy Body, see Appendix B.)

Eleventh Energy Body, Multi-dimensional Experience

The Eleventh Energy Body is quite large and can extend for over one-hundred feet, but typically forms a light field of twenty to forty feet around the body. The physical body begins to change, altering light and sound frequencies. This is an energy body of transfiguration with the ability to simultaneously experience Third, Fourth, Fifth, and Sixth Dimensions. This is the experiential Evolutionary Biome, with bi-location, precipitation, time and multi-dimensional travel. The physical body phases in and out as the consciousness seeks rapport with higher dimensions of experience, other Ascended Beings, ethereal retreats, Shamballa, and the Golden Cities.

APPENDIX T
The Violet Flame

The Violet Flame

Simply stated, the Violet Flame stabilizes past karmas through Transmutation, Forgiveness, and Mercy. This leads to the opening of the spiritual heart and the development of bhakti—the unconditional love and compassion for others. Our Co-creative ability is activated through the Ascended Master's gift of the Unfed Flame in adjunct with the practice of the Law of Love, and the Power of Intention. But the Violet Flame, capable of engendering our greatest spiritual growth and evolution, is spiritual velocity pure and simple.

Invoking the flame's force often produces feelings of peace, tranquility, and inner harmony—its ability to lift the low-vibrating energy fields of blame, despair, and fear into forgiveness and understanding, paves the path to love.

The history of the Violet Flame reaches back thousands of years before the Time of Christ. According to Ascended Master legend, the Lords of Venus transmitted the Violet Flame as a spiritual consciousness during the final days of the pre-Atlantis civilization Lemuria. As one society perished and another bloomed, the power of the Violet Flame shifted, opening the way for Atlantean religiosity. This transfer of power initiated a clearing of the Earth's etheric and psychic realms, and purged the lower physical atmosphere of negative forces and energies. Recorded narratives of Atlantis claim that Seven Temples of Purification sat atop visible materializations of the Violet Flame. The archangels Zadkiel and Amethyst, representing freedom, forgiveness and joy, presided over an Atlantean Brotherhood known as the Order of Zadkiel, also associated with Saint Germain. These Violet Flame Temples still exist today in the celestial realm over Cuba.

The Violet Flame benefits humans and divinities equally. During spiritual visualizations, meditations, prayers, decrees, and mantras, many disciples seek the Violet Flame for serenity and wisdom. Meanwhile, the Ascended Masters always use it in inner retreats—even Saint Germain taps into its power to perfect and apply its force with chelas and students

The Violet Flame, rooted in Alchemic powers, is sometimes identified as a higher energy of Saturn and the Blue Ray, a force leavened with justice, love, and wisdom. Ascended-Master lore explains the Violet Flame's ability to release a person from temporal concerns: Saturn's detachment from emotions and low-lying energies sever worldly connections. That's why the scientific properties of violet light are so important in metaphysical terms. The shortness of its wavelength and the high vibration of its frequency induce a point of transition to the next octave of light and into a keener consciousness.

PHOTONS

Mahatma El Morya
Master Teacher and Hierarch of the Golden City of Gobean.

APPENDIX U
El Morya

El Morya incarnated from a long line of historical notables, including the fabled King Arthur of England; the Renaissance scholar Sir Thomas Moore, author of Utopia; the patron saint of Ireland, Saint Patrick; and a Rajput prince. El Morya is even linked to the Hebrew patriarch Abraham. But in spite of his illustrious lifetimes, El Morya is best known as Melchior, one of the Magi who followed the Star of Bethlehem to the Christ infant.

El Morya first revealed himself to the founder of the Theosophical Society Helena Petrovna Blavatasky—also known as Madame Blavatsky or H. P. B.—during her childhood in London; that mid-nineteenth century meeting forged a lifelong connection with her Master and other members of the Spiritual Hierarchy. Some esoteric scholars recount different, more dramatic scenarios of their initial introduction. Blavatsky herself claimed El Morya rescued her from a suicide attempt on Waterloo Bridge.[1] The gracious Master dissuaded her from plunging into the waters of the Thames River. Others say the two met in Hyde Park or on a London street. According to Blavatsky, El Morya appeared under a secret political cover as the Sikh prince Maharaja Ranbir Singh of Kashmir, who served as a physically incarnated prototype of Master M. Singh and died in 1885.

Metaphysical scholars credit Blavatsky's work as the impetus for present-day theosophical philosophy and the conception of the Great White Brotherhood. Devoted disciples learned of the Hindu teacher from Blavatsky's childhood visions, and later on in a series of correspondences known as the Mahatma Letters, which contained spiritual guidelines for humanity. El Morya's presence in H. P. B.'s life enriched her spiritual knowledge, and she shared this transformation in a prolific body of texts and writings, namely Isis Unveiled and The Secret Doctrine. During a visit with Madame Blavatsky, A.P. Sinnett, an English newspaper editor, found the first of these letters among the branches of a tree. Over the years, the true meaning and authorship of the Mahatma Letters, reportedly co-authored by fellow Mahatma Kuthumi, have spurned controversy; some say Blavatsky herself forged the messages.[2]

Master M. is associated with the Blue Ray of power, faith, and good will; the Golden City of Gobean; and the planet Mercury. A strict disciplinarian, El Morya dedicates his work to the development of the will. He assists many disciples in discovering personal truths, exploring self-development, and honing the practice of the esoteric discipline. El Morya passes this wisdom to his numerous chelas and students. The Maha Chohan—El Morya's Guru, Lord of the Seven Rays and the Steward of Earth and its evolutions—educated him during his Earthly incarnations in India, Egypt, and Tibet. Declining the Ascension a number of times, it is said that El Morya finally accepted this divine passage in 1888, ascending with his beloved pet dog and horse. (Esoteric symbols of friendship and healing.)

---

1. Papastavro, Tellis S., *The Gnosis and the Law* (Tucson, AZ: Group Avatar), page 53.
2. Johnson, K. Paul, *The Masters Revealed: Madame Blavatsky and the Myth of the Great White Lodge* (Suny Series in Western Esoteric Traditions) (Albany, NY: State University of New York Press), page 41.

Akhenaton, Nefertiti, and Two Daughters
Relief of Akhenaton, Nefertiti, and two daughters adoring Aten. 1372-1350 BCE.

APPENDIX V
Akhenaton

Born in 1388 BC, the only surviving son of Amenhotep III, the King of Upper and Lower Egypt, Akhenaton strove to reform the Egyptian priesthood and unite the peoples of Egypt through a monotheist God, Aten. United in marriage at the age of twelve to the Egyptian Queen Nefertiti, Akhenaton was known to have fragile health, was a gentle and loving regent with an inclination to visions and dreams.

At the age of nineteen, Akhenaton broke with the corrupt priesthood of Amen. Historians record this fracture within the ancient Egyptian socio-political scene for several reasons. First, Amenhotep IV, known as Akhenaton, spiritually identified with the principles of Aten—symbolized by the Solar Disc—as a deity of one truth, and one light, who could unite the many secular deities of Egypt. Akhenaton—who had discovered the universal spiritual substance of light, good, and truth while meditating on the cosmic Sun—realized that, "the Sun did not shine upon Egypt alone, nor did its light and heat protect only the cities where it was honored. Its Rays shone beyond the mountains and beyond the deserts. Its light cheered the barbarians and sustained even the enemies of Egypt."[1]

Akhenaton's unfolding consciousness of the ONE and the unity of all life led him to issue orders that the name of Amen, and its implication of hierarchical adversity, be expunged from every inscription in Egypt. His break with the polytheistic religion of the kingdom created problems throughout the cultural state of Egypt, especially in ancient Thebes, the venerated City of his ancestors. To further implement his faith of Aten and his break from the traditional ancient faiths, Akhenaton relocated his capital City of Egypt on the East bank of the Nile River, approximately 160 miles South of present-day Cairo, where he constructed the intentional community of Khut-en-Aten (the Horizon of Aten) at the present-day site of Amarna. This is where Akhenaton oversaw the building of several of the most massive temples of ancient Egypt, including the Temple to the Formless One.[2]

A pioneer of monotheistic religion, Akhenaton embraced the Christ Consciousness, and some esoteric historians view him as a spiritual forerunner who led the way for the incarnation of Jesus, the Christ. Charles Potter in the History of Religion writes, "He was also the first pacifist, the first realist, the first monotheist, the first democrat, the first heretic, the first humanitarian, the first internationalist, and the first person known to attempt to found a religion. He was born out of due time, several thousand years too soon."[3]

According to the Master Teachers, Akhenaton is one of the prior lifetimes attributed to Ascended Master Serapis Bey, and in his lifetime as Akhenaton was able to split his consciousness to physically appear in the Southwest United States. Due to their discovery of an ancient rock-cut cave, esoteric archaeologists theorize that Ancient Egyptians may have left clues to their presence in the Grand Canyon. An April 5, 1909, Phoenix Gazette article alleged that the Smithsonian Institute was financing exploration of the Canyon

---

1. Manly P. Hall, *Twelve World Teachers: A Summary of Their Lives and Teachings*, (Philosophical Research Society, Inc., 1965, Los Angeles, CA), page 21.
2. *Wikipedia*, Akhenaton, http://en.wikipedia.org/wiki/Akhenaton, (2011).
3. Manly P. Hall, *Twelve World Teachers: A Summary of Their Lives and Teachings*, (Philosophical Research Society, Inc., 1965, Los Angeles, CA), page 16.

during the cave discovery: "Discoveries which almost conclusively prove that the race which inhabited this mysterious cavern, hewn in solid rock by human hands, was of oriental origin, possibly from Egypt, tracing back to Rameses. If their theories are born out by the translation of the tablets engraved with hieroglyphics, the mystery of the prehistoric peoples of North America, their ancient arts, who they were and whence they came, will be solved. Egypt and the Nile, and Arizona and the Colorado will be linked by a historical chain running back to ages which stagger the wildest fancy of the fictionist."[4]

The Master Teachers further claim that during this phase of Akhenaton's spiritual development, he studied with the Lord of the Christ Consciousness, Quetzalcoatl. This may explain Akhenaton's spiritual presence among indigenous peoples of the ancient American Southwest.

Akhenaton wrote the celebrated poem, "Great Hymn to Aten," synthesizing many of the religious and spiritual teachings of Atenism:

> How manifold it is, what thou hast made!
> They are hidden from the face (of man).
> O sole god, like whom there is no other!
> Thou didst create the world according to thy desire,
> Whilst thou wert alone: All men, cattle, and wild beasts,
> Whatever is on Earth, going upon (its) feet,
> And what is on high, flying with its wings.
> The countries of Syria and Nubia, the land of Egypt,
> Thou settest every man in his place,
> Thou suppliest their necessities:
> Everyone has his food, and his time of life is reckoned.
> Their tongues are separate in speech,
> And their natures as well;
> Their skins are distinguished,
> As thou distinguishest the foreign peoples.
> Thou makest a Nile in the underworld,
> Thou bringest forth as thou desirest
> To maintain the people (of Egypt)
> According as thou madest them for thyself,
> The lord of all of them, wearying (himself) with them,
> The lord of every land, rising for them,
> The Aten of the day, great of majesty.[5]

---

4. David Hatcher Childress, *Lost Cities of North and Central America*, (Adventures Unlimited Press, 1992, Stelle, IL), page 317.
5. *Wikipedia, Great Hymn to the Aten*, http://en.wikipedia.org/wiki//Great_Hymn_to_the_Aten, (2011).

APPENDIX W
The Will Chakras

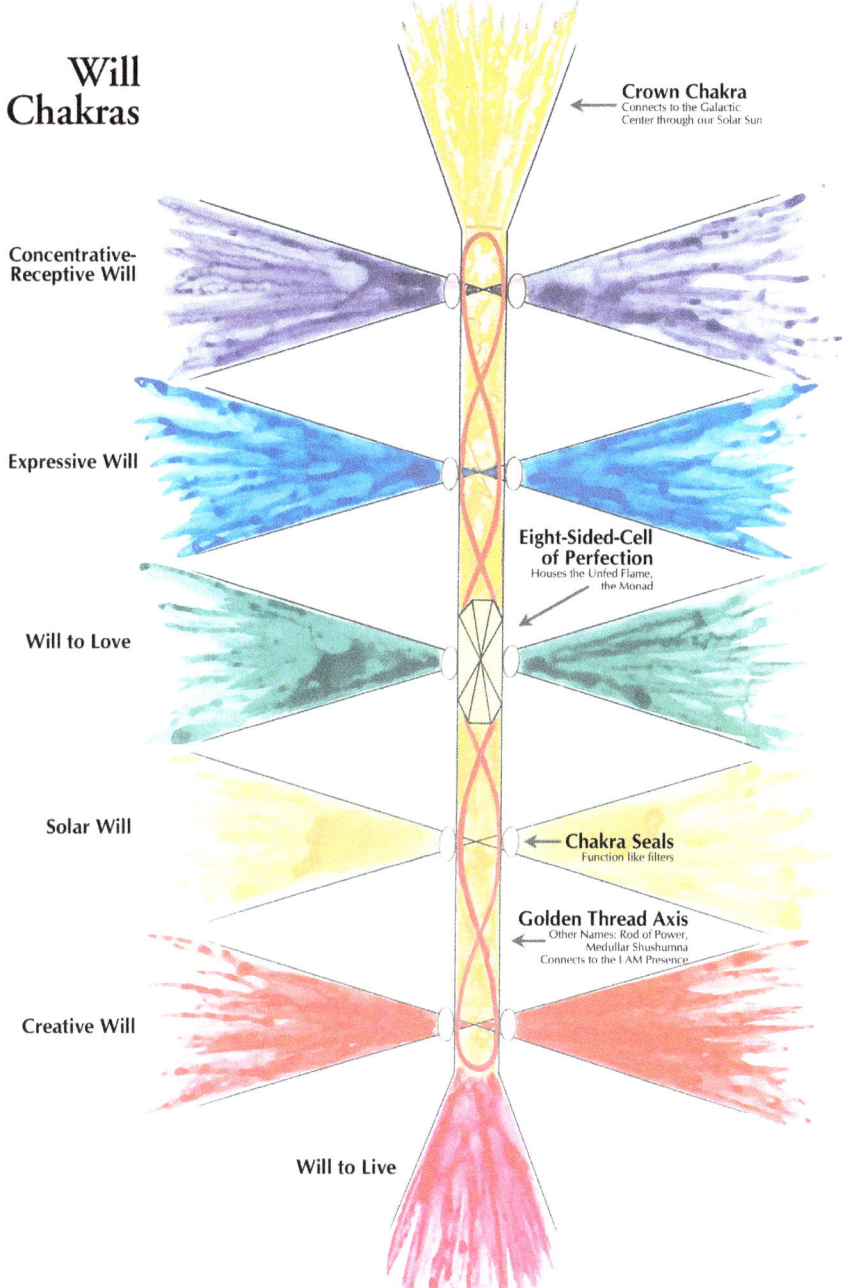

The Will Chakras
The Golden Thread Axis; Eight-sided Cell of Perfection; and the *Will Chakras*.
(Side View: Left represents the back of the body; Right represents the front of the body.)

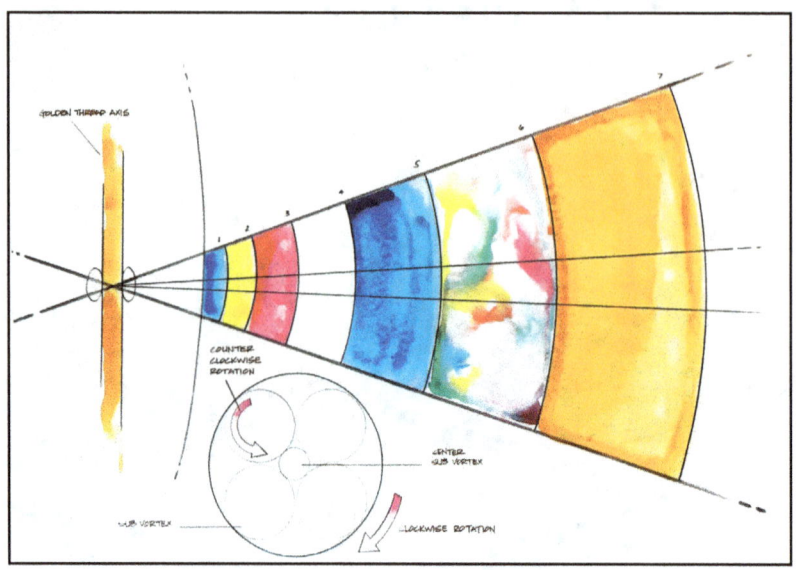

Layers of a Human Chakra
Illustration of the Golden Thread Axis, and cross section of Seven Layers of Light within the chakra. Note sub-Vortices of chakra with clockwise and counterclockwise motions.

Will Chakras

The Will Chakras are a specific series of six chakras located on the back of the human spine and the Root Chakra (kundalini system), and enable the personal actions and choices of the individual. Like the Frontal Chakras, Will Chakras absorb and process light and sound energy from Ray Forces. The entire Human Chakra System affects the Human Aura. A chakra spins, in fact, in Sanskrit chakra literally means, "spinning wheel." The anatomy of a chakra contains both an outer portion and an inner portion. The inner portion of the chakra is comprised of sub-Vortices; the number of sub-Vortices varies according to the type of chakra. Chakra movement absorbs and releases the energy of the Rays. A healthy chakra absorbs Ray Forces through the clockwise movement of the outer chakra and releases the energies through the counterclockwise movement of the sub-Vortices. Will and Frontal Chakras both absorb and release energies; however, when energies enter a Frontal Chakra, the energy exits the Will Chakra; and vice-versa, when energies enter a Will Chakra, the energy exits through the Frontal Chakra. This flow maintains the health of the physical body through the balance of light and sound frequencies present in the Human Aura. Descriptions of the six Will Chakras follow:

Concentrative-Receptive Will: The ability to focus, while remaining open and receptive; centered and sensitive; Masculine and Feminine

Expressive Will: The will to express emotions and thoughts; the ability to communicate with clarity and personal truth; expansive and determined; Masculine

Will to Love: The Heart's Desire; Fulfills goals, aspirations, and desires conceived through the Creative Will. Nurturing and sustaining; Feminine

Solar Will: The ability to interact with others with personal power; receptive and protective; Masculine

Creative Will: The will to create through ideas, intentions, and goals; sensing; Feminine

Will to Live: Root Chakra connects to Mother Earth

APPENDIX X
Agreement Formation

Throughout the Ascension Teachings Saint Germain explains that our Divine Co-creative ability is to reach alignment, balance, and achieve Harmony. You further hone your spiritual practice and enter Fourth Dimension through applying the Law of Agreement.

This is the definition of the Law of Agreement: "The sacred meeting of two minds which on one formative side reflects our intent and commitment. The result of our agreements with others mirrors our choices and our responsible actions which define our life force. Since our actions illustrate our motivations, agreements reflect our ability to effectively Co-create with others, and produce the level of harmony we enjoy from the interaction."

Practice Agreement Formation with the most important person in your life. Start with discussion of common goals and intentions and find one important item you both agree upon. Write your agreement on paper and sign.

Two excerpts about Saint Germain's instructions on Harmony and Agreement Formation from *New World Wisdom, Book One*. The first is: "Choice Reflects Our True Motivations." The second excerpt is: "Harmony, the Law of Agreement."

Choice Reflects Our True Motivations

"Yes, we have work for you to do, as we have always said that there is much to do to continue your work within the light. But we have stressed to you the Laws of Commitment. Stand firm when you make your choice. There is work to do and it must stand as ONE body of work.

We commend and applaud you for what you have achieved, for it has been a monumental task to step as far as you have stepped. It has been a monumental leap to leave what you feel is conventional, to raise your vibration to this level and to extend this to mankind. We applaud you and thank you for the tremendous effort and work. We will continue to dispense the work as you ask and are willing, for, you see, we are not allowed to infringe upon the free will. Through this you will team the responsibility of your energies. For is not the understanding of this work the understanding of the power of the Beloved Mighty I AM working within your life? Perhaps you do not understand how strong this power is. It is a tremendous force, a tremendous force which works on the principle of attraction. Do you understand?

Response: "No, please explain."

He's writing on the board. He has written, 'Commitment -> Agreement -> Choice -> Responsibility -> Action -> Life Force.'

As you see this chart, Dear ones, do you not understand all of your actions come with the original commitment and the original agreement which you have made. Your actions are your true motivations. Does this clarify?

Response: 'Yes, I think so.'

Wonderful! This is truly magnificent! You see, Dear one, this is the way we have interacted with you. We are not allowed to enter into your consciousness for your upliftment without the action of your choice and without the motivation of your pure heart.

Response: 'I've been very aware of how my motivation or intent has changed over the last year or two.'

Good! Your ability to recognize is your ability to carry on the contract with us. Who are we but an extension of the people in your life! We are not allowed

Winter Harmony
John Henry Twatchtman, 1893-1900.

to come into the physical during this transitional time, but our work is being carried out through those whom we call our messengers. And no, we have not positioned them to be glorified, but you must come to the realization that all those within your life are truly messengers! For our energies are of Service and benefit to all.

Your ability to keep your agreement with those about you is important and you must understand this law. This is the true way that we function and communicate. We have formed agreements with you in order to even speak with you. This agreement is made through the Higher Self. Your choice is to have this experience. All that is, is through choice, and the responsibility of choice is yours."

Harmony, the Law of Agreement

"Welcome, my Beloved Brother and Sister, I AM Sananda. I come forth this day to give you continued discourse on what we call the World Project at this time upon your Earth Plane. Do we have permission to enter your energy fields?

Response: "You most certainly have permission to enter my energy field. And I'm sure Lori would give her permission."

Dear ones, we have come forth to offer this project to you, the world changes to occur upon the Earth Plane and Planet. We also have come to bring you discourse or lesson. For you see, this project was originated through Beloved Sanat Kumara many eons ago and this is its completion; for he has expanded on the laws of the cosmos as a creative pattern.

There are, as you understand, several reasons for what has come forth. Change is a continual process, and it is most important that humankind understand that change is the pathway whereby growth is achieved. This is, indeed, the seventh time that the Earth will go through what you call a shift, a shift not only of the poles themselves but of the electromagnetic currents that run through her energy fields.

This shift in energy will occur from her sixth to her seventh body, preparing humankind to enter into what is called the Fourth Dimension. Third Dimensional beings are being prepared to enter into a Fourth Dimension awareness.

As I have stated before, there are Twelve Jurisdictions to accompany this work. The theme of Earth Changes is to be understood in its entire context. I shall recognize those who have helped tirelessly with this effort and work:

Beloved Saint Germain, Sponsor of the Americas.

Beloved Mary, Keeper of what is the Cradleland, also known as South America.

Beloved Kuan Yin, who has stepped forth to sponsor the Asian Continent.

Beloved El Morya, whose directive focus is shared in America and in Europe.

Beloved Kuthumi, who has generously given his light to America and also holds the channel and light for Africa.

There are many more to follow and many more will come forth, many, too numerous to mention. There is indeed, Beloved Nada, who holds her radiance and presence within England. There is also Beloved Paul, who comes to set the seal of his radiance and brilliance in the Central American areas. And, most assuredly, the Seven Beloved Archangels shed their Rays on the entire planet. And who stands at the North and South poles? Beloved Archangel Michael. And who is that who sheds the Ray of Golden Radiance around the equator and surrounds the planet in eternal love, but Archangel Chamuel.

So you see, Dear one, this is a method of cooperation and we work in Harmony, which is, indeed, the topic of our first Jurisdiction, Harmony.

We are All in this Together

Beloveds, you have been brought here to create. Not only are you creative beings, but you must learn to create in full cooperation with one another. You are, at times, like small children in a sandbox, designing your castle. Each of you has the same sand, the same amount of water, and yet, as one designs the building that is his, there is always someone who comes forth to throw sand or to destroy what his Brother or Sister has made. So each person then rebuilds again. It is time for you to let this go! It is time for you to work in cooperation and Harmony! Together, for you are in this truly together. Not only have you shared genetic code, you are on this planet as ONE body of light. It is time for you to come forth and cooperate.

Harmony Maintains Balance

Harmony comes forth for the blending of creative waves. Harmony comes forth when all has achieved balance. We have spoken of alignment and spoken of balance. Alignment must precede balance. Balance is, indeed, the maintenance of alignment. You have yet to achieve this upon your planet. There have, indeed, been times when she has become aligned, but the maintenance of alignment is balance, and this is yet to be achieved. We speak of the directive force within the will itself. For you see, Dear one, mankind has long forgotten that will is to be directed only through love, not through wisdom. Wisdom is the application. But we speak now of direction.

What is the directive force? The directive force of the will is love. To understand this is to become aligned. And to maintain this universal law is to achieve balance. The maintenance of balance, Dear ones, is the nature of our project. Not only is your planet misaligned, it is far from balanced. Earth Changes have been brought forth to provide the creative space and pattern for alignment. You, as human beings, have long understood that all energy, in order to be sustained for creation, must be maintained in balance. To draw from the well of creativity, to drink of its waters, the source must be replenished. And how does the source replenish? Through balance, Dear ones.

Question: 'Balance is the continuous cycle?'

It is the continuous cycle known as Harmony.

And so upon your planet, do you not see the imbalance, the misalignment, and how this has come to be? Each continent is to become aligned. Ascended Beings have come forth to sponsor, to not only keep the alignment, but to hold a focus for maintenance. That is why we are dispensing the information which you know as the energetic bodies of perfection. Man has long known that he was a body of light, but he has refused to recognize this within himself. And now this must be recognized for truly he must be responsible for what he has created.

So you see, Dear ones, you enter into the misappropriation of energy which allows a non-creative force to exist. You have referred to this as a black hole. And eventually, yes, you pull out of this hole into another dimension of creation. It is no mystery to the cosmos that the Earth, through her inhabitants, has created a pattern, a pattern of imbalance, a pattern of disharmony, and a pattern of misalignment. We have stepped forth as members of the Spiritual Hierarchy of the Great White Brotherhood not to duplicate this pattern. We have decided to expand it!

If you are to be a creative planet, Dear ones, create in Harmony. If you are to create Harmony, sustain your creation. We are here to assist you, Dear ones. Harmony is your first lesson. I am here, eternally yours. Are you ready for questions?

The Consciousness of Minerals and Crystals

Question: "Mineral deposits, crystal structures and precious gems, which are crystal structures, they carry the energetic stability of the planet, do they not?"

They have been set forth to hold the creative pattern.

Question: "Then indeed mineral deposits carry consciousness?"

They carry vibration, which, Dear one, is a component of consciousness. Consciousness is a collective vibration.

Question: "Then with reference to the human body and the Earth body comparison, mineral deposits function much the same way as acupuncture meridians do in the human body?"

To the Earth Planet, yes. They also serve as great centers for input and output for the flow of energy, what you have seen on the human body as a chakra point. They assist the planet much as you have understood your nervous system.

Question: "I see. That is the physical mode of how the human nervous system functions. So does the nervous system of the planet function through the mineral deposits?"

The Harmonic Flow of Sound

It does indeed. For this is how light travels, on electromagnetic current, which underneath, if you were to isolate this further, is through sound. For sound precedes light.

Question: 'As the biblical phrase, 'In the beginning,' there was the word?"

This is true.

Question: "In addition, before the word, there was the sound?'

Sound is the building block that light is built upon.

Question: "So all creation is based upon the first primary building block of sound?"

Sound that carries an electromagnetic field.

Question: 'Not all sound carries an electromagnetic field?'

This is true, not all sound is qualified as creative wave.

Question: 'So there are certain sound frequencies which work to create, to rebuild, to align, to restructure, to purify and cleanse?'

This is accurate, for do you not have the division of Rays within light?

Question: 'Yes. Now if we look at the bodies of water on the planet, which do they function on, the sound or the light, or both?'

You see, Dear ones, they function upon a wave and like a wave that comes to the beach, this wave has been predicated by gravitational pull. Beyond the gravitational pull is the energy of light, that streams forth on the electromagnetic current. And what builds the electromagnetic current? Sound. Something as massive as an ocean contains within it the complete harmony and symphony of the Elementals and the Mighty Elohim, those who step forward in Service to the rhythmic, harmonic flow of sound on the electromagnetic wave."

Jesus, Ministered to by Angels
James Tissot, 1894.

APPENDIX Y
Lord Sananda

Lord Sananda

During his paradigm-altering incarnation more than 2,000 years ago, Lord Sananda (above), also known as Sananda Kumara, embodied the Christ Consciousness, as Jesus, son of God. Some esoteric scholars say he's one of the four sons of Brahma—Sanaka, Sanatana, Sanat-Kumara, and Sanandana—his namesake. According to Vedic lore, the foursome possess eternally liberated souls and live in Tapaloka, the dimension of the great sages. Before manifesting in physical form, Jesus belonged to the Angelic Kingdom. His name was Micah—the Great Angel of Unity. Micah is the son of Archangel Michael who led the Israelites out of Egypt.[1] [For more information on the life story of Jesus' life, I recommend reading, Twelve World Teachers, by Manly P. Hall.]

Sananda Kumara revealed his identity to the mystic Sister Thedra. Her Master first contacted her in the early 1960s and instructed her to move to Peru, specifically, to a hidden monastery in the Andes mountains. There, undergoing an intense spiritual training, she kept in constant contact with Sananda, and he shared with her prophecies of the coming Earth Changes. After leaving the abbey, Sister Thedra moved to Mt. Shasta, California where she founded the Association of Sananda and Sanat Kumara. She died in 1992.

Sananda posed for a photograph on June 1, 1961 in Chichen Itza, Yucatan. He told Sister Thedra that though the image is valid, he is not limited by form of any kind; therefore, he may take on any appearance necessary.

Lord Sananda is the Hierarch of the Golden City of Shalahah, located in Idaho, Montana, and Oregon, United States. The Lord of Christ Consciousness also serves as World Teacher in the Shamballa lineage.

---

1. Papastavro, Tellis S., *The Gnosis and the Law* (Tucson, AZ: Group Avatar), page 358.

Tibet, Himalayas.
Nicholas Roerich, 1933.

APPENDIX Z
Saint Germain the Holy Brother

Saint Germain, Ascended Master for the United Brotherhood of Earth

The Lord of the Seventh Ray and the Master of the Violet Flame, Saint Germain, lived numerous noteworthy lifetimes, dating back thousands of years, before incarnating as the Comte de Saint Germainduring Renaissance Europe. He lived as the Englishman Sir Francis Bacon, the sixteenth-century philosopher, essayist, and Utopian who greatly influenced the philosophy of inductive science. His most profound and well-known work on the restoration of humanity, the Instauratio Magna (Great Restoration), defined him as an icon of the Elizabethan era. Research also shows his co-authoring of many Shakespearean sonnets.

According to Esoteric historians, Queen Elizabeth I of England — The Virgin Queen — was his biological mother. Before Bacon's birth, the queen married Earl of Leicester, quieting ideas of illegitimacy. Elizabeth's lady in waiting, Lady Ann Bacon, wife of the Lord High Chancellor of England, adopted him following the stillbirth of her baby. Bacon was, therefore, the true heir to the crown and England's rightful king.[1] But his cousin James I of Scotland succeeded the throne. Sir Bacon described this turn of events in his book, Novum Organo, published in 1620: "It is an immense ocean that surrounds the island of Truth." And Saint Germain often reminds us to this day "there are no mistakes, ever, ever, ever."

Bacon's philosophies also helped define the principles of Free Masonry and democracy. As an adept leader of the Rosicrucians (a secret society of that time), he set out to reveal the obsolescence and oppression of European monarchies.

Eventually, Bacon's destiny morphed. He shed his physical form and sought the greatest gift of all: immortality. And that's what placed him in the most extraordinary circumstances throughout history. Even his death (or lack of) evokes controversy. Some say Bacon faked his demise in 1626 — the coffin contained the carcass of a dog.

According to the author, ADK Luk, Saint Germain ascended on May 1, 1684 in Transylvania at the Rakoczy mansion. He was 123 years old. Some say Saint Germain spent the lost years — from 1626 to 1684 — in Tibet. During this time he took (or may have been given) the name Kajaeshra. Interpreted as God's helper of life and wisdom, it was possibly a secret name and rarely used. Kaja has several interpretations: in Greek it means pure; Balinese, toward the mountain; early Latin (Estonian), echo; Hopi, wise child; Polish, of the Gods;

---

1. Marie Bauer Hall, *Foundations Unearthed*, originally issued as Francis Bacon's Great Virginia Vault, Fourth Edition (Los Angeles: Veritas Press), page 9.

Francis Bacon by John Vanderbank, (1731). Francis Bacon coined the term "New Age" in the seventeenth century. The English philosopher is said to be the last human incarnation of the Ascended Master Saint Germain.

and Hebrew, life. The second part of the name — Eshra (Ezra) — translates into help or aid.

Indeed, Bacon's work would impact centuries to follow. During his time in Tibet, tucked away in silent monasteries, Germain designed a society that eventually created a United Brotherhood of the Earth: Solomon's Temple of the Future. It's a metaphor used to describe the raising of consciousness as the greater work of democracy. Author Marie Bauer Hall studied the life of Francis Bacon. In her book, Foundations Unearthed, she described the legendary edifice: "This great temple was to be supported by the four mighty pillars of history, science, philosophy, and religion, which were to bear the lofty dome of Universal Fellowship and Peace."[2]

But Germain, pictured left, [3] embraced an even deeper passion: the people and nation of America, christening it New Atlantis. He envisioned this land — present-day United States, Canada, Mexico, and South America — as part of the United Democracies of Europe and the People of the World. America, this growing society, held his hope for a future guided by a Democratic Brotherhood.

The Comte de Saint Germain emerged years later in the courts of pre-revolutionary France — his appearance, intelligence, and worldliness baffled members of the Court of Versailles. This gentleman carried the essence of eternal youth: he was a skilled artist and musician; he spoke fluent German, English, French, Italian, Portuguese, Spanish, Greek, Latin, Sanskrit, Arabic, and Chinese; and he was a proficient chemist. Meanwhile, literary, philosophic, and political aristocracy of the time sought his company. French philosophers Jean-Jacque Rousseau and Voltaire; the Italian adventurer Giacomo Casanova; and the Earl of Chatham and statesman Sir Robert Walpole of Britain were among his friends.

In courts throughout Europe, he dazzled royalty with his Mastery of Alchemy, removing flaws from gems and turning lead into Gold. And the extent of Germain's ken reached well into the theosophical realm. A Guru of yogic and tantric disciplines, he possessed highly developed telepathic and psychic abilities. This preternatural knowledge led to the development of a cartographic Prophecy — the Map of Changes. This uncanny blueprint, now in the hands of the scion of Russian aristocracy, detailed an imminent restructuring of the political and social boundaries of Europe.[4]

---

2. M. Hall, *Foundations Unearthed*, page 13.
3. Saint Germain, *The Secret Teachings of All Ages*, Diamond Jubilee Edition (Los Angeles: Philosophical Research Society, Inc.), Manly Hall.
4. K. Paul Johnson, The Masters Revealed: Madame Blavatsky and the Myth of the Great White Lodge (Suny Series in Western Esoteric Traditions) (Albany, NY: State University of New York Press), page 19.

Propel Your Ascension

Farmers, Uncle Sam Asks You to Get Ready for the Census Taker
The author is unknown in this poster depicting Uncle Sam during the World War II effort. This depiction of Uncle Sam was designed for multiple government agencies: the Office for Emergency Management, Office of War Information, Domestic Operations Branch, and Bureau of Special Services. 1943-1945.

Saint Germain
A contemporary portrait of the Ascended Master by Summit Lighthouse.

But few grasped Germain's true purpose during this time of historic critical mass: not even the king and queen of France could comprehend his tragic forewarnings. The Great White Brotherhood — a fellowship of enlightened luminaries — sent the astute diplomat Saint Germain to orchestrate the development of the United States of Europe. Not only a harbinger of European diplomacy, he made his presence in America during the germinal days of this country. Esoteric scholars say he urged the signing of the Declaration of Independence in a moment of collective fear — a fear of treason and ultimately death. Urging the forefathers to proceed, a shadowed figure in the back of the room shouted: Sign that document!

To this day, the ironclad identity of this person remains a mystery, though some mystics believe it was Saint Germain. Nevertheless, his avid support spurred the flurry of signatures, sealing the fate of America — and the beginning of Sir Francis Bacon's democratic experiment.

The Comte de Saint Germain never could shape a congealed Europe, but he did form a lasting and profound relationship with America. Germain's present-day participation in U.S. politics reaches the Oval Office. Some theosophical mystics say Germain visits the president of the United States the day after the leader's inauguration; others suggest he's the fabled patriot Uncle Sam.

Saint Germain identifies with the qualities of Brotherhood and freedom. He is the sponsor of humanity and serves as a conduit of Violet Light — a force some claim is powerful enough to propel one into Ascension.

According to the I AM America Prophecies, Saint Germain says that the people of America have a unique destiny in the New Times. America contains within it a unique anagram:

A M E R I C A = I A M R A C E.

The I AM Race of people is a unique group of souls who lived in America as Atlanteans. But their destiny has evolved since those ancient times. Instead of sinking on a continent destroyed by the misuse of technology and spiritual knowledge, their active intelligence continues to develop in modern times. Their service is focused on the Brotherly love of all nations. In the I AM America Earth Changes Prophecies Saint Germain states, "America will be the first to go through the changes, and then give aid to the rest of the World."

Interpretations of this Prophecy explain why American is possibly the chosen land — the first society to experience dimensional change. Members of this regenerated, enlightened society will share and teach the benefits of this new understanding with the rest of humanity.

Saint Germain identifies with the qualities of Brotherhood and freedom. He is the sponsor of humanity and serves as a conduit of Violet Light — a force some claim is powerful enough to propel one into Ascension. When Saint Germain accepts a chela, the Master appears in physical form. Sometimes, he playfully disguises himself, leaving clues of his identity, most often purple clothing.

Today the essence of Saint Germain — that eternal, eloquent diplomat — fills the world. His presence assures humanity of an alternate path to evolution and growth. In *Changing the Guard* he illustrates this point: "We have spent our time adjusting that Collective Consciousness for the days and the times that are coming. We also would like to remind you that we cannot, at any time, readjust the karma of mankind. For what mankind has created, mankind must now receive. This is the Law of Cause and Effect. But we work with those causes to readjust that plan of the best and highest good." Perhaps our present karma is indeed predestined, but how we work through karmas is engendered in our Free Will and choice.

APPENDIX AA
Timelines and Consciousness

Timeline ONE		Timeline TWO
Third Density	**Fourth Density**	**Fifth Density**
Armageddon	Great Awakening	Golden Age
Earth Changes	Time of Change	Time of Peace
War and Corruption	Justice and Fairness	Harmony and Cooperation
Chemtrails, Weather Modification	Healing of the Elemental Kingdom	Mother Earth—Babajeran
GMOs	Organic Hierloom Seeds and Plants	Monoatomic Plants
Polarity	Composure, Steadiness	Balance
Deception	Transparency	Truthfulness
Spiritual Suppression	Spiritual Awakening	Enlightenment
Greed, Avarice	Generosity, Appreciation	Abundance
Mainstream News	Citizen journalists	Clarity
Depopulation	Birth of the New Children	Immortality of the Soul
Control and Fear	Choice and Love	Empowerment
Globalism	Regionalism	Brotherhood and Sisterhood
Transhumanism	HU-man Development	Ascension
Science vs Religion	Personal Experience	Science of Spirituality
Division	Unity	ONE
Racism	Oneship	Brotherhood and Sisterhood
Class Distinction	Oneness	Group Mind
Corporations	Communities	Individualization
Enslavement	Freedom	Spiritual Liberation
Limitation	Choice	Divine Will
Carbon-based Consciousness	Silicon-based Consciousness	UNANA
Magic	Alchemy	Transformation
Destruction	Healing and Renewal	Co-creation
Artificial Intelligence	I AM Presence	I AM That I AM
Dependency	Self-reliance	Interdependency
Petro gas	Free Energy	Bi-location
Disinformation	Transparency	Truth
Censorship	Freedom of Speech, Self-determination	Sovereignty
Elitism	Rule of Law	Equanimity
"Do what thou wilt."	Karma	Universal Law
Entitlement	Merit	Virtue and Righteousness
Regulation	Self-rule	Empowerment
Pollution	Nature Kingdoms	Stewardship
Environment	Natural Law	Evolutionary Biome

Timeline ONE		Timeline TWO
Third Density	**Fourth Density**	**Fifth Density**
End Times	Time of Change	New Times
Fiat Currency	True State Economy	Precipitation
Banking	Abundance	Universal Substance
Anti-christ	Love	Christ Consciousness
Debt	Energy for energy	Karmic Freedom
Poverty	Gratitude, Prudence	Prosperity
Past lives	Re-membering	True Memory
Crime and Addiction	Self-control	God Control
Disease	Healing	Health
Advice	Inner Guidance	Wisdom
Doubt	Faith	Devotion
Survival	Endurance, Persistence	Strength
Psychic Attack	Intervention, God's Blessing	Consecration
Energy Vampire	Restoration and Renewal	God Expansion
Suppression	Encouragement	Allowing
Attacking	Loving	God Protection
5G	Telepathy	I AM
Ego	Higher Self	I AM Presence
Slavery	Emancipation	Spiritual Freedom
DNA	Light and Energy	Light Bodies
Man	HU-man	Ascended Master
Judging	Forgiveness and Mercy	Compassion
Belief	Experience and Knowledge	Divine Wisdom
Aggression	Diplomacy	Peace within
Confusion	Clarity	Order
Interference	Detachment	Cooperation
Unrest	Nonreactive	Stillness
Bondage	Emancipation, Liberation	Freedom
Decay	Renewal, Regeneration	Wholeness
Conflict	Agreement	Harmony
Ignorance	Education	Knowledge
God outside	Transcension	God within
Spiritual Darkness	Spiritual Awakening	Enlightenment
Bigotry	Tolerance	Brotherhood and Sisterhood
Victim	Choice	Empowered
Original Sin	God's Blessing and Salvation	Innate Divinity
Death	Resurrection	Ascension
Insurance	Trust and Faith	God Protection

Timeline ONE		Timeline TWO
Third Density	**Fourth Density**	**Fifth Density**
Exploitation	Protection and Nurturing	Service
Seven Rays of Light and Sound	Eight Rays of Light and Sound	Nine Rays of Light and Sound
Mind Control	Freedom of Thought	Universal Mind
Medical Treatment	Cure	Health
Lifespan	Longevity	Immortality
Uncertainty	Acceptance	BE-ing
Emotional	Balance	Harmony
Population density	Rural development	Galactic Expansion
Technology	Conscious biology	Evolutionary Biome
Job	Purposeful work	Joy to Serve
Evolution	Evolutionary Biome	Cosmic Being

The Holder of the Cup, Mongolia.
Nicholas Roerich, 1937.

APPENDIX BB
The Cup Ceremony

The Cup Ceremony is a simple Water Ceremony performed by both students and Ascended Masters to pour spiritual blessings upon its participants and to bless Mother Earth, Beloved Babajeran. Cup Ceremony joins chelas and Light Beings into the Group Mind. The ceremony is both activating and purifying, and can anchor benevolent energies into a specific location, particularly a Golden City Adjutant Point. Cup Ceremonies performed on a regular basis at certain locations can increase the energy of a power spot and may open mystical portals to multi-dimensional experience. It can be performed by one person with the help and assistance of spirit guides and Master Teachers, or in groups. A water-filled Cup is passed to each participant who permeates the water with spoken prayers, decrees, and mantras. When the blessing is complete, the prayer-infused water is poured upon the Earth, and it instantly communicates with the Evolutionary Biome.

The Holy Grail

It is claimed that the Cup was originally sent to Earth by the Angels of Neutrality to ease the suffering and extremism of polarity and duality. The Cup is the symbolic Holy Grail, a metaphysical and spiritual symbol that creates Unity with the Creation and the Divine. The Cup is linked to Jesus Christ's Last Supper with his disciples and energies of abundance, alchemy, and restorative healing flow from the Holy Grail. Christ's Cup was said to be entrusted with Joseph of Arimathea — Mary's uncle — and was later buried in a well at Glastonbury, the location of Camelot. According to esoteric researchers, the site at Glastonbury was owned by Joseph, and Christ traveled there to study in his missing years.

A Cupbearer

A ceremonial Cup is considered a sacred relic, and a Cup is given to spiritual students as they complete specific levels of study within the Ascended Master Tradition. Since the Cup can channel emotional energies, it is recommended that an Ascended Master student apply the Violet Flame on a daily basis for two years as a prerequisite to performing Cup Ceremony. A student who has been given a Cup for ceremony is known as a "Cup Bearer." A Cup that has been given as a gift is considered to be more powerful than a Cup that a student has purchased, although Cup Ceremonies of all types are helpful. Cups are considered to be alive and filled with consciousness, and part of the Evolutionary Biome.

The Purification Process

If you purchase a Cup, it is important to purify the Cup for ceremonial use. It is recommended to purify by light, either with an electric light or by candle light. Candle light is preferred, as the flame of the candle contains an elemental life force. Battery-operated candles can also work. Electrical light can be used to reduce the risk of fire. Place your Cup in a sacred location in your home, protected from view and where it will not be disturbed. The best locations are upon altars and in meditation rooms. Surround the Cup with light. You can use two to five candles, and if you are using electrical light, make certain the light is very bright. It is recommended to purify the Cup by light for five to seven days; however, two weeks is often best and these Cups seem to yield the best results. You can also place pictures of various Ascended Masters and Archangels next to the bed or on your personal altar. Burn incense throughout your home. Sandlewood and Nag Champa give good results.

After your Cup has been purified, it is ready for use. You can keep your Cup upon your altar when not in use, or wrap the Cup in silk cloth and place in a dark-colored bag. This helps to insulate and preserve its delicate, subtle energies. Remember that your Cup is very sensitive and can absorb energies: handle it with care, respect, and love.

There is no established way to perform a Cup Ceremony, and each practitioner may vary in their approach. Each ceremony is unique in its setting and participants. The following suggestions are helpful, however, and have been shared in various Ascended Master teachings. If you are traveling to perform Cup Ceremony at a Golden City Adjutant Point or Star location, you may want to purify your Cup again before use. This is especially important if you have driven for several days or have packed and flown with your Cup. Set up a small altar with candles, flowers, and incense. Small pictures of the Masters are helpful, too. Purify the Cup for a minimum of four hours, longer if you have the time.

Your Prayers and Decrees

There are several different approaches to your prayer and decree ceremony. Some ceremonies require privacy, and in this case gather indoors with your Cup. Fill the Cup about two-thirds with water. You can use a few drops of essential oil along with the water, or empower with a special talisman, crystal, or gemstone. Special waters collected from sacred locations and Golden City Adjutant Points can also be used. This, too, can change the spiritual energies and nuance of your Cup Ceremony. Anointing with sacred oil is also suggested, apply any combination you prefer. Lavender, sandalwood, and Sacred Mountain are good. Share the oil with your participants.

When you hold the Cup, place the vessel over your heart and hold it tenderly, like a newborn baby. Call upon the Mighty I AM Presence, chant the OM HUE, and begin your prayers and decrees, and when you are finished pass the Cup to your left. This is the direction used to infuse energies; however, if you are removing negative energies you may pass the Cup counterclockwise to the right. If you are initiating the Cup Ceremony indoors, I suggest that you use a plastic wrap to cover the Cup as you transport the Cup to your outdoor destination. Be careful not to spill the contents.

Once you reach your location, pass the Cup again for prayer. If privacy is an issue, this may not be possible and may require a work-around. Be creative! We have performed many Cup Ceremonies in public places or along the side of the road, yet always seem to find a private alcove in a perfect setting. Call upon the I AM Presence to guide and direct you to the most receptive spot.

Some students use the Awakening Prayer and the Violet Flame. The Violet Flame invocation is good to apply before the use of the Violet Flame. If you are in a private setting it is suggested to use the Violet Flame decree a total of forty-nine times.

Use of the Four Directions

Some Ascended Master chelas place bread to the North, water to the East, salt to the South, and flowers to the West. Any type of flower can be used; however, most students prefer to use red or white roses. If you wish, before

Roses
Red or white roses are traditionally placed in the West during the Cup Ceremony.

beginning your ceremony, a circle of cornmeal, which represents the feminine energies of intuition, along with a circle of salt — the masculine energies of protection, can be sprinkled on the ground. Sage, sweet grass, and incense can all be used, but be aware of fire danger. For this reason, essential oils are best.

Completion and the Evolutionary Biome

After completing your prayers and decrees, gently pour the water on the ground. Leave your Cup upside down on the earth for several minutes to empty all the energies. As beloved Babajeran and the Evolutionary Biome receives the humble gift of your spiritual requests, look for signs. Sometimes you will note an interesting cloud formation, a wildflower, insects, and birds. This is Mother Earth and the receptive Biome communicating with you. If there is a lake or running water nearby, pour some of the contents of your Cup to join its waters. This hastens the reception of your spiritual work. According to the Ascended Masters there would be no life on Earth without the presence of water; it is the "great giver of life." Water instantly responds to human consciousness, and the planes of consciousness are separated by majestic Rivers of Light.

For more information on Cup Ceremony, please see "Evolutionary Biome." The Ascended Masters share many nuances and details regarding the Cup Ceremony and its special use during the annual Shamballa Season throughout this book.

APPENDIX CC
Devas and Elementals

Deva, meaning shining one or being of light, is a Sanskrit word that describes a God, deity, or spirit. Helena Blavatsky, co-founder of the Theosophical Society, introduced these celestial beings, or angels, to the Western World in the nineteenth century. She described them as progressed entities from previous incarnations that would remain dormant until humanity attained a higher level of spiritual consciousness. Devas represent moral values and work directly with nature kingdoms.[1]

Elementals, on the other hand, are an invisible, subhuman group of creatures that act as counterparts to visible nature on terra firma. Medieval alchemist and occultist Paracelsus coined the term for these Elemental spirits. He divided them into the following four categories: gnomes (Earth); undines (water); sylphs (air); and salamanders (fire).

Gnomes: The term comes from the Greek word "genomus" or "Earth dweller." These subterranean spirits work closely with the Earth, giving them immense power over rocks, flora, gemstones, and precious minerals; they are often guardians of hidden treasures. Some gnomes gather in families while others remain indigenous to the substances they serve or guard. Members of this group include elves, brownies, dryads, and the little people of the woods.[2]

Undines: These fairylike pixies, the deification of femininity, synchronize with the earth element, water. Their essence is so closely tied to aquatic milieus that they possess the power to control the course and function of water. Undines, imbued with extraordinary beauty, symmetry, and grace, inhabit riparian environments—rivers, streams, lakes, waterfalls, and swamps. According to mythical lore, these lithe spirits, also known as naiads, water sprites, sea maids, and mermaids, assume male or female identities. Sioux legend says water deities, or wak'teexi in the native tongue, often incarnate as human beings: a telltale blue birthmark on the body will bare their original identities.[3]

Sylphs: The most evolved of the four Elementals, sylphs—often synonymous with fairies and cherubs—are beautiful, lively, diaphanous, yet mortal demigods. They represent the vaporous element of air and the expression of the female essence. Omnipresent, sylphs float in the clouds and in the ether, though their true home lies in mountaintop hamlets. There, they erect sacred sanctuaries for the Gods. This spritely covey, blessed with millennium-passing longevity and highly developed senses of sight, hearing, and smell, are particularly receptive to the voices of the Gods—that's why theosophical scholars believe the ancients used sylphs as oracles. Guided by Paralda, the king of air, and a communal of female sylphs known as sylphides, sylphs occasionally assume a petite human form. They are intelligent, mutable, and loyal to humans.[4]

---

1. Orin Bridges, *Photographing Beings of Light: Images of Nature and Beyond* (Highland City, FL: Rainbow Press, Inc.), page 57.
2. Manly Hall, *The Secret Teachings of All Ages*, Diamond Jubilee Edition (Los Angeles: Philosophical Research Society, Inc.), pages 106-107.
3. Richard Dieterle, *Waterspirits* (Wak'teexi) (http://www.hotcakencyclopedia.com/ho.Waterspirits.html), (2005).
4. Manly Hall, *The Secret Teachings of All Ages*, Diamond Jubilee Edition (Los Angeles: Philosophical Research Society, Inc.), pages 107-108.

Midsummer Eve
Edward Robert Hughes, 1908.

Fire Salamander
Fire contains the Elemental Salamander that thrives and slithers in extreme heat.

Salamanders: Salamanders represent the invisible Elemental spirit of fire and the embodiment of the male divinity; without their existence, warmth wouldn't exist. Working through the blood stream, body temperature, and the liver, salamanders produce heat in humans and animals. Some theosophical scholars say this class of Elementals occupies balmy Southern regions.

The mystical salamander encompasses much more than its amphibious counterparts. According to esoteric teachings, these fabled creatures manifest distinctly different forms. At approximately twelve inches in length, the lizard like salamander is physically tantamount to its terrestrial Urodela cousin. But, unlike earthly species, ethereal salamanders thrive in fire and slither through flames. Lore describes another group of salamanders as a race of giant creatures that wear flowing robes, don protective armor, and emit a fiery, incandescent glow. According to Medieval tradition, the third coterie of these entities are descendents of the great salamander Oromasis—son of the enigmatic Greek, Zarathustra.

But the Acthnici, ruled by the Elemental king Djinn, are the most powerful and feared faction of salamanders. They travel as indistinct globes of light, especially over water. Voyagers and sailors often experience Acthnici at sea as glowing forks of flame on the masts and the riggings of ships. They call this phenomenon St. Elmo's Fire. Scholars and other savants encourage others to avoid these salamanders. The price of knowing them, they say, outweigh the benefits.[5]

---

5. Manly Hall, *The Secret Teachings of All Ages, Diamond Jubilee Edition* (Los Angeles: Philosophical Research Society, Inc.), pages 106-107.

APPENDIX DD
The Heart of the Dove

The Heart of the Dove is not a Golden City; however, this United States location plays an important role for humanity's spiritual development in the New Times. Also known as the *Center of Fire*, this energy anomaly is prophesied to exist Northwest of Kansas City, Kansas and Missouri. Master Teachings claim an umbilicus connection between Earth and the Galactic Center exists, creating time anomalies and the potential for time travel in the New Times. The *Heart of the Dove* is also prophesied to become a spiritual center for learning and self-actualizing the Christ Consciousness, and is sponsored by the immortal Avatar Babaji who claims that, "This is where my heart is." Energies at the Heart of the Dove are restorative and rejuvenating.

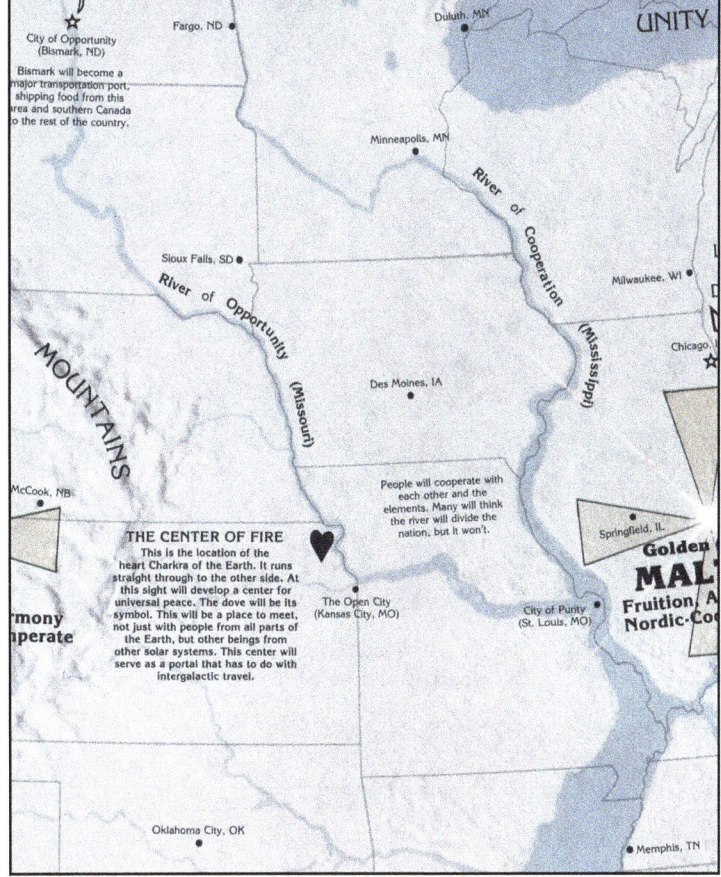

Heart of the Dove

Also known as the *Center of Fire*, this energy anomaly is prophesied to exist Northwest of Kansas City, Missouri. (The center of this portal is near Atchison, Kansas.) It is here that Master Teachings claim an umbilicus connection between Earth, the Galactic Center, and the Galactic Suns exists, creating time anomalies and the potential for time travel in the New Times. The Heart of the Dove is also prophesied to become a spiritual center for learning and self-actualizing the Christ Consciousness. This portal of purity and sanctity radiates restorative, rejuvenating energies that assist Ascension, and it is stewarded by the great Avatar Babaji.

Fire Blossom
Nicholas Roerich, 1924.

APPENDIX EE
Fire Ceremony

Saint Germain recommends lighting a physical fire as a celebration of the Violet Flame or to ceremonially activate an Adjutant Point. After the fire is lit, sit near its flames as you practice breath or meditation technique. This ceremonial fire is equivalent to a puja—a fire ceremony that helps one to shed physical karmas and accelerate the process of spiritual liberation. Plus, fire is cleansing to the chakra system. Leonard Orr writes about fire and its ability to help clear our light fields and achieve physical immortality: "When we sit or sleep near an open flame, the wheels of our energy body (our aura) turn through the flames and are cleaned. The emotional pollution of participating in the world is burned away. Death urges are dissolved by fire and water together as they clean and balance the energy body. Fire is as important as food. Fire may be the highest element of God and requires the most intelligence to use. It is perhaps the most neglected natural divine element of God in our civilization."[1]

Bhumi or bhoomi puja is a Hindu ceremony performed to bless land. This is a fire ceremony that removes obstacles, or any evil associated with land, and blesses the owner and all who inhabit the land. It is performed before construction takes place on raw land, and sacred objects are often buried. These objects may include a blessed conch shell and silver coins. Fruits and flowers are also offered. Bhumi puja cultivates the blessings of Mother Earth.

If you opt to use Fire Ceremony at a Golden City Adjutant Point, never forget the threat of wildfire. If conditions are too dry, go for a Water Ceremony and use essential oils for anointing. In some conditions the simple act of lighting incense or sage is a dangerous fire threat. Remember, your presence at a sacred Adjutant Point celebrates your Oneness with Mother Earth. Please play an attentive role in protecting Babajeran's abundant forests and vulnerable wildlife and ecosystems.

---

1. Orr, Leonard. "Breaking the Death Habit." Rivendell Village, 2 May 2008.

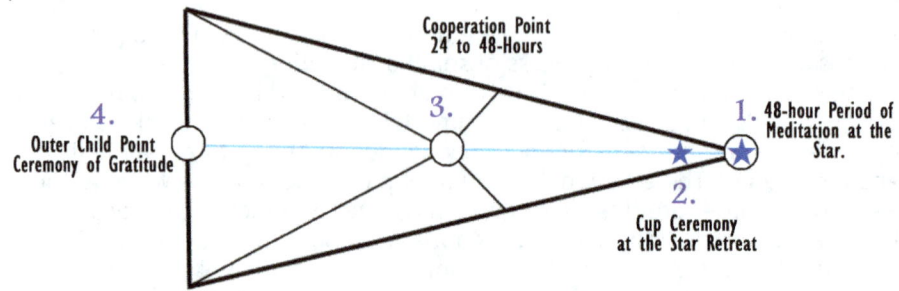

The Golden City Western Door Enlightenment Pilgrimage: Phase One
The First Phase of the Enlightenment Pilgrimage begins in the Star, moves to the Western Star Retreat, onward to the Cooperation Point, and then to the Outer Child (Outer Cardinal) Western Point.

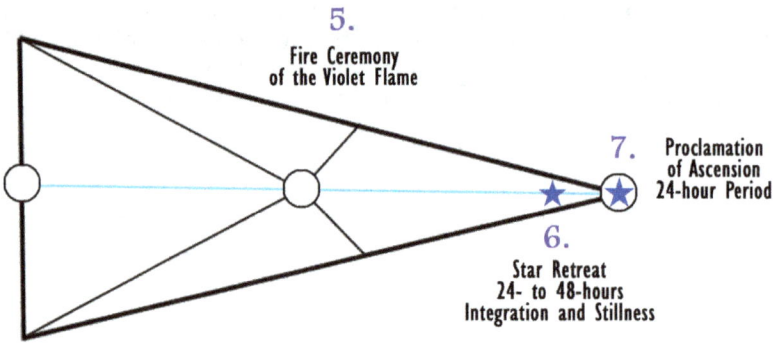

The Golden City Western Door Enlightenment Pilgrimage: Phase Two
The Second Phase of the Enlightenment Pilgrimage moves from the Outer Child Western Point to the Cooperation Point, from there the Pilgrimage moves back to the Western Star Retreat for integration and stillness, and concludes in the Golden City Star. There are seven migrations, total, in this Golden City Pilgrimage.

APPENDIX FF
The Enlightenment Pilgrimage

The Enlightenment Pilgrimage is sponsored by Beloved Saint Germain, Portia, and Archangel Zadkiel for Ascended Master students who wish to reaffirm their dedication to the Right-hand Path and request admittance into the Spiritual Hierarchy of the Great White Brotherhood. It is best to complete this Pilgrimage before the year 2026, as the White Ray is currently in its most benefic location to assist this energetic. This Pilgrimage can, however, be completed at any time to reaffirm our spiritual development, and build the Seamless Garment that is an integral part of the Ascension Process.

Follow the Western Cardinal Lei-line

This Pilgrimage mirrors the Northern Door Pilgrimage (see *Golden Cities and the Masters of Shamballa*), and follows the Cardinal Lei-line of the Western Door. It stops at every important Adjutant Point: the Star, the Star Retreat, the Cooperation Point, and the Outer Child-Cardinal Point. The Migration Pattern travels from the inside out, and then returns, from the most westerly point to the Star. The outer Migration Pattern moves from the Outer Child-Cardinal Point to the Cooperation Point, from the Cooperation Point to the Western Door Star Retreat, and concludes in the Star of the Golden City. Any Western Door of a Golden City will work for this Pilgrimage; however, any Golden City whose predominant Ray Force is the White Ray will intensify the results. Golden Cities of the White Ray are: Klehma—United States, Zaskar—China, Sircalwe—Russia, Arkana—Russia, Sheahah—Australia, and Afrom—Hungary and Romania. (For more information and maps regarding these Golden Cities see *I AM America Atlas*.)

Begin at the Golden City Star

The first Migration begins in the Golden City Star. During your stay of a period of forty-eight hours it is advised to meditate four to six hours per day, for a total of eight to twelve hours, total. The meditations may be broken into smaller, one-hour increments. If you wish to intensify your results, you can meditate for a full forty-eight hours. This, however, will increase the amount of time spent in Spiritual Pilgrimage. During your meditative period you are absorbing the Violet Flame and are over-lighted by Saint Germain, Portia, and Archangel Zadkiel. Visualize the Violet Flame enfolding your light bodies and repeat this decree:

> "Mighty Violet Flame,
> Come forth and free me now,
> To serve Beloved Babajeran,
> As Freedom Star!"

You can travel with a partner or with a small group. It is suggested to use both Cup and Fire Ceremonies, and repeat the Awakening Prayer. Saint Germain advises to call upon the Light Beings of the Inner Earth to assist your Mighty Enlightenment of the I AM, and to travel with you during your Pilgrimage. Saint Germain asks that, "When you feel complete, turn your will over to the Mighty Right-hand Path."

The Western Star Retreat
Your second Spiritual Migration for the Enlightenment Pilgrimage moves to the Western Star Retreat. It is recommended to spend a period of twenty-four hours to integrate the energies of the Violet Flame. Perform Cup Ceremony, along with decrees and prayers.

The Cooperation Point
The third location in Pilgrimage is the Cooperation Point. Spend twenty-four to forty-eight hours at this Migration Point and participate in Group Mind meditations with two or more. There are two important decrees that Saint Germain has given for this step. The first is:

> "Mighty I AM!
> Come forth and produce Cooperation,
> For my Enlightenment Process!"

Saint Germain claims this decree literally infuses the power of the Gold Ray of Cooperation into your cells. The second decree proclaims your freedom in the Ascension through the Right-hand Path. As you say this decree aloud, directly face the West.

> "I AM ONE within the light!
> And I AM free within the light!
> I AM a manifestation of the Right-hand Path,
> And Beloved Freedom Star.
> So be it!"

The Outer Child Point
The Fourth Migration of the Enlightenment Pilgrimage moves to the Outer Child Point, also known as the Outer Cardinal Point. Your stay at this point is for a total of two days—forty-eight hours total. There are two vital initiations that occur at this point. First, you will meditate upon the clarity of the Buddha and then meditate upon the Bodhisattva of Compassion. The Bodhisattva of Compassion can intentionally bear the pain of others and is known as the Amitabha Buddha, and manifests nine divine qualities.

The Nine Qualities of the Buddha
These nine qualities are:
1. Araham: The Arhat who has perfected self and is worthy of homage. At this level of consciousness he has suppressed enemies and avoided corruption. He or she has personally addressed karmic retribution, and is worthy of obedience and respect. The person is blameless and spotless, and void of secretive character.
2. Sammasambuddho: Fully self-awakened.
3. Vija-Carana Sampanno: Insightful, clear vision, aware of all past lives, and embraces the Eight Principles of the Right-hand Path.
4. Sugato: Correct and infallible; harmless and blameless.
5. Lokavidu: Experienced and well-versed with both the physical and spiritual world.
6. Anuttaro Purisa-Damma-Sarathi: A leader who can bring the errant and disobedient into righteousness.
7. Sattha Deva-Manussanam: A teacher of both the Devas and humans.

8. Buddho: Possesses the extraordinary power to teach others.
9. Bhagava: Blessed.[1]

The Gold Ray
During your meditations visualize the Gold Ray moving from your Root Chakra, through your Golden Thread Axis, and into your Crown Chakra.

Angelic Intervention
The next important initiation is to call upon the Violet Flame Angels for their Divine Intervention. The following decrees are from "I AM Angel Decrees, Part Two," from the Saint Germain Press:

"Beloved Mighty I AM Presence and Beloved Saint Germain! Send a group of Violet Flame Angels to keep the Sacred Fire of their love in and around me for this entire day!"

"Beloved Mighty I AM Presence, Archangel Michael, Seven Mighty Archangels, and legions of Angels! I give your full freedom to live in me this day! I AM Come into the World of the Angelic Host! Let your great Angelic Presence blaze its freedom through me and fill my world! I demand my world be the World of the Angelic Host this day!"

"Beloved Mighty I AM Presence and Great Cosmic Angel! Send a group of Violet Flame Angels to stand guard and assist me this day!"

"Beloved Mighty I AM Presence and Great Host of Ascended Masters! I demand the Great Angelic Host's Guarding Flame of Invincible Protection to come forth and hold control of conditions around me and those under this radiation, in the Powers of Nature and Forces of the Elements, in the plant life, or wherever something is planned to be brought forth which is lovely, to bless all."

"Beloved Mighty I AM Presence and Great Angelic Host! I demand legions of the Angels of the Sacred Fire blaze their Cosmic Love, which controls conditions in the Powers of Nature and the Forces of the Elements; bring forth a more balanced condition in outer world affairs and re-establish that which has been thrown out of balance through war, inhumane scientific experiments, and chemtrails! I demand legions of the Angels of the Sacred Fire come to our assistance! I demand all the Angelic Hosts who control the atmosphere of this land and the Powers of Nature, come forth and spread their love over conditions which have been in turmoil, and hold them harmonious and under your control!"

"Beloved Mighty I AM Presence, Beloved Angelic Host, all Angels, Devas, Cherubim, and Seraphim! Come forth and take command of the forces of the Elements! Stand guard over all mankind and annihilate from the Universe all that is not of the light!"[2]

---

1. Thabarwa.org. "Nine Qualities of Buddha." ThaBarWa Centre, August 31, 2021. https://thabarwa.org/9-qualities-of-buddha/.
2. Saint Germain Press. I AM Angel Decrees, Part Two. Chicago, IL: Saint Germain Press, 1974.

Oath of the Right-hand Path

After your Migration to the Outer Child point, you will return to the Cooperation Point. This is your fifth Migration in the Enlightenment Pilgrimage. Light a fire for your Fire Ceremony and invoke the Violet Flame using the Invocation for the Violet Flame. Anoint your Heart, Throat, and Third Eye Chakra with the essential oils of frankincense, myrrh, and lavender—or a combination of them. During your Fire Ceremony raise your right hand, and take the oath of the Right-hand Path:

> "I accept the Sacred Fire within my heart,
> I AM ONE with the Spiritual Hierarchy,
> I AM ONE with Freedom Star.
> So be it!"

Chant the mantra, OM HUE, forty-nine times. This sacred mantra seals your oath.

Integration and Stillness

The sixth Migration of the Enlightenment Pilgrimage is a return to the Western Star Retreat. Spend a minimum of twenty-four to forty-eight hours to still your energies, and integrate with stillness. Perform a Cup Ceremony. This is vital preparation for the final movement to the Golden City Star.

The Proclamation of Ascension

The seventh and final Migration is back to the Golden City Star. This step is your personal proclamation of Ascension. This final process accepts the White Ray throughout your energy fields and Saint Germain suggests meditation on the acceptance of your Divine Seamless Garment of Light, the reciting of the Awakening Prayer, and use of Cup Ceremony. The following decree incorporates the tenets of Mystical Christianity through the recognition of incarnate divinity, spiritual passion, resurrection, Ascension, communion, and the assumption. This statement may be used as your Proclamation of Ascension during your time at the Golden City Star:

Pilgrim
Nicholas Roerich, 1932.

"I AM a Divine HU-man—a BE-ing of Light!
I call forth the Victory of the Violet Flame,
To stream throughout my worldly karmas.
The Ascension heals, restores, glorifies,
And expands my Light!
My Light Ascends to both
Fourth and Fifth Dimensions.
I AM the perfected balance of
Divine Mother and Divine Father!
I AM awakened and realized through
The Christ Consciousness!
I proclaim my Ascension
And eternal Victory!
So be it!
Amen."

After stating your proclamation of Ascension, visualize and receive the anointing of light. Saint Germain reminds us, "All that I give in my teaching is for all the students of I AM America. I share this willingly and from the Great Violet Flame within my heart. This, you see, is a Pilgrimage of Enlightenment that fills you with the Violet Flame of Freedom, it also is a Pilgrimage designed to initiate you into the Great White Brotherhood of Light." The Master of the Violet Flame's final instruction: "Move with haste!"

APPENDIX GG

Spiritual Hierarchy

The term *Spiritual Hierarchy* often refers to the Great White Brotherhood and Sisterhood, however, this term also connotes the spiritual-social structure that exists within the organization, their members, and their various states of evolution. This includes the different offices and activities that serve the Cosmic, Solar, and Planetary Hierarchies. The following outline summarizes the Hierarchy's spiritual infrastructure:

1. Cosmic Hierarchy, the Great Central Sun
    a. The Silent Watcher: Galactic Architect
    b. Cosmic Beings
    c. The Galactic Suns
    d. Galactic Council: the Council of Worlds
    e. Galactic Rays of Light and Sound
2. Solar Hierarchy, our Solar Sun
    a. Solar Rays of Light and Sound
        i. Elohim: Magnetize the Planetary Unfed Flame at the center of Earth
        ii. Archangels: Arch the Rays of Light and Sound to Earth
    b. Solar Manu: oversees the incarnation processes on various planets within this Solar System
    c. Planetary Silent Watcher: Architect of this Solar System
    d. The Cosmic I AM Presence: origination of the I AM Presence in the Creative Hierarchy
3. Planetary Hierarchy
    a. Karmic Board
    b. The Planetary Council
    c. Manu: Protects the current race of humanity
    d. Axis of the Earth: Polaris (North) and Magnus (South)
    e. Earth's Elohim
        i. The Four Elements
        ii. Devas
        iii. Animal and Nature Kingdoms
    f. Earth's Archangels
        i. Seraphim
        ii. Cherubim
        iii. Angels
    g. Shamballa: Rules and balances the magnetism of Earth; keeper of the Rod of Power
        i. Lord of the World
            1. Great White Brotherhood
            2. Lords of Karma
            3. The Right-hand Path

When the Morning Stars Sang Together
William Blake, 1820.

- ii. World Teacher
    1. Spiritual Knowledge and World Religions
    2. Ascension Teachings
    3. The ONE
    4. Christ Consciousness
- iii. The Buddha
    1. World Buddha
    2. Kings of Shambahla: the Earth Protectors
- iv. The Temples of Shamballa
    1. Unity Temple
    2. Nine Temples of the Rays
    3. Temples of the Flame
    4. Temple of the Christ
    5. Temple of the Buddha
    6. Temple of the Violet Flame
- v. The Golden Cities: overseen by Saint Germain
    1. Adjutant Point Ashrams; overseen by each Hierarch
        a. Presiding or predominant Ray Force
        b. Periodic influence
        c. Annual influence
    2. The Temples of Perfection
    3. Star Retreats
    4. The Star
    5. The Evolutionary Fields
        a. Human to HU-man
        b. Eight Principles of the Right-hand Path
        c. The Four Pillars
        d. Activity of the Fourfold Flame
        e. Nine Heavenly Gates
        f. Elohim Evolutionary Fields
- h. Lord of the Rays—Maha Chohan
    - i. Seven Rays of Light and Sound
    - ii. Seven Chohans of the Seven Rays
        1. Etheric Temples
        2. Spiritual Retreats
    - iii. The New Ray Forces for the Golden Age
        1. Gold Ray
        2. Aquamarine Ray
        3. Pastel Green Ray
        4. Orange Ray
        5. Spring Green Ray
        6. Pastel Blue Ray
- i. Heart of the Dove—Babaji

4. Creative Hierarchy (Human)
   a. The Ascended Master: the God-free being
   b. The I AM Presence: descends from the Cosmic I AM Presence as the Electronic Body
      i. Causal Body (Solar Angel)
         1. Abstract Mind
         2. Concrete Mind
      ii. Astral Body
         1. Christ-self
         2. Guardian Angel, Spirit Guides, and Spirit Teachers
   c. The HU-man: the integrated and spiritually evolved human
      i. Master
      ii. Adept
      iii. Arhat
      iv. Initiate
         1. Bodhisattva
         2. Prophet
      v. Chela (disciple)
      vi. Aspirant (student)
   d. The Human
      i. Unfed Flame: the spark of divinity
      ii. Eight-sided Cell of Perfection: the atom of God-perfection
      iii. Flame of Consciousness: the Intellectual Consciousness separates the Human from the Third Hierarchy
      iv. Higher Self: the Holy Spirit
      v. Lower Self: the animal nature

Esoteric historians claim the Spiritual Hierarchy embodies religious principles from Christianity, Hinduism, Buddhism, Neo-Theosophy, and Ascended Master Teachings. However, to correctly understand the provenance of the Spiritual Hierarchy, it is essential to embrace its unique and concurrent Creation Story. The Ascended Masters' chronicle of the mythological formation of our galaxy, our Solar System, and the Earth offers significant insight and knowledge regarding the Spiritual Hierarchy.

A Variety of Solar and Star Systems

According to the Ascended Master legend, the Silent Watcher embraces the Great Central Sun—the Galactic Center. This Cosmic Being is also known as the Galactic Architect who designed the galaxy along with its many Solar Systems. The Galactic Silent Watcher works in tandem with various Solar Silent Watchers who assist in the design of the individual Solar Systems within the galaxy. Scientists theorize that our Sun is one of 200 billion stars in the Milky Way, and so far, astronomers have discovered approximately seventy Solar Systems in our galaxy.[1] The Solar Systems of our galaxy are overseen by the Galactic Silent Watcher and the Galactic Council—comparable to a Galactic United Nations—which comprises many Ascended Cosmic Beings from a variety of solar and star systems, including: the Sirius System, the Pleiades Cluster, the

---
1. "How Many Solar Systems are in Our Galaxy?," http://nasa.gov, (2011).

Arcturus System, the Constellation of Centaurus, the Constellation of Pegasus, the Constellation of Hercules, the Constellation of Volans, the Constellation of Aquila, the Orion System, and representatives from the neighboring DAL or DAHL Universe. At the time of this writing, scientific research discovered that the Earth may in fact originate from another galaxy: the Sagittarius Dwarf Universe.

Researchers surveying the sky with infrared light at the University of Massachusetts mapped a New Star Map, through the use of a supercomputer to sort out a half-billion stars. Through the study of star debris and by pinpointing the exact location of our Solar System—at the crossroads where two galaxies join—they discovered that the Milky Way Galaxy is absorbing smaller galaxies. The Sagittarius Dwarf Universe was discovered by a British team of astronomers in 1994, and in 2003 the Massachusetts team altered their angle of telescopic view to find the Earth in perfect alignment with the smaller galaxy, or what was left of it. Researcher Martin Weinberg believes this process is two-billion years in the making: "After slow, continuous gnawing by the Milky Way, Sagittarius has been whittled down to the point that it cannot hold itself together much longer...we are seeing Sagittarius at the very end of its life as an intact system." Metaphysicians theorize the discovery of the new galaxy may be the basis for the ending of the Mayan Calendar, because the Pleiades Star Cluster—which the calendar is based upon—is no longer a reliable point for celestial navigation as the Earth and its Solar System veer into a new direction.[2]

Elohim and Archangels

The Solar Hierarchy encompasses the Elohim and the Archangels. The Elohim (magnetism) are known as the Universal Builders and with the Archangels (radiation)—the Master conductors of the Rays—jointly formed a Creation Grid. At a central juncture of the grid the center of the Earth was created through the appearance of the Unfed Flame. To this day, the Unfed Flame is claimed to exist in the center of the Earth, and forms the cohesive power for the electrons and atoms of the Four Elements of the Earth.[3] Through the direction of the Rays, the Elohim managed the Four Elements (Virgo, Neptune, Aries, and Helios), the Gods of Mountains and Seas, and Amaryllis—the Goddess of Spring. The Devas created mountains, rivers, valleys, prairies, and lakes. It is claimed that the Ascended Beings Virgo and Pelleur oversaw the creation of the earth element to hold water, and from this substance the human form was ultimately created.[4] The Solar Manu—a Cosmic Being—holds the creative authority to sponsor a generation of incoming lifestreams (approximately 2,000 to 5,000 years). The office of Manu oversees humanity's spiritual evolutionary process throughout various epochs by protecting the current, incoming race. Two Manus protect incarnating souls; the Solar Manu protects the generations of souls incarnating throughout our Solar System, and the Planetary Manu protects souls incarnating on Earth. In the New Times it is prophesied that Mother Mary occupies the Earthly post as guardian of the Seventh Manu—highly-evolved souls currently incarnating on Earth.

---

2. "Scientists Now Know: We're Not from Here!," http://viewzone2.com/milkywayx.html, (2011).
3. A.D.K. Luk, *Law of Life*, (A.D.K. Luk Publications, 1989, Pueblo, CO), Book II, page 206.
4. Ibid., page 207.

Rod of Power

It is said that the gravity of the Earth is held through a mystical Rod of Power, a symbol of the office of Lord of the World that is kept securely in the Golden City of Shamballa. The mysterious wand is said to be constructed of orichalcum—the ancient metal of Atlantis—and encrusted with diamonds on either end.[5]

Hierarchal Offices

The history of Shamballa involves another important position in the Earth's Spiritual Hierarchy, the leader of the Great White Brotherhood: the World Teacher. I AM America Teachings assert Jesus the Christ is the resident of this appointment, and Lord Maitreya is the former World Teacher. The Golden Cities stream through the hierarchal radiance of Shamballa, and their importance for the planet and evolving humanity during the New Times has equal significance to the Earthly hierarchal offices of the World Teacher and the Buddha.

On Earth, the office of the Lord of the Seven Rays is claimed to be held by the Maha Chohan, who oversees the Chohans (Lords) of the activity of the Seven Rays on Earth. The Lord of the Seven Rays is likely the archetypal Mithra. The Lords of the Seven Rays oversee vital Temples and Spiritual Retreats located in both etheric and physical locations on Earth. These spiritual sanctuaries provide a focus for the activity of the Rays of Light and Sound on Earth and shepherd humanity's continued spiritual education and evolution through the Rays. The Maha Chohan—which means the Major Lord—is said to be surrounded by the white light of all the Rays. The Maha Chohan instructs:

> "...the day of Our return into the consciousness of the mankind of Earth looms closer because the door has been opened by Faith and held back by the arms of Love, and the pathway of consciously dedicated energy passing out of your bodies and molded into form is witness before the great Cosmic Tribunal that the mankind of Earth do wish to walk and talk with a free Hierarchy, the Angels, the Devas, and the Gods once more. We come in answer to an invitation from your hearts—we have waited many centuries for such an invitation and Our gratitude to the lifestreams who are able to accept the logic within Our words and counsel cannot be measured by any human concept, but it can be felt, I am sure, by those of you who are now sensitive enough to note the radiation of Our individual Presences."[6]

Creation of the Human Energy System

Ascended Master creation myths place the origination of the human soul from the heart of the Sun God-Goddess who constructs at the end of a Ray the Three-Fold (Unfed) Flame. This generates a Divine Presence, or a God-Flame; a Co-creator with the Source, the Cosmic I AM Presence. According to esoteric historians, some God-Flames choose to remain in the eternal embrace of the loving aura of the parental Sun; those who choose to progress further project their spiritual essence into two Rays—Twin Rays. The Twin Rays develop a new light substance: an electrical light field which separates the Rays into two distinct individuals. The I AM—the individualized presence of God—dwells

---

5. Wikipedia, *Orichalcum*, http://en.wikipedia.org/wiki/Orichalcum, (2011).
6. Tellis Papastavro, *The Gnosis and the Law,* (Group Avatar, 1972, Tucson, AZ), page 119.

within the newly formed soul, and the electrical field of light is known as the I AM Presence.[7]

The Presence of the I AM on Earth forms the nexus of evolution in the Creative, or Human Hierarchy. The Electronic Body of light is formed of both the Causal and Astral Bodies. The Causal Body is known primarily as a mental plane, and many Ascended Masters reside in the higher levels of the Causal Plane during their service to humanity and Earth. In Theosophical texts, the Causal body is known as the Karanopadhi, and its lower manifestation is associated with the causes bringing about re-embodiment on the Earth Plane; however, the Causal Plane is also associated with the Buddhi (Sanskrit for intellect) and the enlightenment of pure consciousness through discrimination between material and spiritual reality.[8] It is also the location of both the abstract and rational mind. The Astral Body or Astral Plane has various levels of evolution and is the heavenly abode where the soul resides after the disintegration of the physical body. Within the Astral Plane lie our individual desires and salvation from their incessant demands—the Christ. This plane of emotional energy becomes the proverbial heaven or hell.

The Ascended Master

The Ascended Master who is free from incarnating on Earth directs the Unfed Flame within the heart and builds a new etheric body focused through the immortal spiritual fire and light. Hence, the unascended are directed by the emotional desires of the Astral Body, symbolized by the earthly element of water. The Ascended Master has dissipated encumbering desires into a living flame; human desire is composed of etheric wandering. The human body is flesh; the Ascended Master is a body of spiritual fire—light. The luminous body of spiritual fire is developed through the use of the Unfed Flame in the physical plane.[9]

Collective Consciousness

Elohim focus their etheric Flame of Consciousness into the pineal gland of the human. This creates the Intellectual Consciousness. An outgrowth of the individual consciousness as thought, feeling, and action is the development of Mass Consciousness. Mass Consciousness is often measured by two methods: Collective Consciousness, the total consciousness of all forms of life currently present on Earth; and the Group Mind. Societal and cultural beliefs are the creators of the Group Mind's collection of thoughts, feelings, and actions.

Spiritual Evolution

The Cosmic I AM Presence of the Solar Hierarchy projects into the Creative Hierarchy through the human heart, and radiates into the Unfed Flame; this is surrounded by the Eight-sided Cell of Perfection. Human growth evolves through basic psychological and physical needs through ongoing spiritual interaction with the Guardian Angel, Spirit Guides, and Spirit Teachers. According to Theosophical thought, a spirit is incorporeal intelligence and can exist in almost limitless ranges of hierarchical classes: highest, intermediate,

---

7. A.D.K. Luk, *Law of Life*, (A.D.K. Luk Publications, 1989, Pueblo, CO), Book II, page 208.
8. *Encyclopedic Theosophical Glossary*, http://www.theosociety.org/pasadena/etglos/etg-hp.htm, (2011).
9. A.D.K. Luk, *Law of Life*, (A.D.K. Luk Publications, 1989, Pueblo, CO), Book II, page 214.

Power of Awakening

and lower.[10] Naturally, these interactions evolve the Lower Self, the animal nature within man, and awaken the Higher Self, as a direct and personal experience of our true nature.[11] Interaction with the Higher Self is also known as the Holy Spirit, a component of the I AM Presence. [Editor's Note: Some esoteric scholars claim that animals are evolved Elemental Beings of the Third Kingdom.]

The Awakened Human evolves to embrace the higher qualities of the Astral Body through the Christ-self (friendship, love, compassion), and the advanced characteristics of the Causal Body through the Solar Angel (leadership, confidence, respect, achievement). The I AM Presence instigates the human need for morality, ethics, Co-creation, and problem solving.

---

10. *Encyclopedic Theosophical Glossary,* http://www.theosociety.org/pasadena/etglos/etg-hp.htm, (2011).
11. "Discovering Your Higher Self," http://www.thevoiceforlove.com/higher-self.html, (2011).

The Pleiades Star System
NASA, 2013.

APPENDIX HH
The DAHL and DERN Universes

DAHL and DERN Universes

The DAHL Universe, also known as the DAL Universe, is mentioned by Billy Meier as a twin parallel universe created simultaneously with our DERN Universe. Meier is a well-known contactee of the Plejaren Federation, from the Pleiades. The early 1970's Pleiadians' mission shared life-enhancing information for humans, such as our true origin and essential laws of creation. Saint Germain affirms many of Meier's disclosures throughout the I AM America Teachings, and asserts that evolved, spiritual beings from both the Pleiades and the DAHL have played significant roles tending to the spiritual needs of humanity at timely junctures. According to Meier's spiritual teachers, the DAL means, "Creation as second born."[1]

Saint Germain suggests that evolved Masters from the DAHL assisted civilizations on the Pleiades through critical junctures of spiritual growth and evolution. Today, cosmic Masters from both the DAHL and the Pleiades support the Golden Age on Earth and the creation of the Golden City Network on Earth's surface. According to Meier's Pleaidian advisors, the DAL "nudges the seventh outer belt of our DERN Universe."[2]

Members from both the DAHL Universe and Pleiades Star system allege advanced technology includes both time and travel portals between the parallel creations.

---

1. DAL Universe." http://futureofmankind.co.uk 21 Aug. 2010. Web. 1 Jan. 2019.
2. Ibid.

Soul's Purpose

APPENDIX II

The Soul Ray of Purpose

(An excerpt from New World Wisdom Three with Master KH)

"Masculine energy rules the appearance of the Soul Ray. It is the determining factor for an individual on our planet according to the position of Mars at the time of birth. The Soul Ray rules purpose and will. As each occult student knows that only the Omnipotent Source of All rules and guides the will. We refer to will in the context of incarnation. The Soul Ray rules the life force within the body, arching energy currents in the direction and with the force required for all subsequent guardians to interchange and interplay. This allows biological functions to begin. It becomes the leading force of the appearance, and sometimes quiet and unnoticed in its reign, directs the energy of the Monad to serve the plan, to align to the will of God.

Ages Seven Through Twenty-Two

The ruling energy of soul keeps most of its leadership roles confined to biological and systematic life until the age of seven, when the child announces sovereign status and begins the steps of its individual journey. Entrusted with the plan, the soul knows and enacts the purpose of all life, directing and guiding the child through the many lessons, perils, and schemes that this schoolhouse provides. Around the age of eleven to fourteen, the awakening occurs, signifying specific biological functions through the Personality Ray, and initiating a pattern which the soul will follow throughout its sojourn on the planet. From the ages fourteen to eighteen, the years of initiation ensue, and the being begins to integrate the great plan of Life he or she must follow. By the twenty-second year, transfiguration occurs. The soul is ready to stand to meet the world and places the plan into the world of forms, utilizing all the attributes of the Personality Ray.

During the period of transfiguration, the soul activates the power of the Monad, and pulsing to optimum capacity (according to the evolution of the soul and its integration with the Personality or feminine Ray) distributes the solar Ray which overshadows it (determined again, at breath of birth). Dispensing a series of waves throughout the Earth Plane, each wave is activated throughout the incarnation of the soul, by the soul. Only the soul recognizes the harmony, synchronism, and sattva (the harmonious response to vibration) required to unlock its life force. There are no exceptions to this rule. Only the soul can rule its own life force and stabilize its own creations.

The Rise of the Spiritual Being

From the twenty-eighth to the thirty-second year, the ascent of the wave and the rise of its purpose is clearly seen by the individual and through union of the guardian Rays, the rise of the spiritual being begins. By the thirty-third year, as the union increases in potency and clarity, the Soul Ray clearly shines, revealing its leadership, gentleness, and attention to the life it serves. [Editor's Note: It is said that Jesus Sananda ascended on his thirty-third year, called a Master Year] This cycle repeats throughout the term of incarnation, although less extreme, due to the continuous integration of the male and female Rays activated in the lifestream. Let me tabulate these stages for your knowledge:

AGE	KEYNOTE	PURPOSE
7	Individualization	Energy becomes sovereign and in service to the plan it serves.
14-18	Initiation	The individual begins to Master the force of the guardian and group Rays, the resulting energy, learning and assimilating the great plan.
22	Transfiguation	Activation of the Monad through the solar Ray emits the waves that only the soul can retrieve, unlock, and utilize. This emission occurs several times during the incarnation; however, the first carrying the greatest impact (as it carries the life purpose of the solar Ray), subsequent emissions supporting that first great emanation.
29-32	Ascension	The ascent of the first wave emitted, the soul learns the value of that which it creates in the world of forms. The ascent of the cresting wave generally runs for four years.
33	Union	The integration of the guardian Rays is seen for the first time, throughout the incarnation. The individual can now draw on the marriage of the female and the male forces, allowing for the gentle leadership of the male and the nurturing support of the female.

The Soul Ray leads the first cycle of the soul's purpose, and on completion of the thirty-third year, finds at its side, the harmonious presence of the Personality Ray. Until that moment, their awareness of one another is limited, as the urgings of the body and outer forms are sometimes in stark contrast to the plan and leadership of the soul. Up to the ascent of union, many individuals fall by the side, choosing to union in the less denser fields of created realities, for example, the astral and the devachan (the ideal heaven state). Perhaps the sattva of their soul will find another opportunity to descend into the world of forms. It is true that only the strongest of steel will temper its consciousness in the world of dual senses. 'It was never promised to be easy,' my Dear teacher would often remind me. I pass these words to you. Hold them and know."

[Editor's Note: The devachan, also known as Summerland, is where the karma (of evil) steps aside for the time being and the karma of good (dharma) is manifested. Each desire quickly manifests its hopeful, optimistic side. In this heaven of our dreams, there are magnificent mountains, lakes, gardens, and thought-forms suited to our individual concepts of Paradise.]

APPENDIX JJ
The New Shamballa Grid Pilgrimage

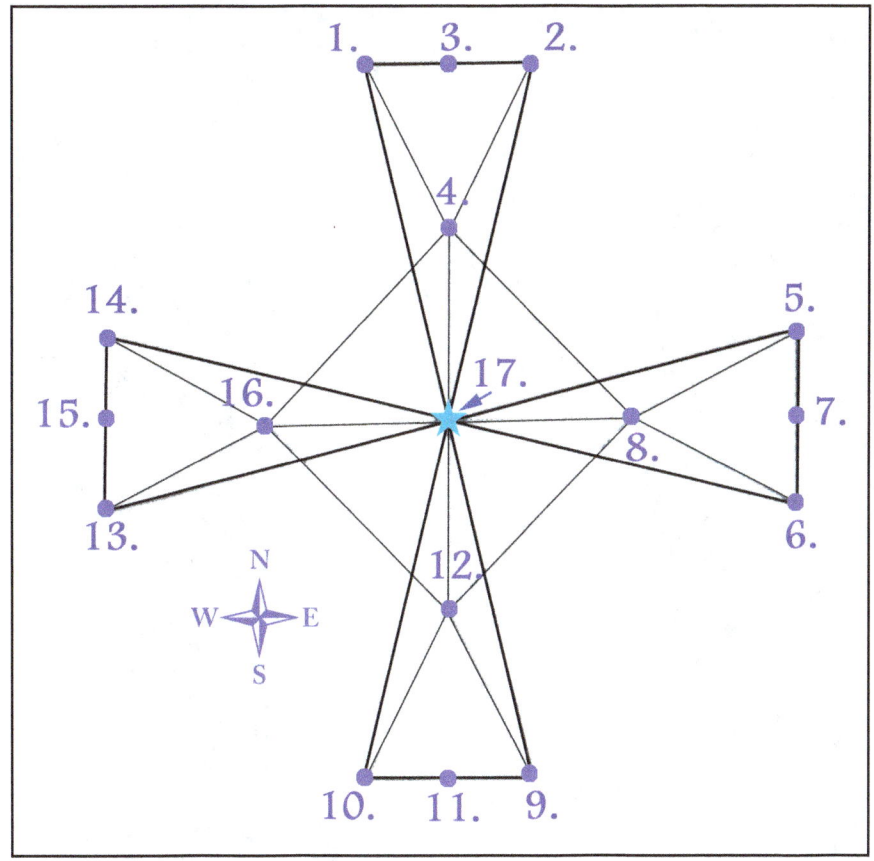

The Seventeen Migrations of the New Shamballa Grid Pilgrimage

The Shamballa Grid Pilgrimage initiates the chela to the mysteries of the Adjutant Points through migration of all of the four doorways and the primary Adjutant Points. This Spiritual Pilgrimage assists both the student and the Golden Cities by building the New Shamballa Grid. It is considered both a service for the Golden Cities and a blessing for the student or chela. The chela travels through a total of seventeen Adjutant Points. This migratory pathway begins at the Northern Door West Adjutant Point, travels onward to the Northern Door East Adjutant Point, then to the Northern Door Outer Cardinal Adjutant Point, and then to the Northern Door Inner Cardinal Adjutant Point. This four-point Pilgrimage concludes the Northern Door.

This spiritual Pilgrimage continues through the East Door and starts in the Eastern Door North Adjutant Point, then to the Eastern Door South Adjutant Point, travels next to the Eastern Door Outer Cardinal Point, and concludes in the Eastern Door Inner Cardinal Point.

The Spiritual Pilgrimage continues onward to the Southern Door and starts in the Southern Door East Adjutant Point, moves to the Southern Door West

Buddhist Monk on Pilgrimage

Adjutant Point, the third stop is the Southern Door Outer Cardinal Adjutant Point, and concludes in the Southern Door Inner Cardinal Point. Again, this four-point Pilgrimage completes the migration through the Southern Door.

The Western Door migration begins at the Western Door Southern Adjutant Point, moves next to the Western Door Northern Adjutant Point, the third migration is to the Western Door Outer Cardinal Point, and onward to the Western Door Inner Cardinal Adjutant Point. This concludes the migratory pathway in the Western Door.

The final migration in the New Shamballa Grid Pilgrimage is to the Golden City's Star. There the spiritual Pilgrimage ends with prayer, ceremony, and meditation in the sublime energies of the Star—where the spiritual light of the four doorways coalesce. This seventeenth point symbolizes the birth of the Christ Consciousness within, integration with the I AM Presence, and the Ascension.

APPENDIX KK
Movement of the Photon as the Golden City

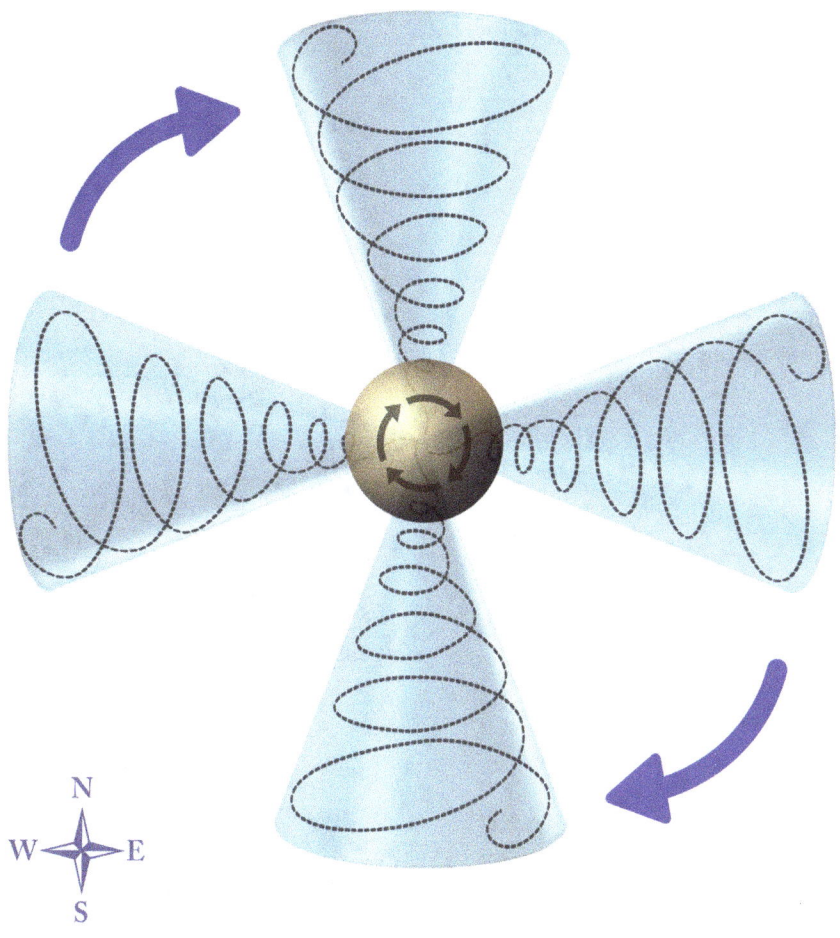

Photonic Movement of the Golden City Vortex

The individual Golden City Doors (Gateways) resemble large chakras that contain a spinning motion. From a three-dimensional viewpoint, they resemble sizeable Vortex funnels that originate at the center (Golden City Star), and each Gateway radiates to the four directions. The Golden City Star (center) is a large rotating sphere. Each Golden City Door functions with a rotation of either a clockwise or counterclockwise direction. The entire Golden City structure rotates clockwise, to take energies in, and counterclockwise to remove energies. Adjutant Points also rotate clockwise or counterclockwise. This simultaneous rotational movement invigorates the Golden City's fundamental energies. There are specific sound pitches for each Adjutant Point that create a harmonic composition for the Ascension Process. Golden City Pilgrimage energizes and restructures your energy fields and vital life force. The Photon is the particle component of light wave frequencies. Albert Einstein theorized this premise in the early twentieth century. Each Photon within the Ray Force rotates in a designated sequence. The White Ray contains all light frequencies and is aligned to the Galactic Center. This movement of the White Ray can appear chaotic.

Examples of the Vortex in Nature

Glossary

Abundance Point: An Evolutionary and Adjutant Point. The second of the Twelve Jurisdictions is the principle of overflowing fullness in all situations, based upon the Law of Choice. In Divine Destiny, Abundance, as a Meta-need, is defined as richness and complexity. Abundance, perceived as an Evolution Point, is synonymous with the Law of Choice, and develops the individual will; hence, the spiritual recognition of Universal Bounty and Manifestation leads the spiritual student to the discernment and the acknowledgement of the Hermetic principles of Cause and Effect through the Law of Attraction. The Abundance Adjutant Point is located in the Golden City Southern Door, and is also known as the Southeast Gateway Point.

Adept: One who has attained Mastery in the art and science of living; a Mahatma.

Adjutant Point Ashrams: The Spiritual Ashrams of Golden Cities fall into four categories: Gateway, Cardinal, Heavenly, and Convergence. Each Golden City contains seventeen Primary Adjutant Points. There are a total of thirty-three Adjutant Points in a Golden City, the balance comprising additional Golden City Ashrams, Temples, and Retreats. Each point has their own distinct energy, guiding Hierarch, Angels, Elohim, and Ray of Focus.

Adjutant Point(s): Power points that form where the lei-lines of the geometric Maltese cross formation of a Golden City, from the holographic energy shape of a photon, traverse or intersect. Adjutant points support the infrastructure of a Golden City, both geometrically and spiritually, and assist and disburse the unique energies held by Babajeran, the Ascended Masters, and the Golden City's Ray Force.

Age of Cooperation: The age humanity is currently being prepared to enter; it occurs simultaneously with the Time of Change.

Agreement Formation: Agreement Formation is an early tenet of the I AM America Teachings, the Law of Agreement is also known as the First Jurisdiction, Harmony. Agreement is the sacred meeting of two minds which on one formative side reflects our intent and commitment. The results of our agreements with others reflect our choices and our responsible actions that ultimately define the quality of our life force.

Akashic Records: The recorded history of all created things from time immemorial, and constructed with the fifth cosmic element: ether.

Alpha Evolutionary Field: This Evolutionary Field is formed from the Faith, Charity, and Creation-Creativity Adjutant Points. It is an acute, isosceles triangle and is one of the three final fields within the Golden City that assists the evolution of the HU-man into the completion of the Ascension.

Anaya: Pleiadean Ascended Master and teacher who serves the Aquamarine and Gold Ray on Earth. Anaya's teachings focus on unity and the cultivation of HU-man Consciousness.

Ancestral Planet: A hidden planet, whose view is obscured by the dark, twin Sun. Its inhabitants are highly evolved Spiritual Beings who assist humanity during times of evolutionary darkness.

Annual (Influence of) Ray Force: Certain Ray Forces that influence all Golden City Doorways on an annual basis. This effect is through the direction of the Maha Chohan, and does not change the Abiding or permament Ray Force of a Temple Point, Retreat Point, or Golden City Star. Nor does it change the assigned Ray Force of an Adjutant Point for a twenty-year period. Annual Ray Forces have a global affect on humanity and their spiritual evolution.

Annual Movement of the Rays: The Rays can move on a yearly basis within a Golden City Doorway; sometimes they move every two to five years. This movement is predicated through the Gold Ray. This effect carries a weight of ten to twenty-five percent influence in the Golden City location.

Anointing of Light: A sacred infusion of light, received during the Enlightenment Pilgrimage. This blessing is given after recitation of the Proclamation of Ascension.

Apollo, Lord: A God of healing, truth, music, and Prophecy. Apollo and Diana serve as the second of the twelve Suns from the lineage of the Alpha-Omega Guardian Suns. The great Apollo is revered as the ancestral father to Saint Germain's heritage of spiritual knowledge and teaching. Additionally, Apollo is a sponsor for the Twelve Jurisdictions.

Aquamarine Ray: A Ray of human ascent, spiritual liberation, and perfection. The Aquamarine Ray is considered a new, yet revolutionary Ray Force and is associated with change and the New Times. The influence of this Ray is destined to develop the higher spiritual qualities of humanity and guide Earth's entrance into the New Times—the Golden Age. This Ray is also associated with Unity Consciousness and is said to originate from the Galactic Center: the Great Central Sun. It is often paired with the Gold Ray to increase its evolutionary affects.

Archangel Chamuel: The Archangel of the Pink Ray serves in the Golden City of Prana, located in India.

Archangel Chrystiel: The Archangel who protects the ongoing spiritual evolution and enlightment of humanity. Chrystiel's angelic complement is the Archeia Clarity who works with the principles of precision and transparency. Chrystiel's color ray is aquamarine and gold. His weapon is a heavenly laser. He serves in the Golden City of Cresta, located in Antarctica.

Archangel Cresta: An archangel of the White and Gold Ray who serves as a Hierarch to one of Gobean's Adjutant Point Ashrams. He is accompanied by the Archeia Christa, who is affiliated with the White and Gold Ray of Purity and the Divine Light of crystals. Cresta and Christa are twin Archangels, brother and sister, who often assist Chrystiel and Clarity, the Archangels of the Gold and Aquamarine Rays.

Archangel Gabriel: The Archangel of the White Ray serves in the Golden City of Arkana, located in East Siberia, Russia.

Archangel Jophiel: The Archangel of the Yellow Ray serves the Golden City of Presching, located in North Korea.

Archangel Michael: Masculine leader of the angels of the Blue Ray, Archangel Michael is the steward of the Golden City of Stienta, located in Iceland. A primary protector of aspiring HU-mans through the Blue White Flame, Archangel Michael is known for binding demons and foreign entities from the Earth Plane and Planet. As an agent of God Protection, he attentively guards the two poles of our Earth.

Archangel Raphael: Archangel of the Green Ray, who serves in the Golden City of Kantan, located in Russia and China.

Archangel Uriel: The Archangel of the Ruby-Gold Ray serves in the Golden City of Gobi, located in the Gobi Desert.

Archangel Zadkiel: Masculine leader of the angels of the Violet Ray, Archangel Zadkiel is the steward of the Golden City of Jeafray, located in Canada. Archangel Zadkiel is associated with the spiritual attributes of transmutation, alchemy, freedom, and mercy.

Arctura and Diana: The twin Elohim of the Violet Ray serve in the Golden City of Arcturus, located in China.

Arhat: The Arhat—one who has overcome antagonistic craving, including the entire range of passions and desires—mental, emotional, and physical. Because of this, the Arhat has undergone and passed arduous spiritual initiations, which make the individual a spiritual teacher and master of meditation and various spiritual techniques.

Ascended Master(s): Once an ordinary human, an Ascended Master has undergone a spiritual transformation over many lifetimes. He or she has Mastered the lower planes—mental, emotional, and physical—to unite with his or her God-Self or I AM Presence. An Ascended Master is freed from the Wheel of Karma. He or she moves forward in spiritual evolution beyond this planet; however, an Ascended Master remains attentive to the spiritual well-being of humanity, inspiring and serving the Earth's spiritual growth and evolution.

Ascension: A process of Mastering thoughts, feelings, and actions that balance positive and negative karmas. It allows entry to a higher state of consciousness and frees a person from the need to reincarnate on the lower Earthly planes or lokas of experience. Ascension is the process of spiritual liberation, also known as moksha.

Ascension Process: Once a soul commits to the Ascension they enter the Ascension Process. This development may ensue until the closure of their current lifetime, or continue into successive lifetimes. Each Ascension Process varies by the techniques and spiritual practices applied through the Ascension Pathway.

Aspirant: A newly awakened spiritual student, whose ambitions create aspiration; the student has yet to find or acquire a guru—a teacher who can assist their evolutionary journey on the spiritual path. The Aspirant is the first level of HU-man development, and occupies the fifth of the Thirteen Evolutionary Pyramids of the Eight-sided Cell of Perfection: Spiritual Awakening.

Astral Body or Plane: The subtle light body that contains our feelings, desires, and emotions. It exists as an intermediate light body between the physical body and the Causal body (Mental Body). According to the Master Teachers, we enter the Astral Plane through our Astral Body when we sleep, and many dreams and visions are experiences in this Plane of vibrant color and sensation. Through spiritual development, the Astral Body strengthens, and the luminosity of its light is often detected in the physical plane. Spiritual adepts may have the ability to consciously leave their physical bodies while traveling in their Astral Bodies. The Astral Body or Astral Plane has various levels of evolution and is the heavenly abode where the soul resides after the disintegration of the physical body. The Astral Body is also known as the Body Double, the Desire Body, and the Emotional Body.

Cardinal Adjutant Point: Adjutant Points located on the arterial directional lei-lines of Golden Cities that oriented to the North, East, South, and West. The Outer Cardinal Point is also known as the *Outer Child*, the Inner Cardinal Point known as the *Inner Child*.

Cardinal Lei-line: A lei-line of directional energy that flows along the cardinal path of North, South, East, and West.

Causal Body: The Fifth Dimensional Body of Light, which is affiliated with thought. Its name is associated with "cause," and is alleged to be the source of both the Astral and physical body. The Causal Body is also defined as the Higher Mind—superior to the Mental Body.

Cellular Awakening: A spiritual initiation activated by the Master Teachers Saint Germain and Kuthumi. Through this process the physical body is accelerated at the cellular level, preparing consciousness to recognize and receive instruction from the Fourth Dimension. Supplemental teachings on the Cellular Awakening claim this process assists the spiritual student to assimilate the higher frequencies and energies now available on Earth. Realizing the Cellular Awakening can ameliorate catastrophic Earth Change and initiate consciousness into the ONE through the realization of devotion, compassion, Brotherhood and the Universal Heart.

Chakra(s): Sanskrit for wheel. Seven spinning wheels of human-bioenergy centers stacked from the base of the spine to the top of the head.

Chela: Disciple.

Choice: Will.

Christ, the: The highest energy or frequency attainable on Earth. The Christ is a step-down transformer of the I AM energies which enlighten, heal, and transform all human conditions of degradation and death.

Christ Consciousness: A level of consciousness that unites both feminine and masculine energies and produces the innocence and purity of the I AM. Its energies heal, enlighten, and transform every negative human condition and pave the way for the realization of the divine HU-man.

City of White: Another name for Shamballa.

Co-creation: Creating with the God-Source.

Collective Consciousness: The higher interactive structure of consciousness as two or more.

Communication Portal: A protected gateway created by an Ascended Master or Being of Light to stream multi-dimensional energy and information through. This Portal can seamlessly connect Third Dimension to both Fourth and Fifth Dimension.

Conscience: The internal recognition of right and wrong in regard to one's actions and motives

Consciousness: Awakening to one's own existence, sensations, and cognitions.

Convergence Adjutant Point(s): Eight Adjutant Points that lie on the intercardinal directions of each Golden City Doorway. They unite the energies of Evolutionary Points, further activating the Evolutionary Biome.

Cooperation Point: An Evolution and Adjutant Point, located in the interior Western Door of a Golden City. As the seventh of the Twelve Jurisdictions advises joint actions, work, and assistance to faithfully adhere with fairness, honesty, and the acknowledgement of the Divine Presence.

Crown Chakra: Also known as the Seventh Chakra, located at the top of or just above the head.

Cup or Cup Ceremony: A symbol of neutrality and grace. The Ascended Masters often refer to our human body as a Cup filled with our thoughts and feelings. Cup Ceremony is a Water Ceremony that blesses Mother Earth.

Cycle of the Elements: According to Taoist understanding the Earth undergoes a cyclic series of nine twenty-year segments. This is known as the Nine Cycles, a total of one-hundred eighty years. A further division of the one-hundred eighty years is the Three Eras—sixty years each, comprising upper, middle, and lower. Universal energy is said to change during each of the Three Eras, and Earth is currently in the Lower Era which started in 1984. Each era contains three cycles of twenty years each, hence the Nine Cycles. According to Taoist philosophy small changes occur between cycles; considerable changes occur between eras. Currently Earth is in the eighth cycle that began in 2004. The ninth cycle begins in 2024. The flow of universal energy significantly changes between each of the Nine Cycles, or every twenty years. The Ascended Masters often refer to the twenty-year cycles of the Earth, and their influence on culture, societies, and individuals. They prophesy a twenty-year period that is likely the Ninth Cycle, in the year 2024, or the Beginning of the Upper Era (first cycle) in 2044, when the spiritual Masters appear on Earth, in physical bodies to teach and heal the masses.

DAHL Universe: The parallel, twin universe to our universe. The DAHL Universe is spiritually and technologically advanced, and it is alleged that members from the DAHL Universe visit our Universe, known as the DERN, at timely junctures for spiritual evolution and intervention.

Decree: Statements of intent and power, similar to prayers and mantras, which are often integrated with the use of the I AM and requests to the I AM Presence.

DERN Universe: The DERN is the twin Universe to the DAHL, the universe where we reside. The DERN was created simultaneously with the DAHL. However, while the DAHL flourished with advanced technologies and spiritual development, the DERN is arrested. It is claimed that the Pleiades resides in the seventh outer belt of the DERN, and is an umbilicus type of portal to the DAHL. Numerous time and travel portals exist between the DAHL and the DERN, as they are twin creations. Venus and Earth are allegedly settlements for the Pleiades, an evolutionary colony for the DAHL.

Deva: A shining one or being of light.

Diamond Mind: A state of consciousness achieved through the Tenth Light Body that purifies and refines desires. It is a powerful energy that assists one to pierce human illusion.

Divine Complement: Each Ascended Master, Divine Being, and Archangel is alleged to be paired with a divine complement of energy. Each divine pair manifests and streams energies into the corporeal worlds through the Hermetic Law of Gender. Hence, one is masculine in quality, while the other is feminine. Similar to a Twin Flame, Divine Complements differ in that they are ascended and purposely divide their efforts to assist Earth and unascended humanity. In the higher realms they are ideally ONE energy, and serve upon one individualized Ray Force.

Doorway of a Golden City or Golden City Doorway: The four doorways of a Golden City. They comprise the North Door (or the Black Door); the East Door (or the Blue Door); the South Door (or the Red Door); the West Door (or the Yellow Door). The center of a Golden City is known as the "Star" and is affiliated with the color white.

Eastern Door: The Blue Door of a Golden City.

Ecological Alchemy: A process of Earth transmutation and transformation. The innate power of Mother Earth restores and heals her own sensitive environments and internal systems. These are currently compromised by global warming and climate change, anthropogenic climate change, and various forms of pollution. This natural, restorative process reinstates the natural cycles and rhythms of Mother Earth and nature, in conjunction with the worldwide appearance of new flora and fauna.

Eighth Energy Body: Known as the Buddha Body or the Field of Awakening, this energy body is initially three to four feet from the human body. It begins by developing two visible grid-like spheres of light that form in the front and in the back of the Human Aura. The front sphere is located three to four feet in front of and between the Heart and Solar Plexus Chakras. The back sphere is located in front of and between the Will-to-Love and Solar Will Chakras. These spheres activate an ovoid of light that surrounds the entire human body; an energy field associated with harmonizing and perfecting the Ascension Process. This is the first step toward Mastery. Once developed and sustained, this energy body grants physical longevity and is associated with immortality. It is known as the first level of Co-creation, and is developed through control of the diet and disciplined breath techniques. Once this light body reaches full development, the spheres dissipate and dissolve into a refined energy field, resembling a metallic armor. The mature Eighth Light Body then contracts and condenses, to reside within several inches of the physical body where it emits a silver-blue sheen.

Eight Principles of the Right-hand Path: These ideals include Right Effort, Right View, Right Conduct, Right Samadhi, Right Mindfulness, Right Livelihood, Right Resolve, and Right Speech.

Eight-sided Cell of Perfection: An atomic-sized cell located in the human heart. It is associated with all aspects of perfection, and contains and maintains a visceral connection with the Godhead and the consciousness of Unana.

Elemental Kingdom: A kingdom comprising an invisible group of beings who act as counterparts to visible nature on Earth and hold an energy focus for the Physical Plane.

Eleventh Energy Body: An Energy Body of transfiguration that creates pronounced differences in perception of reality with the ability to simultaneously experience Third, Fourth, and Fifth Dimension—the Evolutionary Biome. This is the experiential ONE of Fourth, Fifth, and Sixth Dimensions. It is also known as the Stargate, as it is cultivated through time spent in the Star Retreats. This energy body produces the supersenses of the HU-man, with the ability to sense, create, and define numerous Co-creative sounds and pitches.

El Morya: Ascended Master of the Blue Ray, associated with the development of the will. El Morya is the Hierarch of the Golden City of Gobean, located in Arizon and New Mexico, United States.

Elohim: Creative beings of love and light that helped manifest the Divine idea of our solar system. Seven Elohim (the Seven Rays) exist on Earth. They organize and draw forward Archangels, the Four Elements, Devas, Seraphim, Cherubim, Angels, Nature Guardians, and the Elementals. In Ascended Master teaching, the Silent Watcher—the Great Mystery—gives them direction. It is also claimed the Elohim magnetize the Unfed Flame at the center of the Earth. Some esoteric historians perceive the Elohim—also referred to as the Els—as the Ancient Gods, or the Master Teachers of Lemuria and Atlantis. Elohim slow down the light of the Ray Forces to create the material world.

Elohim Evolutionary Field: Four Evolutionary Fields that are served by four pairs of Elohim. Their focus embraces the spiritual principles of Truth—the Blue Ray, Peace—the Ruby-Gold Ray, Freedom—the Violet Ray, and Unity—the Aquamarine and Gold Rays. The Elohim Evolutionary fields are located in the inner directional regions of a Golden City Vortex.

Elohim of Freedom Evolutionary Field: This field of evolutionary energies is created through the Abundance Point, the Service Point, and the Illumination Point of the Golden City. It is located in the inner Southeast region of a Golden City. Its triangular shape is a scalene obtuse triangle, and the Hierarchs of this Evolutionary Field are the Elohim of Freedom, Arctura and Diana.

Elohim of Peace Evolutionary Field: This field of evolutionary energies is created through the Stillness Point, the Faith Point, and the Illumination Point of the Golden City. It is located in the inner Northeast region of a Golden City. Its triangular shape is a scalene obtuse triangle, and the Hierarchs of this Evolutionary Field are the Elohim of Peace, Peace and Tranquility.

Elohim of Truth Evolutionary Field: This field of evolutionary energies is created through the Creation-Creativity Point, the Faith Point, and the Cooperation Point of the Golden City. It is located in the inner Northwest region of a Golden City. Its triangular shape is a scalene obtuse triangle, and the Hierarchs of this Evolutionary Field are the Elohim of Truth, Vista and Virginia.

Elohim of Unity Evolutionary Field: This field of evolutionary energies is created through the Harmony Point, the Service Point, and the Cooperation Point of the Golden City. It is located in the inner Southwest region of a Golden City. Its triangular shape is a scalene obtuse triangle, and the Hierarchs of this Evolutionary Field are the Elohim of Unity, Rainbow and Iris.

Energy-for-energy. The transfer of energies. To understand this spiritual principle, one must remember Isaac Newton's Third Law of Motion: "for every action there is an equal and opposite reaction." However, while energies may be equal, their forms often vary. The Ascended Masters often use this phrase to remind chelas to properly compensate others to avoid karmic retribution, and repayment may take many different forms to maintain balance.

Enlightenment Pilgrimage: This Spiritual Pilgrimage includes migration through a series of seven major Adjutant Points within the Western (Yellow) Door of a Golden City. The Migration Pathway follows the Cardinal Lei-line. This Pilgrimage influses light into the student's cells, and activates Divine DNA. This Pilgrimage includes an intentional set of decrees, water and fire ceremonies, the Oath of the Right-hand Path, and the Proclamation of Ascension.

Evolutionary Biome: The seamless connection, interaction, and cooperation with Creation at multi-dimensional levels through the HU-man senses. The premise of Evolutionary Biome is cultivated through the fractal experience of the Evolution Points in the Eight-sided Cell of Perfection; it is further aided through the Oneness, Oneship, and ONE of the Golden City Adjutant Points, Temples, Retreats, and Stars. The Evolutionary Biome is the evolutionary process that leads Earth and humanity to the Ascended Master state of consciousness known as Unana.

Evolutionary Field(s): A triangular field of energy within a Golden City, created by three specific major Adjutant Points. Each Evolutionary Pyramid is served by a particular Hierarch and Ray Force(s).

Evolutionary or Evolution Points: Stages of spiritual development identified through specific processes that assemble and Co-create Human Consciousness. There are twelve points total, with each phase of development physically manifested and perceptible through the Eight-sided Cell of Perfection. Each of the twelve junctures of spiritual evolution regulate through one of Twelve Jurisdictions, in deliberate sequence.

Evolutionary Pyramids: A triangular field of energy within a Golden City, created by three specific major Adjutant Points. Each Evolutionary Pyramid is served by a particular Hierarch and Ray Force(s). The Evolurionary Pyramid, mirrors the Evolutionary Fields within the Eight-sided Cell of Perfection. This creates a singular, triangular lens, which colors perceptions, insight, and sensitivites. This concentration of energies generates a personal, yet specific internal spiritual process with obtainable, discernable results.

Field of Awakening: The Eighth Energy Body, also known as the *Buddha Body*.

Fifth Dimension: The spiritual dimension of cause, associated with creation, thoughts, visions, and aspirations. This is the dimension of the Ascended Masters and the Archetypes of Evolution, the city of Shamballa, and the templates of all Golden Cities.

Fire Ceremony: The intentional use of the fire element to assist spiritual development and evolution. This can include a simple write-and-burn practice, to an elaborate Hindu Navagraha Ceremony.

Fire Triplicity: Energies from the Great Central Sun, or Galactic Center, triangulate to our Solar System through these three planets: the Sun, Mars, and Jupiter. These three planets are known as the Fire Triplicity and represent three forms of spiritual fire: the Sun is the spiritual leader; Mars is the spiritual pioneer and protector; and Jupiter is the spiritual teacher.

Fourfold Flame: The Threefold Flame exists in the heart and a fourth flame appears as the individual furthers their spiritual evolution. This is known as the Fourfold Flame. The four flames represent Love (pink); Wisdom (yellow); Power (blue); and Desire (of the Source) that evolves into Unity (white).

Fourfold Flame Evolutionary Field: Four Evolutionary Fields that lie to the outer intercardinal edge of a Golden City. Each field is a complement of energy to the Evolutionary Fields of the Four Pillars.

Fourfold Flame of Desire Evolutionary Field: One of four Evolutionary Fields served by Lady Desiree. This field of energy lies to the outer Southwest region of the Golden City and is formed by the Adjutant Points of Harmony, Clarity, and Cooperation. The triangular field is an acute isosceles triangle—a Golden Triangle.

Fourfold Flame of Love Evolutionary Field: One of four Evolutionary Fields served by Lady Miriam. This field of energy lies to the outer Northwest region of the Golden City and is formed by the Adjutant Points of Cooperation, Charity, and Creation-Creativity. The triangular field is an acute isosceles triangle—a Golden Triangle.

Fourfold Flame of Power Evolutionary Field: One of four Evolutionary Fields served by Lady Portia, the Goddess of Justice. This field of energy lies to the outer Southeast region of the Golden City and is formed by the Adjutant Points of Abundance, Love, and Illumination. The triangular field is an acute isosceles triangle—a Golden Triangle.

Fourfold Flame of Wisdom Evolutionary Field: One of four Evolutionary Fields served by Lady Nada. This field of energy lies to the outer Northeast region of the Golden City and is formed by the Adjutant Points of Illumination, Desire, and Stillness. The triangular field is an acute isosceles triangle—a Golden Triangle.

Four Pillars Evolutionary Field(s): Four Evolutionary Fields that are hidden within the intercardinal directions of the Golden Cities. Each field is served by a specific Ascended Master, who works in tandem with the Adjutant Point Hierarchs and Master Teacher of the Golden City. The Four Pillars are masculine in energy and accompanied by their feminine counterparts, the Four Flames.

Fourth Dimension: A dimension of vibration associated with telepathy, psychic ability, and the dream world. This is the dimension of the Elemental Kingdom and the development of the super senses. Awareness of the Fourth Dimension is the first step in Ascension.

Freedom Flame Evolutionary Field: *See Elohim of Freedom Evolutionary Field.*

Freedom Star World Map: The Ascended Masters' map depicts prophesied global Earth Changes and the locations of worldwide Golden City Vortices. This map's spiritual teachings are divided into three unique maps of prophesied social, cultural, and geophysical changes. The Americas Map is composed of Greenland, Canada, the United States, Mexico, Central and South America, and New Atlantis. The Greening Map is composed of India, Pakistan, Afghanistan, Russia, China, Japan, Malaysia, Australia, and New Zealand. The Map of Exchanges is composed of Iceland, Europe, the Middle East, Africa, Antarctica, and New Lemuria. The Map of the Americas, including the I AM America Map, is sponsored by Saint Germain. The Greening Map is sponsored by Kuan Yin, and the Map of Exchanges is sponsored by Lady Nada, Kuthumi, and El Morya.

Each distinctive map depicts the location of seventeen Golden Cities. Three sets of seventeen Golden Cities comprise a total of fifty-one Golden City Vortices. Fifty-one is a pentagonal number and is esoterically connected to Divine Man, Divine Intervention, perfect harmony, and the planet Venus. Gobean, the first Golden City Vortex, was activated in 1981. Cresta, the fifty-first Golden City Vortex, activates in the year 2092 AD.

As the Evolutionary Biome appears and evolves upon Earth, Galactic Light becomes self-sustaining. Earth breaks free from our Solar System and becomes the Freedom Star, and later evolves into a Sun.

Galactic Center: *See Great Central Sun.*

Galactic Light: Energy streams from the Great Central Sun, or Galactic Center, as the Seven Rays of Light and Sound to Earth. Galactic Light calibrates the level of intelligence on Earth through memory function; the ability to absorb, recognize, and respect spiritual knowledge; the length of lifespans; and our ability to access the Akashic Records. The amount of Galactic Light streaming to Earth at any given time is classically measured through the Hindu Puranic timing of the Yugas, and through a contemporary method—the Electric Cycle—advocated by the Eastern Indian guru Sri Yuteswar.

Galactic Web: A large universal, planet-encircling grid created by the consciousness of all things on Earth—humans, animals, plants, and minerals. Magnetic Vortices, namely the Golden Cities, appear at certain intersections.

Gateway Adjutant Points: Eight Adjutant Points that protect the four doorways—gates—of a Golden City. There are two Adjutant Points per Golden City Door, and each point presents a defined gender. Gateway Points are Third Dimensional in nature and expression. They are: Eastern Door, Desire and Love; Southern Door, Abundance. and Harmony; Western Door, Clarity and Charity; Northern Door, Creation-Creativity and Stillness.

Geometric Language: The symbols of sacred geometry.

Gobean, Golden City of: The first United States Golden City located in the states of Arizona and New Mexico. Its qualities are cooperation, harmony, and peace; its Ray Force is Blue; and its Master Teacher is El Morya. Gobean was activated in 1981.

Gobi, Golden City of: Steps-down the energies of Shamballa into the entire Golden City Network. This Golden City is located in the Gobi Desert. It is known as the City of Balance, and means *Across the Star*; its Master Teachers are Lord Meru and Archangel Uriel.

Goddess Ti of the Light: An Ascended Master Hierach of the Abundance Point, located in the Golden City of Gobean. Goddess Ti was embodied in Ancient Egypt as the Queen consort of Akehnaton, Nefertiti.

Godhead of Perfection Evolutionary Field: The Golden City Star. This Evolutionary Field is considered the Temple of the Holy Self, and is the first movement in the sequential Nine Movements of Consciousness.

God Strength Evolutionary Field: Archangel Michael serves this Evolutionary Field, that is also known as the *Fourth Heavenly Gate*. It is located on the north side of the Eastern Door of the Golden City and is composed of the Golden City Star, the Illumination Adjutant Point, and the Desire Adjutant Point. This Evolutionary Field is an obtuse isosceles triangle, and serves the New Children and the Nature Kingdoms.

Golden Age: A peaceful time on Earth that is prophesied to occur after the Time of Change. It is also prophesied that, during this age, human life spans will increase and sacred knowledge will be revered. During this time, the societies, cultures, and the governments of Earth will reflect spiritual enlightenment through worldwide cooperation, compassion, charity, and love. Ascended Master teachings often refer to the Golden Age as the Golden-Crystal Age and the Age of Grace.

Golden Age of Kali Yuga: According to the classic Puranic timing of the Yugas, Earth is in a Kali Yuga period that started around the year 3102 BCE the year that Krishna allegedly left the Earth. During this time period, which according to this Puranic timing lasts a total of 432,000 years—the ten-thousand year Golden Age period, also known as the Golden Age of Kali Yuga, is not a full foce Golden Age. Instead, it is a sub-cycle of higher light frequencies within an overall larger phase of less light energy.

Golden Ball of Light: A sacred geometric sphere of gold light that is the foundation for curative meditation techniques and the formation of Group Mind.

Golden Belt of Golden Light (or Golden Band of Light): This etheric Golden Belt of high-frequency energy was in place since the early 1950s through the efforts of the Ascended Master Saint Germain. It held back catastrophic Earth Changes until humanity has a better chance to evolve. The belt also played a significant role in mankind's spiritual growth. The Golden Belt was dissipated during the Shamballa Season of 2019-2020, and its Golden Threads were woven into each of the fifty-one Golden Cities. This act declares Earth's passage into the Golden Age.

Golden City Doorway: *See Doorway of a Golden City.*

Golden City Hierarch: The spiritual and administrative overseer of a Golden City Vortex. An Elohim, Archangel, or the Spiritual Master directs and protects numerous lei-lines, power points, sub-Vortices, Adjutant Points, Ashrams, Temples, and Retreats throughout a Golden City. The Golden City Hierarch works in tandem with other Angels, Ascended Masters, and Elohim associated throughout their Golden City and within the Golden City Network.

Golden City Network or the **New Shamballa:** The Golden City Network exists throughout our entire planet with affiliated Elohim, Archangels, Angels, Cosmic Beings, and Ascended Masters focused upon humanity's Ascension and spiritual evolution during the Golden Age of Kali Yuga.

Golden City Star and Retreat: The center or apex of the Golden City and location of the Golden City Hierarch's Ashram of Light.

Golden City Temples of Perfection: *See Heavenly Temples of Perfection.*

Golden City Vortex: A Golden City Vortex—based on the Ascended Masters' I AM America material—are prophesied areas of safety and spiritual energies during the Times of Changes. Covering an expanse of land and air space, these sacred energy sites span more than 400 kilometers (270 miles) in diameter, with a vertical height of 400 kilometers (250 miles). Golden City Vortices, more importantly, reach beyond terrestrial significance and into the ethereal realm. This system of safe harbors acts as a group or universal mind within our galaxy, connecting information seamlessly and instantly with other beings. Fifty-one Golden City Vortices are stationed throughout the world, and each carries a different meaning, a combination of Ray Forces, and a Divine Purpose. A Golden City Vortex works on the principles of electromagnetism and geology. Vortices tend to appear near fault lines, possibly serving as conduits of inner-earth movement to terra firma. Golden Cities are symbolized by a Maltese Cross at the two-dimensional level, whose sacred geometry determine their doorways, lei-lines, adjutant points, and coalescing Star energies. They are pyramidal in actual form. Since their energies intensify experiences with both the Fourth and Fifth Dimensions, Golden City Vortices play a vital role with the Ascension Process. The clockwise motion of the Vortex absorbs energy from its Ray Force, Ascended Master Hierarch, the Great Central Sun, and Mother Earth—Babajeran. Its counterclockwise motion releases energy. The spin of the Vortex creates a torsion field.

Gold(en) Ray: The Ray of Brotherhood, Cooperation, and Peace. The Gold Ray produces the qualities of perception, honesty, confidence, courage, and responsibility. It is also associated with leadership, independence, authority, ministration, and justice. The Gold Ray vibrates the energies of Divine Father on Earth. Its attributes are: warm; perceptive; honest; confident; positive; independent; courageous; enduring; vital; leadership; responsible; ministration; authority; justice. The Gold Ray is also associated with the Great Central Sun, the Solar Logos, of which our Solar Sun is a Step-down Transformer of its energies. According to the Master Teachers, the Gold Ray is the epitome of change for the New Times. The Gold Ray is the ultimate authority of Cosmic Law, and carries both our personal and worldwide Karma and Dharma (purpose). Its presence is designed to instigate responsible spiritual growth and planetary evolution as a shimmering light for humanity's aspirations and the development of the HU-man. The Gold Ray, however, is also associated with Karmic justice, and will instigate change: constructive and destructive. The extent of catastrophe or transformation is contingent on humanity's personal and collective spiritual growth and evolutionary process as we progress into the New Times.

Golden Ray Mantra: The Golden Ray Mantra provokes the presence of the Golden Ray in our aura, or enhances the affect of the Ray throughout our lightfields. The structure of the mantra is: "Om Banandra, (2x), Om Hunana, (1x), and Om Sunana, (1x)." Its language is *Owaspee*, the divine language of the Angels, often used by the Master Teachers for specific spiritual phrases and Golden City names. This same mantra can be used to increase longevity, however the arrangement of the words are changed: "Om Hunana, (1x), Om Sunana, (1x), and Om Banandra, (1x)." Hunana invokes the presence of the HU. Sunana invokes the presence of Sanat Kumara. Banandra means *delight*, or *of the light*. The OM steps down the sublime energies of the Great Central Sun.

Golden Thread Axis: Also known as the Vertical Power Current. The Golden Thread Axis physically consists of the Medullar Shushumna, a life-giving nadi comprising one-third of the human Kundalini system. Two vital currents intertwine around the Golden Thread Axis: the lunar Ida Current, and the solar Pingala Current. According to the Master Teachers, the flow of the Golden Thread Axis begins with the I AM Presence, enters the Crown Chakra, and descends through the spinal system. It descends beyond the Base Chakra and travels to the core of the Earth. Esoteric scholars often refer to the axis as the Rod of Power, and it is symbolized by two spheres connected by an elongated rod. Ascended Master students and chelas frequently draw upon the energy of the Earth through the Golden Thread Axis for healing and renewal using meditation, visualization, and breath.

Great Activation: An acceleration of the activation of certain Golden Cities that hastens our entrance into the New Times. Golden Cities participating in the Great Activation are: Braun, Afrom, Ganakra, Mesotamp, Shehez, and Adjatal.

Great Awakening: The time period humanity is currently experiencing marked by political and societal turmoil alongside humanity's collective Spiritual Awakening. As one moves through extreme polarity, the soul awakens to its divine and innate Co-creatorship that initiates the Ascension Process. The Great Awakening transpires concurrently with the turbulent Time of Change.

Great Central Sun: The great sun of our galaxy, around which all of the galaxy's solar systems rotate. The Great Central Sun is also known as the Galactic Center, which is the origin of the Seven Rays of Light and Sound on Earth.

Great White Brotherhood and Sisterhood: A fraternity of ascended and unascended men and women who are dedicated to the universal uplifting of humanity. Its main objective includes the preservation of the lost spirit, and the teachings of the ancient religions and philosophies of the world. Its mission is to reawaken the dormant ethical and spiritual sparks among the masses. In addition to fulfilling spiritual aims, the Great White Lodge pledges to protect mankind against the systematic assaults which inhibit self-knowledge and personal growth on individual and group freedoms.

Greening Map: The second Map of Earth Changes Prophecies. It contains a total of seventeen Golden City Vortices and is sponsored by Ascended Master Kuan Yin. It entails all of Asia, Japan, and Australia. New land is prophesied to appear near New Zealand, New Guinea, Hawaii, and the Easter Islands, and is referred to as "New Lemuria" by the Spiritual Teachers. The Greening Map signifies personal and transpersonal healing of the feminine. It balances Mother Earth through the awakening of Ecological Alchemy. During the Greening Map's Time of Change, Earth is healed and rejuvenated with new flora and fauna appearing throughout the planet.

Green Ray: The Ray of Active Intelligence is associated with education, thoughtfulness, communication, organization, the intellect, science, objectivity, and discrimination. It is also adaptable, rational, healing, and awakened. The Green Ray is affiliated with the planet Mercury. In the I AM America teachings the Green Ray is served by the Archangel Raphael and Archeia Mother Mary; the Elohim of Truth, Vista—also known as Cyclopea, and Virginia; the Ascended Masters Hilarion, Lord Sananda, Lady Viseria, Soltec, and Lady Master Meta.

Group Mind: A conscious intelligent force formed by members of distinguished cultures, societal organizations, and more prominently, by religious church members. The Group Mind is held together by rituals and customs that are typically peculiar to its members; newcomers instantly sense the energies of the atmosphere, and will either accept or reject their influence. The physics of the Group Mind are important to comprehend, as this collective intelligence is purposely formed to aid the Aspirant to raise human consciousness beyond present limitations.

Harmony Point: An Adjutant Point and Adjutant Point Ashram located on the west Gateway Point of the Southern Door. Harmony is the first virtue of the Twelve Jurisdictions based on the principle of agreement.

Healing of the Nations Spiritual Pilgrimage: A series of Migrations through the Southern Door, and the Temples, Retreats, and Star of a Golden City. Through the Evolutionary Biome, this activates both personal healing and global healing for the nations of the world.

Heart Chakra: Known in Sanskrit as the Anahata. The location is in the center of the chest. Its main aspect is Love and Relationships, and includes our ability to feel compassion, forgiveness, and hold our own Divine Purpose.

Heart of the Dove: Also known as the Center of Fire, this energy anomaly is prophesied to exist Northwest of Kansas City, Missouri. It is here that Master Teachings claim an umbilicus connection between Earth and the Galactic Center exists, creating time anomalies and the potential for time travel in the New Times. The Heart of the Dove is also prophesied to become a spiritual center for learning and self-actualizing the consciousness of Quetzalcoatl—the Christ.

Heavenly Temples of Perfection or **Heavenly Points:** There are four Heavenly Adjutant Points per Golden City. These locations manifest where Golden City Third-Dimensional energies shift into Fourth and Fifth Dimension. The four Heavenly Points are: Illumination, Service, Cooperation, and Faith.

Hierarch: The leader and principal spiritual guide, steward, and spiritual teacher of a Golden City Adjutant Point, Temple, Retreat, and Star. Hierarchs can be newly annointed Ascended Masters and seasoned Elohim. Archangels and Angels also serve as Golden City Hierarchs.

HU-man: The God-Man.

HU, or HUE: In Tibetan dialects, the word hue or hu means breath; however, the HU is a sacred sound and when chanted or meditated upon is said to represent the entire spectrum of the Seven Rays. Because of this, the HU powerfully invokes the presence of the Violet Flame, which is the activity of the Violet Ray and its inherent ability to transform and transmit energies to the next octave. HU is also considered an ancient name for God, and it is sung for spiritual enlightenment.

I AM: The presence of God.

I AM America: According to the I AM America Prophecies, Saint Germain claims that the people of America have a unique destiny in the New Times. AMERICA contains within it a unique anagram: IAMRACE.
  The I AM Race of people is a unique group of souls who lived in America as Atlanteans. But their destiny has evolved since those ancient times. Instead of sinking on a continent destroyed by the misuse of technology and spiritual knowledge, their active intelligence continues to develop in modern times. Their service is focused on the Brotherly love of all nations.

I AM America Map: The Ascended Masters' Map of prophesied Earth Changes for the United States.

I AM Presence: The individualized presence of God.

I AM That I AM: A term from Hebrew that translates to, "I Will Be What I Will Be." "I AM" is also derived from the Sanskrit Om (pronounced: A-U-M), whose three letters signify the three aspects of God as beginning, duration, and dissolution—Brahma, Vishnu, and Shiva. The AUM syllable is known as the omkara and translates to "I AM Existence," the name for God. "Soham" is yet another mystical Sanskrit name for God, which means "It is I," or "He is I." In Vedic philosophy, it is claimed that when a child cries, "Who am I?" the universe replies, "Soham—you are the same as I AM." The I AM teachings also use the name "Soham" in place of "I AM."

I AM That I AM Evolutionary Field: This Evolutionary Field helps one to realize the Ascended Master within their personalized Ascension Process. This field is shaped as an acute equilateral triangle and is composed of three Adjutant Points: Faith, Stillness, and Creation-Creativity.

Information or Communication Portal: A multi-dimensional gateway created by an Ascended Master for confidential or one-one-one contact and interaction.

Initiate: The third level of the Ascension Process that relies on personal experience by degree, test, and trial that is encountered both morally and mentally.

Inner Child Point: This Adjutant Point exists at the Faith, Illumination, Service, and Cooperation Point locations of every Golden City. It is the convergence of five arterial lei-lines, and lies halfway between the Outer Child Point and the Golden City Star, located on the Cardinal Lei-line. This Adjutant Point is also known as the *Inner Cardinal Point*.

Inner Earth: Below the Earth's Crust lie many magnificent cities and cultures of various break-away races of humans, evolved HU-mans, and extraterrestrials. The Inner Earth is filled with reservoirs, streams, rivers, lakes, and oceans. According to metaphysical researchers the Earth is honey-combed with pervasive caves and subterranean caverns measuring hundreds of miles in diameter. The center of the Earth is not honey-combed. According to esoteric researchers advanced civilizations inhabit the interior of the Earth along with a smaller interior Sun that emits light and controls spiritual evolution. This viewpoint is held by the Ascended Masters and shared throughout their Earth Changes Prophecies and historical narratives.

Inner Garden Meditation: The Inner Garden is an intentional mind construct that is visualized for peace and comfort during states of meditation. As this state of consciousness strengthens, Spiritual Teachers will often join for instruction in the sanction of this serene setting.

Inner Sun: A smaller Sun that exists in the Inner Earth.

Intention Evolutionary Field: The Evolutionary Field of Ceremony is composed of the three Adjutant Points of Clarity, Cooperation, and the Golden City Star. This is also known as the Western Door. This Evolutionary Field assists right speech and Divine Sound.

Jyotish: Vedic or Hindu Astrology, known as the *Science of Light*.

Kali Yuga: The Age of Iron, or Age of Quarrel, when Earth receives twenty-five percent or less galactic light from the Great Central Sun.

Karma: Laws of Cause and Effect.

Klehma: The fifth United States Golden City located primarily in the states of Colorado and Kansas. Its qualities are continuity, balance, and harmony; its Ray Force is White; and its Master Teacher is Serapis Bey.

Krita Yuga: The Age of Gold, when Earth receives seventy-five to one-hundred percent galactic light from the Great Central Sun. Krita Yuga is also known as Satya Yuga.

Kuan Yin: The Bodhisattva of Compassion and teacher of Saint Germain. She is associated with all the Rays and the principle of femininity.

Kundalini: The coiled energy located at the base of the spine, often established in the lower Base and Sacral Chakras. In Sanskrit, Kundalini literally means coiled, and Kundalini Shatki (shatki means energy) is claimed to initiate spiritual development, wisdom, knowledge, and enlightenment.

Kuthumi: An Ascended Master of the Pink, Ruby, and Gold Rays. He is a gentle and patient teacher who works closely with the Nature Kingdoms.

Lady Luxor: An Ascended Master of the White Ray. She is considered to be the Divine Compliment to Serapis Bey. Lady Luxor assists students to enter and achieve the Ascension. She guards the Golden City Star of every Golden City.

Lady Miriam: Lady Miriam is an Ascended Master of the Green Ray and is considered Lord Sananda's Divine Compliment.

Law of Attraction and Repulsion: Like charges repel; unlike charges attract.

Law of Love: Per the Ascended Master tradition, to consciously live without fear, without inflicting fear on others. Perhaps every religion on Earth is founded on the Law of Love, per the notion of "treating others as you would like to be treated." The Fourth of the Twelve Jurisdictions instructs us that Love is the "Law of Allowing, Maintaining, and Sustainability." All of these precepts distinguish love from an emotion or feeling, and observe Love as action, will, or choice. The Ascended Masters affirm, "If you live love, you will create love." This premise is fundamental to understanding the esoteric underpinnings of the Law of Love. The Master Teachers declare that through practicing the Law of Love, one experiences acceptance, understanding, and tolerance, alongside detachment. Metaphysically, the Law of Love allows different and varied perceptions of ONE experience, situation, or circumstance to exist simultaneously. From this viewpoint, the Law of Love is the practice of tolerance.

Lei-line: Lines of energy that exist among geographical places, ancient monuments, megaliths, and strategic points. These energy lines contain electrical and magnetic points. Golden City Lei-lines extend throughout the Galaxy.

Lemuria: A continent that primarily existed in the Pacific Ocean before it was submerged by Earth Changes. It is deemed to have been the remaining culture and civilization of Mu, an expansive continent that once spanned the entire present-day Pacific Ocean. It is alleged that the lands of Lemuria, also known as Shalmali, existed in the Indian and Southern Pacific Oceans, and included the continent of Australia.

Thus, it is believed to have integrated with the Lands of Rama, and is to be considered one the earliest cultures of humanity. Sri Lanka is alleged to have been one of the empire's capital cities. Esoteric historians theorize that the tectonic Pacific Plate formed this lost continent. Asuramaya is one of the great Manus of Lemuria's Root Race.

Some esoteric writers place the destruction of Mu around the year 30,000 BCE; others place its demise millions of years ago. According to Theosophical history, the Lemurian and Atlantean epochs overlapped. The apparent discrepancy of these timelines is likely due to two different interpretations of the Cycle of the Yugas. It is claimed that the venerated Elders of Lemuria escaped the global tragedy by moving to an uninhabited plateau in central Asia. This account mirrors Ascended Master teachings and Lord Himalaya's founding of the Retreat of the Blue Lotus.

The Lemurian elders re-established their spiritual teachings and massive library as the Thirteenth School. Spiritual teachers claim that the evolutionary purpose of this ancient civilization was to develop humanity's Will (the Blue Ray of Power). Lemurian culture also venerated the Golden Disk of the Sun and practiced the Right-hand Path. It is claimed that these teachings and spiritual records became foundational teachings for the Great White Brotherhood of the mystical lands of His Wang Mu (the Abode of the Immortals) and the Kuan Yin Lineage of Gurus. Present-day Australia—once known by Egyptian gold-miners as the ancient Land of Punt—is considered the remainder of the once great continent of Mu and Lemuria, which likely existed in the time period of Dvapara Yuga, over 800,000 years ago.

Light Being: A Co-creative Human Being, whose evolutionary process involves interaction with the light. Light Beings reside in the Inner Earth and upon the surface of the Earth.

Lighted Stance: A state of light the body acquires during Ascension. This is also known as the Tenth Energy Body.

Lineage of Gurus Evolutionary Field: The Evolutionary Field of Ceremony is composed of the three Adjutant Points of Faith, Stillness, and the Golden City Star. This is also known as the Northern Door. This Evolutionary Field is the principle of *Right Effort*, and contains a visceral connection to Shamballa.

Lords of Venus: A group of Ascended Masters who came to serve humanity. They once resided on the planet Venus.

Love Evolutionary Field: An Evolutionary Field of HU-man Development, contains the Adjutant Points of Harmony, Abundance, and Service. Its shape is an acute equilateral triangle.

Maltese Cross: The Maltese Cross, a symbol often used by Saint Germain, represents the Eight-sided Cell of Perfection, and the human virtues of honesty, faith, contrition, humility, justice, mercy, sincerity, and the endurance of persecution. The shape of a photon is the Maltese Cross.

Malton: The second United States Golden City located in the states of Illinois and Indiana. Its qualities are fruition and attainment; its Ray Force is Gold and Ruby; and its Master Teacher is Kuthumi.

Mantle of Consciousness: Ascending to or attaining a new level of conscious awareness that produces tremendous change.

Map of Exchanges: The Ascended Masters' Map of prophesied Earth Changes for Europe and Africa. Its seventeen Golden City Vortices focus on the self-realization of the HU-man through the exchange of heavenly energies on Earth, which usher in the Golden Age.

Master Teacher: A spiritual teacher from a specific lineage of teachers—gurus. The teacher transmits and emits the energy from that collective lineage.

Meissner Field: A magnetic energy field that does not contain polarity. It is produced during a transitory state of superconductivity. Ascended Master teaching associates this type of energy field with HU-man development, Unana, and Christ Consciousness. This energy field is achieved and sustained in the Ascension.

Mental Body: A subtle light body of the Human Aura comprising thoughts.

Mental Purgatory: The purging of conscious and unconscious fears as the HU-man Consciousness expands into the Ninth Energy Body.

Migratory Pattern or Sequence: A Golden City spiritual pilgrimage that travels through a certain progression of Adjutant Points. The progression of each sacred site may vary, dependent on the desired spiritual result for the chela or initiate. Some sequences focus on healing processes; others focus on integration of Golden City Energies, especially certain Golden City Doorways.

Mineral Kingdom: A Divine Kingdom composed of spiritually conscious beings who embody, comprise, and oversee the many Devas and Elementals of minerals, rocks, crystals, and gemstones.

Modulated Ray Force(s): A Ray Force that contains two or more Color Rays.

Monad: From an Ascended Master viewpoint, the Monad is the spark or flame of life of spiritual consciousness and it is also the Awakened Flame that is growing, evolving, and ultimately on the path to Ascension. Because of its presence of self-awareness and purpose, the Monad represents our dynamic will and the individualized presence of the Divine Father. Ultimately, the Monad is the spark of consciousness that is self-determining, spiritually awake, and drives the growth of human consciousness. The Monad is the indivisible, whole, divine life center of an evolving soul that is immortal and contains the momentum within itself to drive consciousness to learn, grow, and perfect itself in its evolutionary journey.

Mother Mary: Ascended Goddess of the Feminine who was originally of the angelic evolution. She is associated with the Green Ray of Healing, Truth, and Science, and the Pink Ray of Love.

Nada or **Lady Master Nada:** The Ascended Goddess of Justice and Peace is associated with Mastery of speech (vibration), communication, interpretation, and the sacred Word. Nada is also known as a divine advocate of Universal Law and she is often symbolized by the scales of blind justice. She is associated with the Yellow Ray of Wisdom and the Ruby and Gold Rays of Ministration, Brotherhood, and Service. Lady Nada is the hierarch of Denasha, a Golden City located in Scotland.

New Shamballa Grid Pilgrimage: Pilgrimage throughout the seventeen major Adjutant Points of the Golden City.

Nine Heavenly Gates Evolutionary Fields: Nine Evolutionary Fields that include the Golden City Star that are served by the Eight Archangels. The Heavenly Gates mirror the Rays of the Esoteric Color Wheel of the Nine Perfections.

Nine Movements of Consciousness: The movement of energy throughout the Golden City resembles a figure eight, and represents perfect balance.

Ninth Energy Body: An energy field that is developed through uniting dual forces, and requires an in-depth purification of thought. In fact, this energy field causes the soul to face and Master those negative, dark, forces that the Spiritual Teachers refer to as a type of *mental purgatory*. This energy body processes extreme fears and transmutes them. The transmutation completely restructures beliefs, and purifies energies held in the lower mental bodies accumulated throughout all lifetimes.

Northern Door: The Black Door of a Golden City.

Northern Door Pilgrimage: Pilgrimage through the Northern Door that prepares the chela for subsequent Pilgrimage in the Southern Door. This Pilgrimage includes migration through four Adjutant Points that follow the Cardinal Lei-line.

Oath of the Right-hand Path: A sacred oath, taken during the Enlightenment Pilgrimage through the Western Door of a Golden City. The oath: "I accept the Sacred Fire within my heart, I AM ONE with the Spiritual Hierarchy, I AM ONE with Freedom Star. So be it!"

Omega Evolutionary Field: One of the final Evolutionary Fields in HU-man Development. This Evolutionary Field is composed of the Desire, Faith, and Stillness Adjutant Points. The shape is an acute isosceles triangle, and its energies focus upon the attainment of Mastery.

Om Manaya Pitaya or **Om Manaaya Patiya**: This Ascended Master statement has several meanings. Two spiritual translations are: "I AM the Light of God" and "I AM the Seer of the Lord." The Sanskrit translation means: "Amen, honored Lord."

ONE: Indivisible, whole, harmonious Unity.

Oneness: A combination of two or more, which creates the whole.

Oneship: A group or group mind that is based on the notion of whole, harmonious Unity.

Orange (Coral) Ray: This Ray Force is a worldly and grounded energetic and is said to give one a timely blessing or boon that quickly improves one's life. It can enhance money matters and status. At its higher expression the Orange Ray expresses the Coral or Peach Ray, associated with Divine Purpose, joy, and infectious optimism and enthusiasm.

Outer Child Point: This Adjutant Point is exactly halfway between the two Gateway Points of each Golden City Doorway. This Adjutant Point is also known as the *Outer Cardinal Point*.

Overlighting or **Overshadowing:** The process whereby an Ascended Master or being of light follows and monitors a student or chela through a specific phase of spiritual development. This may also include influencing and assisting the student or chela through difficulties with spiritual insight and influencing energies.

Pastel Blue Ray: Attributes of this Ray Force are long-lived, immortality, enduring, problem solving, stewardship, precision, scientific, traditional, respectful, practical and artistic, detached, the New Times and the New Children.

Pastel Green Ray: Attributes of this Ray Force are Co-creative, Mastery of Sound, elevated HU-man culture, vision, originality, etiquette, the realized HU-man.

Peace and Tranquility: The Elohim of the Ruby-Gold Ray who oversee the Evolutionary Field of Peace.

Periodic Adjutant Point Ray Force or **Period Ray Force:** The Ray Force(s) influencing a particular Adjutant Point for a twenty-year phase, based on the Cycle of the Elements.

Permanent (Presiding) Ray Force: The dominant Ray Force of a Golden City. The Hierarch of a Golden City also serves the presiding Ray Force.

Photon Belt: A large current of energy, containing billions of square miles of condensed, monoatomic Photons. This instigates spiritual evolution on many planets, including Earth, and liberates humanity to new levels of spiritual understanding, science, and technology.

Photon(s): A packet or parcel of light, with both multi-dimensional and monoatomic qualities. The Photon has the ability to carry multiple, creative sound and light frequencies.

Pilgrimage: A spiritual journey that assists the evolution or Ascension Process of the spiritual student.

Pineal Gland: A human gland that is located behind the brain's third ventricle that is associated with the Third Eye, rising of the kundalini energies, psychic ability, and many forms of spiritual development and growth. Researchers believe the pineal gland's production of pinoline is responsible for various psychic states of consciousness.

Pink Ray: The Pink Ray is the energy of the Divine Mother and associated with the Moon. It is affiliated with these qualities: loving; nurturing; hopeful; heartfelt; compassionate; considerate; communicative; intuitive; friendly; humane; tolerant; adoring. In the I AM America teachings the Pink Ray is served by the Archangel

Chamuel and Archeia Charity; the Elohim of Divine Love Orion and Angelica; and the Ascended Masters Kuan Yin, Mother Mary, Goddess Meru, and Paul the Venetian.

Planetary Council: The Planetary Council of Justice oversees the Earth's spiritual welfare and development. It has intervened during critical phases of humanity's development, and approved the dispensation of the Violet Flame on Earth to transmute karma. It serves alongside the Karmic Board. Apollo, Sanat Kumara, Kuan Yin, Portia, El Morya, Kuthumi, and the Eight Archangels sit on this important ruling body, alongside other venerated Cosmic Beings of Light.

Plasma Field: A highly charged electromagnetic field of energy comprising condensed galactic light. Each atomic photon is a fractal representation of the Golden City structure, calibrating life spans, intelligence, consciousness, and spiritual development to new levels of evolution.

Pleiades: A seven-star cluster that exists in the same Orion Arm of the Milky Way Galaxy near Earth. Also known as the Seven Sisters, the Pleiades is located in the Taurus Constellation. Its seven stars are: Sterope, Merope, Electra, Maia, Taygeta, Celaeno, and Alcyone.

Portia's Evolutionary Field: Portia, the Goddess of Justice, oversees the Fourfold Flame of Power Evolutionary Field. It comprises the Adjutant Points of Abundance, Love, and Illumination.

Power Evolutionary Field: The HU-man Evolutionary Field of Power comprises the Adjutant Points of Harmony, Service, and Clarity.

Prayer Evolutionary Field: This Evolutionary Field is the principle of *Right Samadhi*. It comprises the Adjutant Points of Abundance, Illumination, and the Golden City Star.

Proclamation of Ascension: This is the final step of the Enlightenment Pilgrimage, the student declares:
"I AM a Divine HU-man — a BEing of Light!
I call forth the Victory of the Violet Flame,
To stream throughout my worldly karmas.
The Ascension heals, restores, glorifies,
And expands my Light!
My Light Ascends to both
Fourth and Fifth Dimensions.
I AM the perfected balance of
Divine Mother and Divine Father!

> I AM awakened and realized through
> The Christ Consciousness!
> I proclaim my Ascension
> And eternal Victory!
> So be it!
> Amen."

Prophecy Evolutionary Field: This is the Evolutionary Field of Right Mindfulness. It comprises the Adjutant Points Harmony, Abundance, and the Golden City Star. This Evolutionary Field is also the Southern Door.

Rainbow and Iris: Elohim of the Aquamarine and Gold Rays.

Ray or Ray Force(s): A force containing a purpose, which divides its efforts into two measurable and perceptible powers, light and sound.

Red Door: The Southern Door of a Golden City.

Red Ray: *See Ruby Ray.*

Right-hand Path: Spiritual teaching based on love, trust, choice, unity, cooperation, and the sanctity of life.

Ruby Ray and **Ruby-Gold Ray**: The Ruby Ray is the energy of the Divine Masculine and Spiritual Warrior. It is associated with these qualities: energetic; passionate; devoted; determination; dutiful; dependable; direct; insightful; inventive; technical; skilled; forceful. This Ray Force is astrologically affiliated with the planet Mars and the Archangel Uriel, Lord Sananda, and Master Kuthumi. The Ruby Ray is often paired with the Gold Ray, which symbolizes Divine Father. The Ruby Ray is the evolutionary Ray Force of both the base and solar chakras of the HU-man; and the Gold and Ruby Rays step-down and radiate sublime energies into six Golden Cities.

Saint Germain: Ascended Master of the Seventh Ray, Saint Germain is known for his work with the Violet Flame of Mercy, Transmutation, Alchemy, and Forgiveness. He is the sponsor of the Americas and the I AM America material. Many other teachers and Masters affiliated with the Great White Brotherhood help his endeavors. Saint Germain serves in the Golden City of Wahanee, a Vortex that helps humanity to spiritually apply justice, liberty, and forgiveness.

Salt Bath: A spiritual healing technique that cleanses the human aura. Its formula is two cups of any type of salt, used in the bath water with essential oils such as lavender or other floral scents.

Sananda, Lord: The name used by Master Jesus in his ascended state of consciousness. Sananda means joy and bliss, and his teachings focus on revealing the savior and heavenly kingdom within. Sananda is associated with Christ Consciousness and the Golden City of Shalahah.

Sanat Kumara: Sanat Kumara is a Venusian Ascended Master and the venerated leader of the Ascended Masters, best known as the founder of Shamballa, the first Golden City on Earth. He is also known in the teachings of the Great White Brotherhood as the Lord of the World, and is regarded as a savior and eminent spiritual teacher. Sanat Kumara is the guru of five of the Twelve Jurisdictions: Service, Cooperation, Charity, Desire, and Stillness. These spiritual precepts are based on the principles of Co-creation, and are prophesied to guide human consciousness into the New Times. These five Jurisdictions reiterate the symbolic revelation of Sanat Kumara's fourfold identity as the Cosmic Christ, which assist humanity's evolutionary process into the New Times. As Kartikkeya, the commander of God's Army, Sanat Kumara teaches Service and Cooperation to overcome the lower mind; as Kumar the holy youth, Sanat Kumara imparts Charity to conquer the darkness of disease and poverty; as Skanda, the son of Shiva and the spiritual warrior, Sanat Kumara offers Desire as the hopeful seed of God's transformation; and as Guha, the Jurisdiction Stillness restores the peace of all hearts.

Sanjana: "In Harmony."

Science of Spiritual Wisdom Evolutionary Field: This is the HU-man Evolutionary Field of the Arhat. It comprises the Adjutant Points Clarity, Cooperation, and Charity.

Seamless Garment: The Ascended Masters wear garments without seams. This clothing is not tailored by hand but perfected through the thought and manifestation process.

Serapis Bey: An Ascended Master from Venus who works on the White Ray. He is the great disciplinarian—essential for Ascension; and works closely with all unascended humanity who remain focused for its attainment. He oversees and serves in the Golden City of Klehma, to promote cooperation and the attainment of Ascension.

Seventh House Evolutionary Field: This Evolutionary Field is associated with marriage and partnership, and is also known as Archangel's Uriel's Heavenly Gate.

Shalahah, Golden City of: The fourth United States Golden City located primarily in the states of Montana and Idaho. Its qualities are abundance, prosperity, and healing; its Ray Force is Green; and its Master Teacher is Sananda.

Shamballa: Venusian volunteers arrived 900 years before their leader Sanat Kumara, and built the Earth's first Golden City. Known as the City of White, located in the present-day Gobi Desert, its purpose was to hold conscious light for the Earth and to sustain her evolutionary place in the solar system.

Shamballa Tradition: Over four weeks (twenty-eight days), esoteric followers, including Ascended Masters, honor the Celebration of the Four Elements during the Shamballa festivities. It begins December 17 — accompanied by lighting of the Eternal Flame Candle, or the Fireless Light — on the altar of the main temple. This etheric celebration is divided into the following four parts:

Week One: December 18 to December 24. Element: Earth. The celebration and thanksgiving offered to Mother Earth. Ceremonies and rituals for Earth Healing are held at Shamballa during this time. Bowls of salt, which represent earth united with spirit, are placed on all the altars in the Temples of Shamballa.

Week Two: December 25 to December 31. Element: Air. Celebrations of gratitude and thanksgiving to the World Teachers and the messengers of the Great White Brotherhood who have selflessly served humanity are held this week. Krishna, Jesus Christ, Buddha, and other well-known avatars and saviors are also lauded. Doves of Peace are symbolically released this week.

Week Three: January 1 to January 7. Element: Water. A thanksgiving for our Soul Families is held during this week. This phase of Shamballa Celebration is about revering love and friendship, and performing Cup Ceremonies. A Cup Ceremony is a water ceremony that celebrates the union of Mother Earth and Soul Families. A cup of water is passed and infused with the prayers of the devoted. The prayer-charged water is then poured on the Earth.

Week Four: January 8 to January 14. Element: Fire. This week is a celebration of Spiritual Fire. This time is set aside for personal purification, intentions, reflection, and meditation for the upcoming year. This is an important period for the Brotherhoods and Sisterhoods of Light to review plans for the following 365 days. Candles for each of the Seven Rays, representing the seven Hermetic Laws, are lit this week.

The Sealing of Divinity: January 15 and 16. Celebrations of Unity — Unana — and the ONE.

The Closing of Shamballa. January 17: the light of the Eternal Flame returns to Venus.

Southern Door: The Red Door of a Golden City.

Spiritual Hierarchy: A fellowship of Ascended Masters and their disciples. This group helps humanity function through the mental plane with meditation, decrees, and prayer. The term Spiritual Hierarchy often refers to the Great White Brotherhood and Sisterhood. However, the term also connotes the spiritual-social structure for the organization, its members, and the various states of member evolution. The hierarchy includes the different offices and activities that serve the Cosmic, Solar, Planetary, and Creative Hierarchies.

Spiritual Liberation: The Ascension Process is also known as moksha in Hindu tradition.

Spiritual Migration: *See Migratory Pattern.*

Spring Green Ray: A new modulated Ray Force whose qualities are hope, renewel, eternal life, perceptive, insightful, mature, subtle, calm, evolutionary, peaceful, self-realization, Divine Earth.

Star: The apex, or center of each Golden City.

Star Retreats: Four retreats that surround the Star of a Golden City at the four cardinal directions.

Step-down Transformer: The processes instigated through the Cellular Awakening rapidly advance human light bodies. Synchronized with an Ascended Master's will, the awakened cells of light and love evolve the skills of a Step-down Transformer to efficiently transmit and distribute currents of Ascended Master energy—referred to as an Ascended Master Current (A.M. Current). This metaphysical form of intentional inductive coupling creates an ethereal power grid that can be used for all types of healing.

Subjective Energy Body: This type of energy is similar to a thought-form, which causes behavioral changes when triggered. They are created through intense emotions, addictive behaviors, and the use of addictive substances, and often contain elements of lower consciousness.

Super senses: Primarily the supernormal powers of telepathy, clairvoyance, and clairaudience, as they naturally unfold through the Law of Love and Unity Consciousness. These are the senses of the developed HU-man.

Temple of Unity: A major temple that exists at the fifth dimensional Golden City of Shamballa.

Temples of Perfection, or Temple Points: *See Heavenly Temples of Perfection.*

Tenth Energy Body: The final level of three protective HU-man light bodies, which is formed through the purification of desires, and is known as the *Diamond Mind*. Because this energy body gathers thought as light, it is a substantive and sizeable light body. The Spiritual Teachers often refer to the three protective HUman energy bodies as the *Triple Gems,* and together they are strong enough to pierce human illusion.

Third Dimension: Thought, feeling, and action.

Third Eye: The inner eye, referring to the ajna (brow) chakra.

Thirteen Evolutionary Pyramids: Thirteen phases of spiritual growth and evolution as the soul proceeds through the Eight-sided Cell of Perfection with the Ascension Process.

Three Standards: A spiritual practice that applies the Violet Flame, the Tube of Light, and the Blue Flame of Protection.

Time Compaction: An anomaly produced as we enter into the prophesied Time of Change. Our perception of time compresses; time seems to speed by. The unfolding of events accelerates, and situations are jammed into a short period of time. This experience of time will become more prevalent as we get closer to the period of cataclysmic Earth Changes.

Timeline: Numerous threads of possible events exist within this measurement of time.

Time of Change: The period of time currently underway. Tremendous changes in our society, cultures, and politics in tandem with individual and collective Spiritual Awakenings and transformations will abound. These events occur simultaneously with the possibilities of massive global warming, climactic changes, and seismic and volcanic activity — Earth Changes. The Time of Change guides the Earth to a new time, the Golden Age.

Transportation Age or Age of Transportation: A prophesied epoch on Earth humanity will experience once we leave the current Information Age (late eighties through the twenty-first century). The Transportation Age will see humanity's consciousness evolve into Mastery beyond the human maxims of time and space. During this period, which is prophesied to run concurrently with several periods of the Golden Age — the Age of Cooperation and the Age of Peace — humanity will begin interstellar travel, alongside leaps in evolutionary growth resulting in telepathic communication, spiritual technologies, and bi-location.

Treta Yuga: The Age of Silver, when Earth receives fifty to seventy-five percent galactic light from the Great Central Sun.

Trinomial Mathematics: Containing three or more components in a mathematical formula.

True Memory: Memory, as defined by Ascended Master teachings, is not seen as a function of the brain, or the soul's recall of past events. Instead, True Memory is achieved through cultivating our perceptions and adjusting our individual perspective of a situation to the multiple juxtapositions of opinion and experience. This depth of understanding gives clarity and illumination to every experience. Our skill and Mastery through True Memory moves our consciousness beyond common experiences to individualized experiences whose perceptive power hones honesty and accountability. The innate truth obtained from many experiences through the interplay of multiple roles creates True Memory, and opens the detached and unconditional Law of Love to the chela.

True North: Use of the geographic North Pole to determine direction.

Tube of Light: Light surges from the tributaries of the Human Energy System: Chakras, meridians, and nadis—to create a large pillar of light. Decrees, prayers, and meditation with the Tube of Light increase its force and ability to protect the individual's spiritual growth and evolution.

Twelfth Energy Body: The energy body of Ascension, cultivated in the Great Silence. Its processes of development are held in mystery, as it is a diverse experience for every spiritual Master on the path of liberation. Once the Twelfth Energy Body is obtained, the shadow presence of duality dissolves, and the Master steps into the vibration and energy of an Ascended Master, forever freed from the need to reincarnate into a physical body upon the Earth.

Twelve Jurisdictions: Twelve laws (virtues) for the New Times that guide consciousness to Co-create the Golden Age. They are: Harmony, Abundance, Clarity, Love, Service, Illumination, Cooperation, Charity, Desire, Faith, Stillness, and Creation/Creativity.

Two Timelines: Two probable scenarios depicted in the I AM America Map. One is based on catastrophic Earth Changes, depopulation, and a physical renewal of Earth. The second is based on the rapid spiritual evolution of humanity, and the self-sustaining light of the Evolutionary Biome forever transforms the Earth.

Umbilicus Connection: The physical and multi-dimensional connection between the DAHL-DERN Universe. This connection emits and controls certain energetics throughout both universes.

Unana: Unity consciousness.

Unfed Flame: The Three-Fold Flame of Divinity that exists in the heart and becomes larger as it evolves. The three flames represent: Love (Pink), Wisdom (Yellow), and Power (Blue).

Vertical Power Current: The Ascended Masters often refer to the Vertical Power Current as the Golden Thread Axis or the Vibral-Core. A portion of this major energy current links the soul to the higher mind and is known as the Hindu Antahkarana. According to the I AM America teachings, the Vertical Power Current connects to our solar Sun and its resident deities Helios and Vesta. Its energies travel to the I AM Presence and stream from the Presence through the Crown Chakra, and flow through the physical spine of the individual (Kundalini), and the current grounds into the center of Earth's core — itself considered a latent, fiery Sun. In Hinduism, the portion of the Antahkarana that enters the physical planes and the Earth's core is known as the Sutratma, or Silver Cord. [See Golden Thread Axis]

Violet Flame: The Violet Flame is the practice of balancing karmas of the past through Transmutation, Forgiveness, and Mercy. The result is an opening of the Spiritual Heart and the development of bhakti—unconditional love and compassion. It came into existence when the Lords of Venus first transmitted the Violet Flame, also known as Violet Fire, at the end of Lemuria to clear the Earth's etheric and psychic realms, and the lower physical atmosphere of negative forces and energies. This paved the way for the Atlanteans, who used it during religious ceremonies and as a visible marker of temples. The Violet Flame also induces Alchemy. Violet light emits the shortest wavelength and the highest frequency in the spectrum, so it induces a point of transition to the next octave of light.

Violet Flame Angels: Legions of Violet Flame Angels are claimed to carry the energies of the transmuting Violet Flame whenever they are called upon. The Angels of the Violet Flame protect the flame in its purity and dispense its transforming vibration.

Vista and Virginia: The Elohim of Truth who serve the Green Ray.

Wahanee: The third United States Golden City located primarily in the states of South Carolina and Georgia. Its qualities are justice, liberty, and freedom; its Ray Force is Violet; and its Master Teacher is Saint Germain.

Western Door: The Yellow Door of a Golden City.

Western Door Pilgrimage: A series of Migrations through the Western Door of a Golden City that awaken the Divine Masculine. This activates the external Evolutionary Biome, creating protection to self and others, alongside developing access to the Seamless Garment, Akashic Knowledge, and telepathic rapport with the Golden City Field of Protection. This Pilgrimage is performed after the Eastern Door Pilgrimage for the Divine Feminine.

White Ray: The Ray of the Divine Feminine is primarily associated with the planet Venus. It is affiliated with beauty, balance, purity, and cooperation. In the I AM America teachings the White Ray is served by the Archangel Gabriel and Archeia Hope; the Elohim Astrea and Claire; and the Ascended Masters Serapis Bey, Paul the Devoted, Reya, the Lady Masters Venus and Se Ray, and the Group of Twelve.

Yellow Door: The Western Door of a Golden City.

Yellow Ray: The Ray of the Divine Wisdom is primarily associated with the planet Jupiter and is also known as the Divine Guru. It is affiliated with expansion, optimism, joy, and spiritual enlightenment. In the I AM America teachings the Yellow Ray is served by the Archangel Jophiel and Archeia Christine; the Elohim of Illumination Cassiopeia and Lumina; and the Ascended Masters Lady Nada, Peter the Everlasting, Confucius, Lanto, Laura, Minerva, and Mighty Victory.

Index

A

Aboundness
  Evolutionary Field 255
Abundance Point 123, 124, 127
  definition 353
Activity of the Fourfold Flame 338
addictions
  Archangel Jophiel 251
Adept 146, 170, 199, 287, 339
  and the Tenth Pyramid 287
  definition 353
Adjutant Point Hierarch(s) 30, 32
  Events of 9-11 85
Adjutant Point(s) 57, 174, 180, 185, 272, 274, 275, 276
  3088 achieve their Ascensions 120
  Adjutant Points with the Annual Ray Forces for 2021-2025 276
  and migratory pathways 349
  Ascension 26
  Calculated Level 159
  Cardinal 359
  Cardinal lei-line 206
  Cardinal Point perimeters 205
  Cardinal Points 206
  Convergence 360
  Cup Ceremony 321
  darkness and light 28
  definition 353
  Developed Energy System 159
  Elemental Kingdom 59
  fractal energy 84
  Gateway 367
  Golden City Gateway 204
  Group Mind 185
  Healing Pilgrimage 191
  Heavenly Points 372
  HU-man Ability 160
  Intuitive-psychic Level 159
  "More energy is flooded into the Earth." 123
  Movemnt as Photon 351
  Music of the Spheres 257
  reorganize DNA 98
  sensing the flux of a Golden City 159
  sensitivity 28
  Sergeants and Lieutenants at Arms 85
  Seventeen Primary Adjutant Points 215
  Spiritual Hierarchy, diagram 339
  Step-down Transformer 111
  Thirty-three Points 215
  Venusians and Pleiadeans 57
  working remotely 137
Age of Cooperation 181
  definition 353
Age of Quarrel 31
Age of Transportation
  definition 385
ages
  twenty-eight to thirty-two
    rise of the spiritual being 347
agreement
  Right-hand Path 46
Agreement Formation 305
  definition 353
Ahura Mazda 163
Akashic Records 41
  definition 353
Akhenaton 124, 300, 301, 302
  Harmony Point, Gobean 124
Alchemical Battles of Ancient Shamans and Spiritual Masters 287
Alpha 201, 202
  Evolutionary Field 220
America
  "As America is free, so is the rest of the world." 64
  "Holds the light for the world." 28
  I AM Race 28
Ameru 287
Anaya
  definition 354
  Elder of Light 53
  Pleiadean teacher 51
Ancestral Planet 80, 92, 99
  behind our Sun 80
  definition 354
Ancient of Days 41, 163
Angelic Kingdom 311
Angel of Miracles
  Zadkiel 248
Angel of Music
  Raphael 247

anger
  transmutation of
    Evolutionary Field 258
animal products 75, 113
Annual Influence of Ray Forces 265
Annual Movement of the Modulated Rays through the Golden City Doorways from 2021-2041 282
Annual Movement of the Rays
  definition 354
Annual Movement of the Rays through the Golden City Doorways from 2021-2041 281
Annual Ray Force
  definition 354
  Golden City 275
Annunciation
  and the Twelfth Evolution Point 202
Anointing of Light
  definition 354
  Enlightenment Pilgrimage 335
Apollo 171
Aquamarine Ray vii, 27, 39, 54, 61, 82, 124, 133, 173, 277, 279, 280, 282, 284, 338
  Anaya 54
  Cup Ceremony 61
  definition 354
Archangel Chamuel
  Evolutionary Field 249
  Heavenly Gate Evolutionary Field 223
Archangel Chrystiel
  Evolutionary Field 252
  Heavenly Gate Evolutionary Field 223
Archangel Cresta 124
Archangel Crystiel
  and the Seventeen Initiations of the Map of Exchanges 271
Archangel Gabriel
  Evolutionary Field 250
  Heavenly Gate Evolutionary Field 223
Archangel Jophiel
  Evolutionary Field 251
  Heavenly Gate Evolutionary Field 223
Archangel Michael 113, 149, 188, 311
  and the binding of entities 31
  and the Seventeen Initiations of the Map of Exchanges 271
  bondage of dark forces 31
  Heavenly Gate Evolutionary Field 223
  in the Map Room 129
Archangel Michael's Blue Flame
  appendix and instruction 113
Archangel Raphael
  Heavenly Gate Evolutionary Field 222
Archangels 288, 336, 340
  Earth's 336
  Star Retreats 214
Archangel Uriel
  Evolutionary Field 250
  Heavenly Gate Evolutionary Field 223
Archangel Zadkiel 68, 139
  Heavenly Gate Evolutionary Field 223
Arctura and Diana 224
  definition 355
  Evolutionary Field 259
Arhat 170, 199, 201, 332, 339, 356
  and the circumvention of the Tenth Pyramid to achieve Ascension 287
  Elemental Kingdom 45
Ascended Master(s)
  appearance of the Masters 88
  aura 145
  builds a new etheric body 342
  definition 356
  Founders of the Golden Age on Earth 148
  I AM That I AM 201
  Sacred Geometry 218
Ascension and Ascension Process 145, 180, 183, 201, 246, 271, 289, 348
  Advanced Light Fields of Ascension 145
  and sound 95
  Archangel Gabriel Evolutionary Field 251
  Ascension Proclamation Enlightenment Pilgrimage 334
  calibration through light 25
  Ceremonial Worship and the Group Mind 156
  Changes within the Human Aura 147
  definition 356
  Divine DNA 55
  Enlightenment 156
  Evolutionary Biome 181
  evolution of light bodies 26
  Field of the Mystic 233
  Golden City 158

    Liberation from the body 156
    Neutral Point 156
    over 10,000 achieved 83
    Rapture 156
    Sacred Fire 158
    Serapis Bey's Evolutionary Field 243
    Spiritual Liberation 156
    the freed chela 85
    White Fire Spiral of Ascension 50
Aspirant 170, 339
    Awakened 201
    definition 356
Assemblage Points 197
Assumption
    and the Eleventh Evolution Point 201
Astral Body 339, 342, 343
    definition 356
    Golden Thread Axis 43
Astral Plane 342
Asuramaya
    Lemurian Manu 375
Atchison, Kansas
    Heart of the Dove 327
Aten 301
    Great Hymn to Aten 302
Atlantis 150, 287, 297, 314, 341
    advanced culture 287
    definition 357
    early civilizations 357
Aurora Borealis
    example of a Plasma Field 154
    plasma 26
Australia
    Land of Punt 375
Avatar Babaji 181
Awakening 27
Awakening Prayer 88, 104, 287, 414
    and the Right-hand Path 287
    Cup Ceremony 322
    definition 357

B

Babajeran 317, 329
    Babaji 64
    Cycle of Ray Forces 265
    definition 358

Babaji 63, 327
    definition 358
    Heart of the Dove 327
Bacon, Sir Francis 313
    portrait by John Vanderbank, 1731 314
Bailey, Alice 163
Ballard, Edna and Guy 88, 259
Beauty of Nature Evolutionary Field 221, 237
    definition 358
Beloved Susan 91, 104, 120
Belt of Golden Light
    definition 368
Besant, Annie 166
    and the Great Plan 239
Bhumi puja 329
Bill of Rights 47
Billy Meier 345
bi-location 146
    Eleventh Energy Body 296
binding of demons and evil spirits 250
Black Door
    definition 358
    Golden City 175
    Lineage of Gurus 232
    of a Golden City 130
Black Magic
    devolutionary path 288
Blake, William 169
    The Ancient of Days 169
    When the Morning Stars Sang Together 337
Blavatsky, Helena 166, 299
Blessing the Americas 193
Blue Door
    definition 358
    Golden City 176
    of a Golden City 130
Blue Flame Angels
    definition 358
    Evolutionary Field 248
Blue Flame of Protection 113, 188
    definition 358
    invoking the Blue Flame for protection 113
Blue Ray 188, 272, 275, 283, 297
    El Morya 299
    Evolutionary Field 249

Bodhisattva of Compassion 339
  Enlightenment Pilgrimage 332
bondage
  of the dark forces 31
Book of Truths 242
Booth, Annice 252, 260
breath and breathing technique 115
  and development of the Eighth Light Body 145
  definition 358
  Evolutionary Field of Prophecy 236
Bronze Age 179
Buddha 145, 168, 173, 338, 341
  definition 358
  Enlightenment Pilgrimage 332
  Mantle of the Buddha 70
  Nine qualities 332
  Right Livelihood 237
Buddha Body 145
Buddha's Noble Eightfold Path
  Evolutionary Fields 221
Buddhi
  Causal Plane 342
Buddhism 165, 287, 339
Bull of Truth
  Cycle of the Yugas 179

C

Cardall, Elaine 83
Cardinal Adjutant Point
  definition 359
Cardinal Lei-line
  definition 359
Castaneda, Carlos
  Assemblage Points 197
Catholic Stations of the Cross-Via Dolorosa 197
Causal Body 339, 342
  definition 359
Cellular Awakening 33, 70, 359, 414
  as the Law of Love 198
  definition 359
Center of Fire 327
Ceremony
  best location 239
  Cup Ceremony 29, 383
  Evolutionary Field 221, 238

chakra(s) and Chakra System 304
  definition 359
  layers 304
  movement 304
  Photon movement 351
  sub-vortices 304
Chamber of the Heart 197
Chamuel, Archangel 150, 223, 249, 255, 263, 269, 270, 307
  definition 355
chela 170, 201, 339
  definition 359
chemtrails 126
choice
  Choice Reflects Our True Motivations 305
  definition 359
  Freedom of Choice 242
  "Is the fulcrum of evolution." 63
  leaving for the higher planes of light 139
Christian 163, 287
Christ or Christ Consciousness 167, 168, 301, 302, 311, 318, 338
  and the Astral Plane 342
  and the Inner Earth 96
  Buddha 71
  consciousness
    Quetzalcoatl 302
  Cosmic 167
  definition 359
  Golden Cities 83
  Heart of the Dove 327
  perfection
    Evolutionary Field 249
  Right Conduct 234
  Spiritual Hierarchy, diagram 338
  trinomial energies 123
Christ-self 197, 339
  the awakened human 343
Chrystiel, Archangel 223, 252
  definition 355
City of the Kumaras 167
City of White 161
  definition 359
Classical Arts
  Spring Green Ray 267
Classical Calculation of the Yugas
  illustration 179

Classical Chinese Feng Shui 180
Co-creation 49
   and the Eighth Light Body 145
   definition 359
   Evolutionary Field 255
Collective Consciousness 48, 112, 185, 186, 316, 342
   a part of Mass Consciousness 342
   definition 360
   Evolutionary Field of Prophecy 236
   timeline shift 56
   water 57
color
   wavelength 101
Color Wheel
   Eight-sided Cell of Perfection 254
Communication (Information) Portal 99, 107, 108
   definition 360
conscience 198
   definition 360
Conscience and Consciousness
   Evolutionary Field 220
Conscious Human 170, 201
consciousness
   definition 360
   mass 342
   Web of Consciousness 115
Convergence Adjutant Point(s) 273
   definition 360
Cooperation Point 332
   definition 360
   Enlightenment Pilgrimage 69
Coral or Peach Ray 123, 266, 378
Cosmic Christ 234, 382
Cosmic Hierarchy 336
Cosmic I AM Presence 336
Creative Hierarchy 339
   the Human Hierarchy 342
Crown Chakra 164, 188, 287
   definition 360
crystals
   consciousness 309
Cupbearer 321
Cup Ceremony 29, 86, 321, 332, 383
   circle of salt 59
   Cooperation Point 70
   definition 360
   Four Directions 322
   Gold and Aquamarine Ray 61
   origins 57
   Prayers and Decrees 322
   Purification Process 321
   Western Door Retreat 72
Cycle of the Elements
   Chinese Calendar 265
   definition 360
Cyclopea and Virginia 257

D

DAHL Universe 30, 36, 40, 47, 50, 55, 56, 57, 59, 60, 65, 82, 92, 94, 97, 99, 101, 102, 114, 265, 340, 345
   appendix 345
dark force(s)
   attacks on freedoms 47
   bound by Archangel Michael 31
death
   dissolved by fire 329
Decree(s)
   Awaken the HU-man 135
   Cooperation Point 69
   Declare Your Freedom 69
   definition 361
   Enlightenment Pilgrimage 332
   Evolutionary Field 221, 240
   Gold Ball of Light 138
   Golden Age 82
   Gold Ray of Cooperation 332
   Healing of the Nations 191, 194
   Moving Into the HU-man 195
   Pillar of Light 140
   Right-hand Path 332
   Right Speech Evolutionary Field 240
   Step-down Transformer 125
   to empower the Ninth Light Body 146
DERN Universe 345
   definition 361
Desiree, or Lady Desiree
   Evolutionary Field 222
devachan 348
Deva(s) and Deva Kingdom 212
   definition 361
   Fourth Dimension 86
Diamond Mind 146, 384
   definition 361

diet 34, 75
  and development of the Eighth Light Body 145
  cleansing impurities 74
  DNA frequencies 34
  during stressful times 34, 75
discipline 175, 288
Divine Blueprint 145
  retrieval 200
Divine Complement 79
  definition 361
Divine DNA
  activation 51
  Eight-sided Cell of Perfection 83
  White Ray 50
Divine Father
  Gold Ray 37
Divine Intercession
  Evolutionary Field 248
Divine Languages 97
Divine Love
  Evolutionary Field 249
Divine Mother 151
Divine Will 188, 317
  Blue Flame 358
Divine Wisdom
  Evolutionary Field 251
DNA 244, 318
  and diet 34
  Divine DNA 44
  Divine DNA and the White Ray 50
  Pleiadean and Elemental Kingdom 44
dolphins 98
Doorway of a Golden City
  and CMYK (colors) 153
  definition 361
Dormition
  and the Ascension Process 201
doubt
  and lower energies 58
duality 145, 147, 386
Dvapara Yuga 179

E

Earth
  ancient geology 124
  becomes Freedom Star 29
  Bhurloka 76
  destiny as Freedom Star 65
  Gold Ray 37
  honey-combed Earth 25
  Inner Sun 47
  passing through Plasma Field 133
  Planetary Council 119, 380
Earth Changes 161, 165, 311, 317
Eastern Door 176
  definition 361
  HU-man Psychology 234
  Pilgrimage 85
Ecological Alchemy
  and the Seventeen Initiations of the Greening Map 269
Egypt 301, 302, 311
Egyptians, Ancient
  presence in the Grand Canyon 301
Eighth Cycle of Earth 265
Eighth Energy Body 70, 110, 188
  definition 362
  First Phase 291
  Second Phase 291
Eight Principles of the Right-hand Path 338
  definition 362
  Evolutionary Fields 232
Eight-sided Cell of Perfection 174, 289, 339, 342
  and the HUE 95
  and the Thirteen Evolutionary Pyramids 202
  and the Will Chakras 303
  Color Wheel 254
  connection to Evolutionary Field 249
  defined 197
  definition 362
  diagram 196
  Divine DNA 83
  Golden City 39
  Nine Movements of Consciousness 253
  Twelve Evolution Points 197

Einstein, Albert
  Photon movement 351
Electric Cycle 182
Elementals or Elemental Kingdom 44, 45, 58, 59, 60, 199, 212, 256, 287, 288, 317
  definition 362
  "One does not live by bread alone..." 287
  Spring Green Ray 266
Eleventh Energy Body 110, 146
  definition 362
  Multi-dimensional Experience 296
elixir
  Energy Technique 34, 75
El Morya 85, 149, 167, 307
  Cup Blessing 122
  definition 362
  Evolutionary Field 222
  Golden City of Gobean 42
  Pillar One Evolutionary Field 241
  Portrait 298
Elohim 170, 185, 189, 212, 288, 336, 340, 342
  Convergence Ashram Point 212
  Elemental Kingdom 45
  Evolutionary Fields 223, 256
  of Earth 336
Elohim Evolutionary Fields 338
  definition 363
Elohim of Freedom Evolutionary Field 224
  definition 363
Elohim of Peace
  Evolutionary Field 224
Elohim of Peace Evolutionary Field
  definition 363
Elohim of Truth Evolutionary Field 224
  definition 363
Elohim of Unity Evolutionary Field 224
  definition 363
Elohim Rainbow and Iris
  Evolutionary Field 260
elves 44
Energy Bodies 145, 146
  development of the new energy bodies 110

Energy-for-energy
  definition 363
  Golden Cities 107
Energy-for-energy Pilgrimage 122, 127
  God Obedience 122
Enlightenment Pilgrimage 331
  definition 364
  overlighting by the Masters 68
  Phase One 330
  Phase Two 330
  "Restores the Will." 85
Enlightenment Process
  Cells and the Photon 70
Enoch 199
essential oils 329
  vibrational frequency 59
Evolutionary Biome 27, 32, 35, 36, 51, 56, 57, 58, 67, 68, 70, 74, 86, 92, 95, 96, 111, 114, 128, 132, 136, 146, 160, 180, 181, 197, 198, 199, 202, 203, 224, 229, 236, 237, 238, 262, 265, 289, 296, 317, 319, 321, 323
  and the Golden Cities 180
  definition 364
  Freedom Star 366
  Unfed Flame 289
Evolutionary Field(s) 217, 338
  Activity of the Fourfold Flame 222
  Archangel Chamuel 249
  Archangel Chrystiel 252
  Archangel Gabriel 250
  Archangel Jophiel 251
  Archangel Michael 248
  Archangel Raphael 247
  Archangel Uriel 250
  Archangel Zadkiel 248
  definition 364
  Eight Principles of the Right-hand Path 221
  Elohim 223
  Golden Triangle 216
  Human to HU-man 220
  Nine Heavenly Gates 222, 247
  Nine Movements of Consciousness 252
  The Four Pillars 221
  Triangles of the Evolutionary Fields 218

Evolutionary Fields of the Elohim 256
  Elohim of Freedom: The Freedom Flame 259
  Elohim of Peace: Cosmic Christ Consciousness 258
  Elohim of Truth: God Vision 257
  Elohim of Unity: Heaven and Earth Unite 260
Evolutionary Pyramid(s) 202
  Conscience and Consciousness 227
  definition 364
  Love, Wisdom, and Power 227
  Mastery 230
  Spiritual Awakening 228
  Spiritual Discipline 228
  Spiritual Wisdom 229
  Strengthen the Soul 230
  Threefold Co-creator 231
  Twelve Jurisdictions 203
  Vision and Compassion 229
Evolution or Evolutionary Point(s)
  definition 364
  Overlaid the Golden City 226
  Twelve Jurisdictions 203
Eye of Horus 198
Eye of Providence
  and the Tenth Evolution Point 200

F

Feng Shui
  Arhat 45
  shape and elements 217
fiat 240
Field of Awakening 145
  definition 364
Fifth Dimension 146, 162, 287
  definition 364
  Master Teachers 86
Fire Ceremony 71, 329
  and the Twilight Breath 329
  definition 365
Fire Triplicity 93
  and arcing of Ray Forces 155
  definition 365
Flame of Consciousness 339
Flame of Love
  Evolutionary Field 249
Flame of Peace
  Evolutionary Field 250
Fleur-de-lis
  iconography of the Ascension and the Unfed Flame 201
form languages 97
Fortune, Dion 237
  Group Mind 185
  White and Black Magic 288
Fouquet, Jean
  Building of the Temple of Jerusalem 172
Four Directions
  Cup Ceremony 322
Four Doorways of a Golden City 175
Fourfold Flame
  definition 365
Fourfold Flame Evolutionary Field(s)
  definition 365
  Evolutionary Fields 244
  Golden City Star
    Lady Luxor 246
  Northeast Region
    Lady Nada 245
  Northwest Region
    Lady Miriam 246
  Southeast Region
    Portia, Goddess of Justice 245
  Southwest Region
    Lady Desiree 244
Fourfold Flame of Desire Evolutionary Field
  definition 365
Fourfold Flame of Power Evolutionary Field
  definition 365
Fourfold Flame of Wisdom Evolutionary Field
  definition 365
Four Kumaras 166, 171, 172
Four Pillars
  Field of the Mystic 233
Fourth Dimension 212
  definition 366
  Evolutionary Biome 57
  Master Teachers 85
  Shaman and Sorcerer 45
frankincense
  anointing oil 59

Frawley, Dr. David 183
freed chela 85
freedom
 decree 69
Freedom Flame Evolutionary Field 259
 definition 366
Freedom Star or Freedom Star Map 80, 162
 definition 366
 Earth's destiny 65
 Evolutionary Biome 181
 Violet Sun 29
Freedom to choose
 the Third Pillar 233
Fu Hsi
 archetype of the Eighth Evolution Point 199

G

Gabriel, Archangel 94, 101, 151, 201, 202, 223, 250, 251, 253, 254, 264, 269, 270
 definition 355
Galactic Center 49, 55, 56, 57, 60, 65, 92, 93, 94, 115, 132, 133, 155, 166, 179, 181, 195, 265, 271, 327, 339
Galactic Council 339
Galactic Light
 definition 366
Galactic Web 39, 43, 132, 143, 160, 219, 271
Garden of Eden 163
Garver, Will L.
 "Brother of the Third Degree" 287
Gateway Adjutant Point(s) 205
 definition 367
genetics
 Elemental Kingdom 44
Geometric Language 217
 definition 367
gnomes 58
Gobean, Golden City of 275
 definition 367
 geology 144
 Temple of the Blue Ray 42
Gobi Desert 162
Gobi, Golden City of 161
 definition 367

Goddess Ti of the Light 123
 definition 367
God-Flame(s)
 the Cosmic I AM 341
Godhead of Perfection
 Evolutionary Field 253
Godhead of Perfection Evolutionary Field
 definition 367
God Obedience
 Archangel Michael 248
God Strength Evolutionary Field 249
 definition 367
Golden Age 162, 179, 180, 181, 182, 183, 184, 213, 273, 317, 338, 345
 "A full force Krita Yuga." 114
 definition 367
 Evolutionary Field 252
 founders 148
Golden Age of Kali Yuga 93, 179, 180, 181, 183, 184
 Brahmavaivarta Purana 183
 definition 368
Golden Ball of Light
 decree 138
 definition 368
 healing technique 138
 meditation 125
Golden (Belt) Band of Light 81
 definition 368
Golden Cities of the Inner Earth 67
Golden Cities of the Pleiades 56
Golden City (Cities) 32, 36, 174, 176, 213
 capacitors of light 133
 Convergence Ashram 210
 Divine Intervention 111
 Eight Golden City Gateway Ashrams 174
 elevation 154
 Five Golden City Star Retreats 210
 Four doorways 175
 functuation 103
 Gateway perimeters 205
 Golden Cities of the Pleiades 56
 Golden City Cardinal Ashrams 209
 Golden City Gateway Ashrams 209
 Golden City Temples of Perfection 210
 Heavenly Ashrams 209
 John's vision 208

living, plasmic light 27
Lord of the Golden Cities, Saint Germain 148
Magnetic North 102
mantras 92
monatomic 134
Movement of the Photon 351
organization 251
overseen by Jesus the Christ 338
permanent Ray Force 275
Photon of Light 60
Presiding Ray Force 265
Ray Force
  calculate overall strength 266
size and dimension 143
Spiritual Ashrams 208
True North 102
United States Golden Cities 142
Vibral Core Axis 92
White Ray 37
White Ray steps-down 65
Golden City Doorway(s)
  Annual influence of the Rays 275
  Chakra movement of Photon 351
  Movement of the Rays 281
  Ray Forces 30
Golden City Hierarch(s)
  definition 368
  Divine Complements 79
Golden City Network 345
  definition 368
Golden City of Afrom
  Beloved Elaine 83
Golden City of Gobi
  Shamballa Grid 112
Golden City Star Retreats 208
Golden City Star(s) 210
  diagram 214
  Evolutionary Field 220, 243
  meditation during Enlightenment Pilgrimage 67
  Photon 351
Golden City Stone Technique
  Appendix K 136
Golden City Temples of Perfection 210

Golden City Vortex or Vortices 161
  electricity 131
  example in nature 352
  gateway 205
  magnetism 131
Golden Disk of the Sun
  Ancient Lemuria 375
Golden Flame
  definition 369
Gold(en) Ray 82, 119, 133, 173, 189, 284, 333, 338
  Annual Influence of Ray Forces 265
  Cup Ceremony 61
  definition 369
  for acceptance and tolerance 94
  Plasma Field 37
Golden Ray Mantra 49
  definition 369
Golden Thread Axis 131, 304
  Astral Body 43
  definition 370
Golden Triangle 216
Great Activation 38, 82
  definition 370
Great Awakening 81, 135, 184, 317
  definition 370
Great Central Sun 49, 155, 161, 179, 336, 339
  definition 370
Great Plan, the 238
Great White Brotherhood and Sisterhood 29, 146, 162, 163, 166, 167, 188, 315, 336, 341, 383
  definition 370
  entrance through the Western Door Enlightenment Pilgrimage 73
  initiation 74
    Enlightenment Pilgrimage 335
  "requires no tests except those which are mental and moral in nature..." 288
Greening Map
  Seventeen Initiations 268
    Archangels Chamuel, Jophiel, Raphael, Gabriel and Uriel 270
  Seventeen Initiations table 269
  sponsor Kuan Yin 148

Green Ray 189, 275, 283
  definition 371
  Evolutionary Field 247, 257
  trend 282
Group Mind 31, 32, 40, 41, 48, 50, 53, 56, 60, 69, 79, 112, 138, 156, 158, 185, 186, 189, 246, 253, 254, 291, 317, 321, 332, 342
  a part of Mass Consciousness 342
  definition 371
  Gold(en) Ball 138
  Violet Flame 40
Group Soul
  Dion Fortune 186
Guardian Angel 339
Guru-chela relationship 198
Guy Ballard
  the refreshing drink 88

H

HAARP 126
Hall, Marie Bauer 314
harmony
  spiritual teachings 308
Harmony Point
  definition 371
  Gobean, Akhenaton 124
Hawkins, Dr. David 32, 36
Healing of the Nations
  decrees 191
  Evolutionary Field of Prophecy 236
Healing of the Nations Spiritual Pilgrimage
  definition 371
Heart Chakra 245
  and the Eighth Light Body 145
  definition 371
Heart of the Dove 131, 327, 338
  Babaji 63
  definition 371
  map 327
  Spiritual Hierarchy, diagram 338
Heart's Desire
  "...is the source of creation." 171
Heaven and Earth
  and the Seventeen Initations of the Map of Exchanges 271

Heavenly Point(s)
  definition 372
Heavenly Temples of Perfection 208
Hierarch(s) 273
  definition 372
Higher Self 339, 343
Hodler, Ferdinand
  The Lady of the Isenfluh 420
Holy Grail
  Cup Ceremony 321
"Holy Science"
  by Sri Yukteswar 181
Holy Spirit
  a component of the I AM Presence 343
  the Higher Self 339
Hudson, David 132
Hughes, Edward Robert
  Midsummer Eve 325
HU-man
  definition 372
Human Aura
  the evolved HU-man 145
HU-man energy bodies
  Diamond Mind 384
human evolution
  seven levels 170
Human Kingdom 288
HU-man Kingdom
  Golden City of Wahanee 49
HU-man or HU-man Consciousness 98, 287, 339
  and the Ninth Pyramid 287
  Diamond Mind 146
  Divine Blueprint 145
  Evolutionary Field 252, 260
  Field of Awakening 145
  levels of development 159
  Light Bodies 84
  multidimensional 135
  the developed God Man 145
HU-man Psychology
  Evolutionary Field 221, 234
human, the
  spiritual outline 339
Human to HU-man 338
HU, or HUE 95, 97, 113, 136, 188
  definition 372

I

I AM 201
blessing food before eating 34, 75
creation of 341
definition 372
immortal consciousness enters 201
Presence 197
Race 28, 316, 372
that I AM 201
I AM America, or I AM America Map
definition 372
Dove of Peace 151
Seventeen Initiations 268
Seventeen Initiations table 268
sponsors Mother Mary and Saint Germain 148
I AM Presence 34, 75, 113, 168, 188, 317, 318, 336, 339, 341, 342, 343
definition 372
elixir technique 34, 75
engendered by Sanat Kumara 168
I AM Race 28, 268
I AM That I AM 113
definition 372
I AM That I AM Evolutionary Field 220
I-Ching 199
Individualization 201, 348
Information or Communication Portal 99
definition 373
Initiate 170, 201, 339
definition 373
initiation 348
Enlightenment Pilgrimage 71
Great White Brotherhood 74
Innate Dvinity
the First Pillar 233
Inner Child Point 66
definition 373
Inner Earth 25, 47, 67, 83
definition 373
Inner Garden Meditation 235, 258
definition 373
Inner Sun 115, 133, 138, 140
definition 373
integration techniques 72
Intellectual Consciousness
creation of 342

Intention
Group Mind 186
Intention Evolutionary Field 221, 232, 238
definition 373
Invocation of the Violet Flame for Sunrise and Sunset 416

J

Jesus Christ 287, 288
Akhenaton, spiritual forerunner 301
and the temptations of Satan 287
Holy Anointing 59
revelation of the Spiritual Hierarchy 288
Jophiel, Archangel 150, 223, 251, 255, 264, 269, 270
definition 355
Joseph of Arimathea
Christ's Cup 321
Jupiter 166, 176, 275
Jyotish 180
definition 373

K

Kabbalah
Tree of Life
the Ten Sephirots (illuminating spiritual processes) 197
Kali Yuga 136, 179, 180, 181, 182, 183, 184, 269
Iron Age 180
Kalki Kings
of Shamballa 165
Karanopadhi
the Causal body 342
karma
"A lessening of karmic burden." 84
definition 374
past 297
shedding karma and the Gold Ray 93
Karmic Board 336
karmic memory
and darkness 31
Kartikkeya 163
Kings of Shambahla
Spiritual Hierarchy, diagram 338

Klehma, Golden City of
  definition 374
  White Ray 50
Knapp, Stephen 184
Krishna or Krishna Teachings
  prophesies a Golden Age in Kali-Yuga 183
Krita Yuga 179
  definition 374
Kuan Yin 307
  definition 374
Kumaras, the 164
Kundalini 199, 287
  Adjutant Points 28
  definition 374
Kuthumi 149, 150, 167, 307
  definition 374
  Evolutionary Field 222
  Pillar Two Evolutionary Field 241

L

Lady Luxor
  definition 376
Land of the Plumed Serpent
  lost history of Mu, Lemuria, and Atlantis 287
Last Waltz of the Tyrants 31, 110
Law of Agreement 305
  Harmony 307
Law of Attraction and Repulsion 111, 130, 198, 353
  definition 374
Law of Choice 353
Law of Energy-for-energy 108
Law of Love
  definition 374
  the Fourth Pillar 233
Leadbeater, C. W. 163
Left-hand Path 288
lei-line(s)
  Adjutant Points 132
  Cardinal Lei-line 73
  Cardinal Lei-lines 66
  Cardinal perimeters 205
  definition 375
  Gateway perimeters 205
  Golden City Gateway Lei-line 204
Lemuria 151, 287, 297

lifespans
  increased 48
light
  Star seeds 34
Light Being 25
  definition 375
  two forms 54
Light Body (Bodies) 26
  Eighth Light Body 145
  Ninth Light Body 145
Lighted Stance 40, 66, 295
  and the attainment of the Seamless Garment 200
  and the Diamond Mind 146
  definition 375
  Pilgrimage 81
Light of Awakening
  and the Sixth Evolution Point 199
Lineage of Gurus Evolutionary Field
  definition 376
lokas of consciousness 76
longevity
  decree 49
Lord Apollo
  definition 354
Lord Gautama 166
  earth's first Buddha 168
Lord Himalaya 149
Lord Maitreya 166, 167, 341
  leader of the Great White Brotherhood 167
  World Teacher 341
Lord Meru 287
Lord of the Seven Rays 338, 341
Lord of the World 336, 338
Lords of the DAHL 82
  Inner Sun 47
Lords of the Flame 162, 167
Lords of Venus 87, 297
  definition 376
  present on Earth 76
Love
  Evolutionary Field 220
Love One Another
  Evolutionary Field 243
Lower Self 343
  the animal nature 339

Luk, A. D. K. 168, 313
Luxor, or Lady Luxor
  Evolutionary Field 222

M

Magi
  *archetype of the Ninth Evolutionary
    Point* 200
Mahabharata
  and Sanat Kumara 164
Maha Chohan 207, 275, 338, 341, 354
  Lord of the Rays 338
Mahatma
  definition 170
Mahatma Letters 299
Maltese Cross 153
  definition 376
  Lady Anaya 53
  Photon 26
  Photon Belt 65
  seed kernal of light 129
  symbolism 152
Malton, Golden City of
  definition 376
  Elemental Kingdom 44
  Thronana 45
Mantle of Consciousness 30
  definition 376
Manu(s) 336, 340
Map of Exchanges
  definition 376
  Seventeen Initiations 270
  Seventeen Initiations table 270
  *sponsors Lady Nada, El Morya, and
    Kuthumi* 148
Map Room 129
marriage and partnership
  Evolutionary Field 254
Mars
  and the Soul Ray 347
masculine
  energy
    and the Soul Ray 347
mass consciousness
  Group Mind 185
Master 170, 201, 339
mastermind 170

Master Teacher
  definition 376
  Evolutionary Field 255
Mastery 288
  Evolutionary Field 220
Master Year 109, 347
Mayan Calendar 340
media 100
meditation 125
  to cleanse toxic vibrations 34, 75
Meissner Field 132
  definition 376
Melchizedek Priests 59
Mental Body 145, 245
  and Co-creation 129
  definition 376
mental equivalent 111
Mental Purgatory 145
  and the Ninth Energy Body 145, 378
  definition 376
Mercury 161, 166, 175, 275
Metatron 199
Micah
  Great Angel of Unity 311
Michael, Archangel 31, 113, 129, 149,
    188, 223, 248, 249, 250, 255, 263,
    271, 307, 311, 333
  definition 355
Middle Way 199
Mighty Christ 234
Migratory Pattern or Sequence
  definition 376
Mineral Kingdom 288
  Golden City of Gobean 49
minerals
  consciousness 309
Miriam, or Lady Miriam
  Evolutionary Field 222
Mithra
  archetypal Lord of the Seven Rays 341
Modulated Ray(s) or Ray Force(s) 266,
    283
  Annual Movement 282
  definition 377
  Gold Ray 266
  Orange, Coral, or Peach Ray 266
  Pastel Blue Ray 267
  Pastel Green Ray 266
  Spring Green Ray 266

Mohammed 149
Monad 289, 347
  definition 377
  Evolutionary Field 241
monoatomic
  Photon 132
Mother Earth 317, 329
Mother Mary 307, 340
  definition 377
Mother Nature
  Beauty of Nature Evolutionary Field 237
Mu 375
Music of the Spheres 257
myrrh
  anointing oil 59
Mysticsm
  Evolutionary Field 221, 233

N

Nada or Lady Master Nada 307
  definition 377
  Evolutionary Field 222
necromancy 287
Nefertiti 300, 301
  Gobean Abundance Point 123
Neptune 133
New Atlantis 271, 314
New Children 317
  Rainbow and Iris 260
New Consciousness
  decree for the Gold Ray 93
New Lemuria 271
New Shamballa Grid Pilgrimage 349
  definition 377
"Night Journey"
  Muhammad's Ascension 201
Nine Cycles
  chart 273
Nine Heavenly Gates 338
Nine Heavenly Gates Evolutionary Fields 247
  definition 377
Nine Movements of Consciousness
  definition 377
  Eight-sided Cell of Perfection 253
  Evolutionary Field 252
Nine Palaces
  Color Wheel 254
Ninth Cycle of Fire 265
Ninth Energy Body 70, 110
  definition 377
  First Phase 292
  Second Phase 293
  Third Phase 294
Northern Door 153, 175, 275
  definition 378
Northern Door Pilgrimage
  definition 378
  Lineage of Gurus 232

O

Oath Ceremony
  Western Door 239
Oath of the Right-hand Path 334
  definition 378
OM 95, 97
Omega 201
  Evolutionary Field 220
Omega Evolutionary Field
  definition 378
Om Manaya Pitaya Hitaka
  definition 378
OM Sheahah 246
ONE
  Adjutant Points and timeline 57
  "All things work together for the ONE!" 94
  and Akhenaten 301
  definition 378
  Evolutionary Field 246
  Nature and Deva Kingdoms 58
Oneness
  definition 378
Oneship 317
  definition 378
Orange (Coral) Ray 123, 266, 284, 338
  definition 378
orichalcum 341
Orr, Leonard 329
Outer Child Point 66, 332
  definition 378
Overlighting or Overshadowing 167
  Enlightenment Pilgrimage 68
Over-soul 197

P

pantheism
  Beauty in Nature 237
parallel universe(s) 345
Pastel Blue Ray 267, 284, 338
  definition 379
Pastel Green Ray 266, 282, 283, 338
  definition 379
Paul 307
Peace and Tranquility 224
  definition 379
Peace of God
  Evolutionary Field 250
Periodic Adjutant Point Ray Force 265
Periodic Adjutant Point Ray Force or Period Ray Force
  definition 379
Period Ray Force 275
  Golden City 275
Permanent (Presiding) Ray Force 272, 274, 275
  definition 379
  Golden City 275
Philosopher's Stone 130
Photon Belt 26, 27, 39, 65, 76, 100, 114, 126, 134, 135, 141, 181
  definition 379
  the atomic Maltese Cross 65
Photon(s)
  activity 131
  definition 379
  holographic energy shape 353
  light within 138
  Maltese Cross 53, 153
  monoatomic 132
  movement 66, 134
  Movement as the Golden City 351
  Photon Hologram 153
  Sacred Geometry 135
  Symbolism of the Photon 152

Pilgrimage 185, 208
  Alignment Process 136
  Aquamarine and Gold Ray 260
  assisted during the opening of Shamballa 81
  Beauty in Nature 238
  Ceremony Evolution Field 239
  Decree Evolutionary Field 240
  definition 379
  Evolutionary Field of Prophecy 236
  Field of Mysticsm 233
  for Christ Consciousness 234
  Golden City 133
  New Shamballa Grid Pilgrimage 349
  Northern Door and Lineage of Gurus 232
  Oath of the Right-hand Path 334
  Peace of God
    Evolutionary Field 258
  Southern Door Healing Pilgrimage 190
  star crafts 127
  Step-down Transformer 257
  test 43
  The Enlightenment Pilgrimage 331
  "Three points at once." 115
  to increase meditative states 235
  Violet Flame 259
Pineal Gland 188
  definition 379
Pink Ray 282, 283
  Atlantis 357
  definition 379
Plane of Reciprocity 235
Planetary Council 119, 380
Planetary Hierarchy 336
Planetary Logos 164
Plant Kingdom
  Evolutionary Field 247
  Golden City of Shalahah 48
Plasma Field vii, 26, 27, 33, 37, 39, 65, 100, 126, 134, 135, 154, 180, 181
  Aurora Borealis 154
  definition 380
Pleiadeans 55
  progenitors 55

Pleiades Star System 30, 36, 40, 47, 50, 54, 55, 56, 57, 59, 60, 65, 76, 82, 91, 92, 94, 95, 96, 97, 99, 101, 102, 103, 339, 340, 344, 345
 definition 380
 Energy steps-down to Earth 57
 Lady Anaya 54
 "Many embodied on Earth." 96
 Masters and Shamballa 82
 Seven Sisters of Shamballa 339, 340, 345
Plejaren Federation 345
Point of Stillness
 and the Eleventh Evolution Point 201
polarity 317
political systems 100
Portia 68
 Evolutionary Field 222
Portia's Evolutionary Field
 definition 380
Power Evolutionary Field 220
 definition 380
Prayer Evolutionary Field 221, 235
 definition 380
Prayers and Decrees
 Cup Ceremony 322
Presiding Ray Force 265
Priesthood of Amen 301
Princes of Darkness
 "have been removed" 31
problem solving
 Pastel Blue Ray 267
Proclamation of Ascension
 definition 380
 Enlightenment Pilgrimage 334
profession
 Evolutionary Field 255
Prophecy 236
Prophecy Evolutionary Field 221, 236
 definition 381
Prophet 339
Puranas 180
purification
 of food and drink, technique 34, 75
Purification of Mind
 the Second Pillar 233

Q

Quetzalcoatl 302

R

Rainbow and Iris 224
 definition 381
Raphael, Archangel 151, 189, 222, 247, 255, 263, 269, 270
 definition 355
Ray(s) and Ray Force(s) 179, 185, 188, 272, 273, 274, 275, 338
 and Golden Cities 155
 Annual Influence of Ray Forces 265
 annual influence on the Golden Cities 275
 definition 381
 Fourteen Ray Forces of the Golden Cities 283
 Golden City Ashrams 273
 Modulated Ray Forces 266
 Periodic Adjutant Point Ray Force 265
 Presiding 265
 Ray Forces through the Doorways for the year 2026 277
 Ray Forces through the Doorways for the year 2030 278
 Ray Forces through the Doorways for the year 2035 279
 Ray Forces through the Doorways for the years 2021-2025 277
 Ray Forces through the Doorways for the years 2027-2029 278
 Ray Forces through the Doorways for the years 2031-2034 279
 Ray Forces through the Doorways for the years 2036-2038 280
 Ray Forces through the Doorways for the years 2039-2040 280
 Ruby
  definition 381
 Strength of the Ray Forces and their Qualities 2021-2041 283
 The New Ray Forces for the Golden Age 338
Red Door
 definition 381
 Golden City 176
 of a Golden City 130

Red Ray 283
relationships
  Pastel Blue Ray 267
religion 301, 314
Resurrection Flame 250
Revelations, Book of
  John's vision 208
Right-hand Path 188, 287, 288, 336
  definition 362, 381
  Evolutionary Fields 232
  initiations and tests 43
  Oath
    Enlightenment Pilgrimage 334
  Sacred Fire Acceptance 72
  Sacred Pact 71
  versus the Left-Hand Path 287
Rinehardt, Rev. Keith 104
Rod of Power 341
Roerich, Nicholas
  And We Are Not Afraid 412
  Christ in Desert 286
  Elijah the Prophet 157
  Fire Blossom 328
  Krishna-Lel 178
  Message from Shambhala 163
  Pilgrim 335
  Song of Shambhala 211
Romania 149
Root Chakra 188
Rosicrucians 313
Ruby-Gold Ray 283
  definition 381
Rule of Law 46

S

Sacred Fire
  acceptance 72
Sagittarius Dwarf Universe 340
Saint Germain 34, 75, 113, 167, 185, 297, 307, 313, 314, 315, 316, 338, 345
  advice on diet 34
  cleansing the physical body 75
  contemporary portrait 315, 323
  Cup Blessing 120
  definition 381
  Evolutionary Field 222
  Golden Belt of Light 56
  Kajaeshra 313

Map of Political Changes 314
  on the Color Rays 265
  Pillar Three Evolutionary Field 242
  spiritual heritage 354
  Uncle Sam 315
Sainthood
  and Ascension 287
Salamanders of Fire 326
salt 75
  Sacred Fire 59
samadhi 235
Sananda, Lord 36, 76, 149, 164, 189, 307, 311
  Cup Blessing 121
  Evolutionary Field 222
  former Lord of the Golden Cities 148
  Pillar Four Evolutionary Field 243
Sanat Kumara 41, 49, 76, 129, 161, 162, 163, 164, 165, 166, 167, 168, 169, 170, 311
  definition 382
  return to Venus 167
  "...your enlightenment has always been." 171
sandalwood
  anointing oil 59
Sanjana
  Ancestral Field 101
  Ancestral Planet 100
  definition 382
Saturn 133, 297
Satyaloka 76
Scheiner, Artur
  Illustration for Vyšehrad 187, 189
School of Beauty
  Evolutionary Field 237
Schrodinger, Erwin 153
Science of Spiritual Wisdom Evolutionary Field 220
  definition 382
Seamless Garment
  and the Diamond Mind 146
  and the Tenth Evolution Point 200
  definition 382
  HU-man Psychology 234
self-actualization
  Evolutionary Field 255
seraphic host 166

Serapis Bey 161, 166, 301
  definition 382
  Evolutionary Field 243
Sermon on the Mount 241
service
  Spiritual Pilgrimage 89
Seven Archangels 307
Seven Chohans of the Seven Rays 338
Seven Rays of Light and Sound 162, 167, 170, 179, 338, 341
  and ancient astrology 179
seventeen
  meaning of the number seventeen 96
Seventh Dimension 119
Seventh Generation Principle 237
Seventh House Evolutionary Field 254
  definition 382
Seventh Manu 340
shadow
  release of 250
shakti 39, 46, 48, 124, 218
Shalahah, Golden City of 48, 311
  geology 144
Shaman
  and the Ninth Evolution Point 200
Shamballa 41, 49
  annual opening and celebration 170
  a state of consciousness 168
  Celebration of the Four Elements 29, 383
  Cup Ceremony 323
  diagram of Temples 173
  Earth's Crown Chakra 164
  energies and Pilgrimage 100
  Eternal Flame 29, 383
  Gatekeeper 41
  in Buddhism 165
  increase of light on Earth 29
  lineage, Lord Sananda 207
  "living in spiritually perfected community" 207
  Nine Temples of the Rays 173
  petitions from the Ashrams of Light 111
  remains open 80, 111
  Rod of Power 336
  Saint Germain's Violet Flame 47
  Seven Temples of the Flame 173
  Shamballa Grid 112
  Temple of Unity 129
  the Temples of Shamballa 338
  timeline 165
  Venusian and Pleiadean Cities of Light 35
Shamballa Tradition
  definition 383
  Evolutionary Field 232
Shapeshifting 200
Silent Watcher 339
Silver Age 179
Sir Francis Bacon 313, 315
Sister Thedra 311
Skanda 382
Solar Hierarchy 336, 340
Solar Manu 336
Solar Plexus 145
Solomon's Temple 314
Son of God
  and the Twelfth Evolution Point 202
soul
  families 383
soul ability 108
Soul Family 29
  Evolutionary Field 254
Soul Ray
  and masculine energy 347
sound 98
  Plasma Field 27
  spiritual teachings 309
  technology 48
Southern Door
  definition 383
  White Ray 36
spacecrafts 56
Spiral
  Evolutionary Field 225
Spirit Guide(s) 342
spiritual
  fire 383
Spiritual Awakening
  Evolutionary Field 220
Spiritual Discipline
  Evolutionary Field 220
Spiritual Evolution
  Thirteen Evolutionary Pyramids 202
Spiritual Experience 201
Spiritual Fire
  week four, Shamballa Celebration 29

spiritual growth
  ages twenty-eight to thirty-two 347
Spiritual Hierarchy
  definition 383
spiritual initiation
  Cellular Awakening 33
Spiritual Liberation 201
  definition 384
Spiritual Master 287
Spiritual Mastery 201
spiritual metabolism 140
Spiritual Migration 185
spiritual practice 32, 36, 74, 75, 113, 287
  overcomes limitation 113
spoken word
  Pastel Green Ray 266
Spring Green Ray 266, 284, 338
  definition 384
Sri Lanka
  Ancient Lemuria 375
Star Retreats 214, 273, 338
  definition 384
  Spiritual Hierarchy, diagram 338
Star(s) of the Golden City 36
  critical points 32, 36
  definition 368, 384
  Golden City Apex 130
  Heavenly Gate Evolutionary Field 222
  meditation technqiue 271
  Shamballa 42
Step-down Transformer 37, 70, 85, 92, 111, 122, 125, 139, 140, 257
  decree 125
  definition 384
  Pillar of Light Decree 140
Stone, Dr. Joshua 164
Strengthen the Soul
  Evolutionary Field 220
Subjective Energy Body 31, 240
  definition 384
Summerland 348
Sun
  companion dwarf star theory 179
Super senses
  definition 384

T

Taj Mahal 184
Taoist philosophy
  Cycle of the Elements 360
telepathy 212
Temple of the Buddha 338
  Shamballa 173
Temple of the Christ 338
  Shamballa 173
Temple of the Violet Flame 338
Temple of Unity 35, 124, 129, 173
  definition 384
Temples of Perfection, Temple Points
  Spiritual Hierarchy, diagram 338
Temples of Shamballa 338
Temples of the Flame 338
Temples of the Rays
  Shamballa and the Golden Cities 32
Temples of the Seven Rays 162
Temple to the Formless One 301
Tenth Energy Body 70, 110, 146
  definition 384
  the Triple Gem 295
Tenth House
  Evolutionary Field 253
Tenth Pyramid of Consciousness
  and soul-trying conflict 287
The Four Pillars 338
The Nine Movements of Consciousness
  Eighth Movement: Worldly Career and Service 255
  Fifth Movement: Children and Co-creation 255
  First Movement: The Holy Temple 253
  Fourth Movement: Family 254
  Ninth Movement: Star of Knowledge 255
  Second Movement: The Divine Path 253
  Seventh Movement: Abundance and Bounty 255
  Sixth Movement: Spiritual Teachers 255
  Third Movement: Marriage and Partnership 254
Third Dimension 145, 212
  definition 385
Third Eye Chakra 188, 245, 257
  definition 385
Third Hierarchy 339

Third Kingdom
of Elemental Beings 343
Thirteen Evolutionary Pyramids
definition 385
growth of the HU-man, illustration 196
Thirteenth School 375
thought-form
Group Mind 185
Three Standards 113
appendix and instruction 113
definition 385
Thronana (gnome)
Earth Kingdom 45
Malton 45
Thunder Strikes
Octagonal Mirror 202
Tiger's Nest Monastery 207
time
freedom from 43
of Changes
  definition 385
Time Compaction 33, 88, 134, 209
definition 385
timeline(s) 92, 126, 161, 165, 181
Apocalyptic 126
Collective Consciousness 57
definition 385
Golden Age 181
"Scramble for the timelines." 109
the Two Timelines 81
Timelines and Consciousness 317
Time of Change 177, 317, 318
time travel 43
Eleventh Energy Body 296
Tissot, James
Jesus, Ministered to by Angels 310
transfiguration 347, 348
transmutation
and the Ninth Light Body 145, 378
Transportation Age 35
definition 385
Treta Yuga 179, 180
definition 385
Triangles
Six Types of Triangles 219

Triangles of the Evolutionary Fields
Acute Triangle 219
Equilateral Triangle 219
Isosceles Triangle 218
Obtuse Triangle 219
Right Angle Triangle 220
Scalene Triangle 218
Trinomial Law of the Biome 116
Trinomial Mathematics 116
definition 385
Triple Gem(s)
and the Tenth Light Body 146, 385
spiritual processes 200
the Unfed Flame 200
True Memory 33
Evolutionary Field 251
True North 102, 103, 104, 113, 114, 131, 137
definition 386
Tube of Light 113
appendix and instruction 113
definition 386
Twelfth Energy Body 110, 146, 386
definition 386
Twelve Evolution Points 198
Point Five: Service 198
Point Four: Love 198
Point Nine: Desire 200
Point One: Harmony 198
Point Seven: Cooperation 199
Point Six: Illumination 199
Point Ten: Faith 200
Point Three: Clarity 198
Point Twelve: Creation-Creativity 202
Twelve Jurisdictions 112, 174, 382
and Sanat Kumara 171
Charity 171
Cooperation: Masculine Principle 171
definition 386
Desire 171
diagram 196
Stillness 171
Thirteen Evolutionary Pyramids and Evolution Points 203
Twenty-year Cycles of the Elements 360
twenty-year periods 265
Twin Rays 341
Two Timelines
definition 386

U

Umbilicus Connection 55, 65, 114, 265, 327
  definition 386
Umbilicus Portal 91, 92, 94, 95
Unana 180, 181
  definition 386
Unfed Flame 168, 173, 197, 289, 297, 336, 339, 340, 342
  and Sanat Kumara 168
  and the Ascended Master 342
  and the Three-Fold Flame Creation Myth 341
  Golden City Star 247
union
  at age 33 348
United States
  Declaration of Independence 315
United States Flag
  blessing 193
Unity Consciousness
  Aquamarine Ray 354
Uriel, Archangel 150, 223, 250, 253, 254, 264, 269, 270
  definition 355

V

Vanderbank, John
  Francis Bacon 314
Van Gogh, Vincent
  Aries View from the Wheat Fields 312, 320
Vastu Shastra 180
Vedic Rishis 179
Vegetable Kingdom 288
Venus 92, 165, 167, 176, 275, 297
  Divine Feminine 285
  Earth's Moon 56
  Golden Cities 102
  Masters and Shamballa 82
  Shamballa 35
  temples of 165
Venus through the Golden City Doors 2021-2065 285
Vertical Power Current
  definition 387
  in a Golden City 92
Violet Fire 387

Violet Flame 75, 113, 119, 146, 173, 188, 213, 297, 312, 313, 320, 329, 338
  appendix and instruction 113
  calling forth the consuming fire 113
  ceremonial fire 329
  Cup Ceremony 322
  definition 297, 387
  Golden City of Wahanee 46
  Group Mind 40
  Healing of Nations 192
  invocation at sunrise, sunset 416
  Invocation of the Violet Flame for Sunrise and Sunset 416
Violet Flame Angels 213
  decrees 333
  definition 387
  Evolutionary Field 248
  for healing 139
Violet Flame Decree
  Ascension 34
  Enlightenment Pilgrimage 331
  for purification 67
  for the Golden Age 82
  Liberty and Freedom 47
  to visualize the Violet Flame throughout your light bodies 68
Violet Flame Temple
  Shamballa 173
Violet Ray 275, 283
  Evolutionary Field 248
Violet Ray Angels 71
Vishvakarma 162
  World Architect 167
Vision and Compassion
  Evolutionary Field 220
Vista (Cyclopea) and Virginia 224, 257
  definition 387
Vortex or Vortices
  example in nature 352

W

Wahanee, Golden City of 275
  definition 387
  Gatekeeper of the Violet Ray 46
water 323
  Dr. Masaru Emoto 86
  Kingdoms of Water 58
  unites the Collective Consciousness 57

Water Ceremony 321
Western Door 153, 176, 272
  definition 387
  Enlightenment Pilgrimage 66
  White Ray 37, 50
Western Door Pilgrimage
  definition 387
Western Star Retreat 332
Wheel of Karma
  Ascended Master 356
White Magic
  and Black Magic 287
White Ray 94, 275, 283
  concentration of 110
  definition 388
  movement of 66
  Photon 351
  Southern Door 36
  Venus 285
  Western Door 37
  Western Doors 50
  Year of Enlightening 65
White Ray Temple
  Golden City of Klehma 50
Will Chakras 145, 304, 362
  and the Golden Thread Axis 303
  Concentrative-Receptive 304
  Expressive 304
  Solar Will 304
  tempering 43
  Will to Live 304
  Will to Love 304
Wisdom
  Evolutionary Field 220
Witness Consciousness 242
World Teacher 338, 341

Y

Yellow Door
  definition 388
  Golden City 176
  of a Golden City 130
Yellow Ray 270, 275, 283
  definition 388
Yogananda, Paramahansa 180, 181
Yuga(s)
  Cycle of 179
  four 179

Yukteswar, Sri 180, 181
  photograph 183
Yukteswar Theory
  of the Yugas 181

Z

Zadkiel, Archangel 40, 68, 73, 139, 149, 192, 223, 248, 255, 263, 268, 297, 331
  and the Seventeen Initiations of I AM America 268
  definition 355
  Order of 297

And We Are Not Afraid
Nicholas Roerich, 1922.

Discography

Toye, Lori

Photons Propel Your Ascension:

A Living Crystal, I AM America Seventh Ray Publishing International MP3. © ℗, December 17, 2020.

Gatekeepers of Light, I AM America Seventh Ray Publishing International MP3. © ℗, January 1, 2021.

Elder of Light, I AM America Seventh Ray Publishing International MP3. © ℗, December 17, 2020.

Enlightenment Pilgrimage, I AM America Seventh Ray Publishing International MP3. © ℗, January 8, 2021.

Free, Humanity Shall Be, I AM America Seventh Ray Publishing International MP3. © ℗, January 15, 2021.

Umbilicus of Light, I AM America Seventh Ray Publishing International MP3. © ℗, February 5, 2021.

Energy-for-Energy, I AM America Seventh Ray Publishing International MP3. © ℗, January 8, 2022.

Pilgrimage of Light, I AM America Seventh Ray Publishing International MP3. © ℗, January 17, 2022.

The Photon, I AM America Seventh Ray Publishing International MP3. © ℗, January 18, 2022.

Awakening Prayer

Great Light of Divine Wisdom,

Stream forth to my being,

And through your right use

Let me serve mankind and the planet.

Love, from the Heart of God.

Radiate my being with the presence of the Christ

That I walk the path of truth.

Great Source of Creation,

Empower my being,

My Brother,

My Sister,

And my planet with perfection,

As we collectively awaken as ONE cell.

I call forth the Cellular Awakening!

Let Wisdom, Love, and Power stream forth to this cell — this cell that we all share.

Great Spark of Creation,

Awaken the Divine Plan of Perfection.

So we may share the ONE perfected cell,

I AM.

Illustrations / Photos Endnotes

"El Morya." Digital image. Summit Lighthouse. 2019. https://summitlighthouse.org/el-morya.

Hall, Manly, *The Phoenix: An Illustrated Overview of Occultism and Philosophy*, Los Angeles, CA: Philosophical Research Society, 1983.

Hall, Manly. "The Secret Teachings of All Ages." Diamond Jubilee Edition. Los Angeles: Philosophical Research Society, 1988.

"Kuthumi." Summit Lighthouse. Accessed July 17, 2021. summitlighthouse.org/kuthumi.

"Lady Master Nada." Digital image. Summit Lighthouse. 2019. https://summitlighthouse.org

"Saint Germain." Summit Lighthouse. Accessed July 17, 2021. summitlighthouse.org/saint+germain.

"Sanat Kumara." Digital image. Sanat Kumara. 2019. https://shekinah-el-daoud.com/2019/01/09/sanat-kumara-shielding-and-setting-boundaries-is-more-important-than-ever-genoveva-cole/.

"Sri Yukteswar." My Dattatreya, 2021. https://mydattatreya.com/sri-yukteswar.

Suvorov, Valdimir. *Archangel Zadkiel*. December 4, 2013. Valdimir Suvorov Art. http://annacatharina.centerblog.net/rub-vladimir-suvorov-art-.html.

"Tiger's Nest." Digital image. Http://www.byronevents.net. 2019.

Invocation of the Violet Flame for Sunrise and Sunset

I invoke the Violet Flame to come forth in the name of I AM That I AM,
To the Creative Force of all the realms of all the Universes, the Alpha, the Omega, the Beginning, and the End,

To the Great Cosmic Beings and Torch Bearers of all the realms of all the Universes,
And the Brotherhoods and Sisterhoods of Breath, Sound, and Light, who honor this Violet Flame that comes forth from the Ray of Divine Love — the Pink Ray, and the Ray of Divine Will — the Blue Ray of all Eternal Truths.

I invoke the Violet Flame to come forth in the name of I AM That I AM!
Mighty Violet Flame, stream forth from the Heart of the Central Logos, the Mighty Great Central Sun! Stream in, through, and around me.

Bibliography

Brennan, Barbara Ann. *Hands of Light: A Guide to Healing through the Human Energy Field: A New Paradigm for the Human Being in Health, Relationship, and Disease.* Toronto: Bantam Books, 1993.

Dale, Cyndi, and Richard Wehrman. *The Subtle Body: An Encyclopedia of Your Energetic Anatomy.* Boulder, CO: Sounds True, 2009.

"David Hudson Discovered Monoatomic Gold Ormus." Monoatomic Orme, 26 July 2016, monoatomic-orme.com/david-hudson/.

Fortune, Dion, and Gareth Knight. *Applied Magic.* York Beach: Weiser Books, 2000.

Fortune, Dion, and Gareth Knight. *The Magical Battle of Britain.* Cheltenham: Skylight, 2012.

Fortune, Dion. *Esoteric Orders and Their Work; the Training and Work of an Initiate.* London: Thorsons, 1995.

Frawley, David. *Astrology of the Seers: A Guide to Vedic/Hindu Astrology.* Twin Lakes, WI: Lotus Press, 2000.

Gurunath, Yogiraj. *Babaji: The Lightning Standing Still.* Alma, CA: Hamsa Yoga Sangh, 2012.

Hall, Manly, *The Phoenix: An Illustrated Overview of Occultism and Philosophy,* Los Angeles, CA: Philosophical Research Society, 1983.

Hall, Manly. *The Secret Teachings of All Ages.* Diamond Jubilee Edition. Los Angeles: Philosophical Research Society, 1988.

Hawkins, David R. *Power vs. Force: The Hidden Determinants of Human Behavior.* Carlsbad, CA: Hay House, 2014.

King Godfré Ray. *Unveiled Mysteries* (Original). Schaumburg, IL: Saint Germain Press, 1982.

Knapp, Stephen. *The Vedic Prophecies: A New Look into the Future.* Detroit, MI: World Relief Networks, 2011.

Luk, ADK. *Law of Life and Teachings by Divine Beings.* Oklahoma City, OK: Luk, 1978.

Papastavro, Tellis S. *The Gnosis and the Law.* Tucson, AZ: Papastavro, 1972.

Prophet, Mark, Elizabeth Clare Prophet, and Annice Booth. *The Masters and Their Retreats.* Corwin Springs, MT: Summit University Press, 2003.

Reichel, Gertraud. *Babaji, Gateway to the Light: Experiences with the Great Immortal Master.* Weilersbach, Ger.: G. Reichel, 1990.

Reichel, Gertraud. *Babaji, the Unfathomable: 108 Encounters.* Weilersbach, Germany: G. Reichel, 1988.

Saint Germain Press. *I AM Angel Decrees,* Part Two. Chicago, IL: Saint Germain Press, 1974.

Saint-Germain, and Manly P. Hall. *The Most Holy Trinosophia of the Comte De St-Germain.* Los Angeles: Philosophical Research Society, 1983.

Stone, Joshua David. *The Complete Ascension Manual: How to Achieve Ascension in This Lifetime.* Sedona, AZ: Light Technology Pub., 1994.

Wong, Eva. *Feng-Shui: The Ancient Wisdom of Harmonious Living for Modern Times.* Boston: Shambhala, 1996.

Yukteswar. *The Holy Science.* Kaivalya Darsanam. Los Angeles: Self-Realization Fellowship, 1972.

Zion, Judi Pope, Ramtha, and J. Z. Knight. *Last Waltz of the Tyrants: The Prophecy.* Orcas, WA: Indelible Ink, 1990.

Illustrations Resources

Earth Changes Maps, Golden City Maps:
I AM America Maps
iamamerica.com

Saint Germain and Visionary Art:
Susan Seddon Boulet
susanseddonboulet.com

El Morya, Saint Germain, Kuthumi, and Spiritual Art:
Summit Lighthouse
summitlighthouse.org

Archangel Gabriel, Astrea, and Visionary Art:
Marius Michael-George
mariusfineart.com

Prince Ragoczy (Saint Germain)**, Symbolic Prints and Posters:**
Philosophical Research School
prs.org

Angelic Art:
Howard David Johnson
howarddavidjohnson.com

Visionary Art:
Celeste Korsolm
artsedona.net

Visionary Art:
Pamela Matthews Art of the Soul
grail.co.nz

Ascended Master Art:
Suvorov Vladimir
artnow.ru

Ascended Masters and Sacred Images:
Saint Germain Press
saintgermainpress.com/pictures

The Lady of the Isenfluh
Ferdinand Hodler, 1902.

About Lori & Lenard Toye

LORI TOYE is not a Prophet of doom and gloom. The fact that she became a Prophet at all was highly unlikely. Reared in a small Idaho farming community, as a member of the conservative Missouri Synod Lutheran church, Lori had never heard of meditation, spiritual development, reincarnation, channeling, or clairvoyant sight.

Her unusual spiritual journey began in Washington State when, as advertising manager of a weekly newspaper, she answered a request to pick up an ad for a local health food store. As she entered, a woman at the counter pointed a finger at her and said, "You have work to do for Master Saint Germain!" The next several years were filled with spiritual enlightenment that introduced Lori, then only twenty-two years old, to the most exceptional and inspirational information she had ever encountered. Lori became a student of Ascended Master teachings.

Awakened one night by the luminous figure of Saint Germain at the foot of her bed, her work had begun. Later in the same year, an image of a map appeared in her dream. Four teachers clad in white robes were present, pointing out Earth Changes that would shape the future United States.

Five years later, faced with the stress of a painful divorce and rebuilding her life as a single mother, Lori attended spiritual meditation classes. While there, she shared her experience; encouraged by friends, she began to explore the dream through daily meditation. The four Beings appeared again, and expressed a willingness to share the information. Over a six-month period, they gave over eighty sessions of material, including detailed information that would later become the I AM America Map. Clearly she had to produce the map. The only means to finance it was to sell her house. She put her home up for sale, and in a depressed market, it sold the first day at full asking price.

She produced the map in 1989, rolled copies of them on her kitchen table, and sold them through word-of-mouth. She then launched a lecture tour of the Northwest and California. Hers was the first Earth Changes Map published, and many others followed including 21 books on Ascended Master teachings, with three more in the works. The maps, as well as the *New World Wisdom Series* (recently updated) became bestsellers.

From the tabloids to the New York Times, The Washington Post, television interviews in the U.S., London, and Europe, Lori's Mission was to honor the material she had received. The material is not hers she stresses. It belongs to the Masters, and their loving, healing approach is disseminated through the I AM America Publishing Company operated by her husband and spiritual partner, Lenard Toye.

Lenard Toye, originally from Philadelphia, PA, pursued his personal interests in alternative healing after a successful career in Europe as an opera singer. He attended Barbara Brennan's School of Healing to further develop the gift of auric vision. Working together with his wife Lori, they formed the *School of the Four Pillars* which included holistic and energy healing and

Ascended Master Teachings. More recently, they have fostered a national and international mentoring program that embraces the teachings Lori has published, the *I AM America Spiritual Teachings*. This transformative information is based on over thirty years of published sessions with the Ascended Masters. Len continues to monitor Lori's channeling sessions and also mentor students.

During the course of the channeling sessions, Lori and Len were directed to build the first Golden City community at Wenima Valley, in Arizona. The *I AM America Atlas* includes those areas called the "Golden Cities." These places hold a high spiritual energy, and are where the Masters encourage the building of a new heaven on Earth; sustainable communities that use solar energy and renewables.

The first community, Wenima Village, has been surveyed over the last twenty years by professionals and Spiritual Masters for the purpose of identifying lots and grids, as well as locating energy points to harness this energy for future spiritual and community development. The surveys have also considered classical feng shui engineering/ infrastructure, indigenous precepts, and astronomical alignments. This achievement has included identification, by numerous master practitioners and shamans, of the dormant indigenous energies on the land. Lei-lines, Earth protectors, and subtle energies have been reactivated and have raised the vibration of the site to herald a future for healing, learning, and spiritual development.

While the Golden Cities are key spiritual locations on the Maps, the other maps show possible Earth Changes. Concerned that some might misinterpret these maps' messages as doom and gloom and miss the metaphor for personal change, or not consider the spiritual teachings attached to the Maps, Lori emphasizes that the Masters stressed that the Maps are a prophecy of "choice." Prophecy allows for choice in making informed decisions and promotes the opportunity for cooperation and harmony. Lenard and Lori's vision is to share the Ascended Masters' prophecies as spiritual guidance to heal, rebuild, and renew our lives.

As such, those who have risen above the noise and polarity of their environment and the current social and political upheaval are already Ascending. We encourage you to work on building one of the Golden Cities, to offer a respite to those souls who have a higher vision and long for a new heaven on Earth. Nothing is static, everything is always changing. The way we embrace the changes is of vital importance. To live in peace and harmony and experience personal growth and self-development is the aim of Ascension.

The I AM America Ascended Master Teachings are available on *Amazon, Barnes & Noble* and other platforms worldwide.

About I AM America

I AM America is an educational and publishing foundation dedicated to disseminating the Ascended Masters' message of Earth Changes Prophecy and Spiritual Teachings for self-development. Our office is run by the husband and wife team of Lenard and Lori Toye who hand-roll maps, package, and mail information and products with a small staff. Our first publication was the I AM America Map, which was published in September 1989. Since then we have published three more Prophecy maps, thirteen books, and numerous recordings based on the channeled sessions with the Spiritual Teachers.

We are not a church, a religion, a sect, or cult and are not interested in amassing followers or members. Nor do we have any affiliation with a church, religion, political group, or government of any kind. We are not a college or university, research facility, or a mystery school. El Morya told us that the best way to see ourselves is as, "Cosmic Beings, having a human experience."

In 1994, we asked Saint Germain, "How do you see our work at I AM America?" and he answered, "I AM America is to be a clearinghouse for the new humanity." Grabbing a dictionary, we quickly learned that the term "clearinghouse" refers to "an organization or unit within an organization that functions as a central agency for collecting, organizing, storing, and disseminating documents, usually within a specific academic discipline or field." So inarguably, we are this too. But in uncomplicated terms, we publish and share spiritually transformational information because at I AM America there is no doubt that, "A Change of Heart can Change the World."

With Violet Flame Blessings,
Lori & Lenard Toye

For more information or to visit our online bookstore, go to:
www.iamamerica.com
www.loritoye.com

To receive a catalog by mail, please write to:
I AM America
P.O. Box 2511
Payson, AZ 85547

I AM America Books:

The I AM America Trilogy

ISBN 978-1-880050-44-6
(Paperback) 235 pages
eBook through Amazon
Audiobook through Audible

BOOK ONE: I AM America Trilogy

A Teacher Appears
An Introduction to the Ascended Masters of the I AM America Teachings

Are you a student who is ready for a teacher? If so, then welcome to *A Teacher Appears*.

As a twenty-two-year-old sales rep in a small town in the Pacific Northwest, Lori Toye had never even thought about meditation, let alone asking spirit teachers for help. But all that changed in 1983 when she got a middle-of-the-night bedside "visit" from Master Saint Germain, an eighteenth-century Frenchman and "Ascended Master" . . . who later returned with four of his friends—teachers in white robes who presented a map of America with a new geography, along with a message: it is time for worldwide healing. Despite her questions and doubts, Lori surrendered to their requests and began disseminating their wisdom and messages—the earliest of which are published for the first time in *A Teacher Appears*.

Why is it helpful to get information from spirit entities? How and why should we change? We've noticed the drama going on in our weather, on the planet, in our culture. What is that about? What about manifesting money; what about fear, social disharmony, and my excruciating headaches? What am I doing here, how can I prepare for my future, and why on earth would spirit entities need *my* help? Lori asked these questions and many more.

A Teacher Appears offers fifty-one small but simple channeled lessons about Earth Change and humanity's opportunity to open to and accept the I AM Presence—your individualized presence of God. All it requires is inspiration, appreciation, love, and a good teacher.

ISBN 978-1-880050-26-2
(Paperback) 196 pages
eBook through Amazon
Audiobook through Audible

BOOK TWO: I AM America Trilogy

Sisters of the Flame
An Introduction to the Ascended Masters of the I AM America Teachings

Imagine sitting around a kitchen table with a small group of women friends asking compassionate Master Teachers—Saint Germain, Kuthumi, Sananda, Kuan Yin, Mary, and others absolutely anything you wanted . . . and getting detailed answers.

Join such a group of women, affectionately named by Master Saint Germain the "Sisters of the Flame." Read transcripts of their question and answer sessions—sessions that took place over the course of many long, hot summer evenings while the crickets sang and air conditioners hummed in the small town of Asotin, Washington. These spiritual teachings focus on the important lessons of Love, Emotion, and the Awakening. Learn about the Angels who serve each of us. Enjoy clear explanations about the roles of minds, bodies, chakras, and sounds. Do you have questions about freewill, collective thought, and cooperation? Here are answers. What about personality and the ONE; fear and safety; science, technology, and healing; Christ and Anti-Christ? Or are you more concerned about jobs, relationships, smoking, or Bigfoot? From the transcendent to the mundane, to the personal and quirky, the lessons in *Sisters of the Flame* provide everyone with a questioning mind and concerns about our future information to help us welcome what many of us perceive to be cataclysmic times. No, say the Masters, it is not a time for despair. Instead, consider it to be a monumental opportunity in this school room we call Earth—an opportunity to become our highest selves. Through *Sisters of the Flame*, you will learn how.

ISBN 978-1-880050-50-7
(Paperback) 196 pages
eBook through Amazon

BOOK THREE: I AM America Trilogy

Fields of Light

An Introduction to the Ascended Masters of the I AM America Teachings

Who are you? Can you really know in an objective way? And how can you grow and change in a healthy way—a way that becomes healing to those around you and our beautiful ailing planet?

In this third book of the I AM America trilogy, mystic Lori Toye blends her entertaining personal love story (with mystic Lenard Toye) and the teachings of Ascended Masters, spirit beings dedicated to helping humanity. Saint Germain, her first Master, visited Lori unbidden and proceeded to school her—giving her visions of a new Earth with altered land and water formations as well as the possibilities of changing, averting the very prophecies of devastation he was sharing.

If you want to know who you are, learn from Saint Germain and his colleagues how the universe mirrors back to us our own thoughts so we can learn discernment, the power of choice, and rewarding responsibility. In twenty lessons you will take a journey to freedom and an experience of perfection and the higher love of a developed soul. Learn acceptance, detachment, sacrifice, and forgiveness. Each lesson from the Spiritual Masters develops and reinforces the inner quest for spiritual expansion—the liberation process better known in these teachings as Ascension. Learn to benefit from challenging partnerships, deal with the inevitable results of our choices, resolve seemingly unsolvable problems, and connect with spirit and the higher realms to find solace, love, resolution, and finally your inner fields of light.

"The world is in need of your light and your love," says Saint Germain. "Come forth in your light and expand to all around you."

Freedom Star
Prophecies that Heal Earth

This book contains detailed and stunning Earth Changes Prophecies for the Americas, Europe, Africa, Japan, Asia, and Australia, as well as a pull-out Earth Changes Map of the World (8 ½ x 11). These prophecies offer spiritual teachings and they map practical and simple solutions to the coming challenges — solutions that, if heeded, can alter the course of the most catastrophic events.

The power of prophecy has always been dependent on the nuance, intelligence, and power of their interpretation. The Oracles of Delphi were surrounded by five interpreters who gave their insights on each prophecy. Native American prophets traditionally utilized one or several steadfast translators to share their messages, and Ancient Hebrew Prophets never allowed prophecy to be heard unless if it had been scrutinized three times. In all cases of ancient prophecies, it was extremely rare for the prophet to interpret or to publicly share the gift of prophecy. In this rare and unique booklet, Lori Adaile Toye acts as prophet, translator, and interpreter, using the Ancient Threefold Technique for the Ascended Masters' World Earth Changes Map — *Freedom* Star.

ISBN 978-1-880050-04-0
(Paperback) 84 pages

Ever Present Now
A New Understanding of Consciousness and Prophecy

With her bestselling *I AM America Maps*, Lori Toye has led and inspired thousands to understand the ongoing "Time of Change" — a period in Earth's history of tumultuous change in society, culture, and politics in tandem with individual and collective spiritual awakenings and transformations. These events occur simultaneously with the possibilities of massive global warming, climatic changes, and worldwide seismic and volcanic activity — Earth Changes. The "Ever Present Now," is a compilation of insights notes, and articles that contain simple reasoning, current anecdotes, in-depth research, and esoteric spiritual teachings. Predictions are for doomsayers, but the nuanced perspective of Prophecy, is carefully explained by well-known mystic and founder of *I AM America* — Lori Toye — through Prophecy's inherent gift of hidden metaphor and its power to guide and change people in unpredictable times. *The Ever Present Now* is a new way of enlightened thinking and understanding — a valuable skill-set for the current times. Learn how collective consciousness can morph and reshape drastic Earth Changes through the Seven Rays of Light and Sound and the Ascended Masters' network of Golden City Vortices. Familiarize yourself with the Fourth Dimension and the evolution of Unity Consciousness and personal transcendence — the Ascension Process. The "Time of Change" is now!

ISBN 978-1-880050-50-7
(Paperback) 174 pages
eBook through Amazon
Audiobook through Audible

New World Wisdom Series

ISBN 978-1-880050-53-8
(Paperback) 386 pages
eBook through Amazon

New World Wisdom, Book One
Teachings from the Ascended Masters

Can we transform our tumultuous society? Is it even possible to save our ailing planet? Yes, say the teachings in this book — channeled wisdom from a team of Ascended Masters, one of whom made his presence known to the young mother and mystic Lori Toye when she least expected it and could do little about it. It took decades to channel, transcribe, and publish the prophecies and counsel in this book, and even more time — and a second revised printing — for Toye to understand the meaning of the material: Prophecies are not predictions! Such messages are both metaphorical and literal. They are warnings with solutions to avoid what is prophesied. The chapters in this book contain information that explains how human consciousness has the ability to change and transform, and how this microcosmic effect literally extends — guiding social and cultural values, physically reshaping the planet's weather, sensitive ecosystems, and geography.

Yes, we can change — by accepting our spiritual virtue and innate goodness; by learning to consciously cultivate the *Twelve Jurisdictions*, shared by the spiritual teachers; by engaging in our own personal Ascension Process. The Spiritual Teachers who contributed their Wisdom call this process the "BE-Coming." Be. Come. Add your effort to engender the growth of a new global, cultural consciousness — the Golden Age. (Formerly *New World Atlas, Volume One.*)

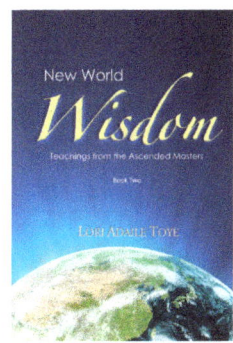

ISBN 978-1-880050-66-8
(Paperback) 344 pages

New World Wisdom, Book Two
Teachings from the Ascended Masters

To keep your light hidden at this time is indeed almost a criminal activity," says the Spiritual Teacher Saint Germain in this channeled book of wisdom, warnings, and prophecies. What are the consequences of choosing ego attractions and aversion over those that come from your heart? Why should we choose heart over ego? How can we tell the difference? Through intimate lectures, Saint Germain, Sananda (Christ), Mother Mary, and Kuan Yin delineate not only the steps to "transfiguration" (when we transform ourselves into beings who function from a place of enlightenment), but they lay out the consequences to Earth and our sensitive environments if we do nothing. In vivid detail, we see a world where land masses have turned into oceans and continents divide. Through Mystic Lori Toye, we hear about a future that has already begun — due to global warming and climatic change. But what beyond use of fossil fuels causes this future? What thought patterns and consequent actions are directing us to behave as we do? This and more is clarified in this second book of a series of three in the *New World Wisdom Series*. Book Two of the New World Wisdom Series contains the prophecies for Japan, China, Australia, and India. This new revision also contains updated prophecies for the United States through the *6-Map Scenario* — six possible Earth Changes scenarios, based upon the insight of the Spiritual Teachers and Earth's potential and possibility for catastrophic change predicated through human collective consciousness.

ISBN 978-1-880050-69-9
(Paperback) 480 pages

New World Wisdom, Book Three
Teachings from the Ascended Masters

New World Wisdom offers a hopeful message: Human consciousness plays a pivotal role in creation, both individually and globally. In other words, "Group consciousness creates climate." The Ascended Masters' teachings in this book, channeled by Lori and Lenard Toye, clarify this, emphasizing that our individual consciousness is not a cause of what is going on, but rather will result in stagnation and destruction of the whole if we choose to do nothing to change our individual movements to affect the dance of group consciousness.

According to the teachings of Ascended Masters, we are in a "Time of Change" — a period of tumult in world societies, environments, climates, cultures, and politics. The good news is that all this upset comes in tandem with individual and collective spiritual awakenings and transformations. These will occur simultaneously with a literally shifting terrain; there will be new lands and oceans. We can experience these changes with fear and loathing, or we can choose to become part of them — literally changing the way we think and behave toward ourselves, each other, and the planet. To do this, we must choose self-knowledge and acknowledgment of the existence of the true self and the consciousness of the ONE — Unana. By sharing the New World Wisdom, we can begin to consciously change, and by doing so, change the group consciousness. Throughout this complex, convoluted time of tipping past almost every point of no return, we most definitely can choose to make a difference. The Spiritual Teachers in this book offer their best advice: it is time for *our* spiritual growth and evolution.

For more information or to purchase, go to:
iamamerica.com

Golden City Series

ISBN 978-1-880050-57-6
(Paperback) 328 pages

BOOK ONE: Golden City Series
Points of Perception
Prophecies and Teachings of Saint Germain

In this time of massive upheaval and transition — through weather and Earth Changes, with governments crashing and new ones being born — is it possible that the words from Genesis, "And it was very good" still apply? Yes, says Saint Germain, an Ascended Master channeled by a gentle and amazing prophet named Lori Toye. Yes!

Learn why what appears to be chaos is actually the beginning of a new harmony and why disasters are necessary. Learn how devastation is an invitation to humanity's new life of love and service. It augurs a time to release guilt and enter into an evolution of consciousness and new creation and new levels of life itself. Learn about Golden Cities — real places with a pivotal role in the prophesied Time of Change.

For people who are new to New Consciousness thinking as well as people who have been studying metaphysics for years, the teachings in *Points of Perception* offer personal instruction. Included in the book are a detailed glossary and appendices featuring contemporary terms, language, and definitions for those who are interested in non-biblical prophecy, the upcoming changes, the New Times, and self-Mastery alongside the Ascension Process.

ISBN 978-1-880050-58-3
(Paperback) 264 pages

BOOK TWO: Golden City Series
Light of Awakening
Prophecies and Teachings of the Ascended Masters

In the year 2000, our planet was flooded by light — albeit extrasensory light that you may or may not believe was sensed by extra-sensed people, one of whom is prophet, channel, and author Lori Toye. What cannot be disputed is that there have since been massive disruptions of the social, political, and economic systems that continue today. According to leading scientists, our earth is experiencing climatic and extreme weather events, geologic change, severe damaging earthquakes, comet and asteroid sightings, and continuous magnetic pole shift — Earth Changes. The same scientists, analysts, economists, and spiritual leaders agree that more drastic change is approaching. In *Light of Awakening*, Lori Toye, channeling wisdom from Ascended Masters, chronicles the critical passage of humanity's evolution into the New Times — a time that is aligned with the hope of Unana (Unity Consciousness) alongside polarizing wars and worldwide economic calamity. Spiritual teachers claim this prophesied period of large-scale difficulty is reference to the return of Christ as the Christ Consciousness. This second volume of the Golden City Series reveals the spiritual lineage that predates Christianity through the Egyptian King Akhenaten (1388 BC) and his association to the Mayan Christ figure, Quetzalcoatl.

Golden City Series *(cont'd)*

Through Toye, the Master Teachers describe prehistoric cataclysms which shaped contemporary occult schools and their spiritual traditions. They connected prophesied Golden Cities to Shamballa, the fabled city of Buddhist lore, which lights the New Grid of Earth. Learn how these sanctuaries expand our psychic energy and increase spiritual awareness to enable us to transcend the destructive End Times.

The steady radiance of Love, Wisdom, and Power that twinkles, glows, flames, and blazes throughout Ascended Master Teaching is known as the classic Seven Rays of Light and Sound. The teachings in this book begin with the metaphoric flicker of the light of a single candle, and end in the brilliant luminosity of a thousand suns: the *Light of Awakening*.

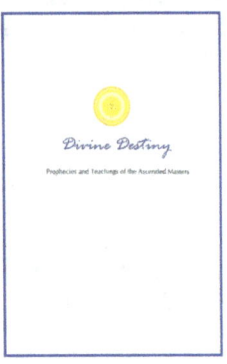

ISBN 978-1-880050-60-6
(Paperback) 334 pages

BOOK THREE: Golden City Series

Divine Destiny
Prophecies and Teachings of the Ascended Masters

Have you ever wondered about Atlantis, or the lost continent of Mu, or the lands of Lemuria? What united the ancient people of earth, and what led them into terrible, divisive wars that depleted their economies and inevitably led to their demise? *Divine Destiny* presents the lands of our myths and legends, with the geologic science that corroborates the prophecies and spiritual teachings of the Ascended Masters.

Lori Toye is best known for the *I AM America Maps of Earth Changes*, however, in 1999 she was contacted by Lord Macaw—an ancient tribal leader within the Toltec nation of Ameru—and given a compelling map of Ancient Earth: *The Map of the Ancients*. The map depicts another time on earth, when men were spiritually realized as divine beings (the HU-man) through the Quetzalcoatl (Christ) energies, and the great kingdoms of Rama, Mu, and Lemuria flourished. *Divine Destiny* shares spiritual teachings from Lemuria that are grounded in the foundational teachings of the lost Thirteenth School and the Right-Hand Path (the right use of energies), and their traditions and spiritual wisdom which were re-established in the New World after world-wide cataclysmic Earth Change.

Divine Destiny assists humanity's passage through 2012 and the critical years ahead, with important insight regarding humanity's upcoming shift in consciousness. This book—the third volume of the *Golden Cities Series*—continues the vital instruction regarding the use of the Golden Cities (the prophesied New Jerusalem) and their role in achieving spiritual initiation through the Ascension Process.

For more information or to purchase, go to:
iamamerica.com

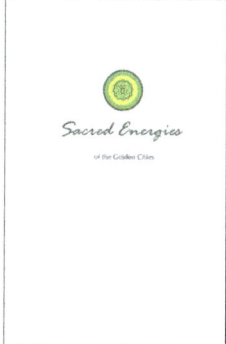

ISBN 978-1-880050-22-4
(Paperback) 290 pages

BOOK FOUR: Golden City Series

Sacred Energies of the Golden Cities

Ascended Master Prophecies and Teachings for Integrating the New Energies

A Guidebook to Right Now—our incredibly turbulent times, our "Time of Testing"

The channeled lectures and study lessons in Sacred Energies tell us exactly what is going on—the big picture—and how to benefit from it: How to perceive it in a way that helps us grow and become our best, loving selves, and how, by appreciating the transcendent nature of what may feel scary and horrible, perhaps we may even experience gratitude.

Take heart: "As the polarity of politics subsides and humanity begins to cultivate and achieve the Christ Consciousness, we enter the neutral point. This neutral point is described as unity and Oneship and ushers in a new period for humanity; poverty is removed as true abundance reigns on Earth."

And, according to channeled Ascended Master Saint Germain, "When darkness seems to produce an all-time low, it is also the greatest opportunity for light."

Sacred Energies features an in-depth study regarding the metaphysics of the Golden Cities—real locations where our spiritual growth can be expedited during the ongoing Time of Change.

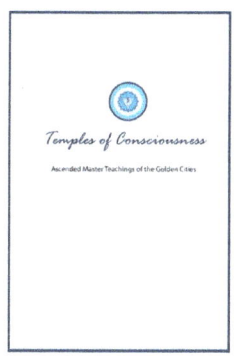

ISBN 978-1-880050-27-9
(Hardcover) 256 pages

BOOK FIVE: Golden City Series

Temples of Consciousness

Ascended Master Teachings of the Golden Cities

A Spiritual Guide for the Great Awakening - the Ascension Teachings for Right Now.

We are now living in the tumultuous Time of Change, a period of worldwide uncertainty and chaos, both physically and spiritually. In this unpredictable time of both global revolution and personal transformation, can we skillfully adjust and thrive while safely acclimating to the ongoing changes?

The Ascended Masters offer a path of spiritual protection and evolution in this fifth book of the Golden City Series, Temples of Consciousness. The journey from our first whiff of self-conscious awareness to life in a state of spiritual liberation is the "Ascension Process"—a process that contains numerous noteworthy spiritual passages that awaken, shock, confirm, align, and inevitably empower the human to HU-man evolution.

This time of personal spiritual growth and global change alongside activating Golden Cities is known as the "Great Awakening." The lessons in these pages help us to nurture and expand our newfound awareness. Learn how to release genetically held fear and how every negative situation we encounter is an opportunity to learn through polarity—making sense out of the senseless and finding balance within turmoil. Also included are suggestions to attune our diet and break negative

Golden City Series (cont'd)

addictions while cultivating compassion, especially for self. Discover and develop your super senses and to identify and feel subtle, heavenly energy. Then travel to a Golden City and enter one of its magnificent doorways to a new age of forgiveness, cooperation, healing, and harmony.

ISBN 978-1-880050-28-6
(Hardcover) 284 pages

BOOK SIX: Golden City Series
Awaken the Master Within
Golden Age Teachings of Saint Germain

Do you yearn for your next precious step of spiritual growth that wholly engages your Ascension Process? Are you ready to transform your Earthly, carbon-centered perceptions into the oneness of telepathic silicon-based consciousness? If so, your time is now.

This is the appointed time that your divine self awakens and spiritually evolves alongside our beloved Mother Earth—Babajeran. And according to the Ascended Master Saint Germain, this global awakening rouses humanity alongside a tenuous backdrop of planetary change and upheaval with the prophetic arrival of the White Star—also known as the planet Nibiru. These invaluable teachings address our current time of chaotic culture, politics, and ecology that were surprisingly received nearly two decades ago by mystic Lori Toye. This published instruction was purposefully held back until this moment, when worldwide events evolved as if to prime our receptivity to listen—waited for our spiritual 'eyes and ears' to be developed enough that we could thoughtfully see and perceptively hear its message. Yes, the time is now!

Whether you have just picked up this book and are new to the I AM America Teachings, or you've been studying for years, you won't find information like this anywhere else. Awaken the Master Within is a manual for students and teachers alike. These teachings are designed to help you to reaffirm your innate divinity via contact with your true self—the Master Within.

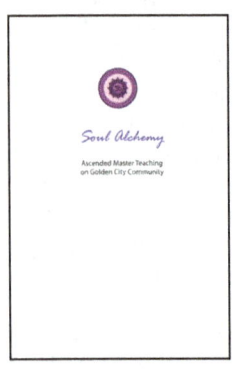

Digital Format Only
Available at the I AM America Bookstore

BOOK SEVEN: Golden City Series
Soul Alchemy
Ascended Master Teaching on Golden City Community

This is the seventh book in the Golden City Series, and recommended for advanced students of the I AM America Spiritual Teachings. Saint Germain, El Morya, and Lord Kuthumi conclude and evolve many of their introductory, yet complex, Golden City Teachings.

How do you build a Golden City Community? Is it based on the loving camaraderie of chelas and initiates of the Ascended Masters, or is it constructed of physical buildings with a carefully planned infrastructure? According to the Spiritual Master El Morya a community is not found within walls, "It is found in hearts!"

The teachings of Soul Alchemy, however, focus on both the spiritual and physical ideal of a Golden City Community. In these channeled spiritual lessons through mystic Lori Toye, the Master Teachers of the I AM America Spiritual Teachings describe and share their knowledge of the Golden Cities and how their transcendent energies can shepherd HU-man Consciousness to new dimensions beyond conventional sensing, a necessary development as we evolve through the Ascension Process. Soul Alchemy features metaphysical knowledge about our environment, describing and delineating the living, breathing energy of mountains and the singing flow of water. Mother Earth—Babajeran—is flourishing, blooming, and buzzing with physical, spiritual, and multi-dimensional energies that channel and define the heavenly energies of Shamballa upon our Earth.

This collection of spiritual teachings features the diverse teachings of Quetzalcoatl—prophet of Christ Consciousness, use of the Vedic Sudharshanna (Victory) and Bhumi (Earth Blessing) puja, and the auspicious Buddhist Windhorse supplication. Teachings on physical remedial measures feature the alchemical Golden City Rock technique, use of energy regulating calibration points, and Lord Kuthumi's mystical "Cup within a Cup," and culminate to the identification of a self-born Shiva Lingam. Undoubtedly, Soul Alchemy is filled with the unveiled mysteries of traditional spiritual knowledge entwined with the promise of Ascended Master wisdom, our HU-man evolution, and Ascension.

I AM America Books and Collections

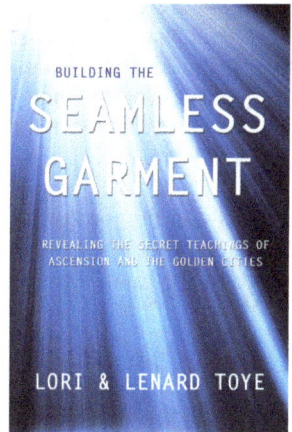

ISBN 978-1-880050-10-1
(Paperback) 288 pages

I AM AMERICA COLLECTION

Building the Seamless Garment
Revealing the Secret Teachings of Ascension and the Golden Cities

Is there a way to master our individual thoughts, feelings, and actions, thereby balancing our inevitable negative and positive karmas? Can we get out of the loop of incarnation-death-reincarnation? Can we conceive of something beyond both the incarnate and the spirit body? According to the channeled teachings of Masters Saint Germain and El Morya, the answer to all these questions is "Yes." The lessons in this book focus on the hidden teachings of Ascension—the spiritual and mental processes and the spiritual techniques that can free us from the confines of the need to reincarnate.

After a conventional Christian upbringing, Lori Toye had her life rocked when she was visited by a spiritual Master, who went on to become her teacher. Over the course of more than thirty years, she has been given information that she shares with others who similarly long to know esoteric truth. In Building the Seamless Garment (the literal growth to final liberation from the reincarnation cycle), Lori and her husband, Len, share detailed soul-freeing techniques and spiritual disciplines for ordinary people who are driven by a longing for Ascension and the dedication to try.

This material is a living text—as alive as you are. Read and reread these words in order to fully comprehend their enlightening message as you begin the soul-transcending journey of building your light bodies of eternal freedom and Ascension.

I AM AMERICA COLLECTION

Sacred Fire
A Handbook for Spiritual Growth and Personal Development

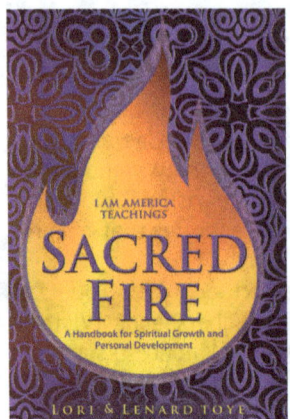

ISBN 978-1-880050-41-5
(Paperback) 288 pages

The soul-freeing process of Ascension is considered the utmost peak of human spiritual development and its precious states of consciousness have been sought by spiritual avatars and adepts of all ages. This book is a practical workbook that explains how to apply numerous Ascension techniques that access this miraculous energy of rejuvenation, strength, and spiritual fortification.

Each lesson in this selection of I AM America Ascension Teachings focuses on methods that set-up dynamic energies that create new HU-man brain connections. Each progressive spiritual technique converges to help you to develop a personal, experiential spiritual practice that evolves both your inner and outer light. As the frequencies of the Earth continue to progress into the Golden Age, you will advance into a seasoned Step-down Transformer of the Gold Ray.

Throughout this unique compilation of channeled lessons received by mystic Lori Toye, Ascended Master Saint Germain focuses many of his teachings on the Violet Flame, the vibrant Sacred Fire of forgiveness and transfiguration and shares numerous insights on how to apply its energies through decree, visualization, meditation, and breath technique. You will also learn about valuable spiritual methods of meditation, specific use of decree and mantra, and how to identify and release karmic patterns.

Sacred Fire contains a unique collection of important prayers and numerous decrees from the Ascended Masters of the I AM America Teachings that fortify and increase your spiritual light during this critical time of collective Spiritual Awakening and worldwide Ascension.

For more information or to purchase, go to:
iamamerica.com

Golden Cities and the Masters of Shamballa
The I AM America Teachings

This book holds the long-kept secrets of the Masters of Shamballa and is your next step on the spiritual path to Ascension. However it's not just a step, but a literal Spiritual Pilgrimage through the words and instruction of the Ascended Masters, to Golden Cities — locations throughout the world where you can accelerate your spiritual development in this Time of Change and Great Awakening.

Through the Adjutant Points, lei-lines, and magical portals described in these pages, you will learn about the growth of HU-man Consciousness and gain entrance into the once guarded knowledge of Master Teachers who aspire for humanity's freedom. You will discover treasured spiritual techniques that rapidly expand and cultivate your Ascension Process while experiencing Spiritual Migration, a real Spiritual Pilgrimage to each Master's Golden City. Migratory patterns help to improve self-awareness, a relationship, or integrate spiritual virtues, like harmony, love, illumination, or charity. But as the teachings of this book progress, you will be trained to enter an umbilicus portal for the world — the Heart of the Dove. Here, through simple straight-forward instruction, you experience the Group Mind with other students to focus energies for specific spiritual intentions and causes. These methods accelerate your Ascension Process, and offer a potent spiritual upgrade to all who enter the ONE of Group Mind.

Golden Cities and the Masters of Shamballa contains the detailed, authentic transcripts from the most recent channeled sessions through mystic Lori Toye, and this book was rushed to print because of recent world events and planetary changes. Filled with easy-to-understand full color illustrations, you will read exact instructions on building the New Shamballa, that is, the Golden Grid of Light that holds and contains the wondrous Golden Cities. You will learn more about the newly revealed Ascended Masters and Teachers who will guide and lead us into the New Times as you are introduced into their Shamballa Lineage of Golden City Teaching. This includes the physical locations of their ashrams, retreats, and temples within a Golden City, the Shamballa provenance, and organizational aspects (Spiritual Hierarchy), as you are guided to apply the spiritual techniques and practices for Ascension.

As the Gold Ray bathes our planet and initiates the Golden Age of Kali Yuga, you are fortunate and privileged to learn this timely, soul-freeing wisdom.

ISBN 978-1-880050-33-0
(Hardcover) Full Color, 412 pages

ISBN 978-1-880050-14-9
(Paperback) Full Color, 412 pages

I AM America Books and Collections (cont'd)

ISBN 978-1-880050-40-8
(Paperback) 230 pages

The Twilight Hours
Teachings for HU-man Development from Saint Germain

In the brief period of Earth's soft transition through dusk or dawn, our planet gains access to the energies of the Fourth Dimension. Spiritual Masters refer to this momentary shift in frequency and light as the heavenly, "Meeting of the Archangels," and leverage this auspicious time with focused spiritual practice and technique.

The Twilight Hours contains specific details regarding the soul-evolutionary methods that rapidly advance your spiritual development into the HU-man—a consciously integrated and telepathic state of Ascension. These teachings progress your Ascension Process through the cultivation of the Twilight Breath of Luminous Light, a rhythmic breath technique designed to drive the sacred, alchemic fire of the Violet Flame to every cell in your body. For those interested in dynamic, experiential Ascended Master Teaching and especially for practitioners of the Violet Flame, this is your next step.

Throughout five insightful channeled lessons received through mystic Lori Toye, Saint Germain describes how to attain the Evolutionary Body, an essential Ascended Master support system that initiates our soul's journey to spiritual freedom. This comprehensive teaching includes the addition of fire ceremony to cleanse chakras and dissolve the death urge, instructive details on the Twilight Breath that transmute fear and open multi-dimensional experience, and a rigorous Spiritual Migration through the four physical doorways of a Golden City Vortex. As you learn each treasured spiritual secret and apply their methods for Ascension, you will evolve into the expansive HU-man. This is our perfect Oneness, and the foundation of Unana—Unity Consciousness.

In this time of entering the unknown, as global economies implode and our worlds wobble and shift through polarized culture in the prophesied Time of Change, take heart, and know that Earth is ascending. The Ascended Masters' wisdom and teaching in The Twilight Hours sheds thoughtful light on darkness, as our inner luminosity initiates a HU-man Revolution of Ascension on Earth.

Evolutionary Biome
The Pilgrimage to Ascension

ISBN 978-1-880050-30-9
(Paperback) Full Color, 492 pages

As the conventional world hurtles uncontrollably through economic uncertainty, pandemic, and constant social and cultural polarity, a new world of abundance, health, harmony, and Oneness offers light to humanity's continuous struggle with shadow. This luminous, creative world is the Evolutionary Biome.

The Evolutionary Biome is the wondrous world around us, from atomic particles to the green grass under our feet. It is contained in all biologic organisms to seemingly inert objects on Earth, from the running water in our kitchen taps to a flowing river during a spring thaw. Its energies are present in all of life. The Master Teachers, as channeled by mystic Lori Toye in the many I AM America books, describe it simply as "Oneness."

Through this book, you will take a journey—literal or meditative—to the worldwide Golden Cities—an evolutionary path enabling us to receive unique and vital energies for the Golden Age. This journey comprises spiritual, mental, and physical forces influenced by the dynamism of Group Mind. On this path you will learn how the Evolutionary Biome seamlessly connects our inner life to the outer life, perfect and imperfect, with sequential chaos and rhythm, beauty and order. With practice and guidance from the many exercises, become a Co-creator of the Golden Age we all long for.

In twenty lessons the Ascended Masters share inspiring and fascinating details that include one of the best collections of contemporary teachings regarding the Western Shamballa Lineage and its invaluable knowledge of the Golden Cities. This spiritual education features Pilgrimages to engage your evolutionary Ascension Process, information regarding Shamballa and its numerous ethereal temples of light, specific instruction on the use of Cup Ceremony, and the rich traditions and legacy of the Ascended Masters that interface the Evolutionary Biome onto our Earth.

Commit to your spiritual evolution and, through the pages of Evolutionary Biome, take an inner and an outer Pilgrimage, intentionally choosing Light that restores and expands our heritage as Light Beings.

I AM America Books and Collections *(cont'd)*

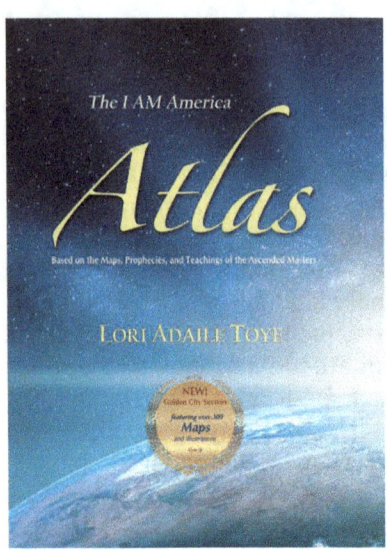

ISBN 978-1-880050-32-3
(Paperback) Full Color, 254 pages

I AM America Atlas
Based on the Maps, Prophecies, and Teachings of the Ascended Masters

How can we navigate the prophesied troubled times ahead? Perhaps by seeing them—literally and metaphorically. A lot has changed since the first presentation of the *I AM America Earth Changes Maps* over thirty years ago, and perhaps we have required that time to fully appreciate what they offer: a look into our possible future, and through contemplation of the literal pictures—land masses, cities, and roads—the opportunity to understand how beliefs create thoughts, that create actions, that create reality. So how can we best create a healthy, humane alternative to the prophesied disaster pictured in this book—changes that the scientific community now acknowledges (global warming) and we are witnessing firsthand as hurricanes and earthquakes besiege us? The *I Am America Atlas* offers perhaps one of the best anthologies of Earth Changes Maps ever produced. In the decades since each Map was received by mystic Lori Toye, our insight has matured. We encourage you to contemplate these Maps. What do they mean to you? How do these pictures arise? What insights arise when you entertain the notion that changing ourselves will change our environment? What are the changes you long to embody? What can you do right now to begin your transformation—and the subsequent transformation of our future maps?

For more information or to purchase, go to:
iamamerica.com

Awakening
Entering the Ascension Timeline of the Golden Age

ISBN 978-1-880050-48-4
(Paperback) Full Color, 628 pages

YOU ARE ON THE VERGE OF SPIRITUAL AWAKENING. In these pages, you will learn that each of us is destined to eventually experience it.

Spiritual Awakening is the transformational process that forever changes life's trajectory. According to Saint Germain, channeled through mystic Lori Toye, "Humanity is on the brink of great evolution and Spiritual Awakening." Through the information presented in this book you will spiritually grow from an ordinary human, and into a developed HU-man—a divinely realized, enlightened, and multi-dimensional BE-ing of Light.

As you discard preconceived ideas and notions that may hinder your spiritual growth you will experience new levels of Awakening as each chapter guides you through many important subtleties and nuances. These teachings include theories about Earth's ancient history, planetary and astronomical wonders, including the true physics of creation. Heal your emotions through the Violet Flame of forgiveness and compassion, then activate your innate divinity with specific meditations, decrees, and positive visualizations.

Awakening: Entering the Ascension Timeline of the Golden Age, is an essential primer and comprehensive encyclopedia of the Ascension Process that describes how to enter the freedom of the Fourth and Fifth Dimension. Detailed knowledge of the worldwide Golden Cities depicts this evolutionary science that distributes and refines the primary Seven Rays of Light and Sound alongside the expansive Gold Ray, instantly recalibrating your light-fields.

Saint Germain explains that multi-dimensional experience is foundational to the HU-man Co-creation of simultaneous realities and multiple timelines. While our culture undergoes turbulent change alongside necessary innovation, assure your stable footing upon the Ascension Timeline. Read and apply this information to become a conscious Co-creator of the hopeful New Times—a Golden Age of enlightenment and spiritual freedom.

This 628-page book is packed with insightful Ascended Master Teaching, accompanied with full color illustrations and charts, including easy to understand explanations that feature important spiritual exercises which help you gain vital, personal experience.